Mastering Cloud-Native Serverless Computing with AWS

Developing full-stack serverless solutions and incorporating modern DevOps practices

Adarsh Krishnamurthy

bpb

www.bpbonline.com

First Edition 2026

Copyright © BPB Publications, India

ISBN: 978-93-65893-724

To View Complete
BPB Publications Catalogue
Scan the QR Code:

Dedicated to

My mom, my wife and my son

Shobha, *Chaithra*, *and Athishq Sampangi*

About the Author

Adarsh Krishnamurthy is a lead consultant and senior solutions architect specializing in cloud computing, helping individuals, teams, and organizations leverage the cloud to solve complex business challenges. His hands-on expertise in infrastructure migration, cloud-native development, and software architecture across diverse technologies makes this book an invaluable resource for readers. Over his 17-year career, Adarsh has delivered innovative solutions across industries, including healthcare, finance, corporate tax, public sector, transportation, automotive, railways, and education. These experiences have shaped his ability to design creative and scalable ways to harness cloud technologies for problem-solving and innovation at scale.

He holds multiple AWS Certifications and actively engages in continuous learning through collaboration, mentoring, and knowledge sharing. His passion for innovation, combined with deep expertise in emerging technologies, positions him at the forefront of the evolving cloud landscape, enabling him to deliver practical, impactful, and forward-looking content to his audience.

About the Reviewer

Nandhakumar Raju is a seasoned technology leader with over 25 years of experience in digital transformation, systems modernization, and innovation across healthcare and public-sector platforms. He currently serves as director of engineering at one of the largest healthcare organizations in the United States, where he leads enterprise-scale initiatives in cloud strategy, AI/ML integration, and digital health infrastructure.

His core expertise includes cloud-native architecture, intelligent automation, system integration, and platform optimization. He is widely recognized for aligning technology with public health goals, improving operational efficiency, and delivering secure, scalable solutions that support population health at scale.

In addition to his leadership role, Nandhakumar is an active mentor, peer reviewer, and published researcher in AI and healthcare innovation. He has authored articles in leading journals and contributed to advancing best practices in digital health. His achievements have earned recognition through multiple industry awards and professional fellowships, including honors from IEEE, the **British Computer Society** (**BCS**), and the Royal Society for Public Health.

Acknowledgement

I want to express my sincere gratitude to everyone who has contributed to the successful completion of this book.

Most importantly, I would like to extend my heartfelt appreciation to my family and friends for providing immense support and believing in the value this book will deliver to readers. The encouragement, love, and guidance have been instrumental in the timely completion of the book and in making it a useful artifact.

I am immensely grateful to BPB Publications for its continuous support, guidance, and trust in this book. BPB's support is paramount in navigating the complexities of the publishing process.

I would also like to acknowledge the reviewers, technical experts, and editors who provided valuable feedback and contributed to the refinement of this manuscript. Their insights and suggestions have significantly enhanced the quality of the book.

Last but not least, I would like to express my sincere gratitude to the readers who have shown interest in the book. Your support and encouragement have been deeply appreciated.

Thank you to everyone who has contributed to making this book a reality.

Preface

Cloud computing has become a buzzword of this decade and has transformed businesses, industries, and most aspects of our modern-day-to-day life.

Cloud computing has become the driving force behind rapid innovation in solving complex challenges, from renting a server in the cloud to deploying sophisticated artificial intelligence capabilities. The cloud has been paving the way for business efficiency, innovation, scale, and resiliency.

Among the various flavors of cloud computing, this book covers an important flavor characterized by reduced management, improved cost efficiency, and effective resource optimization. This book focuses heavily on the serverless paradigm.

This book looks deeper into the cloud computing services provided by the world's largest public cloud provider, **Amazon Web Services** (**AWS**).

This book begins with an appropriate introduction and overview of AWS Serverless services while providing practical use-cases, service limits, and trade-offs in designing and developing applications that are of the highest standard, highly resilient, stable, secure, cost-effective, and scalable.

Chapters 1 to 4 introduce the technology, key terminologies, and their relevance to this paradigm. Chapters 5 to 17 explore key AWS services in detail. Chapters 18 to 20 demonstrate the practical aspects and industrial applications of AWS cloud, showcasing the usecases and capabilities of the AWS cloud. The last four chapters cover a sample application and frameworks that facilitate the design ofbetter-architected applications.

The practical design trade-offs, service limits, and industrial applications, with a deeper and continuous focus on Security, would make this an invaluable book for readers who wish to gain a deeper understanding of the serverless lens of AWS services and their practical applications.

Chapter 1: General Computing and On-premises Systems– This chapter focuses on providing key terminologies of general computing, the evolution of computing, and the common problems that the cloud would try to solve.

Chapter 2: Cloud Computing Paradigms and Common Architecture Patterns– This chapter explores the concepts of virtualization, cloud delivery models, deployment types, cloud providers, and the considerations that organizations must consider when choosing the right service, provider, and delivery model to suit their application and business needs.

Chapter 3: Serverless Systems– This chapter provides an in-depth exploration of the serverless paradigm and how it can be used to solve various business problems with rapid implementation and cost-efficient options. It also explores other related paradigms, such as cloud-native development, and provides examples of services from different public cloud providers.

Chapter 4: Setting Up Your Cloud– This chapter provides a hands-on guide to the local setup of the tools and Software required to run/manage the development and deployment of cloud services (particularly serverless)

Chapter 5: Serverless Compute with AWS Lambda– This chapter is dedicated to one of the most commonly used serverless compute services, AWS Lambda, and how Lambda can be used to connect and interact with a multitude of other AWS services to provide **function as a service** (**FaaS**). It also explores how Lambda has become the backbone for most cloud architectures. The practical examples, use-cases, and exercises help ensure a thorough understanding and the ability to apply the knowledge.

Chapter 6: Serverless Storage with AWS S3– This chapter is dedicated to the oldest AWS service, known for its extremely high durability of 99.999999999%. It covers every aspect of object storage, including methods for storing and managing data. It also explores the constraints and boundless possibilities of storage management with the most mature cloud storage service in AWS. This shows how Amazon S3 has become a cornerstone of modern data innovation.

Chapter 7: Serverless Storage with DynamoDB– This chapter is dedicated to an in-depth exploration of DynamoDB, Amazon's flagship NoSQL database. It showcases the fast and predictable performance and the seamless scalability of DynamoDB while covering its data model, usage, and integration with other AWS services.

Chapter 8: Serverless Storage with Aurora Serverless and EFS– This chapter focuses on two other key storage types offered by AWS for storing and managing relational data and file system storage. It provides a practical framework for understanding structured data with relational databases and the **Elastic File System (EFS)** for managing files.

Chapter 9: Serverless Data Flow and Messaging– This chapter explores serverless messaging and data flow, focusing on three key AWS services: Amazon **Simple Queue Service (SQS)**, Amazon **Simple Notification Service (SNS)**, and Amazon EventBridge. This showcases how these services eliminate the need to manage infrastructure, enabling developers to prioritize innovation and application functionality.

Chapter 10: Serverless Integration and Workflow Orchestration– This chapter explores three key AWS services that enable seamless integration and efficient orchestration among diverse components and workflows through Amazon API Gateway, AWS AppSync, and AWS Step Functions.

Chapter 11: Serverless Security and Authentication– This chapter focuses on the security aspect, with key services provided by AWS to manage every aspect of cloud security. It introduces all aspects of authentication, application and data security, firewalls, and secret management.

Chapter 12: Real-time Systems and User Interfaces– This chapter focuses on AWS services that help build real-time systems and how to create, manage, and deploy user interfaces in a serverless manner in AWS.

Chapter 13: Big Data and Streaming– This chapter focuses on AWS services for managing the efficient storage and ingestion of big data, covering key services such as Amazon Kinesis, OpenSearch, Amazon EMR, and Redshift data warehousing services.

Chapter 14: Machine Learning and Generative AI– This chapter demonstrates the paradigm shift in how businesses can leverage cloud and cloud services to manage **machine learning (ML)** workflows and managed AI services. It also introduces Amazon Bedrock, a new generative AI service by Amazon, and how these services integrate with the AWS ecosystem.

Chapter 15: Mastering Serverless Deployment on AWS– This chapter serves as a cookbook for deploying AWS services, introducing **infrastructure as code (IaC)**, **continuous integration/continuous deployment (CI/CD)**, and AWS-provided services that enable seamless deployment through the use of AWS CloudFormation, CDK, and SAM.

Chapter 16: Monitoring and Observability in AWS– This chapter explores how observability can be achieved through AWS services and the various offerings and interactions with this ecosystem.

Chapter 17: Optimizing Costs in AWS Serverless Architectures– This chapter provides a comprehensive guide to cost optimization in AWS serverless architectures, covering key cost drivers, AWS cost management tools, real-world cost-saving strategies, and anti-patterns that lead to hidden expenses.

Chapter 18: Serverless Applications in Healthcare– This chapter explores how cloud-native and serverless technologies are reshaping healthcare, from claims automation and predictive discharge to remote patient monitoring and AI-driven care

Chapter 19: Serverless Applications in Finance– This chapter examines how serverless and cloud-native technologies are transforming financial applications. It introduces foundational design principles and highlights key AWS services specifically designed for regulated environments.

Chapter 20: Serverless Applications in Industrial and Public Sectors– This chapter examines how AWS serverless services are being leveraged across various industrial and public sector domains to develop predictive, responsive, and mission-critical applications.

Chapter 21: Building a Full-stack Serverless Application– This chapter marks a transition from isolated learning to integrated implementation, reinforcing key architectural principles while producing a functional and scalable application that reflects the qualities expected in production-grade, cloud-native environments.

Chapter 22: AWS Well-Architected Framework– This chapter covers AWS Well-Architected Framework, which provides a structured approach, offering best practices, trade-off considerations, and real-world strategies to design, evaluate, and improve cloud workloads

Chapter 23: Serverless Trends and Emerging Technologies– This chapter introduces emerging trends in serverless computing and highlights how new technologies are shaping cloud-native architectures.

Chapter 24: Beyond Serverless and Limits of Serverless– This chapter provides a comprehensive understanding of serverless computing's limitations and explores strategies to overcome these constraints. This also covers how to move beyond serverless computing to hybrid, complex systems and the future of cloud computing.

Code Bundle and Coloured Images

Please follow the link to download the
Code Bundle and the *Coloured Images* of the book:

https://rebrand.ly/d3f432

The code bundle for the book is also hosted on GitHub at
https://github.com/bpbpublications/Mastering-Cloud-Native-Serverless-Computing-with-AWS.
In case there's an update to the code, it will be updated on the existing GitHub repository.
We have code bundles from our rich catalogue of books and videos available at
https://github.com/bpbpublications. Check them out!

Errata

We take immense pride in our work at BPB Publications and follow best practices to ensure the accuracy of our content to provide with an indulging reading experience to our subscribers. Our readers are our mirrors, and we use their inputs to reflect and improve upon human errors, if any, that may have occurred during the publishing processes involved. To let us maintain the quality and help us reach out to any readers who might be having difficulties due to any unforeseen errors, please write to us at :

errata@bpbonline.com

Your support, suggestions and feedbacks are highly appreciated by the BPB Publications' Family.

Piracy

If you come across any illegal copies of our works in any form on the internet, we would be grateful if you would provide us with the location address or website name. Please contact us at business@bpbonline.com with a link to the material.

If you are interested in becoming an author

If there is a topic that you have expertise in, and you are interested in either writing or contributing to a book, please visit www.bpbonline.com. We have worked with thousands of developers and tech professionals, just like you, to help them share their insights with the global tech community. You can make a general application, apply for a specific hot topic that we are recruiting an author for, or submit your own idea.

Reviews

Please leave a review. Once you have read and used this book, why not leave a review on the site that you purchased it from? Potential readers can then see and use your unbiased opinion to make purchase decisions. We at BPB can understand what you think about our products, and our authors can see your feedback on their book. Thank you!

For more information about BPB, please visit www.bpbonline.com.

Join our Discord space

Join our Discord workspace for latest updates, offers, tech happenings around the world, new releases, and sessions with the authors:

https://discord.bpbonline.com

Table of Contents

CHAPTER 1
General Computing and On-premises Systems

Introduction

This chapter explores key terminologies in general computing, the historical evolution of computing, and the role of **on-premises** systems in enterprise environments. Over the years, virtualization, containerization, and cloud computing advancements have reshaped how organizations manage infrastructure. While traditional on-premises environments offer control and security, modern enterprises rapidly adopt hybrid cloud models that balance flexibility with governance.

The transition from on-premises to cloud-based and hybrid environments has been influenced by factors such as the rise of edge computing, the need for real-time processing, and the cost benefits of scalable cloud solutions. This chapter lays the foundation for understanding how these computing paradigms evolved and why businesses continue to modernize their IT infrastructure. It provides a comparative analysis of on-premises systems, hybrid cloud models, and cloud-native environments, helping readers understand the key considerations for choosing the right computing strategy.

Structure

This chapter covers the following topics:

- Understanding computing
- Personal computers and the evolution of servers
- Computing paradigms
- Common traits for an on-premises system

Objectives

By the end of this chapter, the readers will have a comprehensive understanding of basic computing, how computers and computing solve business problems across different industries, and how they became the foundational blocks for modern computing. The chapter also highlights key historical events with scientific significance, common patterns, and terminologies. It introduces on-premises systems. It also covers what an organization or entity should consider when building a data center and what challenges they face. This provides users with context and foundations upon which the rest of the book will be built.

Understanding computing

Computing is the process of using a machine to complete a task for a purpose. The task could be as simple as adding two numbers (referred to as a calculation), or it could be a complex task involving predicting the course of a weather pattern to help save thousands of lives.

Figure 1.1 shows a generic datacenter/computing infrastructure:

Figure 1.1: A generic computing environment

Computing is done by a machine that follows a set of instructions to produce results. The results could be a simple answer, an operation, a 3-D render, or the launching of a rocket into orbit. It is often not a single machine, but a series of different machines (computers) of different storage and compute capabilities and configurations, often orchestrated by complex intermediate steps and references.

Modern day is heavily dependent on computing, which has become ubiquitous, and computing is now omnipresent. It is present in smartphones, laptops, watches, and cars we drive, from self-driving cars to the televisions we watch, to even the coffee machines that brew coffee.

Origin and evolution of computing

The early origins of computing date to the Abacus (a simple handheld counting tool used in ancient times, 1800s AD), which only consisted of beads that could slide, and the position of those beads would function as a standing memory at any point in time.

Back in the 1700s, the binary system was developed. It helped in converting a series of 0s and 1s into other numbers, letters, and characters, and changed the way machines can interact with their internal systems to produce results. Major events in our world have played a significant role in creating the need to innovate faster and build systems to solve complex problems or save lives.

For example, unprecedented weather events are pushing scientists to develop accurate monitoring systems to predict weather events.

One such event had historical significance and laid a solid foundation for our current computers. It happened in World War II.

When *Hitler* led Nazis built an encryption device called *enigma*, they used it for all major war communications. This had 159 trillion settings and was unbreakable. Later on, *Alan Turing* designed the Turing machine. We now call it a computer. The enigma was broken, and historians believe *World War II* was shortened by two years due to the turing machine. *Figure 1.2* shows bullets representing war and a machine depicting an encryption device:

Figure 1.2: Bullets (depicting war) and a machine (depicting a decoder)

Historical events, natural events, and human survival and thriving have always played a role in evolution and have resulted in faster enablement of technology and computing.

Programming languages and operating systems

Between the 1940s and 1950s, people started implementing and creating high-level languages to interact with machines, but they became commercially available when FORTRAN was developed by a team of experts in 1956 and COBOL in 1959. By the 1900s, many other programming languages like R, Ruby, Python, Java, JavaScript, and PHP came into existence.

On the other hand, mainframe systems (machines capable of meeting small customer needs) became increasingly popular, and COBOL became the mainstream language for mainframe systems. Mainframe systems still exist in this generative AI era, and such was their adaptation.

During the same period, operating systems (programs that can manage intercommunication between physical hardware, programming languages, memory, and processes) gained significance. Some commercial names include Windows 1.0 in 1985 and Unix in 1969.

Personal computers and the evolution of servers

The personal computer (a multi-purpose computer designed to be the assistant for any individual with the required operating system, hardware, storage, and configuration) became more and more prominent and started the digital revolution.

However, individual personal computers were not sufficient to solve business problems, and that is when computers were interconnected to form powerful clusters of computing beasts, and hardware manufacturers started manufacturing these computers with extensive storage, processing power, and speed. This, along with the launch of the World Wide Web (internet) in the 1900s, became the cornerstone for servers.

Servers and on-premises systems

When more organizations started using servers and computer clusters to manage their data, they needed higher levels of control and governance. The security of these systems became paramount, and infrastructure customization was needed to customize to business needs.

This led to the advent of on-premises systems.

In an on-premises system, the computing infrastructure is physically located on the premises of an organization. They are often fed by a dedicated power supply, cooling infrastructure, physical security, and networking.

Data centers for large organizations

A data center is a dedicated physical space or facility used to house computer systems and IT infrastructure (application, networking, and storage), often accompanied by backup power supplies, environmental controls, and security.

A data center could be an on-premises data center, a colocation facility, or even an edge data center (geographically closer to consumers).

Figure 1.3: A standard data center with servers and racks

Data centers play a pivotal role in medium to large-scale organizations for all their IT needs.

Common terminologies

A few terminologies (compute, network, security, and storage), which will be used in the upcoming chapters, are discussed as follows:

- **Algorithm**: A process or set of steps to solve a problem using a finite number of steps. Algorithms are used as specifications for performing calculations and data processing. These instructions should be unambiguous. *Figure 1.4* depicts a user interacting with an algorithm/flow of events:

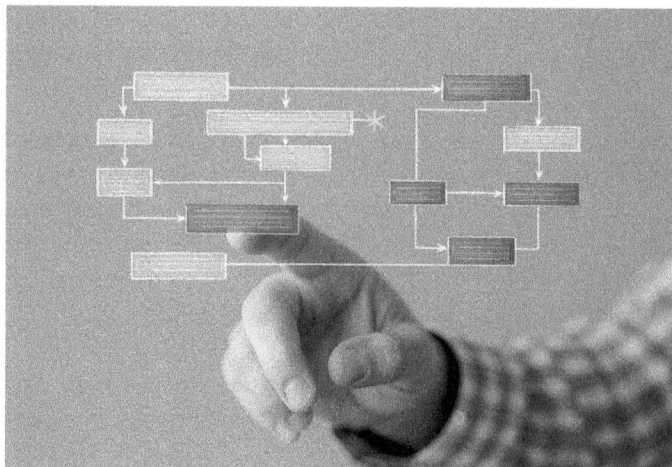

Figure 1.4: Algorithm/flow of events

- **Example:** In e-commerce, recommendation engines like *Amazon's Customers who bought this also bought* feature rely on machine learning algorithms to analyze past purchases and suggest relevant products.

- **Network:** A group of computer systems linked together. A network allows the linked computer systems to exchange information and share resources. If the systems are physically connected, they are called wired or otherwise termed wireless networks. Some computer networks will have a server (a central orchestrator or hub). If a computer is not connected to a network, it can be called a standalone computer.

  - **Example:** Streaming platforms like *Netflix* and *Amazon Prime* depend on global **content delivery networks (CDNs)** to ensure video content is streamed efficiently to users worldwide with minimal buffering.

- **Node:** A node in a computer network represents a system or computer.

  - **Example:** In blockchain networks like Bitcoin and Ethereum, thousands of nodes work together to validate transactions, maintain the ledger, and ensure decentralized trust without a central authority.

- **Firewall:** A system that acts as a gatekeeper for all the traffic in and out of a computer system or network. They inspect data packets and information exchanged between different participating systems. The Firewalls are intended to prevent any malicious activities, attacks, or accidental information and data exposures.

  - **Example:** Banks and financial institutions deploy enterprise-grade firewalls to protect sensitive customer data and prevent cyberattacks like phishing or ransomware.

- **Bandwidth:** The maximum rate at which data can be transferred between two points of a network.

  - **Example:** Video conferencing services like *Zoom* and *Microsoft Teams* require high-bandwidth connections to stream HD video and audio without lag.

- **Latency:** It is the delay between issuing an instruction to transfer a piece of information to its calling program

  - **Example:** Online gaming platforms like **PlayStation Network (PSN)** and Xbox Live require low-latency networks to ensure fast, real-time player interactions.

- **Network topology:** The arrangement of different elements of a network shows a mapping between those elements. It provides a logical and physical structure of a network.

  - **Example:** Large data centers, like **Amazon Web Services (AWS)** regions, use highly redundant mesh topologies to ensure failover and uptime in cloud computing environments.

- **Network protocols:** A set of rules and standards that govern how devices in a network can communicate. The common protocols that will be discussed in this book are:

  - **Management protocols:** SNMP, FTP and Telnet

  - **Communication protocols:** TCP, HTTP, and IP

  - **Security protocols:** TLS, SSL, and IPSec

  - **Example:** Secure e-commerce transactions on websites like Amazon rely on TLS and SSL protocols to encrypt customer credit card details.

- **Local area network vs. wide area network:** A **local area network (LAN)** is a network that connects computers in a specific geographical area (such as a building, library, school, or office) in which each device on the LAN will have its CPU and each device can access other devices connected to the LAN network. A **wide area network (WAN)** generally spans a large geographical area (a country, region, or continent) and often connects multiple LANs.

- **Router, gateway, and modem**: A router manages data communication across networks. They manage the traffic and forward information to the intended destination (machines or systems with dedicated IP addresses). A modem connects networks formed by routers to the Internet. In general, a router connects devices to the LAN, and a modem connects systems to the WAN.

- **IP address**: An IP address is a unique string of numbers and/or letters that uniquely identifies a device in a network.

  o An IP address can be IPv4, which is a range of numbers from 0 to 255 separated by a dot and using a 32-bit addressing scheme. For example, 10.121.20.40 or a 128-bit addressing scheme, which can support up to 340 trillion addresses. For example, 2001:4860:4860::8888 (Google's public DNS Server).

- **DNS**: A system that translates domain names into IP addresses. A DNS works like a phonebook for addresses on the internet and is like a database that can map user-friendly names into unique IP addresses. For example, **www.amazon.com** (DNS) points to the 192.0.2.44 IP address.

Computing paradigms

The following points showcase important paradigms of computing and their evolution over time:

- **Mainframes**: Backbone of the early days of computing, they were capable of hosting extensive processing jobs.

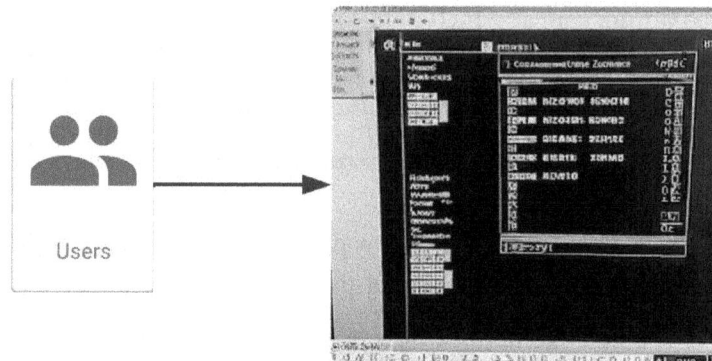

Figure 1.5: A mainframe terminal

- **Personal computers**: A personal device customized and tailored to individual needs. It is often capable of handling many tasks in parallel.

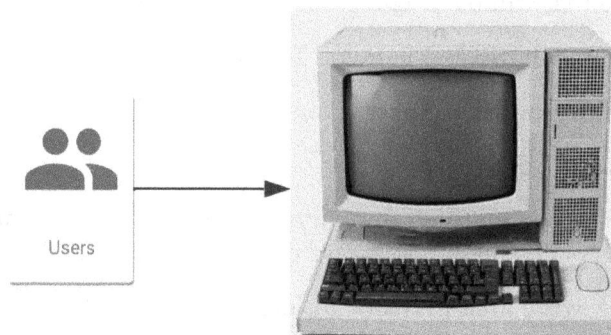

Figure 1.6: An early version of the personal computer/desktop

- **Server-based computing**: A pattern in which much of the data is stored in a central location (server) and allows for centralized management and users to access the same data across devices.

Figure 1.7: *A typical computer connected to a server*

- **Internet-based computing**: Here, servers and computing devices have access to the internet.

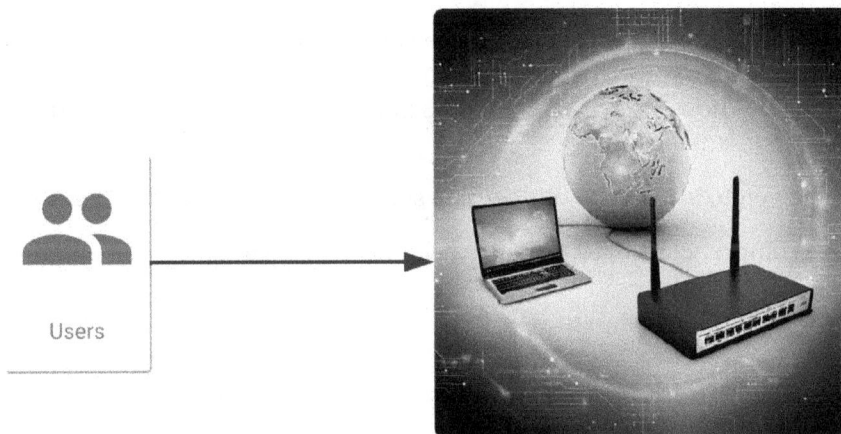

Figure 1.8: *A computer connected to the internet via a standard modem/router*

- **Grid computing**: A type of distributed computing where different computers and networks are connected via shared infrastructure, allowing processing of complex datasets and processes.

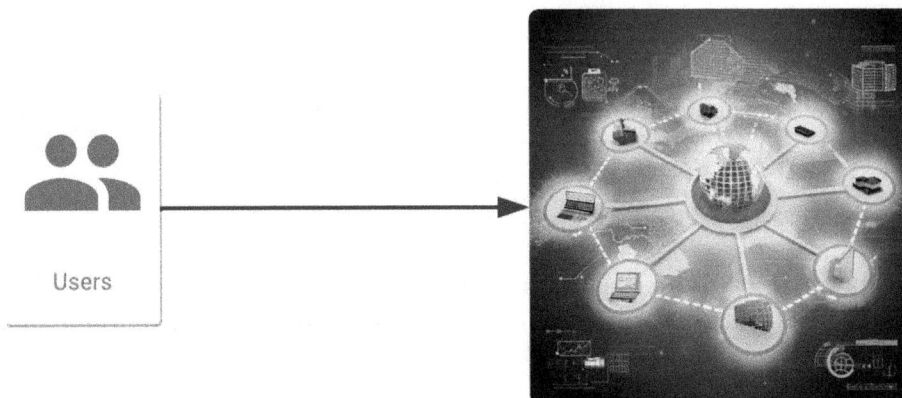

Figure 1.9: *A typical grid computing paradigm*

- **Cloud computing**: A modern paradigm where the resources (compute, storage, networking, software) are all provided by third-party cloud providers over the internet.

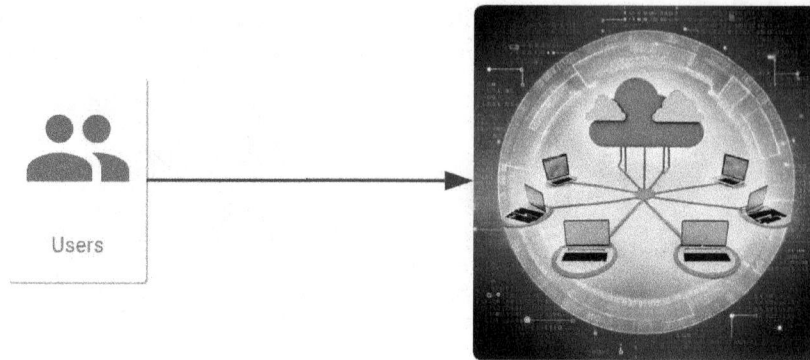

Figure 1.10: *Cloud computing, where resources are connected via the internet to a cloud provider*

Common traits for an on-premises system

When designing and developing a system to be deployed in an on-premises environment, several performance, security, and cost considerations are to be made to ensure that the environment and applications are maintainable. It also includes how the system would be maintained and how to keep the lights on irrespective of the physical and environmental conditions.

The priority should be given to aspects involving data security, resiliency, and disaster recovery.

This section provides a comprehensive list of key considerations when designing an on-premises system.

Ownership

The organization that owns the infrastructure has complete control of the system, including capacity, physical and application security, consumption, and management.

Capital expenditure

Capital expenditure (CapEx) refers to the investments made by an organization in its physical assets (in this case, it refers to infrastructure, including hardware, networking, physical space, storage, and software costs).

Physical security

This refers to the physical security of the infrastructure to ensure no unauthorized access and the positioning of physical security guards to safeguard hardware and related components.

Data security

Security is one of the most critical aspects of managing on-premises infrastructure. Organizations must safeguard data, applications, and networks against cyber threats while ensuring compliance with industry regulations. The details are as follows:

- **Traditional security measures**:
  - **Firewalls**: Act as a gatekeeper by filtering incoming and outgoing traffic to protect systems from unauthorized access.
  - **Encryption**: Protects sensitive data by converting it into unreadable formats, ensuring only authorized parties can decrypt and access it.

o **Access control lists (ACLs)**: Define which users or systems can interact with specific resources, adding an extra layer of security.

While these traditional security controls are effective, modern cyber threats require a more dynamic approach to securing IT environments.

- **Evolving security paradigms**:

  o **Zero Trust Architecture (ZTA)**: The Zero Trust model follows the principle of **never trust, always verify**. Unlike traditional security models that assume users inside a corporate network are trusted, Zero Trust requires continuous authentication and verification for every device, user, and application.

    ▪ **Example**: A financial institution implementing Zero Trust ensures that employees can only access the exact applications needed for their jobs, preventing lateral movement by attackers inside the network.

  o **Secure Access Service Edge (SASE)**: SASE combines network security with cloud-native security frameworks, ensuring secure, policy-based access for remote users. As companies adopt hybrid and multi-cloud models, SASE enables consistent security policies across all environments.

    ▪ **Example**: A global enterprise implementing SASE can enforce secure access controls for remote employees working from various locations, ensuring compliance with organizational security policies.

- **Current security threats in on-premises systems**: On-premises environments face increasingly sophisticated cyber threats, requiring proactive security strategies.

  o **Ransomware attacks**: Malicious software that encrypts critical business data, demanding a ransom for decryption. Enterprises must implement immutable backups, endpoint detection, and network segmentation to prevent large-scale attacks.

  o **Insider threats**: Employees or contractors with access to critical systems can intentionally or unintentionally expose sensitive data. To mitigate risks, organizations must implement strict privilege controls, continuous monitoring, and behavior-based anomaly detection.

  o **Physical security risks**: Unlike cloud-based environments, on-premises data centers are vulnerable to physical breaches. Biometric authentication, surveillance, and restricted access zones ensure that only authorized personnel can access critical infrastructure.

Scalability

Scalability refers to an organization's ability to increase or decrease computing resources based on demand. In an on-premises environment, managing scalability requires proactive capacity planning to ensure sufficient processing power, memory, and storage are available during peak usage periods.

Organizations typically scale their infrastructure using two primary strategies:

- **Vertical scaling (Scaling up)**: Increasing the power of an existing server or machine by adding more CPU, memory, or storage.

- **Horizontal scaling (Scaling out)**: Adding multiple servers or machines to distribute the workload across a larger infrastructure.

Comparing vertical and horizontal scaling

The following table provides a comparison between vertical and horizontal scaling:

Scaling type	Description	Use case	Challenges
Vertical scaling (Scale up)	Increasing the capacity of a single machine by adding CPU, memory, or storage	Used in database-intensive applications, such as financial transaction processing or healthcare data management	Expensive, has hardware limitations, and may lead to single points of failure
Horizontal scaling (Scale out)	Adding multiple servers to distribute workloads	Ideal for web applications, CDNs, and cloud-native architectures	Requires load balancing and distributed computing frameworks

Table 1.1: Comparison of vertical and horizontal scaling

Let us look at some industry-specific examples of scaling:

- **E-commerce (Horizontal scaling)**: E-commerce platforms like *Amazon* and *Shopify* handle massive spikes in web traffic during events like *Black Friday* or *Cyber Monday*. Instead of upgrading a single powerful server (vertical scaling), they deploy multiple web servers across different regions (horizontal scaling), ensuring a seamless user experience.

- **Healthcare (Vertical scaling)**: Hospitals and research institutions rely on large-scale databases to store patient records and medical images. Since these applications require high processing power and low latency, they often scale vertically by upgrading database servers to improve performance.

- **Financial services (Hybrid scaling)**: Banks and trading firms handle real-time financial transactions that require both high processing power (vertical scaling) and distributed computing (horizontal scaling). Trading platforms use high-performance servers for real-time analytics while distributing customer-facing applications across multiple data centers to ensure redundancy.

- **Streaming services (Horizontal scaling with CDNs)**: Netflix and YouTube scale out their infrastructure using CDNs to cache and serve video content from multiple locations, reducing latency and ensuring worldwide smooth streaming experiences.

Disaster recovery

The term disaster refers to any event that can disrupt the normal functional state. They can include natural disasters such as hurricanes, floods, wildfires, earthquakes, volcanoes, tsunamis, or even equipment failures, power outages, cyber-attacks, or internal human errors.

An organization managing on-premises systems must ensure sufficient redundancy and develop systems and processes to quickly recover normal functioning without any data or loss of transactions.

Larger organizations often manage disaster recovery through replication (keeping another copy of data, transaction state) and often involve building backup data centers that will be physically separated (in a neighboring town/city). There will be networking to switch over to the backup system.

Disaster recovery plans are crucial safeguards against downtime in a data center facility and play a critical role in maintaining data center availability.

Software licensing

The licensing required for tools, including software utilities, operating systems, and databases, must be managed by the organization managing the on-premises systems. This also includes routing license renewals, upgrades, and negotiations with vendors for better pricing and volume discounts.

Resource management

This often requires dedicated data center technicians, networking professionals, and IT support to manage all aspects of data center maintenance.

Patching and maintenance

This is another important aspect of managing our infrastructure. An organization's responsibility also includes periodic security scans, software updates, and patching to the overall maintenance of all the resources to ensure optimal availability, safety, and security from any attacks.

Use cases for on-premises systems

An organization may choose to build its data center/maintain its on-premises systems when one/more of the following conditions are greatly satisfied:

- Scenarios where high-speed internet access can only be guaranteed through a dedicated connection.

- An organization is operating in a highly regulated industry dealing with highly sensitive data. Regulations prevent them from exposing data to cloud providers, for example, organizations dealing with the government, military systems, healthcare, and finance.

- An organization requires higher customization of its hardware and policies.

- An organization requires greater ownership of its infrastructure, software, and process controls.

- Complex licensing models prevent them from using those licenses outside of their infrastructure.

- Other regulatory and legal obligations that mandate data to reside within/near the organization.

- Some organizations may have built many legacy systems that would require significant effort to make them cloud-friendly.

Conclusion

In this chapter, we covered how human needs drove the technological revolution and how computers and computing became an integral part of our lives. It laid a strong foundation by covering key concepts and terminologies of computing. It gave a preview of on-premises systems, key considerations when an organization decides to build its data centers, and their advantages. In the next chapter, we are going to build upon the foundation and cover virtualization, an introduction to cloud computing, and its significance.

Join our Discord space

Join our Discord workspace for latest updates, offers, tech happenings around the world, new releases, and sessions with the authors:

https://discord.bpbonline.com

CHAPTER 2

Cloud Computing Paradigms and Common Architecture Patterns

Introduction

Cloud computing has transformed enterprise IT by providing scalable, on-demand services that reduce dependency on traditional data centers. This shift enables businesses to focus on innovation, automation, and operational efficiency instead of infrastructure management.

As organizations migrate to the cloud, hybrid and multi-cloud strategies are becoming dominant trends, driven by regulatory compliance, cost optimization, and risk mitigation.

Hybrid cloud adoption is essential for balancing security and scalability in regulated industries like healthcare and finance. For example, a healthcare provider may store patient health records on a private cloud to meet HIPAA compliance while leveraging public cloud AI services for predictive analytics and diagnostics. Similarly, financial institutions must adhere to data residency laws, keeping transactional data on premises while using cloud providers like AWS or Azure for fraud detection and risk modeling.

In contrast, multi-cloud architectures offer enterprises flexibility by distributing workloads across multiple cloud providers. Organizations can optimize **service-level agreements** (**SLAs**), avoid vendor lock-in, and access specialized cloud-native features by utilizing AWS, Azure, and Google Cloud. This strategy is especially valuable for global enterprises that require redundancy across geographically distributed infrastructure.

This chapter provides a comprehensive overview of cloud paradigms, guiding readers through virtualization, deployment models, and key architectural patterns supporting scalable, secure, and cost-efficient cloud solutions.

Structure

This chapter covers the following topics:

- Virtualization basics
- Introduction to cloud computing
- Cloud computing delivery models
- Cloud deployment and types
- Cloud computing services
- Cloud computing patterns
- Cloud computing paradigms

Objectives

By the end of this chapter, the readers will have a comprehensive understanding of virtualization, ways to deliver software and networking services and solutions over the internet, and how cloud computing aims to make it easy to shift focus from managing infrastructure to solving real business problems. The readers will get an insight into different cloud computing paradigms, cloud providers, and their offerings, and an understanding of what considerations must be taken before choosing a platform or cloud provider and how to choose an option that suits their business needs.

This provides the users with cloud computing foundations upon which the rest of the book will be built.

Virtualization basics

Virtualization is a technology that can create simulated versions of a machine's software or hardware components. This helps in creating multiple environments from a single physical system. Virtualization is managed by a hypervisor, which can be considered the brain of the virtualization system.

This enables abstraction and pooling of resources, enabling sharing of resources (software, hardware, or networking) across a network. Virtualization is a foundational technology that enables cloud computing.

Virtualization is a key enabler of cloud computing, providing **resource abstraction** for compute, storage, and networking. It allows organizations to optimize hardware utilization, reduce operational costs, and improve scalability.

While traditional virtualization focuses on creating multiple **virtual machines** (**VMs**) on a physical server, modern cloud-native applications increasingly rely on containerization for lightweight, portable, and efficient resource management.

Containerization packages applications with their dependencies into isolated runtime environments, ensuring consistent performance across different cloud platforms. Unlike VMs, containers share the same OS kernel, making them lightweight and faster to deploy.

Kubernetes (**K8s**) has emerged as the de facto standard for container orchestration, automating the deployment, scaling, and management of containerized applications. Enterprises leverage Kubernetes on AWS (EKS), Azure (AKS), and Google Cloud (GKE) to deploy and manage microservices architectures efficiently.

Use case example, cloud-native application deployment: A fintech startup may deploy Docker containers for its payment processing service and use Amazon EKS to orchestrate them dynamically.

This setup enables:

- **Auto-scaling** to handle high transaction volumes during peak hours.
- **Zero-downtime deployments** with rolling updates.
- **Multi-cloud portability** to migrate between AWS, Azure, and Google Cloud.

In summary, while traditional virtualization remains relevant for legacy applications, containerization and Kubernetes provide the efficiency, scalability, and automation needed for modern cloud-native architectures.

Server virtualization

This is equivalent to having a magical wand that can create multiple copies of the same resource (server), which can serve different purposes. The core server (physical server) will have a lot of processing power, storage, and memory. This server will use virtualization to split the main server into several small virtual servers. Each virtual server has its own operating system and can run different applications.

The key benefits of server virtualization include the following:

- Reduced operating costs

- Quicker delivery
- High availability of services

Storage virtualization

This presents a logical view of physical storage resources to a host system. This provides a unified view of storage management. Storage virtualization is a way of abstracting or isolating internal functions of storage. Storage virtualization is a way of pooling physical storage from multiple devices and making them appear as a single storage unit.

A classic example of storage virtualization in day-to-day life would be uploading a picture onto a cloud storage (say *Google Drive*); the internal system treats this as a digital suitcase and creates a virtual object inside its portal. The volumes are like shelves for that storage and will be indexed/stacked for easy retrieval.

In this case, if the user uploading pictures needs more space, they do not need to manage the storage. Instead, the provider will allocate from the pool; if there is not enough in the pool, the provider will add more volumes, and this process is abstracted away from the user using this service.

Network virtualization

Network virtualization is a digital playground for networks. It abstracts network resources traditionally delivered in hardware to software. It decouples network services from underlying hardware. The physical network just works as a package-forwarding backplane.

The best way to implement network virtualization is VLAN, which combines computers and printers into a single group regardless of their physical location.

All public clouds use network virtualization to deliver their products and solutions.

This reduces the network deployment effort, which typically takes weeks to a few minutes of configuration.

Introduction to cloud computing

Cloud computing is a game-changing technology that leverages pools of computing resources to minimize cost and maximize efficiency. Cloud computing has emerged as a transformative force that is providing a paradigm shift in IT infrastructure to enable organizations to harness the power of remote servers, storage, networking, and apps over the internet.

This, in simple terms, makes computing resources available over the internet and on demand. These services often work on a pay-as-you-go model. If an organization needs compute resources (say, servers) to process information, it can just rent servers for the duration of the task. It is not just providing hardware virtualization (like servers over the internet) but more of ubiquitous computing covering all key aspects of modern computing (computing, memory, storage, networking, security, and managed services).

Cloud computing has become more of a practice and pervasive to IT, and its emergence is now paving the way for modern-day computing involving machine learning, generative AI, serverless application development, and fully managed **Internet of Things (IoT)** services.

Computing is done by a machine that follows a set of instructions to produce results. The results could be a simple answer, an operation, a 3-D render, or the launching of a rocket into orbit. It is often not a single machine, but a series of different machines (computers) of different storage and compute capabilities and configurations, often orchestrated by complex intermediate steps and references.

The modern world is heavily dependent on computing, which has become ubiquitous. Computing is now omnipresent, present in smartphones, laptops, watches, and cars, from self-driving cars to televisions and even coffee machines.

Characteristics of cloud computing

Cloud computing is a new way of thinking about deploying and making cloud services available to businesses. Cloud services are capable of complex tasks and have many features. The following is a list of key characteristics of a typical cloud computing platform:

- **Disaster recovery and automation**: All software and cloud platforms offer built-in disaster recovery capabilities to ensure 100% of the data and state can be recovered in a matter of minutes to hours.

- **On-demand service**: This is the core principle of cloud computing; it allows renting (provisioning and managing computing resources) based on need. This helps users scale up/ down the resources based on their needs.

  For example, an e-commerce company can scale up the resources during peak sale times or during holidays and scale down the same during off-peak seasons; when they have scaled down, they will not pay for the resources they are not using at any point in time.

- **Globally available**: Cloud computing is delivered over the internet, and the many services have made it possible to deliver services across the world and make applications accessible over the Internet with low-latency access.

- **High availability**: Cloud computing resources are always available and are considered **high availability (HA)**. The cloud provider maintains a very high SLA (often above 99%, and dependent on the type of service)

- **Scalability and performance**: Cloud resources can scale horizontally (adding more servers as required) and vertically (increasing the total capacity of the server). The type of scaling typically depends on the scenario, is seamless in all cases, and provides patterns to manage automatic scaling.

- **Shared responsibility**: The cloud resources work on the principle of shared responsibility. The cloud provider would be responsible for managing the core infrastructure and their physical security (for example, data centers, networking, and preventing any external attacks), and the users would be responsible for managing application-level security, and the cloud providers provide tools to ensure a better security posture of the applications.

- **Resource pooling**: Cloud resources under the hood use shared services, but the pool would be so big that none of them ever matter to the end users.

Cloud computing advantages

Cloud services provide an unparalleled advantage over on-premises-based deployment. Cloud computing may not answer all problems, and it must be done after understanding the workload, cost implications, access patterns, and business fit.

The following are some of the key advantages delivered with cloud computing:

- **Elasticity**: Cloud services are built to be elastic; the services automatically adjust the resources based on demand. It is quite common to automatically add resources during periods of high activity (scale up) and to also de-allocate resources when not in use (scale down). Elasticity is at the core of cloud computing and is applicable for servers as well as managed services.

- **Cost savings**: Cloud computing takes away most of the initial investment required in setting up a datacenter and even buying and setting up servers, storage, and most of the networking. A common paradigm in cloud computing is to rent servers for the duration of need or use serverless services. They are managed services that abstract away the need to maintain any servers and are based on a pay-as-you-go model.

  Cloud computing helps move costs from CapEx to **operating expenses (OpEx)**.

- **Faster time to market**: Since cloud computing provides resources of any type of computing (compute, storage, networking, security, machine learning, or GenAI) with just a few clicks and is served over the internet, there is no time spent on initial hardware procurement, configuration, and setup. Organizations can start working on their core business functions immediately after signing up and hence can release their products faster to market.

- **Improved innovation**: Cloud providers make it easy to access continuous innovations across a broad spectrum of services. They also maintain a marketplace of offerings readily available to use in Enterprise applications. For example, users can leverage the use of GenAI-based services for text summarization in just a few clicks or implement single sign-on with a broad-spectrum third-party identity provider.

- **Disaster recovery**: Cloud providers, by default, provide disaster recovery options included as part of their service offerings. Most cloud providers run their services and provide options for immediate replication of data, such that no data is lost in the event of any natural disaster, and provide strict SLAs for service restoration.

- **Global reach**: Cloud providers provide global services that will help customers to deploy and make the solution available to customers throughout the globe at very low latency. This is possible due to the various edge locations a cloud provider will manage to provide ultra-low latency access to services.

- **Eco-friendly**: Moving workloads from on-premises systems to the cloud, leveraging scale-up/scale-down features, and using shared resources helps reduce carbon emissions and energy consumption. The cloud providers are also investing heavily in making their core infrastructure run on energy-efficient systems, thereby reducing the overall carbon emissions from data centers and helping restore the planet.

- **Maintenance and patching**: Cloud platforms manage automatic updates, ensuring users have full access to the latest and most recent features. The type of maintenance and the level of patching managed depend on the kind of service. If users opt to use serverless services, they do not have to worry about anything. For other use cases involving renting servers, users will still get an option to manage patches.

- **Security and governance**: One of the key advantages of the cloud involves enhanced security. All the cloud systems have enhanced physical security with 24/7 monitoring, automated backups, and dedicated support to ensure and prevent any kind of security attack. Most cloud providers also provide security as a service, tools to customize and manage security for applications in the cloud.

- **Observability**: Most cloud services come with built-in observability frameworks that will help to observe and monitor every request, every business operation, and every transaction, helping businesses to focus on their operations.

- **Analytics**: Cloud providers provide advanced analytics and tools to build complex analytical systems with minimal effort.

- **Generative AI**: Recent developments in machine learning and GenAI have made it possible to provide ready-to-use GenAI services as cloud offerings, enabling businesses to leverage GenAI to solve unique and complex business problems quickly.

  For example, Microsoft Azure provides ChatGPT, and AWS provides Amazon Bedrock, which hosts models from leading GenAI providers like Anthropic, Amazon's own Titan models, Facebook's Llama model, Mistral AI, and many more.

Cloud computing delivery models

A delivery model represents a specific, pre-packaged combination of IT resources offered by a cloud provider. These models define how cloud services are packaged and delivered to users and organizations. There are three primary methodologies in which computing is delivered: SaaS, PaaS, and IaaS.

Software as a service

Software as a service (SaaS) is a fully managed cloud service model, where the provider delivers functional software applications to end users over the internet. The software can be hosted by the cloud provider or a third-party agent, ensuring:

- **Unlimited scalability**: Businesses can scale their user base without managing infrastructure.
- **Continuous and automatic updates**: The provider handles patches and feature updates.
- **Multi-device support**: SaaS applications are accessible via web browsers and mobile apps.
- **Subscription-based pricing**: Pay-as-you-go pricing reduces upfront costs.
- **Real-time collaboration**: Multiple users can work together simultaneously.
- **Reduced IT management**: Organizations need not handle installations or security updates.

Real-world use case

Google Workspace for team collaboration: A multinational enterprise uses Google Workspace (Docs, Drive, Meet) to enable remote teams to collaborate on shared documents, conduct virtual meetings, and securely store files in the cloud.

The following are the key benefits realized in this use case:

- **Instant scalability**: New employees get instant access to collaboration tools.
- **Zero maintenance**: The SaaS provider handles security, patches, and feature updates.
- **Cost-efficiency**: Companies pay per user, reducing software licensing costs.

Platform as a service

Platform as a service (PaaS) provides pre-configured cloud environments for developing, testing, and deploying applications without needing to manage infrastructure.

PaaS ensures the following:

- **Fully managed development environment**: Developers focus on coding rather than hardware management.
- **Flexible hosting**: Supports containerized applications, APIs, and microservices.
- **Auto-scaling**: Adjusts resources dynamically based on demand.
- **Integrated DevOps tools**: Supports automated CI/CD workflows.

Real-world use case

AWS Elastic Beanstalk for mobile app development: A ride-hailing startup builds its backend on AWS Elastic Beanstalk, which manages application servers, auto-scaling, and load balancing.

The following are the key benefits of Paas as realized in this use case:

- **Faster time-to-market**: Developers deploy code without setting up servers.
- **Built-in CI/CD pipelines**: Enable automated testing and deployments.
- **Scalability**: The system scales to accommodate peak traffic during ride requests.

Infrastructure as a service

Infrastructure as a service (IaaS) offers on-demand computing resources, including virtual machines, networking, and storage. Organizations use IaaS to rent IT infrastructure instead of purchasing physical servers.

IaaS ensures the following:

- **Highly customizable**: Users control the OS, applications, security settings, and networking.
- **Scalable on demand**: Can scale up/down based on application needs.
- **Global availability**: Supports multi-region deployments for reduced latency.
- **Cost flexibility**: The pay-as-you-go model eliminates upfront hardware costs.

Real-world use case

Scaling an e-commerce website with AWS EC2: An online retailer experiencing holiday shopping surges uses Amazon EC2 instances to scale dynamically, ensuring smooth operations during peak demand.

The following are the key benefits of IaaS as realized in this use case:

- **Dynamic scaling**: Automatically adjusts server capacity based on traffic spikes.
- **Global reach**: It deploys servers across multiple AWS regions for fast content delivery.
- **Cost optimization**: Only pay for active compute resources, reducing idle costs.

Comparing cloud delivery models

The following figure shows a comprehensive comparison of how the different cloud delivery models differ and compare against each other and to an on-premises implementation. The following figure illustrates that as an organization transitions from an on-premises or data center-based approach to SaaS, the level of responsibility decreases.

The best approach depends on the use case and will be a hybrid approach, with IaaS dominating most of the cloud migration activities for medium—to large-scale organizations for enterprise applications.

On-Premises	IaaS	PaaS	SaaS
Servers	Servers	Servers	Servers
Storage	Storage	Storage	Storage
Networking	Networking	Networking	Networking
Virtualization	Virtualization	Virtualization	Virtualization
OS	OS	OS	OS
Middleware	Middleware	Middleware	Middleware
Runtime	Runtime	Runtime	Runtime
Apps	Apps	Apps	Apps
Data	Data	Data	Data

Figure 2.1: A table showing a comparison of cloud delivery models

Cloud delivery models with an analogy

Let us explore the cloud delivery models, SaaS, PaaS, and IaaS, using your analogy of a multi-day trip:

- **On-premises model**:
    - **Analogy**: Imagine driving your own car for the trip.
    - The explanation is as follows:
        - You plan the entire journey, book hotels, pay road tolls, and tailor the trip according to your preferences.

- This is like managing your own infrastructure, where you manage servers, networking, and software on-site.

- **IaaS**:
  - **Analogy**: Think of renting a car with added conveniences.
  - The explanation is as follows:
    - You rent a car (infrastructure) that comes with built-in GPS (virtualization).
    - The overall pricing includes road taxes (covering networking components), and select locations offer dedicated parking (to accommodate scalability)
    - You focus on driving (applications) while the rental service (cloud provider) manages and handles the infrastructure.

- **PaaS**:
  - **Analogy**: Picture hiring a tourist agent for your trip.
  - The explanation is as follows:
    - The tourist agent (PaaS) takes care of everything:
    - Picks you up (development environment setup).
    - Drives you to attractions (application development and deployment).
    - Arranges hotels (middleware and runtime environment).
    - Includes entry tickets (development tools).
    - You still decide which attractions to visit and how long to stay (customization).

- **SaaS**:
  - **Analogy**: Imagine an all-inclusive guided tour.
  - The explanation is as follows:
    - You book the trip (subscription model), and all services are already included, which are:
    - Flight travel (software applications).
    - Driving around (accessing services via the internet).
    - Tolls, hotels, food, and attraction tickets (fully managed services).
    - Even the return journey (end-to-end solution).
    - Users are not buying or managing any infrastructure (like aircraft or vehicles).

In summary, just as travelers choose different trip styles based on their preferences, organizations can select the right cloud delivery model based on factors like size, skillset, workloads, privacy, security, and customization needs.

Cloud deployment and types

The cloud deployment methodology can vary depending on how the cloud services are provided. It is also defined by how the services are managed and how they take responsibility. Based on this, there are four commonly used cloud deployment types.

Public cloud

This is a type of cloud computing model where computing resources are provided over the public Internet. These cloud providers are generally key players with extensive global reach.

In this model, resources are shared between different individuals and organizations and provided on demand in general, with options to reserve certain types of resources for a specific amount of time.

The advantages and characteristics of the public cloud are as follows:

- Organizations and users share the same infrastructure.
- Nearly infinitely scalable.
- It forms the core of cloud computing and provides a wide range of services, including computing, storage, networking, development, deployment, security, and analytical services.
- Reduced IT operational costs.
- Pay-as-you-go model.

The most common public cloud providers include the following:

- **Amazon Web Services (AWS)**
- Microsoft Azure
- Google Cloud
- Alibaba
- IBM Cloud

Private cloud

This is a type of cloud computing model where the computing resources are dedicated to a single customer.

In this model, no resources are shared between customers and organizations, and it typically follows a single-tenant model. This is also called an internal cloud or corporate cloud.

The advantages and characteristics of the private cloud are as follows:

- Companies and organizations do not share any infrastructure.
- The tenant has exclusive access to dedicated hardware and software resources.
- Isolated Access, hence, offers a higher level of security and privacy.
- Best suited when a strict compliance mandate is required.
- Most used when dealing with **personally identifiable information (PII)**, medical data, financial data, or companies dealing with regulatory, military, and critical affairs.

Hybrid cloud

Hybrid cloud is a cloud computing model that integrates private and public cloud environments, offering scalability, security, and regulatory compliance. It allows organizations to keep sensitive workloads on-premises while utilizing the public cloud for compute-intensive tasks.

Use case

Hybrid cloud in healthcare: A leading healthcare provider needs to process **electronic health records (EHRs)**, which contain sensitive patient data. Due to HIPAA compliance, these records must remain in a private cloud or on-premises data center. However, the provider also wants to utilize AI for predictive diagnostics and to improve patient care.

Hybrid cloud solution: This solution would involve the following core components:

- **Private cloud (On-premises data center)**: Stores sensitive patient records securely, ensuring regulatory compliance.

- **Public cloud (AWS, Azure, Google Cloud)**: Runs AI-driven analytics on anonymized datasets, identifying patterns for early disease detection.

- **Secure VPN and API Gateway**: Ensures secure, controlled data exchange between private and public cloud environments.

Business benefits of hybrid cloud: The following are the key benefits of hybrid cloud in healthcare:

- **Regulatory compliance**: Meets legal data security requirements.

- **AI-powered insights**: Uses public cloud analytics for faster, smarter diagnostics.

- **Cost optimization**: Reduces on-premises infrastructure costs while maintaining **security.**

- **Resiliency and business continuity**: Ensures uninterrupted patient data access.

In summary, the hybrid cloud enables organizations to comply with security requirements while taking advantage of public cloud scalability and analytics. This strategy is particularly critical in the healthcare, finance, and government sectors.

Multi-cloud

This is a type of cloud computing model in which multiple cloud providers are used to deliver business value. In this setup, the resources can be private or public.

The advantages and characteristics of the multi-cloud are as follows:

- This provides flexibility and choice where organizations can choose the best offerings from each cloud provider.

- Provides better cost optimization by choosing the cost-effective products suited for the business operation.

- Eliminates cloud vendor lock-ins, and the setup makes the provider's offerings highly competitive.

GovCloud

This is a type of cloud computing model, GovCloud, which involves cloud computing environments designed specifically for government agencies and organizations. It provides a secure, compliant, and controlled platform for government services, data storage, and applications.

In this setup, the resources can be private or public.

The advantages and characteristics of a GovCloud are as follows:

- **Isolation**: GovCloud operates separately from public cloud services, ensuring data privacy and security.

- **Certifications**: It complies with certifications like FedRAMP (U.S.), IRAP (Australia), HIPAA, and others.

- **Access controls**: Strict access controls limit who can manage and access GovCloud resources.

- **Audit trails**: Detailed logs track user actions for transparency and accountability.

- **Service availability**: GovCloud maintains high availability for critical government services.

Cloud computing services

The following are the core categories of services provided by cloud computing:

- **Compute**: Compute services provide virtualized resources for running applications, processing data, and executing code. These resources include virtual machines, containers, and serverless functions. Users can scale compute capacity up or down as needed.

- o **Use case**: Organizations deploy applications, host websites, and perform data processing.
- o **Examples**: Amazon EC2 (AWS), Azure Virtual Machines, and Google Compute Engine.

- **Storage**: Cloud storage services offer scalable and durable data storage. They allow users to store files, databases, backups, and other data objects. Different storage types include object storage, block storage, and file storage.
  - o **Use case**: Storing files, serving media content, and managing databases.
  - o **Examples**: AWS **Simple Storage Service** (**S3**), Azure Blob Storage, and Google Cloud Storage.

- **Networking**: Networking services enable connectivity between cloud resources. Users can create virtual networks, set up load balancers, configure firewalls, and establish secure connections.
  - o **Use case**: Building secure and reliable network architectures.
  - o **Examples**: Amazon **Virtual Private Cloud** (**VPC**), Azure Virtual Network, and Google VPC.

- **Security**: Cloud security services focus on protecting data, applications, and infrastructure. Features include **identity and access management** (**IAM**), encryption, threat detection, and compliance.
  - o **Use case**: Ensuring data privacy, preventing unauthorized access, and meeting regulatory requirements.
  - o **Examples**: AWS IAM, Azure Security Center, and Google Cloud Security Command Center.

- **Machine learning and AI**: These services provide tools and APIs for building, training, and deploying machine learning models. Users can analyze data, extract insights, and automate processes.
  - o **Use case**: Developing intelligent applications, natural language processing, and predictive analytics.
  - o **Examples**: AWS SageMaker, Azure Machine Learning, and Google AI Platform.

- **Observability and tracing**: Observability services help monitor and understand system behavior. They provide metrics, logs, and distributed tracing to troubleshoot issues and optimize performance.
  - o **Use case**: Diagnosing problems, improving reliability, and ensuring efficient resource utilization.
  - o **Examples**: AWS CloudWatch, Azure Monitor, and Google Cloud Trace.

- **CI/CD and DevOps**: These services support **continuous integration** (**CI**) and **continuous deployment** (**CD**) pipelines. Developers automate code testing, build processes, and deploy workflows.
  - o **Use case**: Streamlining software development, reducing manual tasks, and ensuring rapid releases.
  - o **Examples**: AWS CodePipeline, Azure DevOps, and Google Cloud Build.

Cloud computing patterns

The following are the common architectural patterns in cloud computing. These patterns provide solutions to common challenges faced by architects and developers when designing systems in the cloud. Whether you are building applications on AWS, Microsoft Azure, or Google Cloud, understanding these patterns is crucial for creating robust, scalable, and efficient architectures.

Anti-corruption layer: The anti-corruption layer acts as a bridge between modern applications and legacy systems. By isolating communication and handling data translation, new components remain untangled from existing, often complex, systems. In AWS, consider using custom services or AWS Lambda functions to implement this pattern.

Here is a list of popular computing architectural patterns that will facilitate building scalable and highly efficient systems:

- **Asynchronous request-reply**: Decoupling frontend and backend processing is essential for responsiveness and scalability. The asynchronous request-reply pattern allows backend tasks to be executed asynchronously while providing immediate feedback to users. AWS offers Amazon SQS for reliable message queuing and Lambda for event-driven processing.

- **Backends for frontends (BFF)**: Different client types (web, mobile, etc.) often require tailored APIs. The BFF pattern involves creating separate backend services optimized for specific frontends. In AWS, build custom BFF services using Lambda or Amazon API Gateway.

- **Bulkhead pattern**: To prevent cascading failures, isolate components into pools. The bulkhead pattern ensures that if one part of the system fails, others remain unaffected. AWS provides options like separate EC2 instances or containers for implementing bulkheads.

- **Cache-aside pattern**: Caching frequently accessed data improves performance. The cache-aside pattern involves loading data into a cache on demand. Leverage Amazon Elasticache (Redis or Memcached) or build custom caching solutions.

- **Choreography**: Move away from central orchestrators. With the Choreography pattern, each service decides how and when to process business operations. Use AWS Step Functions or custom event-driven workflows for loosely coupled interactions.

- **Circuit breaker pattern**: Prevent repeated calls to failing services by temporarily opening the circuit. The Circuit Breaker Pattern enhances system resilience. Implement custom circuit breakers or use AWS Lambda for graceful degradation.

Cloud computing paradigms

The paradigms discussed in the following section are commonly used in modern-day cloud computing.

Serverless computing

This is an execution model of cloud computing that utilizes serverless cloud services. Serverless is a concept that includes managed services that do not require intervention from end users while using those services.

Serverless means no servers to manage (for us), but there are always servers under the hood (managed by the cloud/ service provider).

In this paradigm, the services scale up/down automatically based on the demand, and there are no virtual servers/ EC2 instances involved, and obviously no need for any patching requirements. This is becoming increasingly popular due to its low cost and pay-as-you-go model.

For example, AWS Lambda is an offering from AWS that allows us to write code (from a vast majority of supported languages and runtimes) and execute it as required (in response to an event, on a timer, or manually). This Lambda function works in response to a single event or thousands of events. Lambda service can scale to cater to the demand and is only charged for the number of executions and the amount of memory used.

This feature, in which a service can scale automatically and infinitely to cater to demand while following a pay-as-you-go model and providing required customizations to users to suit their business, is a classic example of serverless computing.

Some of the AWS serverless offerings are as follows:
- API Gateway
- Event bridge
- CloudFormation
- CloudFront
- Amazon CodeBuild, CodeDeploy, and CodePipeline

A few Google Cloud serverless offerings are as follows:
- Google Cloud Functions
- Anthos
- Google Distributed Cloud
- Google Kubernetes Engine

A few Microsoft Azure serverless offerings are as follows:
- Azure Functions
- Azure Service Bus
- Azure Service Fabric
- Azure App configuration

Cloud edge computing

This is a type of cloud computing that extends cloud services closer to the data source. The data sources can be devices, sensors, or even users. Edge computing serves as a decentralized extension of cloud computing, bringing computation and data storage closer to the edge devices. Here are the key points:

- **Edge devices**: In edge computing, we focus on devices and networks physically close to the user. These devices function as gatekeepers, managing data flow between service providers and users. Examples include Wi-Fi routers.

- **Edge data centers**: Smaller data centers located near the network edge deliver cloud computing resources to these devices.

- **Local processing**: Edge computing aims to reduce resource requirements by processing data closer to where it is generated. It filters and processes data locally, sending only relevant or compressed information to the cloud for further analysis, archiving, or technical processing. This is opening a whole new world of computing and is the backbone for **Internet of Things** (**IoT**) technology.

- **Use cases**: Edge computing is crucial for scenarios like real-time analytics, IoT, and applications requiring low latency.

Event-driven computing

The **event-driven architecture** (**EDA**) is a software design pattern that allows systems to detect, process, manage, and react to real-time events as they happen. This is applicable to software design but also relevant to cloud computing since most serverless services work alongside real-time events from other sources and are thus highly significant in the world of cloud computing. Additionally, most cloud providers have also provided many managed services and offerings to build event-driven architectures.

The following are the key points:

- **Event detection**: EDA systems continuously monitor events (such as user actions, sensor data, or messages) and react promptly.

- **Real-time responsiveness**: When an event occurs, relevant information is sent to all the apps, systems, and people that need it for immediate action.

- **Applications and use cases**: EDA powers various applications, including multiplayer games, online banking, streaming services, and generative AI.

- **Loose coupling**: EDA systems are loosely coupled, allowing independent development, scalability, fault tolerance, and integration with external systems.

- **Event-driven programming (EDP)**: EDA often involves event-driven programming, where code responds to incoming events.

- **Event processing technologies**: Apache Kafka, a distributed event streaming platform, is commonly used in EDA for efficient communication.

Cloud-native application development

Cloud-native application development refers to the process of creating applications using practices, tools, and technologies optimized for deployment and operation in cloud environments. The following is a concise summary:

- **Definition**: Cloud-native development involves designing, building, and deploying applications in a way that fully leverages the capabilities provided by cloud computing platforms. It emphasizes agility, scalability, resilience, and efficient resource utilization.

- **Key aspects**: Microservices architecture: Cloud-native apps consist of multiple small, interdependent services called microservices. These services work independently and take minimal computing resources to run.

- **DevOps and CD**: Cloud-native development embraces agile practices, automated tools, and modern design culture. Developers use CI/CD pipelines to rapidly build and deploy scalable applications.

- **Cost efficiency**: By avoiding costly physical infrastructure, companies save on operational expenditure.

- **High availability**: Resilient cloud-native applications ensure minimal downtime and can scale resources during peak demand. Cloud-native applications use a collaborative approach, are highly scalable, and adapt well to different platforms.

- **Futureproofing**: Cloud-native development prepares organizations for both the present and the future, ensuring consistent user experiences across public, private, or hybrid clouds.

Conclusion

This chapter covered the fundamentals of virtualization, an introduction to cloud computing, and a comparison of cloud computing to on-premises data center-based approaches. It also showed common delivery models (IaaS, PaaS, and SaaS) to deliver cloud services to customers. The focus shifted to understanding different deployment models (public, private, hybrid, and multi-cloud). Then, the common cloud service-based categorization was shown to make the readers ready to embark on the journey of cloud computing with common architectural patterns.

The next chapter will focus on the serverless paradigm, exploring how serverless services can help businesses and organizations overcome common challenges in rapidly transitioning to the cloud while minimizing infrastructure costs.

CHAPTER 3
Serverless Systems

Introduction

Serverless computing is a cloud execution model where developers focus on writing code while cloud providers handle infrastructure management, scaling, and maintenance. This paradigm enables businesses to build and deploy applications faster while minimizing operational overhead. For instance, companies like *Netflix*, *Coca-Cola*, and *Airbnb* have leveraged the serverless model to reduce infrastructure costs and scale seamlessly to meet customer demands. These examples highlight the transformative power of serverless computing, setting the stage for understanding its core principles, deployment models, and cloud provider offerings.

The chapter also elucidates how these technologies can benefit many entities, including government agencies, non-profit organizations, educational institutions, and research and development sectors. Furthermore, it underscores how the effective deployment of serverless and cloud-native systems can yield substantial advantages in efficiency, scalability, cost-effectiveness, economies of scale, rapid market response, and agility, catering to the needs of entities ranging from individuals to large-scale enterprises.

Structure

This chapter covers the following topics:

- Serverless computing paradigm
- Serverless architecture usage patterns
- Cloud-native systems
- Serverless implementation in AWS
- Serverless implementation in Azure
- Serverless implementation in Google Cloud

Objectives

Upon completing this chapter, readers will have gained a thorough understanding of the core concepts of serverless and cloud native systems. They will have explored the advantages and potential challenges associated with these technologies and learned about their implementation and offerings. Readers will gain insights into the offerings in the serverless and cloud native space provided by leading public cloud service providers such as Azure, AWS, and Google Cloud. This will enable them to visualize how these theoretical concepts are transformed into practical applications.

Furthermore, the chapter provides readers with various use cases and examples, which solidify their understanding and establish a robust foundation for the core concepts and services. The book's subsequent chapters will further expand and explore these foundational concepts. Thus, this chapter serves as a comprehensive guide, providing readers with the necessary knowledge and context to effectively navigate the complex landscape of serverless and cloud native systems.

Serverless computing paradigm

Serverless computing is an application development and execution model that empowers developers to build and run code without the burden of managing infrastructure or paying for idle resources.

Serverless computing revolutionizes industries by enhancing scalability, reducing costs, and accelerating innovation. While common sectors like healthcare and finance are leading adopters, other specialized industries leverage serverless computing for high-performance, event-driven workloads.

The following are some of the examples where industries are uniquely benefiting from serverless computing:

- **Aerospace and defense:** Serverless enables real-time telemetry processing for satellite communications, enhances autonomous drone fleet management, and secures high-frequency data exchanges for mission-critical defense applications.

- **Cryptocurrency and blockchain:** Serverless computing powers real-time transaction validation, fraud detection, and smart contract execution, ensuring decentralized networks remain efficient and scalable.

- **Space exploration:** Agencies like NASA and private space companies use serverless to analyze real-time deep-space data, process massive sensor data from planetary rovers, and simulate astronomical events.

- **Military and cybersecurity:** Military organizations deploy serverless computing for real-time cyber threat detection, AI-driven intelligence analysis, and logistics automation in mission-critical environments.

- **Autonomous vehicles and smart transportation:** Serverless facilitates AI-based traffic predictions, **vehicle-to-infrastructure (V2I)** communications, and fleet telemetry monitoring for connected and self-driving cars.

- **Genomics and biotechnology**: Serverless architectures enable genomic sequencing, real-time DNA analysis, and biomedical research processing, allowing scientists to analyze large datasets without expensive infrastructure overhead.

The serverless offerings provided by leading cloud providers are predominantly cloud-native or directly contribute to building cloud-native systems. By adopting these solutions, institutions and organizations can swiftly reduce resource expenditures on underutilized infrastructure. These resources often spend considerable time on tasks like provisioning, security updates, and custom monitoring.

While cloud providers manage heavy lifting, developers can focus on writing core business logic. Simultaneously, organizations can deliver features to customers, leaving scalability in the capable hands of the cloud providers.

The pay-as-you-go model ensures that costs align with actual usage. No need to manually turn off or shut down resources—the absence of usage incurs no expense.

Once architectural guidelines and security practices are established, new features can be experimented with rapidly, enabling businesses to stay competitive in our ever-evolving digital landscape.

Remember, serverless does not mean no servers. It simply emphasizes that the management of underlying infrastructure is abstracted away from users, whether individuals, organizations, institutions, or enterprises, by the provider.

Key benefits of serverless architectures

The following are the key benefits of serverless architecture, which offer a significant return on investment. While this is applicable, the exact benefit and the amount of benefit depend on the use case:

- **No server management**: This eliminates the total need to manage any servers and their provisioning. The focus will shift to delivering value.

- **Elastic scaling and cost efficiency**: Serverless computing optimizes scalability and cost by dynamically adjusting resources based on demand. AWS Lambda, for instance, scales from zero to thousands of concurrent executions in milliseconds, ensuring that workloads run efficiently without manual intervention. This level of elasticity prevents over-provisioning and eliminates unnecessary costs associated with idle infrastructure.

  Businesses using serverless architectures report up to a 60% reduction in infrastructure costs compared to always-on servers. With a pay-per-use pricing model, organizations only pay for execution time and resource consumption, making serverless computing one of the most cost-effective cloud solutions. This dynamic cost structure benefits industries with spiky workloads, unpredictable traffic patterns, and high seasonal variability, such as e-commerce, gaming, and media streaming.

- **Faster time-to-market**: The serverless-based architectures speed up development and delivery cycles, hence allowing organizations to implement rapid prototyping and quicker release to customers.

- **Event-driven**: Most serverless architectures are event-driven; they respond to events happening in real-time; this is especially useful when dealing with events from IoT and devices (sensors, vehicles, home systems, or medical devices).

- **Microservices friendly**: Serverless technology complements microservice architectures, enabling the modularization of functions and facilitating individualized and infinitely scalable components.

- **Improved scalability**: The serverless systems can scale up (theoretically to infinite capacity) to meet increasing user demand.

- **Coding flexibility**: This is more of a developer productivity improvement that enables developers to write code in most programming languages.

- **Improved capacity planning**: There is little to no capacity planning in a fully serverless application, as there is no need to provision servers and their capacities.

- **High availability**: All the serverless services from major providers are HA by default, and the requests can be fulfilled in a matter of microseconds to seconds, even after an idle state. The backend infrastructure ensures the services are always available.

- **Reduced latency**: Most cloud service providers often provide networking as a service, enabling serverless-based applications to run closer to end-users and diversified geographical locations, ensuring ultra-low latency to end-users

- **CapEx to OpEx**: With serverless architectures, there is no provisioning of physical servers and thus taking away all the CapEx and moving them to OpEx, thus saving significantly on initial investments.

Challenges with serverless architectures

Serverless architectures and cloud adoption have been increasing in industries and verticals, and more than 40% of organizations are using some sort of serverless service. With increasing adoption, there are also some challenges that organizations could face, and here is an insight into some of them:

- **Reduced control**: In a typical serverless implementation, the cloud provider manages everything, from resource provisioning to scaling and maintenance. While this simplicity is advantageous for many use cases, it can be limiting for businesses and organizations that require more granular control over their infrastructure. Areas such as security, networking, storage, and capacity management may fall short in a serverless environment. Consequently, some scenarios deem serverless architectures unsuitable due to the trade-off between convenience and control.

- **Performance impact**: While serverless architectures are inherently highly available, scalable, and low-latency, there is a potential issue known as cold starts. These cold starts can affect the performance of your applications. Imagine it like a car engine taking a moment to warm up before it runs smoothly. Similarly, when a serverless function is invoked after being idle, it might experience a slight delay due to initialization. This latency can impact the responsiveness of your application. Keep this in mind when designing serverless solutions!

- **Vendor lock-in and mitigation strategies**: Vendor lock-in occurs when applications depend on a specific cloud provider's proprietary services. To reduce this risk, organizations can:

  o **Leverage multi-cloud strategies** by designing applications for different providers using Kubernetes (Knative) or cloud-agnostic tools like Terraform and OpenTelemetry.

  o **Utilize open-source serverless frameworks** such as OpenFaaS or Serverless Framework, which enable portability across multiple cloud platforms.

  o **Design modular architectures** that separate cloud-specific functions from business logic, making migrations easier.

- **Cold starts and mitigation strategies**: Cold starts refer to the delay in initializing a serverless function after a period of inactivity. To mitigate this issue, developers can:

  o Use provisioned concurrency (available in AWS Lambda) to keep functions warm and ready to execute.

  o Optimize function code and dependencies to reduce initialization time—smaller packages load faster.

  o Implement periodic warm-up triggers, such as scheduled invocations using CloudWatch Events or Step Functions, ensuring that functions remain active when needed.

By applying these strategies, organizations can enjoy the benefits of serverless computing while effectively managing potential drawbacks.

Serverless architecture usage patterns

Serverless architectures excel in various workloads and scenarios. These components can seamlessly complement on-premises systems or serve as assistants to existing server-based implementations. Additionally, they can be the foundation for fully serverless applications.

Here are some of the common use cases and usage patterns for serverless architectures:

- **Event-driven and trigger-based**: These use cases involve responding to events (internal or external); in this paradigm, a serverless component will wake up (trigger) upon the arrival of the request, complete the assigned task, and release the resources. The cost is only for the amount of resources utilized and the time for which these resources are utilized.

- **APIs**: An **application programming interface (API)** is a framework and guidebook to interact with applications. It defines methods of communication between various software components. APIs enable different software systems to interact with each other, facilitating the sharing of data and functionality. They are at the core of computing because they allow for the creation of complex, feature-rich applications. Without APIs, software systems would be isolated and unable to leverage each other's capabilities, limiting the scope and functionality of software development. APIs function as bridges between different software systems, allowing them to work together and achieve more than they could individually. They are fundamental to the interconnected nature of modern computing systems.

A common use case of serverless is to build these API's. More examples and specific services to build these APIs will be covered in subsequent chapters.

- **Isolated tasks**: Serverless functions provide a straightforward way to run back-end and asynchronous tasks. These tasks could be as simple as formatting an email or transcoding and transcribing from video and audio content. These resources are only required when there is a request.

- **Message orchestration and delivery**: Serverless-based services can be used to manage the orchestration of events and their messages. These can also accumulate, transform, and catalog the data before delivering it to defined targets. Most cloud providers provide multiple offerings of orchestration services to collect, trigger, orchestrate, and deliver messages and events.

- **Storage and archival**: With the complexity of businesses and data growing, there is also an increasing need for various storage options and types of data that we need to manage (it could be objects, audio, video, messages, or even structured and unstructured data). Cloud providers provide ample services to enable data storage and retrieval, and these scale up / down in a serverless fashion.

- **Hosting and user interfaces**: Cloud providers provide services to host websites and applications using serverless paradigms without worrying about the underlying capacity and demand.

- **Content distribution**: Content distribution involves making content available over the internet across geographical boundaries; most of the content distribution services from major cloud providers are serverless. These services will be covered in greater depth in subsequent chapters.

- **Build and deployment tools**: Serverless services also provide options to manage CI/CD pipelines and on-demand build and deployment tools, eliminating the need to manage and procure build servers and thus helping in streamless application deployment processes and practices.

- **Advanced machine learning and generative AI**: Many cloud providers now provide GenAI services on demand and provide these services as an API call, and can scale automatically without the need to fully retrain these machine learning models.

While there are multiple ways to use and leverage serverless services, the exact use case depends on the scenario.

- **Real-time notifications**: Modern businesses rely on real-time notifications and analytics to enhance user experience, improve operational efficiency, and respond to critical events. Serverless computing enables instant data processing, making these capabilities scalable, cost-effective, and event-driven.

The following are some of the use cases that leverage real-time notifications:

  o **Financial services**: Banks and trading platforms use serverless computing to trigger fraud alerts and account activity notifications in milliseconds.

  o **IoT and smart homes**: Serverless functions process sensor data to send instant alerts about fire hazards, security breaches, or appliance malfunctions.

  o **E-commerce and customer engagement**: Serverless, event-driven architectures deliver personalized promotions, order tracking updates, and abandoned cart notifications in real time.

  o **Healthcare and emergency response**: Serverless enables instant alerts for patient vitals monitoring, notifying caregivers when critical thresholds are breached.

- **Serverless-powered monitoring and analytics**: The following provides a list of common use cases for monitoring and analytics:

- o **Security and threat detection**: Organizations deploy serverless **Security Information and Event Management (SIEM)** solutions to monitor log activity, detect anomalies, and respond to cyber threats in real time.

- o **IT infrastructure health checks**: Cloud-native monitoring services (e.g., AWS CloudWatch, Azure Monitor) analyze serverless function performance, API latency, and error rates to ensure high availability.

- o **Business intelligence and data analytics**: Retailers and enterprises stream event logs to services like AWS Kinesis and Amazon OpenSearch, extracting insights on user engagement, operational trends, and predictive analysis.

- o **Industrial IoT and smart manufacturing**: Serverless analytics process machine sensor data, identifying equipment malfunctions, predictive maintenance needs, and production inefficiencies in factories

- • **Process orchestration**: Another common use case involves step-based orchestration (for example, processing a customer order, which could include multiple steps with few waits in steps); a system is required to maintain a state between the steps and to complete subsequent steps automatically. Cloud providers provide a variety of services to enable serverless process orchestration.

Cloud-native systems

Cloud-native is a generic term for modern applications that fully leverage cloud computing potential. They are often comprised of native microservices and services designed to run specifically within the cloud environment with maximum scalability and are built to be flexible, resilient, and highly available. These systems are adaptable to changing business needs, allowing organizations to respond quickly to demand, innovate faster, and provide exceptional user experiences.

Unlike traditional monolithic architectures, cloud-native systems decompose functionalities into loosely coupled services that can be independently developed, deployed, and scaled. They also enable rapid iterations, making them well-suited for dynamic workloads and fast-changing business needs.

These systems are purposely designed with rapid scalability and to harness unique and native features offered by the cloud provider.

Serverless and managed services allow developers to focus on the business and operational logic instead of infrastructure, and they fully embrace CI and CD, enabling frequent updates and releases.

Most cloud-native systems come with a pay-as-you-go model to reduce capital expenditure.

Serverless implementation in AWS

Amazon Web Services (AWS) offers a suite of serverless technologies that allow developers to build and run applications without managing servers. They have serverless and managed services across a broad spectrum of use cases and specializations. The following will cover a high-level view of those categories, but subsequent chapters will cover more details.

Compute

Computing in the context of cloud computing refers to the amount of computational resources that are allocated to run applications. Compute as such encompasses everything required to perform core operations involving processing power, storage, memory, networking, and other resources required for the computational success of any software/program/utility. Compute resources are measurable quantities of computing power that can be requested, allocated, and consumed for computing activities. The services are as follows:

- **AWS Lambda**: AWS Lambda is the most commonly used, cheapest, and most robust serverless service provided by AWS. Lambda runs code, performs operations, and returns results without any user interaction. Lambda is highly scalable, supports a vast majority of programming languages and runtimes, and follows a pay-as-you-go model. This is equivalent to running a function in the cloud on demand and has seamless integration with a majority of AWS services.

- **AWS Fargate**: AWS Fargate can be considered a magic genie, which is a self-contained container wizard that can help us run containers (self-contained software) in a scalable way. Fargate encompasses two services - **Elastic Container Service (ECS)** and Amazon **Elastic Kubernetes Service (EKS)**.

Storage

In the field of serverless computing, storage pertains to the process of securely storing data within a cloud environment. This data resides across multiple interconnected resources within the cloud, ensuring accessibility and scalability. AWS provides a range of serverless storage services, each tailored to specific requirements and use cases:

- **Amazon Simple Storage Service (S3)**: Amazon S3 is an object storage service that offers industry-leading scalability, data availability, security, and performance. S3 is one of the oldest offerings from AWS, and the capabilities of S3 have evolved over the past 10 years, making it the most robust storage solution with seamless integration to every other component and service provided by AWS. This helps us to store data of various kinds and sizes and is infinitely scalable. This also comes with various layers and tiers of how the data and its lifecycle can be managed. This is suited and is the backbone for most applications and types (Mobile, Web, standalone, backup, IoT, big-data analytics, and more.)

- **Amazon Elastic File System (EFS)**: Amazon EFS provides a simple, scalable, elastic file system for Linux-based workloads for use with AWS cloud services and on-premises resources. EFS is a cloud-based storage service that works as a serverless file cabinet and works seamlessly with EC2 instances (AWS servers on the cloud). This is elastic and can scale to petabytes of storage, and scaling is seamless, allowing applications to scale up dynamically.

- **Amazon RDS Aurora Serverless**: Amazon RDS Aurora Serverless is an on-demand, autoscaling configuration for Amazon Aurora. There is some initial configuration required in terms of allocation, which is expressed in **Aurora Capacity Unit (ACU)**, and it can automatically scale up between the bounds specified by the minimum and maximum capacity units. It is perfect for workloads that can be intermittent and infrequent, but RDS also provides provisioned capacity modes for applications that can predict usage and demand. One of the key benefits is the granular per-second billing and easy options to perform data replication, migration, and synchronization.

Content distribution

In the context of cloud computing refers to the process of delivering content from the source to the end-users efficiently. This is often achieved through a distributed network of servers, also known as a **content delivery network (CDN)**, which ensures high availability and performance by serving content to users from the nearest geographical server. AWS offers several serverless content distribution services, each designed to address unique needs and use cases:

- **Amazon CloudFront**: Amazon CloudFront is a fast CDN service that securely delivers data, videos, applications, and APIs to customers globally with low latency and high transfer speeds, all within a developer-friendly environment. This is the go-to option to deploy scalable global websites with ultra-low-latency render times.

- **AWS Elemental MediaPackage**: AWS Elemental MediaPackage is a cloud-based service that manages media preparation and the delivery of media and video content for streaming. The complex process of video packaging is handled and managed by AWS. This empowers content providers to efficiently package, secure, and seamlessly distribute video content accessible across a wide variety of devices and form factors.

- **AWS Elemental MediaLive**: AWS Elemental MediaLive is also a content delivery service aimed at broadcasters and content providers requiring live streaming across platforms. This also allows live media encoding, and the process of provisioning video encoding infrastructure can be done in minutes.

- **AWS Elemental MediaConvert**: AWS Elemental MediaConvert is another variation of other media services but specializes in the creation of on-demand content, often termed **video-on-demand** (**VOD**), and this is serverless, operating at scale.

- **AWS Elemental MediaStore**: This is another serverless media offering aimed at providing low-latency, high-performance, scalable media storage optimized for media-specific workloads and is ideal for building streaming platforms.

- **AWS Elemental MediaTailor**: AWS Elemental MediaTailor, as the name suggests, helps in tailoring and personalizing video content and also allows the inclusion of live content, ads with real-time metrics, and cost dashboards.

Integration

Integration in the context of cloud computing refers to the process of enabling individual computing systems and software applications to function as a coordinated, cohesive whole. This is often achieved by allowing these systems to communicate with each other in a decoupled manner, thereby enhancing scalability and reliability. AWS offers several serverless integration services, each designed to address diverse needs and use cases:

- **Amazon EventBridge**: Amazon EventBridge is a serverless event bus that lets you build event-driven applications at scale across AWS and existing systems. EventBridge can ingest data from a variety of sources, including custom apps running in the cloud and other AWS services, and can publish data to targets. This allows you to create loosely coupled, event-driven architectures that can help you boost agility and build reliable, scalable applications.

- **Amazon Simple Queue Service (SQS)**: Amazon SQS is a fully managed message queuing service that enables you to decouple and scale microservices, distributed systems, and serverless applications. One of the core features of SQS is to decouple various parts of an application; when SQS is introduced between two components, the interacting applications do not have to talk to each other and will not have a direct dependency in terms of scaling or maintenance. One of the components can publish events to an SQS at any time and frequency without having to worry about the availability of the application that reads from the queue. This type of application decoupling forms the backbone of modern microservice and event-driven architectures.

- **AWS Glue**: AWS Glue is an integration/**extract, transform, and load** (**ETL**) service that helps in data discovery and data preparation and is an effortless way to catalog and query big data in real-time. AWS Glue service manages the serverless environment required for end-to-end data transformation, discovery, query, and metrics. The data to AWS Glue can come from multiple sources and formats.

- **API Gateway**: The API Gateway is a managed service that acts as a front door or the main gate to the fortress of AWS applications. This is a fully managed and serverless service offered by AWS, which helps us build and provide API's as services. These APIs can be of multiple types (HTTP, REST, or WebSocket). These APIs help to expose application functionality as an API call with their own access methodologies.

  The API Gateway service manages everything required for the functioning of this service, and users do not have to maintain any API servers. Since all the underlying infrastructure and security are managed by the provider (AWS), this is one of the most common integration of Serverless services.

Notification and real-time communication

In the context of cloud computing, notification and real-time communication refer to the process of sending information or alerts to users or systems and enabling instant, two-way interaction. AWS offers several serverless services in this category, each designed to address unique needs and use cases:

- **Amazon Simple Notification Service (SNS)**: Amazon SNS is a fully managed, serverless pub/sub messaging service that enables you to decouple microservices, distributed systems, and serverless applications. One of the common architectural patterns with SNS is to fan out events and messages to multiple recipients at the same time, which can seamlessly work alongside SQS. It also supports information publishing in various formats, including SMS, Email, and other protocols.

- **AWS AppSync**: AWS AppSync is a fully serverless, managed service that can help us build real-time web and mobile applications and function as a managed GraphQL server that can securely connect to data sources like AWS DynamoDB, Lambda, or any HTTP data source. It supports real-time subscriptions as well as offline access to app data, and hence can be used for real-time updates.

Analytics

In the context of cloud computing, analytics refers to the systematic computational analysis of data or statistics. It involves the discovery, interpretation, and communication of meaningful patterns in data and applying those patterns toward effective decision-making. AWS offers several serverless analytics services, each designed to address diverse needs and use cases:

- **Amazon Kinesis data streams**: It is a fully managed service that enables real-time collection and processing of streaming data at scale. It allows applications to ingest high-throughput data streams and process them with low latency using services like AWS Lambda or custom consumers, making it ideal for event-driven architectures, monitoring pipelines, and analytics use cases.

- **Amazon Redshift Serverless**: Amazon Redshift Serverless is a serverless data warehouse offering that enables users to run analytics without provisioning clusters. It automatically scales capacity and supports complex analytical queries over petabytes of data.

- **Amazon Managed Streaming for Apache Kafka (MSK)**: Amazon MSK is a fully managed service that makes it easy to build and run applications that use Apache Kafka to process streaming data. With Amazon MSK, you can use native Apache Kafka APIs to populate data lakes, stream changes to and from databases, and power machine learning and analytics applications.

- **Amazon EMR Serverless**: Amazon EMR Serverless is a deployment option for Amazon EMR that provides a serverless runtime environment. EMR helps in serverless analytics (with extensive support for Apache Spark and Hive).

Cloud management, logging, and auditing

Cloud management refers to managing and organizing cloud computing products and services that operate in the cloud. It also encompasses processes, strategies, policies, technologies, and controls. Logging and auditing involve recording and storing interactions between systems and the steps a particular system takes to accomplish its job. AWS offers various serverless services to accomplish these tasks:

- **AWS Management Console**: This is the principal place to manage and monitor AWS resources. This provides a web user interface and acts as a dashboard with options to navigate to unique features, services, and categories.

- **AWS CloudWatch**: This is a centralized service to manage metrics covering a vast majority of services. This is extensively used with compute services (like Lambda), but most services use this to log and track system and user-defined metrics.

- **AWS CloudTrail**: This is not an AWS serverless offering, but an offering that will help to control and manage audit trails of all the serverless services and every API call made by every application and interfacing entity.

Infrastructure management and deployment tools

Infrastructure management refers to the process of managing cloud infrastructure, which involves provisioning resources, building deployment pipelines, and automating change management activities. AWS provides many serverless services to manage infrastructure provisioning and deployment:

- **AWS CloudFormation**: This is the backbone that takes care of and is responsible for provisioning every resource (Serverless or Servers) within AWS. CloudFormation allows infrastructure to be defined as code (IaC), allowing us to script building resources while also giving the flexibility to replicate/ configure resource management across different environments.

- **AWS Serverless Application Model (SAM)**: This is an open-source framework for deploying serverless infrastructure and code. AWS SAM provides a shorthand syntax to declare resources and mappings. SAM templates eventually get converted into CloudFormation templates before they are executed.

- **AWS Cloud Development Kit (CDK)**: The AWS CDK is a toolkit and a framework that facilitates **infrastructure as code** (**IaC**) through commonly used programming languages. This makes it easy to define cloud resources in familiar languages in their syntax. The CDK code will eventually be converted into **CloudFormation** (**CFT**) templates before they are executed to create/manage resources.

- **AWS CodeBuild, CodeCommit, and CodeDeploy**: These are the tools and services that enable the development and deployment of applications and the management of pipelines. AWS CodeBuild is a fully managed CI/CD service that compiles source code, runs tests, and produces packages ready for deployment. This is serverless by design, and there is no need to provision build servers. AWS CodeCommit acts as a Git repository, and AWS CodeDeploy orchestrates end-to-end deployment processes.

Security, compliance, and identity services

The services under this category are responsible for managing and providing a means to secure the applications built on the cloud and help protect data both while in transit and while being transferred. AWS provides a comprehensive toolkit of services for managing identity. Here are some of the key services:

- **Identity and access management (IAM)**: IAM acts as a gatekeeper for the kingdom of AWS. It controls who can get in, what that entity can do, and controls all the places that entity can visit or interact with. It has all the tools to manage user permissions, roles, and access keys and can provide fine-grained access to users, systems, services, and entities. It is the backbone for secure cloud applications and is more relevant for Serverless services.

- **AWS Cognito**: This cloud-based service can manage user sign-up, sign-in, and identity management for web/mobile apps. This acts as a backstage for managing user identities and can integrate with existing identity management systems (including Microsoft AD, Google, Facebook Auth, and other similar platforms).

- **AWS Secrets Manager**: This acts as a digital vault to store sensitive information in the cloud; it is highly secure and is ideal for saving passwords, API keys, database credentials, and other confidential data. Cloud components and services can programmatically and securely access AWS Secrets Manager for their operations.

Serverless implementation in Azure

Microsoft Azure is a comprehensive cloud platform offering a wide range of services, including serverless options. It provides robust computing, storage, and networking capabilities. Azure Functions, Logic Apps, and Event Grid are key serverless services that allow developers to build scalable applications without managing infrastructure. Whether you are a student or an expert, Azure empowers you to focus on code and innovation:

- **Compute**:
    - **Azure Functions**: Azure Functions is Microsoft's answer to AWS Lambda, which provides a computing platform for building on-demand and event-driven systems. This is serverless and comes with the option to write code in multiple languages. Azure Functions can automatically scale based on demand and follow a pay-as-you-go model.
    - **Azure Logic Apps**: Logic Apps provide workflow automation through visual design. Create workflows that integrate with numerous services, APIs, and systems. Ideal for orchestrating complex processes and handling business logic.
    - **Azure Container Apps**: Deploy containerized applications without managing complex infrastructure. Write code in your preferred language or framework and scale dynamically based on HTTP traffic or events.
- **Database**:
    - **Azure SQL (Serverless)**: This is a database/storage offering by Microsoft to run database-based workloads (SQL). This is serverless and, hence, can automatically scale to meet increasing/decreasing demand.
- **DevOps and Developer tools**:
    - **Azure Bot Service**: These services help build conversational bots that interact naturally with users across various channels (text/SMS, Skype, Teams, and other tools), which is ideal for creating chatbots and virtual assistants.

Serverless implementation in Google Cloud

Google Cloud offers a suite of serverless technologies designed for simplicity and scalability. Cloud Run, Cloud Functions, and App Engine are prominent offerings. Cloud Run lets you deploy containerized applications, while Cloud Functions enables event-driven functions. App Engine abstracts infrastructure management, allowing developers to concentrate on writing code. Choose Google Cloud for efficient, serverless solutions tailored to your needs:

- **Compute**:
    - **Cloud Run**: Cloud Run provides a fully managed platform for building and deploying serverless applications. Develop using your preferred language or framework and scale automatically based on traffic. You can even deploy applications as containers.
    - **Cloud Functions**: Cloud Functions allow you to write single-purpose functions that respond to events. Ideal for lightweight, event-driven applications. Pay only for execution time.
    - **App Engine**: App Engine is a PaaS model from Google that helps us develop and host web-based applications in the cloud with no infrastructure to maintain. This allows developers to focus on the code and logic while the provider (Google) manages the underlying security and infrastructure. This supports multiple programming languages and frameworks and auto-scales to meet customer demands.

o **Google Kubernetes Engine (GKE) Autopilot**: GKE Autopilot provides a fully managed Kubernetes experience. It abstracts away cluster management, making deploying and managing containerized applications easier.

- **Orchestration**

  o **Eventarc**: This helps in the asynchronous delivery of events from various sources, including Google services, SaaS, and custom applications. It allows us to build event-driven applications without the need to maintain and customize the underlying infrastructure.

- **Storage/database**:

  o **Firestore**: Firestore empowers application developers to create efficient, real-time, and serverless applications. This helps with all kinds of applications, including chat apps, collaborative tools, and content management systems. Firestore automatically scales based on user demand and supports complex querying, indexing, and hierarchical data structures.

Conclusion

In this chapter, we embarked on a comprehensive exploration of the serverless paradigm, uncovering its potential to tackle the critical challenges faced by businesses in today's digital landscape. We looked into the intricacies of serverless concepts, examined diverse implementation modes, and explored the services that leading public cloud providers provide.

Our journey revealed that serverless and cloud-native systems offer many benefits across various domains. These technologies empower entities of all sizes, from government agencies to non-profit organizations, educational institutions, and research sectors.

Our journey revealed that serverless and cloud-native systems provide various benefits across various domains, empowering entities of all sizes, from government agencies to non-profits, educational institutions, and research sectors. These technologies enhance efficiency by streamlining resource allocation, enabling code execution without the operational burden of managing servers. They offer unparalleled scalability with auto-scaling capabilities that dynamically adapt to workload demands. The cost-effectiveness of serverless architectures stems from their pay-as-you-go pricing models, eliminating unnecessary expenses while leveraging economies of scale through shared cloud resources. Furthermore, serverless systems enable rapid market response by facilitating swift development and deployment cycles, helping businesses maintain a competitive edge. With inherent flexibility and agility, they cater to the diverse needs of both individuals and large-scale enterprises.

As we conclude this chapter, remember that successfully adopting serverless and cloud-native approaches hinges on understanding their nuances, selecting the right services, and aligning them with organizational goals. Whether you are building microservices, APIs, or event-driven applications, the serverless paradigm awaits your exploration.

The next chapter provides a guide for setting up an AWS Account and outlines the steps to start the cloud journey. Thus, it provides a solid understanding of the foundational steps to develop in AWS. It covers everything from setting up AWS Accounts and users to navigating the AWS Management Console and setting up a local machine to facilitate rapid development.

CHAPTER 4
Setting Up Your Cloud

Introduction

This chapter is a crucial step in your AWS journey, providing an in-depth guide to setting up your AWS Account and Environment. It will cover the practical aspects of creating a cloud environment for **Amazon Web Services** (**AWS**), the necessary steps to set up AWS accounts and profiles, and the login process to the Management Console. It will also delve into the essential tools and SDKs needed to get started, offering a hands-on approach to cloud setup.

Through this chapter, you will gain a solid understanding of the foundational steps to start developing on the AWS cloud. You will be well-equipped to navigate your cloud environment and be prepared to explore the vast possibilities cloud computing offers, setting the stage for your future AWS endeavors.

Structure

This chapter covers the following topics:

- AWS accounts, organizations, and types
- Signing up for an AWS account
- Navigating AWS Management Console
- Configuring the AWS Command Line Interface
- IAM user login and setup

Objectives

Setting up an AWS environment is the first step in leveraging cloud computing effectively. Whether an individual is exploring AWS for personal use, a startup is launching its first cloud-based product, or an enterprise is managing multiple accounts for compliance and security, understanding the foundational aspects of AWS account setup is crucial. AWS provides flexibility in structuring cloud environments, allowing users to create a single account for consolidated workloads or adopt a multi-account strategy using AWS Organizations to improve governance, security, and cost management. A well-planned AWS setup ensures scalability, operational efficiency, and adherence to best practices.

This chapter explores key concepts such as AWS accounts, IAM roles, and AWS Organizations, helping readers determine when to use single vs. multi-account structures. It also introduces real-world scenarios, such as a financial institution segmenting accounts for compliance or a SaaS provider isolating customer workloads, demonstrating how account structuring impacts security and operational management. Readers will also gain hands-on experience navigating the AWS Management Console, configuring IAM user roles, and utilizing the AWS CLI for efficient resource management.

By the end of this chapter, readers will have a strong foundational understanding of AWS account structures, security best practices, and governance strategies. They will be well-equipped to create, manage, and optimize AWS environments, ensuring an efficient, scalable, and secure cloud setup tailored to their needs.

AWS accounts, organizations, and types

An AWS account is a container or a self-contained vessel that hosts and holds together all the resources required to rent, provision, purchase, or subscribe to services. The services range from a space to upload a file to complex managed systems that can perform complex, multi-step, fully functional actions.

An account has security and provides technical isolation from other accounts. Isolating and managing AWS resources is a go-to strategy for any user or organization. A typical organization will have multiple AWS accounts managing specific actions, and the categorization could be based on business function or structured around operations.

For example, an organization can have one AWS account per development environment (e.g., sandbox, development, acceptance/QA, pre-production, production, and hyper care), or it could be based on operations (e.g., billing account, customer-facing account, auditing account, and similar). However, the exact structure depends on the organization's structure and complexity.

This also provides a clear distinction between costs and billing. Each account will have its own billing and expenses, but with the provision to roll up costs at multiple accounts (which will be covered in subsequent sections).

An AWS account provides a flexible approach to adapting and modifying business processes and needs as they grow. A multi-account strategy is one of the most common and robust ways to scale a business.

AWS Organization and multi-account strategies

AWS Organizations allow businesses to manage multiple AWS accounts under a single entity, enforcing security policies, governance controls, and consolidated billing. This approach provides flexibility for structuring AWS accounts based on operational needs. Organizations typically use one of the following multi-account strategies:

- **Environment-based structure**: Separate accounts for development, testing, and production to enhance isolation, security, and operational control.

- **Business unit segmentation**: Dedicated accounts for different departments or subsidiaries to align with financial, security, and operational policies.

- **Compliance-driven separation**: Isolated accounts for handling regulated workloads (e.g., financial transactions, healthcare data) to meet industry-specific security and compliance standards such as HIPAA or PCI DSS.

Each approach offers benefits in terms of security isolation, cost tracking, and workload management. Companies often implement a hybrid model, combining multiple strategies to balance security, governance, and scalability.

Here is *Figure 4.1*: AWS multi-account structure overview, which visually represents an AWS Organization with separate **Organizational Units** (**OUs**) for security, finance, development, and production with appropriate accounts:

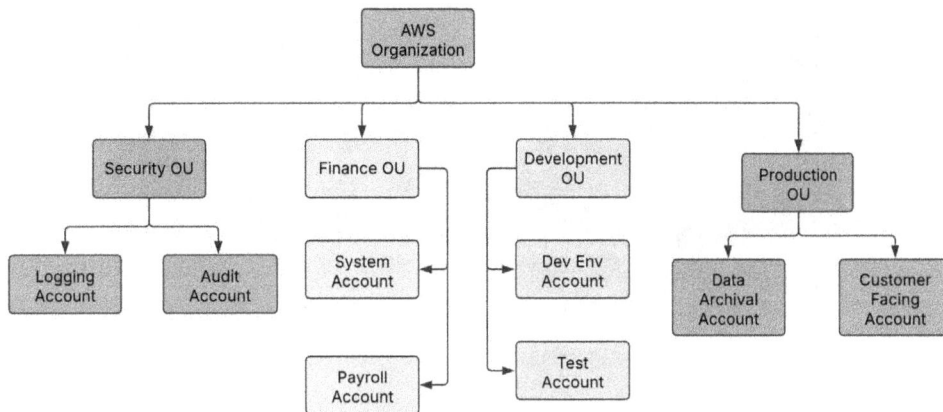

Figure 4.1: AWS multi-account structure overview

AWS account types

The following are the key account types:

- **Management account:** The primary account used to create an organization is a management account. This account is the ultimate owner of the organization, having complete control over security, infrastructure, and finance policies

  This account is also responsible for payments incurred by all the member accounts.

- **Member account:** A member account is part of an organization and can be considered a worker account. At any point in time, it is part of a single management account.

- **AWS personal account:** This is a standalone account used for personal and small-scale purposes and is not part of an organization.

An AWS personal account will be used to cover most of the concepts outlined in this book.

Signing up for an AWS account

Signing up for an AWS account is a straightforward process that involves providing basic personal / business details, payment information, and selecting optional services.

The following are the high-level steps, along with screenshots. This process can be slightly different every time AWS upgrades the Console experience. However, the fundamental principles of the sign-up process remain the same.

The easiest way to start (as a new user) is to create a free tier account and follow the steps below – A free tier provides various AWS services for free with some conditions and boundaries.

1. Using a browser of choice (Google Chrome, Apple Safari, Microsoft Edge, or Mozilla Firefox), navigate to **https://aws.amazon.com/free/**.

   Look at *Figure 4.2* for a reference welcome / placeholder to create a new account:

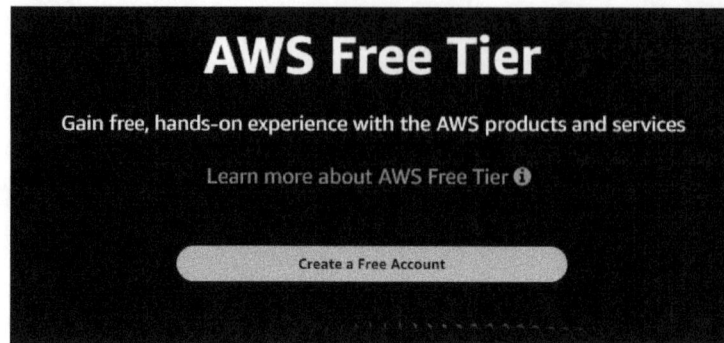

Figure 4.2: Welcome page to open a new AWS account

2. Click on **Create a Free Account**. The system will ask for a root user email and account name.

    a. A root user account is the ultimate identity for managing the account. This superuser, identified by a unique email ID, has complete access to the entire account.

    b. This account should only be used for core administrative purposes, not daily development activities.

    c. The AWS account name is the friendly name on the Management Console. It is more of a friendly identifier/alias that can be updated after the account is created.

    See *Figure 4.3* for a reference screenshot for this step:

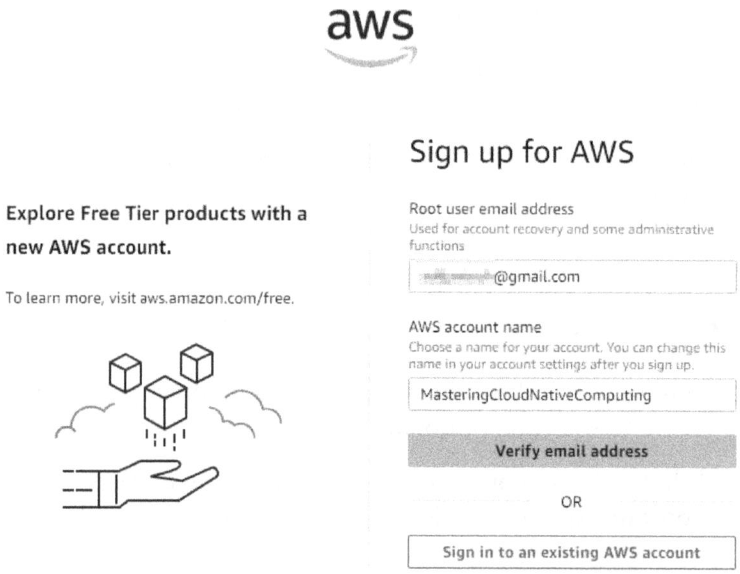

Figure 4.3: Creation of a new AWS free tier account

3. Click on **Verify email address** to get a unique verification code from AWS:

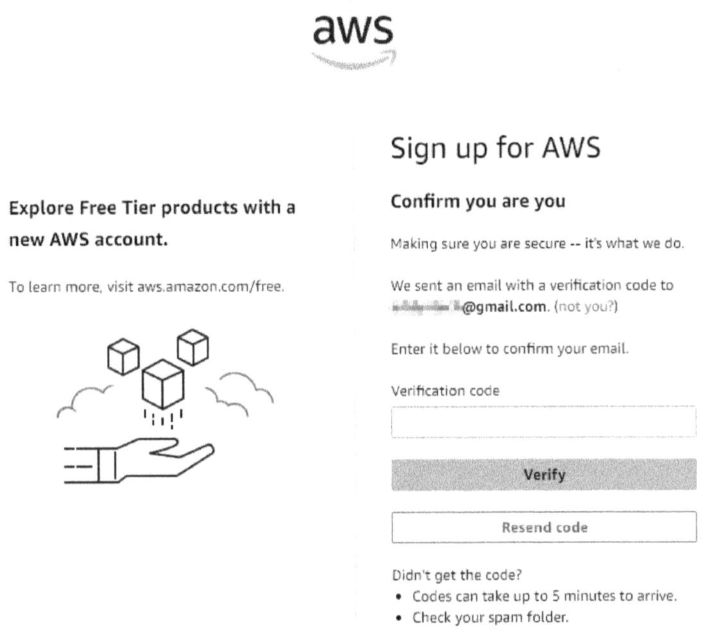

aws

Sign up for AWS

Explore Free Tier products with a new AWS account.

To learn more, visit aws.amazon.com/free.

Confirm you are you

Making sure you are secure -- it's what we do.

We sent an email with a verification code to ━━━ ━ ━@gmail.com. (not you?)

Enter it below to confirm your email.

Verification code

[   ]

[Verify]

[Resend code]

Didn't get the code?
- Codes can take up to 5 minutes to arrive.
- Check your spam folder.

Figure 4.4: Verification page (before verification)

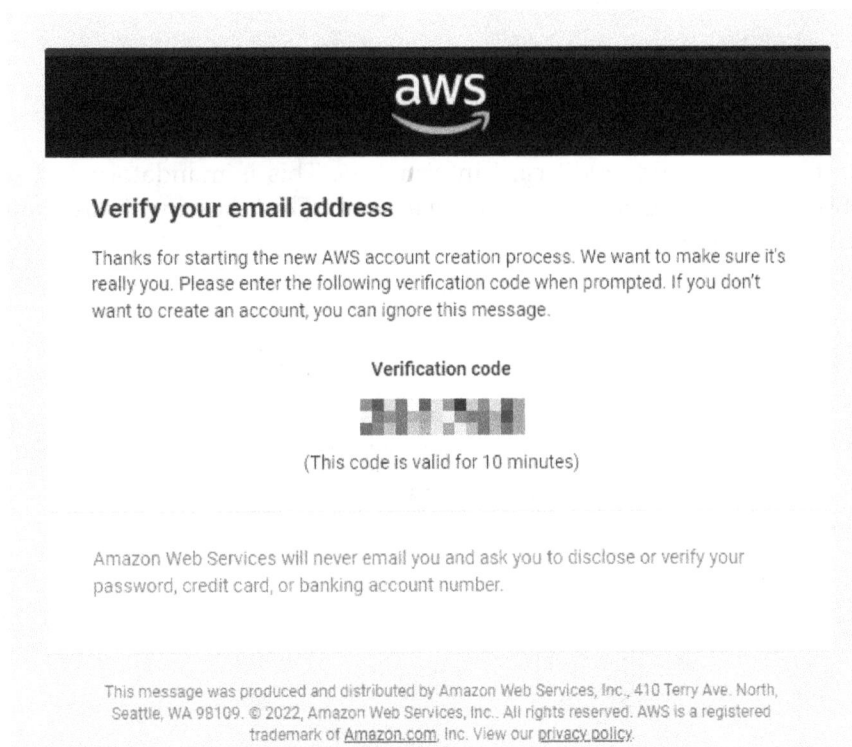

aws

Verify your email address

Thanks for starting the new AWS account creation process. We want to make sure it's really you. Please enter the following verification code when prompted. If you don't want to create an account, you can ignore this message.

Verification code

▓▓▓ ▓▓▓

(This code is valid for 10 minutes)

Amazon Web Services will never email you and ask you to disclose or verify your password, credit card, or banking account number.

This message was produced and distributed by Amazon Web Services, Inc., 410 Terry Ave. North, Seattle, WA 98109. © 2022, Amazon Web Services, Inc.. All rights reserved. AWS is a registered trademark of Amazon.com, Inc. View our privacy policy.

Figure 4.5: Sample verification email with verification code

4. Once successfully verified, it will provide options to complete the sign-up: When asked for a root user password, provide a strong password, and do not share it with any individual. At this step, in the contact information section, the prompt will ask if this account is for **Personal** or **Business** purposes. Select **Personal** to follow this book. See *Figure 4.6* for reference:

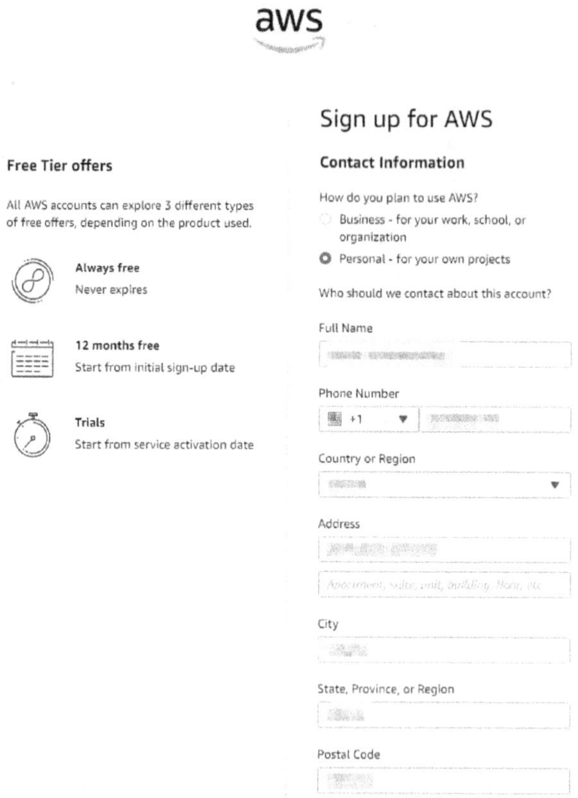

aws

Sign up for AWS

Free Tier offers

All AWS accounts can explore 3 different types
of free offers, depending on the product used.

Always free
Never expires

12 months free
Start from initial sign-up date

Trials
Start from service activation date

Contact Information

How do you plan to use AWS?

○ Business - for your work, school, or
organization

◉ Personal - for your own projects

Who should we contact about this account?

Full Name

Phone Number

🏳 +1 ▼

Country or Region

▼

Address

City

State, Province, or Region

Postal Code

Figure 4.6: Contact information page

At this step, it asks for valid credit card information. This is mandatory and will be the primary
payment option for any charges incurred in that account. The following figure shows how Credit Card
details are collected from users:

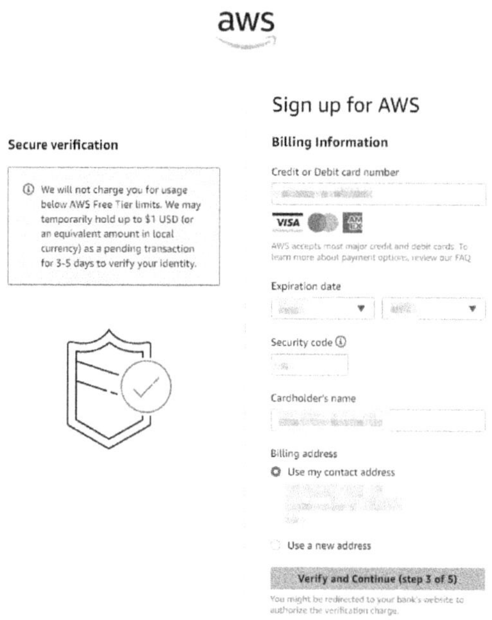

aws

Sign up for AWS

Secure verification

ⓘ We will not charge you for usage
below AWS Free Tier limits. We may
temporarily hold up to $1 USD (or
an equivalent amount in local
currency) as a pending transaction
for 3-5 days to verify your identity.

Billing Information

Credit or Debit card number

VISA

AWS accepts most major credit and debit cards. To
learn more about payment options, review our FAQ

Expiration date

▼   ▼

Security code ⓘ

Cardholder's name

Billing address

◉ Use my contact address

○ Use a new address

Verify and Continue (step 3 of 5)

You might be redirected to your bank's website to
authorize the verification charge.

Figure 4.7: Billing information screen

Additional verification steps (like message verification) could be required. Once the user/identity
verification is complete, the final page will appear, providing an option to select a support plan. Select
Basic support to ensure no additional charges are incurred. See *Figure 4.7* for reference:

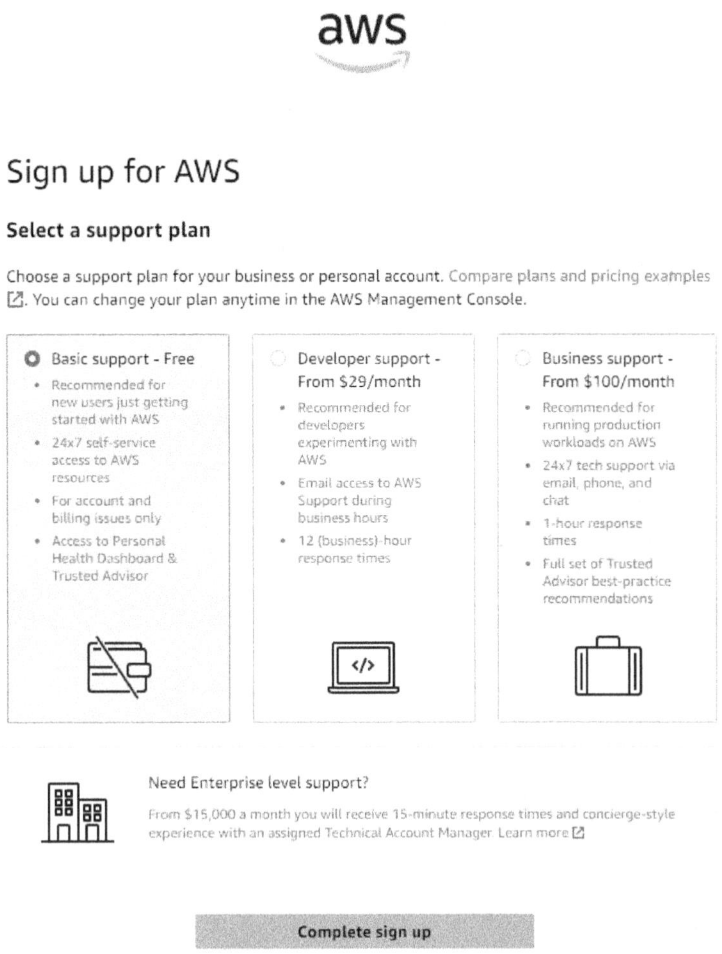

Figure 4.8: Final signup completion page.

Once the sign-up is complete, it is ready to use and often includes a congratulatory page.

Common AWS signup issues and solutions

The following table provides a guideline for common issues that the user may face when signing up for an AWS account:

Issue	Possible cause	Solution
Did not receive email verification code	Email may be in the spam/junk folder	Check spam folder or request a new code
The credit card declined	Bank restrictions or incorrect details	Ensure the card supports international transactions and re-enter details
Phone verification failed	Number format incorrect or carrier restrictions	Use a different phone number or ensure the correct country code
Account activation delayed	AWS performs additional security checks	Check your email for AWS verification request or contact AWS Support

Table 4.1: Table showcasing resolutions to common signup issues

Following this structured signup process and understanding common troubleshooting methods, users can quickly set up an AWS account without unnecessary delays. Once activated, they can access the AWS Management Console and begin deploying cloud resources.

Navigating AWS Management Console

The AWS Management Console is a web-based dashboard that allows users to search for AWS services, configure resources, and monitor cloud workloads in an intuitive graphical interface. It simplifies access to cloud computing, eliminating the need for command-line interactions for basic tasks.

The AWS Console has the following core features for easy navigation:

- **Service search**: Users can type in the search bar at the top of the Console to quickly locate services. For example, entering Lambda will list the AWS Lambda service and related resources like Lambda permissions and function logs.

- **Service menu**: AWS organizes its services into categories, such as compute, storage, networking, security, and databases. Users can explore services by category or access frequently used ones from the Recently Accessed Services list.

- **Cost and usage dashboard**: The Console provides a graphical overview of cloud spending, helping users track expenses across AWS services.

- **AWS health dashboard**: This dashboard displays ongoing maintenance schedules, system outages, and service disruptions in the user's region.

- **AWS regions and availability zones**: The top-right corner of the Console allows users to select the AWS region where their resources are deployed. Regions contain multiple availability zones, separate data centers designed for high availability.

The following section (*Figure 4.9*) shows how to search and navigate to AWS Lambda as a service:

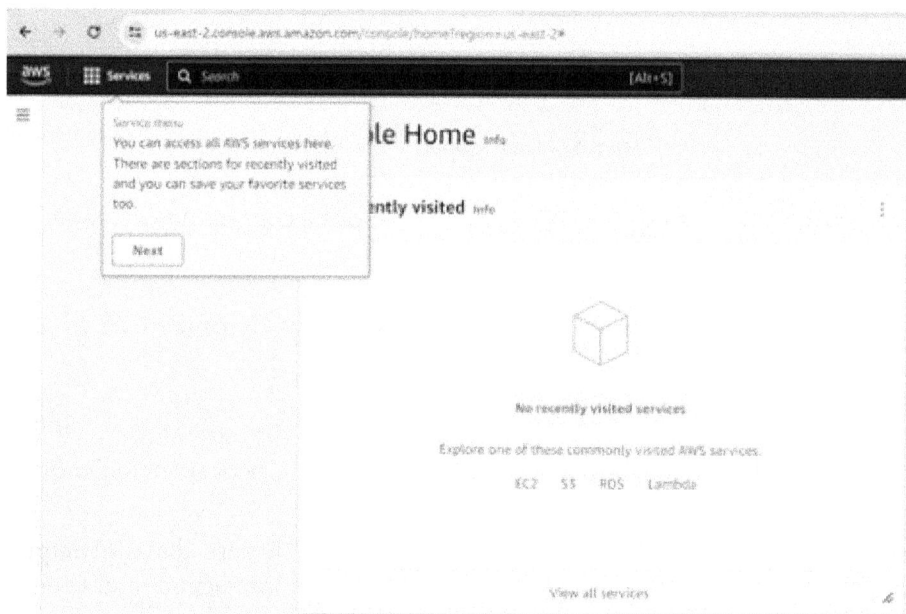

Figure 4.9: AWS Console Home and Service Menu highlighted

The search textbox allows easy search for any service/feature. *Figure 4.10* shows how to search for the text `Lambda function`, which lists many services, including **Lambda** as a service:

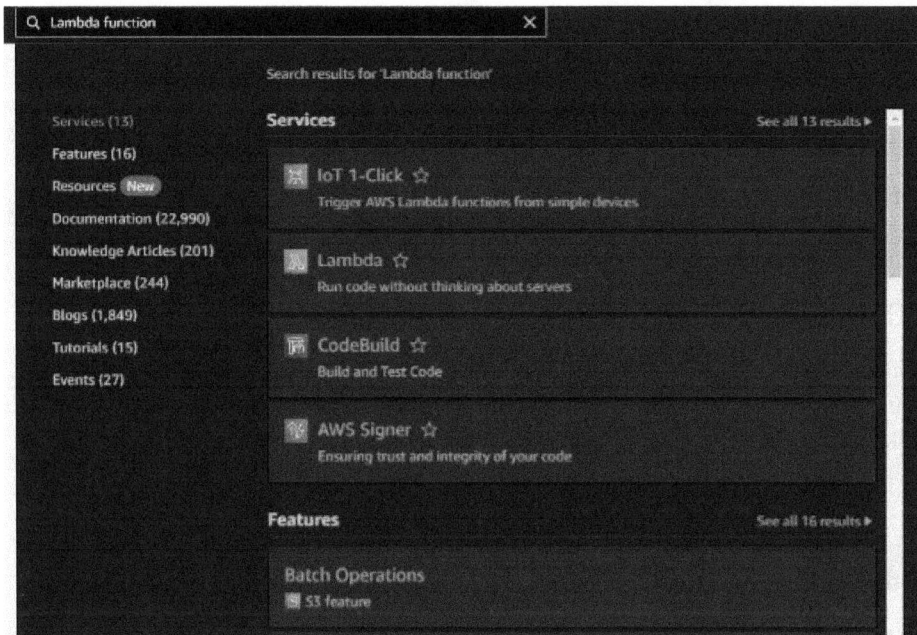

Figure 4.10: Using AWS Console to search for a service/feature

Common AWS services and their functions

AWS provides a broad range of services, but the following are among the most commonly used:

Service	Function
EC2	Virtual servers for hosting applications and workloads.
S3	Scalable cloud storage for files, backups, and static websites.
Lambda	Serverless compute service that runs code in response to events.
DynamoDB	Managed NoSQL database for high-performance applications.
Relational Database Service (RDS)	Fully managed relational databases, such as MySQL and PostgreSQL.
VPC	Custom-defined cloud networking to secure and isolate AWS resources.
IAM	Security service for managing permissions, roles, and authentication.

Table 4.2: Table showing commonly used AWS services

Configuring the AWS Command Line Interface

The **AWS Command Line Interface (AWS CLI)** is a powerful tool for managing AWS resources directly from a terminal. It allows users to create, update, and automate cloud infrastructure without requiring access to the AWS Management Console. AWS CLI supports multiple output formats, including JSON, YAML, text, and table, making it highly flexible for different operational needs.

AWS CLI v1 vs. AWS CLI v2 – Key differences:

AWS CLI v2 introduces several improvements over v1, enhancing security, usability, and functionality. Some key differences include:

- **Built-in AWS SSO support**: AWS CLI v2 natively supports AWS **Single Sign-On (SSO)**, making authentication easier for enterprise users.

- **Automatic pagination**: Unlike v1, AWS CLI v2 automatically paginates output for commands with large datasets.

- **Simplified installation**: AWS CLI v2 provides a self-contained installer, eliminating dependency issues seen in v1.

- **Interactive features**: With v2, users can leverage auto-prompting, which suggests command options, reducing manual errors.

The following section provides high-level steps for installing and configuring AWS CLI for the following systems.

AWS CLI on Windows

To install and configure AWS CLI on a Windows system, it is recommended that you use the latest supported version of Windows (Windows 10 or later) and the latest version of the CLI (version 2 or above at the time of authoring this book).

Administrator privileges are also required to install/modify any Windows component, including AWS CLI installation.

The following are the high-level steps:

1. Find the latest version of AWS CLI compatible with Windows and download it to get a copy of the installable.

   For example, to install CLI on a Windows 64-bit system, install it from **https://awscli.amazonaws. com/AWSCLIV2.msi.**

2. Run the installable to complete the installation

3. Once the installation is successful, validate the installation through the command prompt and use **aws --version** to verify the installed version. If successful, it will display the version of AWS CLI. *Figure 4.11* shows a reference for AWS CLI version 2 on a Windows machine:

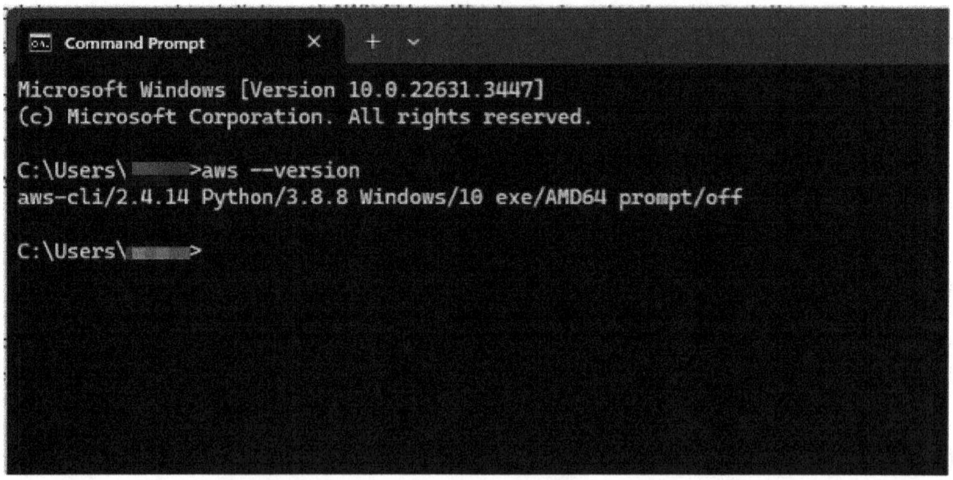

Figure 4.11: AWS CLI version 2.4 on Windows

AWS CLI on macOS

The following are high-level steps to install AWS CLI on a macOS system:

1. Initiate the download of the AWS CLI version for macOS by using the **curl** command: **curl [AWSCLIV2. zip link] -o awscliv2.zip**

2. Once the download is complete, extract the contents of the downloaded zip file with the command **unzip awscliv2.zip**.

3. After extraction, run the installation script with administrative privileges: **sudo ./aws/install**

Alternatively, you can manually download the **AWSCLIV2.pkg** file from the AWS website, open the downloaded file, and follow the instructions provided by the installer.

Replace the **[AWSCLIV2.zip link]** with the actual download link. After the installation, you can confirm it by typing the **aws --version** in your terminal. If installed successfully, the installed version will be returned to the user.

Note that this might require using **sudo** to provide elevated permissions.

AWS CLI on Linux

The following are high-level steps to install AWS CLI on a Linux system:

1. Update the system and install required packages before you start; ensuring your system is up-to-date is good practice. You might also need to install curl and unzip utilities if they have not already been installed.

2. Download AWS CLI. Next, you need to download the AWS CLI installation package. You can do this using the curl command followed by the AWS CLI ZIP file URL.

3. Extract the installation files. After downloading the ZIP file, you need to extract its contents. The file can also be uncompressed and unzipped using the same command, including the **unzip** command.

4. Install AWS CLI. Now that you have extracted the installation files, you can install AWS CLI. Navigate to the extracted files' directory and run the install script with sudo privileges.

5. Verify the installation. Finally, to ensure the AWS CLI has been installed correctly, you can check its version by running the **aws --version** in your terminal.

Remember to replace the placeholders with actual commands or values. Also, the exact commands might vary slightly depending on your Linux distribution.

Sample AWS CLI use case – Listing S3 buckets

Once AWS CLI is installed and configured, users can execute commands to interact with AWS services. Below is an example of listing all S3 buckets in an AWS account:

Command:

```
1. aws s3 ls
```

Expected output:

```
1. 2025-02-01 11:32:45 mastering-aws
2. 2025-02-02 12:21:03 cloud-archival-bucket
3. 2025-02-03 15:05:22 logs-archive-bucket
```

The output displays the creation date and names of all S3 buckets in the AWS account.

By leveraging AWS CLI, users can efficiently manage AWS resources, automate repetitive tasks, and streamline cloud operations. The upcoming chapters will introduce more advanced CLI use cases, covering automation, security management, and serverless application deployment.

IAM user login and setup

Once the root user and AWS account have been created, day-to-day activities must be performed via IAM users. IAM users are identities within the AWS Account with specific permissions to interact with AWS resources. Root users with specific permissions can only create IAM users. The following are the high-level steps to create and provision IAM users:

1. Log in to your AWS account using the root user credentials. The root user is the initial superuser with unrestricted access to all AWS resources.

2. Navigate to IAM. Once logged in, go to the IAM Console. You can find it by typing `IAM` in the AWS Management Console's search bar.

3. In the IAM Console, select **Users** and **Add User**. You will be asked to provide a unique username and specify the new user's access type (programmatic, AWS Management Console, or both).

4. Next, you will define the permissions for the new user. Options include adding a user to a group or attaching policies. AWS makes this process easy by offering a variety of managed policies, such as **AdministratorAccess**, **ReadOnlyAccess**, etc., that you can utilize.

5. After setting up the user and permissions, review the details and click **Create user**. An access key and secret are provided at this time, which are crucial for downloading and securely storing credentials. This credential is only provided once during creation and becomes quintessential for securely saving credentials.

6. Lastly, share the sign-in information with the user. This includes the password and the URL for the account sign-in page.

First-time login and setup

Once the setup for a root user and one or more IAM users is complete, follow the steps to log into the AWS Console as an IAM user:

1. Log in as a root user, navigate to **Account**, and copy the unique **Account ID**, usually a 12-digit number. See *Figure 4.12* for a sample:

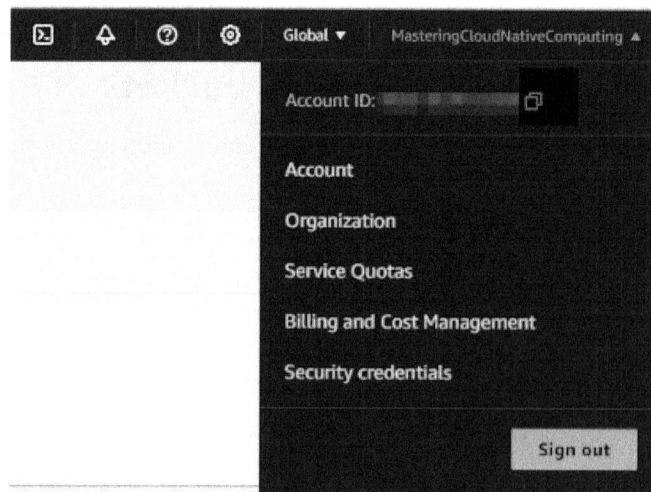

Figure 4.12: Accessing the AWS account number

2. Sign in using an **IAM user** by providing a 12-digit account ID. See *Figure 4.13* for reference. Once prompted, provide the previously saved user ID and password to log in and gain access to the AWS Management Console and the underlying services.

   As a security best practice, it is recommended that both root and **IAM user** accounts be logged into using **multi-factor authentication (MFA)**. Subsequent chapters cover Further details about IAM and access management.

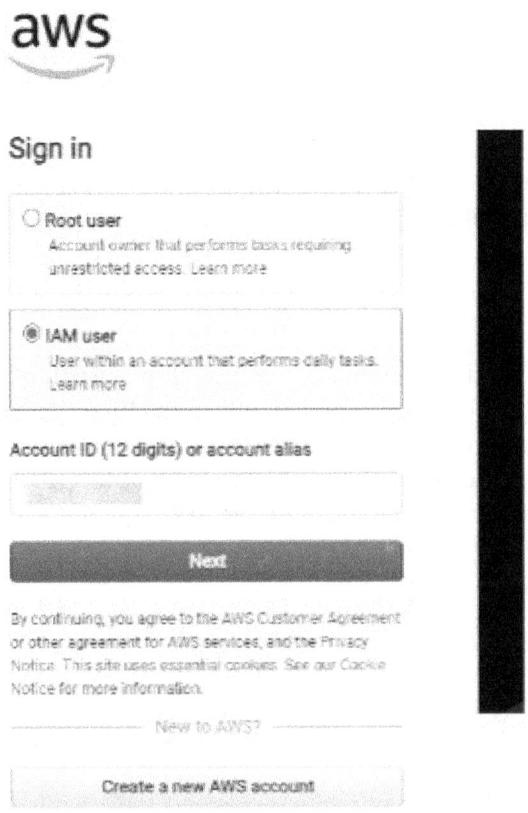

Figure 4.13: Login as an IAM user with Account ID

Understanding IAM roles and permissions

AWS IAM follows **role-based access control** (**RBAC**), where different users are assigned distinct permissions based on their responsibilities. The table below outlines common IAM roles and their associated privileges:

IAM role	Purpose	Common permissions
Root user	Full account control	Unrestricted access (should not be used for daily tasks)
Administrator	Full AWS account management	Manage resources, billing, and security policies
Developer	Build and deploy applications	Create/modify compute resources (EC2, Lambda, S3)
Read-only user	View resources without modification	Read access to AWS services, no write actions
Billing manager	Manage AWS billing and invoices	View and modify billing details

Table 4.3: Table showing common privileges for users

Conclusion

In this chapter, we explored the fundamental steps for setting up an AWS account, creating IAM users, and managing access through AWS Organizations. We examined role-based access control, security best practices, and different AWS account structures, establishing a strong foundation for working in a cloud-native environment. Additionally, we navigated the AWS Management Console, installed the AWS CLI, and learned how to interact with AWS resources efficiently. These core concepts are critical for mastering serverless and cloud-native architectures, ensuring that AWS environments are structured for security, scalability, and operational efficiency.

To build upon this knowledge, readers can explore advanced IAM configurations, such as policies, permission boundaries, and **Service Control Policies** (**SCPs**), which enhance security and governance. Understanding multi-account management through AWS Control Tower can help optimize large-scale cloud deployments, while infrastructure automation using AWS CloudFormation or AWS CDK simplifies provisioning and compliance. Security best practices, including encryption and access key management, further strengthen cloud environments.

With a well-structured AWS foundation in place, the next step is to dive into AWS Lambda, a core component of serverless architectures. The upcoming chapter will introduce Lambda's execution model, event-driven design, and integration with other AWS services. Readers will gain insights into optimizing costs and performance while leveraging the power of serverless computing to build scalable, efficient applications. Mastering Lambda is essential for understanding how AWS enables modern cloud-native development and automation.

Join our Discord space

Join our Discord workspace for latest updates, offers, tech happenings around the world, new releases, and sessions with the authors:

https://discord.bpbonline.com

CHAPTER 5
Serverless Compute with AWS Lambda

Introduction

This chapter comprehensively explores the role and utility of functions in the computing landscape. It looks into creating serverless functions within cloud environments, eliminating the need for server rental, provisioning, and management. This provides a foundational understanding necessary to appreciate the importance of serverless tasks within the context of event-driven systems and serverless computing architectures, making you feel secure in your knowledge.

The chapter introduces AWS Lambda as a service, discussing its setup, opportunities, core concepts, and configurations necessary for its utilization. It also explores AWS Lambda's limitations, use cases, security considerations, monitoring, and deployment options for creating and managing AWS Lambda functions.

As highlighted in recent AWS blog posts, AWS frequently updates Lambda with new capabilities. For instance, AWS introduced Graviton2 support, enabling a 34% better performance ratio than x86-based functions. AWS Lambda is an increasingly compelling choice for cost-conscious, performance-driven serverless applications.

Moreover, this chapter extensively discusses the seamless integration of AWS Lambda with other services. It presents a variety of practical use cases and examples, reinforcing the understanding of serverless computing in the cloud and instilling confidence in your knowledge. Readers will also learn how AWS continues to enhance Lambda's capabilities, making it an evolving and competitive choice for cloud-native applications.

Upon completing this chapter, readers should understand serverless compute, AWS Lambda, a key component of most serverless and event-driven systems, and its position as one of the most cost-effective services within the AWS cloud ecosystem.

Practical examples, use cases, exercises, and questions are provided to further cement the concepts and practical applications of Lambda. This hands-on approach is crucial in ensuring a thorough understanding and the ability to apply the knowledge gained.

Structure

This chapter covers the following topics:

- Functions in computing and IT systems
- Introduction to AWS Lambda

Objectives

This chapter is a comprehensive guide to AWS Lambda, designed to equip readers with a deep understanding of serverless computing and its practical application. By looking into Lambda's core concepts, architecture, and functionalities, readers will gain the knowledge necessary to build efficient, scalable, and cost-effective applications on the AWS platform.

We will explore the fundamental principles of **function as a service** (**FaaS**), positioning Lambda within the broader context of cloud computing. We will cover key terminologies, configuration options, and Lambda's internal workings. Furthermore, readers will learn how to effectively utilize Lambda's various features, including triggers, invocation modes, runtimes, and VPC integration, all in real-world application scenarios.

This chapter showcases Lambda's versatility across different industries, inspiring you to explore the myriad possibilities of serverless applications.

Functions in computing and IT systems

This section provides a foundational understanding of the role of functions in modern computing, empowering you with the knowledge to navigate the complexities of AWS Lambda and other serverless applications.

A function is a fundamental building block in modern computing. It is a block or section of instructions designed to perform a specific task.

An analogy for a function would be that of a magic potion that a wizard can use to light a fire. Instead of rewriting the same spell to light the same fire, the potion can be saved and referred to create the same magic every time.

The magic gets even better! Functions can accept different ingredients (data) to customize their effects. Think of the fire spell; you could add a parameter to control the fire's intensity or color! Functions can also return results, allowing you to use their output in other parts of your program, like chaining spells together for complex magic.

Functions promote code modularity and reusability and significantly reduce errors. They are the backbone of modern programming, and most languages heavily utilize them. Libraries or modules store pre-defined functions, creating a vast spell book for programmers to draw upon!

A function that accepts something from the caller is said to be **parameterized**. The result returned from the function is generally termed as **return value(s)**, and if a function calls itself (it is said to be **recursive**, like a spell casting spell on itself). These functions require an environment to run; this environment could be a server, a browser, or a personal computer, and that is traditional; the next section explains how the same methodology can be extended to the cloud.

Functions in cloud computing

We have explored functions such as reusable mini utilities that can be called tasks/operations. Cloud computing takes this concept further with the idea of serverless functions. A serverless function can generally cater to any number of requests. It can get the execution environment ready when required, thereby eliminating the need to provision servers and resources and also providing customizations.

A cloud function provides all the security guardrails and integrations to work seamlessly with other cloud components, such as databases, storage, utilities, managed services, monitoring, and logging services.

All the major cloud providers have their implementations of serverless functions: Microsoft Azure has Azure Functions, Google Cloud has Google Cloud Functions, and AWS has AWS Lambda.

Other cloud providers, such as Alibaba Cloud and IBM Cloud, offer similar core operations functions.

These cloud functions can be categorized as serverless computing because of the following distinguishing factors:

- **No server management overhead**: There is no server maintenance required from organizations and end-users.

- **Supports event-driven architecture**: Provides hooks to easily connect and respond to events from other components or triggers on a schedule.

- **Massive scaling**: Can cater to sudden spikes in demand and can handle thousands of requests/second.

- **Pay-as-you-go cost model**: There is no upfront cost in setting up servers, and there is no cost involved for idle capacity.

- **No load balancing**: Automatic scaling ensures that load balancing from the calling application is unnecessary.

Function as a service

FaaS is a paradigm for developing and deploying applications. FaaS helps streamline the development process and abstracts away all aspects of server provisioning, maintenance, and patching. The following are the core principles of FaaS systems:

- **Event-driven**: This type supports triggering by actions/events, such as a change in a database, uploading a picture/video/file, or an API request by a web application. Since event-driven eliminates the need to run all the time, it is only required to run when triggered.

- **Focus on code**: The developers can now focus on the core business functions rather than on the underlying infrastructure, server patching, and maintenance.

- **Supports event-driven architecture**: Provides hooks to easily connect and respond to events from other components or triggers on a schedule.

- **Reduced development time**: This accelerates development time since it reduces the time for server provisioning and maintenance.

- **Pay-as-you-go model**: There is no upfront cost in setting up servers, and there is no cost involved for idle capacity.

Introduction to AWS Lambda

AWS Lambda is a serverless computing service that helps bring an idea or functionality to life without the need to provision resources or maintain patches. It eliminates the costs associated with underutilization while accommodating traffic spikes. AWS Lambda is a fully managed serverless offering and one of the longest-standing serverless solutions in the industry. AWS maintains the underlying infrastructure, ensuring high availability across all AWS regions.

Lambda is widely used across industries for various workloads, including real-time data processing, streaming applications, website backends, IoT event handling, and machine learning inferences. It is not just a tool but an integral part of modern cloud-native architectures. Lambda functions execute on demand and support multiple programming languages such as Python, Node.js, C++, Ruby, Go, and Java. Additionally, AWS Lambda allows custom runtimes, enabling developers to execute code in environments beyond the natively supported ones.

An AWS Lambda function can be invoked synchronously or asynchronously, offering flexibility in execution. This versatility allows for greater control, scalability, and security, making it an essential component for event-driven architectures. Functions are stateless by default, meaning each execution is isolated from the previous ones. However, AWS provides various options for maintaining state, such as using Amazon DynamoDB, Amazon S3, or external databases.

AWS Lambda offers key advantages such as event-driven execution, automatic scaling, and cost efficiency. While it traditionally had limitations around cold start latency, AWS introduced SnapStart for Java runtimes in 2024 to optimize performance. SnapStart reduces cold start times by up to 90% by pre-warming execution environments and storing function snapshots. This enhancement significantly improves Lambda's suitability for latency-sensitive Java applications, such as financial transaction processing, e-commerce workloads, and real-time analytics.

Since AWS Lambda functions have access to various AWS services, they can interact with databases, file systems, APIs, or real-time data streams, making them highly versatile for cloud-native applications.

AWS Lambda vs. traditional functions

One of the most significant differences between AWS Lambda and traditional server-based architectures is its event-driven nature. Lambda functions execute only when triggered instead of continuously running a server process, reducing operational overhead and ensuring cost efficiency. The following table compares FaaS like AWS Lambda with traditional server-based models to help readers unfamiliar with the event-driven paradigm understand the key differences:

Feature	FaaS (AWS Lambda, Azure Functions, Google Cloud Functions)	Traditional server-based model
Infrastructure management	Fully managed by cloud provider (no provisioning required)	Requires manual provisioning, scaling, and maintenance
Scalability	Automatically scales based on demand	Requires load balancers and manual resource scaling
Cost efficiency	Pay-per-use (charged only when function executes)	Always-on instances incur costs even when idle
Execution time limits	Short-lived functions (AWS Lambda max: 15 minutes)	Can run indefinitely
Event-driven	Designed for event-driven applications	Typically request-response based, not inherently event-driven
Complexity	Simple to deploy and manage functions	Requires full-stack infrastructure setup
Security and maintenance	AWS handles security patches, runtime updates	Requires manual patching and security updates

Table 5.1: Table showcasing Lambda and traditional function differences

Key terminologies

Key terminologies are as follows:

- **Triggers**: A trigger is an event or message instructing the AWS Lambda service to invoke the assigned Lambda function to perform the task as specified. A wide variety of triggers can invoke/call AWS Lambda functions.

- **Event sources**: Event sources are the sources that can invoke/ initiate the Lambda function to do its task. Common event sources could be a request from an API, a file operation (copy, delete, or modification), an item change in a database, or an event scheduled to run at a particular time (scheduled event).

- **Lambda ARN**: An **Amazon Resource Name** (**ARN**) is a unique identifier for an AWS Lambda function; it is like a digital identity/fingerprint and will precisely refer to a single Lambda function. It follows this pattern:

```
arn:aws:lambda:<region>:<account_id>:function:<function_name> [:version]
```

Here, `<region>` represents which AWS region the services are running—For example, us-west-2 is one of the major regions catering to the western US and Canada.

`<account_id>` is the unique account-id for the function.

`<function_name>` represents the unique name of the function.

- **Handler**: While we commonly refer to AWS Lambda as a Lambda function, it can technically contain many common function/code blocks, supporting a greater degree of modularity. The handler function is the master function that will receive all the incoming events. The handler is like a captain of the ship, and there can only be one handler function for an AWS Lambda function.

- **Runtime**: A Lambda runtime is the interpreter or bridge that seamlessly connects the execution environment, and the code provided in different programming languages. It generally provides language support, context, execution process, and event management.

- **Architecture**: The architecture section denotes the instruction set, representing the computer processor used in the background. This can be an x86-64-based processor or a Graviton-based processor (ARM64). Most common utility functions can be easily interchanged between the two architectures, but if the code contains specific dependencies, it should be set and managed accordingly.

- **Version and alias**: An alias denotes a specific version. It is an identifier for the particular version of the package.

Configuration and capacity management

AWS Lambda follows the serverless philosophy, meaning we do not have to manage servers or allocate resources like CPU and memory. However, the allocation of memory and CPU is based on the configuration. The following are key configuration items:

- **Memory** refers to the amount of memory allocated for the function. The minimum memory allocation for a Lambda function is 128 MB, and the maximum is 10 GB (10,240 MB).

  There is no way to control CPU allocation through configuration in AWS Lambda. However, memory allocation automatically assigns CPU allocation. Accordingly, Increasing the memory automatically and proportionately increases the amount of CPU and, hence, the overall computational power available for the function.

  TIP: **An increase in memory results in an increase in the overall cost of the Lambda.**

  TIP: **When allocating memory when starting a function with evolving requirements, it is better to start with the default configuration (128 MB) and increase as the function progresses.**

- **Ephemeral storage** refers to the temporary file storage available within the execution environment. It manages the intermediate persistence memory while the function is being executed. It is like a cache/scratch memory, released once the function execution is complete.

  Ephemeral storage will be reset to a clean state after every execution, and this slate is never shared between other Lambda executions. The ephemeral storage configuration item allows options to configure this memory. The value ranges from a minimum of 512 MB to a maximum of 10 GB.

  TIP: **Use higher ephemeral storage value when dealing with big datasets requiring storing thousands of records in memory.**

- **Timeout**: This configuration acts as a safety valve/guardrail to prevent a Lambda function from running in an infinite loop. The timeout is the maximum time the function is allowed to run. For example, a timeout of 3 seconds means the Lambda function must finish before 3 seconds. If it is running beyond the timeout specified, the AWS Lambda service will forcibly kill the instance.

This is a configuration and can range from 1 second to 15 minutes (900 seconds).

> TIP: **When choosing Lambda for any task, ensure it can be completed in under 15 minutes; otherwise, Lambda is not the right tool.**

> TIP: **AWS Lambda's timeout property is unsuitable for long-running workloads or batch job operations.**

Internal invocation lifecycle

The invocation lifecycle for an AWS Lambda refers to different phases run in the background to prepare the function for the task. This performs three main phases:

- **Initialization phase**: This involves performing the following activities:

  o **Runtime init**: In this phase, Lambda service allocates resources and starts a new container (an instance to run the logic/code for the intended function).

  o **Extension init**: This involves the initialization of supporting libraries and extensions like logging and tracing functions.

  o **Function init**: The Lambda runtime for the selected runtime is loaded, and the function code is made ready for execution.

  o **Other hooks**: This feature is introduced for SnapStart (Java-based runtimes) to signal other events about being ready for the next step.

- **Invocation phase**: Here, the function is invoked synchronously based on the incoming event, and waiting is involved until the function execution is complete (Successful, failure, or time-out).

  > Tip: **If a Lambda function is asynchronously invoked, the response is immediate since there is no need to wait for the response.**

- **Shutdown phase**: This is an optional phase and involves preparation for shutdown and an opportunity to release resources.

The following figure shows a visual representation of the Lambda lifecycle:

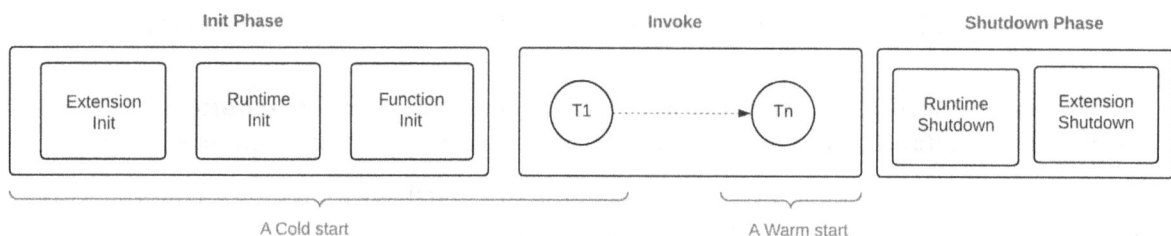

Figure 5.1: A timeline of invocation events

When the Lambda service continuously responds to requests, it does not perform a full initialization step, but it keeps the environment warm so it can quickly respond to other requests. This is a typical scenario when it is processing events continuously, and it is called a **warm start**.

The Lambda environment is only kept warm for a short duration, so the overall execution time when the environment is warm is less, or the execution is said to be fast.

In other scenarios where the environment is not warm, it has to recover from the previous shutdown phase and spin up new containers. This will take additional time, and the phase is called a **cold start**.

A **cold start** is the first request that the new Lambda worker handles.

TIP: **AWS provides an option to keep the environment warm for a limited number of instances. This is called provisioned concurrency. The Lambda service keeps a provisioned concurrency set number of workers in a warm state, thus eliminating cold starts. However, other design aspects need to be considered.**

Triggers

A trigger is an action that starts/invokes the Lambda function to perform its operation. In a typical event-driven system, events from other sources or components within AWS act as a trigger. It is also possible to manually trigger a Lambda function from the AWS Console, AWS CLI, or other SDKs. A few common triggers include the following:

- **API gateway request**: An incoming request (HTTP) from an API can trigger an AWS Lambda function to handle the request, respond with the results, and perform its core operation.

- **DynamoDB stream**: In this case, the change data capture stream of the AWS DynamoDB database can trigger an AWS Lambda to feed on the changes to take further actions.

- **S3 put**: Amazon S3 is the object storage system (covered in detail in subsequent chapters). When a file is copied, the file copy event can trigger a Lambda function to process it further. A classic example would be to enhance a picture as soon as the customer uploads it in a typical photo editing app.

- **CloudWatch events**: Amazon CloudWatch is a monitoring service with event logs for most AWS services. A change in their behavior can trigger an AWS Lambda function to take further action.

- **Scheduled events**: Another common use case is to trigger the Lambda on a schedule. This is a common way for routine and cleanup tasks, often done at a specific time. For example, consolidating all the payments received for the day into a single ledger database at the end of the day.

Invocation modes

The invocation is what happens after a Lambda function is triggered/invoked. The invocation can be either synchronous or asynchronous.

In a synchronous invocation, the Lambda function waits for the function to finish processing the event. Once the function code has finished (successfully/errors out/timed out), the function exists and completes the execution cycle. This is typically used for API-based requests where a client expects an immediate response.

In an asynchronous invocation, the Lambda service places the event in the invocation queue and immediately returns the response. It does not wait for the function processing to be completed, making it ideal for long-running tasks. AWS handles the retry mechanism automatically for failed invocations.

Example workflow of an asynchronous invocation:

Consider an image-processing application where users upload photos, and AWS Lambda automatically resizes the image. In this scenario, an asynchronous invocation is more efficient because the user does not need to wait for the image processing to be immediately completed.

Step-by-step asynchronous workflow is as follows:

1. **User uploads an image**: A user uploads an image to an S3 bucket.
2. **S3 triggers Lambda**: The S3 event automatically triggers an AWS Lambda function.
3. **Lambda places the task in a processing queue**: The Lambda function sends a message to Amazon SQS (or Amazon EventBridge) to queue the processing task.
4. **Processing function executes**: A second Lambda function picks up the job from the queue and processes the image (resizes, compresses, and saves it).

5. **Completion event (optional)**: Once processing is complete, an event can be sent to Amazon SNS to notify the user that the image is ready.

This asynchronous model ensures that the user does not experience delays and that failures can be handled through automatic retries by AWS Lambda.

Tip: **Use synchronous invocation for real-time user interactions, such as when user input is to be validated before submission or payment processing.**

Tip: **Use asynchronous invocation for event-driven tasks like batch processing, data pipeline execution, and background workflows.**

Runtimes and programming languages

In this context, runtime refers to the execution environment provided to an application. This environment is typically self-contained and includes libraries, settings, and environment variables to fully support the software job/task. A simple example of a Python runtime includes built-in functions like the `print()` function. The Python interpreter converts the input Python code into instructions the computer's processor can understand.

In the context of AWS Lambda, runtime is the language interpreter and associated libraries required to execute the function. AWS Lambda provides two primary runtimes:

- **Managed runtimes**: These are prebuilt and managed by AWS (hence the name). Managed runtimes significantly reduce development and setup time. The following are the common runtime options:

  - **Python**: This is one of the most commonly used runtimes, supports a wide range of versions, and is popular among data science, machine learning, and the scientific community.

  - **Node.js**: This is also an equally popular option for cloud-native development because of its typescript support.

  - C# (.NET)

  - Java

  - Ruby

  - Go

- **Custom runtimes**: The AWS Lambda service also allows users to bring their own runtime, which AWS will not manage. This helps when an existing application has to maintain its core dependencies or access exclusive libraries.

In addition, AWS Lambda also supports many third-party community runtimes for other languages like PHP and Swift.

Running in VPC vs. as-is

Lambda can be run in two ways: as-is or inside a **Virtual Private Cloud** (**VPC**).

By default, Lambda executes in a highly available, managed execution environment provided by AWS. This is the as-is execution, and it will get default internet access and default/direct access to other AWS services that run on public endpoints (AWS DynamoDB, AWS S3, and so on).

This setup is fairly simple, with the least latency. However, does not allow access to VPC-only resources like (VPC endpoints, Amazon RDS databases, and so on). The other execution mode is running Lambda inside a VPC. Subsequent chapters will cover more details about VPCs.

In general, when a Lambda is run inside a VPC, it runs within the security context set by the VPC, with greater control over inbound and outbound traffic and direct and low-latency access to VPC-only resources (RDS database and other VPC-only services).

A Lambda running in a VPC generally has a complex security configuration but has greater control. The following table provides a quick comparison between the two options:

Lambda feature	As-is execution	VPC configuration
Execution	AWS managed	Defined by VPC
Access to other AWS services	Public endpoint	VPC endpoints
Latency	Less cold starts	Potentially, more cold starts
Security complexity	Low	High
Internet access	Available	Not available by default
Security	Less secure but has controls	More secure

Table 5.2: Table showing a comparison between as-is and VPC run modes for Lambda

Permission model

AWS Lambda has multiple layers of security, and the permission model and mode depend on the type of usage:

- **IAM policies**: The IAM policies govern who can access Lambda API functions and their layers, and they can be applied to IAM users, groups, or roles.

- **Lambda execution role**: The Lambda execution role is attached to every Lambda function and controls what the Lambda can access.

  In a bare minimum setup, this Lambda execution role would have access to write logs (AWS CloudWatch). For example, if a Lambda function has to read a file from an S3 bucket, it should have an explicit policy. A sample policy is shown as follows:

```json
{
    "Version": "2012-10-17",
    "Statement": [
        {
            "Sid": "VisualEditor0",
            "Effect": "Allow",
            "Action": [
                "s3:GetObjectAcl",
                "s3:GetObject",
                "s3:ListBucket"
            ],
            "Resource": [
                "arn:aws:s3:::arn:aws:s3:::",
                "arn:aws:s3:::arn:aws:s3:::/*"
            ]
        },
```

Figure 5.2: A sample policy to get an object from an S3 bucket

Here, the **Action "s3:GetObject"** on the resource (specified by a bucket ARN) allows Lambda to get any object.

The other **Action "s3:ListBucket"** lists the bucket. Subsequent chapters will discuss IAM policies in detail.

Tip: IAM will be covered in detail in subsequent chapters.

- **Resource-based policies**: This is required to give other AWS accounts and services access to the Lambda function. A classic scenario would be providing access to the AWS S3 service to call an AWS Lambda function to invoke based on an S3-based event.

- **VPC security**: If a Lambda function is configured inside a VPC, its security is controlled by the inbound and outbound rules and is done through VPC security groups.

Tip: AWS strictly follows the principle of shared responsibility. AWS is responsible for the security of the cloud (including infrastructure and the physical security of their data centers), and customers are responsible for the security of the services by ensuring sufficient guardrails are put in place.

Permission flow in AWS Lambda execution

The following figure (*Figure 5.3*) illustrates how permissions work when a Lambda function is invoked:

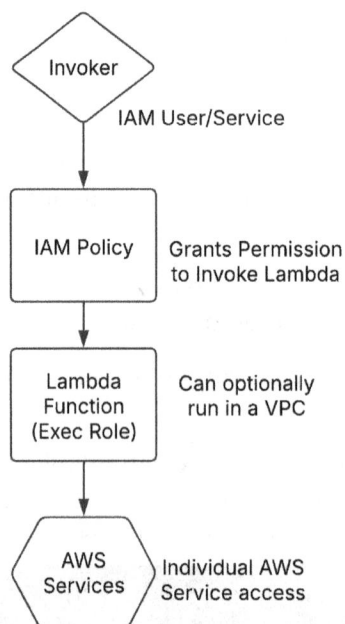

Figure 5.3: AWS Lambda permission flow

Enhancements in IAM permissions boundaries (2023 update)

In 2023, AWS introduced enhanced IAM permission boundaries, restricting IAM role permissions to prevent unintended privilege escalation. This means that administrators can create more controlled IAM roles for Lambda functions, ensuring that roles cannot exceed predefined security constraints. This is especially useful for:

- Preventing excessive API access by limiting Lambda's execution scope.

- Enforcing organization-wide security policies without manual intervention.

- Ensuring that Lambda functions do not accidentally gain access to unauthorized resources.

These updates make IAM permissions more manageable and reduce security risks for Lambda-based architectures.

Monitoring and troubleshooting

Proactively monitoring AWS Lambda functions is essential to guarantee error-free execution and optimal performance. This enables us to anticipate potential scaling challenges and proactively adjust resource allocation, ensuring the ability to handle increased traffic while optimizing costs. The key benefits of monitoring are as follows:

- Cost optimization by identifying inefficiencies
- Predicting costs through historical runs
- Right-size resource allocations
- Track code changes
- Testing function reliability
- Simplify debugging
- Identify errors and exceptions

The following are the main ways to monitor AWS Lambda executions:

- **Amazon CloudWatch**: This is the primary tool for monitoring Lambda functions and can collect and present metrics like Error counts, the number of concurrent invocations, throttles, the duration of the execution, and more.

   Figure 5.4 shows a generic view of CloudWatch metrics for a sample Lambda function. This can provide valuable insights into the execution, user-defined log statements, overall execution timeline, and total memory and time consumed.

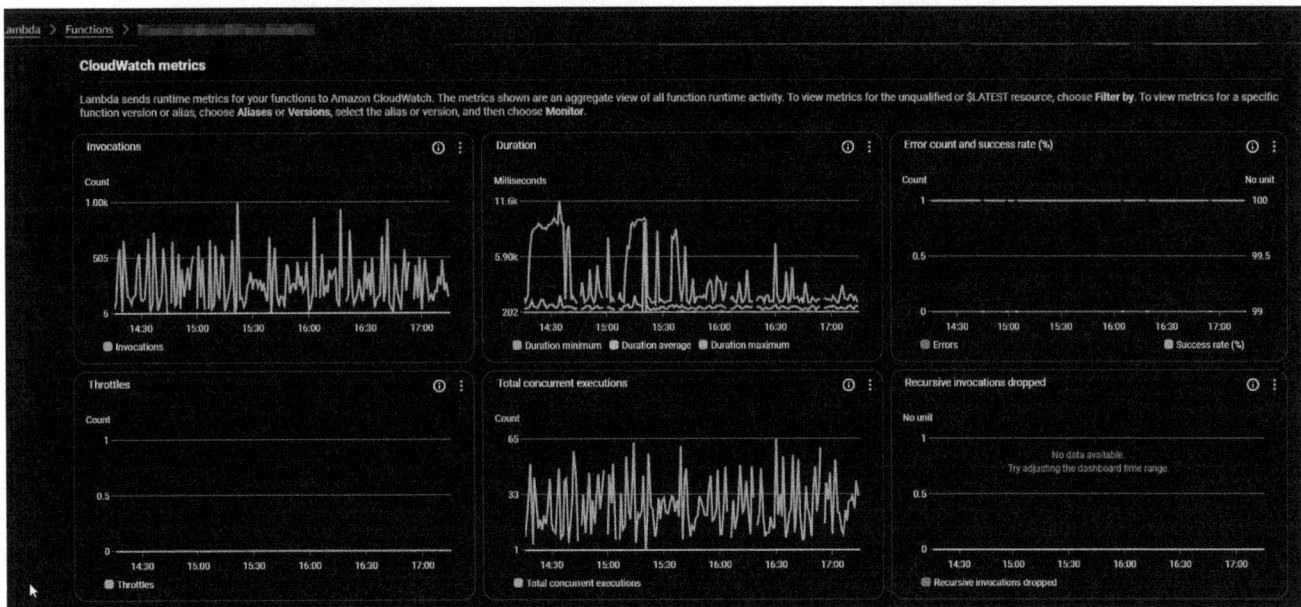

Figure 5.4: Picture showing default CloudWatch metrics for a Lambda function

- **Invocations**: Shows the total number of times this particular Lambda function is invoked/triggered throughout the sample time (represented by the x-axis). By default, this is aggregated at the minute level. For example, there were 308 invocations around 01:50 in the selected time zone.

- **Duration**: Shows the time an invocation takes to complete the job. The y-axis represents milliseconds, providing minimum, average, and maximum duration. An inference from this graph is that most jobs take less than 10 seconds to complete.

- **Error count and success rate**: Shows if there are any errors; in the sample provided, there are no errors.

- **Throttles**: Represents the number of invocations that had to be throttled at any particular instant.

Figure 5.5 shows a sample CloudWatch log for a sample Lambda function:

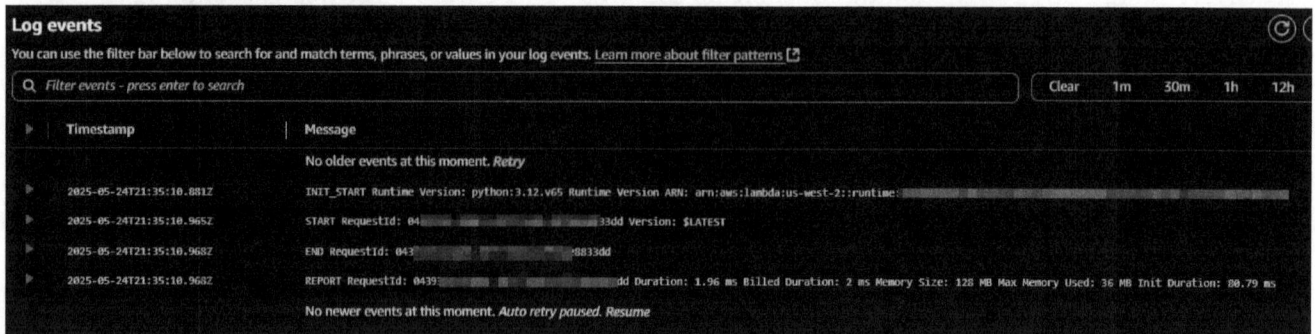

Figure 5.5: Default CloudWatch logs for a sample Lambda function

Here, the Lambda has a unique request ID (obfuscated), and it took 1.47 milliseconds to complete, 32 MB of memory, and 89.92 milliseconds for initialization.

Tip: **There are many more techniques to monitor and troubleshoot in a Lambda function; they are covered in subsequent chapters.**

Deployment patterns

AWS Lambda offers multiple deployment strategies, ranging from manual deployments via the AWS Console to automated **infrastructure as code (IaC)** approaches. The choice of deployment method depends on factors such as scalability, version control, and automation needs.

- **Manual deployment via Console**: This is the simplest option, which involves creating a Lambda function through the AWS Management Console and deploying code through the Deploy button available in the Console.
  - This is best for small-scale development, and proof-of-concept projects.
  - The pros are as follows:
    - Very simple and suitable for initial testing and discovery.
    - Good for personal use cases.
    - Ability to use versions and aliases within the Console.
  - The cons are as follows:
    - Versioning and rollback capabilities are limited.
    - Difficulty in replicating the exact configuration and settings across accounts and environments.
    - Error-prone and repetitive.
  - As a best practice, it is advised to avoid manual deployments for production systems and instead use automated approaches to ensure consistency and reduce operational risks.
- **CloudFormation IaC**: AWS CloudFormation provides a declarative approach to define Lambda as a resource through YAML/ JSON templates.
  - This is best for teams requiring a standard template to create and manage multiple Lambda functions and is a classic approach for managing IaC.
  - The pros are as follows:

- Provides greater control over underlying options and configurations.
- Very easy to replicate in other environments.
- Suited for managing medium to large-scale projects.
  - o The cons are as follows:
    - Includes initial learning curve.
    - Requires additional scripting for complex scenarios.
- **Cloud Deployment Kit (CDK)**: This involves creating Lambda as a resource using a familiar programming language (Python, NodeJS, and a few others). The CDK code finally gets converted into a CloudFormation template.
  - o This is best for organizations requiring programmatical abilities to easily create Lambda functions and their configuration using standard and familiar programming languages. When CDK is used along with AWS CodeCommit or other Git repositories, versioning and rollback capabilities can be introduced for efficient source code management.
  - o The pros are as follows:
    - Ability to use familiar programming languages.
    - Type safety and reduced typos.
    - Integration with other workflows and CI/CD pipelines.
  - o The cons are as follows:
    - Some new resources may not be available in CDK
    - Complex scenarios might require additional setup and programming.
- **AWS Serverless Application Model (SAM)**: This pattern is similar to others, but SAM is a framework specifically designed for building serverless applications. It comes with automated testing and packaging options, which have become complex for hybrid deployments.

Tip: **When AWS SAM and AWS CDK code is compiled, it generates an AWS CloudFormation template (YAML/JSON), the resource attributes, changesets, and the templates can be managed from the AWS CloudFormation service.**

Tip: **When these automated options (AWS SAM/AWS CDK) are used with AWS CodePipeline, the deployment process can be automated, and also provide capabilities of rollbacks, reviews, and even approval processes.**

Cost and concurrency

AWS Lambda is one of the most economical computing services due to its lower execution cost and pay-as-you-go model. The costs are based on the Gigabytes of execution time consumed. If Lambda functions run longer, they are billed more, hence the costs.

There is a request cost as well, regardless of the execution time.

The pricing is subject to change and has many considerations; subsequent chapters will cover more details.

Figure 5.6 shows how Lambda is priced in the AWS region Oregon(us-west-2). This also shows the pricing difference between the two architecture options (x86 and ARM64).

AWS Lambda Pricing

Region:

| US West (Oregon) ▼ |

Architecture	Duration	Requests
x86 Price		
First 6 Billion GB-seconds / month	$0.0000166667 for every GB-second	$0.20 per 1M requests
Next 9 Billion GB-seconds / month	$0.000015 for every GB-second	$0.20 per 1M requests
Over 15 Billion GB-seconds / month	$0.0000133334 for every GB-second	$0.20 per 1M requests
Arm Price		
First 7.5 Billion GB-seconds / month	$0.0000133334 for every GB-second	$0.20 per 1M requests
Next 11.25 Billion GB-seconds / month	$0.0000120001 for every GB-second	$0.20 per 1M requests
Over 18.75 Billion GB-seconds / month	$0.0000106667 for every GB-second	$0.20 per 1M requests

Figure 5.6: Lambda costs in the us-west-2 region

AWS Lambda also comes with a generous free tier, which includes 400,000 GB seconds of compute time every month and free execution for the first million requests.

This free tier is a perfect fit for small-scale business experimentation and is free for 12 months.

The concurrency of a Lambda is the number of execution environments available at any time. Each AWS account has a default limit of 1000 concurrent executions (execution environments at any instant). This limit ensures programs do not go into infinite scaling due to configuration issues or errors, thus preventing unnecessary cost and performance implications.

This is a soft limit, but it is good for most workloads as these execution environments are immediately freed once the execution is complete, and a typical Lambda function takes around a few seconds.

Tip: You can increase the account-level concurrency limits by raising a service request. AWS will review the use cases and then increase them accordingly.

Another important concept is **reserved concurrency**. This option allows you to reserve several execution environments for a particular function. This ensures that the reserved function always has that set number of warm environments and does not have to compete with other Lambda functions. Reserving concurrency to a Lambda function has additional costs, reducing invocations in the account pool.

Other configuration

AWS Lambda is one of the most commonly used AWS services with integration capabilities to connect to a wide variety of services and is used for a range of use cases.

Lambda has many configurations and settings available to fine-tune businesses' varying needs. We will cover a few of the important configuration items and properties:

- **Environment variables**: These are key-value pairs that store function configuration settings. They are accessible with the function code and help configure program behavior without altering the function source code.

A common use case is storing database names, API keys, feature flags, etc., which can change between environments. This is a perfect case for storing environment-specific flags and settings.

- **Tags**: They are user-defined labels that help categorize functions based on project, mode, environment, scenario, or criteria. The billing tag is commonly used to associate Lambda costs with a specific department or entity.

- **Function ARN**: An ARN uniquely identifies a Lambda function and is always unique. A sample ARN has the following format:

  `arn:aws:lambda:us-west-2:99999999999:function:testFunction:v42`

  Here, `testFunction` is the function's name, and `v42` is the version in account `99999999999` in the AWS region `us-west-2`.

- **Function URL**: This is a dedicated HTTPS endpoint for a Lambda function that allows direct invoke of functions from external applications or the internet and can bypass the need for an intermediate API. This helps simplify invocation and is ideal for receiving webhooks from external services.

- **Version**: A version represents a specific snapshot of the function's code (includes configuration) at any point in time, and they are immutable (cannot update versioned code) and help in rollback to any other versioned point in time.

- **Alias**: An alias is a pointer to a specific version that acts as an abstraction, helping to simplify version management, increase flexibility, and improve deployment and testing methodologies.

- **Lambda layers**: Layers help augment additional functionality that may not be readily available in the runtime. For example, if a particular Python function requires a special library to do spatial calculations, it must be imported as a layer.

Limits

Serverless architectures in the cloud generally offer unlimited scalability and flexibility. However, in practice, AWS imposes certain limits and guardrails to prevent unintentional behaviors and cost overruns, and they are also predictable from a service provider's view (AWS in this case). The following are some of the limits at this time (subject to change):

- The maximum memory allocated to a Lambda function is 10 GB and can only be done in 1 MB increments. If a Lambda requires more memory, it is not a valid case for AWS Lambda.

- The maximum duration for which a Lambda function can run is 15 minutes; if a Lambda function takes more than 15 minutes, it is the case for a batch job/asynchronous invocation and requires a redesigned approach.

- The ephemeral storage (temp space) cannot exceed 10 GB.

- The maximum size of a Lambda function cannot exceed 50 MB.

- The total size of environment variables cannot exceed 4 KB.

- The maximum size of a Lambda layer cannot exceed 250 MB.

- The maximum number of concurrent executions in an account is limited to 1000 (can be increased through a service request).

Anti-patterns

While Lambda is a very robust serverless service, it is not the best fit for all scenarios. The following are some of the anti-patterns with AWS Lambda:

- **Monolith**: Lambda is designed and works well for smaller, defined tasks and is best suited for microservice architecture implementation. If more functionality is included in a single Lambda function, it will increase the Lambda's size, increase maintenance complexity, and become unmanageable.

- **Orchestrator Lambda**: A Lambda should not be used to trigger other Lambda functions. Instead, it should be delegated to other managed services like step functions or include services like SQS, which helps with easy and simple orchestration and control.

- **Recursive functions**: This is prone to errors and would result in timeouts.

- **Batch job Lambda**: If a Lambda is doing the job of a long-running job, it is the job of a different AWS service. Lambda can only be used to call a workflow that can handle batch job operations asynchronously.

- **Ignoring cold starts**: Not accounting for cold start times can lead to unexpected performance issues, especially for applications with high latency requirements.

- **Overusing synchronous invocations**: Excessive use of synchronous invocations can impact performance and increase costs due to waiting for function completion.

- **Neglecting error handling**: Proper error handling and retry mechanisms ensure application reliability.

- **Ignoring security best practices**: Improper IAM roles, insecure code, and lack of encryption can expose your application to vulnerabilities.

- **Overlooking cost optimization**: Failing to monitor and optimize Lambda usage can lead to unexpected cost increases.

Build a function via Console

This section covers how a Lambda function can be created within a few steps through the Console and with basic configuration. The steps are as follows:

1. Navigate to **Lambda** service by searching through the **Services** Console. *Figure 5.7* shows how **Lambda** service can be searched from the Console:

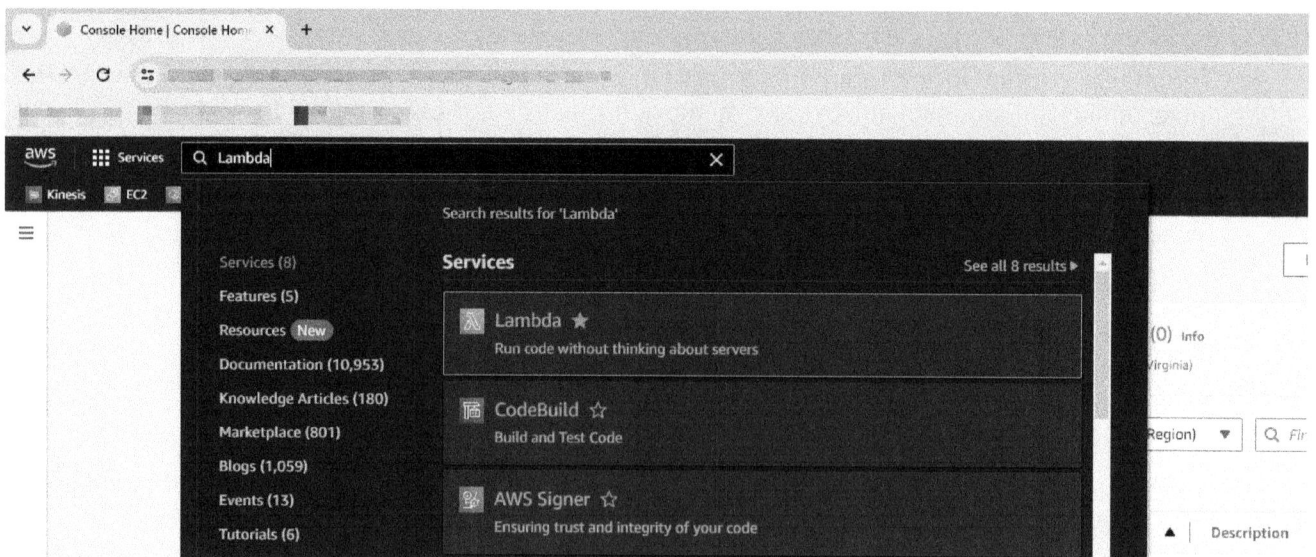

Figure 5.7: Navigating into Lambda service through the Console

2. Create a simple Lambda function by providing a name, selecting a runtime (Python 3.12 and a CPU architecture).

Figure 5.8 shows default options to create a Lambda function and runtime configuration details:

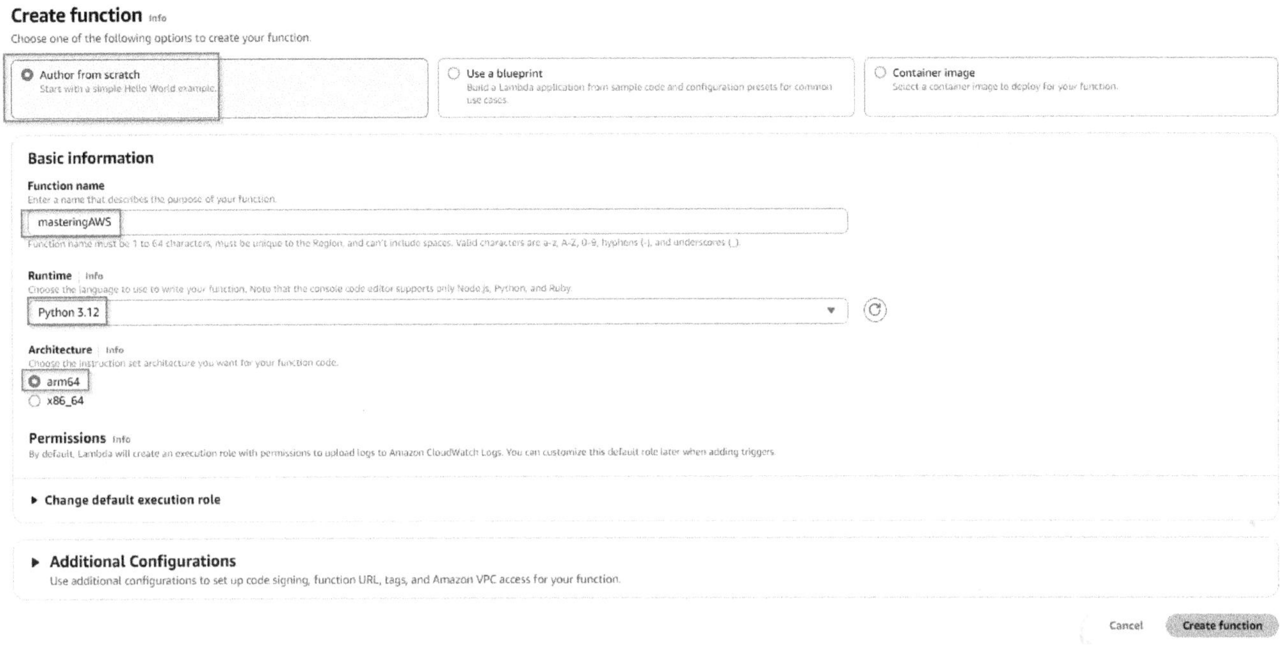

Figure 5.8: Initial runtime selection to create a new function

3. Create a simple hello world/welcome function by editing inline.

   Figure 5.9 shows the Console editor (default), which allows inline development features:

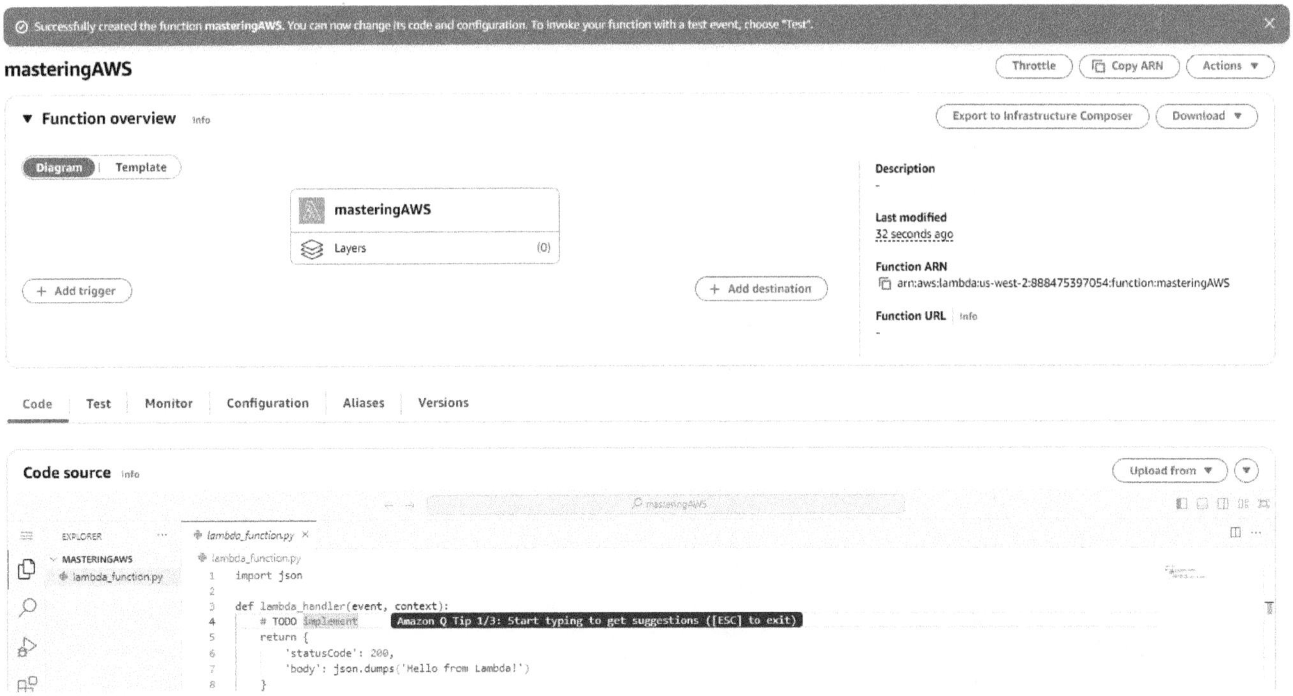

Figure 5.9: A sample source code and the option to deploy code via Console

4. Hit the **Test** button, create a simple test event, and hit **Invoke**.

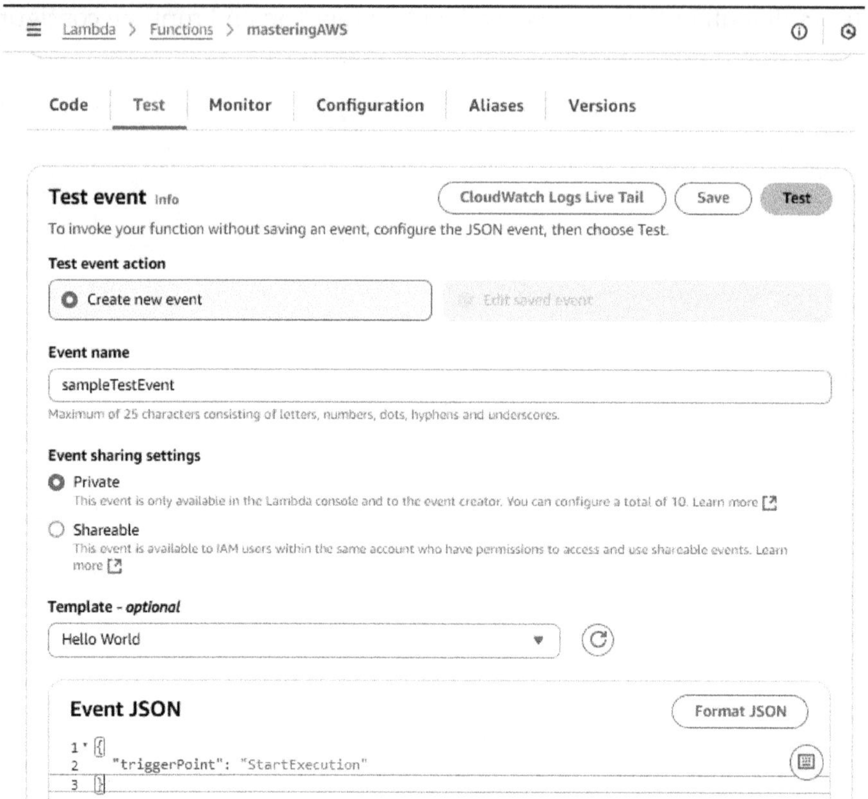

Figure 5.10: A sample test event

5. Verify results from the Console.

    Figure 5.11 shows execution results displayed within the Console for quick validation:

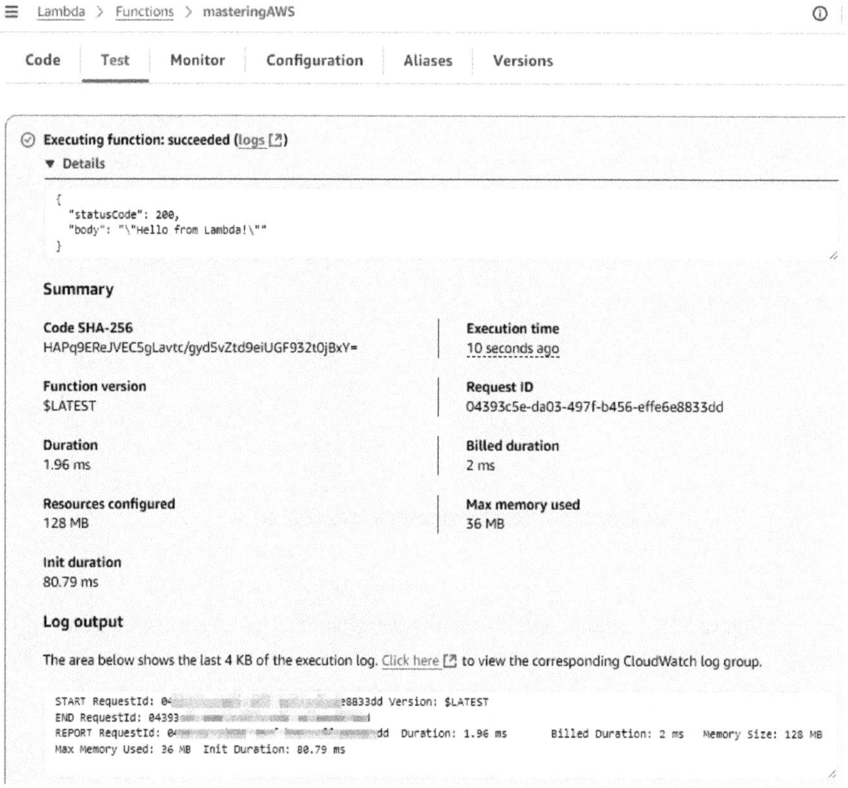

Figure 5.11: A sample test result

Serverless Compute with AWS Lambda 71

6. Navigate to **Monitor** and **View CloudWatch logs**.

Figure 5.12 shows navigation into CloudWatch logs for the test Lambda function:

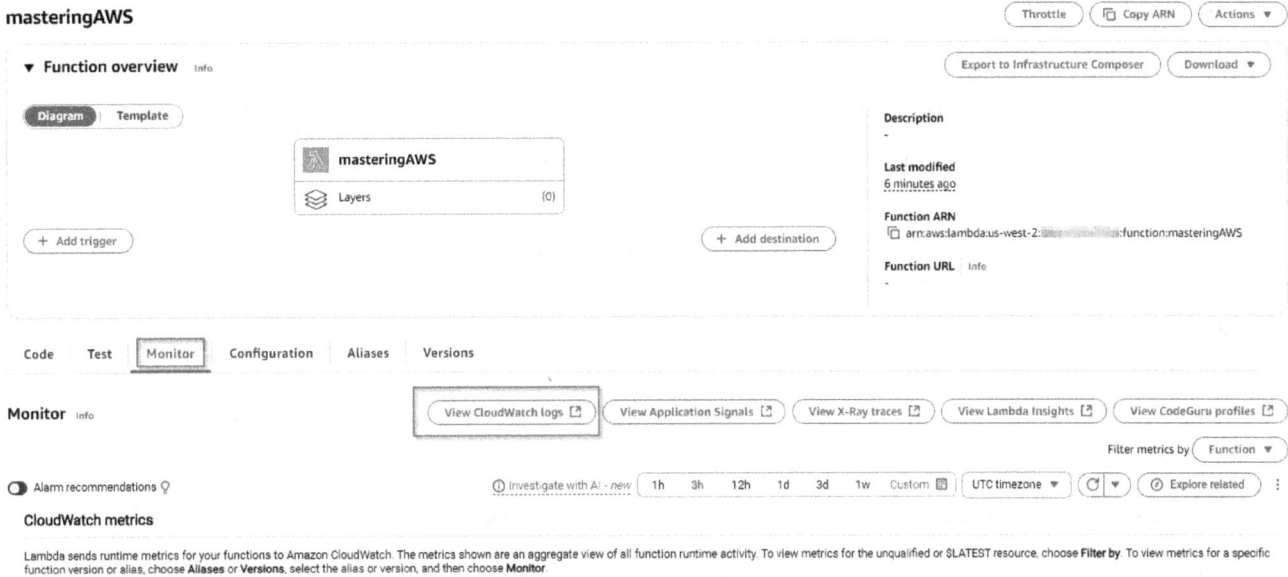

Figure 5.12: *Navigating to CloudWatch logs*

7. Click on the default log group and inspect the log detail.

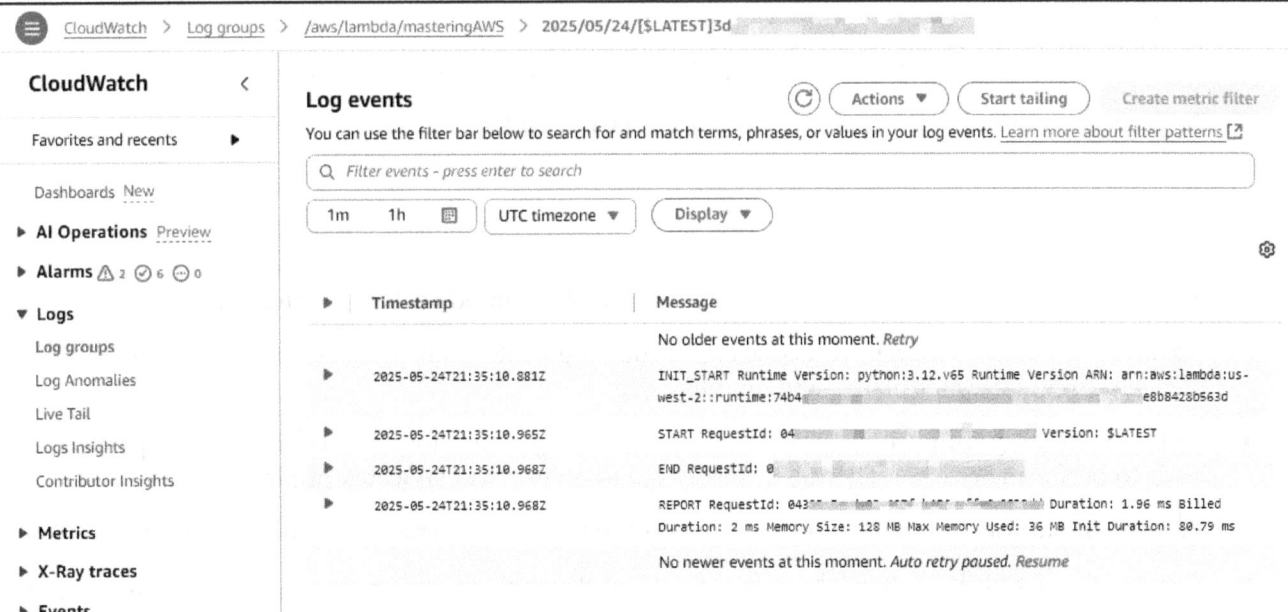

Figure 5.13: *Picture showing a sample CloudWatch Log event*

At this time, we have successfully created a Lambda function by selecting Python runtime; the function prints a welcome statement, tested the function via Console, and verified through CloudWatch logs

Note: As of October 2024, the Lambda editor has been upgraded to provide more capabilities to the AWS Lambda Console and integration with Amazon Q (an AI-powered assistant for rapid development, debugging, and code completion options).

Industry use cases

AWS Lambda is one of the most versatile and highly useful AWS services, which fits into almost all workflows across business domains and verticals; the following are a few examples of how Lambda can be used in different industry domains:

- **Finance**: AWS Lambda can analyze real-time transactions, detect fraud, and identify suspicious activities.

- **Healthcare**: AWS Lambda can analyze patient data, manage medical records, send automated reminders to patients, and manage medication subscriptions.

- **Media and entertainment**: AWS Lambda can generate video encoding, generate thumbnails, manage content, and implement content rights management utilities.

- **IoT**: AWS Lambda is the default choice for managing IoT devices, processing real-time data, analyzing data streams, and enabling analytics.

- **Education**: AWS Lambda can be used for automated grading systems, quizzes, and assignments and process student submissions.

- **Non-profit and social**: To manage online donations, process receipts, and volunteer management.

- **Government**: To process citizen programs, document renewals, tax processing, and automatic request approvals.

- **Retail**: Personalized recommendations, inventory management, fraud detection, and order processing.

- **Manufacturing**: Predictive maintenance, quality control, supply chain optimization, and IoT device management.

- **Gaming**: Game backend logic, leaderboards, matchmaking, and real-time data processing.

- **Telecommunications**: Customer support chatbots, network monitoring, fraud prevention, and billing systems.

Best practices

The following are some of the best practices that will help AWS Lambda achieve better results:

- **Microservice architecture**: Decompose application logic into smaller, focused, targeted functions, and this helps in greater modularity and maintenance

- **Optimal memory allocation**: Overprovisioning leads to additional costs, and under provisioning leads to performance issues; hence, it is essential to review and allocate optimal memory

- **Version and aliases**: Ensure aliases always point to the correct version to avoid unexpected behavior.

- **Secure your Lambda**: Follow the principle of least privilege and provide only the exact required permission for that function to do the assigned task.

- **Cost optimizations**: Review pricing regularly and identify opportunities for cost savings. For example, the recently introduced support for ARM64 processors significantly reduces the cost for medium and complex executions compared to x86 versions.

- **Optimal memory allocation**: While you mentioned the importance of finding the right balance, delve deeper into techniques like profiling your function's memory usage to determine the optimal allocation.

- **Leverage Lambda layers**: Explain how layers can share code and dependencies across multiple functions, reducing function size and improving cold start times.

- **Implement dead-letter queues (DLQs)**: Discuss the importance of DLQs for handling failed messages and retry mechanisms.

- **Utilize provisioned concurrency**: Explain how provisioned concurrency reduces cold starts and improves performance for high-traffic applications.

- **Consider Lambda warm-up strategies**: Discuss techniques for keeping Lambda functions warm, such as using CloudWatch Events or custom warm-up functions.

- **Implement robust error handling**: Emphasize the importance of proper error handling and logging to identify and resolve issues quickly.

Conclusion

This chapter has been your comprehensive guide to AWS Lambda, propelling you from first-time setup to mastering advanced use cases across diverse industries. We have unveiled the powerful features that make Lambda the undisputed champion of cost-effective serverless computing within the AWS arsenal.

We have explored how Lambda empowers the implementation of microservices architectures and event-driven paradigms, fostering agility and responsiveness in your applications. You have also learned to configure Lambda precisely, ensuring it seamlessly integrates into various scenarios. This foundational understanding positions you perfectly to leverage the full potential of serverless computing and unlock a world of innovative solutions.

The next chapter will explore Amazon S3, AWS's cornerstone service for scalable object storage, which plays a critical role in modern cloud architectures. We will look at how S3 stores and retrieves data, its storage classes, lifecycle management, security features, and integration with other AWS services. Additionally, we will address practical use cases and demonstrate how S3 solves key challenges in data storage and management.

Join our Discord space

Join our Discord workspace for latest updates, offers, tech happenings around the world, new releases, and sessions with the authors:

https://discord.bpbonline.com

CHAPTER 6

Serverless Storage with AWS S3

Introduction

In today's interconnected digital world, data has become the lifeblood of progress. It flows through every aspect of our lives, embedded in the devices we carry, the vehicles we drive, and even the food we consume. This ever-growing stream of information drives modern applications, fuels innovation, and shapes industries. Decisions made by companies, financial institutions, and governments are all grounded in the power of data, underscoring its vital role in defining the future.

As technology advances, the sheer volume of data generated by connected devices is reaching unprecedented levels. Storing and managing this data reliably and securely, and doing so at a massive scale, has become a monumental challenge for organizations worldwide. However, scalability and cost are just two aspects of this challenge. Organizations must also consider data durability, compliance, access control, integration with analytics, and lifecycle management when selecting a storage solution. This chapter explores one of the most transformative solutions to these challenges: Amazon S3. S3 provides enterprises with storage and an intelligent foundation for secure, highly available, and event-driven data operations through its versatile architecture.

Amazon S3 is the benchmark for cloud object storage, renowned for its exceptional scalability, durability, and simplicity. Before delving into S3's groundbreaking features, this chapter builds a solid foundation by exploring the evolution of storage solutions. From the physical constraints of on-premises systems to the boundless possibilities offered by the cloud, the journey of storage technology reveals why S3 stands at the forefront.

You will discover how S3's object-based architecture and seamless integration with other AWS services enable businesses to create powerful serverless architectures. Practical examples, real-world use cases, and hands-on exercises will guide you through its capabilities, equipping you to harness S3 for a wide range of applications. Together, we will uncover why Amazon S3 is not just a storage solution but a cornerstone of modern data innovation.

Structure

The chapter covers the following topics:

- Fundamentals of data and storage
- Introduction to cloud storage

- Introduction to Amazon S3
- Operations with S3

Objectives

This chapter provides readers with a solid understanding of cloud storage solutions and the diverse data storage options available through AWS. It begins by introducing the foundational concepts of cloud storage, including the requirements for scalable, secure, and efficient storage systems. Readers will explore the wide range of AWS storage solutions designed to handle various data types and workloads.

A significant focus is placed on Amazon S3, AWS's flagship storage service. The chapter delves into its core principles, including configuration best practices, data security, and strategies to ensure data integrity. Readers will also learn how to implement effective data lifecycle management using S3's built-in automation features, optimizing storage costs and efficiency.

Additionally, this chapter demonstrates how S3 can be applied across industries, showcasing its versatility in enterprise environments. It highlights the integration of S3 into serverless workflows, emphasizing monitoring and governance practices to meet industry standards. The seamless interaction of S3 with other AWS services is also explored, revealing its role in building robust serverless architectures.

Practical examples and real-world use cases are included to ensure that concepts are not only understood but also applied effectively, empowering readers to harness the full potential of Amazon S3 in their storage strategies.

By completing this chapter, readers will be well-positioned to leverage Amazon S3's capabilities for building secure, scalable, and cost-effective serverless applications.

Fundamentals of data and storage

Data is at the core of modern computing; it is the lifeblood of computing and fuels every aspect of our digital lives. Data is present in every aspect of our daily life and is required in every task. Every mobile app, website we visit, appliance/device we use (watch, television, home appliance), and vehicle we drive/commute (airplane, car, bus) has data. This data acts as a raw material for computation and analysis.

Data can be defined as raw information, facts, and statistics collected for the purpose of analytics. Data is the basic unit of information in computing and digital communication.

Data can provide significant insights upon diligent processing, analysis, and interpretation. These insights are instrumental not only for fundamental operations but also for informed decision-making processes. This concept is widely recognized as **data-driven decision-making**.

Data can be broadly categorized into the following types:

Structured data

This data is often organized in a predefined format, making it easily searchable and analyzable.

An example is a relational database storing customer transactions for an e-commerce platform. Each record contains structured fields such as customer ID, purchase date, and order amount, allowing quick queries and analytics. Think of a library with shelves and catalogs storing books by genre, author, and content type.

Figure 6.1 shows a bookshelf, which is analogous to storing structured data:

Figure 6.1: Picture showing a bookshelf in a library for structured data

In computing, data stored in relational database tables and Excel/CSV files are splendid examples of structured data where the data can be indexed, identified, and easily retrieved.

Unstructured data

This data lacks a fixed format or predefined schema, making it difficult to index or analyze without advanced tools. **Example**: Social media platforms generate vast amounts of unstructured data, including tweets, images, and videos. Businesses use AI and machine learning to extract insights from this raw data. An analogy of unstructured data is an attic filled with boxes and belongings, where information is present but not easily searchable.

Figure 6.2 shows an attic with different items and types analogous to unstructured data:

Figure 6.2: Picture showing an unorganized attic representing unstructured data

Semi-structured data

This data has no rigid schema but contains metadata that provides organization. **Examples**: JSON and XML files used in APIs and web applications. These formats structure data using key-value pairs while maintaining flexibility in attributes. A real-life analogy is a hybrid closet, some sections are neatly categorized while others contain scattered items.

See *Figure 6.3* for an example where some items are organized and some are dispersed:

Figure 6.3: Picture showing a semi-structured cabinet

In computing, a **JavaScript Object Notation (JSON)** object/file can be considered semi-structured because the data is still humanly readable (key and value pairs) but does not have a definite structure. The number of JSON keys can vary based on the scenario, and this is one of the most common ways to transmit data between different software systems.

Data storage is a technique that involves using computers and storage devices to store digital and recording media to keep information. The data could be stored/kept temporarily or permanently.

Digital information and data are stored using magnetic, optical, or mechanical media for future operations. Data storage is vital for any business, and every piece of data contains valuable information required for day-to-day operations and to extract valuable insights to help make better business decisions.

A simple example of data storage can be employee records, customer information, financials, patient health records, parts, and assembly instructions in a vehicle manufacturing plant.

When data is stored, the following becomes the building blocks:

- **Fundamental units**: Data is stored as bits (0s and 1s) at the most basic level. Groups of eight bits make a byte, the fundamental unit for storing characters and numbers.
- **Storage devices**: These are the physical devices that store data. They can be hard drives, solid-state devices (persistent storage), or temporary storage devices (Cache storage and RAM).

Evolution of data storage

In the preliminary stages of computing, data was stored in punch cards. The punch cards represented data through patterns, and each card represented a specific informational item.

Another option was to use magnetic drums, which are primarily used for data storage.

The next age of storage was dominated by **hard disk drives (HDDs)** and optical disks, which specialized in storing more information per hardware size and were also portable. This enabled quicker information retrieval and faster access for a fraction of the cost and was a propelling factor for modern-day computing.

In today's world, storage has evolved from HDDs and optical disks into USB flash devices, solid-state devices, and, most importantly, cloud storage.

Cloud storage allows data to be accessed via the Internet. It has revolutionized computing by providing unlimited storage capacity, enhanced fine-grained security, access control, and high availability. The next topic will discuss this in greater detail.

Data storage is a technique that involves using computers and storage devices to store digital and recording media to keep information. The data could be stored/kept temporarily or permanently.

Introduction to cloud storage

Cloud storage can be considered a technique, paradigm, or pattern involving storing data, objects, and files in remote servers managed by a third-party trusted computing provider. The provider is responsible for managing data security, providing data access patterns, and networking within the cloud, while the customer can focus on application development.

Cloud data can be accessed from public and private networks, revolutionizing how data and information are stored, retrieved, and scaled in real time. While cloud storage offers scalability and cost advantages, traditional on-premises storage solutions still have use cases where direct control over data and infrastructure is required.

Table 6.1 provides a quick comparison:

Feature	Cloud storage	Traditional storage
Scalability	Virtually unlimited, scaled on demand	Limited by physical hardware capacity
Cost model	Pay-as-you-go, no upfront infrastructure costs	High upfront costs for purchasing and maintaining servers
Data access	Access from anywhere via the internet	Localized access, which requires direct network connectivity
Deployment time	Instant provisioning, no hardware setup required	Requires time to procure, install, and configure hardware
Security and compliance	Managed encryption, IAM-based access control, and compliance tools	On-premises security requires manual configuration
Reliability and durability	99.999999999% durability (AWS S3) with multi-AZ redundancy	Risk of hardware failure, requires RAID or backups
Maintenance	Fully managed by cloud provider	Requires a dedicated IT team for hardware/software updates

Table 6.1: Table showing comparison of cloud storage and traditional storage

By leveraging cloud storage, businesses eliminate the complexities of hardware management while benefiting from high availability, scalability, and cost optimization. Cloud-based solutions empower organizations to build resilient, serverless applications with seamless data accessibility.

Types of cloud storage

Cloud storage can be broadly categorized based on the type of artifacts it stores into the following storage types.

- **Object storage**: The artifacts/files are stored as storage objects. These objects contain the original data, metadata about the object, and a unique key that identifies the object. The metadata includes critical information about the object (size, purpose, file type, created by, created time, last updated time, encoding, to name a few).

In object storage, files are often stored as they arrive in containers called buckets. Each object is self-contained, with metadata providing an object description.

This storage is better suited for storing unstructured data. Some common examples of unstructured data include images, emails, videos, sensor data, audio files, text files, and spreadsheets.

Some of the common offerings provided by major cloud providers for Object storage include Amazon S3 (by Amazon Web Services), Google Cloud Storage (Google), and Azure blob storage (Microsoft Azure).

- **File storage**: The artifacts are stored in a hierarchical file format. This methodology helps users, applications, and services access data in a shared file system analogous to a centralized shared network drive. It provides a familiar way to store and access data through folder and subfolder-based operations.

  File storage typically offers better performance for frequently accessed files.

  Some common examples from major cloud providers include Amazon EFS, Azure Files, and Google Cloud Filestore. Other examples include Dropbox, Google Drive, and Microsoft OneDrive.

- **Block storage**: Here, data is stored as fixed-size blocks. Applications and file systems regulate how these blocks are accessed, combined, and modified. The original content is divided into smaller pieces and blocks, each stored with a unique identifier. This helps store these blocks across different operating systems.

Choosing the right cloud storage type

In a typical cloud solution involving storage, the type of storage required depends on multiple criteria, including workload requirements, security constraints, and performance expectations. Most architectures typically involve more than one storage type.

Block storage use cases

Since block storage can scale to performance needs, supporting millions to billions of transactions, it is ideal for deploying commercial databases like SQL Server, PostgreSQL, Oracle, and SAP HANA, and also for NoSQL databases like Cassandra, MongoDB, and CouchDB.

Block storage is also ideal for big-data analytics due to its high data persistence and dynamic-performance configuration abilities, making it the ideal candidate for data warehouses and streaming data solutions.

Block storage is the default choice to run mission-critical, highly available, low-latency enterprise applications across industries.

Object storage use cases

Object storage is the go-to for building cloud-native and serverless applications due to the cost-effective storage tiers and the unlimited scalability offered by object storage providers.

Object stores are ideal for building corporate data lakes, which can be used for advanced analytics, running ML workloads, and streaming pipelines.

Amazon AWS storage offerings

AWS provides storage services for all the core storage types (object, block, and file storage):

- **File storage (Amazon EFS)**: Amazon EFS offers a simple, elastic file system that allows file sharing without the need to provide any file servers. This has integrations, making it available within cloud services, and it also works seamlessly with on-premises file systems and resources. Amazon EFS is best suited for offering storage to serverless apps. Web hosting and serving, content management, and database backups.

Amazon EFS is covered in detail in subsequent chapters.

- **Block storage (Amazon EBS)**: Amazon EBS is a high-performance block-storage service designed for Amazon EC2 (cloud servers, which will be covered in detail in subsequent chapters).

  Amazon EBS can create storage volumes and attach them to Amazon EC2 instances.

- **Object storage (Amazon S3)**: This object storage service stores data as objects within containers called **buckets**. It is one of the most versatile and commonly used services for serverless applications, data lakes, mobile apps, IoT devices, big data analytics, and enterprise applications.

Introduction to Amazon S3

Amazon **Simple Storage Service** (**S3**) is an object storage service. This is the oldest offering and the first service offered by Amazon. This was launched on March 14, 2006 (it coincides with Pi Day (3.14)). This service is designed to be secure, durable, highly available, reliable, easy to use, and affordable.

Amazon S3 is a managed service and is considered serverless because there is no need to manage any backend or underlying infrastructure, and it can scale massively. Also, this is the backbone for most serverless applications on the cloud.

This is suited for customers and organizations of all sizes, domains, and industry verticals. It offers high availability and can technically store any amount of data for any use case, such as websites, content management, IoT use cases, big-data analytics, machine learning workflows, transactional data stores, disaster recovery, e-commerce applications, healthcare, and financial analytics, backup and restore services, mobile applications, and as a backbone for most cloud-native and serverless solutions.

Amazon S3 offers 99.999999999% durability, which translates to a potential loss of a single file out of 10 million objects over 10,000 years. This prominent level of durability makes it the most versatile object storage offering by any leading cloud provider. Losing an object from S3, when configured and managed properly, is nearly impossible.

Amazon S3 typically involves storing data as objects inside buckets in an AWS region of choice. There can be more than one bucket/region, and any number of objects in that bucket.

Apart from using S3 as backend storage for serverless applications, S3 can also be fronted with another AWS Service (AWS CloudFront), AWS's **content delivery network** (**CDN**), for serving static files and websites over the Internet.

Amazon S3 offers multiple management features to optimize, organize, and configure access to data to meet specific business needs and compliance requirements.

Interaction with objects in Amazon S3 can be facilitated through various methods, including the AWS Management Console, **software development kits** (**SDKs**), and the AWS **Command Line Interface** (**CLI**). Additionally, it can serve as the underlying infrastructure for numerous services and interfaces.

Amazon S3 is an optimal choice for developing various applications due to several key factors. These include its suitability for cloud-native applications, compatibility with serverless workloads and event-driven systems, and adaptability to hybrid applications. Furthermore, it is an effective website content repository, a robust disaster recovery solution, and a reliable backend for various systems.

The following figure illustrates how Amazon S3 interacts with key AWS services in a typical S3 based datalake:

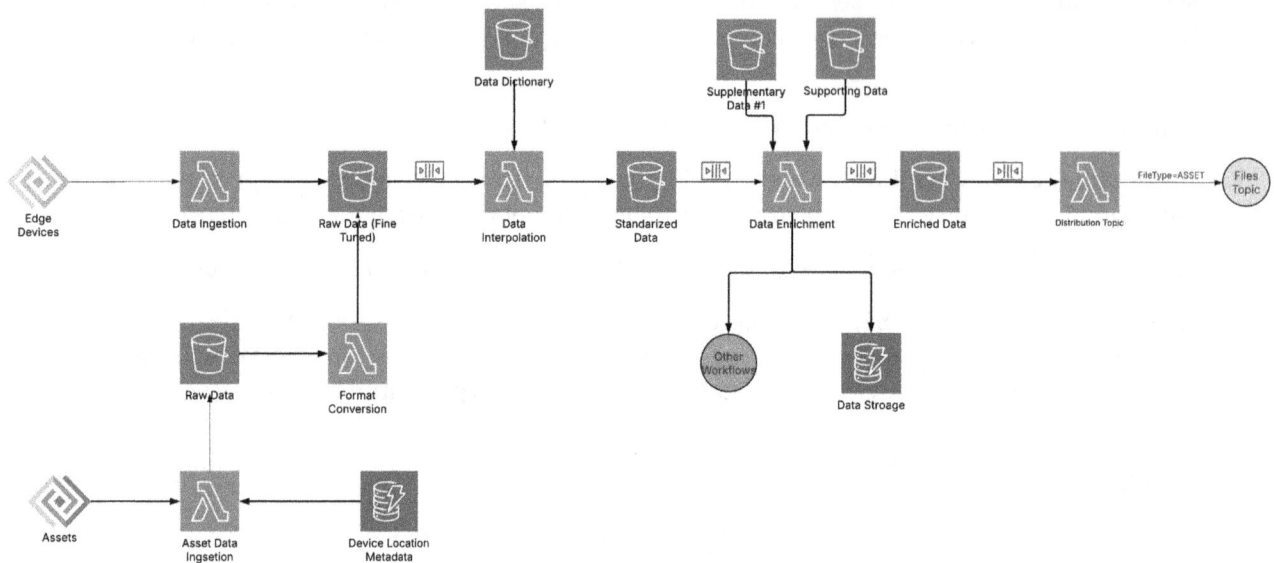

Figure 6.4: *Typical S3 based datalake architecture*

As seen in *Figure 6.4,* a typical data lake architecture involves utilizing Amazon S3 to store data at different stages.

The key features of Amazon S3 are as follows:

- **Fully managed**: Customers do not have to manage any backend infrastructure.

- **Highly scalable**: S3 is infinitely scalable to meet increasing user demands.

- **High availability and durability**: AWS provides 99.999999999 (11 9's of durability), making it the service with the highest reliability.

- **Highly secure**: Provides a wide range of security, guard rails, governance, and audit trails.

- **Seamless integration**: Seamlessly integrates with all of the AWS services.

- **Unlimited storage**: Provides unlimited storage capabilities.

- **Cost-effective**: Economical and also provides storage tiers matching access patterns.

- **Data management and governance**: Provides rich controls for data management and governance controls.

Key terminologies

Some key terminologies used in Amazon S3 are as follows:

- **Data**: Files and objects uploaded to S3 consist of data representing actual information.

- **Metadata**: This represents information about the object. The metadata can be

  o **System-controlled metadata**: Managed by S3 service; some examples include CreationDate, LastModified, eTag, Size, and StorageClass.

  o **User-controlled metadata**: Users have some control over the same; some examples include ContentLength, ContentType, and ServerSideEncryption.

  o **User-defined metadata**: Author, Copyright, CustomTag, SoftwareVersion.

- **Object**: Each piece of data stored can be called an object. Each object has a unique identifier.

- **Bucket**: A bucket is a container or placeholder that holds multiple objects. It is similar to a directory structure. Configurations can be applied at the bucket level to all the objects in that bucket.

  Files and objects can only be placed inside one or more of these buckets, and S3 cannot store objects outside of buckets.

  By default, an AWS S3 bucket is owned by the account and cannot be transferred to other AWS accounts. The bucket name must be unique across all AWS accounts in all AWS regions across partitions. The following are the three partitions for S3:

  - Standard regions (aws)
  - China regions (aws-cn)
  - GovCloud region (aws-us-gov)

  All buckets must conform to bucket naming standards. A few naming rules are listed as follows:

  - The bucket name cannot be less than three characters or more than 63 characters.
  - Must begin with a letter/number.
  - Can only contain lowercase letters, dots, numbers, and hyphens.
  - Bucket names cannot have an IP address format, but can have a fully qualified domain. For example, `testbucket.testdomain.com` is a valid bucket name.

- **Object versioning**: Object versioning in Amazon S3 offers a powerful safeguard against accidental modifications and deletions. This functionality meticulously tracks every change made to objects within a version-enabled bucket, creating a distinct version for each iteration. Each version possesses a unique identifier, enabling clear differentiation and retrieval of past states. This comprehensive history empowers users to:

  - **Recover from unintended deletions**: A misplaced click can lead to the disappearance of critical data. Thankfully, object versioning allows for effortless retrieval from a previous version, eliminating the stress of data loss.

  - **Revert to prior states**: Edits sometimes introduce unforeseen consequences. Object versioning facilitates a seamless rollback to an earlier version, effectively restoring data to its desired state. This proves particularly valuable for configuration files and sensitive documents.

  - **Maintain an immutable audit trail**: Have you ever wondered who modified a file and when? Object versioning is an infallible log, meticulously recording every upload and modification. This transparency is invaluable for regulatory compliance and collaborative projects.

  - **Harnessing the power of versions**: By default, accessing an object through the S3 Console or SDK retrieves the latest version. However, users can leverage version IDs to access any specific version. Additionally, S3 lifecycle management integrates seamlessly with object versioning. This allows for the automated transitioning of older versions to cost-effective storage classes, optimizing storage costs while preserving data history.

  - **A secure future for your data**: Object versioning in S3 safeguards data against accidental edits, deletions, and human error. It empowers users to navigate past states, restore lost data, and maintain a clear audit trail while controlling storage costs. By activating object versioning on S3 buckets, users can experience peace of mind with comprehensive data protection.

- **Storage types**: There are two storage types based on the data usage; they could be:

  - **Active storage**: This is the data that is live (hot / frequently accessed) and must be accessible for transactions. For example, static files for an S3-hosted website.

- o **Archive storage**: This data set is not required to be immediately accessible; this data is rarely accessed but must be maintained. For example, compliance and regulatory data and historical transactions.

- **Storage classes**: These predefined categories determine how data is stored and accessed. They help choose a class that best suits the type of operation being performed. Storage classes are a trade-off between storage cost, speed of access, and data durability. The main storage classes include S3 Standard, S3 Glacier, and S3 Intelligent tiering.

- **Lifecycle management**: A feature that automatically moves files and content between storage classes.

- **Bucket policy**: A JSON formatted policy document that defines entities that can access the specified bucket. It controls how access can be through a resource-based policy approach.

  The following are the key components of a bucket policy:

  - o **Principal**: Specifies who can access the bucket. This can be an IAM user, role, or an AWS account ID.

  - o **Resource**: Identifies the specific S3 bucket to which the policy applies.

  - o **Action**: Defines the operations permitted on the bucket (e.g., GetObject, PutObject, DeleteObject).

  - o **Effect**: Indicates whether to allow (Allow) or deny (Deny) the specified action.

- **Transfer acceleration**: Transferring large datasets to S3 buckets can be sluggish, especially when battling geographical distance or limited bandwidth. S3 transfer acceleration tackles this challenge by establishing numerous connections between your data source and strategically deployed edge locations worldwide. These edge locations act as intelligent intermediaries, efficiently routing your data packets along the optimal path to S3 storage. By leveraging these multiple connections and intelligent routing, S3 transfer acceleration significantly reduces upload times, streamlining the process for large datasets.

  This service offers substantial benefits. You can experience a dramatic reduction in upload times, leading to improved workflow efficiency and potentially lower data transfer costs. S3 transfer acceleration is easy to implement, enable it for your S3 bucket and enjoy the performance boost. This globally available service ensures optimized data transfer speeds regardless of location relative to S3 storage.

Storage classes

AWS S3 storage classes offer a spectrum of options; in simple terms, customers pay more for faster access and pay less for relatively slower retrieval, and these classes provide these trade-offs as options.

The following are the key storage classes offered by Amazon S3:

- **Amazon S3 Standard**: This is the default storage class and often fits most use cases involving frequently accessed data.

  This provides high-performance, low-latency access and is ideal for mission-critical apps, frequently downloadable files, and streaming analytics use cases.

  This has greater access speeds but incurs slightly more cost per GB of data accessed, yet it is cost-effective for frequently accessed data.

- **Amazon S3 Standard-IA**: The data is highly available (like S3 Standard), but data is accessed infrequently. This is a storage class that strikes a balance between cost and access speed. Here, the storage costs are lower but incur a small retrieval fee.

  This best suits backup, disaster recovery, and data archive-based scenarios.

- **Amazon S3 One Zone-IA**: Here, the data is accessed infrequently and is suitable for scenarios where it can be easily recreated when lost. The data is only stored in one of Amazon's **availability zones (AZ)** in that region, so it has the potential for data loss. However, it offers the cheapest pricing in comparison to other storage classes in S3 Standard.

  This is best suited for secondary backups, cross-region replicated data, and scenarios where data can be easily re-created.

- **Amazon S3 Glacier**: This storage class is designed for long-term archiving and compliance. Here, storage costs are significantly lower in comparison to S3 standard storage classes. However, with longer retrieval times ranging from hours to days. This can be further categorized into the following storage classes:

  o **Amazon S3 Glacier: Flexible retrieval**: This follows a balanced approach, balancing between cost and retrieval time. A typical retrieval can take from several hours to days in this class.

  o **Amazon S3 Glacier: Instant retrieval**: This provides faster access times (usually within hours) and hence comes with relatively higher costs than other options in the Glacier class.

  o **Amazon S3 Glacier: Deep archive**: This is the most cost-effective option for rarely accessed data, and a typical retrieval can span from hours to days. The default retrieval time is 12 hours.

- **Amazon S3, Intelligent-Tiering**: This class is best suited in scenarios involving unpredictable data access patterns, and it provides cost efficiencies while automatically managing storage classes based on the access patterns. S3 service ensures cost optimization by moving frequently accessed data to performant tiers and rarely accessed data to lower-cost tiers.

Evolution of S3 as a tabular data store

Amazon S3 has evolved significantly, transitioning from a foundational object storage service to a platform capable of powering complex analytics, machine learning, and AI workloads.

The following shows how S3 usage has evolved from simple object storage to tabular workloads, OpenTable formats, and managed S3 Tables:

- **Object storage**: S3 was initially created to store unstructured data, such as images, videos, backups, and logs. It became the go-to storage solution for its scalability, durability, and cost efficiency, fulfilling the needs of general-purpose data storage.

- **Tabular data storage**: As analytics and machine learning demands grew, S3 began supporting structured data in formats like Apache Parquet, which offered efficient storage and querying. These datasets were organized as files and folders, mapped to S3 objects and prefixes. While this enabled new use cases like meteorological analysis and web traffic tracking, challenges emerged, including the difficulty of schema evolution (e.g., adding or removing columns) and the need for advanced metadata features for versioning and transactions.

- **Open table formats**: To address these issues, open table formats like Apache Iceberg introduced metadata layers for better dataset management.

  These formats brought:
  o Robust transactions for data consistency.
  o Schema evolution for seamless structural updates.
  o Time travel for querying historical data versions.
  o Iceberg improved the scalability of shared datasets and analytics workflows while leveraging S3's reliability. However, its adoption introduced operational complexities, such as increased metadata traffic, compaction needs, and cost burdens from snapshot management.

- **S3 tables**: AWS introduced S3 tables to simplify dataset management, which optimized the benefits of open table formats while addressing their challenges. S3 tables provide:
  o Automated management for tasks like compaction and snapshot optimization.
  o Enhanced performance to handle traffic efficiently.
  o Improved governance with integrated security and policy tools.
  o Cost optimization by reducing the overhead of version control and maintenance.

Lifecycle management

Lifecycle management is a feature in S3 that allows automatic data movement between different storage tiers based on defined rules.

In today's data-driven landscape, organizations are harnessing the power of data to gain valuable insights. As data volumes surge, managing cloud storage becomes paramount. Here is where S3 lifecycle management steps in, offering an automated approach to optimize costs and storage efficiency.

S3 lifecycle management empowers users to define automated rules that govern the movement of their data between different storage tiers within S3 buckets. These rules are based on pre-defined criteria, such as the age of the data or its access patterns. This intelligent automation streamlines data management and ensures leveraging the most cost-effective storage options for your specific needs by effectively utilizing S3 lifecycle management.

The following are some of the key benefits:

- **Reduced storage costs**: Automatically transition less frequently accessed data to lower-cost storage classes, leading to significant cost savings.

- **Simplified data governance**: Define data retention policies and automate the deletion of obsolete data to ensure compliance with regulations.

- **Enhanced storage efficiency**: Organize your S3 buckets by automatically archiving older objects, keeping your storage organized and clutter-free.

- **Streamlined management**: Automate tedious data lifecycle tasks, freeing you to focus on more strategic initiatives.

The key components of a lifecycle policy are as follows:

- **ID**: A unique identifier for the rule within the bucket.

- **Condition**: What triggers the rule (e.g., object age, storage class, the prefix in the object key, user-defined tags)?

- **Action**: What happens to objects meeting the condition (e.g., transition to a different storage class, permanent deletion, delete noncurrent versions)?

The following table provides a sample use case for how lifecycle policies can be implemented to achieve cost efficiencies while maintaining data durability and access requirements:

Log files	**Policy**: Transition log files older than 30 days to Glacier storage class.
	Benefit: Reduces storage costs for log files, which are typically accessed infrequently for troubleshooting purposes.
Media archives	**Policy 1**: Transition media files (e.g., videos) not accessed in the past year to Glacier Deep Archive.
	Policy 2 (Optional): Delete media files older than five years.
	Benefit: Optimizes storage costs for rarely accessed media archives while allowing for potential future deletion of obsolete data.
Backups	**Policy 1**: Transition primary backups to Glacier storage class after 30 days.
	Policy 2 (Optional): Keep the latest backup version indefinitely and delete older versions after seven days.
	Benefit: It maintains readily available primary backups while transitioning older backups to a lower-cost tier for long-term archival. It also ensures backup version control while avoiding unnecessary storage of redundant versions.
Website assets	**Policy**: Exclude frequently accessed website assets (e.g., HTML, CSS, JavaScript) from any lifecycle management rules.
	Benefit: Ensures optimal performance and availability of critical website assets.
Versioned documents	**Policy 1**: Retain the latest version of a document indefinitely.
	Policy 2: Transition older versions of documents to Glacier storage class after one year.
	Policy 3 (Optional): Delete document versions older than five years.
	Benefit: Maintains access to the latest version of documents while archiving older versions for compliance or historical reference purposes. Allows for potential deletion of very old versions to optimize storage costs.

Table 6.2: Lifecycle policies for sample use cases

Security and access control

Amazon S3 provides comprehensive security features that enable fine-grained access control and data protection from unintended and unauthorized access. It also offers flexible ways to easily manage security through policies, immutability options, and access control lists.

The security options and access control management options for S3 ensure the data is protected at rest and during transit while ensuring only trusted entities can access the data. Thus, a Serverless application utilizing S3 becomes highly secure.

The following are the core security options:

- **IAM**: IAM plays an integral role in fine-grained access management and data and access governance. IAM allows the creation of IAM entities with specific permissions. The access policies dictate specific actions users and groups can perform when accessing data. The following are the key IAM components for S3 access control:

  o **IAM Users**: Individual users/entities that can access resources (buckets and objects in S3).

  o **IAM Groups**: A conglomeration of users having the same access, and all entities within a group share the same privileges.

  o **IAM Roles**: Roles provide temporary security credentials to applications and services.

- o **IAM Policies**: Policies are documents that specifically define the permissions associated with users, roles, and groups.

A classic example of granular access could be to allow PutObject and GetObject on the entity for a specific bucket (resource). This will ensure the entity can only get an object or upload an object, but can never delete it.

- **Public vs. private access**: All S3 buckets created after April 2023 will be private by default. This means that entities outside of the account will not be allowed to access the bucket, and that is the default behavior.

There are scenarios where public access to buckets would be required and must be handled on a case-by-case basis.

- **VPC endpoints**: Amazon S3 does not reside in a customer VPC (unlike other services like Amazon RDS), so access goes via the public internet by default even when accessed from inside a corporate network. However, a VPC endpoint for S3 allows resources within the private network to securely access S3 without traversing the public internet. This security feature minimizes the attack surface and strengthens the overall security posture.

- **Bucket policy**: This is a JSON formatted document attached directly to a bucket; this defines access permission to included entities.

- **Access control lists (ACL)**: These allow fine-grained control over who can access specific objects, and the actions allowed (Read, Write, for example).

- **Object lock**: This feature makes objects immutable (they cannot be deleted/destroyed) for a fixed amount of time or for an indefinite interval. It helps in keeping data and auditing transactions for regulatory purposes.

- **Encryption**: This is a process that involves scrambling data before storing it in S3 servers, adding an extra layer of security by making the data unreadable to anyone without the decryption key. The encryption could be:

  - o **Server-side encryption (SSE)**: Here, AWS manages the encryption keys and further allows it in two ways:

    - ▪ **SSE—S3**: Default encryption methodology and here, the data is encrypted at rest (during storage), and this is automatically enabled free of cost for all buckets created after April 20233.

    - ▪ **SSE—KMS**: Here, a master key is created in AWS **Key Management Service** (**KMS**), and that key is used to encrypt content in S3.

  - o **Client-side encryption (CSE)**: Here, the data is encrypted first using a customer-managed key before uploading it into S3.

- **Bucket versioning**: when versioning is enabled for a bucket, any object that gets updated is versioned and kept for reference. This ensures the data's history is maintained.

- **Object ownership**: This controls who owns the objects and is helpful in scenarios where multiple users are uploading data.

- **Logging, monitoring, and trails**: AWS CloudTrail and Server access logging help to track all user activity in S3 buckets.

- **Service control policies (SCP)**: These policies are part of AWS Organizations, which offer a centralized approach to enforce guardrails on IAM permissions for member accounts. SCP can be used to enhance S3 security posture by restricting specific actions or configurations, such as Restricting sensitive actions, enforcing bucket encryption, and preventing public access.

Deployment patterns

Amazon S3, with its scalability, durability, and cost-effectiveness, forms the backbone for many serverless deployments. However, storing your application code or assets in S3 is insufficient. Choosing the right deployment pattern can significantly impact your application's performance, security, and manageability.

At the heart of many serverless architectures lies Amazon S3, a powerful object storage service from AWS due to its scalability, durability, reliability, and ability to seamlessly integrate with serverless services.

This section explores various S3 deployment patterns commonly used in serverless architectures:

- **Static web hosting**: Amazon S3 can be used to host static websites that include web pages with static content, including HTML files, images, videos, and client-side scripts like JavaScript. This is a cost-effective way to host websites that do not require server-side processing.

- **Serverless framework with S3 templates**: S3 can help streamline the deployment of serverless applications, which can refer to S3 as their package and artifact store. For example, AWS CloudFormation, AWS CDK, and AWS SAM seamlessly work with S3.

- **CI/CD pipelines**: S3 can seamlessly integrate with **continuous integration** (**CI**) and **continuous delivery** (**CD**) pipelines, can act as an artifact store (code, libraries, and dependencies), and works well with tools like AWS CodePipeline and Jenkins.

- **Content distribution**: S3, when used in conjunction with Amazon CloudFront (Amazon's own CDN), can serve static content to users across the globe while also providing regional caching capabilities.

- **Data lake and big data analytics**: S3 can be used to build a data lake, which will be a centralized repository for storing data of all kinds (structured, semi-structured, and unstructured). Once the data is cataloged and stored, it can be used in a variety of cloud-native tools like AWS Athena to query, AWS Redshift to build a data warehouse, and AWS Kinesis suite of services to build streaming analytics platforms.

- **Data archiving**: S3 is best suited for long-term data archiving solutions. When moved to the S3 Glacier storage class, this data offers the most cost-effective and service-optimized data storage, archival, and backup for regulatory and compliance requirements.

- **Disaster recovery**: S3 is designed with a very high durability of 99.999999999%, making it an optimal choice for disaster recovery operations.

- **Backup and restore**: S3 provides durable infrastructure to store data redundantly across availability zones. This, coupled with versioning, can help to backup and restore any version of any data for any auditing and operational requirement.

- **IoT store**: S3 can manage the ingestion of and store telemetry and signal data from IoT devices. S3 can be used to ingest massive volumes of data.

- **Machine learning and model training**: S3 can be used to store training data for machine learning models. Most managed ML services, including AWS Sagemaker, can directly access S3.

Comprehensive breakdown of costs

Amazon S3, a cornerstone of the AWS cloud storage landscape, offers a flexible and scalable solution for a wide range of data storage needs. However, understanding the cost structure of S3 can be intricate, with a range of factors influencing the final bill. This comprehensive breakdown looks at the key components of S3 pricing, which help optimize storage strategies and make informed decisions:

- **Core storage costs/storage class**: The primary driver of S3 storage costs is the storage class you choose. S3 offers a tiered storage system catering to different data access frequencies and cost requirements. Understanding these classes is crucial:

o **S3 Standard**: This is the most versatile choice, ideal for frequently accessed data. Pricing is tiered, with costs decreasing as storage volume increases. For example, the first 50 TB stored in a month might incur a charge of $0.023 per GB, while prices can go as low as $0.021 per GB for volumes exceeding 500 TB.

o **S3 Standard-Infrequent Access (S3 Standard-IA)**: This class is optimized for data accessed less frequently but requires occasional retrieval. It offers a lower base price than S3 Standard but incurs retrieval charges for data access.

o **S3 Intelligent-Tiering**: This automated storage class analyzes access patterns and migrates data between S3 Standard, S3 Standard-IA, and a third tier, S3 Glacier Instant Retrieval, based on usage. It helps optimize costs for data with unpredictable access patterns but introduces additional management overhead.

o **S3 One Zone-Infrequent Access (S3 One Zone-IA)**: This regional variant of S3 Standard-IA stores data redundantly within a single AZ at a reduced cost. However, it has slightly higher retrieval fees and reduced durability than multi-AZ storage options.

o **Amazon S3 Glacier**: This class is suited for long-term archival data with minimal access needs. It offers the lowest storage costs but incurs retrieval charges and retrieval request fees. Further subdivisions within Glacier cater to varying retrieval timeframes, with expedited retrievals incurring higher costs.

- **Storage usage**: S3 bills based on the amount of data stored in your buckets, measured in **gigabytes (GB)**. Charges are calculated based on daily snapshots of your storage usage, averaged over the month. This pay-as-you-go model ensures you only pay for the storage you utilize.

- **Additional cost considerations**: While storage class and usage are the primary factors, several other elements contribute to the overall S3 cost:

o **Data transfer**: Costs are associated with data transfer out of S3 buckets. This includes egress charges for data transferred from the AWS region where your bucket resides and inter-region data transfer fees for moving data between regions.

o **Request fees**: S3 charges for specific API requests against your buckets and objects. These include GET, PUT, LIST, and DELETE operations. While generally minimal for standard storage classes, retrieval requests in Glacier can add up significantly.

o **Management features**: Certain S3 features incur additional charges. Examples include S3 Inventory, which provides a detailed listing of objects in a bucket, and S3 Object Tagging, which allows attaching user-defined metadata to objects.

o **Lifecycle management**: While lifecycle policies for automatic data migration between storage classes are free to define, the storage and retrieval costs associated with the target class still apply.

- **Optimizing your S3 costs**: Here are some strategies to control your S3 expenses:

o **Storage class selection**: Carefully choose the storage class that best aligns with your data access patterns. Utilize Glacier for long-term archives and S3 Standard/Standard-IA for frequently accessed data.

o **Lifecycle management**: Leverage lifecycle policies to automatically migrate data between storage classes based on access frequency. This helps transition inactive data to lower-cost tiers.

o **Data transfer optimization**: If users frequently access your data from specific regions, consider transferring data to edge locations using AWS services like CloudFront to reduce egress charges.

o **Monitoring and cost management tools**: Utilize AWS Cost Explorer and Amazon S3 Storage Lens to gain insights into your storage usage and identify potential cost-saving opportunities. Analyzing usage patterns can help refine your storage class selection and data transfer strategies.

Operations with S3

This section covers some basic operations with S3 using the Amazon Management Console:

- **Create a new bucket**: Here, a new bucket will be created using default options as shown in *Figures 6.5*, *6.6*, and *6.7*, and a few salient points to note:
  - o Navigate and search for *S3* in a unified search from the AWS Management Console, and click on **Create bucket** to start this process.
  - o The name chosen should be unique and cannot contain upper-case letters.
  - o ACLs are disabled by default as a starter option.
  - o Public access is blocked by default.
  - o Versioning is enabled in this scenario (not enabled by default).
  - o S3 managed server-side encryption (SSE-S3) is chosen for all objects.

Figure 6.5 shows a generic configuration to create a new S3 bucket from the AWS Console:

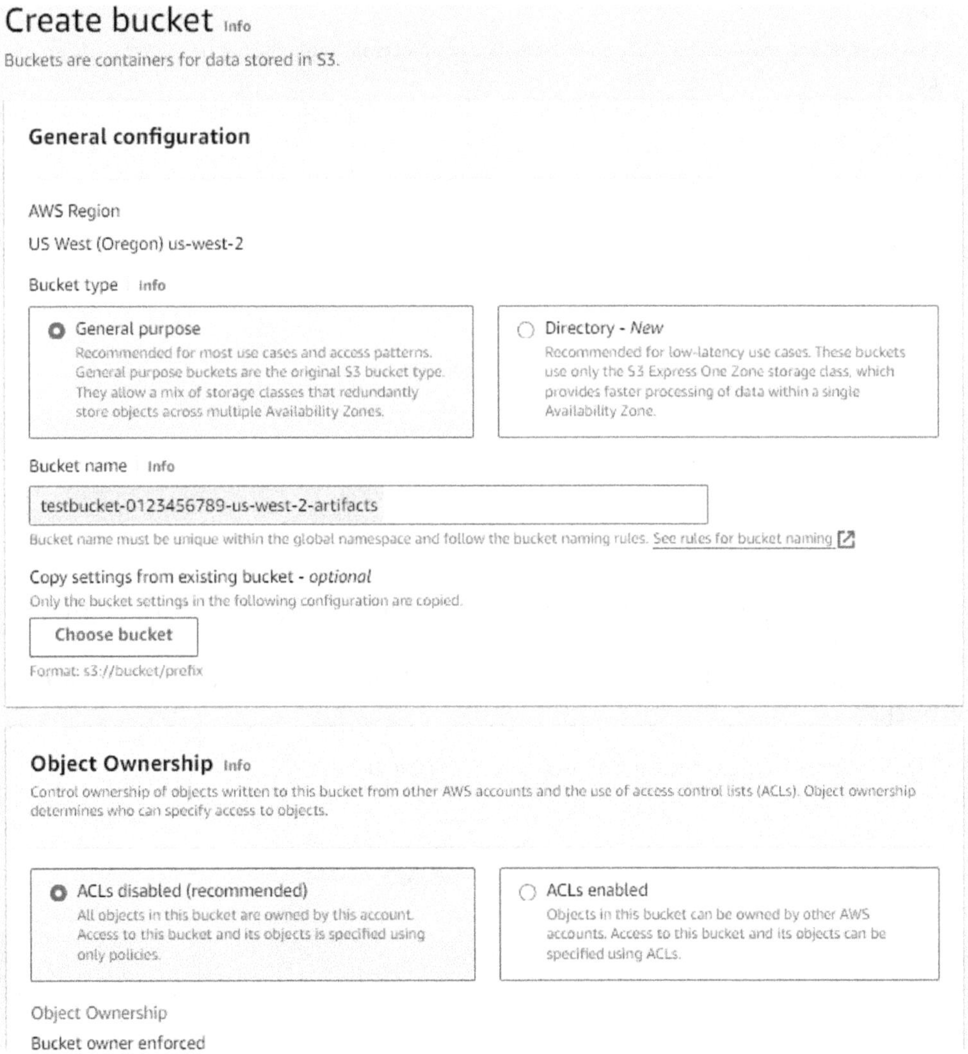

Figure 6.5: Picture showing options to create a new bucket in the region us-west-2

Figure 6.6 shows key bucket creation/configuration settings, highlighting how **Block all public access** is selected:

Block Public Access settings for this bucket

Public access is granted to buckets and objects through access control lists (ACLs), bucket policies, access point policies, or all. In order to ensure that public access to this bucket and its objects is blocked, turn on Block all public access. These settings apply only to this bucket and its access points. AWS recommends that you turn on Block all public access, but before applying any of these settings, ensure that your applications will work correctly without public access. If you require some level of public access to this bucket or objects within, you can customize the individual settings below to suit your specific storage use cases. Learn more [↗]

☑ **Block *all* public access**
Turning this setting on is the same as turning on all four settings below. Each of the following settings are independent of one another.

☐ **Block public access to buckets and objects granted through *new* access control lists (ACLs)**
S3 will block public access permissions applied to newly added buckets or objects, and prevent the creation of new public access ACLs for existing buckets and objects. This setting doesn't change any existing permissions that allow public access to S3 resources using ACLs.

☐ **Block public access to buckets and objects granted through *any* access control lists (ACLs)**
S3 will ignore all ACLs that grant public access to buckets and objects.

☐ **Block public access to buckets and objects granted through *new* public bucket or access point policies**
S3 will block new bucket and access point policies that grant public access to buckets and objects. This setting doesn't change any existing policies that allow public access to S3 resources.

☐ **Block public and cross-account access to buckets and objects through *any* public bucket or access point policies**
S3 will ignore public and cross-account access for buckets or access points with policies that grant public access to buckets and objects.

Bucket Versioning

Versioning is a means of keeping multiple variants of an object in the same bucket. You can use versioning to preserve, retrieve, and restore every version of every object stored in your Amazon S3 bucket. With versioning, you can easily recover from both unintended user actions and application failures. Learn more [↗]

Bucket Versioning
○ Disable
◉ Enable

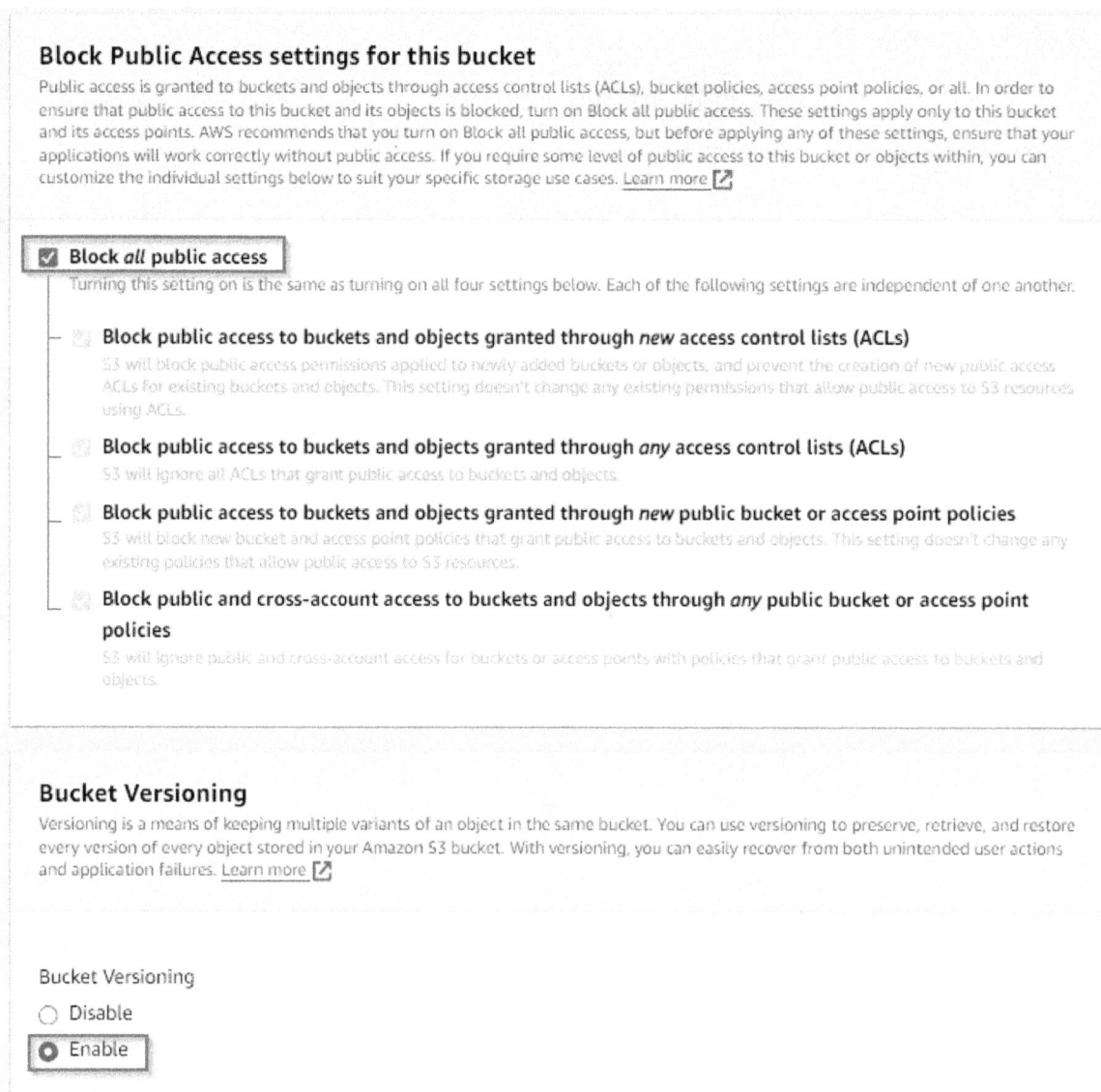

Figure 6.6: *Picture showing additional options, including versioning and public access settings*

Figure 6.7 shows additional configurations, such as tagging and encryption options, when creating a new S3 bucket.

Figure 6.8 shows how to upload an object into the object storage.

Tags - *optional* (1)

You can use bucket tags to track storage costs and organize buckets. Learn more [↗]

Key	Value - *optional*	
Billing	EducationDepartment	Remove

[Add tag]

Default encryption Info

Server-side encryption is automatically applied to new objects stored in this bucket.

Encryption type   Info

◉ Server-side encryption with Amazon S3 managed keys (SSE-S3)
○ Server-side encryption with AWS Key Management Service keys (SSE-KMS)
○ Dual-layer server-side encryption with AWS Key Management Service keys (DSSE-KMS)
  Secure your objects with two separate layers of encryption. For details on pricing, see **DSSE-KMS pricing** on the **Storage** tab of the Amazon S3 pricing page. [↗]

Bucket Key
Using an S3 Bucket Key for SSE-KMS reduces encryption costs by lowering calls to AWS KMS. S3 Bucket Keys aren't supported for DSSE-KMS. Learn more [↗]
○ Disable
◉ Enable

▶ **Advanced settings**

ⓘ After creating the bucket, you can upload files and folders to the bucket, and configure additional bucket settings.

Cancel   **Create bucket**

Figure 6.7: Picture showing tags and encryption settings

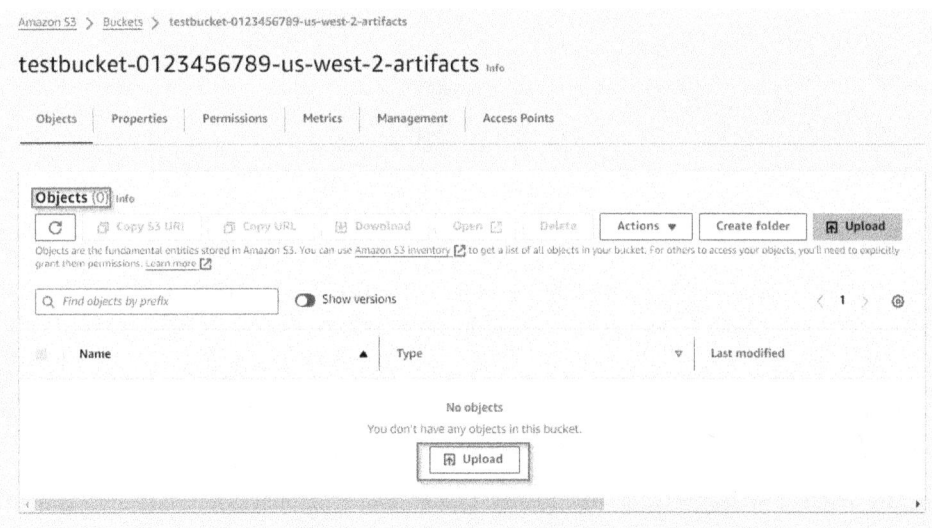

Amazon S3 > Buckets > testbucket-0123456789-us-west-2-artifacts

testbucket-0123456789-us-west-2-artifacts Info

Objects | Properties | Permissions | Metrics | Management | Access Points

Objects (0) Info

[↻] [Copy S3 URI] [Copy URL] [Download] [Open ↗] [Delete] [Actions ▾] [Create folder] [Upload]

Objects are the fundamental entities stored in Amazon S3. You can use Amazon S3 inventory [↗] to get a list of all objects in your bucket. For others to access your objects, you'll need to explicitly grant them permissions. Learn more [↗]

[🔍 Find objects by prefix]   ( ) Show versions   ⟨ 1 ⟩ ⚙

	Name ▲	Type ▽	Last modified

No objects
You don't have any objects in this bucket.

[🔼 Upload]

Figure 6.8: Picture showing a new bucket with no objects

- **Bucket policy to provide fine-grained control for different teams**: As can be seen in *Figure 6.9*:
  - Here, the policy allows the publishers team access to read objects with the **publishers/** prefix.
  - Similarly, the finance team has access to read and write objects with the **finance/** prefix.

  Figure 6.9 shows a sample bucket policy that allows an AWS principal to get/retrieve objects from the S3 bucket:

Amazon S3 > Buckets > testbucket-0123456789-us-west-2-artifacts > **Edit bucket policy**

Edit bucket policy Info Info

Bucket policy

The bucket policy, written in JSON, provides access to the objects stored in the bucket. Bucket policies don't apply to objects owned by other accounts. Learn more [⤤]

Bucket ARN

⬚ arn:aws:s3:::testbucket-0123456789-us-west-2-artifacts

Policy

```
 1 ▼ {
 2      "Version": "2012-10-17",
 3 ▼    "Statement": [
 4 ▼      {
 5          "Effect": "Allow",
 6 ▼        "Principal": {
⊗ 7            "AWS": "arn:aws:iam::<account-id>:group/publishers"
 8          }, "Action": "s3:GetObject",
 9          "Resource": "arn:aws:s3:::test-bucket/publishers/*"
10 ▼      }, {
11          "Effect": "Allow",
12 ▼        "Principal": {
⊗ 13           "AWS": "arn:aws:iam::<account-id>:group/finance"
14          }, "Action": ["s3:GetObject", "s3:PutObject"],
15          "Resource": "arn:aws:s3:::test-bucket/finance/*"
16        },
17 ▼      {
18          "Effect": "Deny",
19 ▼        "Principal": {
20            "AWS": "*"
21          }, "Action": "s3:*",
22          "Resource": "arn:aws:s3:::test-bucket/*"
23        }
24      ]
25  }
```

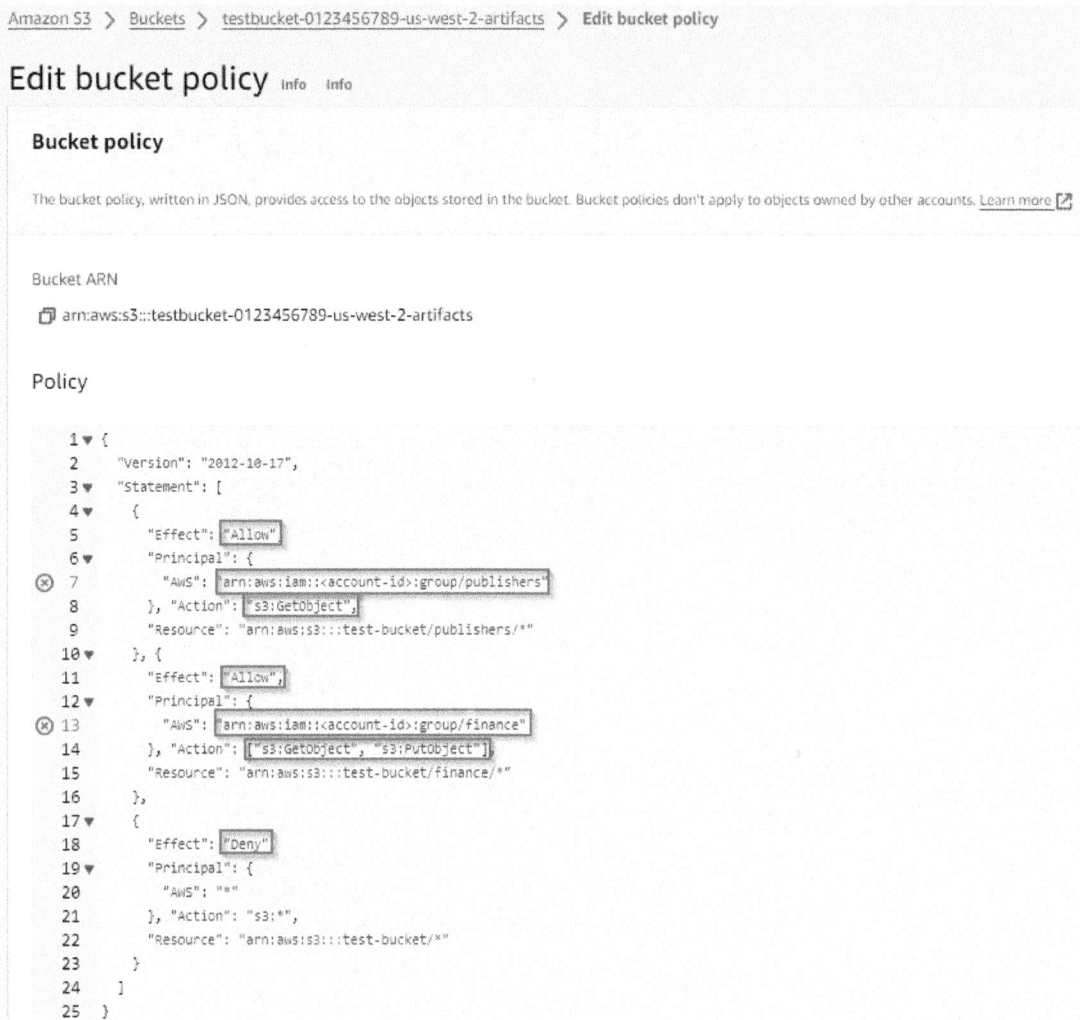

Figure 6.9: Picture showing a bucket policy

Best practices

This section provides key considerations and best practices when using Amazon S3:

- Ensure the default option **Block public access** is enabled for every bucket. If there is a genuine requirement to enable public access, that scenario must be handled after careful consideration and other security guardrails.

- When accessing S3 from inside a VPC, use the S3 VPC endpoint instead of traversing through a public internet-based connection to make it more secure.

- **Choosing the correct storage class**: To ensure better and optimal costs while maintaining data access and speed requirements, choosing the correct storage class becomes paramount. The following are some of the considerations:

  o **Access frequency**: The S3 Standard class offers the fastest access to frequently utilized data and should be the default choice for most workloads. When data is rarely accessed but still required, use Glacier classes.

  o **Budget**: Standard storage has the highest cost / GB, while Glacier offers the lowest cost, with Glacier Deep Archive being the cheapest. Be sure to choose the storage class while keeping the budget in consideration. When the access patterns are unpredictable, choose the S3 Standard, intelligent tiering option.

o **Durability**: All data stored in S3 is highly durable, but some classes offer extra redundancy. S3 Standard / Standard, IA replicates data across multiple AZs with the highest fault tolerance.

o **RTO**: If data is required immediately, choose a class that offers immediate retrieval. S3 Standard is the best option, but in some scenarios, Glacier instant retrieval can help in cost-saving.

o **Criticality**: Choose Standard/Standard-IA for higher durability data and Glacier for less frequently used data.

o **Disaster recovery**: If there is an outage in an AZ, it can disrupt the business; avoid one zone – IA.

The following table can help you choose the correct storage class per use case:

Amazon S3 Standard	Transaction data.
	Websites with static content.
	Frequently accessed log files.
	Configuration files.
Amazon S3 Standard—IA	System backups.
	Files that are rarely accessed but can be retrieved quickly.
Amazon S3 Standard—One Zone—IA	Cross-region replication backups.
	On-premises backups.
	Re-creatable data.
Amazon S3 Glacier—Flexible retrieval	Long-term backups for compliance and auditing.
	Replacement of magnetic tapes.
	Digital media asset archives.
Amazon S3 Glacier—Deep archive	Datasets that must be retained for archival purposes but are rarely accessed.
Amazon S3 Glacier—Intelligent tiering	Unpredictable workloads.

Table 6.3: Storage class and use case mapping

Anti-patterns

AppSync is a powerful tool, but misusing it can lead to performance issues, increased costs, and suboptimal solutions. Here are common anti-patterns:

- **Using for high-frequency transactions**: Due to its scaling constraints, AppSync may not be suitable for applications requiring high-frequency transactions.

- **Using for long-running operations**: AppSync is not designed for long-running operations. Consider using AWS Step Functions or AWS Lambda for such tasks.

- **Over-reliance on real-time features**: While AppSync excels at real-time updates, using it for all data access patterns can be inefficient. Evaluate if traditional REST APIs or other services might be more suitable.

- **Using AppSync for complex business logic**: AppSync is primarily a data access layer. Offloading complex business logic to resolvers can lead to performance and maintainability problems.

- **Misusing subscription features**: Overusing subscriptions or subscribing to unnecessary data can lead to excessive resource consumption and performance degradation.

Limits

The limits are as follows:

- **File size limit**: When authoring this book, each file copied can have a maximum size of 5 **Terabytes (TB)**.

- **Number of buckets**: By default, an AWS account can have a maximum number of 100 buckets. This can be increased by creating a service quota increase.

- **Request throttling**: S3 throttles requests to prevent overload. The following shows the current limit:

  PUT/COPY/POST/DELETE: 3,500 requests per second per partitioned prefix.

  GET/HEAD/LIST: 5,500 requests per second per partitioned prefix.

- **Number of lifecycle rules**: Currently, the maximum number of lifecycle rules supported per bucket is 100.

- **Multipart uploads**: The maximum number of parts allowed in a multipart upload is currently 10,000.

- **Number of objects per bucket**: While there is no hard limit, managing millions of objects without prefixes can impact performance.

- **Bucket ownership**: Once a bucket is created and owned by the creator, it cannot be transferred to another account.

- **Region dependency**: Once a bucket is created in an AWS region, it cannot be moved to another region.

Conclusion

This chapter has served as a comprehensive exploration of Amazon S3, equipping you with the knowledge and skills to leverage its robust object storage solutions capabilities. We have examined the core strengths that position S3 as a foundational element for many cloud architectures: its exceptional scalability, unwavering durability, and cost-effective storage model.

We have looked at S3's robust security features, including granular access control through IAM and encryption options, ensuring your data's confidentiality and integrity. You have also gained insights into S3's seamless integration with other AWS serverless services, unlocking a comprehensive ecosystem for building dynamic and efficient applications.

S3 empowers a diverse range of deployment patterns, from static website hosting to CI/CD pipelines and serverless function deployments. You have explored strategies for perfecting your S3 costs and selecting the most appropriate storage class based on your data access requirements.

The landscape of cloud storage is ever-evolving. As you continue your exploration of S3, stay informed about the latest advancements in its capabilities. Using its expanding functionalities, you can craft innovative and secure storage solutions that propel your applications to the forefront of efficiency and scalability.

The next chapter will focus on DynamoDB, AWS's fully managed NoSQL database tailored for serverless applications. We will explore its architecture, best practices for data modeling, scalability options, and cost structure. The chapter will also highlight its seamless integration with other AWS services and demonstrate practical examples, showcasing how DynamoDB solves common challenges in creating highly scalable and reliable systems.

CHAPTER 7

Serverless Storage with DynamoDB

Introduction

In the dynamic and rapidly progressing realm of technology, the demand for efficient, scalable, and economically viable data storage solutions is paramount. Building upon the foundation in the previous chapter, which focused on object storage, this chapter expands the horizon to accommodate diverse data types, mainly focusing on key-value pair and document-based storage systems. By capitalizing on the robust capabilities of cloud infrastructure, we aim to leverage the benefits of automatic scaling, ensuring high availability and stringent security measures. This approach underscores the significance of these elements in contemporary data storage strategies, thereby reinforcing the comprehensive nature of our exploration into data storage solutions.

This provides a framework for understanding how data can be categorized into relational or key-value pairs (SQL or NoSQL) and how to store, manage, and retrieve it at scale using AWS services.

The chapter starts with an in-depth exploration of Amazon DynamoDB, a NoSQL database service that provides fast and predictable performance with seamless scalability. It covers its key features, flexible data model, built-in security, and automatic scaling. Additionally, we will briefly compare DynamoDB with another AWS NoSQL service, Amazon ElastiCache, to highlight their complementary roles in serverless applications.

This chapter will show how these services interact with other AWS offerings, creating robust, efficient, and powerful serverless architectures. Practical examples, use cases, and exercises are interspersed throughout the chapter to reinforce the concepts and demonstrate the practical applications of these services.

By the end of this chapter, you will have a comprehensive understanding of these serverless storage solutions, their potential applications, and how they can be harnessed to drive innovation and efficiency in your projects. Whether you are an engineering student, a computer professional, or a business audience, this chapter will equip you with the knowledge and skills to navigate the world of serverless storage confidently.

Structure

This chapter covers the following topics:

- SQL vs. NoSQL explained
- Introduction to DynamoDB
- Advanced DynamoDB operations
- DynamoDB security

- DynamoDB integrations
- DynamoDB vs. Amazon ElastiCache
- Anti-patterns
- Best practices
- Limits

Objectives

This chapter is designed to provide a comprehensive understanding of serverless storage solutions with a specific focus on Amazon DynamoDB. By the end of this chapter, readers will have a solid grasp of DynamoDB's core concepts, such as primary and partition keys, indexes, and read/write capacity units, which form the foundation of its NoSQL database architecture.

The chapter looks into DynamoDB operations, offering practical knowledge on creating, reading, updating, and deleting data, as well as performing complex queries and scans. Readers will also gain insight into data management techniques, exploring how to utilize features like automatic scaling, partitioning, and performance tuning to optimize costs and efficiency.

A significant portion of the chapter is dedicated to performance optimization strategies. Best practices, including the use of DynamoDB's on-demand and provisioned modes, **DynamoDB Accelerator (DAX)**, and efficient query design, will empower readers to achieve maximum performance for their applications.

Finally, the chapter reinforces learning through real-world use cases and case studies, demonstrating how DynamoDB can be applied across diverse scenarios. Whether building secure, scalable, or cost-effective serverless applications, this chapter equips readers with the technical knowledge and practical skills to confidently leverage Amazon DynamoDB as a core component of modern architectures.

SQL vs. NoSQL explained

Structured Query Language (SQL) is used by common database systems that manage relational data, such as Oracle, SQL Server, MySQL, and PostgreSQL. These systems are called **relational database management systems (RDBMS)**.

The key strength of an RDBMS system is the capability to manage data attributes and their relationships across various tables. This provides a high degree of flexibility to query, search, index, and categorize data while allowing effortless ways to create new data and relationships, update existing data and relationships, or even remove existing data and their relationships.

A SQL database has the following core characteristics:

- **ACID**: SQL databases follow and make provision for **atomicity, consistency, isolation, and durability (ACID)**, where:
    - **Atomicity**: The goal of an atomic transaction is to prevent half-finished transactions. Here, the complete transaction will either succeed or fail.

      The best example of an atomic transaction is a money transfer between two parties.
    - **Consistency**: Every transaction must transform the database from one valid state to another and adhere to pre-defined rules and constraints. For example, a student must have a Student ID before class participation.
    - **Isolation**: Isolation prevents concurrency issues. If two database transactions are executed simultaneously, they must be isolated from each other without conflicts or interference.
    - **Durability**: This ensures the changes are durable and permanent and will not be lost between failures.

- **Structured**: Data is always structured and organized into tables consisting of rows and columns where each row represents a record/item, and each represents a specific attribute and its value. SQL systems have a defined/fixed schema of fields, and all transactions must adhere to the underlying fields and their types.

  o **Data manipulation language (DML)**: RDBMS tables support SQL, which helps in defining views, data, constraints, and data manipulation

  o **Support for complex queries**: SQL databases provide extensive support to query and aggregate relational data across different tables and schemas to gain valuable insights

A **not only SQL (NoSQL)** database is a different approach to database design that enables the storage and query of data outside of traditional and tabular formats. Data could be document-based, key-value-based, or graph-based. NoSQL databases are becoming increasingly popular in big-data, real-time web applications and applications requiring massive scalability features.

A NoSQL database has the following core characteristics:

- **Flexible/schema-less**: The data is not structured in tabular format, and the NoSQL databases have no rigid schema or relationship constraints. The data can be stored in its original and raw format.

- **Multiple flavors**: A NoSQL database can accommodate heterogeneous data types, such as document storage, key-value pair storage, wide-column base storage, graph databases, and more.

- **High performance**: These are known for providing high performance, speed, agility, and scalability. They are often optimized to handle spikes and can handle many concurrent requests.

Some of the common NoSQL databases include

- **MongoDB** and **CouchDB**, which are document databases.

- **Redis** and **Memcached** are key-value databases optimized for caching. They provide rapid access to frequently accessed data and are ideal for caching.

- **Cassandra** and **HBase,** considered column stores, can store data in columns and are ideal for storing large datasets in data science.

- **Amazon DynamoDB** is a fully managed, serverless, NoSQL database from Amazon that allows for managing multiple kinds of data. It is best suited for use as a key-value store and distributed databases, and can support complex data structures.

SQL databases are generally best suited for dealing with data with complex relationships, and NoSQL databases are best suited for scenarios requiring higher flexibility, dynamic data models, and unstructured and non-relational data.

The following table provides a comprehensive summary of the differences between SQL and NoSQL databases:

Feature	SQL databases	NoSQL databases
Data model	Structured, relational model with tables, rows, and columns	Flexible, schema-less models such as key-value, document, column-family, and graph
Schema	Fixed schema with predefined structure	Dynamic schema, data can evolve without altering existing records
Transactions	ACID-compliant, ensuring strong consistency	**Basically available, soft state, eventually consistent (BASE)** model, optimizing for availability over strict consistency

Scalability	Traditionally vertically scalable (adding more CPU/RAM to a single machine), but cloud-hosted SQL databases (Amazon RDS, Aurora) now support read replicas and partitioning for horizontal scaling	Horizontally scalable by design, distributing data across multiple nodes for large-scale workloads
Performance	Optimized for complex queries, joins, and relational integrity	Optimized for high read/write throughput and low-latency distributed processing
Data relationships	Strictly enforced relationships (foreign keys, normalization)	Flexible relationships, often denormalized for performance optimization
Consistency model	Strong consistency (default)	Eventual consistency (default, with strong consistency options in some NoSQL databases)
Query language	Uses SQL for querying and managing data	Uses specialized query languages (e.g., DynamoDB Query API, MongoDB Query Language, Cassandra CQL) or simple key-value lookups
Use cases	Best for structured data, transactions, financial applications, ERP, CRM, cloud-hosted databases	Best for big data, real-time analytics, IoT, social media, gaming, distributed systems
Examples	MySQL, PostgreSQL, SQL Server, Amazon RDS, Amazon Aurora	Amazon DynamoDB, MongoDB, Cassandra, Redis, Google Bigtable

Table 7.1: Table showing SQL vs. NoSQL databases

Introduction to DynamoDB

Amazon DynamoDB is a serverless offering from AWS that provides a highly scalable, fast NoSQL database service with predictable performance and flexibility. This is a distributed database offering in which AWS fully manages and takes care of all the administrative burden of managing a highly scalable distributed database.

Amazon DynamoDB is serverless; hence, there are no servers to manage or provision from an end-user perspective. It is designed to provide single-digit millisecond response times at any scale. The Flexible schema of Amazon DynamoDB allows an item to have any number and type of attributes.

Amazon DynamoDB is a cloud-native service from AWS that offers built-in security and seamless integration with most other AWS services. It provides fine-grained access control via AWS IAM. The data in DynamoDB can be encrypted at rest and allows for continuous backup.

The following are the key features:

- **Fully managed**: DynamoDB is a fully managed service; users and businesses do not have to worry about server maintenance, patching, or other operations.

- **Serverless**: There are no servers to manage or provision; users do not have to install any software.

- **Performance at scale**: DynamoDB can handle high traffic, spikes, and copious amounts of data with consistent, single-digit millisecond latency.

- **Key-value and document models**: Versatile in supporting key-value pair-based storage and best suited for document data.

- **Flexible data model**: DynamoDB does not require a fixed schema, allowing for flexibility in stored data.

- **Automatic scaling**: DynamoDB can automatically scale up or down to meet the application's capacity requirements.

- **ACID transactions**: DynamoDB supports ACID.

- **Global tables**: DynamoDB provides multi-region, multi-master replication with global tables.

- **On-demand capacity mode**: The customer must only pay for the actual application reads in this mode.

- **Backup and restore**: DynamoDB provides on-demand and continuous backups for your DynamoDB tables.

- **In-memory caching**: DAX delivers in-memory performance for read-intensive workloads.

- **Event-driven programming**: DynamoDB Streams captures table activity, which helps build event-driven workflows.

- **Security and compliance**: DynamoDB is secure by default, encrypting all data at rest and in transit.

- **AWS integrations**: DynamoDB is deeply integrated with other AWS services, such as AWS Lambda, Amazon Redshift, and Amazon SageMaker, making it an omnipresent service in most cloud-native and serverless workflows.

- **Consistent performance**: DynamoDB maintains consistent performance at any scale.

- **Highly available and durable**: DynamoDB replicates data across multiple AZs in an AWS Region, providing built-in high availability and data durability.

- **Point-in-time recovery (PITR)**: DynamoDB can back data with point-in-time recovery.

- **In-place updates**: DynamoDB allows for the modification of items directly in the database without exporting or importing.

- **Data export to S3**: DynamoDB can export table data to an Amazon S3 bucket in a format compatible with other AWS services.

- **Cost-effective**: DynamoDB offers pay-per-use pricing with no upfront costs.

Core concepts of DynamoDB

Amazon DynamoDB is a full database offering features to customize behavior. The following are some of the concepts that help greatly utilize this database's features:

- **Tables, items, and attributes**:

  o In DynamoDB, a table represents a wrapper for information or data collection. For example, a table named Games can have all the games played.

  o An item in a DynamoDB table represents a record/row of a traditional database system and contains information for that item. Thus, an item can be called a collection of information.

  o Attributes are the lowest / fundamental units of information or data elements. An item cannot be broken down further.

- **Partitions**: A partition is a table's core storage unit. It is like a catalog/key that can store and uncover related records. All records with the same partition key hash are stored together in the same partition, ensuring efficient storage and retrieval.

- **Primary key**: A key in a DynamoDB table acts as a magic wand, and a key helps retrieve the entire item. In DynamoDB, a primary key can be composed of a single key item or an aggregator of two items:

o **Partition key**: This type of primary key is composed of a single attribute, and this attribute uniquely identifies the record (when no sort keys are present). This partition key maintains the uniqueness of the row/item/record through an internal hash function, which ensures and manages how the data is stored while maintaining unique values.

o **Partition key and sort key**: Here, uniqueness is guaranteed by combining two attributes (partition key and sort key).

- A table defined with a partition and sort key cannot have multiple records with the same partition and sort keys. However, multiple records with the same partition key but different sort keys can exist.

- This feature is also referred to as a composite key.

- Examples of composite keys are Publisher (partition key) and Title (sort key).

- A publisher can store many titles as separate records/rows in DynamoDB.

- Since DynamoDB allows flexibility, each title row can have various attributes and information.

- **Indexes (global secondary index and local secondary index)**:

  o An index in a DynamoDB table is a catalog that helps query data efficiently. Since DynamoDB relies on the primary key, indexes are crucial in providing different access patterns that suit business needs.

  o The primary key discussed acts as a fundamental/primary index, and every table must have one. Secondary indexes are optional indexes that enable querying data based on attributes outside of primary keys.

  o The secondary indexes can be **global secondary indexes** (**GSI**):

    - A GSI is a secondary index that allows efficient querying based on attributes other than the primary key of your DynamoDB table.

    - It has an independent partition and sort key structure, offering query flexibility beyond the primary key.

    - GSIs on frequently accessed attributes improve query performance when retrieving data.

    - Projected attributes allow you to customize a GSI to include only specific attributes needed for faster retrieval, optimizing storage, and read performance.

    - Using GSIs incurs additional costs for provisioned read and write capacity.

    - DynamoDB uses eventual consistency by default, which might introduce a slight delay in reflecting recently written data in GSI query results.

  o The GSI design should include access patterns, cost implications, performance, and consistency requirements.

  o **Local secondary index (LSI)**:

    - This helps to enhance query performance within a partition in DynamoDB and helps to search for data based on attributes other than the sort key within a partition.

    - This is cost-effective since the LSI is limited to/localized to a single partition, making it ideal for querying based on a specific partition value.

    - A LSI offers a targeted approach to improving query partition within a partition.

    - Imagine a product catalog with a search by type and price range. The product type can be the partition key, and the price range can be the LSI.

- **Consistency model**: DynamoDB offers the following consistency models for data reads.

  o **Strong consistency**: This ensures and guarantees immediate consistency across all replicas and hence comes with slightly higher read delays.

  o **Eventual consistency**: This model focuses on providing results faster, but data may be stale for a short duration since the updates are eventual (not immediate). This model offers higher availability.

- **Provisioned throughput**: This concept and feature help reserve or provision capacity that a table can handle. This concept does not exist with traditional RDBMS systems.

  o If a multi-lane highway represents DynamoDB and if this highway reserves certain lanes for an application, this can be said to be provisioned with that read/write capacity.

  o This is also the maximum capacity that the operations (read/write) can handle.

  o The following are the types of capacity units:

    ▪ **Read capacity units (RCU)**: This determine the number of read requests the table can handle. For example, a table with an RCU of 10 can handle up to 10 requests/second.

    ▪ **Write capacity units (WCU)**: This determines the number of "write requests" a table can handle.

  o RCUs and WCUs help provide predictable performance, ensuring the application has all the resources to manage efficient access. Optimal configuration of capacity units avoids throttling and request slow-downs.

- **Point-in-time recovery (PITR)**: This feature helps restore a database to a specific point in time in the past. It is like a rewind button that ignores changes and returns to a previous clean slate state. This primarily helps recover from accidental and unintended deletions and maintains historical updates.

- **DynamoDB streams**: This feature allows a real-time change data capture feed to be consumed and processed as a data stream. This helps maintain real-time updates and statuses. This feature, when enabled, allows seamless integration with the AWS Lambda service to configure and process the changes (inserts, updates, and deletes).

When a record is updated/deleted, it also sends the previous state, which helps find the exact change and builds data pipelines and real-time alerting workflows.

Core DynamoDB operations

This chapter covers operations that can be done on a DynamoDB table.

The core operations are CRUD, which the DynamoDB API provides to perform common operations:

- **Create operation (DynamoDB PutItem)**: This allows for creating a new entry/item in a DynamoDB table, and the attributes of the items are inserted with the passed values.

  o This supports items of different data types (numbers, strings, lists, and complex types).

  o When this operation is performed from the DynamoDB Console, the Console handles the insert operation by internally calling the putItem API.

  o The key attributes required for this operation are `TableName` and `Item`, but can also have other optional attributes like:

    ▪ **ConditionalExpression**: Allows inserts based on conditions, and the inserts will only succeed if the expression evaluates to true.

- **ExpressionAttributeNames/ExpressionAttributeValues**: This is an optional attribute that allows the provision of more readable names and values within conditional expressions.

- **ReturnValues**: This is optional but generally used, and this can provide the inserted record. The options include **NONE** (no return values) and **ALL_NEW** (return all the inserted attributes of that item).

As seen below, a new entry is made to the table **Publishers**, which has the primary key of **BookID**. – A string value of **1004074** is passed (representing string through **S**), and once the insert is completed, it will return all the attributes (as denoted by **ALL_NEW**).

```json
{
    "TableName": "Publishers",
    "Item": {
        "BookID": {
            "S": "1004074"
        },
        "BookName": {
            "S": "Mastering AWS Serverless"
        },
        "BookPrice": {
            "N": "129.99"
        }
    },
    "ReturnValues": "ALL_NEW"
}
```

  o If the **PutItem** operation is successful, it will return an HTTP status code of 200 and the request data (based on the **ReturnValues**). In case of errors, it will return the corresponding error code.

  o While **PutItem** API is for creating a new record, if an item with the same primary key exists, it overwrites the complete item with new values (update with all values).

- **Update operation (DynamoDB UpdateItem)**: This operation allows modification of an existing item. The update can be done on a specific item/attribute or event to delete other attributes. This operation is targeted and specifically targets a specific item identified by its key. Thus, the following becomes mandatory parameters:

  o **TableName**

  o **Key**

Apart from this, the **ReturnValues** can have a value of **ALL_NEW** (return complete. collection) or **UPDATED_NEW** (returning specified updated attributes).

The following code shows a sample payload for an updated item, which specifically updates/increments the book price:

```json
{
    "TableName": "Publishers",
    "Key": {
        "BookID": {
            "S": "1004074"
        }
    }
```

```
  },
  "UpdateExpression": "SET BookPrice = BookPrice + :incr",
  "ExpressionAttributeValues": {
    ":incr": {
      "N": "139.49"
    }
  },
  "ReturnValues": "UPDATED_NEW"
}
```

- **Read operation (DynamoDB ReadItem)**: This is a simple API to read a targeted item identified by its primary key. This has the following attributes:
  - ○ **TableName**
  - ○ **Key**
  - ○ **ProjectionExpresion**: An optional parameter allowing for the retrieval of specific items.

The following code shows a simple payload for a ReadItem operation on the **Publishers** table:

```
{
  "TableName": "Publishers",
  "Key": {
    "BookID": {
      "S": "1004074"
    }
  },
  "ProjectionExpression": "BookName, BookPrice"
}
```

- **Delete operation (DynamoDB DeleteItem)**: This helps remove an item identified by its primary key. This permanently deletes the item and is a targeted operation.

This has the following parameters:
  - ○ TableName
  - ○ Key
  - ○ **ReturnValues**: Optional parameter which can return attributes from the deleted item. It can return all the values (**ALL_OLD**) or nothing (**NONE**).

The following code shows a sample payload for deleting a single item:

```
{
  "TableName": "Publishers",
  "Key": {
    "BookID": {
      "S": "1004074"
    }
  },
  "ReturnValues": "ALL_OLD"
}
```

Advanced DynamoDB operations

While **GetItem**, **PutItem**, **DeleteItem**, and **UpdateItem** covered individual targeted operations aiming at a particular primary key, there are scenarios where an operation has to be performed to satisfy different business and access criteria.

DynamoDB also provides a broader toolkit for data interaction; the advanced options include:

- **Scan**: This search tool looks at DynamoDB and retrieves everything in the table or a subset based on conditions and filter criteria.

  A filter expression on a DynamoDB scan is only applied after the scan operation is complete. A filter expression only limits the results sent, but does not limit the amount of table scanned. Key request parameters:

  - **TableName**: This is mandatory, specifying which table to perform a scan on.

  - **FilterExpression**: This optional expression filters the scan results and returns matching items.

  - **ExpressionAttributeNames**: An optional parameter to provide easily readable names for attributes.

  - **ExpressionAttributeValues**: An optional parameter that can be used within a filter expression, and it defines values using placeholders.

  - **ProjectionExpression**: This specifies specific attribute names to be projected (returning fields of the scan operation).

  - **Limit**: An upper bound to limit the total number of records returned.

The following code shows the request payload for the scan operation, retrieving all items:

```
[
  {
    "TableName": "Publishers"
  }
]
```

The following code shows the request payload for scan and filter attributes:

```
{
  "TableName": "Publishers",
  "FilterExpression": "BookPrice between :minPrice and :maxPrice",
  "ExpressionAttributeValues": {
    ":minPrice": {
      "N": "89.99"
    },
    ":maxPrice": {
      "N": "399.99"
    }
  }
}
```

Here, the scan operation retrieves all the books from the **Publishers** table with prices ranging from 89.99 to 399.99 (inclusive). It first retrieves the items and then applies the filters.

It is inefficient to do a full scan on a large table, but if the filter expression involves a partition key, the scan operation is limited to that partition.

- **Query**: The query operation makes querying items effective and efficient for most access patterns. A query can get items from a table based on the partition key and an optional sort key (if relevant).

  o The query can also use indexes to further optimize data retrieval, making it a go-to tool for retrieving items from DynamoDB.

The code shows the request payload, which utilizes the query operation on the partition and sort keys:

```
{
  "TableName": "Publishers",
  "KeyConditionExpression": "#BookID = :bookID AND #PublicationYear = :pubYear",
  "ExpressionAttributeNames": {
    "#BookID": "BookID",
    "#PublicationYear": "PublicationYear"
  },
  "ExpressionAttributeValues": {
    ":bookID": {
      "S": "1004074"
    },
    ":pubYear": {
      "N": "2024"
    }
  },
  "ProjectionExpression": "BookID, BookName, Genre, PublicationYear"
}
```

  o The table **Publishers** has a composite primary key (partition key of **BookID** and sort key of **PublicationYear**).

  o This is a targeted operation using the primary key and sort key. This query ensures the query retrieves items where **BookID** is equal to **1004074** and **PublicationYear** is exactly 2024. This query operation is highly efficient

  o The query operation can also be performed on the Indexes, making it the most versatile way to retrieve items from a DynamoDB table.

The code shows the request payload for retrieving items based on the **GenreIndex**, which is done by specifying **IndexName**:

```
{
  "TableName": "Publishers",
  "IndexName": "GenreIndex",
  "KeyConditionExpression": "#Genre = :targetGenre",
  "ExpressionAttributeNames": {
    "#Genre": "Genre"
  },
  "ExpressionAttributeValues": {
    ":targetGenre": {
```

```
        "S": "Sci-Fi"
    }
  },
  "ProjectionExpression": "BookID, BookName, Genre, PublicationYear"
}
```

DynamoDB scan vs. query—Decision flow chart

When choosing between a scan or a query, consider the following decision flow:

A flow chart is added to visually depict when to use query vs. scan based on dataset size, filter criteria, and performance needs. The flow chart follows this logic (see *Figure 7.1*):

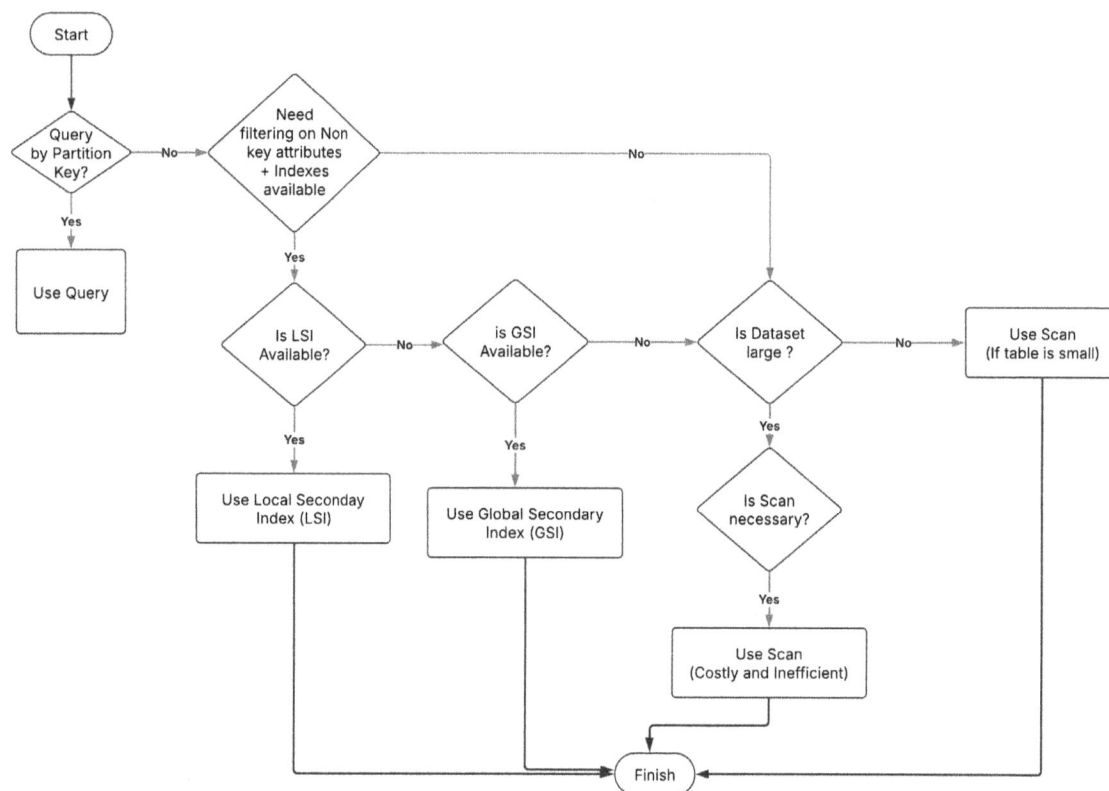

Figure 7.1: Flowchart showing scan vs. query selection flow

Basic operations via the Console

This section covers how a DynamoDB table can be created and how basic operations can be performed via the AWS Management Console:

1. Navigate to the DynamoDB service by searching through the **Services** Console.

    Figure 7.2 shows navigating and searching for the DynamoDB service:

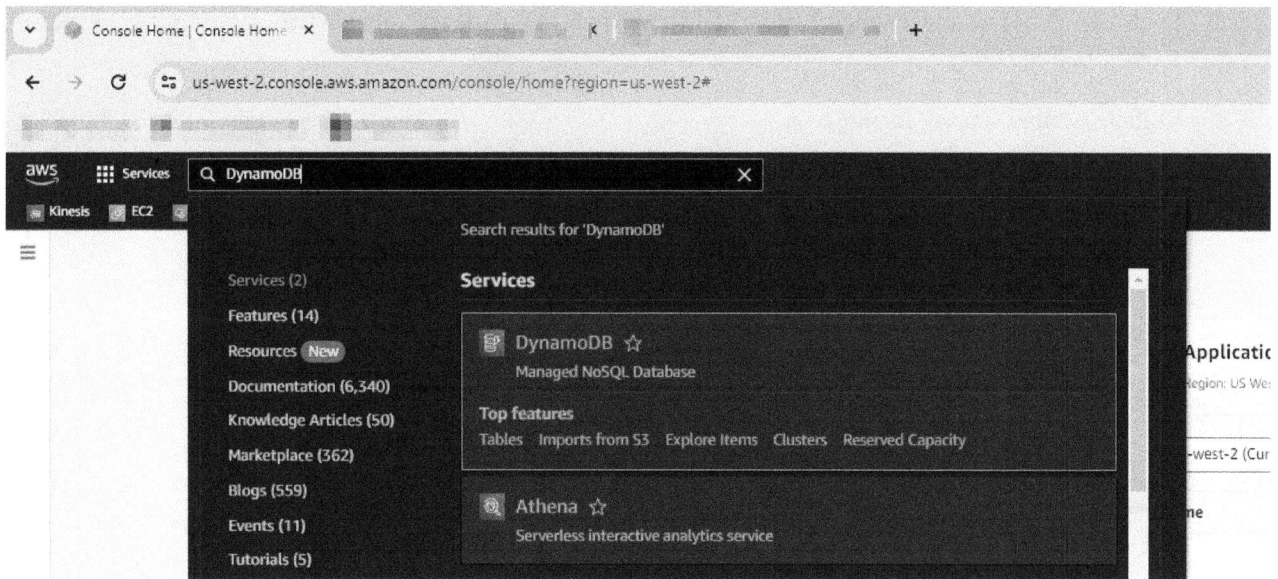

Figure 7.2: Picture showing navigation into DynamoDB service through the Console

2. You can create a new table by selecting **Create Table** on the DynamoDB home page or by navigating to **Tables** and then **Create Table**.

Provide a valid table name, such as **Publishers**, with a partition key of **BookID** and a sort key of **PublicationYear**.

Under options for the **Table** class, select DynamoDB Standard (recommended for general-purpose workloads). For an example, see *Figure 7.3*:

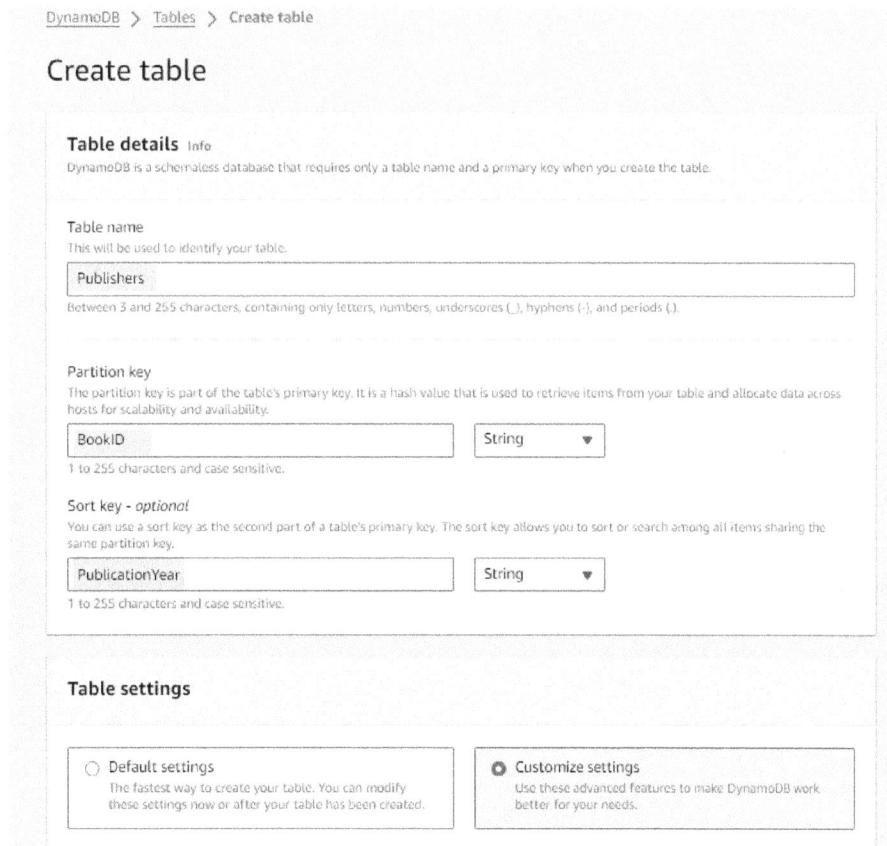

Figure 7.3: Picture showing the creation of a new DynamoDB table

3. Default to **Provisioned** capacity mode and ensure **Read capacity** and **Write capacity** auto-scaling is turned on. See *Figure 7.4* for additional details:

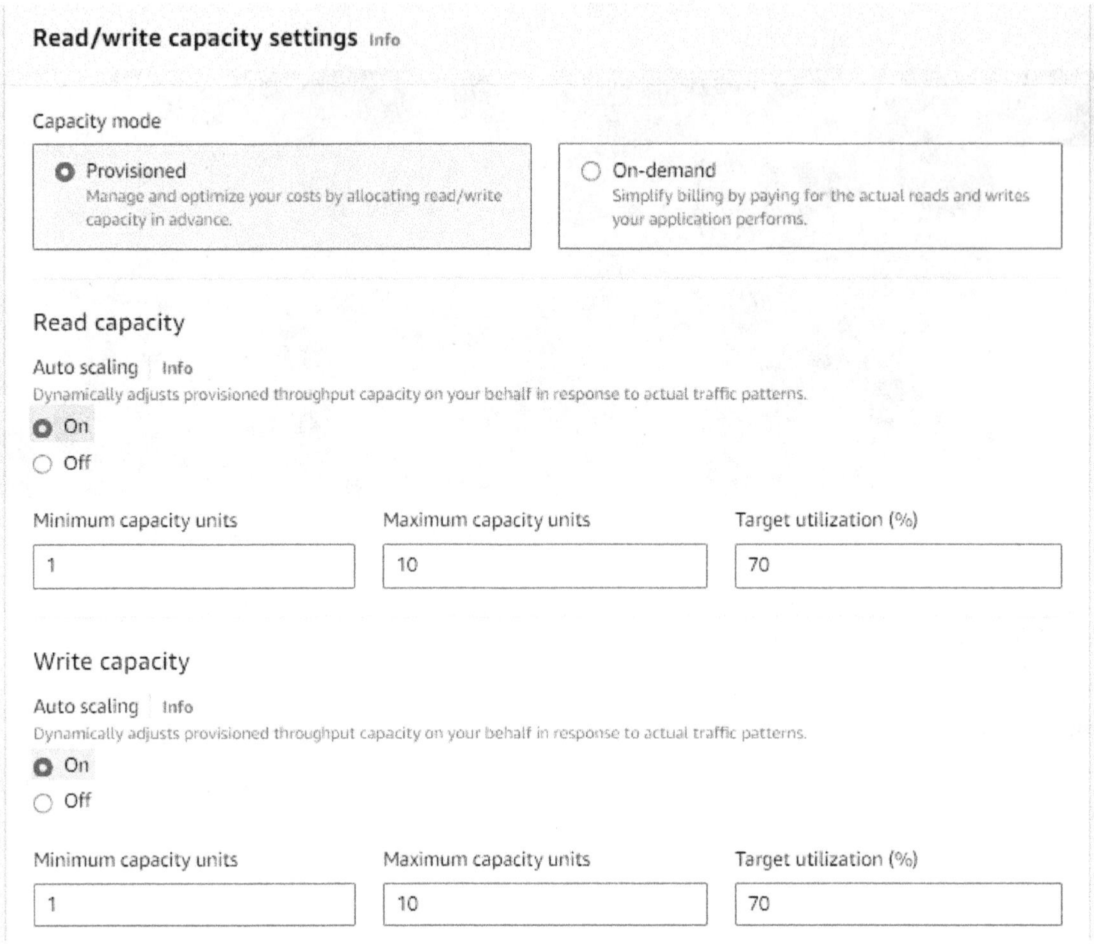

Figure 7.4: Picture showing provisioned mode for the new DynamoDB table

4. Select other customization options and complete the table creation:

- **Estimated read/write capacity cost**: This calculates and provides an average estimated cost based on the mode and capacity units selected in the previous step. This helps assess DynamoDB costs as the table grows; *Figure 7.5* shows an estimate for a table with default RCU and WCU of 1 in the AWS region us-west-2.

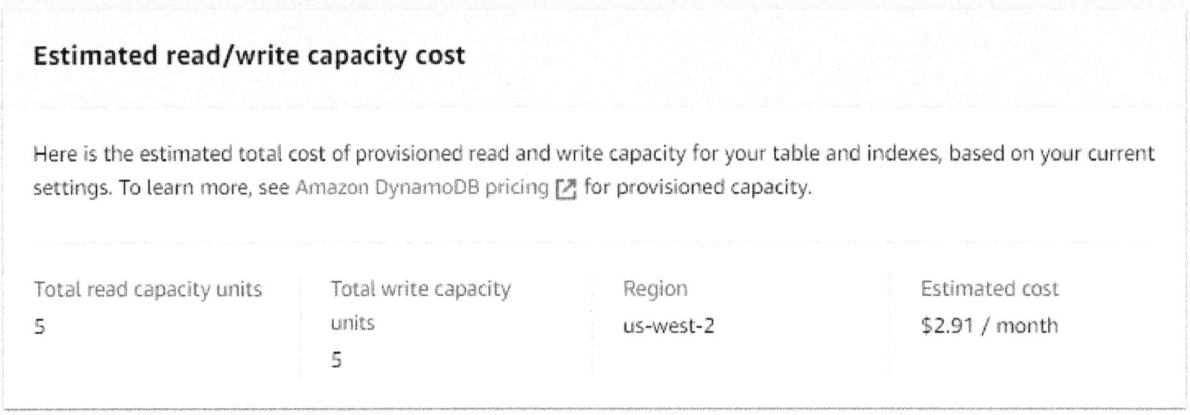

Figure 7.5: Picture showing the estimated cost with default capacity allocation

- **Encryption at rest**: DynamoDB services ensure data encryption at rest and by default. It provides the following options for encryption:

  o **Amazon** DynamoDB managed encryption key: This is the default operation offered free of cost.

  o **AWS managed key**: here, the encryption key is stored within AWS account and is typically from AWS KMS.

  o **Customer managed key**: This gives flexibility for customers to store and manage their own encryption keys.

- **Deletion protection**: This, when turned on, prevents accidental deletion of tables.

- **Resource-based policy**: This is a newly introduced feature allowing external and cross-account access through policy statements.

- **Tags**: This allows adding custom key-value pairs for tagging, such as a specific billing tag, to help identify the source of usage.

5. Once the table is created, click on the table name to review the basic configuration, and click **Explore table item** to start interacting with table data; see *Figure 7.6:*

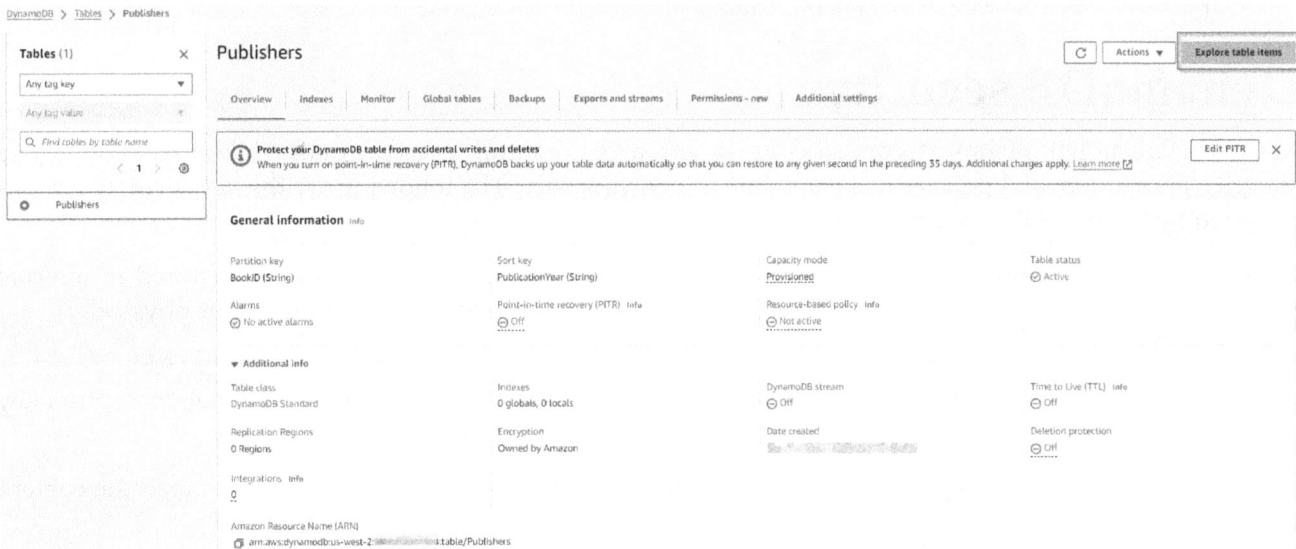

Figure 7.6: Picture showing basic configuration and option to interact with table data

6. Create a new table item by using the options, **Create item**. Complete the JSON payload and ensure **View DynamoDB JSON** is turned off.

Figure 7.7 shows a sample payload to create a new entry:

DynamoDB 〉 Explore items: Publishers 〉 **Create item**

Create item

You can add, remove, or edit the attributes of an item. You can nest attributes inside other a

Attributes ⬤ View DynamoDB JSON

```
1 ▼ {
2    "BookID": "1004074",
3    "PublicationYear": "2024",
4    "BookName": "Mastering AWS serverless",
5    "BookPrice": 129.99,
6    "Genre": "CloudComputing"
7  }
```

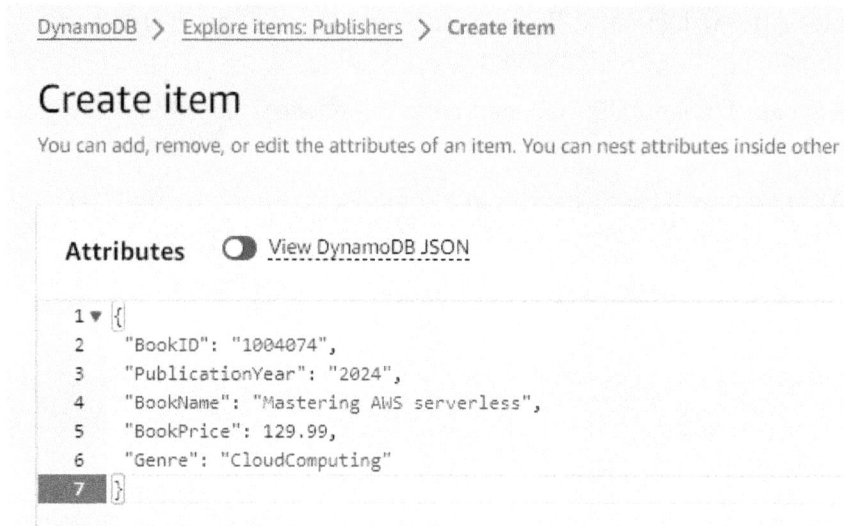

Figure 7.7: Picture showing the creation of a new DynamoDB table

7. Once an entry is created, this entry can be scanned using the **Scan** option or queried by entering the partition key (BookID of 1004074).

DynamoDB security

Amazon DynamoDB offers fine-grained security and access control to access data while maintaining data integrity, encryption, and policies to ensure data is always secure. The following are the key security options provided by DynamoDB service:

- **Encryption at rest**: DynamoDB encrypts all data at rest. This covers stable data stored in internal servers, which is subject to threats from hackers and illegal access (either digitally or physically).

  o When encrypted (typically using a 256-bit advanced encryption methodology (AES-256)), this data is transformed into a format that allows only the entities with the original decryption key to access it. Thus, this feature makes the stored data extremely secure.

  o If an unforeseen circumstance results in access to this data, the hackers cannot read the content without the decryption key.

  o AWS DynamoDB also offers the option to use AWS-managed encryption (free of cost) or AWS KMS to manage and maintain encryption keys. It also allows customers to maintain and manage their encryption keys.

- **Fine-grained access control**: Amazon DynamoDB has seamless integration with AWS IAM and is enabled through the following options:

  o **IAM policies**: To grant permissions only to specific IAM users, roles, or groups.

  o **Condition keys**: These IAM policy conditions can allow/deny access to individual data items and attributes.

  o **Access control**: DynamoDB provides options to selectively hide or expose specific DynamoDB items in a particular table. This can be done either as horizontal access control or vertical access control.

- **Private network connectivity**: AWS PrivateLink allows the creation of Amazon VPC endpoints. These endpoints are directly accessible via a private connection over Amazon Direct Connect through VPC Peering, preventing man-in-the-middle attacks.

- **Network isolation**: The VPC endpoints on DynamoDB provide a secure way to access DynamoDB from resources within the Amazon VPC.

- **On-demand backup and restore**: The on-demand demand and restore help up full tables as backups. This helps manage regulatory compliance requirements and can be restored as required.

- **PITR**: This option helps restore a database table to any previous point in time, thus managing accidental deletes and preventing data corruption.

Security use case of a Saas platform

A **software as a service (SaaS)** company offers a cloud-based HR management system where multiple organizations store employee records, payroll details, and compliance documents in Amazon DynamoDB.

To ensure data isolation, security, and compliance, the following security controls are implemented:

- **Tenant data isolation**:
    - Each customer's data is partitioned using a unique Tenant ID as the partition key.
    - IAM policies enforce strict access control, ensuring organizations can only access their data.

- **Encryption and compliance**:
    - All HR and payroll data is encrypted at rest using AWS KMS with separate encryption keys per tenant.
    - End-to-end TLS encryption ensures secure data transmission between HR applications and DynamoDB.

- **Role-based access control (RBAC)**:
    - IAM condition keys restrict access based on user roles (HR managers, finance teams, auditors).
    - Temporary IAM credentials are issued via AWS STS to prevent long-term access risks.

- **Auditing and security monitoring**:
    - AWS CloudTrail logs all access attempts to detect unauthorized access.
    - Amazon GuardDuty identifies security anomalies, such as mass data downloads or brute-force attempts.

- **Disaster recovery and data integrity**:
    - PITR ensures payroll history can be restored in case of corruption or accidental deletion.
    - Automated daily backups to Amazon S3 provide compliance with labor laws requiring long-term record retention.

DynamoDB integrations

DynamoDB, a heavyweight contender in AWS's NoSQL database arena, boasts scalability, performance, and a rich tapestry of integration possibilities. This in-depth exploration delves into the world of DynamoDB integrations, highlighting various tools and services that seamlessly connect DynamoDB with other parts of AWS infrastructure and beyond.

The integration landscape surrounding DynamoDB offers a diverse orchestra of options, catering to a range of needs and functionalities:

- **AWS services**: A harmonious collaboration exists with numerous AWS services, forming a cohesive cloud ecosystem.

- **Third-party tools**: A vast array of third-party tools and frameworks act as complementary instruments, offering pre-built connectors and functionalities for DynamoDB.

- **Custom integrations**: For truly bespoke creations, you can leverage AWS SDKs and APIs to develop custom integrations tailored to specific needs.

Integrating with the AWS services:

- **AWS Lambda**: This serverless compute service integrates with Lambda functions based on DynamoDB's events (insertions, updates, deletions) to automate tasks like data processing, notifications, or analytics.

- **Amazon Kinesis Firehose**: Stream data from various sources, including DynamoDB change streams, into data lakes (S3) or analytics services (Kinesis Data Analytics) for real-time processing and insights.

- **Amazon S3**: Leverage S3 for storing large objects (e.g., images, videos) referenced by DynamoDB items. DynamoDB is the access conductor that manages metadata and access control for S3 objects, ensuring a cohesive data management strategy.

- **Amazon CloudWatch**: Monitor DynamoDB's health, performance metrics (consumed capacity units, throttling events), and errors using CloudWatch logs and alarms. Gain valuable insights into your DynamoDB deployment's operational efficiency.

- **Amazon Cognito**: Integrate DynamoDB with Cognito for user authentication and authorization. Store user data securely in DynamoDB while leveraging Cognito for access control and identity management within your application.

Beyond the core AWS services, a rich ecosystem of third-party tools offers pre-built connectors and functionalities for interacting with DynamoDB:

- **Data migration instruments**: Tools like AWS **Database Migration Service** (**DMS**) and Stitch facilitate seamless data migration from various sources (relational databases, NoSQL databases) into DynamoDB, simplifying data transfer and adoption.

- **API gateways and backend as a service (BaaS)**: Services like AWS API Gateway and Firebase allow you to build APIs that interact with DynamoDB. This simplifies data access from mobile and web applications without managing complex server infrastructure.

- **Business intelligence (BI) ensembles**: Integrate DynamoDB with BI tools like Tableau or Power BI to visualize and analyze data stored in DynamoDB. Gain valuable insights into trends, user behavior, and **key performance indicators** (**KPIs**).

DynamoDB vs. Amazon ElastiCache

Amazon DynamoDB and Amazon ElastiCache serve different roles in serverless architectures. DynamoDB provides durable, scalable NoSQL storage, while ElastiCache offers high-speed in-memory caching for faster data retrieval. Choosing the right service depends on workload requirements—DynamoDB is ideal for applications needing persistent storage and flexible data models. In contrast, ElastiCache excels in reducing database load and optimizing response times. These services often work together, where DynamoDB stores structured data, and ElastiCache caches frequently access information to enhance performance.

The following table highlights their key differences and recommended use cases:

Feature	Amazon DynamoDB	Amazon ElastiCache
Storage type	Persistent NoSQL storage	In-memory caching (Redis, emcached)
Performance	Single-digit millisecond response time	Microsecond response time

Scalability	Fully managed, auto-scales	Scales horizontally with replicas
Data model	Key-value and document store	Key-value with in-memory structures
Persistence	Durable storage with backups	Volatile storage (unless Redis persistence is enabled)
Best for	Long-term structured/unstructured data storage	Reducing query load and caching frequently accessed data
Use cases	E-commerce, IoT, fraud detection, event logging	API caching, session storage, real-time leaderboards

Table 7.2: Table showing differences between Amazon DynamoDB and ElastiCache

Anti-patterns

While DynamoDB is a robust serverless service, it is not the best fit for all scenarios. The following are some of the anti-patterns with AWS DynamoDB:

- **Overloading single table**: Storing unrelated data in a single table can lead to complex queries and increased latency. For example:

  o A single table storing both user data and product catalog data may require multiple GSIs and complex queries to filter unrelated items.

  o Instead, design separate tables for user data and product catalogs based on their distinct access patterns.

- **Using DynamoDB for complex joins**: DynamoDB is not optimized for complex join operations. For instance:

  o If your application needs to frequently join user orders with detailed product data, using DynamoDB alone may result in inefficient queries.

  o Consider combining DynamoDB with a relational database like Amazon RDS for such workloads, where relational joins are a better fit.

- **Ignoring item size limits**: DynamoDB enforces a strict limit of 400 KB per item. This includes both the attribute names and values, as well as any metadata, once serialized. Exceeding this limit can cause errors and hinder performance. Consider the following solutions to work around item size constraints:

  o **Store large files in S3**: For large objects such as images, videos, or log files, store the file in Amazon S3 and reference it using metadata in DynamoDB. This ensures that only metadata is stored in DynamoDB, keeping the item size below the limit.

  o **Decompose complex items**: Split large, complex data structures into smaller, more manageable items. Use relationships or keys to maintain links between these decomposed items.

  o **Optimize attribute usage**: Avoid storing redundant or unnecessary attributes in DynamoDB items. For instance, compress lengthy text data where feasible or eliminate optional attributes not used in queries.

- **Neglecting indexing**: Failing to use GSIs or LSIs can result in inefficient queries and poor performance. For example:

  o If a table lacks a GSI for a frequently queried attribute (e.g., email), the application will require a full table scan, increasing costs and latency.

    o   Add a GSI to the email to support efficient querying for this attribute.

- **Using scan operations excessively**: Relying heavily on scan operations instead of query operations can lead to high latency and increased costs. For example:

    o   A scan operation on a table with millions of items to filter products by category is inefficient.

    o   Use query operations with GSIs or LSIs to filter data by category and reduce unnecessary reads.

- **Overlooking access controls**: Insufficiently restrictive bucket policies and object ACLs can expose sensitive data.

    o   Ensure IAM policies follow the principle of least privilege, restricting access only to the required resources and operations.

- **Not using DynamoDB streams**: Ignoring DynamoDB Streams for real-time data processing can result in missed opportunities for efficient data handling.

    o   For example, enabling streams can help synchronize data changes with an AWS Lambda analytics system.

Best practices

Amazon DynamoDB offers many features and configuration options to integrate and tailor to individual needs. To gain optimum performance, cost efficiencies, and massive scalability, it is important to follow guidelines and best practices.

- **Data modeling**:

    o   The tables should be designed with appropriate partition keys (primary and sort keys) to satisfy the access patterns required for the application.

    o   When the access patterns require access outside of the primary keys, which leverage primary indexes, secondary indexes must be created.

    o   When faster access is required, utilize the GSI to perform query operations. To speed up and accelerate access to frequently accessed data within a specific partition key value, utilize the LSI.

    o   Avoid table scans as it has to look up the entire table in the most common implementation patterns.

    o   When configuring indexes, set up projected attributes encompassing the required attributes.

    o   When there is a need to retrieve multiple items from one or more DynamoDB tables in a single API call, leverage the BatchGetItem API – This reduces HTTP overhead and can easily retrieve up to 16 MB of data containing 100 items in a single call.

- **Provisioning capacity**:

    o   When the workloads have a predictive load, use reserved capacity.

    o   Leverage read and write auto-scaling based on usage access patterns.

- **Cost optimization**:

    o   Monitor table usage and capacities.

    o   Setup CloudWatch alarms when throughput exceeds set maximums.

- **Security**:

    o   Implement fine-grained access control with IAM policies.

    o   Implement the principle of least privileges to ensure any resource accessing DynamoDB only has that specific access to that action and the resource.

    o   When dealing with access from an organization, try to leverage AWS PrivateLink to prevent man-in-the-middle attacks.

- **Backups and disaster recovery**:
  - o Ensure the database is backed up periodically and per the data needs. Continuous backups to S3 help in managing disaster recoveries.
  - o Ensure PITR is enabled to prevent accidental deletes and immediate recovery from unintentional data corruption.

- **Integration and high-performance access**:
  - o Utilize DynamoDB streams to collect changes and to build event-driven workflows.
  - o When very high-performance access is required, utilize DAX, This in-memory change is fully managed and can provide ultra-high performance. This can help applications scale to millions of requests and cater at blazing milli speeds to microseconds.
  - o In scenarios requiring very high availability across regions, utilize DynamoDB global tables. They are fully managed databases and are serverless and multi-region by default. They have global availability and can provide increased resiliency and business continuity.

Limits

Serverless architectures in the cloud generally offer unlimited scalability and flexibility. However, in practice, AWS imposes certain limits and guardrails to prevent unintentional behaviors and cost overruns, and they are also predictable from a service provider's view (AWS in this case). The following are some of the limits at this time (subject to change).

- **Item size**: Each item in any DynamoDB table cannot exceed 400 KB.

- **Datatype support**: DynamoDB does not support all data types like arrays and hierarchical data structures.

- **GSI limits**: Each table can have a maximum of 20 GSI by default, but there is a provision to increase further through a service request limit increase.

- **LSI limits**: Each table can have a maximum of 5 LSI, with each LSI having a storage limit of 10 GB / partition key.

- **Hot keys**: If a particular partition key receives too many requests, it can result in a hotspot that impacts performance.

- **Capacity limits**: The total capacity (RCU and WCU) cannot exceed 80,000 per table, and the AWS account limit is 400,000.

Conclusion

This chapter has comprehensively explored Amazon DynamoDB, equipping readers with the foundational knowledge and practical skills to leverage its capabilities for robust NoSQL data storage solutions. This has covered core strengths that make DynamoDB a cornerstone for many cloud architectures: its exceptional scalability, high availability, and flexible data modeling capabilities.

The chapter then focused on DynamoDB's robust security features, which ensure the confidentiality and integrity of your data. Granular access control through IAM and encryption options (at rest and in transit) provides a layered security approach. You have also gained insights into DynamoDB's seamless integration with other AWS serverless services like Lambda, unlocking a comprehensive ecosystem for building dynamic and efficient applications.

DynamoDB empowers various deployment patterns, catering to a wide spectrum of data access needs across different application types. The strategies for optimizing DynamoDB costs were explored by choosing the most appropriate billing model: provisioned capacity for predictable workloads or on-demand for more variable access patterns. This ensures efficient resource allocation and cost-effectiveness.

The landscape of NoSQL databases is constantly evolving. As you continue your exploration of DynamoDB, stay informed about the latest advancements in its functionalities. By harnessing its expanding capabilities, you can craft scalable, flexible, and secure data storage solutions that propel your applications to the forefront of performance and efficiency.

The next chapter will explore serverless storage solutions, focusing on Amazon Aurora Serverless and EFS. Aurora Serverless offers a fully managed relational database designed to automatically scale with application demands, delivering cost-efficient performance for variable workloads. In contrast, Amazon EFS provides a scalable, serverless file system ideal for shared access and consistent throughput across multiple applications. This chapter will look into the architecture, use cases, and integration strategies for these services, showcasing how they address diverse storage requirements while ensuring scalability, reliability, and cost-effectiveness in modern cloud environments.

Join our Discord space

Join our Discord workspace for latest updates, offers, tech happenings around the world, new releases, and sessions with the authors:

https://discord.bpbonline.com

CHAPTER 8

Serverless Storage with Aurora Serverless and EFS

Introduction

Traditional data storage methods often require significant upfront provisioning, ongoing maintenance, and manual scaling to accommodate varying workloads. Organizations using on-premises or self-managed cloud databases often struggle with operational complexity, unpredictable costs, and challenges in ensuring high availability and fault tolerance. These issues become more pronounced as businesses scale and demand seamless, efficient, and cost-effective storage solutions.

Serverless storage technologies alleviate these challenges by offering dynamic scalability, automated provisioning, and operational simplicity. This chapter focuses on two essential AWS serverless storage services: Amazon Aurora Serverless and Amazon **Elastic File System** (**EFS**). These services address different storage needs. Aurora Serverless provides an on-demand relational database that automatically scales with application demand, while EFS delivers a fully managed, elastic file storage solution designed for high availability and distributed workloads.

Aurora Serverless supports MySQL and PostgreSQL databases, removing the burden of infrastructure management by scaling seamlessly based on workload fluctuations. It is an ideal choice for applications with unpredictable traffic, intermittent workloads, or infrequent queries. Amazon EFS, in contrast, enables shared file storage that expands and contracts dynamically. It is designed for applications requiring shared access across multiple compute resources, making it well-suited for containerized environments, CI/CD pipelines, and big data processing.

This chapter will provide an in-depth understanding of how Aurora Serverless and EFS solve key challenges in traditional database and file storage management. It will compare their capabilities, explore best practices for integration, and demonstrate real-world scenarios where these technologies optimize cost, scalability, and performance.

Structure

This chapter covers the following topics:

- Challenges in traditional database management
- Databases in the cloud
- Introduction to Amazon RDS
- Key concepts of Amazon RDS

- Introduction to Amazon Aurora
- Cost management in Amazon Aurora Serverless
- Amazon Aurora Serverless security
- Basic operations with Amazon Aurora Serverless
- Integrations and best practices with Amazon Aurora Serverless
- Limits with Amazon Aurora Serverless
- Anti-patterns with Amazon Aurora Serverless
- Real-world applications of Amazon Aurora Serverless
- Introduction to Amazon EFS
- Key concepts in Amazon EFS
- Key integrations with Amazon EFS
- Basic operations with Amazon EFS
- Real-world applications of Amazon EFS

Objectives

This chapter provides a structured approach to understanding serverless storage solutions, focusing on two key AWS services: Amazon Aurora Serverless and Amazon **Elastic File System** (**EFS**). By the end of this chapter, readers will have a clear grasp of when and how to use each service, optimizing them for performance, cost, and security.

Readers will first explore Amazon RDS and its various database engines, emphasizing Aurora Serverless, a fully managed, auto-scaling relational database. The chapter will cover Aurora's architecture, capabilities, use cases, cost management strategies, and security best practices, helping readers evaluate its suitability for cloud-native database workloads.

The second part of the chapter focuses on Amazon EFS, a serverless, scalable file storage system that provides seamless access across multiple AWS compute services. Readers will gain insights into EFS architecture, integration best practices, and cost optimization strategies.

This chapter will equip readers with the skills to integrate Aurora Serverless and EFS into cloud architectures effectively through practical use cases, hands-on exercises, and real-world scenarios. Focusing on best practices, cost optimization, and security considerations, readers will develop a strategic approach to selecting and implementing serverless storage solutions in AWS.

Challenges in traditional database management

Managing relational databases in traditional on-premises or self-hosted environments presents several challenges, particularly in high-growth industries such as e-commerce, financial services, and healthcare. Organizations must handle complex infrastructure provisioning, manual scaling, security management, and high operational costs to maintain database performance and reliability.

The following real-world challenges illustrate the limitations of traditional database management:

- **Scaling constraints in e-commerce**: Online retailers experience traffic spikes during seasonal sales events (e.g., Black Friday, Cyber Monday). Traditional databases require manual scaling, often resulting in downtime, slow response times, or over-provisioned resources that remain idle during off-peak periods.

- **Operational overhead in financial services**: Banks and financial institutions must comply with strict security and data governance policies. Manually managing database security, encryption, and access control mechanisms requires dedicated teams and high operational costs, making traditional setups inefficient.

- **Infrastructure burden in healthcare**: Hospitals and telemedicine providers handle massive patient records and imaging data volumes. Traditional database storage struggles with elasticity, requiring administrators to constantly provision additional storage hardware, which increases costs and delays scaling efforts during high-demand periods.

These real-world pain points highlight why organizations are increasingly migrating to serverless database solutions like Amazon Aurora Serverless. These solutions offer automatic scaling, managed security, and cost-efficiency without the complexity of traditional database management.

Databases in the cloud

By leveraging the cloud for databases, organizations can effectively address the challenges traditional on-premises systems face. There are two primary approaches in data management and migration: Database migration and cloud database solutions.

The database migration process is a strategic move that involves transferring or moving existing on-premises databases and their underlying schema into a cloud environment. It is akin to lifting and shifting the existing database to the cloud infrastructure.

Some of the key advantages of this approach include the following:

- **Granularity in control**: This type of migration provides granular control over the underlying infrastructure with options to tailor configurations, security controls, and performance optimizations.

- **Compatibility with legacy systems**: If complex legacy systems are intricately tied to existing on-premises databases, this approach can help keep the current structure and functionalities while providing the benefits of cloud computing

- **Data ownership and security**: Complete data ownership and control lie within the organization and could be a major factor for regulatory and data privacy laws.

- **Training**: This option requires relatively less training and upskilling for existing database professionals to manage database systems.

While this option solves many problems with on-premises databases with cloud infrastructure, it has some challenges and disadvantages, explained as follows:

- **Higher upfront costs**: This process typically involves upfront costs for migration services and potentially additional licensing fees for cloud-based database software (not all licenses can be transferred to their cloud deployment equivalent).

- **Limited scalability**: Some scaling levels are inherently possible after a database is migrated to the cloud. However, choosing a fully managed cloud database solution is not as seamless and automated.

- **Operational maintenance**: In this approach, the primary responsibility of managing database infrastructure remains with the organization or customer. This involves routine backups, security patches, upgrades, backup management, data disaster recovery, and security guardrails.

- **Additional considerations**: This option requires additional consideration into IT team expertise in managing migration, vendor lock-ins, and resource-intensive migration processes.

Cloud database solutions: This is a managed offering and an alternative where a cloud provider provides and oversees most aspects of database administration, management, security, and scalability.

All the major cloud service providers (AWS—Amazon RDS, Microsoft Azure—Azure SQL, and Google Cloud—Cloud SQL) offer this managed database offering.

The key advantages of this approach include the following:

- **Reduced operational costs**: Managed solutions generally offer a pay-as-you model. This eliminates initial capital expenditures in the procurement and maintenance of database servers. In this approach, users pay only for actual resource consumption, which often does not include separate licensing costs.

- **Agility, simplicity, and speed**: The cloud provider does the heavy lifting in managing the cloud infrastructure, so setting up databases is simple and easy and can be performed with minimal configuration overhead. This helps organizations quickly and immediately provision cloud databases and stay ahead of the game.

- **Scaling**: Managed cloud database solutions provide flexibility and control to scale up/down based on traffic. They also come with different service tiers that can make this process seamless.

- **Data security and disaster recovery**: A managed cloud database offers built-in and automatic fault tolerance, data replication, backup mechanisms, and encryption, which helps keep the data secure while providing disaster recovery options to recover from any data loss or disaster immediately. This feature can take off much of the burden of securing and managing data backups and replication processes with an on-premises database or other data migration options to the cloud.

- **Security**: The cloud provider solutions have built-in security controls, including firewalls, intrusion detection, and data encryption. The cloud provider is also responsible for the physical security of the infrastructure.

- **Easy maintenance**: The cloud provider manages the software updates, routine management, and maintenance tasks, thus ensuring the database is up-to-date with the most recent security patches.

Introduction to Amazon RDS

Amazon **Relational Database Service** (**RDS**) is a fully managed database offering from AWS. It is easy to use and built for speed, agility, security, and cost-effectiveness while leveraging all the benefits of a relational database and cloud computing.

RDS, as a service, handles all maintenance and management tasks, including server provisioning, data security (at rest and during transit), maintenance (upgrades and patching), and recovery (failures and disasters).

RDS offers on-demand pricing for database services with a granularity of up to seconds (billing at the second level), so customers will only pay for the exact number of seconds they have used the database. This service also offers flexibility and options to purchase the database as a service for a term (1 year to 3 years) at a much lower price point on a long-term scale.

Amazon RDS supports many database engines and seamlessly integrates into other AWS services, including IAM. Thus, it is a default choice for most cloud solutions (including serverless, event-driven, and cloud-native workloads).

Some of the key benefits of RDS include the following:

- **Versatile engine offerings**: RDS offers flexibility to choose from a wide range of database engines that are commonly used, popular, and have proven for complex use cases. The common engines supported include:
  - MySQL
  - PostgreSQL
  - MariaDB
  - Oracle
  - SQL Server

o IBM DB2

o Aurora

Using familiar database engines eases development processes, helps leverage existing skillsets, and allows one to pick the one that best suits the workload.

- **High availability (HA)**: Amazon RDS offers high availability through multi-AZ deployments. The database replicas are created and managed in geographically separated zones. In an AZ outage, the failover mechanisms ensure that the data is restored from other zones with minimal downtime and interruptions.

- **Security**: Amazon RDS offers built-in security and promotes best practices for safeguarding databases. Security features include data encryption at rest and in transit, continuous monitoring, authentication, fine-grained access controls, and comprehensive auditing capabilities.

- **Backup and recovery**: Amazon RDS automates regular backups of your database, enabling point-in-time recovery. This means you can restore your database to a specific state in case of accidental data deletion, application errors, or other unforeseen events. Additionally, you can create manual database snapshots for further control and disaster recovery purposes. These snapshots can be easily restored to create a new database instance, offering flexibility and peace of mind.

- **Cost-efficiency**: Amazon RDS utilizes a pay-as-you-go pricing model, meaning you only pay for the resources your database consumes. This eliminates the upfront costs of purchasing and managing your database hardware. Optimizing resource allocation with features like auto-scaling can reduce costs and ensure you are not paying for unused resources.

- **Read replicas**: Amazon RDS offers read replicas for high-read traffic applications. These are read-only copies of your primary database instance that can distribute read operations across multiple servers. This offloads read traffic from the primary database, improving overall performance and scalability for read-heavy workloads. Read replicas are also cost-effective as they typically use smaller computing resources than the primary instance.

- **Ease of management**: Amazon RDS offers multiple ways to set up and manage databases, AWS Management Console, RDS CLI, and SDKs, and helps create a production-ready database system in minutes.

- **AI/ML integrations**: RDS offers many capabilities that allow for easy integration and building of AI/ML workflows. When Amazon Aurora for PostgreSQL is used, it comes with an open-source extension called **pgvector**, which can store vector embeddings, enabling similarity searches.

- **Amazon RDS:** It can also store vector embeddings from other AI services, such as Amazon SageMaker and Amazon Bedrock.

Key concepts of Amazon RDS

Amazon RDS offers a robust and managed database service for various workloads. While it removes the burden of managing the underlying infrastructure, understanding core concepts like database engines, instances, and scaling is essential for building secure, performant, and cost-effective database solutions on AWS. Let us look further into these key concepts to empower you to leverage Amazon RDS's full potential:

- **Database engine**: A Database engine is the master orchestrator that manages all aspects of data organization and is responsible for creating, managing, securing, and manipulating data stored in a structured format. It provides functionalities for data definition, data retrieval, and data administration.

The following are the engine options available in Amazon RDS:

o **MySQL**: An open-source relational database management system known for its ease of use, flexibility, and wide community support.

- o **PostgreSQL**: Another open-source relational database engine known for its advanced features, data integrity, and object-relational capabilities.
- o **MariaDB**: A community-developed fork of MySQL, offering high compatibility and improved scalability.
- o **Oracle database**: A powerful and commercially licensed relational database system known for scalability, security features, and complex data types.
- o **SQL Server**: Microsoft's popular relational database engine, known for its integration with other Microsoft products and strong transaction processing capabilities.

- **Database instance**: A database instance is a server preconfigured to run a specific database engine. An instance is a container for database files, configurations, and running processes.

  Users can select a different instance class suited to the workload (memory-optimized, compute-optimized), storage allocation, and AZ during the instance creation process.

- **AZ**: This is a geographically isolated data center within an AWS region. These zones are physically isolated with independent power, cooling, and network connectivity.

  A multi-AZ deployment of the RDS database ensures high availability by replicating the primary Database into a standby instance in a different AZ.

  If the primary instance fails, RDS automatically promotes the standby instance to the primary role during a failover, ensuring minimal downtime.

- **Read replicas**: A read replica is an additional copy of the primary database to handle read traffic. Its key benefit is that it can offload read queries from the primary instance, thus improving overall performance.

  This also helps improve scalability, as read replicas can handle read-heavy workloads.

  This is best suited for analytics, reporting, and other workloads demanding read-heavy processing.

- **Amazon RDS network isolation**: The RDS database resides in a VPC, enabling fine-grained network access control.

  This also offers additional security controls:
  - o **Security groups**: Control inbound and outbound access and traffic from RDS instances. They act as a firewall and first line of defense, which allows for fine-grained control over specific entities that can access databases (for example, a particular IP range over a specific database network port).
  - o **Parameter groups**: Allowing configuration of database-specific settings at the instance level.
  - o **IAM authentication**: IAM Roles to manage access.
  - o **Encryption**: Supports encryption at rest (Using AWS KMS) and SSL/TLS for data in transit.

Introduction to Amazon Aurora

Amazon Aurora is another flavor of Amazon RDS. It is a fully managed MySQL and PostgreSQL compatible relational database.

Amazon RDS is architecturally similar to installing database engines on Amazon EC2 and leveraging provisioning and maintenance from AWS. Amazon Aurora's database storage has six copies in three different AZs, thus providing higher and more consistent performance than Amazon RDS.

Amazon Aurora has better durability and higher availability due to its unique storage model, which provides faster backup and recovery operations. Here, data is always durable by design and spread across AZs.

Some of the key differentiating factors of Amazon Aurora include:

- **Failover**: Failover in Aurora is automatic and faster than Amazon RDS (where it is manual).

- **Replication**: Aurora allows up to 15 replicas, whereas RDS provides up to 5 replicas. Replication in Aurora is faster and often takes a few milliseconds.

- **Scalability**: RDS and Aurora allow vertical scaling. Aurora also provides an option for auto-scaling, enabling you to dynamically adjust the number of replicas for an Aurora DB cluster using single-master replication.

- **Backups**: Aurora offers continuous and incremental data backups with no performance impacts to reads/writes.

- **Resiliency**: Aurora offers higher resiliency, can recover faster, and has minimal latency compared to RDS.

Amazon Aurora offers a compelling solution for businesses seeking a high-performance, reliable, and scalable database service on AWS. Its unmatched performance, robust availability, and effortless scalability make it ideal for mission-critical applications and demanding workloads.

Amazon Aurora types

While renowned for its high performance and scalability, Amazon Aurora offers different configurations to cater to specific needs. Here is a breakdown of the key Aurora types:

- **Aurora MySQL compatible edition**: This edition is ideal for existing applications that leverage MySQL, requiring a seamless transition to the cloud. This ensures compatibility with most MySQL-based tools and libraries, minimizing code modifications during migration.

- **Aurora PostgreSQL compatible edition**: This edition provides a familiar development environment within the robust Aurora framework. It delivers Aurora's performance and scalability while maintaining compatibility with existing PostgreSQL tools and functionalities.

- **Aurora Serverless**: This serverless offering eliminates the need for manual capacity planning. Aurora Serverless automatically scales compute resources (CPU, memory) up or down based on real-time application demands. This ensures optimal performance during traffic spikes without incurring overspending during low-activity periods. It is a perfect fit for applications with fluctuating workloads.

Choosing the right Aurora type

The selection process hinges on your existing development environment and application needs. Here is a quick guide:

- **For existing MySQL applications**: The MySQL-compatible edition offers a smooth migration path.

- **For existing PostgreSQL applications**: The PostgreSQL-compatible edition leverages your skillset and tools.

- **For applications with unpredictable workloads**: Aurora Serverless ensures cost-efficiency with its auto-scaling capabilities.

Cost management in Amazon Aurora Serverless

One of the most appealing aspects of Amazon Aurora Serverless is its inherent cost-efficiency. However, strategies can still be employed to further optimize the cloud database budget. Here is a look at the cost management considerations for Aurora Serverless:

- **Billing model**:
  - o Amazon Aurora Serverless operates on a flexible pay-per-use model, where costs are based on the **Aurora Capacity Units (ACUs)** consumed per second. This approach eliminates the expense of overprovisioning during periods of low traffic. Aurora Serverless features fine-grained scaling, adjusting resources in increments as small as 0.5 ACUs to meet workload demands efficiently without unnecessary resource allocation.
  - o Users can leverage AWS CloudWatch to monitor database utilization and schedule resource downscaling during idle periods using AWS Lambda to optimize costs further. Additionally, AWS Cost Explorer provides actionable insights into usage patterns and budgeting, enabling organizations to refine cost management strategies and enhance efficiency.

- **Optimizing resource consumption**:
  - o **Fine-grained scaling**: Aurora Serverless automatically scales resources in increments of 0.5 ACUs, providing a highly granular level of control compared to traditional provisioning methods. This ensures customers are not paying for more resources than their application needs.
  - o **Right-sizing ACUs**: While Aurora Serverless automatically scales, there is an initial configuration step. Selecting the appropriate starting ACU size can significantly impact costs. Analyze your application's typical workload to choose an initial size that accommodates most use cases without overprovisioning.
  - o **Identify idle periods**: Analyze your application's usage patterns to identify periods of low activity. Consider implementing scheduled scaling using AWS Lambda functions to scale down ACUs automatically during these times. This can further reduce your overall serverless database costs.

- **Monitoring and cost insights**:
  - o **AWS CloudWatch**: Leverage CloudWatch to monitor your Aurora Serverless database metrics, including ACU utilization, storage usage, and database calls. This data helps you identify resource usage trends and potential areas for optimization.
  - o **Cost explorer**: Utilize AWS Cost Explorer to gain deeper insights into your Aurora Serverless costs. It allows you to visualize cost breakdowns by dimensions, such as period, usage type (ACUs, storage), and specific databases. This granular visibility empowers you to identify potential cost outliers and make informed decisions for future optimization.

- **Additional considerations**:
  - o **Bursting vs. provisioned instances**: Aurora Serverless might be more cost-effective for workloads with frequent, short-lived bursts of activity. However, a provisioned instance might offer better cost predictability for sustained high workloads. Analyze your workload patterns carefully to make the right choice.
  - o **RIs for predictable workloads**: If you have predictable workloads, consider using Amazon Aurora **Reserved Instances (RIs)**. RIs offer significant discounts compared to Aurora Serverless' on-demand pricing. However, they have a fixed upfront cost and require a commitment to a specific usage level.

Amazon Aurora Serverless security

Security in Amazon Aurora Serverless is designed to meet the stringent requirements of modern applications, particularly in finance, healthcare, and e-commerce, where data protection, regulatory compliance, and access control are critical. Below, we examine real-world security applications, Aurora's core security features, and best practices for strengthening database security.

Real-world use cases of security in action

The following real-world use cases illustrate how Aurora Serverless security features are applied in production environments, ensuring data protection, compliance, and secure access management.

Security in financial services

Financial institutions must implement strict access control mechanisms to prevent unauthorized access to sensitive financial records. Given the industry's regulatory nature, ensuring that only authorized personnel can query transactional data is critical to maintaining security and compliance.

- A global financial institution using Aurora Serverless for transactional workloads ensures that only specific IAM roles can query customer data.

- Instead of static database credentials, the organization implements IAM authentication, which enforces fine-grained access control through AWS IAM.

- Security Measure Applied: IAM authentication eliminates password-based access, ensuring only authorized roles or federated users can connect, reducing the risk of insider threats and credential leaks.

Security in healthcare systems

Data privacy and compliance with HIPAA regulations are mandatory in healthcare. Medical institutions must ensure that patient records remain encrypted at all times, reducing the risk of unauthorized exposure.

- A telemedicine provider stores and processes sensitive patient records using Aurora Serverless, subject to HIPAA compliance.

- To secure **protected health information** (**PHI**), the company encrypts all data at rest and in transit using AWS **Key Management Service** (**KMS**) and SSL/TLS encryption.

- Security measure applied:
  - AES-256 encryption ensures data confidentiality even if unauthorized access occurs.
  - SSL/TLS encryption protects data in transit, preventing unauthorized interception.
  - KMS-managed encryption keys enforce strict access control over decryption operations, ensuring only authorized services and roles can access sensitive data.

Security in e-commerce applications

E-commerce platforms process millions of transactions daily, making them prime targets for DDoS attacks and unauthorized access attempts. Implementing robust security controls is essential to prevent service disruptions and unauthorized data breaches.

- A large online retailer uses Aurora Serverless as part of its real-time inventory system, where API-driven queries handle thousands of requests per second.

- To prevent unauthorized database access, they configure AWS Security Groups to allow only requests originating from their approved VPC subnets.

- Additionally, the AWS **Web Application Firewall** (**WAF**) blocks malicious queries such as SQL injection or automated bot attacks.

- Security measure applied:
  - VPC isolation ensures only internal AWS services can interact with the database.
  - Security groups enforce IP-based access control.
  - AWS WAF mitigates common web threats, ensuring a secure API layer.

Basic operations with Amazon Aurora Serverless

This section covers how an Aurora table can be created and how basic operations can be performed via the AWS Management Console. The steps are as follows:

1. Navigate to the **RDS** service by searching through the **Services** Console.

   Figure 8.1 shows how to locate and search for RDS service:

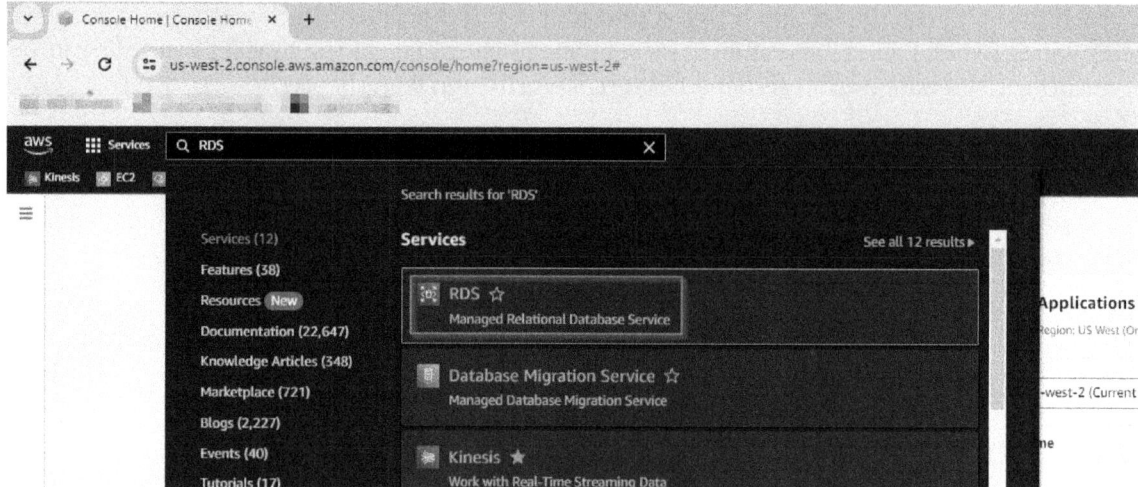

Figure 8.1: Search and navigate into RDS service through the Console

2. Create a new database by navigating to **RDS**, **Databases**, **Create Database**.

3. Create a new table by selecting **Create Table** under the RDS home page or navigating into **Tables** and then **Create Table**.

   a. Select **Standard Create** for the basic and pre-filled common configuration.

   b. Select **Aurora PostgreSQL** to create an Aurora Serverless database cluster.

   Figure 8.2 shows provide shows different database engines available:

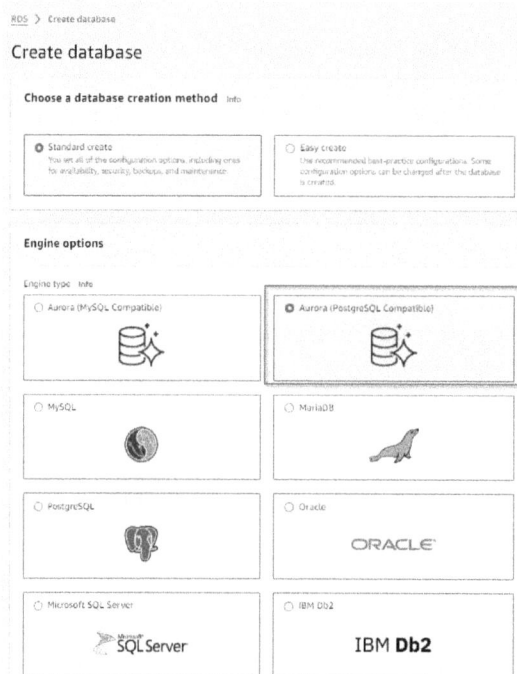

Figure 8.2: Selection of Aurora (PostgreSQL compatible) database

4. When prompted to select the engine version, default to the currently available major version and ensure dev/test is chosen for initial setup and non-production workloads.

   a. The DB cluster identifier is a unique identifier in an AWS account and provides a meaningful name.

   b. The credentials help in logging in and accessing the database, defaulting to Postgres, and allowing AWS Secrets Manager to manage the secrets

Figure 8.3 shows additional settings when creating a cluster (including engine version and instance identifier):

Figure 8.3: Additional options when creating a new database

5. For **Credentials management**, default to AWS Secrets Manager to store secrets.

As shown in *Figure 8.4*, select **Aurora Standard**, which provides the most cost-effective option for database storage using Aurora Serverless:

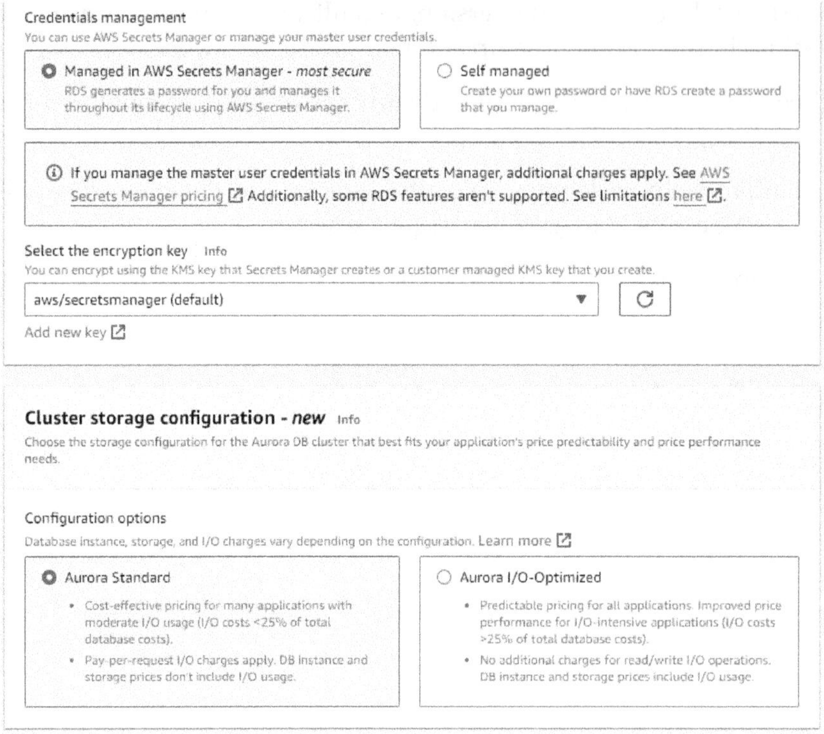

Figure 8.4: Cluster configuration and credentials management for Aurora

6. **Instance configuration**: Choose **Serverless v2** for DB Instance class and default capacities. This option of **Serverless v2** makes the cluster an Aurora Serverless Cluster. This can be seen in *Figure 8.5*:

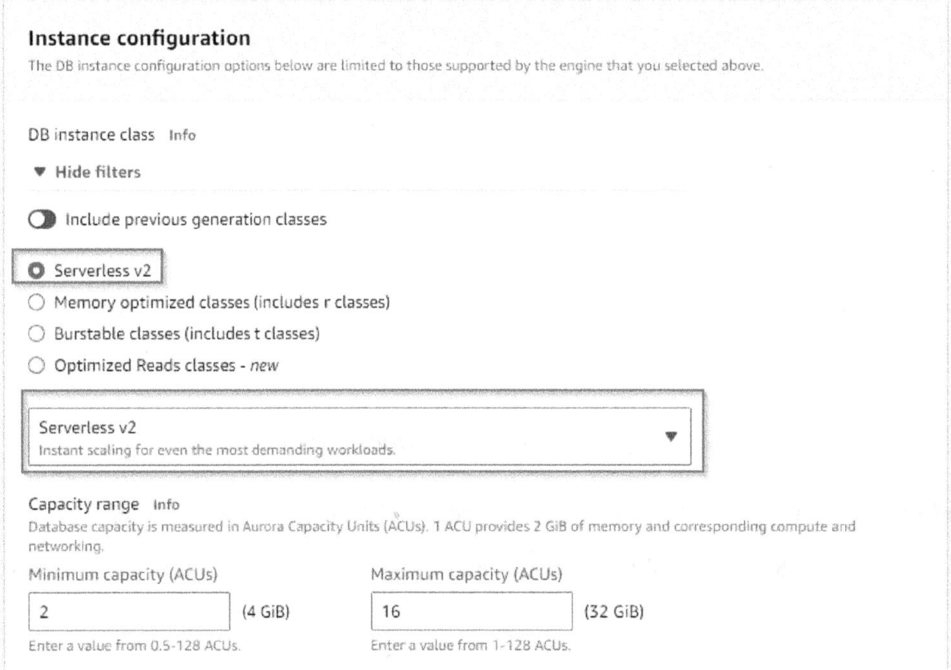

Figure 8.5: Instance configuration and type selection

7. Click on **Create Database**. Once the database is created, it creates a regional cluster and a reader instance (as can be seen in *Figure 8.6*).

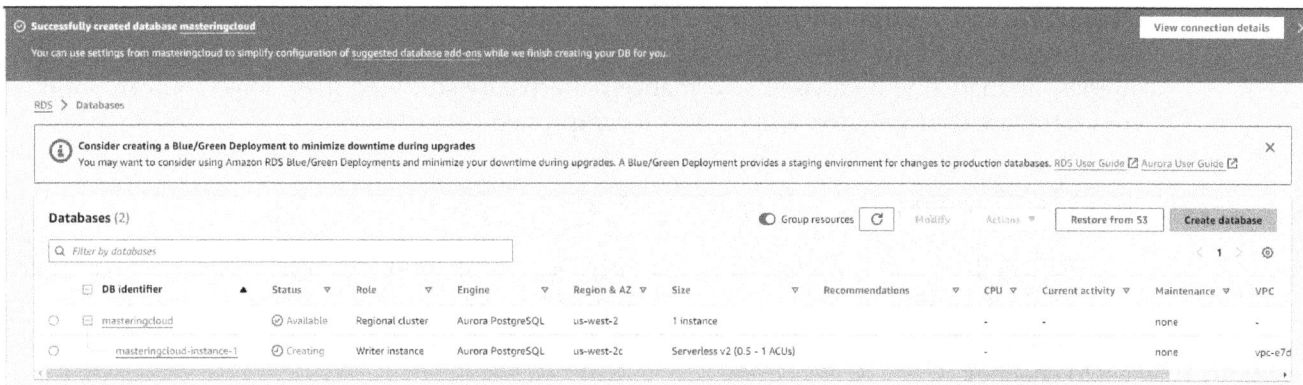

Figure 8.6: DB Cluster created successfully

8. Once the DB cluster is created, all the cluster properties can be viewed by clicking on the cluster/ instance, and any desktop utility can be used to connect to the database instance.

For credentials, use the username selected during setup and retrieve the password from the AWS secrets manager.

Integration capabilities with Amazon Aurora Serverless

Amazon **Relational Database Service (RDS)** shines for its managed database capabilities and seamless integration with other AWS services. This tight integration allows you to build robust and efficient data-driven applications within the AWS cloud. Here is a look at some key integrations:

- **Amazon S3 (Simple Storage Service)**:
    - **Backups and restore**: RDS simplifies database backups by offering automated backups to S3. You can schedule regular backups and easily restore your database from a specific point in time in case of failures or accidental data modifications. S3's durability and scalability ensure the backups are secure and readily available for restore operations.
    - **Data migration and analytics**: S3 can also serve as a staging ground for large data sets. You can migrate data into your RDS instance from S3 for further processing and analysis. Conversely, you can offload processed data from RDS to S3 for long-term archival or use it with analytics services like Amazon Redshift for large-scale data exploration.
- **AWS Lambda (Serverless Functions)**:
    - **Event-driven data processing**: RDS integrates with AWS Lambda to enable event-driven architectures. You can configure Lambda functions to trigger based on specific database events, such as data insertions or updates. This allows for real-time processing of database changes, such as sending notifications, kicking off downstream workflows, or performing data transformations.
    - **Cost-effective data processing**: By leveraging serverless Lambda functions, you can avoid constantly running servers for data processing tasks triggered by RDS events. This translates to cost savings, as you only pay for the compute resources used during the Lambda invocation.
- **Amazon CloudWatch**:
    - **Monitoring and alerting**: CloudWatch provides comprehensive monitoring capabilities for your RDS instances. You can monitor key metrics like database queries, throughput, and connection errors. CloudWatch allows you to set up custom alarms that trigger notifications when specific thresholds are breached, helping you identify potential issues and proactively address performance bottlenecks within RDS databases.

    o **Debugging and performance optimization**: CloudWatch logs detailed information about your RDS instance activity. These logs can be invaluable for debugging issues, identifying slow queries, or analyzing database performance patterns. By studying these logs, you can optimize your database configuration and queries for improved performance.

Limits with Amazon Aurora Serverless

Serverless architectures in the cloud generally offer unlimited scalability and flexibility. However, in practice, AWS imposes certain limits and guardrails to prevent unintentional behaviors and cost overruns, and they are also predictable from a service provider's view (AWS in this case). The following are some of the limits currently (subject to change):

- **Storage size**: Aurora Serverless clusters can scale up to 128 TB of storage.

- **Instance classes**: Aurora Serverless supports specific instance classes, and you cannot use other instance types.

- **Scaling constraints**: Aurora Serverless provides automatic scaling, but scaling events typically take a few seconds to minutes, making it unsuitable for real-time analytics or ultra-low-latency applications. Storage is capped at 128 TB per cluster, and the service supports specific MySQL and PostgreSQL versions only. Connection limits vary by workload intensity, and scaling timeouts can impact applications with strict availability requirements. Additionally, Aurora Serverless may not be available in all AWS regions, necessitating careful planning for multi-region deployments.

- **Connection limits**: The maximum number of connections is determined by the instance class and can vary.

- **Timeouts**: Aurora Serverless has a timeout limit for scaling operations, which can impact applications with high availability requirements.

- **Region availability**: Aurora Serverless may not be available in all AWS regions.

- **Backup retention**: The maximum backup retention period is 35 days.

- **Parameter group limits**: Aurora Serverless uses specific parameter groups, and not all parameters are adjustable.

- **Read replica limits**: Create up to 15 read replicas for each Aurora Serverless cluster.

- **Database engine versions**: Aurora Serverless supports specific versions of MySQL and PostgreSQL, and you cannot use other versions.

Anti-patterns with Amazon Aurora Serverless

While Aurora Serverless offers auto-scaling and on-demand capacity, it is essential to avoid these common pitfalls:

- **Unsuitable for real-time analytics**: Aurora Serverless V1 suffers from scaling delays that range from seconds to minutes, making it unsuitable for real-time analytics where immediate scalability and low-latency responses are critical. While Aurora Serverless V2 significantly reduces scaling latency with fine-grained adjustments occurring in milliseconds to seconds, it may still not be the best choice for real-time analytics. Purpose-built services such as Amazon Redshift or Amazon Kinesis Data Analytics are better suited for these scenarios due to their specialized architecture designed to handle real-time data processing and analytics at scale.

- **Ineffective for high-frequency transactions**: Applications with consistently high transaction rates may experience delays during scaling operations, potentially causing performance bottlenecks. Provisioned Aurora clusters or Amazon DynamoDB are better alternatives for such use cases.

- **Cold start delays**: Applications requiring ultra-low latency may face issues during Aurora Serverless cold starts, where resources take time to initialize. Analyze your workload patterns carefully to determine if Aurora Serverless aligns with your performance expectations.

Real-world applications of Amazon Aurora Serverless

Amazon Aurora Serverless provides auto-scaling, cost efficiency, and high availability, making it ideal for applications that experience unpredictable workloads or require flexible scaling. The following real-world examples demonstrate its scalability and cost-saving benefits.

Scaling e-commerce during peak seasons

Retail businesses experience massive traffic spikes during holiday seasons, sales events, and promotional campaigns. A scalable and cost-efficient database is essential to handle this surge while maintaining low costs during off-peak periods.

The following challenges arise when handling seasonal demand:

- Over-provisioning databases leads to high costs during non-peak times.
- Manual scaling causes delays in processing transactions, affecting customer experience.
- Unexpected traffic surges can overload the database, resulting in slow checkouts and abandoned carts.

By using Aurora Serverless, retailers achieve:

- Instant scaling from a few ACUs to over 100 ACUs, adjusting to real-time demand.
- Cost reduction of up to 60% by scaling down automatically when demand drops.
- High availability and smooth transactions, ensuring a seamless customer experience during sales events.

Outcome: The retailer handles millions of transactions without downtime, ensuring fast checkouts and a great shopping experience while optimizing infrastructure costs.

Managing traffic for news and events

Media and news platforms see unpredictable traffic surges when breaking news, global events, or viral content attracts millions of concurrent users. They need a scalable and cost-effective solution to deliver real-time updates without delays.

Media platforms face the following challenges:

- Manual database scaling results in delays when traffic spikes unexpectedly.
- Keeping a database active 24/7 leads to wasted costs during slow news cycles.
- Slow queries and performance bottlenecks impact reader engagement during major events.

By implementing Aurora Serverless, news platforms benefit from:

- Auto-scaling that supports sudden traffic surges, handling millions of requests efficiently.
- Cost savings of up to 70%, as the database scales down when demand is low.
- Optimized query performance, allowing fast content updates even under high traffic loads.

Outcome: The platform ensures seamless news delivery during peak events while optimizing database costs in off-peak periods.

Optimizing development and testing environments

Software companies often require temporary databases to test new features, run QA cycles, or simulate production environments. Aurora Serverless provides an on-demand solution, eliminating manual setup and unnecessary costs.

Development teams face common challenges such as:

- Manually provisioning and shutting down databases, leading to operational inefficiencies.
- Keeping unused databases running, increasing unnecessary infrastructure costs.
- Delays in spinning up environments, slowing down software releases.

With Aurora Serverless, development teams can:

- Quickly activate and deactivate databases, avoiding manual intervention.
- Reduce testing costs by up to 65%, eliminating idle database expenses.
- Speed up feature testing, improving release cycles and team productivity.

Outcome: The company streamlines development workflows, reducing operational overhead while ensuring faster product delivery.

Introduction to Amazon EFS

Amazon EFS is a serverless file system that can automatically scale up/down to meet application file needs. Amazon EFS works seamlessly with cloud-native applications, making it one of the most used services when shared file-based access is required in applications.

With EFS, the administrative overhead of managing file servers, configuring RAID arrays, and investing in anticipated demands are no longer a problem. Amazon EFS is fully managed and is designed to be scalable, durable, and cost-effective with pay-as-you-go models.

Amazon EFS also supports multiple AZ deployments, making it fault-tolerant and able to recover from any undesired outages immediately.

Developers can focus on the business logic when Amazon EFS is a storage layer.

Amazon EFS is best suited for the following scenarios:

- **Shared file systems**: EFS is optimal when multiple instances (EC2 instances) require concurrent access to the same file system. This provides distributed access to a common file system and is essential in application clustering and load-balancing scenarios.

  Application Clustering is a process where multiple instances must work together and access the same files. With Amazon EFS, this complex task is made simple as it fully manages data access, conflict management, and data synchronization, giving you confidence in its capabilities.

- **Content management/web sharing**: EFS is ideal for frequently updating content from various servers on a shared backend. When static content is to be served, Amazon S3 is recommended instead of Amazon EFS.

- **Software development/testing environments**: Amazon EFS can be a perfect fit for providing a shared environment for code repositories, application binaries, and test data. It ensures seamless access to these shared datasets, offering the necessary convenience.

- **Legacy application migrations**: Amazon EFS is your reliable partner when legacy applications involving file share accesses must be moved to the cloud. It helps and facilitates migrating on-premises applications without refactoring existing code to suit the cloud environment and settings, providing relief.

Key concepts in Amazon EFS

Amazon EFS is an elastic NFS file system offering seamless file share and collaboration capabilities for cloud or on-premises applications. Thus, it is a useful toolkit/service for building modern applications requiring massive scalability, durability, collaboration, and security.

The following are the key concepts required to master Amazon EFS and gain benefits through integrations:

- **Amazon EFS and VPC**: Amazon EFS lies inside a VPC, and hence, access to EFS is governed by the VPC access controls and in-built security built for EFS.

- **Mount target**: A mount target is a critical bridge between VPC and the EFS file system. It is not an access point for individual resources (like a mount point on an EC2 instance) but rather the access point within the VPC that resources can utilize.

  o A mount target provides an endpoint within the VPC, allowing authorized resources to connect to the EFS file system. Each mount target has a unique DNS name and IP address for connection.

  o Each mount target lies in a specific availability zone, and all connections to the EFS go through mount targets by providing a centralized access control.

  o A single EFS file system can have multiple mount targets, thus enabling access from various resources within the same VPC.

- **Mount target security group**: Each mount target is associated with a security group that controls inbound and outbound access by providing restrictions through rules. If an AWS service requires access to an EFS file system, the mount point should explicitly allow access, thus providing additional security and access control capabilities.

- **Mount point**: Mount points provide access points within a VPC and interact with individual resources like EC2 instances.

  o A mount point is a directory path on the EC2 instance's operating system, and it establishes a connection between the local directory in the EC2 instance and the EFS file system (via mount target).

  o A mount point is created using the operating system's **mount** command. It also requires details like the mount target's DNS name/IP address and the local directory to be designated as the mount point.

  o Mount points provides a familiar way to interact with EFS file systems, leveraging existing knowledge of file systems for application development. Applications can access and interact with file systems through mount points as if they were accessing a local storage directory.

  o A mount point does not store any data; the underlying data/files are always in EFS. The mount point can be configured to stay persistent between EC2 server restarts.

  o In summary, a mount target acts as a VPC-level access point controlling inbound traffic, and a mount point is a local directory path connecting the EFS file system.

- **EFS file system types**: Amazon EFS provides two file system types that cater to different application needs by providing varying levels of durability, availability, and cost:

  o **EFS regional file system**: This option provides very high availability by storing data across multiple AZ in an AWS region, hence the name regional file system.

    This is the recommended approach for all production-critical workflows, and it ensures immediate failover in case an AZ is down or hardware fails.

- o **EFS on-zone file system**: One-zone EFS offers a cost-effective way to use EFS. The data resides in a single AZ, making it susceptible to data loss and limited availability.

- o One zone file system is best suited for development/testing workflows or scenarios where workloads can tolerate short periods of downtime.

- **EFS storage classes**: Amazon EFS goes beyond just file system types. It offers a range of storage classes, allowing you to optimize costs based on how frequently your data is accessed. Here is a breakdown of the three main storage classes providing varying levels of durability, availability, and cost:

  - o **EFS Standard**: This class is built for applications craving high performance. Under the hood, it utilizes high-speed SSD storage and provides sub-millisecond latency for frequently accessed files. This is ideal for storing active/transactional application data, rapid development environments, and real-time analytics.

  - o **EFS Infrequent Access (IA)**: This storage class provides better cost efficiencies by trading durability with cost. The data is still available but is better suited for less frequently accessed data like backups, logs, and historical records.

    EFS IA is best suited for historical transaction management and version control systems.

  - o **EFS archive**: This budget-friendly option is a vault for seldom-accessed information.

    This is best suited to managing legal and regulatory mandates for older data and storing and disaster recovery backups.

In summary, choose EFS Standard when blazing fast durable access is required, use EFS IA when data is accessed infrequently, and use EFS archive for long-term storage and archival needs.

- **File system ID**: A file system ID is a unique identifier that acts as a name tag assigned by AWS to recognize and manage EFS resources.

  This is the primary way to reference the EFS file system when interacting with AWS services or tools and forms part of the DNS name used to access the EFS file system.

- **Throughput configuration**: Amazon EFS offers three flexible throughput modes to manage the amount of data a file system can process per second, catering to different workload requirements:

  - o **Bursting throughput**: Designed for workloads with irregular or unpredictable access patterns, this mode provides a baseline throughput level that depends on the file system's size, supplemented by a burstable credit system. Similar to a prepaid data plan, EFS accumulates credits over time, enabling temporary bursts of higher throughput when needed. However, if credits are exhausted, performance reverts to the baseline level.

  - o **Provisioned throughput**: Ideal for predictable workloads requiring consistent performance, this mode allows you to specify a fixed throughput level in MiB/s during the creation or modification of the file system. While it ensures stable performance, it incurs a fixed cost, regardless of actual usage.

  - o **Elastic throughput**: The most dynamic and recently introduced option, elastic throughput eliminates the need to balance between bursting and provisioned modes. It automatically adjusts throughput in real-time based on your application's needs, within the minimum and maximum thresholds you define. This mode is particularly well-suited for workloads with highly variable or unpredictable throughput demands, ensuring both cost-efficiency and optimal performance.

In summary:

- For workloads with unpredictable and fluctuating access patterns, bursting throughput is an ideal choice as it balances performance and cost dynamically

- Choose provisioned throughput when workloads are predictable and consistency is key.

- Choose elastic throughput when dealing with dynamic access patterns and workloads in an AWS region that supports elastic throughput mode.

Key integrations with Amazon EFS

Amazon EFS has seamless integration with various AWS services. Some of the key integrations include:

- **EC2 integration**: Integrating Amazon EFS with EC2 instances within an AWS architecture provides a scalable, elastic, and durable solution for shared file storage that can be accessed concurrently by EC2 instances. Understanding how this integration fits within an AWS architecture involves looking at network setup, security, data flow, and management.

  Both Amazon EFS and EC2 reside in a VPC:

  - EFS and EC2 instances do not necessarily reside in the same subnet.
  - An EC2 instance can access EFS through a mount target in an AZ.
  - Each EFS file system can have up to one mount target per AZ.

  An EC2 instance in a subnet of a different AZ can still communicate with EFS in another AZ. Still, since all the communication can only happen through mount targets, it is recommended to have mount targets in each AZ where communication is intended.

- **AWS Lambda integration**: AWS Lambda is ephemeral (the execution environment is restarted, and resources are freed after every run). However, EFS integration with AWS Lambda can provide persistent and reliable file storage.

  Also, multiple Lambda function instances can access the EFS file system concurrently, enabling rapid and dynamic collaboration and shared data access. The Lambda function must reside inside a VPC for this integration, and the EFS mount target must be created.

  In addition, EFS can also overcome another limitation with AWS Lambda (Package size limitations).

  The maximum size of a Lambda deployment package is 50 MB zipped (250 MB unzipped). By integrating AWS Lambda with EFS, the large reference artifacts can be stored in EFS, and Lambda can dynamically refer to them as needed.

- **ECS integration**: Containerized workloads are naturally ephemeral. EFS integration provides shared access, ensuring files are updated and data stored are accessible after task/container restarts. Leveraging EFS as a file gateway can auto-scale to match the demand while adopting a pay-as-you-go model.

See *Figure 8.7*, which provides a high-level architecture of how AWS Lambda, AWS ECS Task, and an EC2 instance communicate with Amazon EFS via mount targets.

All the services must reside in a VPC to communicate and access the EFS service. Since an AWS Lambda does not reside in a custom VPC by default, it has to be configured to reside inside the same VPC for the communication to work.

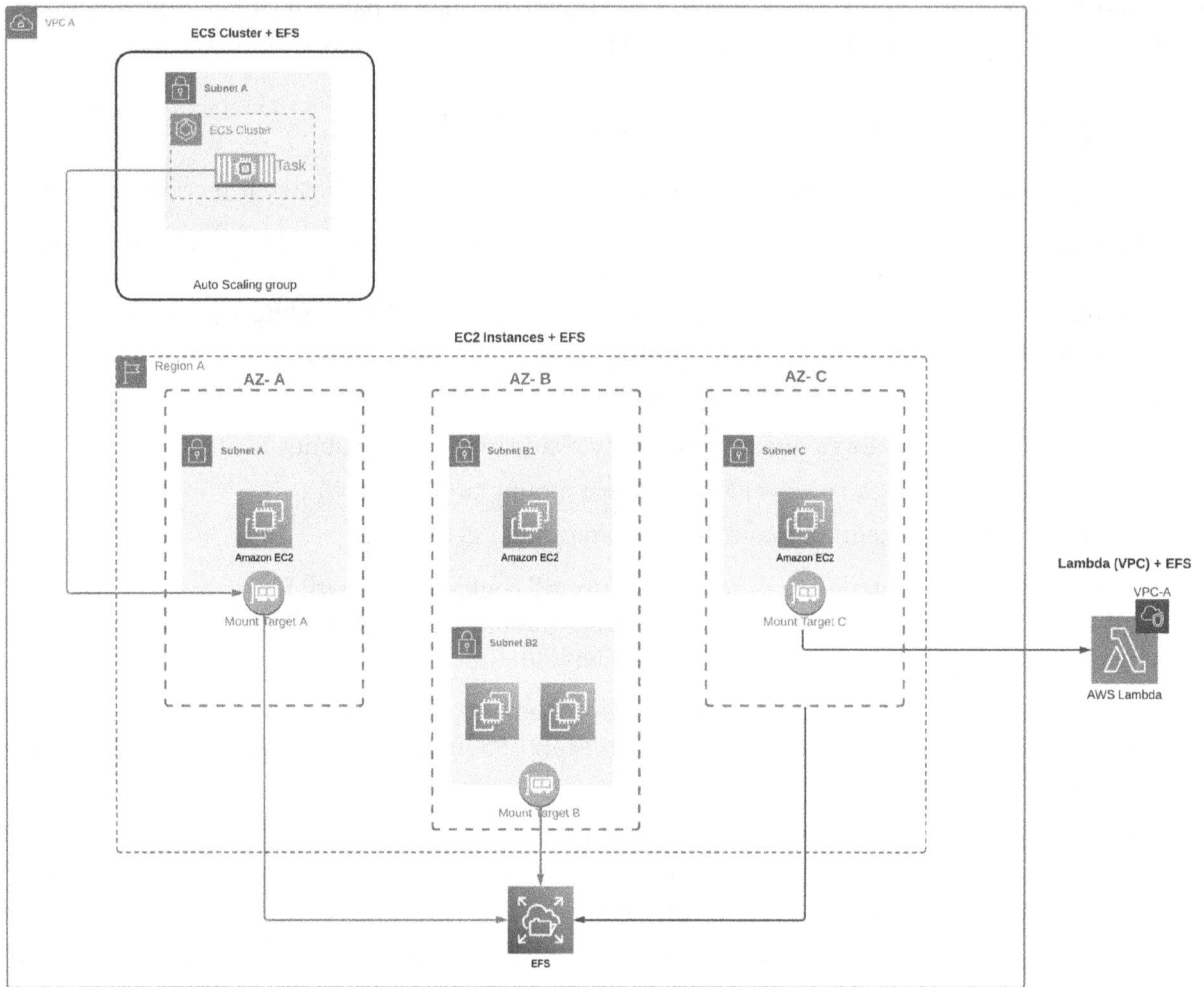

Figure 8.7: Architecture representing integrations with AWS Lambda, ECS, and EC2 Instances

Basic operations with Amazon EFS

This section covers how an EFS file system can be created and how basic operations can be performed via the AWS Management Console. The steps are as follows:

1.　Navigate to **EFS** service by searching through the **Services** Console (See *Figure 8.8*):

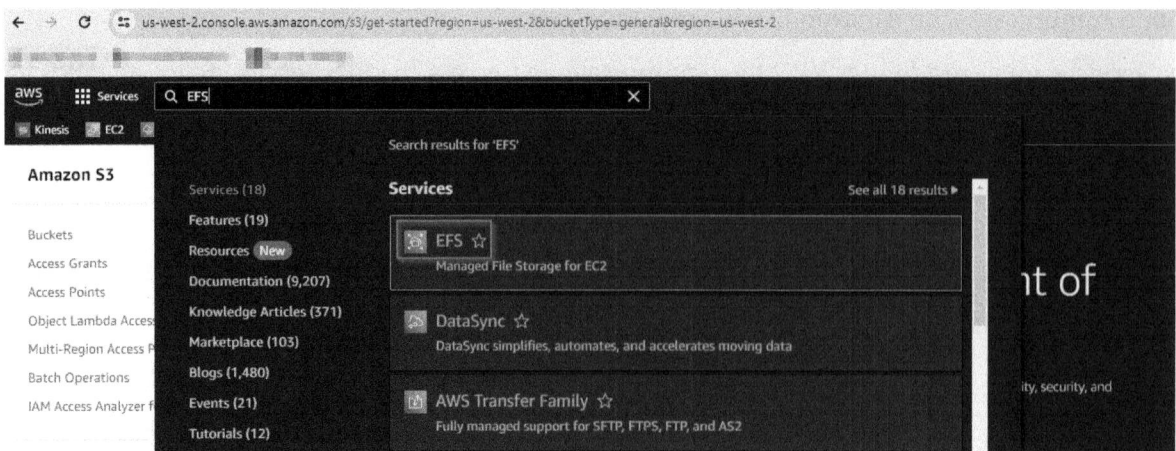

Figure 8.8: AWS Management Console access to Amazon EFS

2. Click on **Create File System** to create a new file system, provide a meaningful name, select the VPC where you want the file system to be designed, and then **Customize**.

This is shown in *Figure 8.9*:

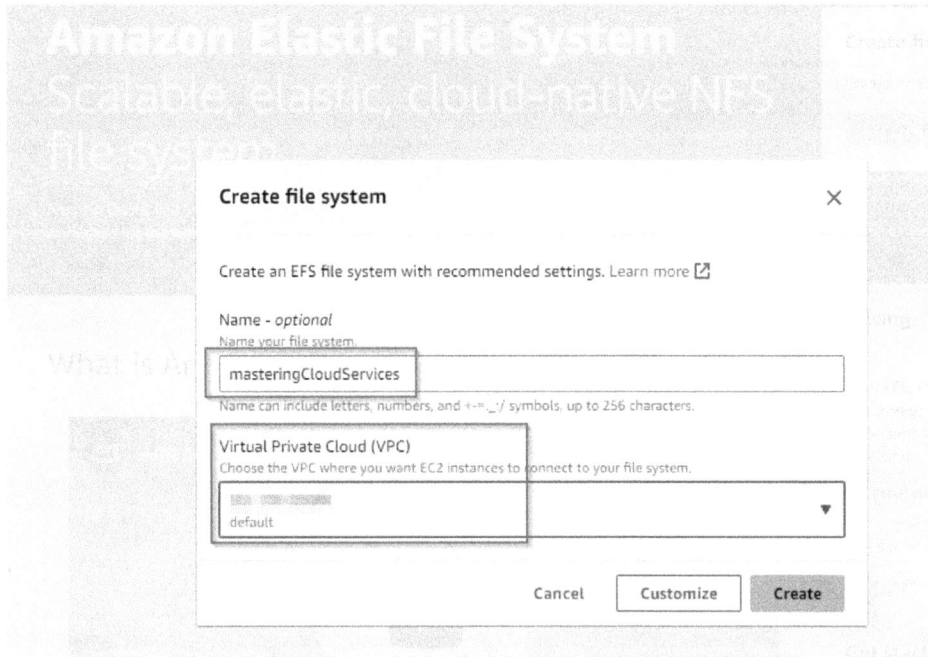

Figure 8.9: Initial Configuration for creating EFS file system

Select **Regional** to create a durable, highly resilient, highly available file system with multi-AZ support within that AWS region.

Provide customization options for backups and lifecycle management to move older files to lower access tiers (cost management).

It is a good practice always to encrypt data at rest; see *Figure 8.10* for more information:

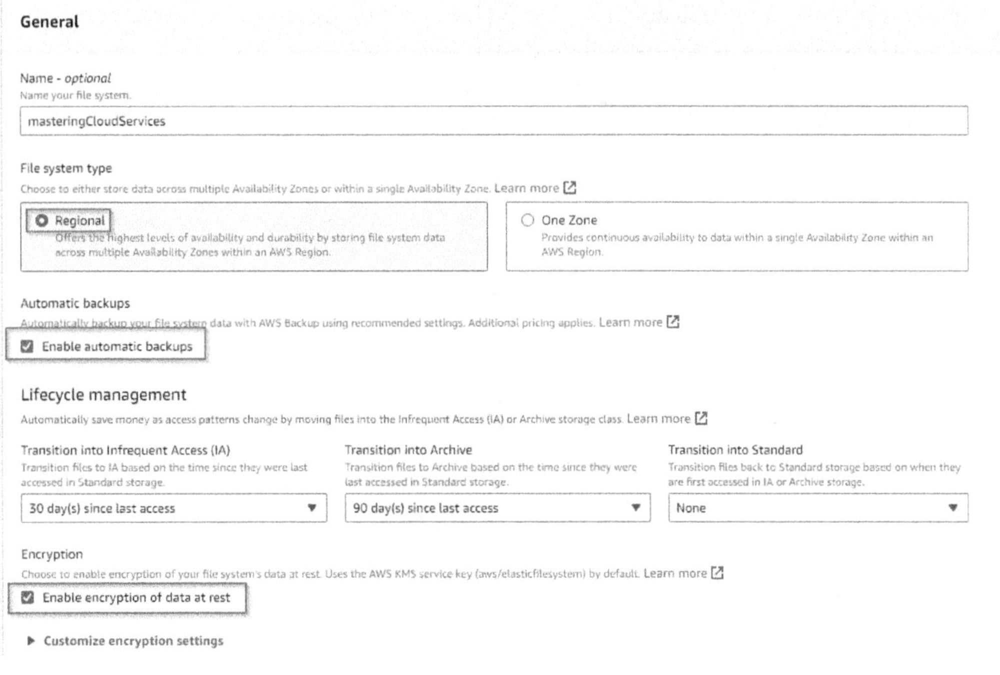

Figure 8.10: File system type, backups, and encryption settings when creating an EFS file system

3. Select a suitable performance throughput mode, Select **Elastic** if it is available in the region where the workload will reside, and select **Next** to navigate to **Network Access** (see *Figure 8.11*).

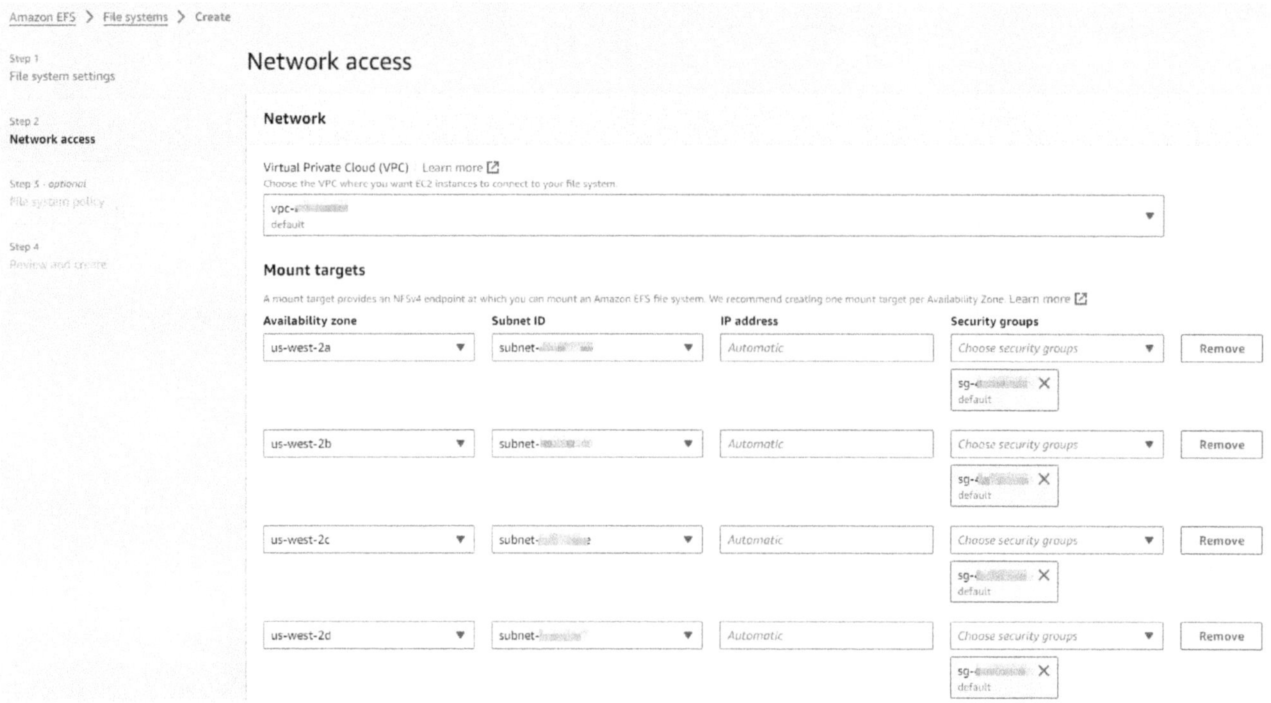

Figure 8.11: *Network access and configuration while creating an EFS file system*

a. Depending on the region, mount targets will be automatically created by default in each AZ. In *Figure 8.11*, four availability zones exist in this region; hence, four mount targets will be created with the default configuration.

b. Each mount target has an option to assign a security group and will be defaulted to the VPC default security group, with an option to assign a relevant security group.

4. In the next step (as shown in *Figure 8.12*), a file system policy can be created in JSON, and additional options can be provided to customize access. When you navigate to the next step, a full review of all the selected configurations will be displayed.

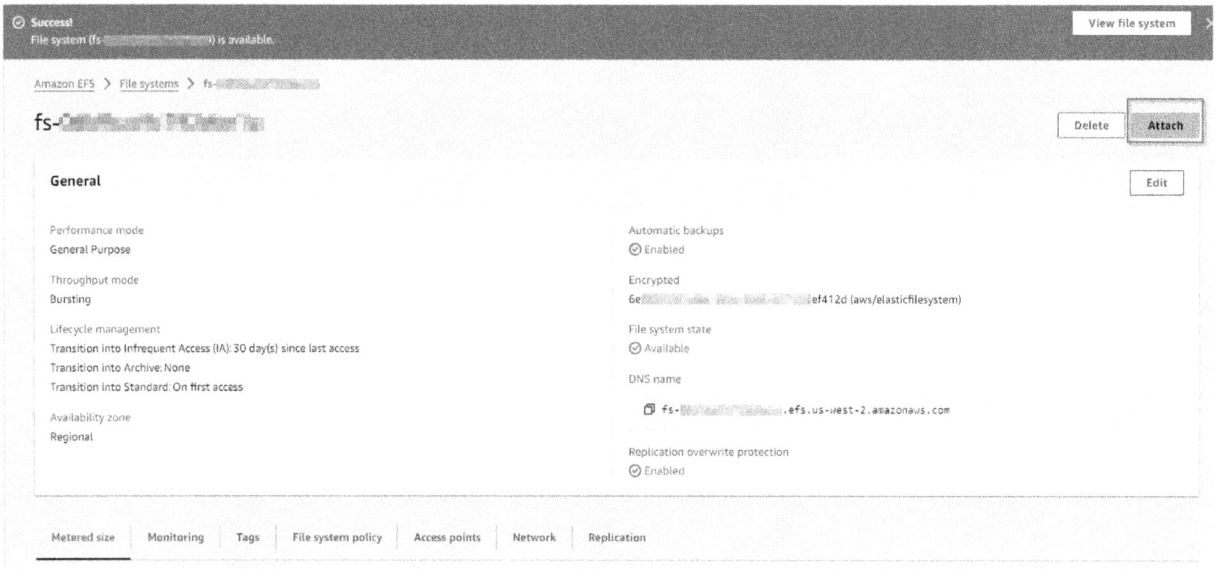

Figure 8.12: *Basic configuration showing file system ID and file system information*

Once the creation is complete, AWS EFS will assign a unique file system ID with options to mount to an EC2 instance.

Limits of Amazon EFS

Serverless architectures in the cloud generally offer unlimited scalability and flexibility. However, in practice, AWS imposes certain limits and guardrails to prevent unintentional behaviors and cost overruns, and they are also predictable from a service provider's view (AWS in this case). The following are some of the limits currently (subject to change):

- **File system size**: Amazon EFS file systems can scale up to petabytes of data, but there are practical limits based on usage patterns and performance requirements.

- **File size**: The maximum size for a single file in EFS is 52 TB.

- **Throughput limits**: EFS offers two throughput modes (bursting and provisioned), and each has its limits. Bursting mode is based on the size of the file system, while provisioned mode allows you to specify the throughput.

- **Performance modes**: EFS supports two performance modes (general purpose and max I/O), and each has its own limits and use cases.

- **Mount targets**: Each file system can have up to 1,000 mount targets.

- **Concurrent connections**: EFS can handle thousands of concurrent connections, but performance may vary based on the workload.

- **Region availability**: EFS is not available in all AWS regions.

- **Backup and restore**: EFS supports AWS Backup for creating backups, but there are limits on the number of backups and retention periods.

- **Access points**: Each file system can have up to 1,000 access points.

- **File system policies**: EFS supports file system policies for access control, but the complexity and number of policies are limited.

Anti-patterns of Amazon EFS

While Aurora EFS is a handy and mature service, it is essential to avoid these common pitfalls:

- **Inefficiency with small files**: EFS's pricing model is based on storage size and I/O requests, which can make it costly for workloads with a large number of small files. For such scenarios, Amazon S3 offers a more cost-effective alternative.

- **Neglecting throughput limits**: EFS performance is tied to throughput configurations, and overlooking these can cause performance degradation. For predictable workloads, use the provisioned throughput mode to avoid bottlenecks.

- **Inappropriate for high-performance databases**: EFS is not optimized for transactional database workloads or applications requiring low-latency, high-throughput performance. For these needs, consider Amazon RDS or Amazon FSx for Lustre, which provides higher performance and reliability.

Real-world applications of Amazon EFS

Amazon EFS provides fully managed, scalable, and highly available file storage, making it ideal for applications that require shared storage across multiple environments. Unlike traditional file systems, EFS automatically scales, ensuring applications have the necessary storage capacity without over-provisioning. The following examples highlight how organizations benefit from EFS's scalability, performance, and cost efficiency.

Scalable storage for content management

Web applications and content management systems require highly available shared storage for large media files, static content, and digital assets. Ensuring consistent file access across multiple servers is crucial for performance and reliability.

Challenges in content-heavy applications:

- Managing high volumes of content requires scalable storage.
- Multiple servers accessing files simultaneously can cause performance bottlenecks.
- Storage limitations lead to manual interventions and downtime.

With EFS, organizations can achieve the following:

- Seamless scaling, ensuring storage adjusts automatically with demand.
- Faster content delivery, as files are accessible across multiple servers in real time.
- Lower administrative overhead, eliminating manual storage provisioning.

Outcome: Businesses can ensure high availability, faster content access, and improved website performance with less storage management effort.

Efficient machine learning and big data workflows

AI and data analytics workloads require shared access to large datasets for distributed training, real-time processing, and collaborative model development.

Challenges in machine learning and big data workflows:

- Duplicating datasets across instances increases storage costs and processing delays.
- Local instance storage limitations slow down distributed training workloads.
- Manually transferring datasets creates bottlenecks in workflow automation.

With EFS, data-driven teams benefit from:

- Concurrent access to shared datasets, eliminating data duplication.
- Optimized data retrieval speeds, improving processing times and workflow efficiency.
- Seamless AWS service integration supports automated data processing.

Outcome: Organizations can reduce processing delays, improve collaboration, and streamline large-scale data workflows.

Supporting high-performance computing

Research, financial modeling, and large-scale simulations require low-latency, high-throughput storage to support parallel computing workloads.

Challenges in high-performance computing:

- Data-intensive simulations demand high-speed, scalable storage.
- Local storage constraints limit real-time processing capabilities.
- High storage costs impact compute-heavy workloads.

With EFS, research and HPC teams achieve the following:

- Fast, concurrent data access, reducing processing bottlenecks.
- Seamless scaling, ensuring storage grows with workload demands.
- Optimized storage costs, as infrequently accessed data moves to lower-cost tiers.

Outcome: Organizations can process large datasets faster, optimize computing resources, and reduce storage costs.

Conclusion

Amazon Aurora Serverless and Amazon EFS provide powerful, scalable storage solutions for cloud-native applications, enabling seamless scalability, automation, and cost optimization. By leveraging Aurora Serverless, organizations can eliminate manual database scaling and reduce costs, while EFS offers managed, elastic file storage for distributed workloads. These services simplify infrastructure management, ensuring that businesses can focus on innovation rather than operational complexity.

Throughout this chapter, we explored the challenges of traditional database and file storage solutions and how serverless storage overcomes them. Aurora Serverless enables organizations to build highly available, automatically scaling relational databases without over-provisioning resources, making it ideal for unpredictable workloads. Its cost-efficient model and automated maintenance allow businesses to maintain performance without unnecessary infrastructure overhead. Similarly, EFS delivers fully managed, scalable file storage, integrating seamlessly with AWS compute services to support high-performance applications, containerized workloads, and large-scale data processing.

Now that we have established a solid foundation in serverless storage, the next chapter will explore AWS messaging services, which play a crucial role in event-driven architectures. Services like Amazon SQS, Amazon SNS, and Amazon EventBridge enable serverless applications to communicate efficiently, ensuring decoupled workflows that scale dynamically based on demand. Understanding messaging patterns and best practices is essential for designing resilient cloud-native applications that can react to real-time events while maintaining system reliability.

As we transition from serverless storage to event-driven messaging, you will gain a deeper understanding of how to architect scalable, cloud-native systems that respond to changes efficiently. This next step will provide the knowledge required to integrate serverless storage with messaging services, enabling highly flexible and responsive application architectures that leverage the full potential of AWS serverless technologies.

Join our Discord space

Join our Discord workspace for latest updates, offers, tech happenings around the world, new releases, and sessions with the authors:

https://discord.bpbonline.com

CHAPTER 9
Serverless Data Flow and Messaging

Introduction

In today's digital landscape, efficient and scalable communication forms the backbone of modern applications. Traditionally, messaging systems relied on dedicated infrastructure requiring manual provisioning, maintenance, and scalability planning. These conventional approaches often suffered from issues such as limited scalability, increased latency, complex resource management, and higher operational costs.

In contrast, this chapter explores modern serverless messaging and data flow solutions through three pivotal AWS services: Amazon **Simple Queue Service (SQS)**, Amazon **Simple Notification Service (SNS)**, and Amazon EventBridge. These services offer significant improvements by abstracting infrastructure management, automatically scaling to demand, and providing built-in fault tolerance and high availability. This serverless approach not only reduces the operational burden but also enhances application resilience and responsiveness.

Specifically, readers will gain insights into distinct use cases for each service: SQS supports decoupled, asynchronous communication ideal for microservices, SNS excels at broadcasting messages in pub/sub scenarios, and EventBridge provides centralized event routing for diverse applications.

Practical examples will illustrate how these AWS services integrate seamlessly with other serverless components, such as AWS Lambda, Amazon S3, and Amazon Kinesis Firehose. Additionally, the chapter emphasizes built-in security and reliability, addressing encryption, access control, and message deduplication.

Through real-world scenarios, including IoT data ingestion and real-time analytics, readers will understand how serverless messaging enhances responsiveness and scalability, preparing them to build robust, agile, and future-ready cloud solutions.

Structure

This chapter covers the following topics:

- Fundamentals of message queuing
- Introduction to Amazon SQS
- Fundamentals of pub/sub messaging
- Introduction to Amazon SNS
- Fundamentals of event-driven orchestration

- Core concepts in Amazon EventBridge
- Amazon EventBridge best practices
- Amazon SQS vs. SNS vs EventBridge

Objectives

This chapter explores AWS messaging and event-driven architecture, focusing on three transformative services: Amazon SQS, Amazon SNS, and Amazon EventBridge. It demystifies core concepts like message queuing, pub-sub messaging, and event-driven workflows, enabling you to build scalable, decoupled cloud applications.

Readers will look into the functionalities of Amazon SQS to understand message queues, visibility timeouts, and **dead letter queues** (**DLQs**). The chapter also covers access control, cost-optimization strategies, and integrating SQS with other AWS services like Lambda.

For Amazon SNS, you will explore core features like topics, subscriptions, and message filtering while learning to integrate SNS with mobile push notifications and serverless applications for real-time communication. Security best practices and cost-management techniques are also included.

Finally, Amazon EventBridge takes center stage as the hub for routing events and automating workflows. This section covers event buses, rules, and schemas, as well as advanced capabilities like scheduling tasks, API destinations, and external application integration.

By the end of this chapter, you will have the knowledge and skills to leverage AWS messaging and event-driven services to orchestrate efficient, secure, and cost-effective cloud solutions.

Fundamentals of message queuing

In the dynamic world of cloud applications, ensuring seamless communication between various components is paramount. However, situations arise where applications do not require real-time interaction. This is where message queuing steps in, providing a robust mechanism for asynchronous processing. This section looks at the core concepts of message queuing, equipping users to understand its functionality and benefits.

The following are the key features of any messaging system:

- **Synchronous communication**: Traditionally, applications use synchronous communication analogous to a conversation. An application waits for a response from the communicating application before proceeding. This approach can be inefficient, especially for slow-responding applications or high message volumes.

- **Power of asynchronous communication**: Unlike waiting for a response, Asynchronous communication involving message queuing introduces a decoupled approach. Applications send messages (packets of data and information) to a queue, a temporary storage location. Receiving applications and retrieving messages at their own pace, fostering independence, and eliminating the need for constant back-and-forth communication.

- **Essential components of a message queue**:
  - **Message**: The core message element is a data unit stored in the queue. It can contain text, code, or any information requiring exchange.
  - **Queue**: This is similar to a waiting line. Queues can be of multiple types. If messages are added (enqueued) at one end and retrieved (dequeued) from the other in a first-in, first-out manner, they can be called **first-in-first-out** (**FIFO**) queues, and here, the order is preserved. In the case of standard (non-FIFO) queues, the messages do not retain order.

- o **Producer**: The application responsible for sending messages to the queue.

- o **Consumer**: An application or a component that retrieves, processes, and deletes messages from the source queue.

- o **Message broker (optional)**: This software manages the queue, ensuring reliable message delivery, routing, and security. (Not all implementations utilize a dedicated broker.)

Introduction to Amazon SQS

Amazon SQS is one of the fundamental building blocks for creating scalable, fault-tolerant applications in the AWS Cloud. As a distributed message queue, it provides a reliable and efficient way to decouple and coordinate software components. With SQS, events and messages can be exchanged between components at any scale, ensuring high availability and durability.

Amazon SQS is a fully managed, serverless messaging solution that leverages a pay-as-you-go pricing model, eliminating the need for upfront infrastructure investments. Amazon SQS provides two types of queues: standard queues and FIFO queues. Standard queues offer high throughput and guarantee message delivery at least once, making them suitable for most asynchronous workflows where strict ordering isn't critical.

FIFO queues, however, maintain strict message ordering and guarantee exactly-once processing, which is essential for sensitive applications such as financial transactions and order processing. A critical advantage of FIFO queues is their built-in message deduplication mechanism, which prevents duplicate messages from being processed more than once. This ensures data accuracy and message integrity, especially when repeated message processing can result in significant errors or inconsistencies.

Combining these robust features positions Amazon SQS as an essential component for scalable, reliable, and efficient serverless architectures.

Key features of Amazon SQS include:

- **Reliable delivery**: Standard queues provide at least once delivery with potential duplicates, while FIFO queues ensure exactly once processing and strict message order.

- **Application decoupling**: SQS fosters modularity by decoupling producers and consumers, allowing each to scale independently.

- **Cost effectiveness**: With pay-per-use pricing, SQS is one of the most economical services in the AWS Cloud, charging only for messages sent and received.

- **Message redelivery**: Ensures no messages are lost during application issues by allowing redelivery.

- **Visibility controls**: Enables fine-grained control over message visibility, facilitating horizontal scaling by allowing multiple consumers to process messages concurrently.

Amazon SQS integrates seamlessly with other AWS services, making it a critical tool for building responsive, scalable, and cost-efficient applications.

Key concepts in Amazon SQS

Amazon **Simple Queue Service (SQS)** is an essential tool for enabling reliable, asynchronous communication in distributed systems. Mastering its key concepts is crucial for designing scalable, fault-tolerant applications. The following are the foundational elements that make SQS an invaluable service:

- **Queue types**: SQS provides two main queue types: standard queues and FIFO queues.

- o **Standard queues**: These are suited for most use cases and offer at least one delivery. While messages might occasionally be delivered more than once or out of order, the queue ensures eventual delivery to consumers.

o **FIFO queues**: These queues guarantee exact-once delivery and maintain strict message ordering, making them ideal for critical operations like financial transactions or stock updates.

- **Visibility timeout**: This parameter defines how long a message remains invisible to other consumers after being retrieved by one consumer. If a consumer fails to process the message within this period, the message becomes available for reprocessing by other consumers. Configuring an appropriate timeout ensures efficient error handling without message loss.

- **DLQs**: DLQs handle messages that consistently fail processing due to errors or invalid data. Failed messages are routed to a designated DLQ for analysis, retries, or manual intervention, preventing them from clogging the primary queue and maintaining message flow.

- **Fanout vs. point-to-point delivery**:

  o **Fanout**: A single message is broadcast to multiple consumers, enabling parallel processing or simultaneous notifications.

  o **Point-to-point**: Messages are delivered to a single consumer, ensuring unique processing for scenarios requiring strict handling or avoiding duplicate tasks.

  o **Polling vs. long polling**: Traditional polling involves consumers frequently querying the queue for new messages, which can be inefficient during low activity. Long polling, by contrast, reduces overhead by allowing consumers to wait for messages over a configurable duration (up to 20 seconds), optimizing resource usage and improving efficiency.

  o **Server-side encryption (SSE)**: SQS ensures data security with server-side encryption. Messages are encrypted both at rest and in transit, protecting sensitive information from unauthorized access. Decryption occurs only when delivered to authorized consumers, providing robust security.

  o **Approximate receive count and purging**: Due to SQS's distributed architecture, it provides an approximate receive count API for estimating the number of messages in the queue. Additionally, purging allows administrators to clear unwanted messages, manage queue size, and maintain optimal message flow.

Amazon SQS queue types

Amazon SQS provides two primary queue types: standard queues and FIFO queues. Each queue type is designed to address different messaging needs, and understanding their features is critical for selecting the right solution. Let us study the details of these queue types to explore their unique strengths and practical applications:

- **Standard queues**:

  o **Delivery model**: Standard queues are designed for maximum scalability and throughput, making them ideal for handling high-volume workloads. These queues operate with an at-least-once delivery model, where messages may be delivered one or more times. This non-deterministic behavior works well in scenarios where strict message ordering is not required and occasional duplicates are acceptable.

  o **Use cases**: Standard queues are versatile and excel in these scenarios:

  o **Background tasks**: Ideal for triggering asynchronous processes, such as image processing or data analysis, based on application events or user actions.

  o **Fan-out workflows are suitable** for distributing messages to multiple consumers simultaneously, enabling parallel processing or broadcasting updates efficiently.

  o **Microservice communication**: Facilitates loosely coupled interactions between independent microservices, allowing them to scale independently while maintaining seamless communication.

o **Considerations**: While standard queues are highly scalable, keep these factors in mind:

- **Eventual consistency**: Since standard queues use an at-least-once delivery model, the order of message processing may not always match the order in which messages are sent. Implementing idempotent operations in consuming applications ensures that actions are executed only once, even if messages are reprocessed.

- **Duplicate handling**: Standard queues do not eliminate duplicate messages. To address this, consumers can implement deduplication techniques, such as tracking message IDs, to ensure accurate processing.

- **FIFO queues**:

o **Delivery model**: FIFO queues prioritize maintaining message order, guaranteeing that messages are processed in the exact sequence they are sent. These queues ensure exactly one delivery, meaning each message is delivered and processed only once by a single consumer. This makes FIFO queues indispensable for applications where strict sequencing is critical.

o **Use cases**: FIFO queues excel in scenarios requiring strict order and exactly-once delivery:

- **Financial transactions**: Ensures sequential processing for stock trades or fund transfers, preserving data integrity.

- **Inventory management**: Guarantees the correct sequence of inventory updates, preventing overselling or inaccuracies.

- **Log processing**: Maintains the chronological order of log messages, aiding debugging and compliance audits.

o **Considerations**: While FIFO queues provide robust guarantees, some factors to consider include:

- **Throughput**: FIFO queues have a lower throughput than standard queues due to the additional overhead required to maintain strict message order.

- **Visibility timeout**: Proper visibility time-out configuration is necessary to avoid disrupting message order. If messages take too long to process, they may be redelivered, causing delays in downstream operations.

- **Consumer availability**: FIFO queues require at least one active consumer to process messages. If no consumer is available, messages can accumulate, potentially impacting performance.

Demystifying message deduplication in SQS

Amazon SQS provides a powerful messaging solution, but certain applications demand strict control over duplicate message processing. Message deduplication ensures that even in cases of retries or multiple submissions, messages are processed only once. Let us examine effectively leveraging deduplication in SQS to maintain data consistency and avoid duplicate processing.

Understanding the need: Consider a scenario where a mobile app submits an order multiple times due to poor network connectivity. In a standard SQS setup, each submission might be processed independently, resulting in duplicate orders. Message deduplication mitigates this by ensuring a message is handled only once, even if it is sent repeatedly within a short interval.

Approaches to deduplication include the following:

- **Content-based deduplication**: With content-based deduplication, SQS automatically generates a deduplication ID using a SHA-256 hash of the message body content. If another message with the same ID arrives within the deduplication interval (default: 5 minutes), it will not be processed again.

This approach works best when the message content itself guarantees uniqueness, such as timestamps or transactional data.

- **Explicit deduplication**: Explicit deduplication allows greater control using custom message attributes. For example, a unique identifier, such as an order ID, can be included in a message attribute. Consumers can verify the identifier against previously processed messages before handling it. This method is particularly useful for scenarios where message content does not inherently ensure uniqueness.

Considerations for deduplication:

- **Deduplication interval**: Messages with the same deduplication ID that arrive after the interval expires will be processed again. To minimize unnecessary processing, configure this interval in alignment with your application's retry logic.

- **Redelivered messages**: If a message delivery fails, retries within the deduplication interval might result in reprocessing attempts. Using mechanisms like exponential backoff helps prevent retry storms, ensuring eventual successful delivery without overwhelming the queue.

Use cases: Message deduplication is essential for maintaining data accuracy in the following scenarios:

- **E-commerce transactions**: Prevents duplicate processing of orders, even when users resubmit due to connectivity issues.

- **Idempotent operations**: Ensures operations like updating user profiles are executed only once, regardless of repeated triggers.

- **Event sourcing**: Guarantees that events are processed in sequence without unnecessary repetitions, preserving the accuracy of system state reconstruction.

Cost management in Amazon SQS

Amazon SQS is a cost-effective and scalable messaging service, but a deeper understanding of its pricing model and associated cost factors is essential for optimizing expenses. By implementing best practices, you can reduce unnecessary charges and make the most of this serverless messaging solution. Let us explore how to manage costs effectively in Amazon SQS.

Understanding the pay-as-you-go model

SQS operates on a **pay-as-you-go** pricing model, where you are charged only for the resources you use. There are no upfront costs or long-term commitments, making it an economical choice for workloads of all sizes.

Cost factors to consider: Several factors influence the cost of using Amazon SQS. Understanding these can help you identify areas to optimize:

- **Number of requests**: Each interaction with SQS, such as sending, receiving, deleting, or purging messages, is counted as a request. Minimizing redundant or unnecessary requests can significantly reduce costs.

- **Data transfer**: Charges apply for data transferred into and out of SQS queues. Larger message payloads lead to higher data transfer costs, so keeping payloads efficient is crucial.

- **Storage**: The amount of data stored in SQS queues affects your bill. Implement mechanisms to remove processed or expired messages periodically to optimize storage usage.

- **API requests**: Calls to SQS APIs, like retrieving queue attributes or using the ApproximateNumberOfMessages API, incur costs. Be mindful of how frequently you invoke these APIs to avoid unnecessary charges.

- **Cost-saving strategies**: Implementing the following strategies can help you optimize costs while ensuring efficient messaging workflows.

- **Batching requests**: Combine multiple operations into a single API call using batch actions for sending, receiving, or deleting messages. This reduces the number of requests and lowers overall costs.

- **Optimizing message size**: To reduce data transfer charges, keep message payloads as small as possible. If applicable, use data compression techniques to minimize payload size further.

- **Utilizing long polling**: Configure long polling so consumers can wait up to 20 seconds for messages to arrive. This reduces the number of empty receive requests, lowering costs associated with unnecessary polling.

- **Implementing DLQs**: Route failed messages to DLQs for later analysis or retries. This prevents unprocessable messages from occupying storage space in the main queue and incurring unnecessary charges.

- **Monitoring and cost analysis**: Amazon Cost Explorer and CloudWatch are used to monitor SQS usage metrics. These tools provide insights into request patterns, data transfer, and storage consumption, helping you identify opportunities for optimization and resource allocation.

By applying these cost-saving strategies and continuously monitoring usage, you can effectively manage your SQS costs while maintaining efficient and reliable messaging workflows.

Security considerations with Amazon SQS

Amazon SQS provides robust security features to protect your data and ensure safe communication between application components. However, securing an SQS implementation requires careful planning, adherence to best practices, and a clear understanding of AWS's shared responsibility model. Let us explore the key security considerations that can help you maintain a strong security posture when using Amazon SQS:

- **Shared security model**: In the shared responsibility model, AWS handles the physical security of its cloud infrastructure, while customers are responsible for securing their data and configuring SQS access controls. This means customers must actively manage permissions, encryption, and logging to ensure the security of their SQS resources.

- **Encryption at rest and in transit**: Amazon SQS supports **server-side encryption** (**SSE**) to protect messages. You can choose between SSE-KMS or SSE-SQS for encryption. SSE ensures that your messages are encrypted at rest (when stored on SQS servers) and in transit (when transmitted between services).

- **AWS IAM**: IAM is central to controlling access in AWS. Through IAM policies, define granular permissions, specifying who can send or receive messages from specific SQS queues. This ensures that only authorized users or applications have access to your data.

- **Least privilege principle**: Adopt the least privilege principle when configuring IAM policies. This means granting users and applications only the minimum permissions necessary to perform their tasks, reducing the risk of unauthorized access.

- **Auditing and logging**: Enable AWS CloudTrail to log all API calls made to SQS. This provides a detailed audit trail of queue activity, allowing you to monitor access patterns and identify suspicious behavior. Logs can also help with compliance and incident response.

- **Network security**: Consider placing your SQS queues within a VPC for additional security. A VPC enables you to create a logically isolated network segment within AWS, providing tighter control over network traffic. You can further restrict access to queues using security groups, ensuring only trusted resources can interact with them.

Security is a constantly evolving field. Review your security configurations regularly to stay informed about the latest AWS best practices and known vulnerabilities. Implement recommended security patches promptly to maintain a secure messaging environment.

By leveraging these security features and adhering to best practices, you can build a secure messaging environment using Amazon SQS. Remember, security is an ongoing process that requires regular monitoring, adaptation to new threats, and vigilance in maintaining a strong security posture.

Key integrations with Amazon SQS

Amazon SQS is not just a robust messaging service; it enables seamless integration with other AWS services, creating scalable, efficient, and serverless workflows. By leveraging this interconnected ecosystem, developers can unlock new possibilities for building dynamic applications. However, it is essential to understand the latency and cost implications when integrating SQS with other AWS messaging services, ensuring optimal performance and cost efficiency.

SQS and Amazon S3

Traditional message queues face limitations when handling large files but integrating Amazon SQS with Amazon S3 provides an efficient and scalable solution. Together, they enable a two-step process that combines lightweight messaging with secure object storage:

- **Secure storage in S3**: Large files are uploaded directly to an S3 bucket, where S3's scalability and durability ensure reliable storage for further processing.

- **Lightweight notification via SQS**: SQS acts as a notification system, sending messages containing the S3 object key instead of the file itself. This reduces message size and improves throughput.

- **Latency considerations:** Polling frequency in SQS directly influences notification latency. Short polling intervals decrease latency but can slightly increase API request frequency and associated costs. Optimize this setting based on your application's specific latency requirements.

- **Cost considerations:** Leveraging S3 for larger payloads significantly reduces message size, lowering messaging costs and improving overall cost efficiency.

Example use cases are as follows:

- **Scientific data processing**: Massive telescope data files can be uploaded to an S3 bucket in a research institution. SQS sends a message with the S3 object key to a queue, triggering a Lambda function. The function retrieves the file from S3, processes it, and stores the results in another S3 bucket for analysis. This integration streamlines large-scale data workflows with remarkable efficiency.

SQS and AWS Lambda

Traditional approaches for handling data streams often involve inefficient polling or scheduled tasks. By combining Amazon SQS and AWS Lambda, developers can create a dynamic and serverless solution:

- **Enqueue the workload**: Messages are added to an SQS queue, decoupling data arrival from processing.

- **Trigger the worker**: Lambda functions, configured to process the queue, are triggered on-demand to handle incoming messages.

The considerations are as follows:

- **Latency considerations**: Message processing latency typically ranges from milliseconds to seconds, impacted by Lambda cold starts and SQS polling configurations. Optimizing Lambda concurrency and memory settings significantly reduces latency.

- **Cost considerations**: Batching multiple SQS messages per Lambda invocation minimizes function calls, directly reducing Lambda execution costs and overall expenses.

Example use case: Real-time image processing:

In an e-commerce platform, when a user uploads an image:

1. A message containing the image location and processing instructions is added to the SQS queue.

2. A Lambda function retrieves the message, processes the image, and stores the result.

This integration enables scalable, event-driven applications that efficiently handle real-time data streams.

Expanding SQS functionality with additional integrations

Amazon SQS extends its capabilities as a messaging service by integrating seamlessly with other AWS tools:

- **Data streamlining with Kinesis Data Firehose**: SQS queues can feed data into Kinesis Data Firehose, transforming and delivering the data to destinations like S3, Redshift, or Elasticsearch for storage and analytics.

- **Latency considerations**: Batch intervals and sizes in Kinesis influence processing latency. Shorter intervals provide reduced latency but may increase API usage.

- **Cost considerations:** Optimize batch frequency and size to balance latency and cost effectively, minimizing data transfer and API call costs.

- **Scalable notifications with Amazon SNS**: SQS integrates with SNS to enable high-volume notifications, delivering targeted messages from queues to a large subscriber base.

The considerations are as follows:

- **Latency considerations**: Integrating SNS introduces minimal latency (typically milliseconds). Effective SNS message filtering reduces unnecessary latency due to unwanted message processing.

- **Cost considerations**: Efficient message filtering through SNS subscriptions significantly reduces unnecessary message volume, directly lowering messaging costs.

Amazon SQS limits

Understanding Amazon SQS's operational limits is essential for designing efficient, scalable applications. These limits define message size, throughput, queue configurations, and other critical parameters. Let us explore these limits and their practical implications:

- **Message size**: The maximum message size, including the message body, attributes, and metadata, is 256 KB.

    Applications requiring larger payloads can split data into smaller chunks or store it in Amazon S3 and send a reference through SQS.

- **Message rates**: SQS regulates the rate of sending, receiving, and inflight messages:
    - **Send rate**: 300 messages per second per account (quota increases available upon request).
    - **Receive rate**: 1,000 messages per second per queue (varies with message size and other factors).
    - **Inflight messages**:
        - **Standard queues**: Up to 120,000 messages (received but not yet deleted).
        - **FIFO queues**: Recently increased to 120,000 messages, supporting greater concurrency while maintaining order.

- **Queue limits**:
    - **Number of queues**: There is no fixed limit, but managing many queues can be operationally complex.

- o **Queue name length**: Maximum 80 characters.

- **Visibility timeout**: Defines how long a message remains invisible to other consumers after being retrieved:

  - o **Minimum timeout**: 0 seconds

  - o **Maximum timeout**: 12 hours—Appropriate configuration prevents premature retries or unprocessed messages from lingering too long.

- **Long polling**: Maximum wait time: 20 seconds—Long polling reduces unnecessary polling requests by waiting up to 20 seconds for messages to become available.

- **DLQs**: Dead Letter Queues inherit limits from the associated queue type:

  - o **Standard queues**: Up to 120,000 messages.

  - o **FIFO queues**: Recently increased to 120,000 messages.

DLQs help manage unprocessable messages by isolating them for troubleshooting without disrupting the primary workflow.

Throughput enhancements for FIFO queues: Amazon SQS now offers high throughput mode for FIFO queues, increasing processing rates significantly:

- **US East (N. Virginia), US West (Oregon), Europe (Ireland)**: Up to 18,000 transactions per second per API action.

- **Asia Pacific (Singapore, Sydney)**: Up to 9,000 transactions per second per API action.

- **Other regions**: Varies between 2,400 and 4,500 transactions per second per API action.

High throughput mode is ideal for high-volume, order-sensitive applications like real-time analytics or transactional processing.

Amazon SQS anti-patterns

While Amazon SQS is a powerful messaging service, certain misuse patterns can lead to inefficiencies or suboptimal system performance. Avoiding these anti-patterns ensures you leverage SQS effectively for your applications:

- **Overloading a single queue**: Using a single queue for multiple unrelated message types can create processing bottlenecks and make managing or debugging message flows harder. Instead, use separate queues tailored to specific message categories.

- **Ignoring message visibility timeout**: Improperly configuring the visibility timeout can result in unintentional message reprocessing or loss. Always align the visibility timeout with the expected processing duration to ensure messages are handled reliably.

- **Using for long-term storage**: SQS is not designed for long-term message retention. For durable, scalable storage, services like Amazon S3, which are purpose-built for data retention, are used.

- **Using for real-time processing**: SQS is optimized for decoupling and buffering workloads, not real-time processing. For applications requiring real-time data streaming, consider Amazon Kinesis or similar services.

Amazon SQS best practices

Implementing best practices ensures efficient, secure, and cost-effective use of Amazon SQS. These guidelines help you optimize your workflows while avoiding common pitfalls.

- **Use DLQs**: Configure DLQs to capture and isolate messages that cannot be processed. This prevents message loss and provides a clear path for analyzing and resolving issues with unprocessable messages.

- **Enable server-side encryption**: Protect your messages with AWS **Key Management Service (KMS)**. Server-side encryption ensures data is secure at rest and in transit, meeting compliance and security standards.

- **Monitor costs**: Use tools like Amazon CloudWatch and Cost Explorer to monitor your SQS usage and identify optimization opportunities. Regular reviews help avoid unexpected expenses.

- **Set visibility timeout**: Configure the visibility timeout to align with your processing times. This prevents messages from being reprocessed while ensuring unprocessed messages are retried within a reasonable timeframe.

- **Use short polling**: Short polling reduces response times for scenarios requiring low-latency processing. While long polling is cost-effective for most use cases, it is suitable for near real-time applications.

Fundamentals of pub/sub messaging

Communication between numerous application components can be challenging, especially in distributed systems. **Publish/subscribe (pub/sub)** messaging offers a robust solution by enabling asynchronous communication and decoupling producers and consumers. Let us explore the key elements of this paradigm, its benefits, and its practical applications.

The core components of pub/sub messaging are as follows:

- **Publishers**: Publishers create and send messages, acting as the originators of information. Messages can range from simple text to complex data structures. Publishers send these messages to a central hub known as the message broker.

- **Subscribers**: Subscribers register their interest in specific topics or message categories. They only receive messages relevant to their subscribed topics, ensuring targeted and efficient communication.

- **Message broker**: The message broker is the backbone of the pub/sub system. It manages the flow of messages, delivering them from publishers to the appropriate subscribers based on their topic subscriptions.

The key benefits of pub/sub messaging are as follows:

- **Scalability**: Supports high-volume message exchanges in distributed environments.

- **Loosely coupled systems**: Publishers and subscribers operate independently, reducing dependencies and enhancing system flexibility.

- **Real-time responsiveness**: Enables near real-time data dissemination, ensuring subscribers quickly receive updates.

Platforms offering pub/sub functionality

Several platforms provide pub/sub messaging capabilities, including:

- Amazon SQS
- Apache Kafka
- Google Cloud Pub/Sub
- RabbitMQ

Pub/sub messaging is a cornerstone for building scalable, loosely coupled, and real-time responsive applications. By embracing this paradigm, developers can simplify communication in distributed systems and create robust, efficient solutions tailored to modern software challenges.

Introduction to Amazon SNS

Amazon SNS is a versatile messaging service designed for efficient, scalable notification delivery within AWS applications. Using a pub/sub model, SNS enables publishers to broadcast messages to multiple subscribers simultaneously across various communication channels, including email, SMS, and mobile push notifications.

A key capability of SNS is its built-in **message filtering**, allowing subscribers to define criteria and selectively receive only relevant messages based on message attributes. By applying subscription filters, systems can significantly reduce unnecessary notifications, optimize resource usage, and improve subscriber responsiveness. For example, an e-commerce platform can use message filtering to deliver targeted promotional notifications only to customers who meet specific criteria, such as geographic location or user preferences.

Leveraging this powerful filtering capability enhances the effectiveness of messaging workflows, reduces costs associated with irrelevant message processing, and ensures that subscribers receive timely, relevant notifications, further solidifying SNS as an essential service for building intelligent, efficient notification systems.

The key features of Amazon SNS are as follows:

- **Fan-out delivery**: Publish a single message to an SNS topic and deliver it to all subscribed endpoints. This broadcast-style delivery is ideal for scenarios like system alerts or updates.

- **Targeted delivery**: Subscribers can filter messages based on attributes, ensuring they only receive relevant notifications. This enables precise, audience-specific communication.

- **Mobile push notifications**: SNS integrates seamlessly with mobile push services to deliver real-time updates to user devices, fostering timely application engagement.

- **Email and SMS notifications**: Leverage traditional communication channels by sending messages via email or SMS. This ensures outreach to audiences across various platforms.

- **Decoupled delivery**: Publishers and subscribers operate independently, improving responsiveness by separating message publication from notification delivery.

- **Scalability and reliability**: SNS supports high message volumes and ensures reliable delivery across all subscribed endpoints.

- **Security**: SNS offers encryption and access controls to safeguard messages, ensuring secure and compliant notification delivery.

Key concepts in Amazon SNS

Understanding the core concepts of Amazon SNS is essential for designing scalable, distributed, and fault-tolerant systems. Let us explore the fundamental components and features that make SNS an invaluable service:

- **Pub/sub model**: The pub/sub model is the backbone of Amazon SNS. Publishers send messages (publish) to topics, and subscribers register their interest (subscribe) to receive messages from those topics.

- **Topics**: Topics act as central communication hubs where publishers send messages. Subscribers register with specific topics to ensure they only receive relevant notifications, enabling precise and efficient communication.

- **Subscription filters**: Subscribers can define filters based on message attributes, ensuring they only receive notifications that match their specific criteria. This targeted delivery reduces noise and improves efficiency.

- **Attributes**: Attributes are additional data points included with messages. They enable targeted delivery, routing, deduplication, and more, enhancing the flexibility of SNS messaging workflows.

- **Delivery mechanisms**: Amazon SNS supports multiple delivery methods to suit various use cases:

  - **Fan-out delivery**: Delivers a single message to all topic subscribers.

  - **Targeted delivery**: Filters messages based on subscriber preferences or attributes.

  - **Mobile push notifications**: Sends notifications directly to mobile devices.

  - **Email and SMS notifications**: Utilizes traditional communication channels to reach users.

- **Delivery policies**: SNS delivery policies provide control over message handling:

  - **Retries**: Configure retry attempts for failed deliveries.

  - **DLQs**: Define destinations for undelivered messages after retries.

  - **Maximum delivery delay**: Set time limits for holding messages before delivery.

Key integrations with Amazon SNS

Amazon SNS becomes even more powerful when integrated with other AWS services. These integrations foster robust notification workflows, allowing developers to streamline communication, improve scalability, and deliver messages to the right audience through the most appropriate channels. Let us explore some key integrations that unlock SNS's full potential.

Amazon SNS and Amazon SQS

Amazon SNS and Amazon SQS, while serving distinct purposes, complement each other to create scalable notification workflows. Together, they enable:

- **Decoupled delivery**: SNS decouples message publishing from notification delivery. For example, when a user signs up, an SNS message can publish the event to a topic, which triggers an SQS queue to stage notifications for processing.

- **Fan-out vs. targeted delivery**:

  - **Fan-out notifications**: Send the same message to multiple subscribers via an SQS queue.

  - **Targeted delivery**: Use filters within the SQS queue to process only relevant messages for specific subscribers.

- **Scalability and cost-effectiveness**: SQS efficiently handles high message volumes, acting as a buffer for SNS. This reduces the load on SNS, optimizes message handling, and can lower costs.

- **Example use case**: In an e-commerce platform, an SNS message for order confirmation triggers an SQS queue. The SQS queue processes the order details, sending a receipt to the customer and a notification to the warehouse. This approach ensures notifications are delivered promptly while efficiently utilizing SNS and SQS.

Amazon SNS and AWS Lambda

Integrating SNS with AWS Lambda allows for seamless, event-driven serverless workflows:

- **Event-driven workflows**: Publish an SNS message on a topic based on specific application events.
- **Lambda function trigger**: Configure the topic to trigger a Lambda function when receiving a message.
- **Dynamic processing**: The Lambda function processes the message, performs necessary actions (e.g., database updates or data transformations), and may trigger further workflows.

- **Example use case**: When a user uploads an image to a social media platform, an SNS message triggers a Lambda function. The function resizes the image, applies watermarks, and stores it in an S3 bucket—all without requiring a dedicated server.

Amazon SNS and Kinesis

For high-volume data streams and real-time analytics, SNS integrates effectively with Amazon Kinesis:

- **Fan-out for stream processing**: Publish SNS messages containing data points to a topic.
- **Kinesis data streams**: Subscribe a Kinesis data stream to the SNS topic to enable continuous data flow.
- **Real-time analytics**: Process and analyze streaming data using Kinesis Data Analytics or other AWS services.
- **Example use case**: IoT sensors send SNS messages for each reading. A Kinesis data stream processes the data in real-time, identifying trends and anomalies or generating alerts based on pre-defined conditions.

Security considerations with Amazon SNS

Amazon SNS prioritizes security by providing robust features to safeguard message privacy, data protection, and message integrity. These features help ensure that sensitive data remains secure while delivering notifications reliably within AWS applications:

- **VPC Endpoints and AWS PrivateLink**: Amazon SNS supports **VPC Endpoints** through **AWS PrivateLink**, enabling secure communication within your Amazon VPC. Messages published to topics remain entirely within the VPC, avoiding the public internet. This eliminates exposure points, enhances privacy, and bolsters data security.

- **Message data protection**: SNS provides advanced data protection policies to identify and manage sensitive information within messages, ensuring compliance with standards like HIPAA, GDPR, PCI, and FedRAMP. Key capabilities include:

  o **Audit incoming messages**: Analyze inbound messages to detect sensitive data.

  o **Block delivery**: Prevent messages containing sensitive data from being delivered to downstream subscribers.

  o **Redact or mask data**: Sanitize sensitive data within the payload while preserving the overall message structure.

  By offloading data protection logic to SNS, you simplify application architecture while maintaining regulatory compliance.

- **Message encryption**: SNS supports encrypted topics for secure event messaging. When publishing to an encrypted topic:

  o Messages are encrypted using a 256-bit AES-GCM algorithm.

  o Encryption is managed via a KMS key - previously called **Customer Managed Key** (**CMK**) in AWS KMS. Messages remain encrypted at rest and are decrypted only when delivered to authorized endpoints (e.g., SQS queues, Lambda functions, email addresses).

- **Additional security considerations**:

  o **IAM policies**: Define fine-grained IAM policies to control who can publish messages, subscribe to topics, and perform actions like modifying subscriptions. This ensures that only authorized users interact with SNS resources.

o **Monitoring and logging**: Enable monitoring and logging for your SNS topics and subscriptions using tools like Amazon CloudWatch and AWS CloudTrail. These features allow you to track activity, detect anomalies, and proactively address potential security threats.

Leveraging these security features helps create a robust and reliable notification system. Amazon SNS empowers you to protect sensitive data, maintain message confidentiality, and ensure secure interactions, fostering a safe and dependable communication environment within your AWS infrastructure.

Amazon SNS limits

Amazon SNS enforces specific limits to maintain service stability, optimize resource allocation, and ensure consistent performance. Below is an overview of the key limitations to consider when using SNS:

- **Topic limits**:
  o **Standard topics**: Up to 100,000 topics per account (increases available through AWS Support).
  o **FIFO topics**: Up to 1,000 topics per account (increases available upon request).

- **Subscription limits**:
  o **Standard topics**: Support up to 12,500,000 subscriptions per topic (increases available upon request).
  o **FIFO topics**: Allow up to 100 subscriptions per topic (increases available upon request).

- **Message size**:
  o **Maximum message size**: Messages can be up to 256 KiB, including payload and attributes.

The SNS Extended Client Library supports messages up to 2 GB for larger payloads, leveraging Amazon S3 for storage.

- **Message publishing rates**:
  o **Standard topics**: Support up to 30,000 messages per second per topic.
  o **FIFO topics**: Allow up to 3,000 messages per second or 20 MB per second per topic, whichever is smaller. For cross-region delivery, FIFO topics support up to 1,000 messages per second or 6 MB per second per topic.

- **Message attributes**:
  o **Maximum number of attributes**: Up to 10 attributes per message.
  o **Maximum combined attribute size**: Up to 1 KiB.

- **Delivery policies**:
  o **Maximum retry attempts**: Configurable, up to 15 attempts for message delivery retries.
  o **Maximum delivery delay**: Configurable, up to 15 minutes before delivery.

- **Tagging limits**:
  o **Maximum tags per SNS resource**: Up to 50 tags per resource.
  o **Tag key length**: Up to 128 characters.
  o **Tag value length**: Up to 256 characters.

Amazon SNS anti-patterns

While Amazon SNS is a robust and versatile messaging service, certain misuse patterns can result in inefficiencies and suboptimal performance. Avoid the following anti-patterns to ensure effective implementation:

- **Overloading a single topic**: Using a single topic for multiple unrelated message types complicates filtering and processing, making it harder for subscribers to handle relevant messages efficiently.

- **Ignoring subscription filtering**: Failing to use subscription filters forces all subscribers to process every message, regardless of relevance, increasing processing costs and inefficiencies.

- **Misusing SNS for synchronous communication**: Amazon SNS is optimized for asynchronous messaging. Using it for synchronous operations can result in latency, reduced reliability, and potential message delivery delays.

- **Using SNS for long-term storage**: Amazon SNS is not designed for long-term message retention. For durable, scalable storage, consider Amazon S3 or other AWS storage services tailored for data persistence.

- **Using SNS for real-time processing**: Amazon SNS is ideal for decoupling and message distribution, but is not intended for real-time processing. Amazon Kinesis is a more appropriate solution for scenarios requiring real-time data analysis.

Amazon SNS best practices

To maximize the efficiency, reliability, and scalability of Amazon SNS, follow these best practices:

- **Leverage subscription filters**: Use subscription filters to deliver messages only to subscribers who need them. By filtering messages based on attributes, you can reduce processing overhead and ensure targeted delivery.

- **Implement DLQs**: Set up DLQs to capture undeliverable messages for analysis and resolution. DLQs help prevent message loss and enable troubleshooting of failed deliveries without impacting active workflows.

- **Enable message deduplication**: Enable deduplication for FIFO topics to ensure that duplicate messages are not processed more than once. Deduplication prevents redundant processing, enhancing system efficiency and reliability.

- **Organize topics logically**: Structure topics logically by grouping related message types or use cases. Logical organization simplifies message routing, improves management, and ensures subscribers can easily connect to relevant topics.

- **Monitor SNS metrics**: Monitoring tools like Amazon CloudWatch can track SNS metrics, such as delivery success rates, subscription activity, and message processing delays. Set up alerts to detect anomalies early and address potential issues before they escalate.

Fundamentals of event-driven orchestration

Event-driven orchestration (EDO) is a modern approach to building software. It replaces monolithic applications with loosely coupled microservices that communicate through events.

- **Events as triggers**: Events signal that something important has happened. They trigger specific actions within microservices that are subscribed to them.

- **Loose coupling for flexibility**: Microservices operate independently and communicate only through events. This allows for:
  - **Scalability**: Individual microservices can be scaled as needed.
  - **Maintainability**: Changes to one microservice have minimal impact on others.
  - **Flexibility**: New microservices can be easily integrated.

- **Event brokers**: Event brokers store and route events to the appropriate microservices.

- **Event consumers**: Microservices that listen to events are known as consumers. They trigger actions based on the events they receive.

  Benefits of EDO are as follows:

- **Scalability and agility**: Applications can easily adapt to changing demands.

- **Resilience**: If one microservice fails, others can continue processing events.

- **Maintainability**: Modular design simplifies development and maintenance.

- **Real-time processing**: Events enable faster and more responsive applications.

EDO offers a powerful way to build modern software. Developers can create adaptable, resilient, responsive applications using events and decoupled microservices.

Core concepts in Amazon EventBridge

Amazon EventBridge is the central nervous system for event-driven architectures on AWS. It streamlines the ingesting, filtering, and routing of events between diverse sources and targets. Events in EventBridge broadly fall into two categories: AWS service events and custom events.

- **AWS service events** are automatically generated by AWS resources when certain actions occur. For example, an event can be triggered when a new file is uploaded to Amazon S3 or when an EC2 instance changes state. These built-in events require no additional configuration other than setting event rules to route them effectively.

- **Custom events** are user-defined and explicitly published by your applications or third-party integrations. Custom events allow greater flexibility, enabling you to define event structures and payloads tailored to your application's logic or business workflows.

To leverage custom events, the event rules must be defined. These rules specify the conditions (event patterns) under which events trigger downstream actions. Effective custom event rules should:

- Clearly specify unique identifiers or attributes in the event pattern to ensure accurate event matching.

- Keep event patterns concise to simplify maintenance and improve performance.

- Leverage event payload details to filter events precisely, avoiding unnecessary event triggers.

For instance, if you are building a retail application, you might create a custom event called `OrderPlaced`. The event payload could include attributes such as `orderID`, `customerRegion`, and `orderTotal`. Your event rule can then route events specifically for high-value orders (`orderTotal` above a certain threshold) or orders from particular regions (`customerRegion` set to `Europe`) to relevant processing services, optimizing your workflow.

Clearly distinguishing between AWS service events and custom events and mastering the creation of effective custom event rules significantly enhance one's ability to design efficient, responsive, and tailored event-driven architectures.

Amazon EventBridge simplifies the process of ingesting, filtering, and routing events between sources and targets, enabling robust, scalable, and responsive applications. Let us explore the core concepts of EventBridge in detail:

- **Events**: Events are the foundation of EventBridge, capturing significant system occurrences as self-contained messages. Each event typically includes:
  - **Event type**: A unique identifier representing the nature of the event (e.g., `OrderPlaced`, `UserLoggedIn`).
  - **Event payload**: The associated data payload, such as order details or user information.
  - **Timestamp**: The exact time when the event occurred.

- **Event sources**: EventBridge ingests events from multiple sources, providing seamless integration across AWS and external systems:
  - o **AWS services**: AWS services like S3, DynamoDB, or SQS automatically publish events based on specific triggers.
  - o **Custom applications**: Use the AWS SDK or EventBridge API to publish custom events from your applications.
  - o **SaaS applications**: Leverage EventBridge integrations with third-party SaaS partners to ingest events from external applications.
- **Event bus**: The event bus acts as the central conduit for managing and routing events:
  - o **Event ingestion**: The bus collects events from all configured sources.
  - o **Event filtering**: Apply event patterns to filter events based on specific payload attributes, ensuring only relevant events are routed.
  - o **Event delivery**: Filtered events are sent to the designated targets for processing.
- **Event targets**: EventBridge supports a variety of targets to process events, enabling flexible and scalable workflows:
  - o **AWS Lambda**: Trigger serverless functions to execute custom code in response to events.
  - o **SQS queues**: Deliver events to queues for asynchronous processing by downstream applications.
  - o **Amazon ECS**: Trigger containerized applications in response to events.
  - o **Step functions**: Orchestrate complex workflows using event triggers.
- **Rules**: Event rules define how events are routed to targets:
  - o **Event pattern**: Specifies the criteria an event must match, such as event type, source, or payload attributes.
  - o **Targets**: Determines the destinations for matched events. A single rule can route an event to multiple targets, enabling versatile workflows.
- **Event replay**: EventBridge's replay functionality enhances testing and debugging capabilities:
  - o **Testing rules**: Replay historical events to validate whether your rules trigger the intended actions.
  - o **Debugging workflows**: Investigate workflow issues by replaying events and monitoring target behavior.

Amazon EventBridge integrations

Amazon EventBridge is the backbone of event-driven architectures, enabling seamless connections between AWS services and external applications. The following are its key integrations:

- **AWS Lambda functions**: EventBridge triggers AWS Lambda functions in response to events, enabling real-time processing. Lambda executes custom logic, such as transforming data, updating databases, or initiating downstream workflows, without managing servers.
- **Amazon SQS queues**: EventBridge integrates with Amazon SQS to enable asynchronous event processing. Events published to SQS queues allow applications to retrieve and process messages at their own pace. This decoupling is ideal for high-volume event streams or non-critical workflows.

- **Amazon SNS topics**: With Amazon SNS, EventBridge enables event-driven notifications. Events sent to SNS topics are distributed to subscribers via email, SMS, or mobile notifications, making it suitable for broadcasting information to multiple recipients.

- **AWS Step Functions**: EventBridge integrates with AWS Step Functions to orchestrate complex workflows. Events trigger Step Functions workflows, executing sequences of tasks across AWS services, enabling reliable orchestration of intricate processes.

- **Amazon CloudWatch Events**: EventBridge consolidates rules from Amazon CloudWatch Events, providing a unified platform for event routing. This integration simplifies monitoring and streamlines event management.

- **AWS API Gateway**: EventBridge integrates with AWS API Gateway to invoke API endpoints based on events. This enables the creation of real-time APIs that respond to events dynamically, perfect for highly responsive applications.

- **AWS CodePipeline**: EventBridge automates deployment workflows through AWS CodePipeline. Events can trigger pipeline executions, facilitating CI/CD workflows and ensuring seamless integration and delivery processes.

Amazon EventBridge use cases

Amazon EventBridge empowers developers to design dynamic, event-driven architectures by integrating AWS services and external applications. The following are its key use cases:

- **Real-time serverless applications**: EventBridge triggers AWS Lambda functions in real-time for events such as file uploads, database modifications, or API invocations. This facilitates immediate responses and real-time processing, ideal for building interactive, highly responsive applications.

- **Event-driven monitoring and auditing**: Use EventBridge for event-driven monitoring and auditing across AWS resources. By capturing API activity from AWS CloudTrail, EventBridge can trigger automated actions such as initiating security audits, running compliance checks, or detecting anomalies. This approach enhances proactive monitoring and accelerates responses to potential security threats.

- **Streamlined data pipelines**: EventBridge streamlines data processing pipelines by triggering workflows across AWS services. For example, it can initiate AWS Glue jobs for data transformation or send events to Amazon Kinesis Data Streams for real-time analytics. This enables efficient data ingestion, transformation, and analysis, helping organizations derive actionable insights from their data.

- **Automated microservices orchestration**: EventBridge enables automated microservices orchestration by acting as a central conductor for event-driven communication. One microservice publishes events for processing to the appropriate consumer microservices. This fosters loose coupling, independent scalability, and faster development cycles, making transitioning from monolithic to modular architectures easier.

- **Automated CI/CD workflows**: Integrate EventBridge with AWS CodePipeline to automate CI/CD workflows. Events like new code commits or successful test completions can trigger deployments, streamlining application delivery. This integration accelerates release cycles and enhances reliability in the deployment process.

- **Hybrid and multi-cloud integration**: EventBridge facilitates hybrid and multi-cloud integrations by connecting with external applications and SaaS providers through custom events. These events can trigger workflows.

Amazon EventBridge limits

Amazon EventBridge enforces specific limits to ensure reliable performance and resource allocation across your event-driven applications. Understanding these constraints is essential for designing scalable and efficient architectures. The following are the key limits to consider:

- **Rules per Event Bus**: Each Event Bus can support a limited number of rules. This limit varies depending on your AWS region, but it is crucial to plan your rule configurations thoughtfully to avoid reaching this threshold.

- **Targets per rule**: A single EventBridge rule can have a maximum number of targets. While this is usually sufficient for most use cases, complex workflows requiring numerous targets may need additional rules to distribute the workload effectively.

- **Event pattern size**: The size of an event pattern, which defines the criteria for matching events, is restricted to a specific character limit. To avoid exceeding this limit, ensure your event patterns are concise while capturing all necessary matching criteria.

- **API rate limits**: EventBridge enforces rate limits on API calls, such as the maximum number of event publishing requests per second. These limits can vary by region and type of operation, so applications with high event throughput must account for these constraints to prevent throttling.

- **Event Buses per account**: You can create a limited number of Event Buses per AWS account. For organizations requiring a large number of event buses, careful planning and consolidation strategies are necessary to stay within this limit.

It is important to design your application with these limits in mind to prevent performance issues or unexpected behavior. Monitor usage metrics, optimize rule configurations, and distribute workloads effectively across event buses and rules. When necessary, consider alternative strategies or architectures to meet growing application demands.

Amazon EventBridge anti-patterns

Amazon EventBridge provides a robust platform for building event-driven architectures, but improper usage can lead to inefficiencies, increased costs, and maintenance challenges. Avoid these common anti-patterns to ensure optimal performance and scalability:

- **Overly complex event patterns**: Overcomplicating event patterns by including excessive matching criteria or nested conditions can degrade performance and increase debugging difficulty. Complex patterns are harder to maintain and adapt as application requirements evolve. Instead, aim for clear, concise patterns focusing on essential matching attributes. Simplified patterns improve readability, ease troubleshooting, and enhance long-term maintainability.

- **Excessive rule count**: Creating an unnecessarily large number of rules on an Event Bus can strain system performance and lead to higher costs. This approach also increases the complexity of managing configurations and debugging workflows. When possible, consolidate similar rules into broader patterns and ensure each rule has a specific purpose. Thoughtful rule design reduces administrative overhead and keeps your architecture streamlined.

- **Misusing EventBridge for synchronous communication**: EventBridge is optimized for asynchronous event handling, where events are processed independently of the sender. Using it for synchronous workflows can introduce latency due to the time taken to route events through the Event Bus. Additionally, this usage pattern can compromise reliability in scenarios requiring immediate feedback. For synchronous communication needs, consider alternatives like AWS API Gateway or AWS AppSync, designed for real-time interactions.

Amazon EventBridge best practices

Adopting best practices is essential to maximizing Amazon EventBridge's efficiency, scalability, and reliability. These recommendations ensure optimal performance and help maintain robust, cost-effective, event-driven architectures:

- **Define precise event patterns**: Craft event patterns that match only the desired events to prevent unnecessary triggers and reduce system noise. Clear and precise patterns improve event routing efficiency, lower operational costs, and minimize the risk of triggering unintended actions.

- **Use DLQs**: Configure dead letter queues to capture events that fail to reach their target due to errors or delivery issues. DLQs ensure that no events are lost and provide a mechanism for analyzing and troubleshooting failed deliveries. This practice is crucial for maintaining data integrity and addressing workflow issues promptly.

- **Optimize rule count**: Keep the number of rules on your Event Bus to a minimum while maintaining functionality. Consolidate similar rules into broader patterns to reduce performance overhead, lower costs, and simplify system management. A streamlined rule configuration enhances the maintainability of your architecture.

- **Monitor and set alerts**: Leverage tools like Amazon CloudWatch to monitor EventBridge metrics, including event throughput, rule invocations, and error rates. Set up alerts to detect anomalies early and address issues proactively. Continuous monitoring helps maintain the health of your event-driven workflows and prevents disruptions.

Amazon SQS vs. SNS vs. EventBridge

Having explored Amazon SQS, SNS, and EventBridge in detail, this section consolidates your understanding by providing clear decision-making criteria to choose the appropriate messaging service for your application. Each AWS service has its own strengths, making it critical to understand how they align with specific scenarios and technical requirements. The following comparative overview summarizes key capabilities, practical usage patterns, and common scenarios, equipping you with actionable insights to determine which service best meets your needs with confidence.

The following table shows the difference:

Decision criteria	Amazon SQS	Amazon SNS	Amazon EventBridge
Typical usage scenario	Decoupled, asynchronous tasks	Real-time notifications, alerting and fan-out scenarios	Event routing and orchestration
Communication pattern	Point-to-point (queues)	Publish-subscribe(fan-out)	Event-driven (rule-based)
Message ordering	Supports FIFO queues for strict ordering	**Standard topics**: No inherent ordering **FIFO topics**: Strict ordering, deduplication	Supports ordered delivery (FIFO buses)
Message filtering	Not supported	Subscription-based filtering	Advanced filtering via event patterns
Message durability and retries	High durability, built-in retry, and DLQs	Limited retry policies, no DLQ	Automatic retries, integrates DLQs
Integration capabilities	Primarily direct (Lambda, EC2, etc.)	Multiple targets (email, SMS, Lambda, etc.)	Extensive AWS and third-party integrations

Latency expectations	Moderate latency, optimized durability	Low latency, near real-time	Near real-time event propagation
Scalability and throughput	High scalability for message buffering	High throughput for message fan-out	High scalability for event routing
Cost considerations	Pay-per-request (economical buffering)	Pay-per-notification (efficient broadcasts)	Pay-per-event (cost-effective)
Best-fit application examples	Microservices, job scheduling, background processing	Real-time notifications, mobile messages, ordered message broadcasting	Complex workflows, multi-service integrations

Table 9.1: Table showing the difference between Amazon SQS, SNS, and EventBridge

Conclusion

This chapter explored the critical components of serverless, event-driven architectures on AWS: Amazon SQS, Amazon SNS, and Amazon EventBridge. These services address distinct aspects of event-driven communication, forming the backbone of scalable, reliable, and efficient applications.

Amazon SQS offers a dependable message queueing service designed to decouple application components and manage asynchronous tasks. Its high availability and scalability ensure seamless message buffering and consistent performance, even under heavy workloads.

Amazon SNS serves as a versatile pub-sub messaging service, delivering notifications efficiently. With its fan-out capabilities, SNS enables messages to reach multiple subscribers simultaneously, while targeted delivery ensures specific notifications are sent to intended recipients, making it a powerful tool for real-time communication.

Amazon EventBridge acts as the backbone of event-driven workflows, seamlessly ingesting events from various sources and routing them to downstream targets. Its rich integration options allow developers to design adaptive and scalable architectures, orchestrating complex workflows effortlessly. Together, these services empower applications to respond dynamically to real-time changes, with SQS ensuring reliable buffering, SNS facilitating efficient notifications, and EventBridge orchestrating workflows across the infrastructure.

Looking ahead, the next chapter introduces API management with Amazon API Gateway and AWS AppSync, focusing on key concepts, security, integrations, and best practices. Additionally, it explores AWS Step Functions for workflow orchestration, equipping readers to design scalable APIs, leverage GraphQL, and build efficient, stateful workflows for modern applications.

Join our Discord space

Join our Discord workspace for latest updates, offers, tech happenings around the world, new releases, and sessions with the authors:

https://discord.bpbonline.com

CHAPTER 10

Serverless Integration and Workflow Orchestration

Introduction

Modern serverless applications thrive on seamless integration and efficient orchestration across diverse services. This chapter explores three key AWS services that enable such workflows: Amazon API Gateway, AWS AppSync, and AWS Step Functions. Together, these services empower developers to build scalable, secure, and dynamic serverless solutions by eliminating the need for server and infrastructure management. Serverless integration offers a cost-effective, highly available approach to constructing responsive applications, allowing developers to focus on core application logic and accelerate development cycles.

Amazon API Gateway acts as the single entry point for serverless applications, enabling secure and scalable RESTful APIs while effortlessly managing traffic, authentication, and authorization. AWS AppSync extends these capabilities with flexible GraphQL-based data querying, allowing efficient retrieval from multiple sources. With real-time subscriptions and offline capabilities, AppSync is ideal for creating interactive applications.

AWS Step Functions orchestrates multi-step workflows visually, ensuring reliable execution, sequencing, and built-in retries. In contrast, AWS Lambda orchestration suits simpler, event-driven processes requiring minimal state handling. Step Functions simplifies complex workflows with precise state management, visual monitoring, and declarative error handling, whereas Lambda orchestration typically involves manual implementation of conditional logic and retries.

Structure

This chapter covers the following topics:

- Fundamentals of API management
- Introduction to API Gatewayt
- Introducing AWS AppSync and GraphQL
- Amazon API Gateway and AWS AppSync
- Understanding workflow orchestration
- Introduction to AWS Step Functions

Objectives

This chapter equips readers with the knowledge and skills necessary to design seamless, scalable APIs and orchestrate efficient workflows using key AWS services—Amazon API Gateway, AWS AppSync, and AWS Step Functions. By diving into the fundamentals of API management with Amazon API Gateway, readers will learn how effective API strategies can enhance development efficiency and streamline communication in cloud-native applications. Additionally, the chapter explores how to leverage API Gateway and the flexible querying capabilities of AWS AppSync to unlock the potential of serverless and GraphQL APIs. Readers will gain the ability to design cost-effective, scalable APIs tailored to modern application needs while providing developers with a robust GraphQL-powered interface.

The chapter also looks into the capabilities of AWS Step Functions, enabling readers to orchestrate stateful workflows confidently. Through practical examples, such as order processing or data pipeline automation, readers will learn how to design and implement complex workflows that execute tasks in sequence and recover gracefully from failures. By the end of this chapter, readers will have a clear understanding of how to select the appropriate service for their specific needs, whether it is API Gateway for RESTful APIs, AppSync for complex GraphQL queries, or Step Functions for workflow orchestration. With these insights, they will acquire the skills to design scalable integrations, construct robust workflows, and securely connect serverless applications, unlocking the full potential of AWS's serverless ecosystem.

Fundamentals of API management

In today's interconnected digital landscape, applications rely heavily on **application programming interfaces (APIs)** to exchange data, functionality, and services between components and systems. APIs serve as intermediaries, enabling seamless communication in a structured, secure, and standardized manner. They are foundational to modern application integration, akin to a waiter in a restaurant who takes orders (requests), communicates with the kitchen (backend), and returns the prepared dish (data) to the customer.

APIs generally follow these widely adopted methodologies, each tailored to specific use cases:

- **RESTful APIs**: REST APIs are the most popular style for modern integrations. They are built around resources, representing data entities like users or orders, and use standard HTTP verbs (e.g., GET, POST, PUT, DELETE) for interaction. For example, GET retrieves data (like asking for a menu), POST creates new entries (placing an order), PUT updates existing data (modifying an order), and DELETE removes entries (canceling items). RESTful APIs are:
  - **Simple and familiar**: Based on standard HTTP, they are intuitive for developers.
  - **Scalable and flexible**: Suitable for diverse applications handling complex requests.
  - **Widely supported**: Supported across most programming languages and frameworks.

- **WebSockets**: WebSockets offer a persistent, bidirectional communication channel, ideal for real-time applications like live chat or stock tickers. Unlike RESTful APIs, WebSockets maintain a continuous connection, enabling instant data exchanges. WebSockets are:
  - **Real-time**: Deliver updates instantaneously.
  - **Low latency**: Reduce delays in communication.
  - **Bidirectional**: Allow simultaneous data transmission between client and server.

- **API security**: API security uses robust authentication, authorization, and encryption mechanisms to protect against unauthorized access, data breaches, and malicious attacks.

- **API lifecycle management**: Managing an API involves overseeing its lifecycle, from design to decommissioning. This process includes development, testing, deployment, monitoring, and retirement to ensure optimal performance, security, and alignment with business goals.

Introduction to API Gateway

Amazon API Gateway is a fully managed service that simplifies the process of building, publishing, securing, monitoring, and deploying APIs. Supporting multiple API types, REST, HTTP, and WebSockets, API Gateway acts as the single entry point for external applications to access backend functionalities. API Gateway ensures efficient and seamless interactions between systems by translating incoming API requests, routing them to appropriate services, and returning responses.

A cornerstone of modern application development, Amazon API Gateway enables the creation of highly resilient, customizable, and secure APIs. These APIs power serverless, cloud-native, and event-driven workflows across various industries and use cases. The service offers robust integration with several programming languages through SDKs, covering web, mobile, and native applications, enhancing versatility and developer productivity.

API Gateway's standout features include:

- **Cost-effectiveness**: As a serverless service, API Gateway eliminates the need for infrastructure management, allowing you to pay only for the API resources consumed.

- **Effortless scalability**: It automatically scales to handle traffic fluctuations, ensuring consistent performance even during peak demand.

- **Enhanced developer experience**: API Gateway provides intuitive tools for creating, testing, and deploying APIs, streamlining the development process.

- **Robust security**: With features like authentication, authorization, and throttling, API Gateway protects APIs from unauthorized access and malicious threats, ensuring secure and reliable interactions.

By leveraging Amazon API Gateway, developers can create secure, scalable, and responsive APIs that meet evolving application needs.

Key concepts in Amazon API Gateway

Amazon API Gateway is a fully managed service that is the entry point for applications to access and share data, content, and resources securely. It provides a reliable, scalable, and efficient interface for managing APIs, like a gateway to endless possibilities. Understanding its core concepts is essential for building distributed, scalable, and fault-tolerant systems. Let us explore these foundational components:

- **Resources and methods**: In API Gateway, resources represent the logical entities in your API structure, defined by specific paths such as **/books** or **/users**. Resources serve as the foundation of API design, organizing endpoints logically. Paired with methods—HTTP operations like GET, POST, PUT, and DELETE—they define what actions can be performed on each resource.

  For example, in a bookstore API, the **/books** resource might have a GET method to retrieve book details and a POST method to add a new book. Resources like **/books/{book_id}/authors** can also be nested to represent hierarchical data relationships. Proper structuring of resources and methods is crucial for designing intuitive and easy-to-maintain APIs.

  Integrations bridge the API Gateway and backend services, defining how API methods interact with these services. API Gateway offers several types of integrations:

  o **HTTP integrations**: Enable APIs to call public HTTP endpoints or microservices running on EC2 instances.

  o **AWS service integrations**: Directly connect APIs to AWS services like S3 or DynamoDB, enabling seamless data operations.

  o **Lambda integrations**: Trigger AWS Lambda functions to execute business logic, returning processed results to clients.

o **VPC Link integrations**: Provide secure access to resources within a VPC, such as private databases or internal APIs.

These integrations enable flexible and powerful connections between APIs and backend services, forming the backbone of API Gateway's functionality.

- **Stages**: Stages in API Gateway represent different environments, such as development, testing, or production. Deploying an API to a stage makes it available through a specific URL. Each stage can have unique caching, logging, throttling, and more settings, allowing fine-grained control over API behavior across environments. Efficient stage management helps streamline version control and lifecycle management.

- **Throttling**: Throttling limits the rate at which requests are processed to ensure API reliability and prevent backend services from being overwhelmed. This mechanism is particularly critical during high-demand periods, protecting resources and maintaining consistent performance.

  Throttling controls the processing rate of API requests to protect backend systems and ensure reliable performance, particularly during traffic spikes. Amazon API Gateway implements throttling through multiple layers, including account-level, method-level, and per-client controls. Account-level throttling sets a global maximum for requests per second across all APIs within an account, providing a high-level safeguard against resource overload.

  Method-level throttling defines specific limits for each API method, allowing fine-grained control over performance. Additionally, per-client throttling restricts the request rate for specific API keys or client applications, effectively managing and balancing consumer resource usage. Combined, these mechanisms provide comprehensive and precise management of API traffic, preventing resource exhaustion and maintaining optimal performance during peak demand.

- **Mapping templates**: Mapping templates transform incoming requests and outgoing responses, ensuring data compatibility between clients and backend services. Using **Velocity Template Language (VTL)** and JSON path expressions, mapping templates enable flexible data transformations to meet backend requirements or customize response structures. They provide control over data formatting, enhancing API flexibility and usability.

API types in API Gateway

Amazon API Gateway is a versatile service that facilitates seamless communication between applications and backend services. By supporting multiple API types, API Gateway caters to a wide range of use cases, each with its strengths and specific applications. Understanding these API types is essential for building efficient, scalable, responsive systems.

- **RESTful APIs**: RESTful APIs are the classic choice for building APIs, adhering to the well-established principles of REST architecture. They use standard HTTP verbs like GET, POST, PUT, and DELETE to perform operations on resources, such as `/users` or `/products/{productid}`.

  These APIs offer a structured approach to designing endpoints. Each resource represents data entities, and methods define the allowed actions. For example, `GET /users` retrieves a list of users, while `POST /products` creates a new product. RESTful APIs are widely used for web applications and database interactions due to their simplicity and seamless integration capabilities.

- **WebSocket APIs**: WebSocket APIs enable real-time, two-way communication between clients and servers, making them ideal for applications requiring live updates. Unlike traditional HTTP requests, WebSockets maintain a persistent connection, eliminating the need to establish new connections for frequent data updates repeatedly.

  WebSocket APIs excel in event-driven architectures, allowing servers to push data to connected clients whenever relevant events occur. This makes them a powerhouse for use cases like chat applications, stock market tickers, and collaborative tools.

- **HTTP APIs**: HTTP APIs offer a lightweight and flexible alternative to RESTful APIs. They allow for custom HTTP methods, path parameters, and headers, providing greater flexibility in API design. Unlike RESTful APIs, HTTP APIs do not strictly adhere to REST principles, reducing overhead and simplifying integrations with microservices or serverless functions.

  HTTP APIs are particularly well-suited for scenarios requiring straightforward data exchange and minimal protocol constraints. They enable clean, efficient communication between components.

Choosing the right API type

Selecting the appropriate API type depends on your application's needs:

- **RESTful APIs**: Best suited for structured data access and traditional web application development.

- **WebSocket APIs**: Ideal for real-time updates and interactive applications requiring continuous communication.

- **HTTP APIs**: A streamlined choice for integrating with microservices or serverless functions where simplicity and flexibility are key.

By understanding the strengths of each API type, you can design APIs tailored to your specific communication patterns and application requirements.

Security considerations in API Gateway

Amazon API Gateway is a powerful frontline defense for backend services, enforcing access control and protecting against threats. This section explores its key security features:

- **Authentication**: Authentication ensures that only verified users can access your API. Supported mechanisms include:

  o **API Keys** for identifying users.

  o **IAM Roles** for fine-grained access control.

  o **Amazon Cognito User Pools** for managing user registration and login.

  o **OAuth 2.0** for secure third-party integration.

- **Authorization**: Authorization governs user actions within APIs. Key mechanisms include:

  o **IAM Policies** for defining access rules.

  o **Resource-based policies** for resource-level access control.

  o **Method-level authorizers** for fine-grained control of API methods.

- **Throttling and quotas**: To prevent overuse:

  o **Rate limiting** caps requests per user or IP address.

  o **Quotas** limit total data usage, managing costs, and ensuring fair access.

- **Data encryption**: All communication with the API Gateway is encrypted via HTTPS, ensuring data integrity during transmission.

- **CORS**: **Cross-origin resource sharing** (**CORS**) ensures secure communication across domains by specifying allowed origins, methods, and headers. This mitigates unauthorized access and prevents XSS attacks.

  By leveraging these features, Amazon API Gateway enables you to build secure, reliable, and resilient APIs.

Integrating AWS services with API Gateway

Amazon API Gateway is a versatile bridge connecting applications to various AWS services and external resources. Its integration capabilities simplify the development of scalable APIs by reducing the need for complex backend infrastructure. This section explores the key integration types supported by API Gateway:

- **AWS service integrations**: AWS service integrations allow APIs to interact directly with AWS resources, streamlining workflows and eliminating the need for a backend application.

    o **Amazon S3**: Enable secure uploading, downloading, and managing objects stored in S3 buckets.

    o **Amazon DynamoDB**: Perform CRUD operations on DynamoDB tables for seamless interaction with scalable NoSQL databases.

    o **AWS Lambda**: Execute serverless functions to implement complex business logic without managing servers.

    o **Amazon SNS**: Publish messages and trigger notifications to subscribers in event-driven architectures.

    o **Amazon SQS**: Add or retrieve messages from SQS queues for asynchronous communication and decoupled workflows.

- **HTTP integrations**: HTTP integrations enable APIs to make external HTTP requests, broadening their functionality:

    o **Microservices**: Invoke microservices directly to support distributed, modular architectures.

    o **Public APIs**: Leverage third-party APIs to enhance your API's capabilities.

    o **On-premises resources**: Securely interact with private resources in data centers or VPCs, facilitating hybrid cloud solutions.

By leveraging these integrations, developers can build powerful APIs that connect seamlessly with AWS services and external systems, creating scalable and robust solutions for modern applications.

Understanding limits in API Gateway

Amazon API Gateway imposes specific limits to ensure reliable performance and scalability. While some limits are fixed, others can be adjusted by requesting an increase in service limit through AWS Support. Since these limits may evolve, always refer to the official AWS documentation for the latest updates:

- **Request and payload size**: API Gateway supports a maximum request size of 10 MB, including headers, URL parameters, and payload. However, integrated services like AWS Lambda may impose stricter limits, such as Lambda's 6 MB payload limit.

- **Throttling limits**: Throttling helps maintain API performance by restricting the number of requests processed:

    o **Account-level throttling**: Regional quotas govern the number of API requests per second. Contact AWS Support for detailed information or adjustments.

    o **Per-method throttling**: Set maximum request rates for specific API methods.

    o **Per-client throttling**: To control usage, define throttling limits for API keys or client applications.

- **Other limits**: Other notable API Gateway limits include:

    o **Integration timeout**: API Gateway waits for backend responses for up to 29 seconds, with longer durations affecting throttling limits.

- o **API limits**:
  - ▪ **Number of APIs**: Up to 500 APIs per region.
  - ▪ **Methods per API**: Maximum of 10,000 methods per API.
  - ▪ **Authorizers**: Up to 10 per API for authentication purposes.
  - ▪ **Model size**: Request/response models are limited to 400 KB.
  - ▪ **Header size**: Private APIs support headers totaling up to 8 KB, not applicable to public APIs.
  - ▪ **Stage tags**: Up to 50 tags for organizing deployment environments per stage.
- o **Mapping template loops**: #foreach loops in mapping templates are limited to 1000 iterations.
- o **ARN length**: ARNs in authorized methods are capped at 1600 bytes.

Developers can design scalable and reliable APIs by understanding and effectively managing these limits while adhering to operational constraints.

Common anti-patterns in Amazon API Gateway

Amazon API Gateway is a powerful tool for building and managing APIs, but it is not a one-size-fits-all solution. Misusing it in certain scenarios can lead to suboptimal performance, increased costs, or security vulnerabilities. Here are common anti-patterns to avoid:

- **Handling large payloads**: API Gateway is not optimized for processing large file uploads or downloads. Amazon S3 provides a more efficient and scalable solution for these scenarios, allowing seamless handling of large files with reduced overhead.

- **WebSockets with high throughput**: API Gateway WebSocket APIs are suited for moderate data transfer and typical client-server communication patterns. However, services like Amazon Kinesis or AWS IoT Core offer better performance and reliability for high-throughput, low-latency use cases, such as streaming large volumes of data in real-time.

- **Long-running operations**: Tasks that require extended execution times are not well-suited for API Gateway. For such operations, AWS Step Functions or AWS Lambda provide robust alternatives, enabling orchestration and serverless execution of long-running processes.

- **Ignoring security best practices**: Neglecting proper security practices, such as authentication, authorization, and encryption, can expose your APIs to vulnerabilities. Following AWS security best practices is critical to safeguarding your API infrastructure.

By avoiding these anti-patterns and leveraging the right AWS services for specific use cases, you can design more efficient, scalable, and secure APIs.

Best practices for Amazon API Gateway

Adhering to best practices ensures your APIs built with Amazon API Gateway are secure, scalable, and efficient. The following are key recommendations for optimizing your API Gateway implementation:

- **Throttle and quotas**: Set throttling limits and usage quotas to protect your API from abuse and ensure fair resource allocation. These measures prevent overuse and safeguard backend systems from being overwhelmed.

- **Efficient API design**: Design APIs with well-structured and optimized resources, adhering to RESTful principles. This approach enhances performance, simplifies maintenance, and improves the developer experience by ensuring consistency and scalability.

- **Caching for performance**: Leverage API Gateway's caching capabilities to store frequently accessed data. Caching reduces response times, lowers backend load, and improves user experience, particularly in read-heavy scenarios.

- **Custom domain names**: Configure custom domain names to provide user-friendly and professional URLs for your APIs. Custom domains improve branding, usability, and integration with existing web platforms.

- **Rate limiting**: Apply rate limits to prevent excessive API requests and ensure fair client usage. Rate limiting protects your infrastructure from sudden traffic spikes and enables predictable system performance.

- **Performance monitoring**: Use tools like Amazon CloudWatch to monitor API usage and performance metrics, such as latency, error rates, and throughput. Proactively identifying and resolving issues ensures seamless user experiences and maintains API reliability.

By following these best practices, developers can optimize their API Gateway implementations, delivering high-performance, secure, and scalable APIs tailored to their users' needs.

Introducing AWS AppSync and GraphQL

In today's rapidly evolving application development landscape, efficient data access and manipulation are critical for building robust solutions. AWS AppSync and GraphQL combine to create a powerful foundation for building flexible, scalable, and developer-friendly APIs. This section explores their core functionalities, showcasing how they streamline modern application development and enhance overall performance:

- **AWS AppSync**: A Managed GraphQL API Service:

  o AWS AppSync is a fully managed, serverless GraphQL API service that provides a unified entry point for accessing and managing data from diverse sources. By eliminating the complexities of server management, AppSync enables developers to focus on their application's core logic. It simplifies creating and deploying GraphQL APIs, making delivering secure, scalable solutions easier.

- **GraphQL**: A flexible query language for APIs:

  o GraphQL is a query language for APIs that empowers clients to request exactly the data they need, offering several distinct advantages:

    ▪ **Flexibility**: Clients can retrieve only the necessary data fields, avoiding over-fetching and improving overall performance.

    ▪ **Simplified data access**: Nested queries allow fetching multiple pieces of related data in a single request, reducing the need for multiple API calls.

    ▪ **Enhanced developer experience**: A single, unified GraphQL schema provides a clear view of all available data, simplifying API usage and eliminating the need to track multiple endpoints.

By leveraging AWS AppSync and GraphQL, developers can build modern APIs optimized for performance, scalability, and usability, making them ideal for today's dynamic application requirements.

Exploring API types in AWS AppSync

AWS AppSync offers two distinct API types, GraphQL and pub/sub, each designed to address specific application needs. Understanding their unique strengths and use cases is crucial for building efficient and scalable solutions:

- **GraphQL**: Flexible data fetching powerhouse:
  - GraphQL APIs enable client-driven data retrieval, offering unparalleled flexibility and efficiency:
    - **Client-driven data access**: Clients request the data fields they need, reducing unnecessary data transfer and improving performance.
    - **Simplified data relationships**: Nested queries allow related data to be fetched in a single request, eliminating multiple API calls.
    - **Schema as a contract**: A GraphQL schema clearly defines the API's data structure, operations (queries and mutations), and relationships, ensuring consistency and clarity.
  - **Benefits of GraphQL**:
    - **Improved performance**: Minimizes data transfer compared to REST APIs.
    - **Granular control**: Clients have fine-grained control over the data they retrieve.
    - **Streamlined development**: Consolidates related data retrieval, simplifying API logic.
- **Pub/sub**: Real-time data delivery:
  - Pub/sub APIs enable real-time communication through an event-driven publish-subscribe model:
    - **Pub/sub model**: Clients subscribe to specific data channels, and updates are pushed to subscribers in real time.
    - **Event-driven updates**: Data changes trigger events, ensuring clients receive the latest information without frequent polling.
    - **Real-time use cases**: Ideal for applications like chat systems, live dashboards, and collaborative editing tools.
  - **Benefits of pub/sub APIs**:
    - **Real-time notifications**: Provides instant updates for a dynamic user experience.
    - **Scalable communication**: Eliminates constant polling, reducing server load.
    - **Targeted updates**: Sends data only to interested subscribers, optimizing efficiency.

Choosing the right API type:

- **GraphQL**: Best for applications needing flexible, client-driven data retrieval and efficient handling of nested queries.
- **Pub/sub** is ideal for real-time applications requiring immediate updates, such as chat platforms or live dashboards.

By selecting the right API type, developers can leverage AWS AppSync to create optimized, scalable, and user-friendly applications.

Key concepts in AWS AppSync

AWS AppSync enables developers to build flexible, serverless GraphQL APIs. Understanding its core concepts is essential for creating efficient and scalable APIs:

- **Schema**: The schema defines your API's structure, outlining data types, operations, and relationships:
  - **Data types**: Specify API entities (e.g., User, Product, Order) and their fields.

- o **Queries**: Retrieve data mapped to specific fields.

- o **Mutations**: Modify data, including creation, updates, and deletion.

- o **Subscriptions**: Enable real-time updates for clients.

- **Resolvers**: Resolvers fetch and process data requested by GraphQL queries. They:

  - o **Respond to queries**: Triggered when queries request specific schema fields.

  - o **Incorporate logic**: Allow custom logic for data manipulation, authorization, and multi-source integration.

  - o **Integrate seamlessly**: Work with diverse data sources like DynamoDB, Lambda, and HTTP APIs.

- **VTL**: VTL scripts resolve logic, enabling:

  - o **Data transformation**: Handles request and response formatting.

  - o **Conditional processing**: Supports decision-making within resolvers.

  - o **Contextual integration**: Accesses user identity, authorization details, and query arguments.

- **Other key concepts:**

  - o **Data sources**: AppSync integrates with DynamoDB, S3, Lambda, and more for versatile API building.

  - o **Authorization and authentication**: IAM secures APIs through robust role and policy configurations.

  - o **Mapping templates**: Simplifies data transformation between source responses and schema formats.

  - o **Caching**: Optimizes performance by storing frequently accessed data.

  - o **Subscriptions**: Supports real-time data updates, ideal for live or collaborative applications.

By mastering these key concepts, developers can unlock the full potential of AWS AppSync to build modern, scalable APIs.

Key integrations in AWS AppSync

AWS AppSync is more than a GraphQL API service; it is a central hub for seamless integration with AWS services and external data sources. Developers can build secure, scalable, and efficient APIs by leveraging their integrations. The following are some key integrations that enhance AppSync's functionality:

- **Data source powerhouse**: AppSync connects your APIs to a variety of data sources, enabling unparalleled versatility:

  - o **AWS native services**: Integrate directly with DynamoDB for NoSQL storage, S3 for scalable file management, and Lambda for serverless computing within workflows.

  - o **External APIs and microservices**: Use HTTP resolvers to integrate with external systems, consolidating diverse functionalities into a single API.

  - o **Relational databases**: Efficiently connect to relational databases through resolvers, bridging modern APIs with traditional data architectures.

- **Fort Knox security**: AppSync integrates with AWS IAM to enforce robust access control. IAM roles and policies ensure that only authorized users and services can interact with your API resources, safeguarding sensitive data.

- **AWS Cognito**: Simplified user management:

    o AppSync seamlessly integrates with AWS Cognito for user authentication and authorization. This simplifies user registration, login, and access control, reducing development overhead while ensuring secure API interactions.

- **Lambda**: Offloading complex workflows:

    o AppSync's integration with AWS Lambda allows you to delegate complex business logic to serverless functions. This keeps resolvers lightweight and efficient, improving API performance and simplifying maintenance.

- **Unlocking AppSync's full potential**: By mastering these integrations, developers can build robust APIs that leverage AWS's ecosystem for secure data access, efficient processing, and enhanced user experiences. Whether it is connecting to diverse data sources, ensuring top-tier security, or offloading complex tasks, AppSync empowers modern application development.

Securing APIs with AWS AppSync

Amazon AppSync prioritizes security by offering a comprehensive suite of features to protect your APIs and data. Here is how these capabilities ensure robust protection for your applications:

- **Authentication and authorization with IAM**: AppSync integrates with AWS IAM to enforce fine-grained access control. IAM roles and policies define permissions for API resources, specifying actions such as reading, writing, or deleting data. This ensures that only authorized users and applications can interact with your APIs.

- **API key management**: AppSync provides built-in API key management, enabling developers to define key lifetimes, assign specific permissions, and revoke keys. This simplifies API credential management and reduces the risk of unauthorized access.

- **Data encryption**: AppSync protects sensitive data through encryption:

    o **At rest**: Data stored in DynamoDB is encrypted using AWS KMS for secure key management.

    o **In transit**: HTTPS connections encrypt client-to-API communication, ensuring data integrity during transmission.

- **Context-aware access control**: AppSync supports fine-grained access control through VTL resolvers. Developers can implement dynamic access rules based on user identity or roles, tailoring permissions to specific users or groups.

- **AWS Cognito for user authentication**: For user authentication, AppSync integrates seamlessly with AWS Cognito. Cognito manages user pools, simplifying user registration, login, and group role assignments. This integration reduces development complexity and enhances security.

- **Building a strong security posture**: By leveraging these features, developers can secure their APIs and build user trust. Regularly review IAM policies, API key practices, and AppSync security updates to maintain a robust and proactive security posture for your applications.

Limits AWS AppSync

AWS AppSync is a powerful tool for building GraphQL APIs, but it comes with certain limits designed to ensure optimal performance and resource allocation. Understanding these limits is critical for designing scalable and efficient applications. The following are the key constraints to keep in mind:

- **API limits**: Number of APIs: Each AWS region supports up to 25 AppSync APIs per account. This limit can often be increased for larger-scale projects by submitting a request to AWS Support.

- **API key limits**: Number of API keys: Each API can have 50 API keys simultaneously. API keys are essential for managing access, and expired keys count against this limit until they are deleted.

- **Subscription limits**: Maximum subscriptions: Subscriptions enable real-time data updates, but the number of subscriptions per API depends on the backend and region-specific service quotas. Monitoring this limit is essential to avoid exceeding capacity.

- **Schema size limit**: GraphQL schema size: The maximum size of a GraphQL schema is 1 MB. This limit includes all type definitions, queries, mutations, and subscriptions.

- **Resolver count limit**: Maximum resolvers: An AppSync API can support up to 200 resolvers. Resolvers define how data is fetched or manipulated, and careful planning is required to stay within this constraint.

- **Data source limits**: Number of data sources: Each API supports a maximum of 50 data sources, which include DynamoDB tables, Lambda functions, S3 buckets, HTTP endpoints, and more.

- **VTL mapping template limits**: Size limits:

  o   Maximum size of a VTL mapping template: 64 KB.

  o   Maximum evaluated size after execution: 5 MB.

  o   VTL templates allow for dynamic transformations and logic but should be optimized to fit within these size constraints.

- **Nested resolvers**: Iterations in loops: The number of iterations for each loop within VTL templates is limited to 1,000. This prevents excessive computational complexity and ensures efficient API execution.

- **Design considerations**: While these limits are in place to maintain scalability and performance, they can influence design decisions in your application. For example:

  o   Use modular schemas to stay within the schema size limit.

  o   Combine data sources or optimize resolvers to reduce overall counts.

  o   Monitor real-time subscription usage to stay within backend thresholds.

For limits that may restrict your use case, consider requesting a service quota increase through AWS Support. Always refer to the AWS Service Quotas page for the most up-to-date information.

Avoiding common anti-patterns in AWS AppSync

AWS AppSync is a powerful tool for building GraphQL APIs, but misusing its features can lead to inefficiencies, increased costs, and suboptimal solutions. The following are some common anti-patterns and recommendations for avoiding them:

- **High-frequency transactions**: AppSync is not designed for workloads involving extremely high-frequency transactions, such as real-time trading systems or high-volume e-commerce applications. For such use cases, consider alternatives like Amazon API Gateway or specialized transaction processing services that offer lower latency and higher throughput.

- **Long-running operations**: Tasks that require extended execution times, such as batch processing or complex workflows, are not well-suited for AppSync. Use AWS Step Functions to orchestrate workflows or AWS Lambda to handle long-running operations efficiently.

- **Over-reliance on real-time features:** While AppSync's subscription capabilities are ideal for real-time updates, overusing them for static or rarely updated data can lead to inefficiencies and unnecessary costs. REST APIs or traditional backend services are more suitable and cost-effective for such data access patterns.

- **Complex business logic in resolvers**: AppSync functions best as a data access layer. Adding complex business logic to resolvers can degrade API performance and make your solution harder to maintain. Delegate intricate processing tasks to AWS Lambda or other backend services for better scalability and manageability.

- **Misusing subscription features**: Subscriptions should be used judiciously for high-priority, real-time updates. Subscribing to unnecessary or broad datasets can lead to resource overconsumption and performance degradation. Design targeted subscriptions to ensure optimal resource utilization.

- **Design smarter with AWS AppSync**: Avoiding these anti-patterns ensures that your AppSync-based solutions remain efficient, scalable, and cost-effective. By leveraging the right AWS services alongside AppSync, you can build robust APIs tailored to your application's specific needs.

Best practices for AWS AppSync

AWS AppSync provides a powerful platform for building GraphQL APIs. Adopting best practices ensures your APIs are efficient, secure, and scalable. Here are key recommendations to optimize your AppSync implementations:

- **Optimize your data graph**: Design a well-structured GraphQL schema that reflects your data relationships. Simplify the schema to minimize query complexity, improve performance, and enhance the developer experience. A clean, intuitive data graph is the cornerstone of an efficient API.

- **Prioritize API performance**: Enhance performance and reduce operational costs by using the following techniques:

  o **Caching**: Store frequently requested data to reduce backend load.

  o **Batching**: Consolidate multiple queries into a single request to minimize network latency.

  o **Efficient resolvers**: Optimize resolver logic to reduce unnecessary processing and streamline data retrieval.

- **Strengthen API security**: Protect sensitive information by implementing comprehensive security measures:

  o **Authentication and authorization**: Use AWS IAM or Cognito to control user access.

  o **Data encryption**: Secure data at rest using AWS KMS and in transit via HTTPS.

  o **Fine-grained controls**: Leverage VTL scripts to implement context-aware access control based on user roles or attributes.

- **Monitor and refine your API**: Proactively manage and improve your APIs by:

  o Monitoring API usage to identify and optimize heavily accessed resources.

  o Analyzing performance metrics to detect and resolve bottlenecks.

  o Logging error rates and troubleshooting with tools like Amazon CloudWatch.

  o Regular refinements based on these insights ensure continuous performance improvement.

- **Leverage offline capabilities**: Utilize AppSync's offline features to enhance user experience in low-connectivity environments. Local caching and synchronization allow users to continue interacting with your application offline, and changes sync automatically when reconnected.

- **Elevate your AppSync solutions**: By following these best practices, you can build secure, high-performance APIs that provide a seamless user experience and are well-suited to modern application requirements. Continuous monitoring and iterative improvements are key to maximizing the value of AWS AppSync.

Amazon API Gateway and AWS AppSync

The following table provides a comprehensive overview highlighting the differences between the two:

Feature	Amazon API Gateway	AWS AppSync
API type	Primarily RESTful	Primarily GraphQL
Data fetching	Traditional request methods (GET, POST, PUT and DELETE)	Client-driven, specific fields requested in queries
Data transformation	Limited transformational capabilities	Flexible data transformation through VTL scripting within resolvers
Real-time updates	Only available through WebSockets and polling	Optional (Subscriptions for real-time data delivery)
Offline functionality	No built-in support	This can be achieved with client-side caching strategies
Development complexity	Generally simpler for basic RESTful APIs	It can involve a steeper learning curve due to GraphQL and Resolvers
Performance	Optimized for high traffic and low latency	Can offer improved performance due to reduced data transfer with GraphQL
Scalability	Highly scalable to handle large volumes of API requests	Designed for scalability with serverless architecture
Security	Integrates with IAM for user authentication and authorization	Integrates with IAM for authentication and authorization, with context-aware access control through VTL
Integration flexibility	Integrates with a wide range of AWS services for external APIs using plugins	Integrates with various data sources (DynamoDB, Lambda functions, relational databases)
Data source agnostic	Yes	Yes
Monitoring and logging	CloudWatch integration for monitoring and logging API requests and responses	CloudWatch integration for monitoring API requests, responses, and resolver execution
Pricing model	Pay-per-use based on API calls and data transfer	Pay-per-user based on API calls and **provisioned capacity units** (**PCUs**)
Ideal for	Traditional RESTful API's Microservices architectures Integration with multiple data sources	GraphQL APIs Mobile and **single-page applications** (**SPAs**) Real-time data requirements Efficient data fetching Flexible data access control

Table 10.1: Key differences between API Gateway and AppSync

Understanding workflow orchestration

Workflow orchestration is systematically coordinating and automating tasks within a business process. Acting as a central controlling system, orchestration ensures tasks are executed in the correct sequence, handles state transitions, and manages dependencies and data flow across functions, applications, and services. This approach enables seamless execution of complex workflows, improving efficiency and reducing manual intervention.

Workflow automation, a key orchestration aspect, replaces repetitive manual steps with automated processes. Minimizing human input enhances productivity, reduces error rates, and drives operational efficiency.

Manufacturing, retail, finance, healthcare, and insurance industries rely on workflow automation to optimize their processes.

Core benefits of workflow orchestration:

- **Enhanced efficiency**: Automating repetitive tasks lets teams focus on strategic, high-value activities.
- **Higher accuracy**: Reduces human error, ensuring consistent and reliable process execution.
- **Streamlined operations**: Eliminates bottlenecks and ensures smooth task sequencing for faster workflows.
- **Improved visibility**: Provides actionable insights through real-time monitoring, enabling better decision-making.
- **Scalable automation**: Efficiently adapts to increasing workloads and evolving business demands.

Applications across industries

Workflow orchestration drives efficiency and innovation across various sectors:

- **Manufacturing**: Improves production workflows, reduces waste, and increases output.
- **Retail**: Automates inventory management, order processing, and supply chain logistics.
- **Finance**: Facilitates loan approvals, fraud detection, and compliance processes.
- **Healthcare**: Enhances patient scheduling, claim processing, and medical record management.
- **Insurance**: Speeds up policy approvals and claims handling, improving customer satisfaction.

From fundamentals to implementation

This foundational knowledge equips readers to explore tools like AWS Step Functions, which bring workflow orchestration to life. AWS Step Functions automate complex processes, optimize task execution, and enable organizations to scale operations while improving efficiency and reducing costs.

Introduction to AWS Step Functions

AWS Step Functions is Amazon's answer to serverless, cloud-native, highly scalable, reliable, secure workflow orchestration and automation service.

AWS Step Functions emerges as a powerful tool for coordinating and automating complex workflows. It acts as a visual workflow service, enabling users to design and manage multi-step applications as state machines. These state machines define a sequence of steps, each representing a task or decision point within the workflow.

Here is a glimpse into the core functionalities of AWS Step Functions:

- **Visual workflow design**: Step Functions boasts a user-friendly graphical interface. Users can construct workflows by dragging and dropping pre-defined building blocks. This visual approach streamlines workflow creation and fosters better collaboration between developers and operations teams.
- **Integration powerhouse**: Step Functions seamlessly integrates with a vast array of AWS services, including Lambda functions, S3 buckets, and DynamoDB databases. This integration capability empowers users to leverage the strengths of various AWS services within their workflows, fostering a cohesive and automated application environment.
- **State Machine Orchestration**: Workflows in Step Functions are modeled as state machines. Each state represents a specific stage in the workflow, such as invoking a Lambda function, waiting for user input, or branching based on certain conditions. Transitions between states are triggered by events, ensuring a clear and controlled execution flow.

- **Robust error handling**: Step Functions incorporate robust error handling mechanisms. In the event of failures, it can automatically retry tasks, notify users, or redirect the workflow down alternative paths. This built-in resilience safeguards the overall execution of workflows and fosters reliable automation.

- **Scalability and cost-effectiveness**: Step Functions is a serverless offering, eliminating the need for infrastructure provisioning and management. This translates to cost efficiency as users are only charged for the number of state transitions their workflows incur. Moreover, Step Functions scales effortlessly to accommodate an increasing volume of workflows.

AWS Step Functions combines ease of use, seamless integration, and powerful automation to streamline workflow orchestration. Whether building serverless applications, automating backend processes, or managing complex systems, Step Functions provides the tools to create scalable, resilient, and cost-effective workflows.

Key concepts in AWS Step Functions

AWS Step Functions simplifies workflow orchestration and automation in a serverless environment. By modeling workflows as state machines, Step Functions enables users to efficiently manage complex processes like data processing, parallel workflows, and ETL tasks. Here are the key concepts to understand:

- **Workflow types**
  - **Standard workflows**: Suitable for long-running, mission-critical processes requiring durability and precise execution.
  - **Express workflows**: Optimized for short-duration, high-throughput workloads like real-time data processing and event-driven architectures.

- **States and tasks**: Workflows are modeled as state machines, with states categorized into:
  - **Task states**: Perform work like invoking AWS Lambda functions or interacting with services like S3 and DynamoDB.
  - **Decision states**: Enable conditional execution by routing workflows based on predefined logic.

- **Events and transitions**: Events drive workflow execution, triggering state transitions based on success, failure, or timeouts. This ensures a controlled and predictable flow.

- **Execution history and visibility**: Step Functions track execution history, including state transitions, input/output data, and errors. This visibility enables monitoring, troubleshooting, and gaining insights.

- **Integrations and data flow**: Step Functions integrates seamlessly with AWS services like Lambda, S3, and DynamoDB, enabling efficient workflows and seamless data flow.

- **Error handling and retries**: Robust error-handling mechanisms allow retry strategies, alternative paths, and notifications, ensuring workflow resilience and reliable automation.

- **Asynchronous execution**: Workflows run asynchronously, enabling long-running tasks to execute independently without blocking other processes.

Key integrations in AWS Step Functions

AWS Step Functions stands out for its seamless integration with various AWS services, allowing users to build cohesive workflows that automate complex processes. These key integrations highlight its versatility:

- **AWS Lambda functions**: Step Functions integrates with Lambda to execute serverless tasks within workflows. Input data is passed to Lambda functions, and their output feeds subsequent steps. This integration facilitates the following:

- o **Modular workflows**: Encapsulate discrete logic into reusable Lambda functions for better code maintainability.

- o **Separation of concerns**: Offload specific tasks to Lambda, keeping orchestration distinct from business logic.

- **Amazon S3 buckets**: Step Functions interacts with S3 for file storage and retrieval. Tasks can upload, download, or process files stored in S3, enabling workflows to:

  - o **Leverage S3 data**: Trigger workflows on new file uploads or retrieve data for subsequent steps.

- **Amazon DynamoDB**: Workflows can query or update data in DynamoDB using task states, enabling workflows to:

  - o **Leverage DynamoDB**: Use DynamoDB for data persistence, decision-making, and result storage.

- **Amazon SNS and SQS**: Step Functions connect with SNS and SQS for advanced communication workflows:

  - o **SNS**: Publish messages to trigger downstream processes or send notifications.

  - o **SQS**: Retrieve and send messages to enable event-driven workflows.

These integrations support:

- **Event-driven processes**: Trigger actions after workflow completion or on specific events.

- **Reactive architectures**: Respond dynamically to events through SQS queues.

Troubleshooting failed Step Functions

Troubleshooting AWS Step Functions effectively ensures reliable and stable workflow execution. AWS provides integrated troubleshooting tools like execution histories, visual workflow diagrams, and Amazon CloudWatch logs to diagnose and address failures quickly. Execution histories help rapidly pinpoint errors at specific workflow states while visual diagrams clarify problematic transitions. Additionally, enabling CloudWatch Logs integration captures detailed diagnostics at each step, significantly streamlining troubleshooting.

The following are AWS Step Functions-specific limits that can affect workflow execution:

- **Exceeding state payload limit (256 KB)**:
  - o Store large data payloads in external services like Amazon S3 or DynamoDB.
  - o Reference these external data sources using identifiers or URLs within workflow states.

- **Execution history event limits (25,000 events)**:
  - o Simplify complex workflows by breaking them into smaller, chained state machines to prevent reaching event limits.

The following are the common mistakes in Step Functions workflows and the section below shows how to mitigate them.

- **Incorrect IAM permissions for task states**:
  - o Review and ensure accurate IAM roles and policies are attached to each state, verifying service-specific permissions.

- **Lack of robust error handling (retries and catch blocks)**:
  - o Define clear retry policies for transient failures.
  - o Implement catch blocks to handle permanent errors gracefully, redirecting workflows to recovery states.

- **Inefficient workflow complexity**:
  - o Modularize workflows by separating complex logic into reusable components or smaller state machines, simplifying debugging and improving maintainability.

Addressing these common issues proactively helps improve the reliability and scalability of Step Functions workflows.

Limits in AWS Step Functions

AWS Step Functions has several defined limits that impact the design and execution of workflows. Understanding these constraints ensures efficient and reliable orchestration. The following are the key limits to consider:

- **State size**: The maximum payload size for a state in a workflow execution is 256 KB, including all data passed between states. Consider using external storage services like Amazon S3 to manage payloads for workflows requiring large data exchanges.

- **Execution history**: Step Functions tracks each workflow's execution history, with a limit of **25,000 events** per execution. This includes all state transitions, making it essential to account for this limit in workflows with numerous states or frequent transitions.

- **Concurrency**: The maximum concurrency for a workflow execution is 1000, meaning up to 1000 tasks (e.g., Lambda invocations) can run simultaneously. Applications requiring higher concurrency should optimize workflow design or request a quota increase.

- **State machine versions**: Each state machine can maintain up to 1000 published versions. AWS Support can increase this quota upon request for projects requiring extensive versioning.

- **State machine aliases**: State machines can have up to 100 aliases, enabling workflows to reference specific versions for testing, staging, or production environments. This feature simplifies version management and workflow updates.

- **Execution duration**: Workflows can run for a maximum of one year. Long-running workflows should be carefully designed to complete within this limit, or they should be considered broken into smaller, manageable workflows.

Anti-patterns of AWS Step Functions

AWS Step Functions provide a powerful framework for orchestrating complex workflows. However, improper usage or design choices can result in inefficiencies, increased costs, and performance bottlenecks. Understanding and avoiding the following anti-patterns ensures optimal use of Step Functions:

- **Overuse for simple workflows**: Step Functions may be unnecessarily complex for linear or simple workflows. Alternatives like AWS Lambda with direct service integrations or AWS EventBridge can be used for straightforward processes, reducing cost and design complexity.

- **Misuse for high-throughput workloads**: Step Functions are not optimized for real-time, high-throughput workloads like event-stream processing. Instead, leverage services like Amazon Kinesis or AWS Lambda with EventBridge that are specifically designed for these scenarios.

- **Data storage abuse**: Avoid using Step Functions as a primary data store. Large state payloads can increase costs and reduce performance. Use dedicated storage services like **Amazon S3** or **DynamoDB** to manage and persist data, reserving Step Functions for workflow orchestration.

- **Neglecting error handling**: Failure to implement robust error-handling strategies can disrupt workflows. Utilize Step Functions' built-in features to:

- o Define retry mechanisms for transient failures.

- o Add fallback states for graceful recovery.

- o Trigger notifications for monitoring and issue resolution.

- **Ignoring cost optimization**: Inefficient workflows can lead to unnecessary costs. To optimize costs:

- o Minimize state transitions where possible.

- o Reuse business logic through Lambda functions.

- o Monitor resource usage regularly to identify opportunities for optimization.

- **Design smarter workflows**: By recognizing and addressing these anti-patterns, users can design efficient, cost-effective, and resilient workflows. When used appropriately, AWS Step Functions become a cornerstone of scalable, serverless application architectures.

Best practices of AWS Step Functions

Adopting best practices ensures that AWS Step Function workflows are efficient, resilient, and cost-effective. The following recommendations can help you maximize the value of your state machines:

- **Optimize state machine design**: Simplify state machines to improve readability and maintainability. Select appropriate state types (e.g., Task, Choice, Wait) to enhance performance and create intuitive, easier-to-debug, and modified workflows.

- **Implement robust error handling**: Integrate error-handling mechanisms such as:

- o **Retry strategies**: Automatically retry tasks on transient errors.

- o **Catch blocks**: Redirect workflows upon failure to handle issues gracefully.

- o **Fallback states**: Provide alternative paths to ensure workflows remain resilient and fault-tolerant.

- **Leverage result path**: Using ResultPath, manage data flow efficiently within the state machine. This feature controls how output data merges with input data, avoiding unnecessary data duplication, reducing payload sizes, and improving workflow performance.

- **Monitor and optimize performance**: Utilize tools like Amazon CloudWatch to track workflow execution metrics, including:

- o **Execution times**: Identify slow states or bottlenecks.

- o **Error rates**: Detect and resolve recurring failures.

- o **Cost metrics**: Optimize state transitions and minimize costs.

- o Regular monitoring and analysis ensure workflows remain efficient and scalable.

- **Implement state machine versioning**: Version your state machines to manage updates without disrupting active workflows. Test changes in isolated environments before deploying them to production, ensuring smooth transitions across development, testing, and live systems.

Conclusion

This chapter explored serverless integration and workflow orchestration within the AWS ecosystem, focusing on its transformative benefits, including cost savings, scalability, and operational efficiency. It highlighted three core AWS services essential for serverless applications: Amazon API Gateway, AWS AppSync, and AWS Step Functions. Amazon API Gateway provides a secure and unified entry point for backend services, AWS

AppSync offers a managed GraphQL service for efficient data fetching and manipulation, and AWS Step Functions enables the orchestration of complex workflows across serverless components.

The chapter demonstrated how these services integrate seamlessly with AWS offerings like Lambda functions, DynamoDB, and S3, allowing developers to build sophisticated, interconnected serverless applications for various business needs. It also addressed the limitations of each service, equipping architects with insights to design effective workflows within defined parameters.

Serverless integration and workflow orchestration, powered by these AWS tools, offer a robust framework for building scalable, cost-effective applications. By leveraging these services, organizations can streamline operations, manage complex workflows, and unlock the potential of serverless computing to drive innovation in an evolving digital landscape.

Looking ahead, the next chapter looks into securing serverless architectures. It covers essential tools and strategies, including AWS IAM for access control, Amazon Cognito for authentication, Amazon KMS and AWS Secrets Manager for sensitive data management, and AWS WAF and AWS Inspector for safeguarding applications against threats, ensuring robust and secure serverless environments.

Join our Discord space

Join our Discord workspace for latest updates, offers, tech happenings around the world, new releases, and sessions with the authors:

https://discord.bpbonline.com

CHAPTER 11
Serverless Security and Authentication

Introduction

Modern serverless applications demand robust security measures to protect sensitive data and ensure seamless functionality. Unlike traditional environments, serverless architectures present unique security considerations that require a tailored approach. This chapter provides readers with essential knowledge and practical guidance to navigate the intricacies of serverless security and authentication on AWS. By leveraging the right tools and services, developers can focus on core application functionalities while maintaining confidence in the security of their systems.

This chapter covers security fundamentals in serverless environments, including access control, encryption, and identity management. Readers will gain insight into critical AWS services, such as IAM, Amazon Cognito, AWS WAF, AWS KMS, Secrets Manager, AWS Inspector, and CloudTrail, designed to safeguard serverless applications. Authentication and authorization mechanisms, including API keys, token-based authentication (JWT), and user identity management, are explored to ensure secure resource access. Additionally, strategies for securing serverless functions, such as handling sensitive data, managing secrets, and implementing robust logging, are examined in detail.

Structure

This chapter covers the following topics:
- Building a secure foundation
- Mastering AWS IAM concepts
- Introduction to Amazon Cognito
- AWS Key Management Service
- AWS Secrets Manager
- Amazon Macie
- AWS CloudTrail
- AWS Web Application Firewall
- AWS Inspector
- AWS Shield
- AWS Trusted Advisor

- AWS Security Token Service
- AWS Security Hub
- IAM Access Analyzer
- Service limits in AWS Security Services
- AWS Security best practices
- Security checklist for serverless developers

Objectives

This chapter explores serverless security and authentication on AWS, equipping you with the tools to build secure and reliable applications. Serverless architectures present unique security challenges compared to traditional environments, requiring specialized approaches and services. This chapter introduces AWS tools designed to address these challenges, enabling you to fortify and protect your applications from potential threats.

You will gain a strong foundation in essential security concepts like access control, encryption, and identity management. Key services like IAM allow granular permission management, while Amazon Cognito simplifies user authentication through social logins and username-password combinations. Cognito Authorizers ensure only authorized users access APIs, and AWS KMS safeguards sensitive data by securely managing encryption keys. Secrets manager protects credentials like API keys and passwords, reducing risks associated with embedding them in code.

CloudTrail logs API calls to enhance monitoring and help detect security breaches. Macie provides data classification and analysis to protect sensitive S3 bucket data. AWS Shield defends applications against **distributed denial-of-service** (**DDoS**) attacks, and AWS WAF filters malicious traffic, protecting web applications from common exploits.

By the end of this chapter, you will understand how these services work together to secure serverless applications, enabling you to design functional, secure, and resilient solutions.

Building a secure foundation

The cloud's elasticity and scalability drive modern application development, but maintaining a secure environment remains paramount. This section establishes the foundational principles of cloud security and introduces the shared responsibility model—an essential framework dividing security responsibilities between AWS and customers.

AWS follows a well-defined shared responsibility model, where security roles are split between AWS (responsible for the cloud infrastructure) and customers (responsible for securing applications and data within the cloud).

Table 11.1 clearly illustrates how the responsibilities differ between AWS and the customer:

Area of responsibility	AWS (provider) responsibility	Customer responsibility
Physical security	Data center physical security (guards, CCTV, access control, networking)	N/A
Network and infrastructure	Infrastructure protection, network isolation, DDoS mitigation	Security groups, firewalls, VPC configuration
Server management	Server provisioning, patching, maintenance	Managed services configuration, function deployments

Application security	Security of underlying managed service infrastructure	Code quality, secure coding practices, IAM policies
Data security	Infrastructure level encryption capabilities	Data encryption configuration, key rotation, and management
IAM	Platform access mechanisms	Definition and management of user permissions and roles

Table 11.1: AWS and customer responsibilities

Example: Consider a serverless application using AWS Lambda, Amazon S3, and API Gateway. AWS manages the physical servers, Lambda execution environments, and encryption of S3 storage infrastructure. The customer is responsible for configuring access permissions via IAM, setting encryption for sensitive data stored in S3 buckets, and ensuring that the Lambda function code follows secure coding best practices.

Understanding this clear delineation of responsibilities helps cloud architects implement comprehensive security practices tailored to serverless applications on AWS.

Cloud security essentials

Imagine a digital fortress safeguarding your applications and data. Cloud security relies on a multi-layered defense strategy to protect cloud-based assets:

- **Fortress gates**: **Access control**: Access control acts as the first line of defense, ensuring that only authorized users and resources can enter. Similar to a fortress, secure gates block unauthorized access to your environment.

- **Treasure vaults**: **Data security**: Sensitive data must be protected at rest, in transit, and during use. Encryption and other security measures serve as virtual vaults, shielding valuable assets from threats.

- **Swift response**: **Incident response**: A robust incident response plan ensures that security incidents are quickly identified, contained, and resolved to minimize potential damage.

- **Following the rules**: **Compliance**: Following security regulations and standards ensures your cloud environment operates within a trusted framework.

Shared responsibility via collaborative approach

The shared responsibility model is the cornerstone of cloud security, defining the division of security duties between cloud providers and users. It emphasizes collaboration to maintain a secure cloud ecosystem:

- **Cloud provider's role**: **Guardian of infrastructure**: The cloud provider manages the underlying infrastructure, including physical security, network security, and virtualization. Their responsibility extends to protecting the cloud services they offer.

- **Your role**: **Securing your digital realm**: As a cloud user, your responsibility lies in securing applications, data, and configurations within your environment. This includes applying the **principle of least privilege** (**PoLP**), which grants users and resources only the minimal permissions required to perform their tasks.

Advantages of the principle of least privilege

Implementing PoLP within a serverless environment offers several benefits:

- **Reduced attack surface**: Minimal permissions limit the potential entry points for malicious actors, containing damage even if a function or user account is compromised.

- **Enhanced security posture**: Restricting access reduces the risk of unintended data exposure or unauthorized modifications, strengthening overall security.

- **Improved compliance**: Many regulations emphasize least privilege as a best practice, and implementing it demonstrates your commitment to meeting compliance standards.

Implementing PoLP in serverless on AWS

AWS provides tools to enforce PoLP in serverless environments:

- **IAM policies**: Define fine-grained permissions to control users' and resources' actions on AWS services.
- **Lambda function permissions**: Restrict serverless functions to only access the necessary resources, ensuring tighter security.
- **Amazon Cognito user pools**: Cognito is used to define granular access control based on user roles, enhancing authentication and authorization in serverless applications.

Mastering AWS IAM concepts

Building secure and reliable applications on AWS requires a well-defined IAM strategy. AWS IAM establishes the foundation for trust and controlled access to resources within the AWS cloud. Its core principles are crucial for workflows of all kinds, especially serverless applications.

AWS IAM is a fully managed service that enables fine-grained access control to services and resources, including interactions between components and resources. Understanding these core IAM concepts is essential for designing and developing secure AWS applications:

- **Identities and permissions:**
  - **IAM users**: Individual accounts with credentials (usernames, passwords, or access keys) that grant access to AWS resources. It is recommended that dedicated IAM users be created for specific purposes. The root user, created during account setup, has unrestricted access to all AWS services and resources but should not be used for daily tasks due to its critical level of access.
  - **IAM groups**: IAM groups simplify permission management by allowing you to assign users to groups and attach permissions to those groups. This approach is particularly effective when multiple users require similar access levels.
  - **IAM roles**: Temporary security credentials that users or applications can assume. They provide specific permissions without requiring long-term credentials. For instance, a service account accessing an S3 bucket for a particular task can use a role instead of permanent access keys.
  - **Policies**: Documents defining permissions for users, groups, or roles. Policies dictate what actions (e.g., launching an EC2 instance) can be performed on which resources (e.g., an S3 bucket). Granular policies ensure users only have the access they need.

- **Service roles and instance profiles**:
  - **Service roles**: These roles are designed for AWS services and grant permissions to the services themselves. For example, a Lambda function requiring access to an S3 bucket would use a service role. These roles provide the exact permissions the service needs to perform its tasks.
  - **Instance profiles**: Instance profiles attach IAM roles to EC2 instances. When an EC2 instance launches, it assumes the role associated with the instance profile, granting temporary permissions to its applications. This allows the applications running on the instance to interact with AWS resources securely.

- **Security groups and IAM policies**: A symphony of security:
  - IAM controls access to AWS resources at the identity level, while security groups define network access rules for resources like EC2 instances. Together, these form a robust security framework:

IAM determines who can access a resource, and security groups define how they can access it (e.g., specific IP addresses).

Table 11.2 helps compare IAM users, Roles, and policies:

Aspect	IAM users	IAM roles	IAM policies
Definition	Individuals with AWS credentials	Temporary access entities for users/services.	JSON documents defining permissions.
Use case	More relevant for individuals accessing the system (Developers, admins, etc..)	More relevant for applications, AWS services or temporary access for users.	Attached to users, roles or groups to define access
Best practice	Avoid creating IAM users, Use IAM Roles where possible. Enforce MFA for necessary IAM users.	Use IAM roles instead of hardcoded credentials. Assign roles with minimal permissions based on job function.	Follow the least privilege by granting only the necessary actions on specific resources.
Authentication	Requires login (username, password and MFA / access keys)	Assumed by users/services with required permission (temporary credentials)	Not an identity. This is applied automatically when attached to a user / role.
Security risk	Compromised user credentials can lead to privilege escalation.	Overly permissive roles can cause unauthorized access to AWS resources.	Misconfigured policies can lead to excessive or unintended permissions.
Example scenario	A DevOps engineer accesses AWS Console with IAM user + MFA enabled	A Lambda function assumes an execution role to access S3 securely.	An IAM policy restricts access to an S3 bucket to specific IP addresses only.

Table 11.2: *Difference between IAM entities (users, roles, and policies)*

By mastering these core IAM concepts, developers can create secure applications on AWS with strong access control and resource management. Security is an ongoing process, and regular reviews of IAM configurations are necessary to align with evolving application needs and best practices.

AWS IAM, implementation, and integrations

AWS IAM is the fundamental authority for security within the AWS cloud environment. It is the gatekeeper for users, applications, and resources, ensuring secure interactions with your data and infrastructure. This section explores how IAM integrates with AWS services, focusing on serverless architectures and beyond:

- **The serverless powerhouse:**

  o **Lambda and API Gateway**: IAM is vital in securing serverless applications. IAM roles attached to Lambda functions define their access permissions. API Gateway can use IAM for authorization, ensuring users have the necessary permissions before invoking Lambda functions.

- **Storage and data havens**:

  o **S3 and DynamoDB**: IAM policies control access to S3 buckets and objects with fine-grained permissions for reading, writing, and deleting data. Similarly, for DynamoDB, IAM dictates who can query, update, or delete data.

- **Guarding the gates of machine learning**:

  o **Amazon SageMaker**: IAM secures ML pipelines by granting SageMaker notebooks access to specific resources, such as S3 buckets for training data or ECR repositories for model deployment.

- o **Amazon Rekognition and Amazon Transcribe**: IAM controls access to features and data sources for Rekognition (image analysis) and Transcribe (speech recognition), ensuring secure interactions.

- **Enabling secure big data workflows**:

  - o **Amazon Kinesis and Amazon EMR**: IAM policies govern access to data streams, S3 buckets, and EMR clusters for real-time streaming (Kinesis) or batch processing (EMR).

  - o **Amazon Redshift and Amazon Athena**: IAM defines who can query specific datasets in Redshift (data warehouses) and Athena (serverless data querying).

- **Serverless ETL workflows**:

  - o **AWS Glue and AWS Lake Formation**: For data cataloging and ETL processes, IAM grants Glue access to data sources like S3 and databases, while Lake Formation enhances data lake security.

- **Messaging and notification fortresses**:

  - o **SQS and SNS**: IAM secures messaging services by governing who can send, receive, or delete messages in SQS queues and publish or subscribe to SNS topics.

- **Security and management bastions**:

  - o **CloudTrail and CloudWatch**: IAM ensures secure access to CloudTrail (API call logging) and CloudWatch (logs and metrics). Only authorized users can view audit data and manage log groups or metrics namespaces.

Beyond the serverless realm

IAM's integration extends beyond serverless architectures to virtually all AWS services:

- **Compute services**: IAM controls access to resources like Amazon EC2 for launching and managing instances.

- **Database services**: IAM manages permissions for actions in services like Amazon RDS.

- **Networking services**: IAM secures resources like Amazon VPC.

- **Developer tools**: IAM facilitates secure Console and programmatic access via AWS SDKs.

- **Cost management**: While IAM does not directly control costs, it restricts access to the AWS Billing Console or billing settings.

- **Mobile development**: AWS Amplify integrates IAM for authentication and authorization in mobile apps.

IAM is indispensable for building secure and compliant AWS environments. Integrating IAM with your services helps protect data and resources. Security is an ongoing process; regularly revisit IAM configurations to adapt to evolving needs and maintain robust protection.

Limits in AWS IAM

AWS IAM includes several limits that balance performance, scalability, and security. While these limits are generous, understanding them is essential to avoid unexpected constraints and ensure smooth operations.

The following are the limits and considerations when designing security using IAM:

- **User and group limits**: IAM does not impose a strict default limit on the number of users or groups you can create. However, extremely large numbers may introduce performance considerations. It is recommended that users and groups be structured efficiently to minimize unnecessary overhead.

- **Policy limits**: IAM policies are central to access control, and their usage comes with specific size and complexity limits:

    o **Policy size**: Inline policies vary depending on the entity they are attached to (user, role, or group) and typically range between 2,048 and 10,240 characters.

    o **Number of managed policies per role**: By default, up to 10 managed policies can be attached to a role, but this limit can be increased to a maximum of 20 upon request.

    o **Policy complexity**: Although there's no strict numerical limit on policy complexity, policies must adhere to AWS syntax rules, which can impact their design.

- **Password restrictions**: Password requirements, length, complexity, and expiration depend on the AWS account's security policies. These settings allow organizations to enforce stringent password management practices tailored to their needs.

- **Session duration limits**: The duration of sessions for IAM roles is configurable. The default duration is often several hours, but administrators can extend or shorten it based on specific requirements to improve security or usability.

- **API call throttling**: IAM's API calls are subject to dynamic throttling limits, which vary based on account activity, the specific AWS service used, and the region. While no fixed default limit applies, staying within these thresholds ensures optimal performance and prevents service disruptions.

Introduction to Amazon Cognito

Managing user authentication and authorization securely is a top priority in the dynamic landscape of web and mobile applications. Amazon Cognito is a robust solution within the AWS ecosystem, offering developers a comprehensive toolkit for secure identity management. This section explores what Cognito is, the challenges it addresses, and its security-centric features.

Amazon Cognito is a fully managed user identity and access management service. It enables developers to implement user signup, sign-in, and access control functionalities seamlessly within their applications. Cognito's scalable and feature-rich design addresses basic and advanced authentication needs.

Key features of Amazon Cognito are as follows:

- **User pools**: A secure repository for storing user data, including usernames, passwords, and other attributes.

- **Social sign-in**: Integration with popular social identity providers, such as Google, Facebook, and Apple, for streamlined user authentication.

- **MFA**: Adds a security layer to protect user accounts from unauthorized access.

- **Temporary security credentials**: Provide users and applications with time-limited access to AWS services based on their assigned permissions.

Problems solved by Cognito:

- **Reduced development time**: Cognito eliminates the need to build and maintain custom authentication systems, saving significant development effort and resources.

- **Scalability**: As a fully managed service, Cognito scales automatically to handle high user volumes and authentication requests.

- **Enhanced security**: Built-in features like password hashing, MFA, and activity monitoring bolster user account protection.

- **Centralized management**: Cognito provides a unified platform for efficiently managing user data and access control policies within AWS.

Cognito's security features

Security is central to Cognito's design, ensuring robust protection for user data and applications:

- **Strong password hashing**: Cognito uses industry-standard hashing algorithms to securely store user passwords, transforming them into unreadable strings that are resilient to data breaches.

- **MFA integration**: Users can be required to verify their identity with MFA, which combines a username, password, and a one-time code from an authenticator app or SMS.

- **Customizable user pools**: Administrators can configure user pool settings to enforce password policies (e.g., minimum length, complexity requirements), enable MFA selectively, and restrict login attempts to mitigate brute-force attacks.

- **Access control with IAM**: Cognito integrates with AWS IAM, enabling fine-grained policies that define which users or groups can access specific resources based on roles and permissions.

- **Identity federation**: Cognito supports external **identity providers (IdPs)** using standards like SAML and OpenID Connect, allowing users to authenticate with their existing corporate credentials and reducing the need for multiple logins.

Amazon Cognito simplifies authentication while prioritizing security, making it an indispensable tool for developers building secure, scalable applications.

Core concepts in Amazon Cognito

Amazon Cognito is a cornerstone of secure user management within AWS, providing a powerful toolkit for user authentication and authorization. Understanding its core concepts is essential to maximizing its potential. This section explores these foundational elements, enabling you to build secure, scalable user experiences within your AWS applications:

- **User pools**: User pools are the central repository for user data in Amazon Cognito. They securely store usernames, passwords, and attributes like email addresses and profile information. Administrators can define password strength requirements, enable MFA for added security, and configure verification methods (e.g., email or phone) to validate user authenticity. User pools can also integrate with social IdPs like Facebook, Google, or Amazon, simplifying signup and sign-in processes.

- **Identity pools**: Identity pools provide temporary credentials for accessing AWS resources. Depending on the configuration, these credentials can be issued to both authenticated and anonymous users. Identity pools support authentication through user pools, social identities, or external IdPs using SAML or OpenID Connect. By integrating with IAM policies, identity pools allow administrators to define which users or groups can access specific AWS resources and actions, ensuring secure resource access.

- **Authentication and authorization**: Amazon Cognito authenticates users through various methods, such as username/password combinations, social sign-ins using IdPs, or custom authentication challenges. Once authenticated, Cognito integrates with IAM to enforce fine-grained access control policies. This layered approach ensures that only authorized users can access specific resources, creating a robust security model.

- **Social IdPs**: Cognito integrates with trusted social identity providers, enabling users to log in with their existing social media credentials. Popular providers like *Google*, *Facebook*, and *Apple* are supported, simplifying user authentication while reducing the need for users to manage multiple passwords.

- **MFA**: MFA enhances security by requiring a second verification factor during user authentication. This could be a one-time code generated by an authenticator app or SMS, used alongside a username and password. Administrators can enforce MFA for all users or specific user groups, significantly reducing the risk of unauthorized access.

- **User activity logs**: Amazon Cognito tracks detailed logs of user sign-in attempts, access requests, and other activities. These logs provide invaluable insights for security monitoring, enabling administrators to detect suspicious login attempts and analyze user access patterns. Additionally, user activity logs can help optimize application functionality and enhance user experiences.

- **Custom attributes**: User pools allow for the storage of custom attributes beyond standard data like usernames and passwords. These attributes include user preferences, profile details, or application-specific data. Custom attributes are valuable for access control decisions or personalizing the application user experience.

Amazon Cognito's core concepts form the foundation of secure, scalable user management in AWS applications. By leveraging these features, developers can create seamless and secure user experiences that meet the highest security and performance standards.

Key AWS integrations with Amazon Cognito

Amazon Cognito is a cornerstone of user management in AWS, offering robust functionalities for secure authentication and authorization. However, its true potential is unlocked when integrated strategically with other AWS services. These integrations extend Cognito's capabilities, enabling organizations to build secure, streamlined, and scalable user experiences across their AWS applications.

Essential integrations for bolstered security:

- **AWS IAM**: IAM is the cornerstone of access control within AWS. After Cognito authenticates a user, IAM policies enforce granular access control by defining which resources and actions the user or group can access. This integration ensures that only authorized users can access sensitive data and perform specific actions within the AWS environment.

- **AWS directory service**: AWS Directory Service bridges the gap between existing directory services and AWS applications. For organizations using Active Directory or Microsoft **Active Directory Federation Services (AD FS)**, this integration allows users to authenticate with their existing credentials. This eliminates the need for separate logins, enhancing the user experience while maintaining security.

- **AWS IAM Identity Center (successor to AWS SSO)**: AWS SSO simplifies user authentication by providing a centralized sign-in experience. Users gain seamless access to multiple AWS applications after a single login by integrating with Cognito. This reduces credential management burdens and strengthens security by minimizing the risks associated with various logins.

- **Social IdPs**: Cognito integrates with trusted social identity providers like Google, Facebook, and Amazon, enabling users to authenticate using their existing social media credentials. This simplifies the signup process, reduces password fatigue, and enhances security. Organizations can also leverage advanced features some IdPs offer, such as MFA, to further strengthen user authentication.

- **Amazon CloudFront**: Cognito integrates with Amazon CloudFront, AWS's **content delivery network (CDN)** service, to extend secure authentication to the network edge. This integration enhances performance by offloading authentication tasks from application servers and supports features like CloudFront signed URLs, ensuring only authorized users can access specific content.

- **Cognito Authorizer**: Cognito Authorizer is a gatekeeper for API endpoints created with AWS API Gateway. When a user requests an API, the Cognito Authorizer verifies the user's identity and access token by interacting with the Cognito user pool. Based on the token's claims, the authorizer determines whether access to the requested resource should be granted. This integration enforces fine-grained access control and simplifies security management for APIs.

By leveraging these integrations, organizations can create a robust, secure, and scalable user management system for their AWS applications. Staying updated on the latest AWS services and their Cognito integrations empowers organizations to optimize their security posture and user experience within the AWS ecosystem.

AWS Key Management Service

AWS **Key Management Service (KMS)** is a fully managed, serverless solution that simplifies cryptographic key management within the AWS cloud environment. As a secure vault for cryptographic keys, KMS enables data encryption and decryption while ensuring its integrity. It supports encryption at rest across multiple AWS services and provides tools for signing and verifying data. This comprehensive approach safeguards sensitive information's confidentiality and integrity.

Managing cryptographic keys has traditionally been a complex and error-prone process. AWS KMS addresses these challenges by offering:

- **Centralized management**: A unified platform to create, rotate, and manage cryptographic keys, ensuring consistent security practices across your AWS environment.

- **Granular access control**: This feature leverages IAM and key policies to restrict access, ensuring that only authorized users and applications can use specific keys.

- **Hardware security module (HSM) protection**: Keys are protected using tamper-resistant hardware security modules, which add a layer of defense against attacks.

Key rotation in AWS KMS

Key rotation is a critical security practice that ensures encryption keys remain secure and reduces the risk of compromise. AWS KMS provides two methods for key rotation, depending on the use case:

- **AWS-managed automatic key rotation**: AWS KMS supports automatic key rotation for customer-managed symmetric KMS keys. AWS rotates the key every 365 days when enabled, generating a new cryptographic version while maintaining access to previously encrypted data.

  o **Best practice**: Always enable automatic key rotation for customer-managed symmetric keys to ensure long-term security without manual intervention.

- **Manual key rotation using key aliases**: A manual rotation approach is recommended for compliance-driven applications that require more frequent or asymmetric key rotations (which AWS does not automatically handle).

  o **Best practice**: Use key aliases to abstract key changes in applications, ensuring seamless transitions between old and new encryption keys without modifying application code.

- **Key rotation in a sample application**: Consider a serverless application that encrypts user data in an Amazon DynamoDB table using a KMS key. When rotating keys:

  o Enable automatic key rotation for standard security requirements.

  o If regulatory requirements demand frequent key changes, use manual key rotation and update the DynamoDB encryption key reference via KMS key alias updates.

By following key rotation best practices, organizations can maintain compliance with industry security standards (PCI DSS, GDPR, HIPAA) while ensuring encryption remains effective against emerging threats.

KMS integrations with AWS services

AWS KMS integrates seamlessly with many AWS services to enhance data security across your cloud environment:

- **Amazon S3**: Encrypts objects stored in S3 buckets, ensuring data at rest remains secure.

- **Amazon EBS**: Protects data volumes attached to EC2 instances with encryption.

- **Amazon DynamoDB**: Secures table data through encryption using KMS keys.
- **AWS CloudTrail**: Logs all key usage activities, providing a complete audit trail for compliance and security monitoring.

Key concepts in KMS are as follows:

- **KMS key types**: AWS KMS supports multiple key types:
  - **Symmetric keys**: Used for encryption and decryption.
  - **Asymmetric keys**: Enables signing and verifying data.
  - **HMAC keys**: Provides message authentication using hash-based message authentication codes.
- **Data key management**: KMS generates and manages data keys for specific encryption tasks, isolating them from master keys to enhance security.

Benefits of AWS KMS

By adopting AWS KMS, organizations gain a centralized, secure, and scalable solution for cryptographic key management. This strengthens the overall security posture of cloud environments, empowering developers to focus on building applications while ensuring their data remains protected.

AWS Secrets Manager

In the dynamic world of cloud computing, protecting sensitive information like access credentials is crucial. AWS Secrets Manager is a managed service designed to safeguard cloud secrets, offering a secure, centralized solution for storing, retrieving, and rotating credentials and other sensitive data. By automating secret management, Secrets Manager eliminates the need for manual handling, reducing the risk of exposure and improving overall security.

Concepts and functionalities are as follows:

- **Secret storage**: Secrets Manager is a centralized vault for storing sensitive information, such as database credentials, API keys, OAuth tokens, and other secrets. These are encrypted using AWS KMS to ensure maximum security, and they are never stored in plain text.
- **Secret rotation**: Automates credential rotation, a critical security practice that reduces the risk associated with compromised keys. Even if a secret is exposed with automated rotation, it becomes invalid quickly.
- **Fine-grained access control**: Granular IAM policies and resource-based policies restrict access to secrets, ensuring that only authorized users or applications can retrieve them.
- **Secret retrieval**: Applications can securely retrieve secrets at runtime using the Secrets Manager API, removing the need to hardcode credentials into application code, a common security vulnerability.

Use cases and benefits are as follows:

- **Improved security posture**: Centralizing and encrypting secrets significantly reduces the attack surface and minimizes the risk of unauthorized access.
- **Simplified application development**: Secrets Manager enables developers to retrieve secrets securely at runtime, eliminating the need to handle credentials and streamlining application development manually.
- **Enhanced compliance**: Meets stringent compliance requirements for secure storage and access control of sensitive information, helping organizations adhere to regulations like GDPR, PCI DSS, and SOC 2.

Integrations and ecosystem are as follows:

- **AWS services**: Secrets Manager integrates with services like Amazon RDS, Lambda, and Elastic Beanstalk to inject secrets into applications automatically. This simplifies application deployment and ensures secrets remain secure throughout their lifecycle.

- **CI/CD pipelines**: Seamlessly integrates with CI/CD workflows to manage secrets during the development and deployment stages. This prevents inadvertent exposure of sensitive information in code repositories or deployment artifacts.

Benefits of AWS Secrets Manager

By adopting AWS Secrets Manager, organizations gain a secure, centralized solution for managing sensitive information. It empowers developers to focus on building applications while strengthening security and ensuring compliance with regulatory standards. Let AWS Secrets Manager be your trusted guardian, safeguarding your secrets in the ever-evolving world of cloud computing.

Amazon Macie

Sensitive data often goes unnoticed in an expansive AWS cloud environment, creating potential security and compliance risks. Amazon Macie is a fully managed data security and privacy service that leverages machine learning to identify, classify, and protect sensitive data stored in Amazon S3. By illuminating hidden risks, Macie empowers organizations to make informed security decisions and maintain compliance with data privacy regulations.

Key functionalities of Amazon Macie are as follows:

- **Automated data discovery**: Macie uses machine learning to scan S3 buckets, automatically detecting sensitive data like **personally identifiable information** (**PII**), financial records, and intellectual property. Users can define customizable detection rules tailored to organizational needs.

- **Actionable insights**: Macie generates detailed findings and reports highlighting the type and location of sensitive data. These insights allow organizations to prioritize remediation efforts and implement targeted data protection measures.

The benefits and use cases are as follows:

- **Enhanced security**: By proactively identifying sensitive data, Macie enables organizations to implement precise access controls, reducing the risk of data exposure and breaches.

- **Compliance enablement**: Macie helps ensure compliance with data privacy regulations such as GDPR, HIPAA, and CCPA by managing and protecting sensitive data.

The integration and ecosystem entails:

- **AWS Security Hub**: Macie integrates seamlessly with AWS Security Hub, providing a unified view of security findings across AWS services. This centralization enhances visibility into an organization's overall security posture.

By adopting Amazon Macie, organizations gain a proactive tool for uncovering sensitive data and mitigating risks associated with its storage and access. Its automated discovery capabilities and integrations with other AWS security services make it indispensable to a modern cloud security strategy. Let Amazon Macie serve as your guardian, shedding light on the hidden risks within your cloud environment.

AWS CloudTrail

Maintaining visibility into user activity is essential in the dynamic realm of cloud security. AWS CloudTrail is a log recorder service designed to provide a comprehensive view of actions taken within your AWS account. By capturing API calls, role usage, and service interactions, CloudTrail enables organizations to monitor activity, detect threats, and ensure compliance with security regulations.

The key benefits of AWS CloudTrail are as follows:

- **Threat detection and investigation**: CloudTrail logs create a detailed audit trail of all activity within your AWS account. Security teams can use these logs to identify suspicious behavior, investigate unauthorized access attempts, and analyze unusual API calls. They can swiftly detect and remediate potential security incidents by correlating these events.

- **Compliance adherence**: Many regulatory frameworks require detailed logging of user activity. CloudTrail simplifies compliance by maintaining readily available logs demonstrating adherence to standards like GDPR, HIPAA, or SOC 2.

- **User accountability**: CloudTrail logs capture the who, what, and when of actions taken within your account. This level of detail fosters accountability among users and simplifies auditing practices to verify proper access control and resource utilization.

Security-focused functionalities are as follows:

- **Management events vs. data events**: CloudTrail can capture two primary types of events:

  o **Management events**: Track actions that modify your AWS environment, such as creating an S3 bucket or altering IAM permissions.

  o **Data events**: Provide visibility into read and write operations on specific resources, like S3 objects or Lambda function invocations, enabling a more granular view of activity.

- **CloudWatch integration**: CloudTrail integrates with Amazon CloudWatch to enable real-time log analysis and monitoring. Security teams can set up alerts for suspicious activity, ensuring a rapid response to potential threats.

- **S3 bucket delivery**: CloudTrail logs can be securely delivered to an S3 bucket in your account for long-term storage. These logs can be analyzed using security tools or log management platforms, enabling detailed forensic investigations and advanced insights.

Benefits of AWS CloudTrail

By leveraging AWS CloudTrail, organizations gain a powerful tool for monitoring and securing their AWS environment. The service provides detailed audit trails that empower security teams to detect threats, investigate incidents, and ensure compliance with regulatory standards. Let AWS CloudTrail serve as your vigilant watchtower, illuminating activity within your cloud and safeguarding your critical data.

AWS Web Application Firewall

AWS **Web Application Firewall** (**WAF**) is a managed service that protects web applications from common web exploits and malicious traffic. By filtering and monitoring HTTP(S) requests, WAF helps safeguard applications against vulnerabilities such as SQL injection, **cross-site scripting** (**XSS**), and DDoS attacks. AWS WAF empowers organizations to enhance application security while maintaining performance and availability.

The core functionalities of AWS WAF are as follows:

- **Security rule groups**: AWS WAF uses pre-configured security rule groups that block common attack patterns, such as SQL injection and XSS. Additionally, WAF allows organizations to create fine-grained custom rules tailored to specific application needs.

- **Web traffic filtering**: WAF inspects incoming web traffic as a protective filter and blocks requests that violate configured security rules. This functionality helps mitigate malicious attempts, including DDoS attacks, and ensures that only legitimate traffic reaches the application.

- **Integration and automation**: AWS WAF integrates seamlessly with services like Amazon CloudFront and API Gateway, enabling centralized security management for web applications. WAF also supports automated security rule updates, ensuring defenses stay current against evolving threats.

Security benefits of AWS WAF are as follows:

- **Enhanced application security**: AWS WAF reduces the risk of exploited vulnerabilities by proactively protecting applications and sensitive user data from common web threats.

- **Improved availability**: By filtering out malicious traffic and mitigating DDoS attacks, WAF ensures high availability for legitimate users and maintains an uninterrupted user experience.

- **Simplified security management**: AWS WAF's managed nature offloads complex security tasks, such as rule creation and web traffic filtering, allowing organizations to focus on innovation rather than infrastructure management.

Benefits of AWS WAF

AWS WAF provides organizations a robust toolset to strengthen their web application security posture. By leveraging automated filtering, pre-configured rules, and seamless integrations, WAF shields applications from common threats, empowering teams to focus on building and delivering exceptional user experiences without compromising security.

AWS Inspector

Undetected vulnerabilities within an AWS environment can pose significant security risks. AWS Inspector is a managed vulnerability management service that continuously scans workloads for known software vulnerabilities and unintended network exposure. By automating vulnerability assessments, AWS Inspector helps organizations strengthen their security posture and safeguard cloud workloads.

The core functionalities of AWS Inspector are as follows:

- **Automated vulnerability scanning**: AWS Inspector automatically scans Amazon EC2 instances, container images in Amazon ECR, and AWS Lambda functions to identify known software vulnerabilities.

- **Network configuration insights**: Although earlier versions of AWS Inspector emphasized network configuration assessments, the redesigned Inspector, relaunched in April 2021, focuses primarily on vulnerability management for EC2 instances, ECR images, and Lambda functions. While network configurations remain an essential security aspect, the updated service prioritizes identifying and managing software vulnerabilities.

- **Detailed findings report**: After each scan, AWS Inspector generates comprehensive reports that detail identified vulnerabilities. These reports provide actionable insights, enabling security teams to prioritize remediation efforts effectively.

The security benefits of AWS Inspector are as follows:

- **Proactive vulnerability management**: By continuously scanning workloads, AWS Inspector empowers organizations to address vulnerabilities before they can be exploited.

- **Improved security posture**: The actionable findings from AWS Inspector allow teams to prioritize and remediate vulnerabilities, ultimately strengthening their overall security posture.

- **Streamlined compliance**: AWS Inspector integrates with AWS Security Hub to facilitate compliance audits and demonstrate adherence to security best practices through detailed findings and reports.

Benefits of AWS Inspector

By adopting AWS Inspector, organizations gain a proactive and automated approach to vulnerability management. Its continuous scanning and actionable findings empower security teams to identify and remediate risks effectively, safeguarding critical cloud workloads and ensuring compliance with security standards.

AWS Shield

In the ever-evolving threat landscape, DDoS attacks pose significant risks to web applications, potentially causing downtime, operational disruption, and reputational damage. AWS Shield is a managed DDoS protection service designed to safeguard web applications and maintain their availability during attacks. With always-on monitoring and automated defenses, AWS Shield empowers organizations to deliver secure and resilient user experiences.

The core functionalities of AWS Shield are as follows:

- **Always-on protection**: AWS Shield continuously monitors web traffic, automatically detecting and mitigating DDoS attacks in real-time. This ensures applications remain accessible to legitimate users, even during an active attack.

- **Multi-layered defense**: Shield combines network-layer protection and application-layer defenses to effectively counter a wide range of DDoS tactics.

- **Scalability and elasticity**: AWS Shield automatically scales its defenses to handle even the most significant DDoS attacks, ensuring uninterrupted application access.

The security benefits of AWS Shield are as follows:

- **Enhanced application availability**: Shield's always-on protection and real-time mitigation capabilities preserve application uptime and user experience during attacks.

- **Reduced downtime and costs**: By mitigating DDoS attacks, Shield minimizes service disruptions and the associated revenue losses, protecting operational continuity and business reputation.

- **Simplified security management**: AWS Shield offloads the complexities of DDoS mitigation as a managed service, allowing teams to focus on core business functions instead of managing attack responses.

AWS Shield Advanced

For enhanced protection, **AWS Shield Advanced** offers:

- **DDoS Response Team (DRT)**: 24/7 access to expert support for proactive attack assistance and mitigation.

- **Detailed diagnostics**: Comprehensive insights into attack patterns and metrics for better understanding and resolution.

- **Cost protection**: Safeguards against unexpected costs from increased resource usage during an attack.

Benefits of AWS Shield

AWS Shield provides a reliable and scalable solution to defend against DDoS attacks. Its automated defenses, continuous monitoring, and optional advanced features enable organizations to maintain application availability and secure their cloud environment. With AWS Shield, businesses can confidently deliver resilient user experiences, even in the face of evolving threats.

AWS Trusted Advisor

Continuous optimization is essential in a dynamic and complex AWS environment to maximize efficiency, reduce costs, and enhance security. AWS Trusted Advisor is your copilot, providing real-time assessments and actionable recommendations to streamline cloud operations.

The key features of AWS Trusted Advisor are as follows:

- **Comprehensive assessments**: Trusted Advisor evaluates your AWS environment across five key categories:
    - **Cost optimization**: Identifies opportunities to reduce costs, such as unused resources or underutilized instances.
    - **Security**: This section highlights potential security risks and offers recommendations to improve protection, such as closing unused ports or enabling encryption.
    - **Performance**: Suggests optimizations to enhance the efficiency of workloads, such as adjusting instance types or scaling configurations.
    - **Fault tolerance**: Ensures applications remain resilient by identifying potential points of failure and recommending backups or failover configurations.
    - **Service limits**: Monitors service quotas and usage to help prevent disruptions caused by reaching limits.
- **Actionable insights**: Trusted Advisor prioritizes its recommendations to deliver the greatest impact. For example, it might flag hidden cost-saving opportunities or critical security vulnerabilities for immediate action.
- **Plan flexibility**: Trusted Advisor offers different levels of service:
    - **Basic and developer support plans**: Focus on cost optimization and service limits.
    - **Business and enterprise support plans**: Expand coverage to include security, performance, fault tolerance, and operational excellence, offering a more holistic view of your AWS environment.

Benefits of Trusted Advisor

AWS Trusted Advisor empowers organizations to make informed decisions, enabling proactive security, cost efficiency, and performance improvements. By leveraging its insights, you can build a well-optimized, secure, and cost-effective AWS environment, freeing your team to focus on innovation rather than cloud management.

AWS Security Token Service

Long-lived credentials can pose significant security risks by increasing the potential damage if compromised. AWS **Security Token Service (STS)** addresses this challenge by providing temporary, time-limited credentials for secure access to AWS resources. This approach enhances security while maintaining flexibility for users and applications.

The key features of AWS STS are as follows:

- **Temporary credentials**: AWS STS issues temporary credentials that allow users or applications to access AWS resources for a specific duration. Once expired, these credentials are no longer valid, minimizing the impact of a potential compromise.

- **Role assumption**: STS enables users or applications to assume specific roles with defined permissions. For instance, a developer needing temporary S3 bucket access can assume a role created for this purpose. After completing the task, the credentials automatically expire, reducing security risks.

The benefits of AWS STS are as follows:

- **Reduced risk**: Temporary credentials significantly limit the potential impact of compromised access, as the credentials expire automatically after a defined duration.

- **Granular control**: Administrators can define specific permissions for temporary roles, ensuring users or applications can access only the resources and actions required for their tasks.

- **Improved compliance**: By enabling temporary, purpose-specific access, STS supports adherence to security best practices and regulatory requirements for minimizing credential exposure.

Benefits of AWS STS

AWS STS empowers organizations to enhance their security posture by replacing long-lived credentials with temporary access solutions. This minimizes the attack surface while enabling secure and efficient collaboration across teams. By leveraging STS, organizations can fortify their AWS environment with flexible, time-limited access tailored to their needs.

AWS Security Hub

Monitoring and managing your AWS security posture across multiple services can quickly become overwhelming. AWS Security Hub is a centralized command center that provides a unified view of security findings from various AWS services and third-party tools. By aggregating and prioritizing potential security risks, Security Hub simplifies cloud security management and enhances your organization's overall security posture.

The core features of AWS Security Hub are as follows:

- **Unified dashboard**: Security Hub aggregates security findings from AWS services like Amazon GuardDuty, Inspector, and Macie, as well as third-party security solutions. This eliminates the need to navigate individual services, offering a single view of potential risks.

- **Risk prioritization**: Findings are automatically analyzed and ranked by severity, enabling teams to focus on addressing the most critical issues first.

- **Automation capabilities**: Security Hub supports automation by integrating with AWS services like AWS Lambda and Systems Manager. For instance, it can trigger automated remediation actions for high-risk vulnerabilities or compliance violations.

- **Collaboration tools**: The service enables the sharing of security findings across your organization, fostering collaboration and improving response efficiency.

The benefits of using AWS Security Hub are as follows:

- **Centralized security management**: Security Hub consolidates security findings into a single platform, making monitoring, analyzing, and responding to potential threats easier.

- **Enhanced workflow efficiency**: Automated workflows reduce manual effort by streamlining the remediation process for high-priority issues.

- **Improved security posture**: By providing real-time insights and prioritizing risks, Security Hub empowers organizations to address vulnerabilities proactively and maintain compliance with security best practices.

Benefits of AWS Security Hub

AWS Security Hub offers a centralized, user-friendly platform for managing your cloud security. By unifying findings, prioritizing risks, and automating workflows, Security Hub helps organizations strengthen their security posture while enabling effective collaboration across teams.

IAM Access Analyzer

Managing granular IAM permissions in AWS can be challenging. AWS IAM Access Analyzer simplifies this process by providing powerful tools to analyze and optimize IAM configurations. Identifying overly permissive access and potential security risks empowers organizations to enforce the principle of least privilege and enhance their cloud security posture.

The key features of IAM Access Analyzer are as follows:

- **Advanced policy analysis**: IAM Access Analyzer leverages advanced logic to analyze existing IAM policies, simulating potential user actions based on assigned permissions. This helps identify whether resources are accessible by unauthorized users or external entities.

- **Proactive risk identification**: The service automatically flags risks associated with overly permissive policies, enabling teams to mitigate vulnerabilities before they can be exploited.

- **Insights for least privilege**: IAM Access Analyzer provides actionable insights to help organizations refine IAM configurations and enforce the principle of least privilege, ensuring users and applications have only the permissions they need.

The benefits of IAM Access Analyzer are as follows:

- **Streamlined analysis**: Automates the complex process of IAM policy analysis, saving time and reducing the likelihood of human error.

- **Proactive risk mitigation**: Identifies potential security risks early, enabling organizations to address vulnerabilities before they become incidents.

- **Enhanced security posture**: Access Analyzer strengthens overall cloud security and reduces the attack surface by facilitating the enforcement of the least privilege.

Need for using IAM Access Analyzer

AWS IAM Access Analyzer simplifies security analysis and empowers organizations to effectively enforce least privilege principles. Proactive risk identification and actionable insights help secure your cloud environment, ensuring your IAM configurations align with security best practices and organizational policies.

Service limits in AWS Security Services

AWS services operate within predefined quotas, formerly known as limits, to ensure optimal performance, resource allocation, and fair usage. Understanding these constraints is crucial for managing your AWS environment effectively and avoiding disruptions. Here is an overview of key service limits across user management, security, compliance, and general operations.

User and identity management quotas:

- **Amazon Cognito**:
  - **User pools**:
    - Maximum of 50,000 users per pool by default.
    - Up to 50 custom attributes per user pool.
    - API call rate limits, such as 50 requests per second for user authentication, vary by operation and region.
  - **Identity pools**:
    - API rate limits for operations like GetId (default 10 requests per second).
- **AWS IAM**:
  - Maximum of 5,000 users and 300 groups per account.
  - Up to 1,000 roles and 1,500 managed policies per account.
  - Session duration for roles can be configured up to 12 hours.
  - Custom password policies support the enforcement of complexity and rotation rules.

Security, compliance, and data protection quotas:

- **Amazon Macie**: Designed for analyzing S3 data sources, with constraints on API usage and resource configurations.
- **AWS KMS**:
  - Maximum of 100,000 customer-managed keys per region.
  - Up to 50 aliases and 50,000 grants per key.
- **AWS Secrets Manager**: Supports an unlimited number of secrets but enforces limits on versions and rotation intervals.
- **Amazon Inspector**: No hard limits on assessment template runs or findings, but effective use depends on resource availability.
- **AWS WAF**: Maximum of 100 Web ACLs per account and 1,500 rules per Web ACL.
- **AWS Shield**: Limits vary based on protected resource types. Shield advanced includes additional support for diagnostics and response.

General service constraints:

- **API call rate limits**: Most AWS services enforce rate limits to prevent abuse and ensure fair resource distribution. These limits vary by service and operation, and adjustments can be requested via the AWS Service Quotas Console or AWS Support.

Understanding these quotas allows organizations to plan resource usage effectively and avoid disruptions. AWS offers tools like the Service Quotas Console to monitor usage and request limit increases where needed. Staying within quotas ensures seamless performance and resource availability while complying with AWS best practices.

AWS Security best practices

In the ever-changing landscape of cloud security, adhering to best practices is essential for safeguarding sensitive data and ensuring the integrity of applications within the AWS ecosystem. The following are 25 key security practices organized by critical AWS services to help bolster your security posture:

- **IAM**:

  o **Principle of least privilege**: Grant users and roles only the permissions necessary for their tasks. This reduces the potential impact of compromised credentials and prevents unauthorized access to resources.

  o **MFA**: Enforce MFA for all IAM users, particularly those with root or administrative access. MFA adds a layer of security beyond a username and password.

  o **IAM roles over credentials**: Replace long-lived credentials with IAM roles for applications and services. Roles provide temporary credentials, reducing the risk associated with exposed keys.

  o **Regular policy review**: Periodically review IAM policies to ensure they align with current access requirements and revoke unnecessary permissions.

  o **Strong password policies**: Enforce password complexity and rotation requirements through IAM password policies. This minimizes the risk of brute force attacks and reduces credential misuse.

- **Amazon Cognito**:

  o **Robust password policies**: Set stringent password policies for Cognito user pools, including minimum length and complexity requirements.

  o **MFA**: Enable MFA for user sign-ins to add an extra layer of security, protecting against compromised passwords.

  o **WAF integration**: Protect the Cognito user interface with AWS WAF to block SQL injection, XSS, and other common exploits.

  o **Suspicious activity monitoring**: Regularly monitor Cognito user activity logs for unusual patterns, helping to identify unauthorized access attempts.

  o **Data encryption**: Use strong encryption for data at rest and in transit to protect sensitive user information stored within Cognito.

- **AWS Shield**:

  o **Automatic DDoS mitigation**: Enable AWS Shield Standard for all internet-facing applications to protect against common DDoS attacks.

  o **Enhanced DDoS protection**: Consider AWS Shield Advanced for additional protections, including 24/7 AWS DRT access.

  o **DDoS preparedness testing**: Conduct regular tests to evaluate your application's resilience against DDoS attacks.

  o **Real-time security monitoring**: Integrate AWS Shield with Amazon CloudWatch to monitor attacks and evaluate mitigation strategies.

  o **Attack pattern analysis**: Use AWS Shield logs to analyze attack patterns and refine your defense mechanisms.

- **Amazon Macie**:

  o **Automated data discovery**: Leverage Macie to automatically identify sensitive data in your S3 buckets, such as PII.

  o **Custom data identification**: Create custom rules in Macie to identify data specific to your organization's security and compliance requirements.

  o **Data protection measures**: Apply access controls and encryption based on data classification to secure sensitive information.

- o **Prioritized security efforts**: Use Macie's findings to focus on securing the most critical data and addressing compliance risks.

- o **Continuous effectiveness**: Regularly update Macie settings to ensure ongoing accuracy as your data landscape evolves.

- **Additional security measures**:

  - o **AWS KMS**: Centralize encryption key management with KMS to safeguard data at rest and in transit. Rotate keys regularly for enhanced security.

  - o **AWS Secrets Manager**: Use Secrets Manager to securely store and manage sensitive information like passwords, API keys, and database credentials.

  - o **CloudTrail Logging**: Enable AWS CloudTrail across all regions to maintain a comprehensive audit trail of user activity. CloudTrail logs are critical for forensic analysis in the event of a breach.

  - o **AWS WAF**: Protect your web applications with AWS WAF by blocking malicious traffic and implementing custom security rules to address vulnerabilities.

  - o **Routine security audits**: To maintain a robust security posture, perform regular security audits of your AWS environment, including permissions, resource configurations, and log analysis.

Security checklist for serverless developers

The following security checklist for developers provides actionable guidance for securing serverless applications on AWS:

- **Access management and authentication**:

  - o **Use IAM roles instead of IAM users**: Lambda functions, API Gateway, and serverless workloads should assume IAM roles instead of using hardcoded credentials.

  - o **Apply the PoLP**: Limit Lambda function execution roles to only the required permissions.

  - o **Secure API Gateway with Cognito or IAM authorization**: Avoid public APIs unless necessary.

  - o **Use AWS Secrets Manager or SSM Parameter** Store to securely store and retrieve API keys, database credentials, and sensitive configurations.

  - o Enable MFA for AWS Console and CLI Users to prevent unauthorized account access.

- **Data security and encryption**:

  - o **Encrypt all data at rest and in transit**: Use AWS KMS for Lambda, S3, and DynamoDB encryption.

  - o Enable automatic key rotation for KMS keys to reduce cryptographic risks.

  - o Never store secrets in Lambda environment variables; use AWS Secrets Manager instead.

  - o Mask or anonymize PII before storing it in databases or logs

- **Network and API security**:

  - o **Restrict API Gateway and Lambda Networking**: Use VPC endpoints and resource policies.

  - o **Enable AWS WAF on API Gateway and CloudFront**: Block malicious requests and bot traffic.

  - o Enforce rate limits in API Gateway to protect against DDoS and API abuse attacks.

- o **Disable unauthenticated requests**: Require IAM authentication or token-based authorization.

- o Use Amazon CloudFront Signed URLs for static content, prevent unauthorized access.

- **Serverless-specific security hardening**:

  - o **Limit Lambda execution permissions**: Apply fine-grained IAM permissions per function.

  - o **Enable CloudWatch Logging for all Lambda functions**: Track errors and execution anomalies.

  - o Monitor for suspicious behavior with AWS Security Hub and GuardDuty.

  - o **Implement API Gateway request validation**: Reject malformed or oversized API requests.

  - o **Use layers and runtime controls**: Ensure only trusted dependencies are used in Lambda.

- **DDoS and threat protection**:

  - o **Enable AWS Shield Standard for API Gateway and CloudFront**: Protect against automated bot attacks.

  - o **Use AWS Firewall Manager for multi-account security**: Enforce security controls on scale.

  - o Detect anomalous API behavior with Amazon GuardDuty to prevent data exfiltration risks.

  - o **Prevent excessive function invocations**: Use Lambda concurrency limits to avoid DoS risks.

- **Monitoring and automated security response**:

  - o Enable AWS CloudTrail Logging for API Calls: Track all AWS API activity.

  - o **Set up CloudWatch alarms for unauthorized API requests**: Alert security teams in real time.

  - o **Use AWS Config to detect policy violations**: Prevent misconfigurations before they become security incidents.

  - o **Automate security incident response**: Trigger Lambda functions based on AWS Security Hub findings.

Conclusion

This chapter explored the comprehensive suite of security services AWS offers, providing a robust foundation for building and maintaining a secure cloud environment. Starting with IAM, we detailed its role in controlling user resource access. Services like Amazon Cognito and Amazon Macie were highlighted for their user authentication and data security capabilities. Monitoring and auditing tools such as AWS CloudTrail and Amazon Inspector were discussed for their ability to track and analyze activity. The chapter also covered AWS KMS for encryption and AWS Secrets Manager for secure credential storage. Network-layer security was addressed through AWS WAF and AWS Shield, which were designed to protect against web application attacks and DDoS threats. Organizations can build a strong and scalable security posture for their AWS infrastructure by understanding and utilizing these services.

The next chapter explores the dynamic realm of real-time systems and user interfaces, focusing on AWS tools like Amplify and CloudFront. You will learn about building and deploying modern user interfaces, leveraging AWS for scalability, key concepts, integrations, and use cases. This chapter emphasizes creating responsive, secure, scalable applications, bridging the gap between real-time interactions and user-friendly design.

CHAPTER 12

Real-time Systems and User Interfaces

Introduction

The year is 2050, and *Mars* has its first fully operational autonomous colony. Hundreds of robotic rovers and drones navigate the Martian landscape, collecting geological samples, monitoring atmospheric conditions, and maintaining solar farms while communicating to Earth in near real-time. In this environment, every second counts. A delayed system update could mean failing to detect a solar storm in time, risking catastrophic damage to infrastructure. The entire operation depends on real-time event processing, ensuring that data from Mars reaches mission control on Earth instantly. At the same time, advanced user interfaces provide astronauts and engineers with actionable insights, predictive alerts, and automated countermeasures.

Real-time event processing has transitioned from a technological advantage to a cornerstone of modern digital ecosystems. This capability enables systems to process events as they occur, facilitating immediate responses vital for diverse applications. From supporting instant communication on messaging platforms to delivering live updates in online gaming and enabling feedback-driven mechanisms, real-time processing ensures systems remain responsive, adaptive, and relevant. It is no longer just a technical enhancement but an essential component for providing seamless user experiences and maintaining high-performance standards.

Similarly, **user interfaces (UIs)** extend beyond visual or interactive elements to be the pivotal link between users and a system's core functionalities. A well-crafted UI shapes user engagement, enhances task efficiency, and drives overall satisfaction. In today's digital-first world, where interactions are predominantly virtual, the need for intuitive and user-centric UIs has never been more critical. A carefully designed UI boosts usability and unlocks the system's full potential, amplifying its value to end-users.

Structure

This chapter covers the following topics:
- Introduction to real-time systems
- Developing and deploying modern user interfaces
- Scaling a Dynamic UI for live events
- Introduction to AWS Amplify
- Introduction to AWS CloudFront
- Serving static content in an internal web app

Objectives

This chapter explores how developers and architects can design and deploy real-time user interfaces using AWS serverless technologies. While deep expertise in UI development is not required, familiarity with AWS services such as API Gateway, Lambda, and event-driven architectures will help you understand key concepts and implementation strategies.

Readers will learn how to integrate real-time data updates into applications to enhance interactivity and responsiveness while leveraging AWS-managed services to eliminate infrastructure management. AWS Amplify simplifies UI development with pre-built components, authentication, and hosting, while AWS AppSync enables real-time updates through GraphQL subscriptions. Amazon CloudFront ensures fast, secure content delivery by caching assets at global edge locations, and API Gateway with WebSockets facilitates bidirectional real-time communication. AWS Lambda processes real-time events efficiently, supporting highly scalable, event-driven architectures without dedicated servers.

The chapter also introduces two deployment strategies. Static site generation with Amplify Hosting enables pre-rendered UI components while allowing real-time updates through AppSync subscriptions. Client-side rendering using Amplify libraries provides highly interactive updates, ensuring a dynamic user experience. By the end of this chapter, readers will understand how to build, deploy, and optimize real-time interfaces on AWS while implementing best practices for scalability, security, and operational efficiency in a serverless environment.

Introduction to real-time systems

Real-time event processing powers modern interactive applications, ensuring seamless communication between clients, servers, and devices. Imagine an advanced space station orbiting a distant planet. Its autonomous systems must exchange data with Earth and onboard AI assistants in real time, adjusting life support, rerouting solar energy, and detecting environmental changes instantly. A delayed response could mean catastrophic failure. Just as this space station relies on high-speed, reliable communication to function, digital applications require real-time event processing to ensure instant interactions, automated decision-making, and uninterrupted user experiences.

AWS provides several real-time communication paradigms, each designed for different scenarios:

- **Web Real-Time Communication (WebRTC)** operates like neural pathways in a human brain, allowing direct, uninterrupted communication between two points without external routing. Just as neurons rapidly transmit sensory data between different body parts, WebRTC enables peer-to-peer, low-latency video calls, live interactions, and real-time collaborative editing without a centralized server. While AWS does not provide a managed WebRTC service, implementations can be built using Amazon EC2, ECS, or EKS.

- **Server-sent events (SSE)** function like an automated weather station, continuously broadcasting one-way updates to receivers without expecting a response. Like a weather sensor that transmits real-time climate data to meteorological centers, SSE enables streaming updates for stock tickers, live sports scores, and real-time notifications. AWS services like Lambda, API Gateway, and ALB can be used to implement SSE-based architectures.

- **WebSockets** act like a high-frequency trading system, where transactions must happen instantaneously in both directions with zero delay. Just as financial markets rely on constant back-and-forth communication between traders and stock exchanges, WebSockets allow full-duplex communication, making them essential for real-time chat applications, collaborative whiteboards, and multiplayer games. AWS offers managed WebSocket support through:

  o API Gateway, which keeps persistent, bidirectional connections without infrastructure overhead.

  o AWS AppSync leverages WebSockets for GraphQL subscriptions that keep UI components updated without polling.

- **gRPC** mimics an interconnected swarm of drones, where every unit in the swarm must continuously exchange structured data to stay synchronized and respond collectively. Just as drones in a surveillance network share positional data, battery levels, and mission updates in real-time, gRPC enables efficient machine-to-machine communication for highly distributed microservices. AWS does not provide a managed gRPC service, but deployments can leverage:
  - **Application load balancer (ALB)** to route gRPC traffic over HTTP/2.
  - Amazon EC2 is used to run dedicated gRPC servers with custom configurations.
  - Amazon ECS and EKS for orchestrating scalable, containerized gRPC microservices.

By understanding these paradigms and their practical applications, developers can select the most efficient real-time communication strategy while leveraging AWS to simplify implementation, scalability, and security.

Developing and deploying modern user interfaces

Frameworks promoting modular UI construction enable developers to break interfaces into reusable components, fostering consistency and efficiency. Responsive design principles ensure seamless adaptation to various screen sizes, providing a smooth device experience.

The following provides additional context on the factors to be considered while developing modern user interfaces:

- **Importance of real-time communication**: An intuitive UI becomes even more critical in real-time applications. Users must comprehend dynamic interactions effortlessly, minimizing reliance on tutorials or support. Scalability is equally important, enabling the system to seamlessly handle sudden traffic surges or future growth. Real-time UIs depend on efficient, continuous data exchange between users and servers, demanding a robust backend. Cloud-based solutions and serverless architectures are pivotal in meeting these demands by providing flexibility, reliability, and scalability.

- **Managing the real-time challenge**: Developing the real-time communication layer of these UIs presents unique challenges. Persistent two-way connections via technologies like WebSockets must be meticulously managed to maintain reliable performance for large user bases. Misconfigurations can disrupt connections or degrade performance, causing latency or downtime. GraphQL servers, often preferred for efficient real-time data fetching, require continuous optimization to handle complex queries and ensure low latency.

  Traditional infrastructure approaches typically involve extensive manual oversight, making it difficult to scale seamlessly with fluctuating traffic. These complexities can lead to bottlenecks, reducing the effectiveness of real-time interactions.

- **Deployment challenges**: Deploying UIs using traditional server-based methods introduces additional hurdles. Manual server provisioning and management can be time-consuming and rigid, making adapting to changing traffic patterns difficult. Scaling servers to accommodate spikes in demand requires constant monitoring and intervention, often resulting in bottlenecks or degraded performance during unexpected traffic surges. These limitations make it challenging to deliver a smooth and responsive real-time user experience consistently.

Real-time IoT monitoring in smart cities

Consider a smart city dashboard that monitors real-time environmental conditions such as air quality, water levels, and energy consumption. Sensors deployed across the city continuously send updates, and the UI must instantly reflect changes. This allows city officials to take immediate action on anomalies such as hazardous air pollution or water shortages. Critical insights would be delayed without real-time synchronization, leading to inefficient responses.

AWS services address these challenges effectively. AWS IoT Core is the backbone, managing incoming sensor data and securely routing it to AWS services. WebSockets via API Gateway provide a direct channel to stream real-time updates to the dashboard. AWS AppSync with GraphQL subscriptions ensures that every sensor reading seamlessly updates the UI without requiring manual refreshes. DynamoDB Streams track real-time data changes, triggering AWS Lambda functions to process and push updates dynamically. Amazon CloudFront accelerates content delivery, ensuring smooth visualization for users across different locations. The UI is deployed with AWS Amplify, providing a scalable front-end hosting solution that can handle fluctuations in data loads efficiently.

This example highlights how AWS services enable real-time UI updates for IoT applications while addressing the core challenges of real-time data ingestion, backend synchronization, and scalability in smart city monitoring systems.

Scaling a Dynamic UI for live events

Deploying modern, real-time UIs requires infrastructure that can scale dynamically, handle high availability, and ensure low latency for optimal user experience. AWS provides a suite of services to address these needs.

The following section explores a real-world scenario: A live-streaming and event booking platform that serves thousands of concurrent users worldwide.

A global live-streaming platform must support high-traffic events such as concerts, sports games, and virtual conferences. Users must be able to purchase event tickets, watch live streams, and interact with real-time chat—all within a seamless, responsive UI. The platform must support sudden traffic surges while maintaining performance and minimizing costs.

The AWS-powered solution is as follows:

- **Frontend deployment with AWS Amplify**: The UI is built using React and hosted on AWS Amplify, which provides automatic CI/CD pipelines and a globally distributed frontend without requiring manual infrastructure management.

- **Live video streaming via Amazon CloudFront**: The video streams are delivered using Amazon CloudFront, ensuring fast, low-latency playback for global audiences by caching and distributing content through edge locations.

- **Dynamic event ticketing with AWS AppSync**: Ticket availability must update in real-time to prevent overbooking. AWS AppSync with GraphQL subscriptions allows the UI to reflect instant seat availability changes without requiring page refreshes.

- **User authentication and profiles via Amazon Cognito**: Amazon Cognito handles secure sign-ups, logins, and personalized recommendations, ensuring a seamless and scalable authentication system.

- **Handling traffic spikes with AWS Auto Scaling**: The backend APIs, hosted on AWS Fargate and API Gateway, automatically scale during high-demand ticket sales. AWS Auto Scaling ensures cost-effective resource allocation and avoids over-provisioning.

- **Data storage and analytics with DynamoDB**: User interactions, event registrations, and chat messages are stored efficiently in Amazon DynamoDB, allowing real-time analytics and trend forecasting.

The outcome of the solution is as follows:

- By leveraging AWS services, the platform handles real-time updates, low-latency streaming, and secure user interactions while dynamically scaling to meet demand. This ensures a highly available and engaging UI experience for thousands of concurrent users across the globe.

This chapter also explores how to host websites using Amazon S3, AWS Amplify, and Amazon CloudFront, providing options for integrating real-time features to enhance interactivity and user experience.

Introduction to AWS Amplify

AWS Amplify is a comprehensive toolset designed to simplify and accelerate the development and deployment of modern web applications on AWS. More than just a hosting solution, Amplify streamlines both backend and frontend development processes, enabling developers to focus on delivering exceptional user experiences.

Consider a fitness tracking application that requires real-time updates, secure authentication, scalable data storage, and a responsive UI capable of handling dynamic data inputs from multiple users. Users need to log workouts, track live heart rate data, and receive AI-driven insights—all while ensuring fast and seamless interactions. Managing this manually with traditional infrastructure would be complex, requiring significant backend configuration, API management, and security policies.

Amplify simplifies these challenges by providing a fully managed framework that integrates essential backend functionalities such as:

- **User authentication**: Amazon Cognito, integrated through Amplify, enables secure user sign-ups and login flows, offering **multi-factor authentication** (**MFA**) and social sign-ins.

- **Data storage**: Amazon DynamoDB, abstracted by Amplify's backend services, stores workout history and AI-generated insights, ensuring high availability with low-latency access.

- **Real-time data streaming**: AWS AppSync manages GraphQL subscriptions, allowing users to see live updates on workout metrics like steps, calories burned, and heart rate.

Beyond backend integration, Amplify empowers developers to create performant and visually appealing UIs. It offers pre-built UI components that adhere to modern design standards and best practices, ensuring applications remain both functional and user-friendly.

To enhance performance, Amplify integrates seamlessly with Amazon CloudFront, providing low-latency, global access to static UI assets. This is particularly beneficial for fitness tracking applications that require real-time responsiveness across multiple regions. By caching frequently accessed assets at edge locations, CloudFront minimizes load times, delivering a smooth and uninterrupted user experience.

AWS Amplify is designed to simplify every stage of the development lifecycle for modern web applications. Whether building a real-time fitness tracker, a collaborative document editor, or an e-commerce storefront, Amplify enables developers to focus on innovation rather than backend maintenance, ensuring scalability, security, and efficiency in cloud-native applications.

Core concepts in AWS Amplify

AWS Amplify empowers developers to streamline the development of modern web and mobile applications on AWS by offering an integrated toolset for both frontend and backend development. This section explores Amplify's core concepts, highlighting its feature-rich ecosystem and how it simplifies the development lifecycle:

- **UI component library**: AWS Amplify provides a comprehensive library of pre-built UI components designed to adhere to modern design principles. These components accelerate development by offering reusable building blocks that ensure consistency and align with best practices, enabling developers to create intuitive and polished user experiences efficiently.

- **Simplified backend integration**: Amplify simplifies backend integration by offering pre-built components and libraries that seamlessly connect to essential AWS services. For example, Amazon Cognito supports secure user authentication, Amazon DynamoDB provides scalable data storage, and API Gateway facilitates API management. This abstraction reduces complexity, enabling developers to focus on core functionality rather than infrastructure setup.

- **Data management with abstraction layers**: Amplify's libraries abstract interactions with data storage services, offering a consistent syntax that eliminates the need to master specific query languages. Optional offline capabilities allow applications to function seamlessly without an internet connection, ensuring reliability and accessibility in diverse scenarios.

- **GraphQL integration and real-time data**: Amplify supports automatic GraphQL schema generation based on data models, simplifying API creation. Developers can choose flexible data storage options, including DynamoDB for NoSQL databases, S3 for object storage, and Aurora for relational data. Optional real-time data updates enhance user experience by enabling dynamic interfaces that react to changes instantly.

- **Secure user authentication**: Amplify integrates with Amazon Cognito to provide secure and customizable authentication solutions. Features include user registration, login, password management, and advanced options such as MFA, social logins, and custom challenges. Fine-grained authorization is achieved through AWS IAM, offering developers precise control over user access to resources.

- **Continuous delivery and deployment**: Amplify integrates with services like AWS CodePipeline and Amazon CloudFront to facilitate continuous delivery and hosting of web applications. Automated workflows streamline the process of building, testing, and deploying applications, reducing manual effort and accelerating development cycles.

- **Amplify CLI**: The Amplify **command line interface (CLI)** simplifies the development process by enabling developers to:

  o Initialize projects, configure resources, and deploy applications to AWS infrastructure.

  o Set up backend services like authentication, data storage, and API access through an intuitive guided interface.

  o Manage local development environments with mock functionalities, allowing developers to simulate services like authentication and data storage without deploying to the cloud.

- **Amplify generational differences**: AWS Amplify has evolved to meet the needs of modern development:

  o **Generation 1 (Legacy)**: Focused on web application development with libraries for AWS service integration and UI construction. It required more manual configuration, making it less intuitive for developers accustomed to modern frameworks.

  o **Generation 2 (Current)**: Offers a unified experience for both web and mobile applications, emphasizing compatibility with modern frameworks such as React, Angular, and Vue.js. This generation introduces a more declarative, code-driven approach, streamlining the configuration process and reducing development overhead.

- **Data modeling**: Amplify includes tools to define data models that represent the application's structure, enabling code generation and serving as a central definition for data across the application. This feature accelerates development by aligning backend and frontend data layers.

- **Hosting and deployment options**: Amplify supports diverse hosting and deployment needs, including:

  o **Static site hosting**: Deploy simple websites or landing pages directly from a Git repository for fast and efficient delivery.

  o **Backend API deployment**: Host server-side logic to handle complex application needs.

  o **Custom domain support**: Enhance user experience and brand recognition by integrating custom domains for hosted applications.

Integrations using AWS Amplify

AWS Amplify seamlessly integrates with various AWS services, enabling developers to build feature-rich web and mobile applications with greater efficiency. This section provides a detailed overview of these key integrations and how they simplify application development:

- **Amazon Cognito (authentication and authorization)**: AWS Amplify integrates with Amazon Cognito to deliver secure user authentication and authorization functionalities. Cognito supports user registration, login, and password management while offering advanced features like social logins, MFA, and custom authentication challenges. Amplify enhances this integration by providing pre-built UI components, such as login and signup forms, that developers can embed directly into applications. These components streamline user management and allow seamless configuration of IAM for granular access control, ensuring secure interactions with application resources.

- **Amazon S3 (Storage)**: Amazon S3 serves as a robust storage solution for user-uploaded files, images, and static assets. Amplify simplifies interactions with S3 by offering libraries for file upload, download, deletion, and management. This integration abstracts the complexities of bucket configuration and access control, allowing developers to focus on building the core application. S3's scalability and reliability make it an ideal choice for managing static content efficiently.

- **Amazon DynamoDB (Data storage)**: For data storage, AWS Amplify integrates with Amazon DynamoDB, a fully managed NoSQL database. Amplify provides an abstraction layer that simplifies **create, read, update, delete** (CRUD) operations, eliminating the need for developers to learn DynamoDB's complex query language. By defining data models in Amplify, developers can automatically generate the required DynamoDB tables and manage data persistence with ease.

- **Amazon CloudFront (CDN)**: AWS Amplify enhances application performance through seamless integration with Amazon CloudFront. CloudFront accelerates content delivery by caching static assets and API calls at globally distributed edge locations, ensuring reduced latency and faster load times for users. Amplify automates CloudFront configuration, enabling developers to leverage its CDN capabilities effortlessly.

- **Amazon API Gateway (Backend APIs)**: AWS Amplify simplifies the creation and deployment of secure backend APIs by integrating with Amazon API Gateway. Amplify allows developers to define APIs declaratively within their application code, automatically provisioning and configuring resources in the API Gateway. This integration streamlines the process of building scalable APIs while ensuring secure communication between the front-end and back-end.

- **AWS AppSync (Data interaction)**: Amplify integrates with AWS AppSync to enable flexible data querying and real-time updates through GraphQL. Developers can define data models directly in Amplify, which generates a GraphQL schema and integrates it with AppSync. This eliminates the need for manual schema definition and simplifies the creation of GraphQL APIs, ensuring seamless data interaction and dynamic user experiences.

- **Amazon Pinpoint (User engagement)**: AWS Amplify works with Amazon Pinpoint to facilitate user engagement through targeted notifications and in-app messaging. Amplify libraries simplify the integration of Pinpoint, allowing developers to define user segments based on behavior, location, or preferences. Pinpoint enables the delivery of push notifications, SMS, and in-app messages, enhancing engagement and promoting relevant content. Additionally, clickstream analytics provide insights into user behavior and campaign effectiveness, helping refine communication strategies.

- **Amazon Kinesis Firehose (Data streaming)**: While AWS Amplify does not directly manage data streaming with Amazon Kinesis Firehose, it can integrate with it indirectly. Amplify libraries can capture relevant data points within an application, such as user interactions or sensor data, and send them to Kinesis Firehose using the AWS SDK. Kinesis Firehose then delivers the data to destinations like Amazon S3, Amazon Redshift, or Amazon OpenSearch Service, facilitating real-time analytics and data-driven decision-making.

Limits in AWS Amplify

AWS Amplify enforces service quotas to ensure performance, resource efficiency, and system stability. While these limits are designed to balance scalability and security, they can introduce challenges in real-world applications. Understanding their impact and implementing effective workarounds can help developers optimize their deployments.

The common AWS amplify limits and their real-world impact are explained as follows:

- **Apps per region (25 apps per AWS Region):**
  - ○ **Impact:** Organizations managing multiple environments (e.g., development, staging, production) or deploying numerous micro-apps may find this limit restrictive.
  - ○ **Workarounds:** Use feature branches within a single Amplify app, leverage separate AWS accounts for different environments, or request a quota increase via the AWS Service Quotas Console.

- **Branches per app (50 branches per Amplify app):**
  - ○ **Impact:** Large teams working on various features, testing, and hotfixes may approach this limit quickly.
  - ○ **Workarounds:** Archive or delete inactive branches, integrate external Git-based CI/CD workflows, or manage builds separately with AWS CodeBuild.

- **Concurrent build jobs (5 jobs at a time):**
  - ○ **Impact:** High-development velocity teams may experience build queue delays, slowing down the release cycle.
  - ○ **Workarounds:** Stagger build schedules, utilize multiple Amplify apps for modular builds, or request an increase for additional concurrency.

- **Custom domains per app (5 domains per Amplify app):**
  - ○ **Impact:** Businesses with multiple brand identities or regional versions of their applications may find this limit constraining.
  - ○ **Workarounds:** Use AWS Route 53 for domain management and URL path-based routing to serve multiple applications under a single domain.

- **API request rate limits (20,000 requests per second per region):**
  - ○ **Impact:** High-traffic applications with real-time updates, such as streaming dashboards or chat applications, may experience throttling.
  - ○ **Workarounds:** Implement caching via Amazon CloudFront, reduce API calls by optimizing request patterns, and leverage AWS AppSync for more efficient real-time data handling.

- **Build and cache artifact size limits (5GB each):**
  - ○ **Impact:** Applications with large assets or dependencies may struggle with storage constraints.
  - ○ **Workarounds:** Minimize dependencies, store static assets in Amazon S3, and optimize builds by removing unused code.

Staying updated on AWS Amplify limits

AWS regularly reviews and updates service quotas, meaning these limits may change over time. Developers should monitor the AWS Amplify Service Quotas documentation and use the AWS Service Quotas Console to track limits and request increases where applicable.

By proactively managing these constraints and leveraging AWS best practices, developers can ensure scalable, high-performing applications while staying prepared for evolving service limitations.

AWS Amplify anti-patterns

AWS Amplify is a robust framework for developing web and mobile applications, offering tools to streamline development and deployment. However, understanding Amplify's limitations and avoiding common anti-patterns is essential for building efficient and scalable solutions. Misusing Amplify can lead to performance bottlenecks, increased costs, and suboptimal architecture. The following are key anti-patterns to be aware of:

- **Using Amplify Hosting for heavy static content**: Amplify Hosting is designed for hosting lightweight applications with minimal static content. Using it to serve large-scale static assets, such as video files or high-resolution images, can strain resources and lead to higher costs. For these scenarios, combining Amazon S3 with Amazon CloudFront is a more cost-effective and performant solution, as they are optimized for large-scale static content delivery.

- **Misusing Amplify for data storage**: While Amplify provides tools for data storage, such as integration with Amazon S3 and DynamoDB, these options are best suited for lightweight or moderately complex data requirements. For applications with large-scale, highly structured data needs, using dedicated database services like Amazon RDS or DynamoDB directly ensures better performance, scalability, and query optimization.

- **Overusing Amplify for server-side rendering (SSR)**: Amplify is not inherently designed for complex SSR workflows. While it can handle basic SSR use cases, frameworks like Next.js or Gatsby are better suited for building sophisticated SSR applications. These frameworks provide greater flexibility, advanced features, and optimized performance for rendering dynamic content on the server.

- **Ignoring Amplify's limitations for large-scale applications**: Amplify excels in rapid prototyping and smaller-scale applications but may struggle to meet the needs of large-scale enterprise applications with complex workflows and high user demand. For enterprise-level solutions, a combination of AWS services, such as AWS Lambda, API Gateway, and managed databases, may provide a more scalable and robust architecture.

- **Over-reliance on Amplify for backend logic**: While Amplify simplifies backend development, relying solely on it for complex business logic can lead to inefficiencies. For intricate workflows, consider using AWS Lambda for event-driven logic, Amazon API Gateway for API management, or Step Functions for orchestrating multi-step workflows. These services provide greater flexibility and scalability for handling complex backend requirements.

Building real-time systems with AWS Amplify

This section outlines a reference architecture for building a real-time web application powered by AWS Amplify. Developers can integrate their chosen UI framework (e.g., React) with backend AWS services to build scalable, cloud-native applications. AWS Amplify simplifies the development process by offering abstractions for managing persistent connections and real-time data updates.

Real-time communication is enabled using GraphQL-based subscriptions provided by AWS AppSync. These subscriptions maintain persistent connections between the client and the backend, ensuring real-time notifications whenever the underlying data changes. Amplify libraries handle these complexities, enabling seamless integration for web and mobile applications.

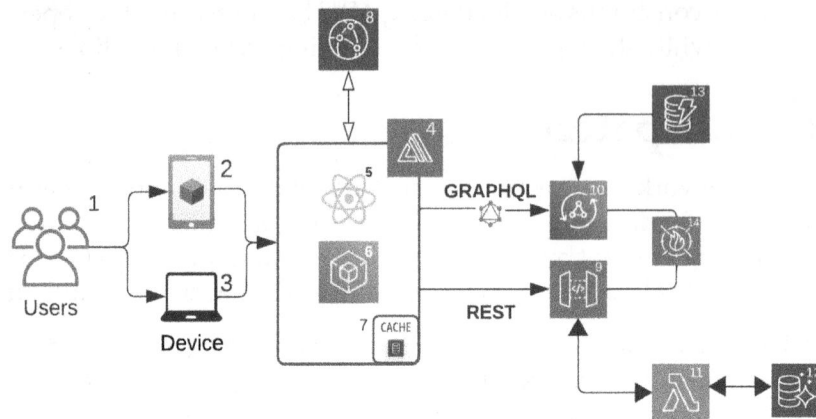

Figure 12.1: *Reference architecture for AWS Amplify with AWS AppSync*

The architecture from *Figure 12.1* demonstrates how AWS services interact to deliver real-time data to web and mobile applications, ensuring scalability, low latency, and secure content delivery. The following is a detailed explanation of the components in *Figure 12.1*:

- **Users**: End-users access the real-time web application via their browsers or mobile devices. Their interactions initiate requests for content and updates.

- **Devices**: Represents the users' devices, such as smartphones, tablets, or desktops, running the Amplify-based web or mobile application. These devices act as the interface for user interactions.

- **AWS WAF**: Provides security by applying predefined or custom rules to filter malicious traffic and prevent threats like SQL injection and DDoS attacks. WAF ensures secure communication at the edge.

- **AWS CloudFront**: Delivers web content from Amazon S3 or backend systems with low latency. It caches static assets at edge locations to optimize performance and reduce load on origin servers.

- **React web app**: The frontend of the web application is built using React and hosted in Amazon S3. The application provides a user-friendly interface and interactive functionality.

- **AWS Amplify libraries**: Simplifies integration with AWS backend services, enabling seamless authentication, data storage, and API management.

- **Offline capabilities**: Provides local caching to ensure that the application remains functional even when users experience connectivity issues.

- **AWS AppSync**: Enables real-time communication by managing GraphQL-based subscriptions. AppSync fetches data from the underlying backend systems and provides real-time notifications to all connected clients.

- **DynamoDB**: Serves as the NoSQL backend for real-time applications, storing application data in a highly scalable and durable manner.

- **API Gateway**: Manages REST API calls for additional application needs, such as retrieving non-real-time content or interacting with legacy systems.

- **AWS Lambda**: Processes API requests and retrieves data from backend systems like Amazon Aurora RDS for PostgreSQL. It provides serverless computing functionality to handle custom logic.

- **Aurora RDS**: A fully managed relational database that stores structured application data and supports complex queries required by backend systems.

- **IAM roles and policies**: Enforce secure access control across the architecture, ensuring only authorized components interact with services like AppSync, DynamoDB, and Lambda.

- **Security layer**: AWS WAF and IAM roles together ensure that the application and its data remain secure from unauthorized access or malicious threats.

Serverless and cloud-native architecture

This architecture demonstrates a fully serverless and cloud-native approach, leveraging AWS services such as Amplify, AppSync, DynamoDB, API Gateway, and Aurora RDS. These managed services allow developers to focus on building real-time application logic while AWS handles the underlying infrastructure, scaling, and security.

Scalability and flexibility

The architecture is designed to support a variety of real-time communication scenarios, including notifications, live updates, and collaborative tools. By utilizing AWS-managed services, the solution ensures scalability to handle high user traffic, flexibility to adapt to evolving business requirements, and robust security to protect sensitive data.

Introduction to AWS CloudFront

AWS CloudFront is a fully managed, serverless CDN offering from AWS. It plays a pivotal role in modern web application architectures by accelerating the delivery of static and dynamic content to users worldwide. Acting as a global digital courier, CloudFront ensures ultra-low latency and high performance, making it an indispensable component for scalable web applications.

CloudFront integrates seamlessly with numerous AWS services, enabling efficient distribution of static files and dynamic content. Its pay-as-you-go pricing model provides cost-effectiveness while ensuring the scalability to handle surges in demand.

Benefits of CloudFront's serverless architecture

One of the most significant advantages of AWS CloudFront is its serverless nature. Users do not need to manage the underlying infrastructure, such as servers, load balancers, or content distribution software. The serverless model brings several key benefits:

- **Reduced management overhead**: CloudFront automatically handles server provisioning, scaling, and maintenance, allowing developers to focus on application functionality instead of infrastructure management.

- **Cost-effectiveness**: CloudFront's pay-as-you-go pricing ensures that customers only pay for the data transferred (data egress) and requests served. There are no fixed costs or fees for unused resources, making it an economical choice for businesses of all sizes.

- **Increased scalability**: CloudFront's global edge network automatically scales to handle traffic spikes, ensuring consistent performance even during high-demand periods.

- **Faster loading times**: By caching content at edge locations geographically close to users, CloudFront reduces latency, significantly improving website performance and user experience.

Working of AWS CloudFront

Traditional web content delivery often involves multiple network hops, leading to slower response times. AWS CloudFront optimizes this process by leveraging its global edge network. The following key features are responsible for the working of CloudFront distribution:

- **Content distribution**: CloudFront caches copies of static assets such as HTML, CSS, JavaScript, images, and videos across its network of edge locations.

- **Geographic proximity**: When a user requests content, CloudFront directs the request to the nearest edge location, ensuring the shortest possible data transfer distance.

- **Enhanced speed**: This approach minimizes delays caused by long-distance data transmission, providing a seamless and responsive user experience.

- **Dynamic content handling**: In addition to static files, CloudFront can handle dynamic content by integrating with AWS services like Lambda@Edge, enabling real-time processing and customization of content closer to the user.

Key concepts in AWS CloudFront

In today's digital landscape, the speed and security of content delivery are paramount for providing an exceptional user experience. AWS CloudFront, a robust CDN from AWS, ensures that data is delivered swiftly and securely to users worldwide. As a cornerstone of serverless computing and scalable application architectures, CloudFront offers several key concepts critical to its functionality. Let us explore these concepts to understand how CloudFront enhances performance and security:

- **CDN**: At the core of AWS CloudFront lies its global network of edge locations. These edge locations cache static and dynamic content, ensuring that user requests are served from geographically proximate locations. By reducing the distance between users and content, CloudFront significantly minimizes latency, leading to faster load times and improved user satisfaction.

- **Origin**: The origin refers to the source location of your content, such as an Amazon S3 bucket, MediaPackage channel, or an HTTP server. CloudFront retrieves original content from the origin when it is not cached at an edge location, ensuring that the latest version is delivered to users.

- **Content caching**: CloudFront caches content at edge locations to serve subsequent requests more efficiently. When a user requests content, CloudFront first checks the cache at the nearest edge location. If the content is available, it is delivered instantly, reducing latency and origin server load.

- **Origin Shield**: Origin Shield is an additional layer of caching within CloudFront that further reduces the load on your origin. By centralizing content requests to a single edge location before contacting the origin, Origin Shield minimizes duplicate requests and optimizes cache efficiency.

- **Request routing**: CloudFront intelligently routes user requests to the nearest edge location using advanced algorithms that consider factors like geography and network conditions. This ensures that content is delivered quickly and reliably.

- **Behaviors**: Behaviors in CloudFront allow fine-grained control over how specific paths or URLs are handled. For example, you can define different cache settings, apply security restrictions, or configure custom headers for various content types.

- **Key groups and public keys**: To enhance content security, CloudFront supports key groups and public keys. You can create key groups containing trusted public keys and associate them with your distribution. Content is encrypted with these public keys and can only be decrypted by viewers possessing the corresponding private keys.

- **Distribution**: A CloudFront distribution is the virtual configuration container for your CDN. It defines key settings, such as the origin, behaviors, security certificates, and caching policies for your content.

- **Cache invalidation**: Cache invalidation ensures that users receive updated content when changes are made. You can manually invalidate cached content or configure automatic invalidation policies based on application requirements.

- **Restricting access with custom headers**: Custom headers allow you to control access to content in your CloudFront distribution. This is particularly useful for scenarios such as pay-per-view models or protecting sensitive data.

- **Custom SSL/TLS certificates**: CloudFront supports the use of custom SSL/TLS certificates to enable HTTPS communication between users and edge locations, ensuring secure data transfer and compliance with modern security standards.

- **Lambda@Edge functions**: AWS CloudFront integrates with Lambda@Edge, allowing developers to execute serverless functions at edge locations. This enables advanced use cases, such as content transformation, dynamic personalization, and implementing custom authentication at the edge.

- **Field-level encryption**: Field-level encryption enables granular data protection by encrypting specific fields within content objects while leaving other parts unencrypted. This ensures compliance with stringent data security requirements.

- **HTTP methods and headers**: CloudFront allows customization of HTTP methods (e.g., GET, POST) and headers, enabling tailored behavior for different use cases. This flexibility helps optimize content delivery workflows.

- **Geo restriction**: Geo restriction allows you to control access to content based on the user's geographic location. This feature is essential for adhering to regional regulations or tailoring content delivery to specific markets.

- **Geo-targeting**: CloudFront supports geo-targeting, enabling optimized content delivery to specific geographic regions. Users are routed to the nearest edge location for faster delivery and improved performance.

Integrations via AWS CloudFront

AWS CloudFront seamlessly integrates with a range of AWS services, enabling developers to enhance content delivery, improve security, and streamline operations. These integrations unlock powerful functionalities that elevate the scalability and performance of modern web applications. The following is a breakdown of key integrations that developers and content delivery professionals can leverage:

- **Amazon S3**: CloudFront integrates directly with Amazon S3 to deliver both static and dynamic content stored in S3 buckets. By offloading content delivery to CloudFront, S3 can focus on storage, while CloudFront ensures improved scalability and reduced latency. This combination is ideal for hosting websites, media assets, and application data.

- **Amazon MediaPackage**: For video content delivery, CloudFront works seamlessly with Amazon MediaPackage. MediaPackage optimizes video streams for different devices and internet speeds, while CloudFront accelerates delivery to global viewers. This integration ensures smooth, buffer-free playback, even during peak traffic periods.

- **AWS WAF**: Integrating CloudFront with AWS WAF enhances security by enabling developers to create rules that block malicious traffic, mitigate DDoS attacks, and prevent common web vulnerabilities. By deploying these rules at edge locations, CloudFront ensures threats are neutralized before reaching the origin, safeguarding content and infrastructure.

- **AWS Lambda@Edge**: AWS Lambda@Edge takes content manipulation and customization to the next level. These serverless functions execute at edge locations, enabling dynamic content transformation and user-specific experiences. Examples include:
  - Resizing images dynamically.
  - Modifying headers to implement custom authentication.
  - Delivering personalized content based on user location or preferences.

- **Amazon Kinesis**: Integrating CloudFront with Amazon Kinesis enables real-time data streaming and analysis of user requests and content delivery metrics. Developers can capture data, such as user behavior patterns and request trends, to optimize CloudFront configurations, enhance cache efficiency, and improve overall performance.

- **Amazon CloudWatch**: Amazon CloudWatch provides deep visibility into CloudFront distributions, allowing monitoring of metrics like:

  o **Cache hit rate**: Measures the efficiency of cached content delivery.

  o **Request latency**: Tracks the speed of content delivery to users.

  o **Origin fetches**: Monitors the frequency of requests sent to the origin. By identifying performance bottlenecks and usage trends, CloudWatch ensures CloudFront distributions operate at peak efficiency.

- **Amazon KMS**: CloudFront integrates with Amazon KMS to provide robust encryption for data in transit and at rest. Developers can use KMS to encrypt sensitive content stored in S3 buckets or secure data as it is delivered to viewers via HTTPS. This integration ensures compliance with stringent data security requirements.

- **Amazon Route 53**: Amazon Route 53 offers a reliable and scalable DNS solution that works seamlessly with CloudFront. Route 53 intelligently routes user requests to the nearest CloudFront edge location, optimizing content delivery and reducing latency.

Limits in AWS CloudFront

AWS CloudFront is a robust and scalable CDN, but understanding its service quotas is essential for designing efficient, cost-effective solutions. These limits define the boundaries within which CloudFront operates and ensure the system delivers optimal performance. The following is an overview of the key limits associated with CloudFront:

- **General limits**:

  o **Distributions per account**: You can create up to 200 distributions per AWS account.

  o **Alternate Domain Names (Canonical Names, which are referred to as CNAMEs)**: A single distribution supports up to 100 alternate domain names.

  o **Maximum data transfer rate**: Each distribution can handle up to 150 Gbps of data transfer.

  o **Request rate**: CloudFront supports up to 250,000 requests per second per distribution, making it highly suitable for high-traffic applications.

- **Cache behavior limits**:

  o **Cache behaviors per distribution**: Each distribution can define up to 25 cache behaviors. Cache behaviors allow you to customize how specific content is cached, routed, and served.

  o **Custom cache policies**: You can create up to 20 custom cache policies per account, with each policy supporting up to 10 query strings, headers, and cookies.

- **Origin and connection limits**:

  o **Origins per distribution**: Each distribution supports up to 25 origins. This enables content delivery from multiple sources, such as Amazon S3 buckets, HTTP servers, and MediaPackage channels.

  o **Connection timeout**: The connection timeout for each origin can range from 1 to 10 seconds, ensuring timely responses from the origin server.

- o **Keep-alive timeout**: CloudFront maintains a maximum keep-alive timeout of 20 seconds per origin to optimize persistent connections.

- **Invalidation limits**:

  - o **Invalidation requests**: You can submit up to 1,000 invalidation requests per distribution each month without incurring additional charges.

  - o **Paths per invalidation request**: Each invalidation request can include up to 3,000 paths, allowing for efficient cache updates across multiple objects.

- **Lambda@Edge limits**:

  - o **Functions per account**: Each AWS account can create up to 100 Lambda@Edge functions.

  - o **Maximum function size**: Lambda@Edge functions are limited to 1 MB of compressed code.

  - o **Execution timeout**: Each function can execute for a maximum of 5 seconds.

- **WebSocket limits**:

  - o **Concurrent WebSocket connections**: CloudFront supports up to 1,000,000 concurrent WebSocket connections per distribution, enabling scalable real-time communication.

  - o **Connection duration**: Each WebSocket connection can remain active for up to 2 hours.

- **Data transfer and cache size limits**:

  - o **Data transfer limits**: While there is no fixed cap on data transfer, the total volume is subject to billing tiers and pricing models.

  - o **Cache size**: Implicitly determined by the popularity of the cached content and the selected pricing plan.

- **Geo-restriction and price class limits**:

  - o **Geo-restriction**: Content delivery can be restricted based on geographic regions to comply with regulatory requirements or licensing agreements.

  - o **Price class**: CloudFront offers three pricing classes, low, medium, and high. The selected price class impacts both performance and costs, as it determines the number of edge locations available for content delivery.

AWS CloudFront anti-patterns

AWS CloudFront is a powerful CDN that enhances the speed and security of content delivery. However, misusing CloudFront can lead to inefficiencies, increased costs, or suboptimal application performance. The following are common anti-patterns to avoid:

- **Using CloudFront for dynamic content**: CloudFront is optimized for delivering static content like HTML, CSS, JavaScript, images, and videos. While it can support dynamic content with caching strategies or Lambda@Edge integration, relying on CloudFront for highly dynamic, compute-intensive operations is inefficient. Services such as AWS API Gateway or Lambda@Edge are better suited for handling dynamic content delivery.

- **Over-reliance on CloudFront for origin shielding**: CloudFront's Origin Shield helps reduce the load on origin servers by centralizing content requests. However, this is not a substitute for implementing robust security at the origin. Ensure origin servers are protected using AWS WAF for malicious traffic filtering, secure IAM configurations, and properly managed network access controls.

- **Ignoring cache invalidation**: Failing to invalidate cached content properly can result in outdated data being served to users, especially during frequent updates or deployments. Implement automated cache invalidation processes to ensure users always receive the most up-to-date content while minimizing manual intervention.

- **Misusing CloudFront for application logic**: CloudFront is designed for content delivery, not executing application logic. Using it for complex computations or heavy data processing creates inefficiencies. Lightweight logic, such as header manipulation or request modification, can be handled by Lambda@Edge. For resource-intensive operations, origin servers or backend services like AWS Lambda are more appropriate.

- **Ignoring regional edge caches**: Regional edge caches act as intermediate layers between CloudFront's global edge locations and origin servers. Not leveraging these caches can increase the origin server load and latency, reducing performance. Enable regional edge caches to optimize request handling and improve content delivery efficiency.

- **Using CloudFront for long-running operations**: CloudFront is not suitable for handling long-running operations such as workflows or background processing. Tasks requiring extended execution times are better managed with AWS services like Lambda or Step Functions, which are purpose-built for these workloads.

Serving static content with AWS CloudFront

This section outlines a reference architecture for hosting and delivering static websites using AWS S3 and Amazon CloudFront. The content of the website is securely stored in an S3 bucket, while CloudFront ensures efficient global delivery with ultra-low latency. The **Origin Access Identity** (**OAI**) feature of CloudFront protects the S3 bucket by preventing direct external access, ensuring that content is securely distributed.

In addition to static content delivery, the architecture supports dynamic content retrieval from backend systems, including cloud-based and on-premises databases. This hybrid approach combines static hosting with dynamic data generation, leveraging services like API Gateway, AWS Lambda, and Amazon Aurora RDS.

The architecture depicted in *Figure 12.2* illustrates the interaction between various AWS services and components involved in serving static and dynamic content:

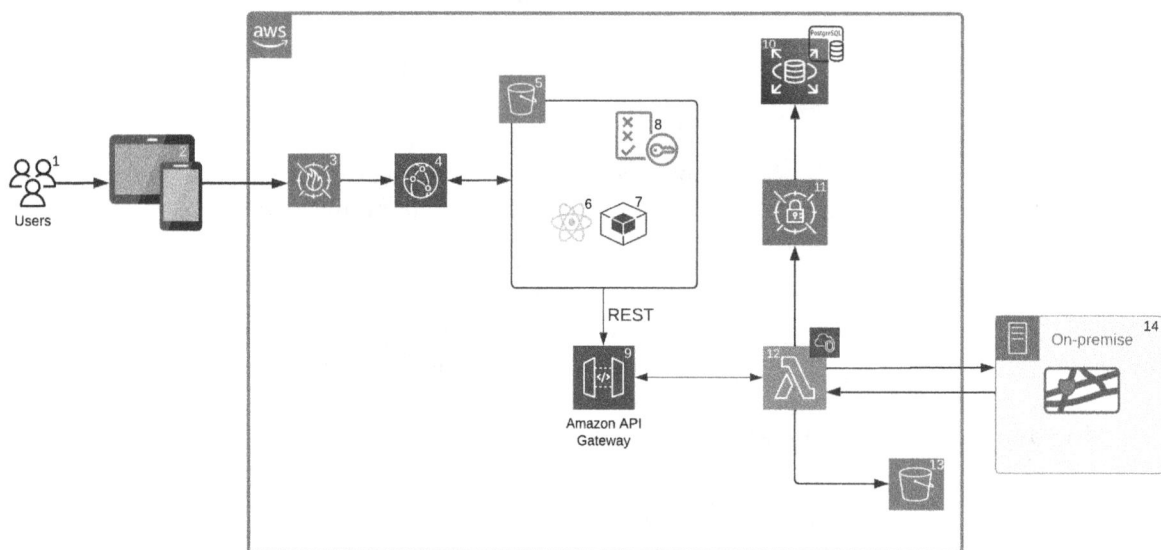

Figure 12.2: *Reference architecture for AWS CloudFront with S3 Static Hosting*

The following is an explanation of each numbered component:

- **Users**: The end-users who access the website using their devices, such as laptops, smartphones, or tablets. Their requests initiate the workflow by navigating to the website or interacting with its features.

- **Devices**: Represents the user's devices, which send requests through a web browser or application to access the website content. These devices act as the interface between users and the system.

- **AWS WAF**: Provides security at the edge by applying predefined or custom rule sets to filter malicious traffic and protect against threats such as SQL injection and DDoS attacks. WAF ensures that only legitimate requests are forwarded to CloudFront.

- **CloudFront**: A CDN that retrieves static content from Amazon S3 and serves it to users with low latency. It caches the content at edge locations, ensuring fast delivery while reducing the load on the origin servers.

- **S3 bucket holding static content and Amplify artifacts**: The primary storage location for static website files, such as HTML, CSS, and JavaScript, as well as Amplify artifacts. The bucket is configured to be private and accessed only via CloudFront using OAI for enhanced security.

- **React web app**: The frontend of the website is developed using React and hosted in the S3 bucket. The web app provides the user interface and functionality for interacting with the application.

- **AWS JavaScript SDK**: A library included in the React web app that facilitates seamless integration with AWS services. It provides abstractions for tasks such as data retrieval, API calls, and managing AWS resources from the frontend.

- **IAM roles and policies**: Enforce security and permissions throughout the architecture. IAM roles are assigned to resources like Lambda and API Gateway, ensuring controlled access to databases, storage, and other AWS services.

- **API Gateway**: Acts as the frontend for dynamic content requests. It receives API calls from the React web app and routes them to the appropriate backend services, such as Lambda or other AWS resources.

- **Amazon RDS for PostgreSQL**: A managed relational database that stores dynamic application data. It serves as the backend for the web application's dynamic content and is accessed securely by Lambda functions.

- **AWS Secrets Manager**: Ensures the secure storage and management of sensitive information, such as database credentials and API keys. Secrets Manager allows Lambda functions to access these secrets securely, avoiding hardcoding sensitive data.

- **Lambda**: A serverless compute service used for processing API requests and retrieving data from Amazon RDS or other backend systems. In this architecture, Lambda is deployed within a VPC to ensure secure connectivity to the RDS instance

Serving static content in an internal web app

This section describes a reference architecture for hosting internal-only websites that are restricted to users within an organization's secure network. The architecture leverages AWS services to provide secure, scalable, and low-latency access to content, ensuring compliance with internal regulations that prohibit hosting or managing data outside the organization's private network.

The solution uses AWS Direct Connect to establish a private connection between the organization and AWS, ensuring traffic remains within the secure network. This architecture is ideal for internal portals, dashboards, or content management systems where access is strictly limited to intranet users.

See *Figure 12.3* for detailed architecture:

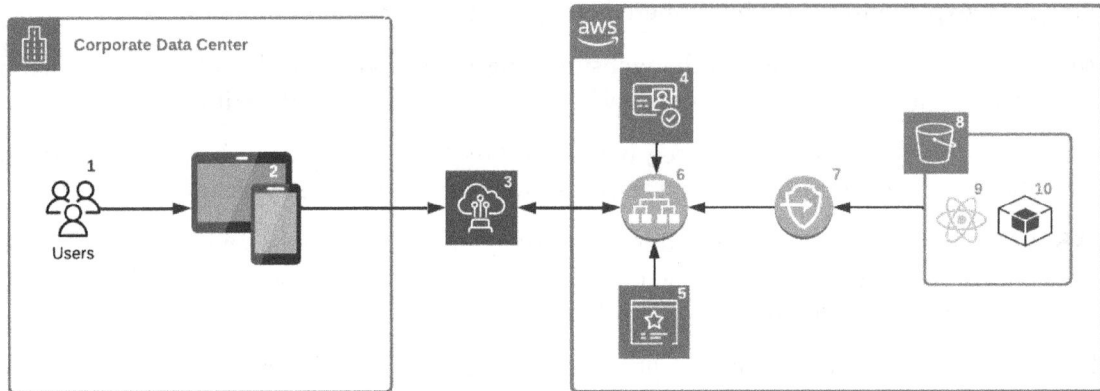

Figure 12.3: Reference architecture for hosting internal sites using ALB

The components and workflow are as follows:

1. **Users**: Employees or authorized personnel access the internal website using browsers or devices connected to the organization's intranet. Their requests initiate the workflow within the secure network.

2. **Device browsers**: The browsers or devices used to request access to the internal web app. These devices operate within the organization's secure network.

3. **AWS Direct Connect**: Provides a dedicated, private connection between the organization's network and AWS. This private link ensures that data never traverses the public internet, reducing latency and enhancing security by minimizing the attack surface.

4. **Amazon Cognito**: Handles user authentication by enabling secure login, multi-factor authentication, and role-based access control for internal users.

5. **AWS Certificate Manager (ACM)**: Manages SSL/TLS certificates for secure communication. ACM ensures that all traffic between users and the internal web app is encrypted.

6. **ALB**: Distributes incoming user requests across backend resources. The ALB is deployed as an internal-only resource within the organization's VPC, ensuring it is inaccessible from the public internet.

7. **VPC Private Endpoint for S3**: Connects the internal ALB with the S3 bucket storing the website content. The private endpoint ensures that S3 content is accessible only within the organization's VPC and not exposed to the public internet.

8. **Amazon S3**: Hosts the static website files, such as HTML, CSS, and JavaScript. The S3 bucket is configured with fine-grained access control, ensuring content is available only via the VPC private endpoint.

The flow logic is explained as follows:

1. Users initiate requests to access the internal website using browsers or devices connected to the intranet (Points 1 and 2).

2. Traffic from the users is routed through the secure private connection established by AWS Direct Connect (Point 3), bypassing the public internet entirely.

3. Amazon Cognito (Point 4) authenticates users, ensuring only authorized personnel gain access.

4. The ALB (Point 6), configured as an internal VPC resource, routes the authenticated requests.

5. The ALB retrieves static content from Amazon S3 (Point 8) via the VPC private endpoint for S3 (Point

7), ensuring data remains within the secure network.

6. SSL/TLS encryption provided by ACM (Point 5) ensures secure communication between all components.

The key benefits of the architecture are as follows:

- **Enhanced security**: By leveraging AWS Direct Connect, traffic is contained within the private network, reducing exposure to external threats.

- **Compliance with internal policies**: The architecture ensures content is hosted and accessed within the organization's secure network, adhering to regulatory requirements.

- **Low latency**: Direct Connect minimizes latency by providing a high-speed, dedicated link between the organization and AWS.

- **Scalability**: Amazon S3 and the Application Load Balancer ensure scalability to handle varying levels of traffic without compromising performance.

This architecture serves as a robust framework for hosting secure, internal-only websites, ensuring a seamless, compliant, and efficient user experience.

Conclusion

This chapter provided a comprehensive guide to building real-time web applications using serverless and cloud-native technologies. It explored the fundamentals of real-time systems and user interfaces, emphasizing the importance of delivering responsive and engaging experiences. AWS Amplify and AWS CloudFront emerged as key enablers, simplifying serverless UI deployment while optimizing content delivery through global caching and acceleration. The discussion also highlighted practical use cases, including hosting static websites with S3 and CloudFront and deploying internal real-time applications, demonstrating how AWS services enhance performance, security, and scalability.

As technology advances, real-time systems will continue evolving with trends such as edge computing, AI-powered interfaces, and 5G connectivity. These innovations will push computation closer to users, reducing latency and enabling dynamic, adaptive UI experiences. Developers must design architectures that embrace scalability and cost efficiency while maintaining resilience in distributed environments. Leveraging AWS's serverless offerings allows developers to offload infrastructure management while ensuring high availability and secure data flow. Implementing caching strategies, asynchronous processing, and real-time monitoring will further optimize system performance, balancing responsiveness with long-term sustainability.

The next chapter shifts focus to big data, exploring AWS tools for large-scale data processing and analytics. Developers will learn how services like Amazon EMR, Amazon Redshift, and the Amazon Kinesis family

Join our Discord space

Join our Discord workspace for latest updates, offers, tech happenings around the world, new releases, and sessions with the authors:

https://discord.bpbonline.com

CHAPTER 13
Big Data and Streaming

Introduction

Big Data refers to the massive, complex datasets generated at high velocity from diverse sources such as IoT devices, social media platforms, financial transactions, and machine logs. These datasets are characterized by the three Vs, volume, variety, and velocity, making them challenging to store, process, and analyze using traditional architectures. As organizations strive to extract meaningful insights from this data, they face scalability, cost, and real-time processing challenges.

AWS offers the most comprehensive and high-performance suite of big data services, enabling businesses to build scalable, cost-effective pipelines capable of handling hundreds of terabytes daily. With seamless integration across storage, processing, and analytics services, AWS simplifies big data management across structured, semi-structured, and unstructured data formats. Enterprises can eliminate infrastructure overhead by leveraging serverless and fully managed solutions while ensuring high availability, security, and real-time analytics capabilities. This flexibility makes AWS a preferred choice for organizations seeking to drive large-scale internet analytics, machine learning workloads, and real-time decision-making.

This chapter explores how AWS Serverless technologies can be leveraged to construct end-to-end big data architectures. It covers essential storage solutions, data ingestion pipelines, real-time stream processing, scalable analytics, and best practices for managing serverless big data applications.

Structure

The chapter covers the following topics:
- Introduction to big data
- Big data processing challenges and approaches
- Essential services for storing big data
- Essential services for processing big data
- Essential services for streaming big data
- Introduction to Amazon OpenSearch Serverless

Objectives

This chapter provides a comprehensive guide to handling big data in a serverless architecture on AWS, covering storage, processing, streaming, and analytics. Readers will explore the fundamental characteristics of big data and its role in modern cloud-native applications.

The chapter introduces AWS storage solutions, including Amazon S3 for scalable object storage and DynamoDB for NoSQL workloads, ensuring efficient data management. It then looks into serverless big data processing, featuring AWS Glue for ETL workloads, Amazon EMR for distributed data processing, and Amazon Redshift for data warehousing and analytics.

For real-time data streaming, readers will gain insights into Amazon Kinesis services, including Kinesis Data Streams and Firehose, to enable high-throughput ingestion and low-latency processing. Additionally, the chapter covers Amazon OpenSearch for real-time search and analytics and Kinesis Data Analytics for transforming streaming data into actionable insights.

By the end of this chapter, readers will be equipped to architect scalable, serverless big data pipelines on AWS, making informed decisions about storage, processing, and analytics tools to extract meaningful insights from both batch and real-time data streams.

Introduction to big data

Big data refers to the vast and continuously growing datasets generated from diverse sources such as IoT devices, social media, financial transactions, and machine logs.

For example, platforms like Twitter process millions of real-time messages per second, requiring scalable streaming architectures to analyze sentiment, detect trends, and filter spam in real time.

These datasets are defined by three core characteristics, commonly known as the 3Vs of big data:

- **Volume**: The sheer quantity of data generated daily, ranging from terabytes to exabytes, makes traditional storage solutions inadequate.

- **Variety**: The diverse formats of data, including **structured** (databases, spreadsheets), **semi-structured** (JSON, XML, logs), and **unstructured** (videos, images, free-text documents).

- **Velocity**: The speed at which data is produced and must be processed, from real-time event streams to high-frequency transactional data.

The following sections will explore how AWS services can be leveraged to build high-performance big data architectures, from storage and batch processing to real-time analytics and machine learning applications.

Big data processing challenges and approaches

Processing big data efficiently requires balancing speed, scalability, and cost-effectiveness. Depending on the workload, organizations must choose between batch processing for large-scale analytics and real-time processing for immediate insights. Each approach presents unique challenges, requiring specialized solutions to efficiently handle large volumes of diverse data.

Challenges in processing big data

Traditional data processing systems struggle with modern big data workloads due to the following challenges:

- **Massive data volumes**: Datasets often scale from petabytes to exabytes, requiring distributed computing frameworks for parallel processing.

- **Unstructured and semi-structured data**: Traditional relational databases cannot efficiently process logs, sensor data, or multimedia content.

- **Low-latency processing needs**: Some applications, such as fraud detection and monitoring, require sub-second response times.

- **Scalability and cost efficiency**: Managing on-premises data clusters is resource-intensive, leading to high operational costs and infrastructure complexity.

Batch vs. real-time processing

Big data processing typically falls into two categories: batch processing and real-time processing. Each method serves different business needs and requires different AWS services.

The following table shows how different AWS services can be leveraged for different processing types:

Processing type	Best use cases	Key characteristics	AWS services
Batch processing	Data warehousing, periodic analytics, log processing	Processing large datasets over minutes to hours	Amazon EMR, AWS Glue, Amazon Redshift
Real-time processing	Fraud detection, IoT sensor data streaming, market analysis	Processes continuous data streaming with sub-second latency. Time series data ingestion could be a feature.	Amazon Kinesis, Apache Flink, and AWS Lambda

Table 13.1: Table showing batch and real-time processing comparison

AWS services for scalable big data processing

To address these challenges, AWS provides cloud-native processing solutions that integrate batch and real-time workloads with minimal infrastructure management.

The following are the core solutions and services:

- **Storage solutions**: Storage services like Amazon S3 and DynamoDB provide scalable, high-availability data lakes and structured data storage.

- **Batch processing solutions**: Amazon EMR, AWS Glue, and Amazon Redshift provide distributed computing, ETL, and scalable data warehousing.

- **Real-time processing solutions**: Amazon Kinesis, Apache Flink, and AWS Lambda enable real-time, event-driven workloads with automatic scaling.

- **Hybrid processing**: Some workloads require a mix of batch and real-time processing (e.g., processing real-time IoT data while storing aggregated results for analytics in Redshift).

The following sections will explore how AWS storage, processing, and streaming services can be used to build an end-to-end big data architecture.

Essential services for storing big data

The exponential growth of data in today's digital landscape demands scalable and efficient storage solutions. AWS provides a suite of cloud-native storage services designed to meet the challenges of high-volume, high-velocity, and diverse data formats, ensuring reliability, flexibility, and cost-effectiveness.

The following AWS storage services form the backbone of a scalable big data infrastructure.

Amazon S3 for scalable object storage

Amazon **Simple Storage Service** (**S3**) is the primary storage solution for big data workloads. It offers unlimited capacity, high durability, and multiple storage classes to optimize costs.

The following are the key features for S3.

- **Data lake foundation**: Stores raw, structured, and unstructured data for analytics.
- **Lifecycle management**: Automatically moves data to lower-cost storage tiers.
- **Scalability and durability**: Designed for 99.999999999% durability (11 nines).

Example use case: IoT and Log Data Storage: Organizations collect petabytes of raw logs and sensor data in S3 for later analysis using services like Athena, EMR, or OpenSearch.

Amazon DynamoDB for NoSQL workloads

Amazon DynamoDB is a fully managed serverless NoSQL database optimized for real-time applications requiring low latency and high throughput.

The following are the key features of Amazon DynamoDB.

- Schema-less design supports semi-structured and unstructured data.
- Auto-scaling dynamically adjusts to traffic spikes.
- Integrated caching via **DynamoDB Accelerator** (**DAX**) for ultra-fast access.

Example use case: E-commerce and real-time analytics: Retailers process millions of customer transactions per second and store them in DynamoDB for instant lookup and recommendation systems.

Key differences between S3 and DynamoDB

The following table provides the key differences between S3 and DynamoDB:

Feature	Amazon S3 (Object storage)	Amazon DynamoDB (NoSQL database)
Data type	Unstructured and semi-structured data	Key-value and document-based data
Best use cases	Data lakes, backup, and static content	Real-time analytics, caching, transactions
Latency	Higher (milliseconds to seconds)	Low latency (single-digit milliseconds)
Scalability	Virtually unlimited	Scales with workload demand
Cost model	Pay-per-storage and requests	Pay-per-read/write or provisioned capacity

Table 13.2: Table showing Amazon S3 and Amazon DynamoDB differences

Choosing the right service

The following list helps identify core services for common processing paradigms:

- Use Amazon S3 for static files, backups, and large datasets that do not require low-latency access.
- Use DynamoDB when real-time performance and millisecond response times are required, such as in web, gaming, or IoT applications.

- Many AWS architectures combine both—storing historical data in S3 while using DynamoDB for high-speed transactional lookups.

Amazon EBS for high-performance storage

Amazon **Elastic Block Store** (**EBS**) provides persistent, high-performance block storage for compute-intensive workloads running on Amazon EC2.

The following are the key features of Amazon EBS:

- Optimized for databases and analytics workloads requiring frequent read/write operations.
- Supports encryption and snapshots for secure backup and disaster recovery.
- Configurable IOPS for **high-performance computing** (**HPC**) use cases.

Example use case:

Data warehousing with Amazon Redshift: Organizations run high-performance ETL operations on structured datasets using EBS-backed EC2 instances.

Amazon S3 Glacier for data archiving

Amazon S3 Glacier and S3 Glacier Deep Archive offer ultra-low-cost storage for long-term data retention and compliance needs.

The following are the key features of S3 Glacier:

- Cost-effective archival storage with retrieval options (Expedited, Standard, Bulk).
- Seamless integration with Amazon S3 for automatic data Tiering.
- Immutable backups for compliance-heavy industries (e.g., finance, healthcare).

Example use case:

Regulatory compliance: Financial institutions store customer transaction logs for seven or more years using S3 Glacier Deep Archive, ensuring regulatory compliance at minimal cost.

Essential services for processing big data

Once data is stored efficiently, it is processed to extract meaningful insights. AWS provides several scalable and cost-effective solutions to handle large-scale data processing, each optimized for different workload types, whether batch processing for high-volume analytics or real-time streaming for continuous event-driven insights.

Batch processing is best suited for structured analysis, running large-scale transformations at scheduled intervals. In contrast, real-time processing is essential for workloads requiring low-latency, high-frequency data ingestion, such as fraud detection or IoT analytics.

To choose the right AWS service for processing big data, it is important to distinguish between batch processing and real-time streaming analytics based on latency, data volume, and computational requirements.

The following table provides an insight into how to choose the right services for the processing type:

Processing type	Best for	AWS services
Batch processing	Large-scale ETL jobs, data warehousing, periodic reports	EMR, Glue, Redshift, Athena
Real-time streaming	Continuous event-driven data processing, low-latency analytics	Kinesis, MSK, Lambda

Table 13.3: AWS service choice for processing type

Batch processing services

Batch processing handles large-scale datasets that do not require immediate analysis. These workloads process data at scheduled intervals or in large chunks, ensuring efficient use of computing resources:

- **Amazon Elastic MapReduce (EMR)**: A managed Hadoop and Spark framework, allowing organizations to run large-scale data transformations in parallel using Python, Scala, and SQL-based tools like Hive and Presto.

- **AWS Glue**: A serverless ETL service that automates data preparation and schema transformations. Ideal for processing raw data before analytics.

- **Amazon Redshift**: A fully managed, SQL-based data warehouse optimized for querying exabyte-scale datasets efficiently. Best suited for **business intelligence** (**BI**), reporting, and historical data analysis.

- **Amazon Athena**: A serverless, on-demand query engine that enables analysts to run SQL queries directly on Amazon S3 data lakes without provisioning infrastructure.

Example use case: A retail company runs nightly batch jobs using Amazon EMR to process large customer purchase datasets and stores structured results in Amazon Redshift for daily business reports.

Real-time streaming and analytical services

Real-time processing is designed for applications that ingest and analyze data streams with minimal latency. These services allow organizations to process and respond to data as it is generated:

- **Amazon Kinesis**: AWS's real-time data streaming platform, consisting of:
    - **Kinesis Data Streams**: Captures high-speed streaming data for processing within milliseconds.
    - **Kinesis Firehose**: Delivers real-time streaming data to AWS destinations like S3, Redshift, and OpenSearch.
    - **Kinesis Data Analytics**: Allows users to run SQL queries on streaming data in real time.

- **Amazon Managed Streaming for Apache Kafka (MSK)**: A fully managed Kafka service optimized for ultra-low latency, high-throughput event streaming. Ideal for real-time fraud detection, anomaly detection, and financial transactions.

- **AWS Lambda**: A serverless compute service that triggers processing workflows based on real-time events, commonly used for log processing, image transformations, and streaming enrichments.

Example use case: A financial services company uses MSK to stream fraud detection logs, process them using AWS Lambda, and trigger real-time alerts when anomalies are detected.

The following table provides a general guideline that helps in choosing the right services based on the processing needs:

Use case	Recommended AWS service
Batch processing (ETL, ML training)	Amazon EMR, AWS Glue
SQL-based data warehousing	Amazon Redshift
Ad-hoc queries on S3 Data	Amazon Athena
Event-driven data processing	AWS Lambda
Real-time stream processing	Amazon Kinesis, MSK

Table 13.4: Table showing use case and AWS service mapping

The following sections provide a detailed breakdown of each AWS service, highlighting their capabilities, best use cases, and how they fit into batch and real-time processing workflows.

Amazon EMR for distributed data processing

Amazon EMR is a fully managed service that simplifies the execution of large-scale distributed computing frameworks like Apache Hadoop, Apache Spark, Presto, and HBase. It enables organizations to process, analyze, and transform petabyte-scale datasets without managing infrastructure complexities.

EMR cluster architecture and task execution

An EMR cluster consists of three types of nodes:

Node type	Function
Primary node	Managers Cluster orchestration, job scheduling, and resource allocation.
Core nodes	Execute processing tasks and store intermediate data using HDFS or Amazon S3
Task nodes	It handles additional computational workloads but does not store data.

Table 13.5: Table showing EMR node type and intended function

EMR supports multiple resource managers, depending on the workload:

- **Yet Another Resource Negotiator** (**YARN**) for Hadoop and Spark-based processing.
- Kubernetes for containerized big data applications.
- Mesos for multi-cluster scheduling and flexible resource management.

Task execution is handled through:

- Spark **Directed Acyclic Graphs** (**DAGs**) for optimized parallel processing.
- MapReduce Jobs for large-scale batch transformations.
- Presto Queries for distributed, low-latency SQL-based analytics.

This automated task distribution allows organizations to scale efficiently while optimizing performance for batch processing, machine learning pipelines, and real-time analytics workflows.

Simplified processing and analytics usability

Amazon EMR abstracts the complexity of big data processing by providing pre-configured frameworks, auto-scaling, and managed cluster tuning. Analysts and engineers can leverage familiar programming languages like SQL, Python (PySpark), Scala (Spark), and Java (MapReduce) to run computations efficiently.

EMR integrates seamlessly with AWS services like Amazon S3 (data lakes), AWS Glue (schema discovery), Redshift (data warehouses), and OpenSearch (search analytics), ensuring compatibility with a variety of big data use cases.

For interactive data exploration, EMR Studio and EMR Notebooks offer a Jupyter-based development experience, allowing data scientists to perform ad-hoc queries, visualize datasets, and develop machine learning models directly within EMR.

The key features of Amazon EMR are as follows:

- **Auto-scaling clusters**: Automatically adjusts compute resources based on workload demand.
- **Multi-framework support**: Runs Apache Hadoop, Spark, Presto, and HBase, offering flexible processing options.
- **Seamless AWS Integration**: Connects with Amazon S3 (data lakes), DynamoDB (structured storage), Redshift (data warehouses), and OpenSearch (search analytics).
- **Cost optimization**: Supports Spot and Reserved Instances for reducing costs in batch processing.
- **EMR notebooks**: Provides an interactive Jupyter-based notebook environment for data scientists using Spark.

Amazon EMR is used for a wide range of big data processing applications, including:

- **Large-scale log analysis**
  - A telecom company processes billions of network logs daily to detect performance bottlenecks.
  - EMR runs Apache Spark to aggregate, cleanse, and analyze log data stored in Amazon S3.
- **Machine learning on big data**
  - A healthcare AI company uses Apache Spark on EMR to train ML models on genomic sequencing data.
  - Processed results are stored in Amazon Redshift for researchers to access in real time.
- **Clickstream data processing**
  - An e-commerce company processes millions of user interactions per hour to optimize product recommendations.
  - Apache Presto on EMR queries structured and semi-structured data across S3 and DynamoDB.
- **Financial risk analysis**
  - A bank analyzes historical stock market trends using Apache Hadoop on EMR.
  - The system ingests raw financial data from Kinesis, aggregates it in EMR, and stores insights in Amazon Redshift for reporting.

Cost optimizations in Amazon EMR

The following strategies help in optimizing costs in EMR:

- **Spot instances**: Leverage discounted EC2 instances for non-critical workloads.
- **Cluster auto-scaling**: Dynamically adjust node count to prevent over-provisioning.
- **AWS savings plans**: Reduce costs for long-running workloads with reserved compute pricing.
- **EMR serverless**: Removes Cluster management overhead.

AWS Glue for serverless data preparation

AWS Glue is a fully managed ETL service that automates data preparation for analytics and machine learning.

The key features are as follows:

- **Automated schema discovery**: Detects data structures in S3, Redshift, DynamoDB, and RDS.
- **Serverless architecture**: No need to provision or manage infrastructure.
- **Built-in Apache Spark Engine**: Executes ETL jobs efficiently.
- **Data catalog**: A centralized metadata repository for discovering and managing data sources.

Example use case:

Retail data aggregation: AWS Glue merges customer transactions, CRM data, and web interactions into a structured dataset for real-time business intelligence in Amazon Redshift.

Amazon Redshift for data warehousing

Amazon Redshift is a managed cloud data warehouse for complex analytical queries on structured data.

The key features are as follows:

- **Massively Parallel Processing (MPP)**: Distributes queries across multiple nodes for fast execution.
- **Columnar storage and compression**: Optimized for high-performance SQL analytics.
- **Federated query support**: Can query data across S3, DynamoDB, and relational databases.
- **Auto-scaling clusters**: Dynamically resizes based on workload.

Example use case is as follows:

- **Marketing analytics**: An advertising firm aggregates customer engagement data across social media platforms, storing structured reports in Redshift for real-time campaign performance tracking.

Amazon Athena for ad-hoc querying

Amazon Athena enables users to run SQL queries directly on S3 without provisioning infrastructure.

The key features are as follows:

- **Serverless query execution**: No cluster management is required.
- **Pay-per-query pricing**: Costs are based on the amount of data scanned.
- **Supports open data formats**: Works with Parquet, ORC, JSON, and Avro.

Example use case is as follows:

- **Healthcare research**: A bIoTech company analyzes patient genome sequences stored in S3 using Athena SQL queries to identify mutation patterns in genetic disorders.

Choosing the right processing service

The following table will help choose the right processing service for the use case:

Service	Best use case	Key benefits
Amazon EMR	Large-scale distributed computing, Spark, and Hadoop analysis	Scalable clusters, integrates with S3, Glue, and DynamoDB
AWS Glue	ETL, data cleansing, schema transformation	Serverless, automated schema discovery, seamless integration with Redshift
Amazon Redshift	Data warehousing, BI reporting, advanced SQL analytics	High-performance queries, MPP, columnar storage
Amazon Athena	Ad-hoc SQL queries on S3, cost-efficient analytics	Serverless, no cluster management, pay-per-query pricing

Table 13.6: Table showing AWS service, use case, and benefit mapping

Essential services for streaming big data

Big data is no longer confined to static datasets; the modern data landscape encompasses real-time streaming, where data flows continuously from sources like social media, IoT devices, and application logs. Traditional batch processing struggles to keep pace with this dynamic flow. Still, AWS offers a robust suite of services tailored for big data streaming and real-time analytics, often leveraging serverless architectures.

Big data streaming challenges

Handling real-time streaming data presents several challenges:

- **High throughput needs**: Managing **millions of events per second** from IoT sensors, stock market feeds, or security logs.
- **Low latency requirements**: Processing data in **sub-second timeframes** for **real-time fraud detection, monitoring, and alerts.**
- **Data order and consistency**: Ensuring **event sequencing** and accuracy across multiple shards.
- **Scalability and fault tolerance**: **Auto-scaling to handle peak traffic** and ensuring event durability against failures.

AWS provides fully managed streaming solutions that simplify real-time ingestion, transformation, and analytics.

AWS empowers organizations to manage and analyze real-time data streams efficiently, transforming raw streams into actionable insights and enabling data-driven decision-making in near real-time.

Amazon Kinesis family

The growing complexity of big data demands solutions capable of handling continuous, real-time streams of information. Traditional batch processing methods often fall short when faced with the relentless influx of data from sources such as social media, IoT devices, and application logs. The Amazon Kinesis family addresses this challenge with a suite of services designed to capture, process, and analyze streaming data efficiently. This section explores the key components of the Kinesis family, focusing on their functionalities and how they contribute to robust real-time data pipelines.

Overview of the Kinesis family

Amazon Kinesis serves as an umbrella term for AWS's real-time data streaming services. While Kinesis itself does not directly process data, it provides the framework and essential capabilities for constructing real-time data pipelines. Key services within the Kinesis family include Kinesis Data Streams and Kinesis Firehose, each designed for specific use cases in big data streaming.

The core concepts in Kinesis are as follows:

- **Data streams**: At the heart of Kinesis lies the concept of data streams—ordered sequences of data records flowing continuously from producers to consumers. These streams enable real-time data movement for further processing.

- **Sharding**: To support scalability and fault tolerance, Kinesis splits data streams into horizontal partitions called shards. Each shard handles a portion of the data, enabling parallel processing and scaling to accommodate growing workloads.

- **Serverless integration**: While Kinesis is not inherently serverless, it integrates seamlessly with serverless services like AWS Lambda, enabling event-driven stream processing.

The functionalities supporting big data processing are as follows:

- **Stream management**: Kinesis simplifies stream management by offering capabilities like access controls, data retention policies, and efficient handling of large datasets.

- **Producer and consumer integration**: The service bridges data producers (sources generating data) and consumers (applications processing data), ensuring horizontal scalability and seamless communication.

- **Integration with complementary services**: Kinesis is the backbone of real-time data pipelines, enabling tight integration with its sibling services, Kinesis Data Streams and Kinesis Firehose, which are tailored for data ingestion and transformation tasks.

By leveraging the Amazon Kinesis family, organizations can design scalable, real-time data pipelines that process and analyze streaming data effectively, unlocking insights at the speed of business.

Introduction to Amazon Kinesis Firehose

Amazon Kinesis Firehose is a serverless service designed to simplify the delivery of real-time data streams to various destinations. It enables organizations to process, transform, and store streaming data efficiently, making it a critical tool for big data workloads. By managing the complexities of data delivery and transformation, Firehose empowers users to build streamlined, scalable data pipelines.

The core features of Kinesis Firehose are as follows:

- **Delivery destinations**: Firehose provides seamless integration with key AWS services, offering multiple pre-configured destinations for data streams:
  - **Amazon S3**: For scalable, cost-effective storage of raw or transformed datasets.
  - **Amazon Redshift**: For analytics and data warehousing at scale.
  - **Amazon OpenSearch Service (formerly Elasticsearch Service)**: For search and real-time analytics optimized for large datasets.
  - **CloudWatch Logs**: For monitoring and troubleshooting purposes.

- **Data transformation**: Firehose allows users to transform data in real-time before delivery. This includes:
  - Filtering unnecessary data points to optimize storage and processing.
  - Converting record formats to ensure compatibility with the destination.
  - Compressing data to minimize storage costs.

- **Serverless integration with AWS Lambda**: Firehose integrates with AWS Lambda, enabling custom, serverless transformation logic. This eliminates the need for standalone processing steps and reduces the operational burden, making it ideal for big data pipelines.

Building effective workflows with Kinesis Firehose

Even without prior knowledge of Kinesis Data Streams, Firehose can be used independently to deliver and transform data for big data use cases. For example:

- Data can be ingested directly from event sources like AWS CloudWatch Events, application logs, or IoT devices.

- Transformed and optimized data can be delivered to services like S3 or Redshift for storage and analytics.

When introduced later in the workflow, Kinesis Data Streams enhances real-time ingestion and processing capabilities. Together, these services create a cohesive pipeline, with Kinesis Firehose focusing on delivery and transformation while other services address ingestion or analytics tasks.

Limits in AWS Kinesis Firehose

Amazon Kinesis Firehose provides a robust and serverless way to deliver streaming data to various destinations, but it operates under specific limitations. Understanding these constraints is essential for designing efficient and cost-effective data pipelines. The following are the key limits associated with Kinesis Firehose:

- **Record size**: A single record sent to Kinesis Firehose can have a maximum size of 1 MB. Data exceeding this limit must be split or pre-processed to fit within the allowed size.

- **PutRecordBatch limits**: The PutRecordBatch API call is limited to a maximum of 500 records or 4 MB of data per request. Workflows generating higher volumes of data must batch or segment their records appropriately to stay within this threshold.

- **Delivery stream limits**: While there is no predefined limit on the number of delivery streams per account, each stream is subject to regional or account-specific resource quotas. For workloads requiring additional streams, users can request an increase in the quota from AWS.

- **Throughput limits**: The throughput of a delivery stream is governed by the number of shards, with each shard supporting up to 1 MB/sec or 1,000 records/sec. Exceeding these limits may result in throttling or data delivery delays.

- **Destination-specific limits**: Destinations such as Amazon S3, Redshift, and OpenSearch Service have their own constraints:
  - For Amazon S3, factors like bucket size, object size, and write throughput can impact delivery performance.
  - Redshift destinations may impose limits on the frequency or volume of data ingestion.

- **Error handling limits**: Kinesis Firehose retries failed deliveries up to a maximum number of attempts before routing the data to a pre-configured backup destination, such as an S3 bucket. The retry count and backup configurations are customizable to balance reliability and cost.

AWS Kinesis Firehose anti-patterns

Amazon Kinesis Firehose is a powerful tool for delivering streaming data, designed for near real-time ingestion, transformation, and delivery. However, improper usage can lead to performance issues, increased costs, and even data loss. To maximize the efficiency of Kinesis Firehose, it is essential to avoid the following common anti-patterns:

- **Using Firehose for real-time analytics**: Firehose is optimized for near real-time data delivery, not real-time analytics or processing. Attempting to use Firehose for millisecond-level latency tasks can result in delays and unmet expectations. For real-time analytics, Amazon Kinesis Data Streams is the better choice.

- **Overloading a single delivery stream**: Aggregating multiple, unrelated data sources into a single Firehose delivery stream may seem convenient, but it can lead to performance degradation and complicate stream management. Segmenting data ingestion into multiple delivery streams is best to prevent bottlenecks and improve clarity and scalability.

- **Neglecting buffer size configuration**: Small buffer sizes (e.g., 1 MB) can slow ingestion, creating delays in data delivery. Conversely, overly large buffers (e.g., 128 MB) can increase latency before data is written to storage. The choice of buffer size should align with workload characteristics, ensuring an optimal trade-off between throughput and real-time processing.

- **Lack of partitioning and scaling considerations**: Proper partitioning of data streams is necessary to ensure efficient scaling. Failing to segment data appropriately can overload a single stream, causing throttling and performance degradation. Designing partitions based on data ingestion rates and destination constraints helps maintain reliable performance.

- **Attaching too many Firehose delivery streams to a single S3 bucket**: While Firehose integrates seamlessly with Amazon S3, assigning multiple delivery streams to the same S3 bucket can lead to write contention, increased request latencies, and potential failures. To avoid these issues, distribute workloads across multiple destination buckets based on logical data segmentation.

- **Over-reliance on Firehose for complex data processing**: While Firehose integrates with AWS Lambda for lightweight transformations, it is not intended for complex ETL workflows. Services like AWS Glue, AWS EMR, or Step Functions offer greater flexibility for advanced data transformations.

- **Ignoring data transformation**: Failing to preprocess data before delivery can degrade data quality and hinder downstream processing. Leveraging Firehose's Lambda integration allows for format conversion, filtering, and enrichment, improving the usability of ingested data.

By understanding and avoiding these anti-patterns, organizations can harness Amazon Kinesis Firehose's full potential while maintaining performance, cost efficiency, and data reliability.

Sensor data ingestion via Kinesis Data Firehose

This section outlines a reference architecture for ingesting and processing sensor data from field devices such as temperature sensors, water level sensors, wind sensors, or motion detectors. These devices generate a series of readings at regular intervals, requiring buffering and micro-batching for aggregation and cleaning before feeding the data into downstream systems for reporting, notifications, and insights.

The reference architecture for sensor data ingestion is represented in *Figure 13.1*:

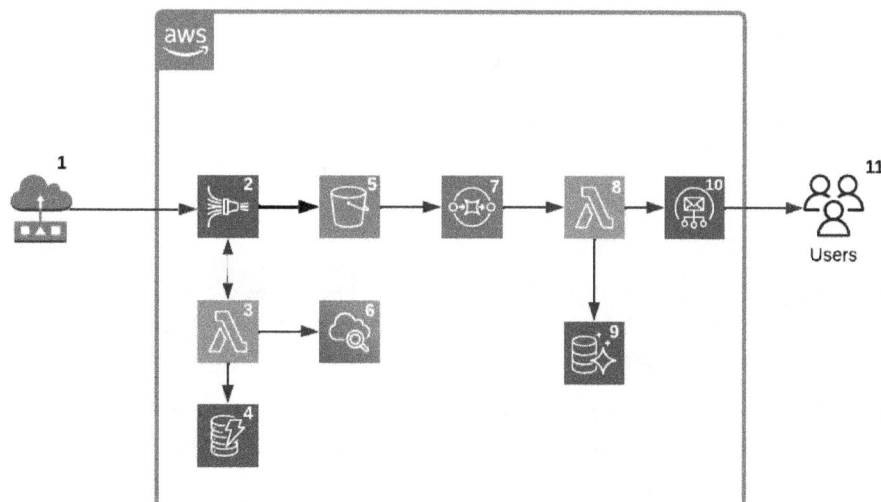

Figure 13.1: Reference architecture for sensor data ingestion via Kinesis Data Firehose

The following is a step-by-step explanation of the components illustrated in *Figure 13.1*:

- **Sensor data transmission (1)**: Sensors send periodic signals and readings, such as temperature updates every second.

- **Data ingestion with Kinesis Data Firehose (2)**: The sensor readings are ingested into Kinesis Data Firehose, which buffers the data based on predefined conditions, such as reaching a specific size (e.g., 128 MB) or a time interval (e.g., 5 minutes).

- **Pre-processing with AWS Lambda (3)**: Kinesis Firehose invokes an AWS Lambda function to pre-process the batched data. This often includes transforming MQTT messages from sensors into standardized formats such as JSON.

- **Metadata storage in DynamoDB (4)**: The Lambda function can reference a metadata store, such as Amazon DynamoDB, to enrich the data with additional contextual information.

- **Storage in Amazon S3 (5)**: Aggregated and pre-processed data is stored in Amazon S3 for long-term archival and further analysis.

- **S3 event notifications to Amazon SQS (7)**: Once the data is stored in S3, an event notification is triggered to send a message to Amazon SQS. This message serves as a payload for downstream processing.

- **Processing and insights with AWS Lambda (8)**: Another AWS Lambda function consumes the SQS message, processes the payload, extracts insights, and prepares the data for further actions.

- **Data storage in Amazon Aurora Serverless (9)**: Insights derived from the Lambda function are stored in Amazon Aurora Serverless, providing a scalable and cost-effective relational database solution.

- **User notifications via Amazon SES (10)**: Processed data triggers Amazon **Simple Email Service (SES)** to send email notifications to relevant users.

- **User interaction (11)**: Notifications provide actionable insights to users, enabling them to make informed decisions based on the processed sensor data.

This architecture showcases how Kinesis Data Firehose, combined with other AWS services, creates an efficient and scalable pipeline for ingesting, processing, and analyzing sensor data in real-time.

Introduction to Amazon Kinesis Data Streams

Amazon Kinesis Data Streams is the powerhouse at the core of real-time data processing on AWS. This scalable and serverless service enables high-throughput ingestion and processing of continuous data streams in real-time, making it a perfect fit for big data workloads.

The key concepts in Kinesis Data Streams are as follows:

- **Data records**: A data record represents an individual piece of information within a data stream. Each record can include attributes such as a timestamp and metadata, making it suitable for complex big data analysis and workflows.

- **Partition key**: Producers specify a partition key when sending data records into the stream. Kinesis uses this key to assign records to specific shards, optimizing data distribution and ensuring efficient organization for big data pipelines.

- **Record sequence number**: Every record within a shard is assigned a unique sequence number, ensuring that data remains ordered, even in scenarios with high network latency. This guarantees data integrity, which is critical for consistent processing in big data workflows.

- **Serverless processing**: Kinesis Data Streams integrates seamlessly with AWS Lambda, enabling serverless processing of data streams. Lambda functions can be used to define custom logic for tasks such as transformation, filtering, and enrichment, eliminating the need for server management while scaling automatically with data volume.

The usability patterns in Kinesis Data Streams are as follows:

- **Real-time data ingestion**: Use the Kinesis SDK or producer libraries to ingest data streams from various sources, such as IoT devices, application logs, or social media feeds. This allows for handling large data volumes in diverse use cases.

- **Stream processing with AWS Lambda**: Integrate AWS Lambda with Kinesis Data Streams to process ingested data in real time. Lambda functions can apply transformations, filter data, or enrich records on the fly, providing a serverless approach to big data processing.

- **Scalability**: Kinesis Data Streams scales automatically by adding or removing shards based on data volume. This eliminates the need for manual provisioning, ensuring cost efficiency and optimal resource utilization.

Kinesis Data Streams serve as the backbone for real-time big data processing workflows. Its scalability, serverless capabilities, and seamless integration with other AWS services make it an indispensable tool for building dynamic, efficient big data pipelines.

Amazon Kinesis Data Streams limits

Amazon Kinesis Data Streams is a powerful service for real-time data ingestion and processing, but it operates under specific limits that impact stream configuration, performance, and scalability. Understanding these constraints is critical for designing efficient and reliable data pipelines. The following are the key limits associated with Kinesis Data Streams:

- **Shard limits**:

  o **Maximum shards per data stream**: The number of shards allowed per data stream varies by region and account but typically ranges in the hundreds.

  o **Maximum shards per account**: The total shard count across all streams also varies by region and account, often reaching into the thousands. For higher limits, users can request an increase in their quota from AWS.

- **Record size**: Each data record can have a maximum size of 1 MB before base64-encoding. Larger records must be split into smaller chunks to comply with this limit.

- **PutRecords limits**: The PutRecords API supports a maximum of 500 records or 4 MB of data per request. Applications must batch records efficiently to stay within these thresholds.

- **GetRecords limits**:

  o A single GetRecords request can return up to 10,000 records.

  o The maximum data retrieved per request is capped at 10 MB. Applications requiring higher throughput should optimize shard usage or leverage enhanced fan-out.

- **Read provisioned throughput**: Each shard provides a maximum read capacity of 2 MB/sec or 2,000 records/sec. Exceeding these limits may result in throttling or delayed data processing.

- **Write provisioned throughput**: Write operations are limited to 1 MB/sec or 1,000 records/sec per shard. Workloads with high ingestion rates may require additional shards to distribute the load effectively.

- **Retention period**: The maximum retention period for data in a stream is 365 days, allowing for the extended availability of historical data. By default, the retention period is 24 hours, but it can be adjusted based on use case requirements.

- **Enhanced fan-out limits**: Enhanced fan-out allows streams to support up to 20 registered consumers per stream, enabling high-speed data delivery without impacting shared throughput.

Amazon Kinesis Data Streams anti-patterns

While Amazon Kinesis Data Streams is a robust service for real-time data processing, improper usage can lead to performance degradation, increased costs, or data loss. To optimize performance and reliability, avoid the following common anti-patterns:

- **Incorrect shard count**: Misconfiguring the number of shards in a data stream can have significant consequences:

  o **Too few shards**: This leads to bottlenecks as data volume exceeds shard capacity, causing throttling and delayed processing.

  o **Too many shards**: Increases operational costs unnecessarily without delivering proportional benefits.

- **Inefficient partition key usage**: Selecting a poor partition key can result in uneven data distribution across shards:

  o **Hot partitions**: A large portion of the data being routed to a single shard causes bottlenecks.

  o **Solution**: Use partition keys that evenly distribute data across shards, such as hashed values or unique identifiers.

- **Neglecting data retention settings**: Improperly configuring the data retention period can lead to:

  o **Data loss**: Short retention periods may result in data expiring before it is processed.

  o **Increased costs**: Extending retention unnecessarily inflates storage costs.

  o **Best practice**: Align retention settings with specific use case requirements.

- **Ignoring record size limits**: Exceeding the maximum record size of 1 MB (before base64 encoding) causes errors, impacting system reliability. Always validate record sizes before sending them to the stream.

- **Overusing consumer instances**: Deploying an excessive number of consumer instances can result in:

  o **Higher costs**: Each consumer adds to resource usage and expenses.

  o **Potential performance issues**: Overlapping consumer processing can reduce efficiency.

- **Insufficient error handling**: A lack of robust error-handling mechanisms can lead to data loss or system downtime.

  o Implement retry logic, DLQs, and alerts for failed processing scenarios.

- **Misusing Kinesis for batch processing**: Kinesis is designed for real-time streaming, and using it for batch processing undermines its efficiency and increases costs. Services like Amazon S3 or AWS Glue may be more suitable for batch workloads.

- **Ignoring data skew**: Unbalanced data distribution across shards leads to hot partitions, causing uneven performance.

  o Mitigate skew by using dynamic partition keys or evaluating data distribution periodically.

Amazon Managed Service for Apache Flink

Amazon Managed Service for Apache Flink (**AMSF**) leverages Apache Flink's powerful architecture to provide businesses with a scalable, user-friendly solution for real-time data analytics. With its ability to process massive data volumes with low latency, AMSF empowers organizations to gain actionable insights from streaming data efficiently.

The key features of AMSF are as follows:

- **Simplified stream processing**: AMSF enables users to process streaming data with familiar SQL queries, eliminating the need for advanced coding expertise in languages like Java or Scala. This intuitive interface allows data engineers and analysts to focus on deriving insights rather than dealing with complex programming.

- **Real-time analytics at scale**: Inheriting Apache Flink's distributed processing and state management capabilities, AMSF handles large-scale data streams with low latency. Businesses can analyze streaming data from diverse sources in real-time, supporting faster, data-driven decision-making.

- **Automatic scaling and cost-efficiency**: AMSF automatically adjusts resources to match fluctuations in data flow, ensuring optimal performance and cost-efficiency. By eliminating manual provisioning and infrastructure management, businesses can focus on analytics without worrying about cluster scaling or maintenance.

- **Flexible data destinations**: Processed data can be seamlessly directed to various destinations within the AWS ecosystem, including:
  o **Amazon S3** for scalable storage,
  o **Amazon Redshift** for data warehousing and advanced analytics,
  o **Amazon OpenSearch Service** (formerly Elasticsearch Service) for real-time search and visualization. This flexibility enables businesses to design workflows that meet their unique data storage and analysis requirements.

- **Pre-built integrations**: AMSF integrates with other AWS services, such as:
  o **Kinesis Data Streams** for data ingestion,
  o **Kinesis Data Firehose** for data delivery, and
  o Pre-built connectors for integrating with various data sources and sinks. These integrations simplify pipeline creation, streamlining end-to-end data processing workflows.

- **Focus on business logic**: By managing the infrastructure and offering pre-built integrations, AMSF allows businesses to concentrate on developing business logic for their streaming applications. This focus accelerates time-to-insight and frees up resources for innovation rather than infrastructure management.

Business applications of AMSF

AMSF supports real-time analytics across various industries, enabling organizations to unlock the full potential of streaming data. Common use cases include:

- **Fraud detection in finance**: Identify fraudulent transactions in real-time by analyzing financial data streams.

- **Sensor data analysis in IoT**: Process and monitor sensor data to detect anomalies or track environmental conditions.

- **Customer behavior analysis in e-commerce**: Gain insights into customer actions to improve personalization and optimize user experiences.

By offering a managed, scalable, and cost-effective platform, AMSF provides businesses with the tools to turn raw data streams into actionable intelligence. Detailed use cases will be explored in future sections to showcase AMSF's potential across diverse business scenarios.

Kinesis for fraud detection in online gaming

This section presents a reference architecture for detecting fraud in real-time gaming data using AWS services. The architecture demonstrates how data from various game servers and databases can be aggregated, transformed, and processed in rea-time to detect behavioral deviations, enabling timely notifications to relevant personnel. Refer to *Figure 13.2* for the architectural flow:

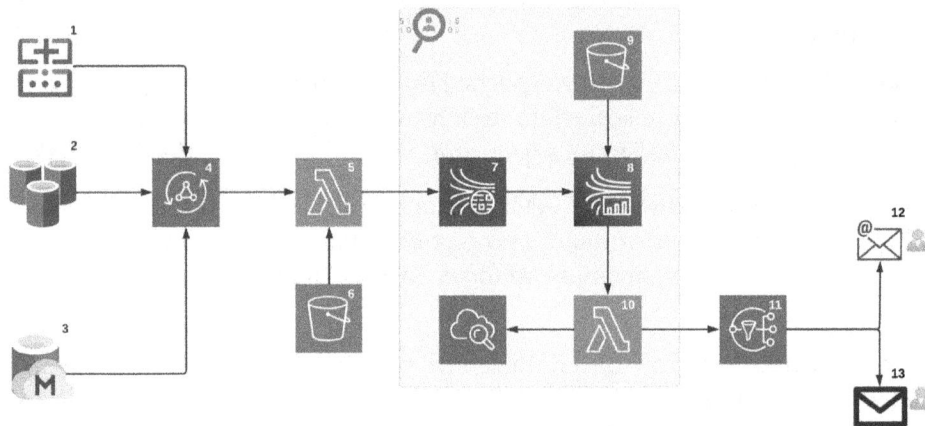

Figure 13.2: Fraud detection via Kinesis Data Streams and Amazon Managed Service for Apache Flink

The following are the components and their purpose in the use case:

- **Data ingestion and streaming**:
  - **Game data sources (1, 2, 3)**: Real-time data is sourced from game servers or databases that log player activity, such as in-game transactions, gameplay statistics, and session details.
  - **AWS AppSync (4)**: Acts as the entry point for ingesting gaming data, using a GraphQL API to retrieve data from the game data sources.
  - **AWS Lambda (5)**: A serverless compute service triggered by AppSync events. It transforms raw game data into a standardized format suitable for real-time processing by downstream services like Amazon Kinesis.
  - **Amazon Kinesis Data Streams (7)**: Serves as the real-time data pipeline. Transformed data from Lambda is ingested into Kinesis Data Streams, which buffers the data and makes it available for real-time analytics.
- **Real-time analytics and fraud detection**:
  - **Amazon Managed Service for Apache Flink (8)**: Processes the data stream from Kinesis Data Streams. Using Apache Flink's stateful processing capabilities, it performs continuous analytics to detect anomalies and suspicious patterns.
  - **Behavioral deviation detection (9)**: AMSF identifies anomalies in player behavior, such as unexpected spikes in experience points, abnormal currency accumulation, or unusual gameplay actions, which may indicate fraudulent activity.
  - **Further analysis with Lambda (Optional)**: AMSF can invoke an additional Lambda function to enrich or validate the flagged data before confirming it as fraudulent.

- **Notification and alerting (11, 12, 13):**

  o **Amazon SNS (Simple Notification Service) (11):** When potential fraud is detected, AMSF publishes a message to an SNS topic, enabling downstream notifications.

  o **Email and SMS notifications (12, 13):** Subscribers to the SNS topic receive fraud alerts via email or SMS. This ensures timely intervention by security teams to investigate and mitigate suspicious activity.

This architecture demonstrates the power of AWS services in creating a scalable, real-time fraud detection system for online gaming platforms. By integrating Kinesis Data Streams and AMSF, organizations can continuously analyze gaming data streams, identify anomalies, and respond promptly to potential fraud, ensuring a secure and fair gaming experience for all players.

Introduction to Amazon OpenSearch Serverless

Imagine instantly searching and analyzing massive datasets without the complexity of managing infrastructure. That is the promise of Amazon OpenSearch Serverless. Built on the robust capabilities of OpenSearch, a popular open-source search and analytics engine, this fully managed service provides scalable, high-performance search capabilities while eliminating the burden of infrastructure management.

The key features of Amazon OpenSearch Serverless are as follows:

- **Effortless search at scale**

  o **Serverless simplicity:** OpenSearch Serverless removes the need for provisioning or managing clusters. AWS handles infrastructure management, allowing you to focus solely on analyzing data and building applications.

  o **Automatic scaling:** The service scales resources automatically based on search demand, ensuring optimal performance during peak usage while avoiding overprovisioning and controlling costs.

  o **Pay-as-you-go pricing:** With a pricing model based on usage, OpenSearch Serverless is a cost-effective solution for businesses of all sizes.

- **Powerful search and analytics:**

  o **Seamless integration:** OpenSearch Serverless integrates effortlessly with AWS services like Kinesis Data Firehose for data ingestion and Amazon S3 for storage. This simplifies data pipelines and accelerates the process of preparing searchable datasets.

  o **Advanced analytics:** Perform complex searches and aggregations on your data using features such as faceted search, geospatial analysis, and real-time dashboards. These capabilities enable deeper insights into your data.

  o **Customizable dashboards:** Create interactive dashboards to visualize trends, patterns, and anomalies. Share these dashboards with teams for collaborative decision-making.

- **Real-world applications:**

  o **Log analysis:** Analyze and troubleshoot application logs in real-time to identify anomalies or issues.

  o **Security threat detection:** Gain insights into potential threats by analyzing security logs and events, enabling proactive threat mitigation.

  o **Customer behavior analytics:** Explore website clickstreams and search queries to understand customer preferences. Use these insights to personalize user experiences and refine marketing strategies.

o **Operational efficiency**: Monitor system performance and resource utilization to identify bottlenecks and optimize your infrastructure.

Amazon OpenSearch Serverless model unlocks the potential of real-time data analytics. Its scalable, effortless search capabilities and seamless integration into the AWS ecosystem empowers organizations to transform data into actionable insights, whether for troubleshooting, security, or customer engagement.

Climate data analytics with Amazon OpenSearch Serverless

Real-time data analysis has become indispensable in understanding the complexities of climate change. Amazon OpenSearch Serverless enables climate scientists to process and analyze vast data streams from satellites and sensors, offering critical insights into weather patterns and climate anomalies. Refer to *Figure 13.3* for the reference architecture:

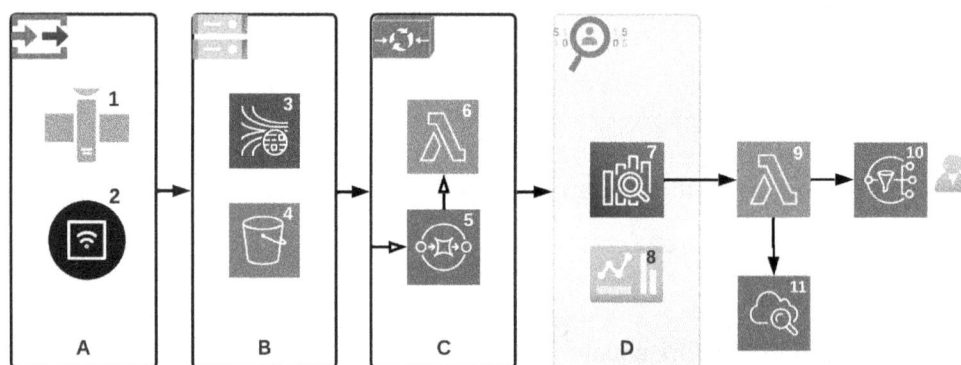

Figure 13.3: Reference architecture for climate data analytics using Amazon OpenSearch Serverless

The following are the key components in the reference architecture:

- **Real-time data feeding**:
  - o **Continuous acquisition (1)**: Satellites and sensor networks worldwide generate massive amounts of climate data, including temperature, precipitation, and atmospheric composition readings, continuously feeding into the system.
  - o **Low-latency streaming (2)**: OpenSearch Serverless processes these incoming data streams with minimal latency, ensuring that scientists receive near real-time updates for prompt analysis and response.

- **Ingestion and cataloging**:
  - o **Stream transformation (3)**: **Amazon Kinesis Data Firehose** acts as an intermediary, transforming raw data streams by filtering irrelevant information or converting formats, making them ready for ingestion by OpenSearch Serverless.
  - o **Delivery and indexing (4)**: Transformed data is delivered by Kinesis Data Firehose to an OpenSearch Serverless domain, where it is indexed and cataloged for efficient search and retrieval.

- **Advanced processing and anomaly detection**:
  - o **Enriched transformations (6)**: OpenSearch Serverless enhances data processing by deriving additional metrics, calculating averages or deviations, and performing geospatial referencing for location-specific analysis.
  - o **Real-time search and analytics (7)**: Scientists use OpenSearch Serverless to perform real-time complex searches and aggregations, identifying trends, correlations, and meaningful insights across multiple climate variables.

- o **Custom anomaly detection (8)**: Custom anomaly detection algorithms built within OpenSearch Serverless analyze historical data and identify deviations in real-time. These anomalies may signify significant climate events requiring deeper investigation.

- **Visualization and insights**: OpenSearch Serverless integrates with customizable dashboards that enable scientists to visualize trends and anomalies in climate data. These dashboards facilitate informed predictions and collaboration among researchers, allowing them to identify critical patterns and make timely decisions to protect the environment.

Research institutions analyzing climate change rely on OpenSearch Serverless to index and query massive sensor datasets. A leading research team indexed petabytes of satellite data in real time, allowing scientists to perform complex searches across 500 billion rows to detect climate anomalies and greenhouse gas patterns. They visualized data trends by leveraging OpenSearch Serverless dashboards, enhancing predictive modeling and global environmental research.

By leveraging Amazon OpenSearch Serverless, climate scientists can process and analyze real-time data streams precisely and efficiently. This architecture empowers researchers to detect climate anomalies, gain actionable insights, and contribute meaningfully to the fight against climate change.

Conclusion

This chapter has provided a comprehensive overview of AWS big data services, showcasing how they address every stage of the big data lifecycle, from scalable storage and processing to real-time streaming and analytics. Solutions like Amazon S3 and Amazon EBS offer secure and cost-effective storage, while tools such as Amazon EMR and Amazon Redshift enable efficient processing and analysis of large-scale datasets. For real-time data management, the Amazon Kinesis suite empowers organizations with data stream ingestion, transformation, and analytics, enabling use cases like social media sentiment analysis.

Strategically combining these services unlocks powerful real-time analytics capabilities. For instance, Amazon OpenSearch Serverless allows climate scientists to analyze real-time satellite and sensor data, while Kinesis Data Firehose transforms sensor data streams to support instant decision-making across industries.

Mastering AWS big data services empowers organizations to convert raw data into actionable insights, driving innovation and enabling informed decisions across domains.

The next chapter explores machine learning and generative AI and their applications on AWS. Beginning with foundational concepts, it looks into Amazon SageMaker, covering its key features, integrations, and common anti-patterns. The chapter also introduces advanced tools like Amazon Bedrock, Amazon Rekognition, Amazon Transcribe, and Amazon Comprehend, offering a roadmap for building intelligent, scalable solutions on AWS. The chapter also introduces services like Amazon Bedrock, Amazon Rekognition, Amazon Transcribe, and Amazon Comprehend, highlighting their roles in enabling generative AI solutions. Additionally, it discusses service limits and quotas, offering a comprehensive guide to building intelligent, scalable solutions on AWS.

Join our Discord space

Join our Discord workspace for latest updates, offers, tech happenings around the world, new releases, and sessions with the authors:

https://discord.bpbonline.com

CHAPTER 14
Machine Learning and Generative AI

Introduction

Machine Learning (ML) and **Artificial Intelligence (AI)** have fundamentally transformed how businesses derive insights and foster innovation. Generative AI represents a revolutionary advancement, not only automating complex tasks but also enabling the creation of entirely new content, text, images, and beyond. However, effectively leveraging these technologies requires a nuanced understanding and sophisticated tools. AWS SageMaker simplifies this challenge by equipping businesses and developers with intuitive solutions for model training, deployment, and optimization. Companies such as Anthropic, which leveraged SageMaker to advance constitutional AI that adheres to societal values, and *RAIC Labs* (formerly *Synthetaic*), which applied it to enhance healthcare with compassionate clinical language models, exemplify its transformative potential in real-world applications.

This chapter explores the core AWS services that power generative AI workflows. Amazon SageMaker lays the foundation with its fully managed capabilities, simplifying model training, tuning, and deployment while integrating seamlessly with serverless technologies for scalable operations. Building upon this, Amazon Bedrock accelerates the adoption of state-of-the-art generative AI models by providing a curated selection of foundational models, eliminating infrastructure complexities, and enabling rapid experimentation.

Serverless computing plays a pivotal role in generative AI by delivering unmatched scalability, agility, and cost-efficiency. These benefits free development teams to focus on innovation and algorithm refinement without being constrained by infrastructure management. In addition, specialized services like Amazon Rekognition, Amazon Transcribe, and Amazon Comprehend extend generative AI capabilities into areas such as image recognition, speech processing, and natural language understanding.

This chapter provides practical insights into building and scaling generative AI solutions with AWS, helping businesses unlock the true potential of artificial intelligence.

Structure

The chapter covers the following topics:

- Machine learning on AWS
- Introduction to Amazon SageMaker
- Key concepts in Amazon SageMaker
- Amazon SageMaker components

- Amazon SageMaker integrations
- Amazon SageMaker anti-patterns
- Amazon SageMaker limits
- Generative AI on AWS
- Introduction to Amazon Bedrock
- Introduction to Amazon Rekognition
- Introduction to Amazon Transcribe
- Introduction to Amazon Comprehend
- Service limits and quotas

Objectives

The digital era is characterized by an overwhelming influx of data, offering organizations unparalleled opportunities to derive insights and drive innovation. AI, with ML and generative AI at its core, fuels breakthroughs across industries by automating complex tasks and unlocking new possibilities.

AWS leads the cloud AI space by democratizing AI access and simplifying model deployment at scale. While Google Cloud AI offers advanced models requiring extensive customization, and Microsoft Azure AI integrates well with enterprise systems but presents fragmented workflows, AWS provides a fully managed, scalable, and production-ready AI/ML ecosystem that eliminates infrastructure overhead, allowing organizations to focus on innovation.

ML enables systems to analyze vast datasets, uncover patterns, and make accurate predictions, transforming decision-making across industries. Generative AI goes further by creating entirely new content—text, images, music, and more—expanding creative potential and enhancing automation.

In this chapter, readers will understand these transformative technologies comprehensively, key considerations for robust AI deployment, and insightful coverage of AWS services like Amazon SageMaker and Bedrock, which streamline the machine learning and generative AI lifecycle.

Machine learning on AWS

The digital era has unleashed an unprecedented surge of data, offering businesses vast opportunities to derive actionable insights. ML, a pivotal branch of AI, is a beacon in navigating this data deluge. ML transforms processes traditionally reliant on human intervention by enabling machines to analyze complex datasets and make data-driven predictions. For instance, algorithms can now analyze customer behavior, uncover trends, and optimize marketing strategies in real-time.

At its core, ML operates through a continuous cycle:

- **Decision-making**: Algorithms process input data, whether labeled or unlabeled, to identify patterns and generate predictions.

- **Error evaluation**: Predicted outcomes are assessed for accuracy using error functions that compare results against known benchmarks.

- **Model optimization**: Discrepancies are iteratively addressed by refining algorithmic parameters, enhancing model performance over time.

Building and deploying ML models has traditionally required significant infrastructure management, creating bottlenecks that slow innovation. AWS has redefined this process with Amazon SageMaker, a fully managed platform that simplifies model training, tuning, and deployment.

Organizations across industries have leveraged SageMaker's capabilities to drive AI innovation. Anthropic, an AI research company, used SageMaker to develop Constitutional AI, ensuring models adhere to ethical guidelines while scaling efficiently. Similarly, RAIC Labs, a leader in healthcare AI, integrated SageMaker to enhance medical language models, improving clinical documentation and decision support. These success stories underscore how SageMaker democratizes AI, enabling enterprises to deploy models at scale while maintaining compliance and accuracy.

Beyond SageMaker, AWS offers specialized AI services tailored to unique workloads. Amazon Rekognition provides powerful image and video analysis, unlocking applications such as automated content moderation and facial recognition. Amazon Transcribe enables speech-to-text conversion, making call center analytics and real-time transcription more accessible. Seamlessly integrated with SageMaker, these services empower organizations to build full-scale AI-driven solutions with minimal operational overhead.

Introduction to Amazon SageMaker

In an era of data abundance, extracting actionable insights from vast information stores remains a significant challenge. ML offers a powerful solution, but building, training, and deploying models often requires complex and resource-intensive workflows. Amazon SageMaker addresses this challenge by providing a comprehensive, fully managed platform designed to simplify and accelerate the entire ML lifecycle on AWS.

SageMaker delivers a managed service experience, abstracting the complexities of server provisioning, configuration, and scaling. While not strictly serverless, its fully managed nature enables users to focus entirely on building and deploying ML models without the burden of infrastructure management.

Democratizing machine learning

Amazon SageMaker democratizes machine learning by removing infrastructure complexity, allowing businesses of all sizes to build, train, and deploy ML models efficiently.

Unlike alternatives such as Google Vertex AI, which require extensive manual tuning and pipeline orchestration, SageMaker provides an end-to-end managed experience, seamlessly integrating with AWS services like CloudWatch, Lambda, and S3. This ensures scalability and automation, making model development accessible even to teams without dedicated ML infrastructure expertise.

One of SageMaker's most powerful features is automated hyperparameter tuning, which optimizes model performance by systematically adjusting parameters. In a traditional ML setup, this requires manual iterations and significant expertise. With SageMaker, users can define a tuning job, and AWS automatically selects the best parameters based on pre-defined objectives. This process accelerates model training, reduces computational overhead, and ensures accuracy without requiring deep ML expertise.

SageMaker streamlines every stage of the ML lifecycle, ensuring businesses can focus on innovation rather than infrastructure management. With features like pre-built ML frameworks, automated scaling, and integrated model deployment, organizations can efficiently transition from development to production, realizing AI-driven insights faster than ever.

Accelerating business success

SageMaker offers transformative advantages:

- **Faster time-to-insight**: Automation in model building, training, and deployment reduces development cycles, enabling businesses to respond rapidly to emerging opportunities.

- **Enhanced productivity**: By eliminating the need to manage infrastructure, SageMaker enables data scientists and developers to concentrate on innovation, accelerating the delivery of impactful ML solutions.

- **Scalable workflows**: SageMaker's scalable architecture adapts to evolving data demands and model complexity, ensuring future growth and business resilience.

Through its intuitive interface and comprehensive capabilities, Amazon SageMaker empowers businesses to unlock the true potential of ML. SageMaker helps organizations make confident, data-driven decisions that drive innovation and success by eliminating infrastructure bottlenecks and fostering a productive environment for data science teams.

Key concepts in Amazon SageMaker

Amazon SageMaker simplifies the complexities of the machine learning lifecycle by providing tools and services that address key challenges in building, training, and deploying models. Understanding its core concepts is essential for leveraging its full potential and achieving impactful results.

Algorithms and frameworks

Amazon SageMaker offers an extensive library of pre-built algorithms tailored for diverse machine learning tasks, including classification, regression, recommendation systems, and **natural language processing** (**NLP**). These algorithms provide a strong foundation for developing models quickly. For more advanced use cases, SageMaker integrates seamlessly with popular ML frameworks like TensorFlow and PyTorch. This integration enables experienced practitioners to bring custom algorithms to the platform, offering flexibility and adaptability:

- **Hyperparameter tuning**: Hyperparameters are critical to a model's performance, influencing how it learns and generalizes from data. SageMaker provides advanced hyperparameter tuning capabilities, allowing users to experiment with different configurations and optimize model performance efficiently. Users can leverage built-in tuning algorithms or incorporate their own tailoring optimization strategies to meet specific objectives.

  o **Hyperparameter tuning in SageMaker:** Amazon SageMaker streamlines hyperparameter tuning through automated model tuning, eliminating the need for manual iterations. Instead of developers manually adjusting parameters like learning rate, batch size, or number of layers, SageMaker runs multiple training jobs with different configurations, analyzing results and selecting the optimal combination. This not only accelerates model convergence but also reduces computational costs by focusing resources on the most promising configurations.

  o **Hyperparameter tuning workflow in SageMaker:** The following figure shows generic steps on how to do hyperparameter tuning:

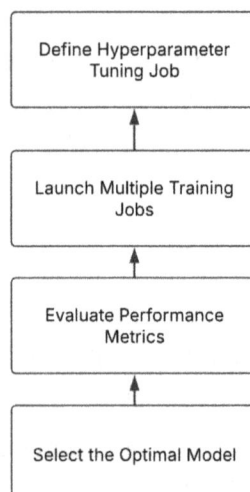

Figure 14.1: Picture showing hyperparameter tuning steps

o **Define a hyperparameter tuning job**: Users specify which hyperparameters need optimization, such as learning rate or activation functions.

o **Launch multiple training jobs**: SageMaker automatically runs multiple parallel training jobs, each with different hyperparameter values.

o **Evaluate performance metrics**: SageMaker selects the best model by analyzing accuracy, loss functions, or other predefined objectives.

o **Select the optimal model**: The best-performing configuration is finalized for deployment, reducing the time required for manual tuning.

This automation enables businesses to accelerate model development while reducing infrastructure overhead.

- **Model packaging and deployment**: SageMaker facilitates seamless packaging and deployment once models are trained. It supports real-time and batch inference endpoints, enabling applications to access model predictions easily. SageMaker handles the underlying infrastructure, ensuring scalability and reliability while users focus on integrating models into their applications.

- **Monitoring and explainability**: SageMaker includes robust tools to monitor deployed models in production. Metrics such as accuracy, latency, and cost are tracked, enabling users to detect potential issues and maintain model performance. Features for explainability provide insights into model predictions, fostering transparency and trust in AI-driven decisions.

Explainability in AI: SHAP and LIME

Beyond optimization, explainability plays a crucial role in ensuring AI transparency and trustworthiness. SageMaker integrates with **SHapley Additive exPlanations (SHAP)** and **Local Interpretable Model-Agnostic Explanations (LIME)**—two widely adopted techniques that help interpret complex ML models.

- **SHAP**: SHAP quantifies each feature's contribution to a model's prediction, making it ideal for high-stakes applications like financial risk modeling and fraud detection.

- **LIME**: LIME creates local surrogate models to approximate a model's decision boundaries, providing human-interpretable justifications for individual predictions—widely used in medical diagnostics and automated decision-making systems.

These tools enable organizations to detect biases, improve fairness, and comply with regulatory requirements, ensuring AI models are both effective and ethically sound.

Amazon SageMaker components

The following are the key components of SageMaker that help utilize the service to its fullest:

- **Amazon S3 integration**: Amazon SageMaker uses Amazon S3 as the primary storage for training data, model artifacts, and experiment results. This integration ensures scalable and cost-effective storage while providing seamless access to data throughout the machine learning lifecycle.

- **SageMaker notebooks**: SageMaker notebooks offer a cloud-based Jupyter Notebook environment tailored for data science workflows. These notebooks provide an interactive platform for experimenting with code, visualizing data, training models, and evaluating their performance. Integrated with Amazon S3, they enable efficient access to and analysis of large datasets.

- **Training jobs and compute resources**: SageMaker orchestrates training through dedicated jobs defining algorithms, hyperparameters, and data locations. The platform automatically provisions compute instances optimized for various workloads, eliminating the need for manual server management and ensuring efficient resource utilization.

Advanced features for mastering AWS SageMaker

The following advanced features help further enhance the power of this indispensable machine-learning service:

- **SageMaker Studio**: SageMaker Studio offers a unified interface consolidating all stages of the machine learning lifecycle, including data exploration, model development, training, deployment, and monitoring. Studio enhances collaboration through tools like code notebooks, project tracking, and experiment management, fostering productivity and efficiency.

- **SageMaker Autopilot**: SageMaker Autopilot automates model creation and deployment, catering to users with limited machine-learning expertise. It analyzes datasets, selects appropriate algorithms, and tunes hyperparameters, delivering high-quality models with minimal manual effort.

- **Multi-model endpoints**: SageMaker supports deploying multiple models behind a single endpoint. This is particularly useful for scenarios requiring different models for varying applications or offering multiple prediction options. SageMaker automatically routes requests to the appropriate model, simplifying endpoint management.

- **Pipelines**: Amazon SageMaker Pipelines provides a structured and automated approach to ML workflow orchestration, streamlining the transition from data preprocessing to model training, validation, and deployment. Unlike traditional ML workflows, which often rely on manual scripts, ad hoc model training, and independent processing steps, Pipelines enables a fully managed, scalable, and reproducible process.

  In a traditional ML workflow, data preprocessing, training, and deployment may be handled using separate scripts, notebooks, or manual interventions, making the process error-prone and difficult to track. In contrast, SageMaker Pipelines automates workflow execution, defining each stage using a declarative approach that ensures:

  o **Reproducibility**: Every step in the ML lifecycle is trackable and version controlled.

  o **Scalability**: Pipelines leverage AWS infrastructure to process large-scale ML workflows efficiently.

  o **Automation**: Instead of managing ML processes manually, Pipelines orchestrate training and deployment seamlessly.

  For organizations dealing with frequent model retraining, CI/CD for ML, or large-scale data ingestion, SageMaker Pipelines outperforms traditional approaches, ensuring faster iterations, reduced operational overhead, and improved governance.

- **Model Monitor**: SageMaker Model Monitor tracks the performance of deployed models in real-time. By establishing baseline metrics like accuracy and recall, it can detect deviations caused by data drift or model degradation. This proactive monitoring helps ensure model reliability and effectiveness.

- **Model Debugger**: SageMaker Debugger provides invaluable insights during model training by capturing metrics and data at various stages. It helps diagnose overfitting or underfitting, enabling users to fine-tune models for improved accuracy and performance.

Amazon SageMaker integrations

Amazon SageMaker integrates seamlessly with various AWS services, creating a unified ecosystem for machine learning workflows. These integrations enhance scalability, flexibility, and efficiency, enabling businesses to tackle complex ML challenges. The following is an overview of key integrations and how they contribute to SageMaker's capabilities:

- **Amazon S3**: SageMaker relies on S3 for highly scalable, cost-effective object storage to manage training data, model artifacts, and experiment results, ensuring smooth data access throughout the ML lifecycle.

- **AWS Lambda**: Lambda enables the deployment of trained models as serverless functions, making it ideal for real-time predictions or scenarios with minimal computing requirements. By eliminating infrastructure management, Lambda simplifies deployment and scaling.

  For model deployment, AWS Lambda plays a key role in enabling event-driven inference. Instead of maintaining long-running inference endpoints, organizations can configure Lambda functions to invoke SageMaker models dynamically, reducing infrastructure costs while scaling inference workloads on demand. This approach is particularly useful for real-time applications, such as fraud detection, personalized recommendations, or IoT-based decision-making, where low-latency, cost-efficient model execution is critical.

  By combining SageMaker, Lambda, and AWS Step Functions, businesses can orchestrate end-to-end ML workflows—from data ingestion to model inference and continuous retraining—without managing persistent infrastructure. This architecture enables AI-driven innovation with high availability, cost efficiency, and operational simplicity.

- **Amazon CloudWatch**: CloudWatch provides detailed monitoring and logging for training jobs, endpoint invocations, and model deployments. It ensures ML workflows remain healthy by tracking performance metrics and identifying potential issues.

- **Amazon Elastic Compute Cloud (EC2)**: For specialized workloads requiring custom configurations, SageMaker integrates with EC2, allowing users to launch tailored instances for unique training needs.

- **Amazon Elastic Container Service (ECS)**: ECS facilitates managing containerized ML workflows, particularly for deploying complex models or running multi-container workflows in production environments.

- **Amazon Kinesis**: Kinesis integrates real-time data streams into SageMaker, enabling continuous model training with dynamic datasets and ensuring models remain adaptable to evolving patterns.

- **Amazon Rekognition and Amazon Transcribe**: These pre-trained AI services enhance SageMaker workflows. Rekognition supports tasks like image and video analysis, while transcribing enriches data preparation for NLP and speech-related applications.

- **Amazon VPC**: Running ML workloads within a VPC enhances security and network control by isolating resources from the public internet and configuring custom security settings.

- **IAM**: SageMaker uses IAM roles to manage access control. Roles with specific permissions ensure secure resource access for training jobs and model deployments.

- **Vector databases**: These databases enhance similarity searches and semantic queries, supporting advanced AI applications such as recommendation systems and natural language understanding.

- **Inference optimization**: Techniques like model quantization and caching improve inference speed and reduce costs, enhancing application responsiveness and efficiency.

- **Model versioning**: SageMaker supports robust MLOps practices with model versioning, enabling users to track, compare, and roll back versions of fine-tuned models when necessary.

- **Prompt templates**: Predefined templates simplify and standardize input structures for foundational model interactions, improving consistency across deployments.

- **Output filtering and moderation**: SageMaker includes tools for controlling and sanitizing model outputs, ensuring safety and appropriateness in public-facing applications.

- **Cost management**: SageMaker follows a pay-as-you-go pricing model, supplemented by cost-monitoring tools and reserved capacity options to optimize expenses and provide predictability.

- **Experiment tracking**: SageMaker enables logging and comparison of model runs, facilitating iterative development, optimization, and team collaboration.

Amazon SageMaker anti-patterns

Amazon SageMaker is a powerful tool for managing the entire machine learning lifecycle. However, failing to use it effectively can result in inefficiencies, increased costs, or poorly performing models. The following are some common anti-patterns, along with why avoiding them is critical for long-term success:

- **Overreliance on pre-built algorithms**: While SageMaker provides a range of pre-built machine learning algorithms, relying solely on them can limit customization and model performance. For unique datasets or specialized use cases, training custom models can yield significantly better results.

- **Neglecting hyperparameter tuning**: Optimizing model parameters is essential for accuracy and generalization. Ignoring this step can result in overfitting (performing well on training data but poorly on real-world data) or underfitting (failing to capture meaningful patterns).

- **Inadequate data preprocessing**: Poorly prepared data can severely impact model effectiveness. Missing values, skewed distributions, or unnormalized data can distort model performance, leading to misleading results.

- **Overfitting models**: Overfitting occurs when models become too tailored to training data and fail to generalize to unseen data. This can be mitigated using techniques like regularization, dropout layers, and cross-validation.

- **Misusing SageMaker for batch inference**: SageMaker offers batch inference capabilities, but for large-scale jobs, AWS services like AWS Batch or Lambda may be more cost-effective and scalable.

- **Ignoring cost optimization**: Without resource monitoring and optimization, organizations may over-provision instances, leading to unnecessary expenses. Leveraging spot instances and auto-scaling can help manage costs effectively.

Amazon SageMaker limits

Amazon SageMaker operates within certain limits to ensure optimal performance and scalability for machine learning workflows. These limits, often called quotas, govern the resources and services available to users. Understanding these constraints is essential for planning and executing successful ML projects:

- **Resource quotas**:
  - **Compute instances**: SageMaker limits the number of compute instances that can be launched concurrently. By default, the limit is 100 instances per account, though this can be increased by submitting a request through the AWS Service Quotas Console. These quotas ensure efficient resource allocation and prevent overuse.
  - **Storage volume size**: SageMaker utilizes Amazon S3 for storage, which offers unlimited capacity for training data, model artifacts, and experiment results. However, the practical volume size for datasets used in SageMaker-managed training jobs is limited to 16 TB per volume.
  - **Network bandwidth**: Data transfer rates between SageMaker and other AWS services depend on the selected instance type and region. While not explicitly limited, these rates vary and should be accounted for during model training and deployment.

- **Service-specific limits**:

- o **Notebook instances**: Each account has a default limit of 100 notebook instances. Limits can be adjusted to meet specific needs through quota increase requests. Instance types and storage configurations are also subject to predefined constraints.

- o **Training jobs**: SageMaker generally supports up to 100 concurrent training jobs. Training job durations and instance types may vary depending on workload requirements, but default limits can be extended upon request.

- o **Endpoint configuration**: SageMaker allows up to 200 endpoint configurations per account. This includes real-time and batch inference endpoints, providing flexibility for diverse deployment strategies.

- o **Model registry**: The registry supports up to 1,000 models and associated versions. This helps teams manage versions, track experiments, and maintain an organized ML pipeline.

- **Data and model size**:

  - o **Dataset size**: While Amazon S3 supports large-scale datasets, individual training jobs within SageMaker are optimized for up to 2 TB datasets. Efficiently processing larger datasets may require specialized strategies, such as partitioning or distributed training.

  - o **Model size**: The maximum deployable model size varies by instance type and region. Selecting appropriately sized instances ensures smooth model hosting and inference performance.

- **Feature availability**:

  - o **Region-specific features**: Not all SageMaker features are available in every AWS region. Users should consult the AWS regional services list to verify the availability of desired features.

  - o **Algorithm and framework support**: SageMaker supports many algorithms and frameworks, though performance may vary. Choosing compatible frameworks that align with workload requirements and SageMaker capabilities is important.

- **Cost considerations**:

  - o **Compute costs**: Training and deploying models involve compute costs, which vary based on the type and duration of instance usage. Selecting optimized instance types can help manage costs effectively.

  - o **Storage costs**: Storing datasets and models in Amazon S3 incurs charges based on storage volume and duration. Monitoring and optimizing storage usage can significantly reduce costs.

Generative AI on AWS

Generative AI represents a transformative leap in creativity and innovation, enabling businesses to explore new content creation, data enhancement, and more frontiers. AWS provides a comprehensive suite of tools and services that empower organizations to harness this technology effectively. This section explores how AWS supports generative AI development, deployment, and responsible use:

- **Building the foundation**:

  - o **Pre-trained AI services**: AWS accelerates generative AI projects with pre-trained services like Amazon Comprehend and Amazon Translate. Comprehend simplifies natural language processing, generating engaging and contextually accurate text. Translate seamlessly integrates multilingual capabilities, allowing businesses to expand their global reach easily.

  - o **EC2 and Amazon SageMaker**: For businesses seeking full control, Amazon EC2 offers granular compute resources for building custom generative AI models. Alternatively, Amazon SageMaker provides a streamlined solution for managing the machine learning lifecycle, offering tools for training, tuning, and deploying models. SageMaker allows teams to focus on their creative vision by handling infrastructure complexities.

- o **Amazon S3 storage**: Generative AI relies on robust data management, and Amazon S3 delivers scalable, cost-effective storage for training data, model artifacts, and AI-generated content. Its seamless integration with AWS services ensures consistent data accessibility throughout development and deployment.

- o **Amazon Bedrock**: Amazon Bedrock simplifies the creation and deployment of generative AI applications by providing access to high-performing **foundation models (FMs)** from leading providers. These models accelerate innovation by serving as starting points for custom applications. Bedrock also supports the integration of custom models, offering businesses the flexibility to tailor solutions to their specific needs.

- **Empowering creation**:

  - o **Text generation**: Generative AI enables businesses to craft compelling narratives, personalized marketing copy, and engaging scripts. Organizations can fuel innovative content strategies and elevate user experiences by leveraging pre-trained services or foundation models through Bedrock.

  - o **Image and video synthesis**: AWS empowers businesses to develop generative models for creating dynamic images and videos. Whether producing product mock-ups, generating training data for AI models, or crafting visual effects for media and entertainment, these tools open new avenues for creativity.

  - o **Music and audio generation**: The potential of generative AI extends to music composition, sound effects, and personalized audio experiences. Businesses like gaming, advertising, and entertainment can revolutionize their offerings by integrating generative AI capabilities.

- **Beyond creation**:

  - o **Data augmentation**: Generative AI addresses the challenges of limited data availability by creating synthetic datasets. These enhanced datasets improve the performance of machine learning models, particularly in scenarios where real-world data is scarce.

  - o **Anomaly detection**: Generative models analyze typical data patterns, enabling the identification of anomalies or outliers. This capability enhances proactive decision-making by detecting potential issues or fraudulent activities.

- **Ensuring responsible AI**:

  - o **Bias mitigation with Rekognition and Transcribe**: Pre-trained AI services like Amazon Rekognition and Amazon Transcribe support ethical AI practices. Businesses can analyze generated content to identify and address potential biases, ensuring inclusivity and fairness.

  - o **Explainability tools**: Transparency builds trust in AI. AWS offers tools to interpret how generative models make decisions, allowing businesses to understand and validate their outputs. This fosters confidence in AI-driven processes.

  - o **Amazon Guardrails with Bedrock**: Bedrock provides built-in guardrails that enforce responsible AI principles. Businesses can define safety parameters and ensure ethical use of pre-trained and custom generative models, maintaining control over their applications.

AWS empowers businesses to unlock innovation through generative AI, from crafting unique content to enhancing data-driven strategies. By leveraging the capabilities of services like SageMaker, Bedrock, and S3 and adhering to responsible AI practices, organizations can explore the limitless possibilities of generative AI while shaping a future defined by creativity and ethical AI use.

Introduction to Amazon Bedrock

Amazon Bedrock is a fully managed service that streamlines the complexities of developing and deploying generative AI solutions. By abstracting the intricacies of machine learning, Bedrock empowers developers to harness the potential of FMs without requiring deep ML expertise. This groundbreaking service enables innovation across industries, providing seamless access to cutting-edge AI capabilities and accelerating the adoption of generative AI.

To fully leverage Bedrock's capabilities, it is essential to understand its core offerings, including access to foundation models, customization options, and seamless integration features. These elements form the backbone of Bedrock, enabling businesses to create impactful generative AI applications with greater efficiency:

- **Leveraging FMs**: Bedrock's defining feature is its curated selection of high-performing foundation models from leading AI providers, including Anthropic, Cohere, Stability AI, and Amazon's models. These pre-trained models, accessible through a single API, allow businesses to incorporate the latest advancements in generative AI into their applications. Bedrock eliminates traditional barriers to AI access, empowering organizations of all sizes to adopt state-of-the-art capabilities.

- **Customizing and fine-tuning models**: Bedrock goes beyond pre-trained models by enabling developers to fine-tune them or integrate their own custom solutions. This flexibility ensures that generated content aligns precisely with specific business needs, allowing organizations to create specialized AI applications tailored to unique tasks and domains.

- **Streamlined development and integration**: As a fully managed service, Bedrock handles server provisioning, scaling, and configuration, freeing developers to focus on building impactful generative AI solutions. Its seamless integration with other AWS services allows businesses to efficiently incorporate generative AI into their existing workflows, bridging the gap between innovation and real-world implementation.

- **Driving innovation with Bedrock**: Amazon Bedrock delivers a range of benefits that help organizations unlock the potential of generative AI:

  - **Accelerated development cycles**: Pre-trained models and streamlined tools significantly reduce the time required to build and deploy generative AI applications, helping businesses respond quickly to emerging trends.

  - **Enhanced productivity**: By eliminating infrastructure challenges, Bedrock allows developers to focus on creativity and model refinement, fostering rapid innovation.

  - **Ethical AI practices**: Integrations with services like Amazon Rekognition and Amazon Transcribe enable analysis of generated content for biases, ensuring responsible use of generative AI in applications.

- **Advancing innovation with responsible AI**: Amazon Bedrock provides an intuitive platform for developing generative AI applications. It combines access to advanced foundational models with flexible customization and seamless AWS integration. By supporting responsible AI practices and enhancing developer productivity, Bedrock empowers businesses to drive innovation and shape the future of creativity ethically and effectively.

Key concepts in Amazon Bedrock

Generative AI is revolutionizing industries by enabling the creation of entirely new data, opening pathways for innovation that were once unimaginable. However, developing and deploying generative AI applications involves navigating significant complexities. Amazon Bedrock simplifies this journey by providing a robust, fully managed platform tailored to streamline generative AI workflows on AWS.

Core concepts for generative AI success:

- **FMs**: Amazon Bedrock's heart lies in its curated pre-trained FMs collection. These models, trained on massive datasets, are designed to handle diverse tasks such as creative text generation, image-to-text translation, and more. Supporting text, image, and multimodal formats, FMs serve as the cornerstone for generative applications. Examples include advanced models like Claude, Jurassic-1, Stable Diffusion, and Amazon's own Titan.

- **Unified model access**: Amazon Bedrock provides a single API interface to access various foundation models. This user-friendly approach simplifies integration and development, enabling scalable model inference across high-volume applications. Bedrock supports synchronous and asynchronous requests, making it adaptable to diverse operational needs.

- **Diverse model providers**: Bedrock's unique strength is its access to FMs from multiple industry leaders, including Anthropic, AI21 Labs, and Stability AI. By combining these offerings with Amazon's models, businesses can choose the most suitable tools for their specific use cases.

- **Fine-tuning capabilities**: Bedrock can fine-tune pre-trained models with domain-specific data for advanced users. This customization improves model performance for targeted applications, ensuring outputs are optimized for unique business needs.

- **Knowledge bases for enhanced accuracy**: Bedrock allows users to build custom knowledge bases as specialized repositories for domain-specific data. These knowledge bases can be queried during generative tasks, enriching FM outputs with precise, relevant information to enhance accuracy and context.

- **Retrieval-augmented generation (RAG)**: RAG combines FMs' generative capabilities with external knowledge sources, enabling real-time access to up-to-date information. This technique improves content accuracy and reduces the likelihood of factual errors, making it a critical component for dynamic and reliable AI applications.

Essential components for streamlined development:

- **AI agents for workflow automation**: Agents in Bedrock revolutionize the development of complex, multi-step workflows. These AI-powered entities can combine Bedrock functionalities, such as model inference, knowledge base queries, and external API interactions. For example, an agent could generate creative content, answer questions using internal knowledge, or automate tasks based on specific business logic.

- **Prompt engineering**: Effective communication with FMs is key to generating high-quality outputs. Prompt engineering equips developers with techniques to structure inputs and guide models toward desired results. Mastering this practice ensures optimal model performance and maximizes the value of generative AI applications.

- **Model evaluation tools**: Choosing the right foundation model for a specific task is essential for achieving the best outcomes. Bedrock provides evaluation tools and performance metrics, enabling users to assess models objectively and make informed decisions to refine their AI applications.

- **Security and governance**: Bedrock strongly emphasizes security and responsible AI development. Features such as private endpoints for secure API access, data encryption, and IAM integration for granular access control ensure robust protection. Audit logging and monitoring capabilities also provide comprehensive oversight, enabling businesses to maintain compliance and accountability.

Amazon Bedrock

Powering the future of generative AI, Amazon Bedrock equips organizations with the tools needed to harness the transformative potential of generative AI. From its powerful foundation models and fine-tuning capabilities to advanced security and governance features, Bedrock streamlines the development and deployment of AI applications. By reducing complexity and enhancing accessibility, Bedrock empowers businesses to innovate confidently and responsibly.

Key integrations with Amazon Bedrock

The true power of Amazon Bedrock lies in its seamless integration with a wide range of AWS services. These integrations enable Bedrock to function as part of a cohesive ecosystem, enhancing its capabilities and extending its potential across diverse workflows. By combining Bedrock with other AWS tools, businesses can build robust, secure, and scalable generative AI solutions tailored to their needs.

Key integrations for generative AI workflows:

- **Amazon S3**: Amazon S3 provides the foundation for securely storing and managing training data, knowledge base information, and model artifacts. Its scalability ensures sufficient storage capacity for projects of any size, making it an indispensable resource for Bedrock-powered applications.

- **Amazon EC2**: Amazon EC2 offers on-demand computing resources for computationally intensive tasks like large-scale model inference. This flexibility supports high-performance processing for scenarios involving complex workflows or large datasets.

- **Amazon DynamoDB**: Amazon DynamoDB is ideal for managing knowledge bases that fuel Bedrock's generative processes. Its scalable, NoSQL database architecture allows businesses to store domain-specific data efficiently, enriching AI outputs with precise contextual information.

- **Amazon RDS**: Structured data can be managed through Amazon RDS, which supports knowledge base storage, experiment results, and other critical datasets. Its relational database capabilities ensure efficient querying and data management, complementing Bedrock's generative applications.

- **Amazon SageMaker**: Integrating Bedrock with Amazon SageMaker empowers users to handle the entire machine learning lifecycle. SageMaker can preprocess training data, fine-tune FMs for domain-specific tasks, and manage workflows with Bedrock's generative capabilities.

- **Amazon QuickSight**: Amazon QuickSight enhances Bedrock's analytical potential by visualizing and interpreting generated content. Users can leverage QuickSight's data visualization tools to uncover trends, evaluate generative model effectiveness, and guide iterative improvements.

- **Amazon Athena**: For ad-hoc querying and detailed exploration of Bedrock's outputs, Amazon Athena provides a serverless, interactive query service. This allows businesses to analyze generated content directly and make informed decisions to optimize generative workflows.

- **AWS IAM**: IAM facilitates fine-grained access control, ensuring security within the Bedrock environment. Businesses can maintain compliance and prevent unauthorized access by defining permissions for accessing FMs, training data, and other resources.

- **AWS CloudTrail and Amazon CloudWatch**: Monitoring and observability are crucial for maintaining the health of generative AI applications. CloudTrail logs API activity, offering visibility into Bedrock's operations, while CloudWatch provides real-time metrics and performance monitoring for proactive management and troubleshooting.

Empowering generative AI ecosystems

These integrations enable Bedrock to seamlessly operate within a broader AWS environment, unlocking powerful possibilities. For instance, intelligent chatbots can draw on knowledge bases stored in DynamoDB, while marketing content can be automatically generated using customer data housed in S3. By leveraging these integrations, businesses can craft AI-driven solutions tailored to specific use cases, data sources, and operational requirements within AWS's familiar and secure infrastructure.

Amazon Bedrock limits

Amazon Bedrock is a powerful service for generative AI, offering seamless access to FMs and robust integration with AWS services. However, like any platform, it operates within defined limits and constraints.

Understanding these limitations is crucial for optimizing workflows, managing costs, and ensuring the efficient operation of your AI initiatives:

- **Resource quotas:**

  o **Model invocation quotas:** Amazon Bedrock enforces quotas on the number of model invocations per account to maintain service performance and ensure equitable resource distribution. These quotas vary by model and region, accommodating the specific requirements of different applications. Users can monitor and manage these limits through the AWS Service Quotas Console, and for unmodifiable quotas, AWS account managers can provide guidance.

  o **Adjustable quotas:** Many Bedrock limits, such as token throughput or request volumes, are adjustable based on project needs. Users can submit requests to increase quotas via the AWS Service Quotas Console, allowing scalability as workflows evolve.

- **Service-specific limits:**

  o **Provisioned throughput:** Amazon Bedrock offers provisioned throughput to address high throughput needs. This service enables users to reserve a fixed number of **model units** (**MUs**), ensuring consistent performance during high-demand operations. Pricing for provisioned throughput is tied to the specific model and the number of reserved MUs, making it a scalable option for demanding applications.

  o **Model requests and tokens processed:** Different models limit the number of requests and tokens they can process per minute. For example, some models support up to 400 requests per minute or process up to 300,000 tokens per minute. These constraints depend on model complexity and are essential for optimizing application performance.

- **Data and model size constraints:**

  o **Dataset size:** The efficiency of dataset processing depends on the model and regional capabilities. While Amazon Bedrock supports substantial datasets, it is important to structure and preprocess data for optimal performance, especially for complex generative tasks.

  o **Model size:** The size of deployable models varies based on the chosen foundation model and the compute resources available in your region. Selecting appropriate instance types ensures smooth operation and scalability for inference workloads.

- **Feature availability:**

  o **Regional access:** Not all Amazon Bedrock features are available in every AWS region. Businesses should verify the availability of desired features and foundation models in their target regions to ensure compatibility with operational requirements.

  o **Algorithm and framework support:** While Bedrock supports a variety of algorithms and frameworks, specific limitations or performance variations may exist depending on the model and use case. Businesses should evaluate compatibility and performance benchmarks before deploying large-scale applications.

- **Cost considerations:**

  o **Inference and customization costs:** Using Bedrock for model inference incurs costs based on the volume of input and output tokens. Businesses can also opt for Provisioned Throughput to ensure consistent performance during peak demands. Pricing is model-specific, providing flexibility for managing expenditures.

  o **Guardrails pricing:** Amazon Bedrock integrates guardrails to support responsible AI practices, such as filtering inappropriate content or redacting **personally identifiable information** (**PII**). Recently, AWS significantly reduced the costs of guardrails, making them a more accessible option for maintaining ethical and secure AI deployments.

Optimizing your Bedrock workflow

By understanding these limits and constraints, businesses can better plan their generative AI projects, ensuring efficient resource allocation and cost management. Whether scaling operations, fine-tuning foundation models, or deploying AI applications globally, Amazon Bedrock offers the flexibility and capabilities to support your goals within defined parameters.

Introduction to Amazon Rekognition

Amazon Rekognition is a serverless, cloud-native service designed to revolutionize image and video analysis at scale. By leveraging the power of the AWS cloud, Rekognition enables businesses to extract actionable insights from visual data with ease, enhancing decision-making and accelerating innovation. Its seamless integration, scalability, and advanced capabilities make it a cornerstone for building intelligent, visual-data-driven applications.

The following are the key characteristics of Amazon Rekognition service:

- **Effortless integration for rapid development**: Amazon Rekognition eliminates the complexities of infrastructure management, allowing developers to focus on innovation. As a fully managed service, it simplifies integration through its user-friendly API, enabling teams to embed advanced visual analysis into existing applications quickly. Rekognition reduces overhead costs and accelerates development cycles by removing the need for manual infrastructure provisioning.

- **Scalability for demanding workloads**: Built natively for the cloud, Rekognition offers automatic scalability to handle workloads of any size or complexity. Whether processing high-resolution images or analyzing extensive video datasets, Rekognition maintains consistent performance without requiring capacity planning or manual scaling. This frees IT teams to focus on other strategic priorities, enhancing operational efficiency.

- **Pre-trained intelligence for accelerated value**: Rekognition is powered by a comprehensive dataset of pre-trained knowledge, enabling it to recognize a wide range of objects, scenes, and activities. It can even identify celebrities within visual content. This pre-trained expertise eliminates extensive custom training, allowing businesses to derive value quickly and deploy visual analysis capabilities with minimal setup.

- **Customizable capabilities for tailored solutions**: While Rekognition offers robust pre-trained functionality, it also supports customization to meet unique business needs. Organizations can fine-tune Rekognition using their specific datasets to align outputs with domain-specific requirements. This flexibility simplifies the customization process by removing the need for separate training infrastructure, making it easier to achieve highly targeted results.

- **Transforming insights into action**: Amazon Rekognition generates actionable insights from visual data, enabling businesses to enhance applications and processes. For example, product images in an e-commerce platform can be automatically tagged, customer behavior can be analyzed in video surveillance stored in S3, or content can be moderated for appropriateness. By integrating these insights into cloud-based applications, businesses can drive better outcomes through data-driven decision-making.

- **Unlocking the potential of visual data**: Amazon Rekognition's serverless architecture, scalability, and customizable capabilities make it a critical tool for unlocking the value of visual data. Rekognition empowers businesses to transform images and videos into powerful, actionable insights within the robust and secure AWS environment by enabling rapid integration, providing pre-trained intelligence, and supporting fine-tuned customization.

Introduction to Amazon Transcribe

In a world where information flows faster than ever, converting spoken language into text has become a vital capability for modern businesses. Amazon Transcribe is a fully managed, cloud-native service that simplifies **automatic speech recognition (ASR)** on AWS. Transcribe provides a scalable, cost-effective platform for transforming audio data into actionable insights by removing the need for on-premises solutions or complex infrastructure management.

The following are the key characteristics of Amazon Transcribe:

- **Effortless integration and managed service**: Amazon Transcribe's intuitive API enables seamless integration into existing applications, allowing developers to focus on innovation rather than infrastructure management. As a fully managed service, Transcribe ensures automatic updates and continuous access to the latest ASR capabilities, eliminating the burden of software maintenance. This streamlined approach reduces overhead costs and accelerates application development lifecycles.

- **Cloud-native scalability**: Built for the cloud, Amazon Transcribe is designed to handle workloads of any size or complexity. Its ability to automatically scale ensures consistent performance, whether processing large audio datasets or handling bursts in demand. By leveraging AWS's elasticity, businesses can process audio data without capacity concerns, eliminating the need for costly upfront hardware investments.

- **Advanced speech recognition**: Transcribe harnesses the power of Amazon's cutting-edge machine learning models to deliver highly accurate transcriptions. It supports a wide range of audio formats, accommodates diverse accents, and effectively filters background noise, ensuring reliability across various use cases. Hosting these models in the cloud minimizes the infrastructure footprint, allowing businesses to focus resources on delivering value to their customers.

- **Flexibility for diverse applications**: Amazon Transcribe offers flexibility in real-time and asynchronous speech-to-text scenarios. Businesses can stream live audio for immediate transcription or upload pre-recorded files for batch processing. This versatility makes Transcribe suitable for a broad spectrum of use cases, from enhancing accessibility in live video conferences to analyzing historical audio data for insights.

- **Domain-specific customization**: Transcribe allows organizations to integrate domain-specific knowledge, enhancing transcription accuracy for specialized terminology or industry jargon. Businesses can tailor the service to their unique requirements by creating custom knowledge bases within AWS. This domain-specific customization eliminates the need for separate knowledge management infrastructure, streamlining operations while improving the quality of outputs.

- **Actionable insights from transcriptions**: Beyond generating text, Amazon Transcribe provides detailed outputs that include timestamps, speaker identification, and sentiment analysis. These enriched insights enable businesses to build advanced applications that derive deeper meaning from audio data. For example, identifying sentiment trends in customer service calls or automating workflows based on transcription metadata becomes seamless with Transcribe's comprehensive output capabilities.

- **Transforming audio data into value**: Amazon Transcribe empowers businesses to unlock the potential of spoken language data by providing a scalable, flexible, and intelligent platform. With its cloud-native design, advanced speech recognition, and actionable insights, Transcribe enables organizations to streamline workflows, enhance accessibility, and gain meaningful insights from their audio content. This is achieved within the robust and secure AWS environment, making Amazon Transcribe an indispensable tool for modern businesses.

Introduction to Amazon Comprehend

In the era of big data, where unstructured text constitutes a significant portion of information, uncovering valuable insights from textual data is both a challenge and an opportunity. Amazon Comprehend, a fully managed, serverless NLP service, empowers businesses to unlock the hidden potential within their text data. By eliminating the complexities of NLP infrastructure and machine learning expertise, Comprehend allows organizations to focus on deriving actionable insights from their textual content.

The following are the key characteristics of Amazon Comprehend:

- **Effortless integration and managed service**: Amazon Comprehend offers a straightforward API that integrates seamlessly into existing applications, enabling developers to incorporate advanced NLP capabilities without managing infrastructure. As a fully managed service, it ensures automatic updates, bug fixes, and continuous access to cutting-edge NLP advancements. This reduces maintenance overhead, accelerates development lifecycles, and allows businesses to focus on innovation rather than operational complexities.

- **Cloud-native scalability**: Designed as a cloud-native service, Amazon Comprehend scales automatically to handle large and complex datasets. Whether analyzing customer feedback from millions of reviews or processing legal documents for key insights, Comprehend delivers consistent performance without needing manual scaling or upfront hardware investments. The elasticity of the AWS cloud ensures that businesses can effortlessly meet surges in text processing demands.

- **Pre-trained NLP capabilities**: Comprehend leverages pre-trained machine learning models, built on extensive datasets of text and code, to perform a wide range of NLP tasks out of the box. These capabilities include:

    o **Sentiment analysis**: Identify the emotional tone of the text, such as customer feedback or product reviews.

    o **Entity recognition**: Extract entities like names, locations, dates, and monetary values.

    o **Key phrase extraction**: Highlight essential concepts within the text.

    o **Topic modeling**: Group similar documents based on underlying themes.

By leveraging pre-trained models, businesses can quickly deploy NLP functionalities into their workflows without needing custom training, reducing development time and infrastructure costs:

- **Customization for domain-specific insights**: While the pre-trained capabilities are robust, Amazon Comprehend allows businesses to tailor NLP outputs to their unique requirements. Custom entity recognition and domain-specific tuning enable organizations to achieve higher accuracy in niche use cases. For example, a healthcare organization can train Comprehend to identify medical terminologies, streamlining tasks like patient record analysis or medical research.

- **Actionable insights for business impact**: Amazon Comprehend transforms unstructured text into structured, actionable insights that can be integrated directly into applications. For example:

    o **Customer support optimization**: Automatically classify and route customer support tickets based on sentiment or topic to improve resolution times.

    o **Legal document analysis**: This process extracts critical information from contracts, such as clauses, dates, and parties, enabling faster review and compliance checks.

    o **Content moderation**: Analyze user-generated content on social platforms to identify inappropriate language or offensive material.

Real-world use case

A leading global e-commerce company implemented Amazon Comprehend's sentiment analysis to analyze customer reviews, support tickets, and social media conversations in real time. Before integrating Comprehend, customer feedback processing was manual, making it difficult to detect emerging issues or track sentiment trends efficiently.

By deploying Amazon Comprehend's real-time sentiment analysis, the company was able to:

- **Identify negative sentiment trends early**: Customer dissatisfaction related to product quality was flagged automatically, allowing proactive intervention.

- **Optimize product features**: Insights from sentiment analysis led to targeted product improvements, reducing return rates by 20%.

- **Enhance customer service efficiency**: Support teams prioritized negative feedback, leading to a 30% faster resolution time and 15% higher customer satisfaction scores.

- **Boost sales and retention**: By responding dynamically to sentiment-driven insights, the company saw a 12% increase in repeat purchases and an 18% reduction in customer churn.

Through seamless AWS Lambda integration, sentiment data was processed instantly, triggering automated business workflows that directly influenced product development, marketing, and customer engagement strategies.

Unlocking the power of text data

Amazon Comprehend empowers businesses to transform unstructured text into actionable insights with ease. Its serverless, cloud-native architecture, robust pre-trained models, and customization capabilities make it an indispensable tool for automating NLP workflows. Whether enhancing customer experiences, streamlining operations, or improving decision-making, Comprehend enables organizations to derive maximum value from their text data, all within the secure and scalable AWS environment.

Service limits and quotas

AWS services provide robust machine learning and AI workload capabilities, but understanding service limits and quotas is critical to optimizing performance and ensuring smooth operations. The following is a summary of key constraints for Amazon SageMaker, Amazon Bedrock, Amazon Rekognition, Amazon Transcribe, and Amazon Comprehend:

- **Amazon SageMaker**:
  - **Model endpoints**: Limits on concurrent endpoints vary by account and region, typically ranging from tens to hundreds.
  - **Training jobs**: Concurrent training jobs are quota-limited, depending on instance type and region, ranging from a few to dozens.
  - **Notebook instances**: Running notebook instances are capped per account, with limits often ranging from tens to hundreds.
  - **Instance types**: Specific memory, storage, or vCPU constraints apply to different instance types, requiring careful selection based on workload needs.

- **Amazon Bedrock**:
  - **Knowledge bases and models**: Quotas govern the number of knowledge bases and models per account, varying by account type and pricing tier. Higher tiers allow more flexibility for large-scale deployments.

- **Amazon Rekognition**:
  - **Image analysis**: Limits exist for **transactions per second** (**TPS**) and monthly image analysis volumes. Free tiers have lower TPS, while higher tiers support increased processing capacity.
  - **Image size and format**: Specific image formats and large file sizes may have processing limitations.

- **Amazon Transcribe**:
  - **Character limits**: Transcriptions are capped at a specific number of characters to ensure efficiency and manageable output files.
  - **Concurrent jobs**: Limits apply to simultaneous transcription jobs, based on account type and tier.
  - **Audio length and quality**: Highly compressed or lengthy audio may require segmentation and can impact transcription accuracy.

- **Amazon Comprehend**:
  - **Documents per request**: Depending on account and tier, limits range from dozens to hundreds of documents per call.
  - **Monthly quotas**: Total documents analyzed per billing period are capped, varying by pricing tier.
  - **Document size and format**: Constraints apply to file size and format; not all large or uncommon formats are supported.

Service limits are designed to ensure fair usage and performance. Quotas can be adjusted in many cases through the AWS Service Quotas Console or by contacting AWS Support. Regularly reviewing usage and limits allows you to scale efficiently while avoiding disruptions.

Conclusion

AWS stands as a trusted leader in artificial intelligence, providing a comprehensive suite of cloud-native and serverless AI services that empower businesses to accelerate their machine learning and generative AI initiatives. By abstracting infrastructure complexities, AWS enables organizations to focus on innovation, ensuring that AI workloads scale dynamically, integrate seamlessly, and drive measurable business impact.

Services like Amazon SageMaker and Amazon Bedrock offer fully managed, scalable platforms for building, training, and deploying machine learning and generative AI models. These services unlock transformative capabilities, from automated content generation to intelligent decision-making, allowing businesses to extract actionable insights, optimize workflows, and enhance customer experiences. Seamless integration with AWS's ecosystem ensures operational efficiency, eliminating overhead while optimizing cost and resource utilization.

By adopting AI-driven automation, organizations can streamline operations, improve predictive analytics, and enhance innovation across industries. AWS's managed AI services, coupled with robust security and compliance frameworks, provide the flexibility and scalability required for modern AI architectures. Businesses leveraging these tools can deploy AI solutions rapidly, iterate efficiently, and maintain high availability in dynamic cloud environments.

The next chapter explores **infrastructure as code (IaC)** and its role in automating and managing cloud resources efficiently. Tools like AWS CloudFormation and AWS CDK, combined with key DevOps principles, enable organizations to implement scalable, repeatable, and resilient infrastructure deployments. As AI adoption grows, integrating AI workloads with IaC ensures consistent environments, optimized resource allocation, and streamlined deployment pipelines, bridging the gap between intelligent applications and automated cloud management.

Join our Discord space

Join our Discord workspace for latest updates, offers, tech happenings around the world, new releases, and sessions with the authors:

https://discord.bpbonline.com

CHAPTER 15

Mastering Serverless Deployment on AWS

Introduction

Deploying serverless applications effectively is a cornerstone of building scalable, resilient, and cost-efficient solutions on AWS. With the rise of serverless computing, deployment practices have evolved significantly, prioritizing automation, IaC, and **continuous integration and continuous deployment (CI/CD)** workflows. These modern practices streamline operations and enhance application reliability, security, and speed to market, empowering teams to focus on innovation.

AWS offers a robust ecosystem of tools and services tailored to meet the diverse needs of deployment workflows, particularly for serverless architectures. Tools such as AWS CloudFormation, AWS **Cloud Development Kit (CDK)**, and AWS **Serverless Application Model (SAM)** enable developers to define infrastructure programmatically with precision. In parallel, the AWS Code suite, which includes CodePipeline, CodeBuild, and CodeDeploy, facilitates the creation of highly automated, scalable, and repeatable deployment pipelines. Together, these tools ensure consistency and flexibility, making them invaluable for managing serverless and hybrid deployments.

This chapter looks at the principles, tools, and techniques necessary for deploying serverless applications on AWS. It begins with an overview of IaC progresses into detailed hands-on examples using AWS CloudFormation, CDK, and SAM, and explores CI/CD workflows leveraging the AWS Code suite. Readers will also gain insight into deployment best practices, troubleshooting techniques, and strategies for optimizing costs and security, all of which extend beyond serverless workloads.

Structure

The chapter covers the following topics:

- Introduction to deployment automation
- Infrastructure as code
- Introduction to AWS CloudFormation
- Introduction to AWS Cloud Development Kit
- Introduction to AWS Serverless Application Model
- Continuous integration and continuous deployment
- Best practices for serverless deployments
- Troubleshooting common deployment issues

- Real-time sensor data ingestion case study
- Future trends

Objectives

This chapter equips readers with the knowledge and tools to master the deployment of serverless applications on AWS, emphasizing automation, efficiency, and scalability. It introduces foundational concepts such as IaC, enabling readers to programmatically define and manage serverless infrastructure using AWS CloudFormation, AWS CDK, and AWS SAM. By integrating these IaC tools with AWS's comprehensive ecosystem, readers will learn to create robust deployment pipelines that enhance consistency and reliability.

The chapter looks at the AWS Code suite, CodePipeline, CodeBuild, and CodeDeploy, showing how to automate application build, test, and deployment workflows. With hands-on examples, readers will gain practical experience deploying serverless architectures, from simple microservices to complex, multi-tiered applications.

Critical best practices are emphasized throughout, including security, scalability, and cost optimization strategies. Real-world case studies provide additional context and lessons learned, demonstrating successful serverless deployment strategies in action.

Finally, this chapter explores future trends in serverless deployments, including event-driven architectures, edge computing, and AI-enhanced CI/CD workflows. By the end, readers will be equipped to confidently deploy serverless applications, automate critical processes, and adopt emerging technologies to build deployment strategies that are resilient, scalable, and future-ready.

Introduction to deployment automation

Deploying applications in today's fast-paced, cloud-native environments demands a high degree of automation. As businesses scale and innovate, manual deployment processes fall short, introducing inconsistencies, delays, and risks of human error. For serverless architectures, where deployments can involve multiple interdependent resources such as APIs, databases, and functions, automation is no longer a luxury but a necessity.

Challenges of manual deployments

Manual deployments are manageable for small-scale projects, but quickly become error-prone and inefficient as complexity grows. The challenges include:

- **Increased risk of errors**: Misconfigurations during resource creation can lead to downtime, security vulnerabilities, or system failures.

- **Time-intensive processes**: Repetitive tasks consume valuable time, delaying feature releases and increasing operational overhead.

- **Inconsistencies across environments**: One critical issue with manual deployments is the inability to replicate infrastructure consistently across multiple environments. Discrepancies can arise between development, staging, and production configurations, leading to unpredictable production behavior and making troubleshooting difficult.

- **Scalability bottlenecks**: Managing deployments across multiple regions or environments becomes increasingly cumbersome without automation.

Benefits of automated deployments

Automated deployments address these challenges by standardizing and streamlining the process. Key advantages include:

- **Consistency across environments**: Automation ensures all environments are provisioned identically, reducing the risk of configuration drift.

- **Reduced errors**: By eliminating manual steps, automation minimizes configuration mistakes and enhances reliability.

- **Faster iterations**: Automated workflows enable rapid deployments, helping teams deliver features and fixes more quickly.

- **Scalability**: Automation effortlessly manages increasing workloads and environments, supporting organizational growth.

- **Improved collaboration**: Using IaC and automated pipelines fosters collaboration by integrating deployment processes into version control systems.

Automation and serverless applications

Serverless architectures amplify the need for automation due to their dynamic nature. Functions, event triggers, APIs, and storage systems must work seamlessly together. Automated deployments ensure these interconnected components are deployed accurately and efficiently, reducing downtime and enabling teams to focus on innovation rather than infrastructure management.

Key automation tools on AWS

AWS provides a robust suite of tools to support deployment automation:

- **IaC**: Tools like AWS CloudFormation, AWS CDK, and AWS SAM enable programmatic resource definitions, ensuring repeatability and control.

- **CI/CD**: The AWS Code suite (CodePipeline, CodeBuild, and CodeDeploy) orchestrates automated workflows for building, testing, and deploying applications.

For serverless applications, deployments often involve intricate configurations, For example:

- Event-driven triggers between services like Amazon S3 and AWS Lambda.

- Integration with managed services like API Gateway or DynamoDB.

- Security roles and policies for each component.

Automation ensures these configurations are deployed accurately, avoiding misalignments that can lead to runtime failures.

Automated deployments align with DevOps principles, bridging the gap between development and operations teams. They enable rapid innovation cycles, reduce operational overhead, and enhance organizational agility. By adopting deployment automation, teams can not only meet but exceed the demands of modern serverless workloads.

Infrastructure as code

IaC is a transformative approach to cloud resource management, enabling developers to define and manage infrastructure through code. By automating configurations, IaC ensures consistent, scalable, and error-free deployments across environments. In dynamic serverless architectures, where rapid deployments are essential, IaC forms the backbone of operational efficiency.

Core principles of IaC

IaC integrates software engineering practices into infrastructure management, making it a cornerstone of modern deployments. Key principles include:

- **Declarative configurations**: Define the desired state of resources (e.g., an S3 bucket or Lambda function) while the underlying tools handle the implementation details.

- **Repeatability**: Ensure consistent infrastructure setups across development, staging, and production environments.

- **Version control**: Store IaC templates or code in version control systems like Git, enabling collaboration, auditability, and rollbacks to previous configurations.

By adopting these principles, organizations can achieve reliable and efficient infrastructure provisioning that aligns with DevOps practices and continuous delivery workflows.

AWS IaC tools

AWS offers a comprehensive suite of IaC tools tailored to different use cases, each providing unique benefits to serverless deployments.

- **AWS CloudFormation**: CloudFormation is a declarative IaC tool that uses YAML or JSON templates to define and manage AWS resources. It is ideal for predictable and repeatable configurations, allowing teams to group resources into stacks and reuse them through nested stacks. The following are the key features of AWS CloudFormation:

  o **Drift detection**: Identify changes made outside the IaC framework, ensuring configurations remain consistent.

  o **Resource dependencies**: Automatically manage relationships between resources during deployments.

  o **Cross-region deployment**: Use StackSets to deploy resources across multiple regions.

CloudFromation helps in standardizing infrastructure in large-scale environments that require consistent setups across teams and environments.

- **AWS CDK**: AWS CDK offers a developer-friendly, code-first approach, allowing teams to define infrastructure using popular languages like Python or TypeScript. This flexibility is ideal for projects requiring dynamic logic and reusable components.

The CDK on compilation results in CloudFormation templates which can be executed to create and manage resources.

The key difference between the CDK and CFT-based approach involves the ease of management and provisioning of resources with familiar programming languages. The following are the core features of CDK.

  o **Dynamic logic**: Use loops, conditions, and variables for flexible configurations.

  o **Construct library**: Leverage pre-built constructs for common resources to simplify development.

  o **Language support**: Write infrastructure code in widely used programming languages.

AWS CDK helps in achieving highly customizable deployments for teams familiar with programming and needing dynamic logic.

- **AWS SAM**: AWS SAM extends CloudFormation with a serverless-specific syntax, simplifying the deployment of Lambda, API Gateway, DynamoDB, and more. The SAM CLI provides tools for local testing and debugging, making it ideal for serverless-first projects. The following are the salient features of AWS SAM:

  o **Simplified syntax**: Define serverless resources concisely with reduced boilerplate.

    o   **Local testing**: SAM CLI can be used to emulate Lambda functions and API Gateway locally.

    o   **Integration with CI/CD**: Seamlessly integrates with automated pipelines.

AWS SAM helps in the rapid development and deployment of serverless applications with a focus on simplicity.

Common limits in IaC

While IaC tools streamline deployment workflows, they come with specific constraints:

- **CloudFormation template size**: Limited to 1 MB for uploads and 51 KB for embedded SAM templates.

- **Resource limits per stack**: A maximum of 500 resources per stack, extendable via service quota requests.

- **Nested stack depth**: Limited to five levels, requiring careful planning for modular designs. Understanding these limits helps developers design efficient IaC templates that avoid operational bottlenecks.

Anti-patterns with IaC

To fully leverage IaC, it is essential to avoid common pitfalls:

- **Hardcoding secrets**: Do not embed sensitive information like API keys or credentials in templates. Use AWS Secrets Manager or Systems Manager Parameter Store instead.

- **Monolithic templates**: Avoid overly complex templates with too many resources, as they are harder to maintain and deploy.

- **Ignoring drift detection**: Failing to monitor changes outside the IaC framework can lead to inconsistencies between intended and actual resource states.

Best practices

To maximize the potential of IaC, readers should adhere to the following best practices:

- **Modular design**: Break infrastructure into smaller, reusable templates or constructs to simplify maintenance.

- **Parameterization**: Use parameters and mappings to adapt templates to multiple environments, such as development and production.

- **Validation tools**: Leverage tools like cfn-lint or SAM CLI to validate templates before deployment and catch syntax or configuration errors.

- **CI/CD integration**: Store IaC configurations in version control and automate deployments using AWS CodePipeline to ensure consistency and scalability.

IaC is fundamental to managing and deploying serverless applications at scale. Tools like AWS CloudFormation, AWS CDK, and AWS SAM empower teams to achieve consistent, automated, and repeatable workflows. By following best practices and avoiding common anti-patterns, organizations can ensure robust and scalable deployments, enabling them to innovate confidently and efficiently.

Introduction to AWS CloudFormation

AWS CloudFormation is a foundational tool for IaC on AWS. It enables developers to define and provision infrastructure in a predictable and repeatable manner using declarative templates written in YAML or JSON. By treating infrastructure as code, CloudFormation simplifies resource management, enhances consistency, and integrates seamlessly into CI/CD pipelines.

With CloudFormation, resources are grouped into stacks, which can be deployed, updated, or deleted as a single unit. The tool also provides advanced features such as changesets for previewing updates, parameters for dynamic configurations, and outputs for sharing values between stacks or with external systems.

The core concepts are as follows:

- **Templates**: The blueprint that defines the desired resources and configurations.
- **Stacks**: A collection of AWS resources created and managed as a unit.
- **Changesets**: A mechanism to preview and validate changes before applying them to a stack.
- **Parameters**: Allow customization of templates by providing dynamic values during stack creation or updates.
- **Outputs**: Enable sharing of important resource attributes, such as ARNs or URLs, across stacks or with external tools.
- **Drift detection**: Identifies discrepancies between the stack's template and the actual deployed resources.

Hands-on example with CloudFormation

This hands-on example demonstrates how to use AWS CloudFormation to deploy an S3 bucket and a Lambda function. The Lambda function will be triggered whenever a file is uploaded to the S3 bucket. The step-by-step instructions are as follows:

1. **Write the CloudFormation template**: Create a `cft-s3-lambda.yml` file with the following content, as represented here:

```yaml
AWSTemplateFormatVersion: '2010-09-09'
Description: Deploy an S3 bucket and a Lambda function triggered by file uploads.
Resources:
  MyS3Bucket:
    Type: AWS::S3::Bucket
    Properties:
      BucketName: my-serverless-s3-bucket
  MyLambdaFunction:
    Type: AWS::Lambda::Function
    Properties:
      FunctionName: MyS3TriggerLambda
      Runtime: python3.9
      Handler: index.handler
      Role: !GetAtt LambdaExecutionRole.Arn
      Code:
        ZipFile: |
          import json
          def handler(event, context):
              print("Event: ", json.dumps(event))
              return {«statusCode»: 200, «body»: «File processed successfully»}
  LambdaExecutionRole:
    Type: AWS::IAM::Role
```

```
      Properties:
        AssumeRolePolicyDocument:
          Version: '2012-10-17'
          Statement:
            - Effect: Allow
              Principal:
                Service: lambda.amazonaws.com
              Action: sts:AssumeRole
        Policies:
          - PolicyName: S3AccessPolicy
            PolicyDocument:
              Version: '2012-10-17'
              Statement:
                - Effect: Allow
                  Action:
                    - s3:GetObject
                    - s3:PutObject
                  Resource: !Sub "${MyS3Bucket.Arn}/*"
  S3BucketPermission:
    Type: AWS::Lambda::Permission
    Properties:
      FunctionName: !Ref MyLambdaFunction
      Action: lambda:InvokeFunction
      Principal: s3.amazonaws.com
      SourceArn: !GetAtt MyS3Bucket.Arn
Outputs:
  BucketName:
    Value: !Ref MyS3Bucket
    Description: Name of the S3 bucket
  LambdaFunctionName:
    Value: !Ref MyLambdaFunction
    Description: Name of the Lambda function
```

For production environments, it is recommended to store Lambda function code in a versioned S3 bucket or use container images for better maintainability and security. Below is a revised example referencing external code from an S3 bucket instead of using inline code:

```
Code:
  S3Bucket: my-lambda-code-bucket
  S3Key: lambda-code.zip
```

2. **Deploy the Stack via AWS Management Console**:

   a. Log in to the **AWS Management Console** and navigate to the **CloudFormation** service.

   b. Click **Create Stack | With new resources (standard)**.

   c. Upload the `cloudformation-s3-lambda.yml` file.

d. Specify stack details:

    i.   **Stack name**: S3-Lambda-Trigger.

e. Review the configuration and click **Create Stack**.

3. **Monitor the deployment**:

a. Navigate to the **Events** tab in the CloudFormation stack details page to monitor resource creation.

b. Once the stack status is **CREATE_COMPLETE**, check the **Outputs** tab for the S3 bucket name and Lambda function name.

4. **Test the setup**:

a. Upload a test file to the newly created bucket using AWS S3 Console.

b. Navigate to CloudWatch logs and verify that the function is created.

The following are some of the best practices when dealing with AWS CloudFormation:

- **Modular design**: Break complex infrastructure into smaller, reusable templates (nested stacks).

- **Secure parameter handling**: Use AWS Secrets Manager or Systems Manager Parameter Store for sensitive data instead of hardcoding values in the template.

- **Rollback strategies**: Enable stack rollback to avoid incomplete or faulty deployments in case of errors.

Introduction to AWS Cloud Development Kit

The AWS CDK provides a powerful, programmatic approach to defining cloud infrastructure using familiar programming languages like Python, TypeScript, Java, C#, and Go. With CDK, developers can use reusable constructs, write dynamic logic, and leverage native programming constructs like loops and conditions to manage infrastructure efficiently. CDK abstracts the complexity of AWS resource configurations, making it particularly valuable for serverless deployments.

The core concepts are as follows:

- **Constructs**: High-level building blocks that represent AWS resources.

- **Stacks**: Logical units of infrastructure that are deployed together.

- **App lifecycle**: CDK applications are organized into stacks, and stacks are synthesized into CloudFormation templates before deployment.

- **Dynamic logic**: Use loops, conditions, and programming constructs for flexible resource creation.

Hands-on example with AWS CDK

This hands-on example demonstrates how to use the AWS CDK to programmatically deploy a REST API backed by AWS Lambda and DynamoDB. The API allows users to perform **create, read, update, delete** (**CRUD**) operations on a DynamoDB table.

The step-by-step instructions are as follows:

1. **Set up your environment**:

a. Install the AWS CDK CLI.

b. Initialize a new CDK project (TypeScript is used in this example).

c. Set up a Python virtual environment and install CDK libraries as follows:

```
npm install -g aws-cdk
mkdir cdk-rest-project && cd cdk-rest-project
cdk init app --language python

python3 -m venv .venv
source .venv/bin/activate

pip install aws-cdk.aws-lambda aws-cdk.aws-dynamodb aws-cdk.aws-apigateway
```

2. **Define the resources**: After setting up the CDK project, the next step is to define the infrastructure resources that form the backbone of the serverless API. These include:

   - A DynamoDB table for storing data.

   - A Lambda function for handling API logic.

   - An API Gateway for exposing HTTP endpoints.

All these resources will be defined in the **cdk_rest_api/cdk_rest_api_stack.py** file. This file acts as the blueprint for your stack, specifying what infrastructure will be created and how they are interconnected.

Below is the code implementation for this serverless stack:

```python
from aws_cdk import (
    Stack,
    aws_dynamodb as dynamodb,
    aws_lambda as _lambda,
    aws_apigateway as apigateway
)
from constructs import Construct
class CdkRestApiStack(Stack):
    def __init__(self, scope: Construct, construct_id: str, **kwargs) -> None:
        super().__init__(scope, construct_id, **kwargs)
        # Create a DynamoDB Table
        dynamo_table = dynamodb.Table(
            self, "InformationTable",
            partition_key=dynamodb.Attribute(name="id", type=dynamodb.AttributeType.
STRING),
            billing_mode=dynamodb.BillingMode.PAY_PER_REQUEST  # Added best practice
        )
        # Create a Python Lambda Function for processing
        information_lambda = _lambda.Function(
            self, "InformationFunction",
            runtime=_lambda.Runtime.PYTHON_3_12,
            handler="index.lambda_handler",  # Corrected for Python
            code=_lambda.Code.from_asset("lambda"),  # Ensure this directory exists
            environment={
                "TABLE_NAME": dynamo_table.table_name
            }
        )
        # Grant Lambda Function access to DynamoDB Table
```

```python
        dynamo_table.grant_read_write_data(information_lambda)
        # Create an API Gateway REST API
        information_api = apigateway.RestApi(
            self, "InformationAPI",
            rest_api_name="Informational Service"
        )
        # Define a resource and method for the Information API
        information = information_api.root.add_resource("information")
        information.add_method("POST", apigateway.LambdaIntegration(information_
lambda))
        information.add_method("GET", apigateway.LambdaIntegration(information_
lambda))
```

3. **Add Lambda function code**: Create a Lambda directory in your project root and add an **index.py** file for the Lambda function:

```python
import os
import boto3
import json
from botocore.exceptions import BotoCoreError, ClientError


dynamodb = boto3.resource("dynamodb")
table = dynamodb.Table(os.getenv("TABLE_NAME", ""))


def handler(event, context):
    try:
        if event["httpMethod"] == "POST":
            body = json.loads(event["body"])
            if not isinstance(body, dict) or "id" not in body:
                return {"statusCode": 400, "body": json.
dumps({"message": "Invalid input"})}
            table.put_item(Item=body)
            return {"statusCode": 201, "body": json.dumps({"message": "Item added"})}

        if event["httpMethod"] == "GET":
            return {"statusCode": 200, "body": json.dumps(table.scan(Limit=10).
get("Items", []))}

        return {"statusCode": 400, "body": json.
dumps({"message": "Unsupported method"})}

    except (BotoCoreError, ClientError) as e:
        return {"statusCode": 500, "body": json.
dumps({"message": f"DynamoDB error: {str(e)}"})}
    except json.JSONDecodeError:
        return {"statusCode": 400, "body": json.dumps({"message": "Invalid JSON"})}
    except Exception as e:
```

```
        return {"statusCode": 500, "body": json.
dumps({"message": f"Error: {str(e)}"})}
```

4. **Deploy the stack**: Bootstrap your environment (only required for the first deployment) and run the **cdk deploy** as shown here:

```
cdk bootstrap
cdk deploy
```

5. **Test the API**: Note the API Gateway endpoint from the deployment output and test the **POST** method as follows:

```
curl -X POST "https://abcd1234.execute-api.us-west-2.amazonaws.com/prod/information" \
  -H "Content-Type: application/json" \
  -d '{"id": "4", "Information_type": "Basic Information"}'
```

The following are the best practices to keep in mind when using AWS CDK to define AWS resources:

-   **Reusable constructs**: Group common resource configurations into reusable constructs to simplify stack definitions.

-   **Environment variables**: Use environment variables to pass resource details (e.g., table names) to Lambda functions.

-   **CI/CD integration**: Automate CDK deployments using pipelines like AWS CodePipeline.

-   **Secure permissions**: Grant minimal IAM permissions to resources to follow the principle of least privilege.

Introduction to AWS Serverless Application Model

The AWS SAM is a framework specifically designed for deploying serverless applications. It extends AWS CloudFormation with simplified syntax, making it easier to define serverless resources such as AWS Lambda, API Gateway, and DynamoDB. SAM accelerates development workflows with features like local testing, debugging, and integration with CI/CD pipelines.

The core concepts are as follows:

-   **SAM templates**: Define serverless resources using simplified YAML syntax.

-   **SAM CLI**: Provides commands to build, deploy, and test serverless applications locally and in the cloud.

-   **Event sources**: Define triggers such as HTTP requests (via API Gateway) or DynamoDB streams.

-   **Environment variables**: Pass dynamic configuration values to Lambda functions.

Hands-on example with AWS SAM

The steps are as follows:

1. **Install and set up SAM**:

    a. Download the appropriate installer for your operating system from the

        i.   **Windows**: Download the **.msi** installer.

        ii. **macOS**: Download the **.pkg** installer.

        iii. **Linux**: Follow the instructions for **.tar.gz**.

b. Follow the installation steps provided in the guide for your OS:

    i. **Windows**: Double-click the installer and follow the wizard.

    ii. **macOS**: Open the **.pkg** file and follow the guided instructions.

    iii. **Linux**: Extract the package and move the binary to a directory in your **$PATH**.

c. Verify the installation:

```
sam --version
```

2. **Initialize the SAM Application**:

a. Create a new SAM application:

```
sam --init
```

b. Choose the following options when prompted:

    i. **Template source**: AWS Quick Start Templates

    ii. **Runtime**: python3.12

    iii. **Application template**: Hello World Example

    iv. **Project name**: sam-crud-API

3. **Modify the SAM template**: Edit the **template.yaml** file to define the resources for the CRUD API:

```yaml
AWSTemplateFormatVersion: '2010-09-09'
Transform: AWS::Serverless-2016-10-31
Description: SAM Stack
Resources:
  InformationTable:
    Type: AWS::DynamoDB::Table
    Properties:
      TableName: Information
      AttributeDefinitions:
        - AttributeName: id
          AttributeType: S
      KeySchema:
        - AttributeName: id
          KeyType: HASH
      BillingMode: PAY_PER_REQUEST
  InformationFunction:
    Type: AWS::Serverless::Function
    Properties:
      Handler: index.lambda_handler
      Runtime: python3.12
      CodeUri: lambda/
      Environment:
        Variables:
          TABLE_NAME: !Ref InformationTable
      Policies:
        - DynamoDBCrudPolicy:
```

```
            TableName: !Ref InformationTable
    InformationAPI:
      Type: AWS::Serverless::Api
      Properties:
        Name: Informational Service
        StageName: prod
        DefinitionBody:
          swagger: "2.0"
          info:
            title: "Information API"
          paths:
            /information:
              post:
                x-amazon-apigateway-integration:
                  type: aws_proxy
                  uri: !Sub arn:aws:apigateway:${AWS::Region}:lambda:path/2015-03-31/
functions/${InformationFunction.Arn}/invocations
                  httpMethod: POST
                  passthroughBehavior: when_no_match
              get:
                x-amazon-apigateway-integration:
                  type: aws_proxy
                  uri: !Sub arn:aws:apigateway:${AWS::Region}:lambda:path/2015-03-31/
functions/${InformationFunction.Arn}/invocations
                  httpMethod: GET
                  passthroughBehavior: when_no_match
Outputs:
  ApiEndpoint:
    Description: "API Gateway endpoint URL"
    Value: !Sub "https://${InformationAPI}.execute-api.${AWS::Region}.amazonaws.com/
prod/information"
```

4. **Add Lambda function code**: Create an **app.py** file in the root directory to implement the Lambda function and use the following code:

```python
import os
import boto3
import json
from botocore.exceptions import BotoCoreError, ClientError


dynamodb = boto3.resource("dynamodb")
table = dynamodb.Table(os.getenv("TABLE_NAME", ""))


def handler(event, context):
  try:
    if event["httpMethod"] == "POST":
```

```
body = json.loads(event["body"])
if not isinstance(body, dict) or "id" not in body:
    return {"statusCode": 400, "body": json.dumps({"message": "Invalid input"})}
table.put_item(Item=body)
return {"statusCode": 201, "body": json.dumps({"message": "Item added"})}


if event["httpMethod"] == "GET":
    return {"statusCode": 200, "body": json.dumps(table.scan(Limit=10).
get("Items", []))}


return {"statusCode": 400, "body": json.dumps({"message": "Unsupported method"})}


except (BotoCoreError, ClientError) as e:
    return {"statusCode": 500, "body": json.
dumps({"message": f"DynamoDB error: {str(e)}"})}
except json.JSONDecodeError:
    return {"statusCode": 400, "body": json.dumps({"message": "Invalid JSON"})}
except Exception as e:
    return {"statusCode": 500, "body": json.dumps({"message": f"Error: {str(e)}"})}
```

5. **Build and deploy the application**:

   a.   Build the SAM application.

   b.   Deploy the application using the **sam deploy** command and when prompted, use the following:

   - **Stack name**: sam-crud-API-stack

   - **Region**: Your preferred AWS Region

   - **Confirm changes before deployment**: Y

   - **Save arguments to samconfig.toml**: Y
     ```
     sam build
     sam deploy –guided
     ```

6. **Test the API**:

   a.   Note the API Gateway endpoint from the deployment output.

   b.   Test the endpoints using **curl** or **Postman**.

The following are the best practices when dealing with AWS SAM:

- **Environment variables**: Use environment variables to pass dynamic configuration details like table names or regions.

- **Local testing**: Use the SAM CLI's **sam local invoke** command to test Lambda functions locally.

- **Secure policies**: Use least-privilege IAM policies for Lambda functions, granting only the necessary permissions.

- **Template modularity**: Break complex templates into smaller, reusable pieces using nested stacks or separate templates.

Continuous integration and continuous deployment

Modern application development thrives on agility, efficiency, and reliability, qualities that CI/CD workflows deliver. CI/CD enables teams to automate the build, test, and deployment processes, ensuring faster iterations and reducing the risk of errors. For serverless applications on AWS, CI/CD pipelines are invaluable for managing dynamic, scalable resources while maintaining consistency across environments. The explanations are as follows:

- **CI**: Automates the integration of code changes into a shared repository. CI ensures that every commit is validated through automated builds and tests, identifying issues early in the development lifecycle.

- **CD**: Extends CI by automating the deployment of validated code to production or staging environments. This eliminates manual steps, accelerates delivery, and maintains consistency across environments.

Together, CI/CD forms the backbone of DevOps, promoting faster feedback loops, improved collaboration, and reduced time to market.

The key benefits of CI/CD for serverless applications are as follows:

- **Automation**: Automates repetitive tasks, such as packaging and deploying Lambda functions, saving time and reducing errors.

- **Consistency**: Ensures environments are provisioned identically using IaC, reducing configuration drift.

- **Faster iterations**: Speeds up development cycles, allowing teams to focus on innovation rather than infrastructure management.

- **Scalability**: CI/CD pipelines seamlessly handle the dynamic nature of serverless resources, such as API Gateway endpoints or DynamoDB tables.

- **Resiliency**: Automated testing and rollback mechanisms ensure production deployments are reliable and recoverable.

CI/CD tools on AWS

AWS provides powerful tools designed specifically to simplify and enhance CI/CD pipelines for serverless applications. Some of the tools are as follows:

- **AWS CodePipeline**: Orchestrates the end-to-end CI/CD process by automating the movement of code through defined stages (e.g., source, build, test, and deploy). It integrates with tools like GitHub, AWS CodeBuild, and AWS CodeDeploy.

- **AWS CodeBuild**: A fully managed build service that compiles source code, runs tests, and produces deployable artifacts. It supports custom-build environments via `buildspec.yml`.

- **AWS CodeDeploy**: Automates deployments across environments, supporting various strategies (e.g., canary, linear, all-at-once) to minimize downtime.

- **Third-party integrations**: AWS CI/CD tools integrate seamlessly with GitHub, Bitbucket, Jenkins, and other popular DevOps tools, enabling flexibility in pipeline design.

CI/CD pipeline sample for a serverless application

These hands-on examples help in creating a CI/CD pipeline for deploying a serverless application (AWS Lambda + API Gateway) using AWS CodePipeline, CodeBuild, and CodeDeploy. The steps are as follows:

1. **Prepare the source repository**:
   a. Push your Lambda application code and **template.yaml** (SAM template) to a GitHub repository.
   b. Ensure the repository includes:
      - **Source code**: Python-based Lambda function.
      - **SAM template**: Defines the Lambda function and API Gateway resources.

2. **Define the CI/CD pipeline**:
   a. Navigate to the AWS CodePipeline Console and create a new pipeline.
   b. Configure the following stages:
      - Source stage:
         i.   Select GitHub as the source provider.
         ii. Connect your repository and specify the branch to monitor for changes.
      - Build stage:
         i.   Choose AWS CodeBuild as the build provider.

      Use a **buildspec.yml** file for the build instructions. Below is a sample file used in AWS CodeBuild to build and package a SAM-based serverless application.

```
version: 0.2
phases:
  install:
    runtime-versions:
      python: 3.12
    commands:
      - pip install aws-sam-cli  # Installs the AWS SAM CLI to enable build
and packaging
  build:
    commands:
      - sam build  # Compiles the application and prepares dependencies in
.aws-sam directory
      - sam package --output-template-file packaged.yaml --s3-bucket
<your-s3-bucket>
        # Packages the compiled application and uploads it to the specified
S3 bucket
artifacts:
  files:
    - packaged.
yaml  # The transformed template that will be used for deployment
```

      - Deploy stage:
         i.   Select AWS CloudFormation as the deploy provider.
         ii. Use the **packaged.yaml** file to deploy the stack.

3. **Test the pipeline**:
   a. Commit a code change to the monitored GitHub branch.
   b. Observe the pipeline execution in the CodePipeline Console:
      - **Source stage**: Detects the code change and triggers the pipeline.

- **Build stage**: Builds the Lambda function and generates a deployable package.

- **Deploy stage**: Deploys the updated Lambda function and API Gateway configuration.

c. Verify the deployment by accessing the API Gateway endpoint.

Best practices for CI/CD in serverless workflows

The following guidelines will help in getting the most out of the pipelines.

- **Automate testing**: Automated testing is essential for CI pipelines in serverless applications. This includes unit tests, integration tests, and regression tests, all of which should be integrated seamlessly into the build phase. AWS CodeBuild offers robust support for automating these tests, ensuring early detection of errors and reliable deployments.

- **Enable rollbacks**: Configure automatic rollbacks in CodeDeploy to revert to the previous version in case of deployment failures.

- **Use least privilege IAM roles**: Assign only the necessary permissions to CI/CD components to enhance security.

- **Monitor pipelines**: Leverage Amazon CloudWatch and AWS CodePipeline logs to monitor pipeline execution and troubleshoot issues.

- **Optimize artifact storage**: Use Amazon S3 for storing build artifacts and ensure proper lifecycle policies to manage storage costs.

Deployment strategies

AWS CodeDeploy supports several deployment strategies for serverless applications:

- **Canary**: Deploy updates to a small subset of users first and gradually roll out to all users.

- **Linear**: Deploy updates in fixed increments over a defined period.

- **All-at-once**: Deploy updates to all users simultaneously (ideal for non-critical changes).

CI/CD pipelines are essential for modern serverless workflows, ensuring faster, more reliable deployments while minimizing manual effort. By leveraging AWS CodePipeline, CodeBuild, and CodeDeploy, along with best practices, teams can automate their entire development lifecycle, delivering high-quality applications with confidence.

Best practices for serverless deployments

Deploying serverless applications effectively requires adherence to best practices that optimize performance, maintain scalability, and reduce operational risks. These practices are essential for ensuring deployments are consistent, cost-efficient, and compliant with organizational policies. The following section describes the key practices:

- **Ensuring idempotency in IaC templates**: Idempotency is a critical principle for IaC templates. It ensures that repeated deployments of the same template produce consistent results, avoiding unintended changes or resource duplication. For serverless deployments, idempotency is crucial for maintaining infrastructure integrity across environments.

  o **Avoid hardcoding resource names**: Use dynamic naming conventions or parameters to ensure templates can be reused across environments (e.g., development, staging, production).

  o **Leverage resource dependencies**: Define dependencies explicitly in IaC templates to control the creation order of resources.

o **Use ChangeSets and drift detection**:

- Preview changes before applying them using CloudFormation ChangeSets.

- Regularly run drift detection to identify discrepancies between the deployed infrastructure and the template.

- **Using automated testing and validation tools**: Automated testing and validation tools ensure that IaC templates and deployments are error-free and adhere to best practices. These tools help identify issues early in the development lifecycle, reducing deployment risks.

o **CloudFormation Linter (cfn-lint)**: Validate CloudFormation templates for syntax errors and resource configuration issues before deployment.

o **SAM CLI validation**: Use the `sam validate` command to ensure that SAM templates are correctly structured and follow best practices.

o **AWS Config rules**: Leverage AWS Config to enforce compliance rules for serverless resources. For example:

- Ensure S3 buckets have versioning enabled.

- Verify that Lambda functions use secure runtime environments.

o **Example rule**: `lambda-function-settings-check` ensures that Lambda functions are configured securely.

- **Leveraging resource tagging for cost and performance monitoring**: Tagging resources systematically help monitor and optimize costs, track performance, and implement access controls. AWS supports tagging for nearly all serverless resources, including Lambda, API Gateway, and DynamoDB.

o **Standardized tagging conventions**: Use a consistent tagging strategy to categorize resources by environment, owner, or application. Example tags:

- **Key**: Environment, **Value**: StagingArea

- **Key**: Owner, **Value**: ServerlessTeam

- **Key**: Project, **Value**: SensorDataApp

o **Monitor costs using AWS cost explorer**: Filter costs by tags to identify high-spending resources and optimize usage.

o **Performance analysis**: Use tags to group and analyze resource metrics in Amazon CloudWatch. For example:

- Tag Lambda functions with service names and monitor invocation metrics collectively.

- **Additional best practices**:

o **Enable logging and monitoring**: Use Amazon CloudWatch for tracking logs, metrics, and alarms for serverless resources.

Enable AWS X-Ray for distributed tracing of Lambda invocations and API Gateway requests.

o **Secure deployment pipelines**: Assign least privilege IAM roles to CI/CD pipelines to limit unauthorized access to critical resources.

o **Minimize cold starts**: Configure Lambda functions with appropriate memory allocations and use provisioned concurrency for latency-sensitive workloads.

o **Adopt modularity in templates**: Break large templates into smaller, reusable components (e.g., nested stacks in CloudFormation).

By adopting these best practices, organizations can ensure their serverless deployments are reliable, secure, and optimized for performance and cost. Idempotent IaC templates, automated validation tools, and systematic tagging lay the foundation for scalable and maintainable serverless architectures. These practices not only reduce operational risks but also empower teams to innovate with confidence.

Troubleshooting common deployment issues

Deploying serverless applications often involves challenges such as resource conflicts, IAM misconfigurations, and deployment drift. Resource conflicts, like overlapping S3 bucket names, arise from hardcoded resource names or simultaneous deployments targeting shared resources. To mitigate this, dynamic naming conventions and rollback mechanisms in CI/CD pipelines ensure unique and recoverable deployments. IAM misconfigurations, often caused by insufficient or overly restrictive permissions, can prevent services like Lambda from accessing required resources. These issues can be addressed by auditing policies with AWS IAM Access Analyzer, validating configurations with the AWS Policy Simulator, and adhering to the principle of least privilege.

Deployment drift occurs when deployed resources differ from IaC definitions, often due to manual updates. AWS CloudFormation drift detection identifies these discrepancies, enabling teams to realign resources with IaC templates. Regular re-deployments further ensure consistent infrastructure across environments.

AWS offers powerful tools to debug and resolve deployment issues. AWS X-Ray enables distributed tracing, helping teams identify bottlenecks and errors across API Gateway, Lambda, and downstream services. Amazon CloudWatch Logs centralizes logs, providing detailed insights into unhandled exceptions and invalid requests. CloudWatch Insights simplifies log queries to quickly identify critical issues. For local testing, the AWS SAM CLI allows developers to simulate events like HTTP requests or S3 uploads and provides detailed error traces for debugging.

To proactively avoid deployment issues, teams should integrate monitoring, validation, and version control into their workflows. Detailed monitoring in CloudWatch tracks metrics like Lambda invocation errors and API Gateway latencies, while alarms notify teams of anomalies. Tools like cfn-lint and sam validate ensure template accuracy, and version control systems like Git enable efficient tracking and rollback of IaC changes. By addressing common issues and leveraging AWS debugging tools, teams can ensure reliable, scalable serverless deployments.

Real-time sensor data ingestion case study

Deploying a scalable and reliable real-time data ingestion pipeline is a critical use case in industries such as manufacturing, agriculture, and transportation. Organizations need deployment strategies that ensure consistency across environments, handle infrastructure updates seamlessly, and enable rapid scaling. AWS serverless services provide a robust foundation for deploying such pipelines while simplifying operations.

Scenario

A precision agriculture company deploys IoT sensors across vast farmlands to monitor soil moisture, weather conditions, and crop health. These sensors generate real-time data that informs irrigation schedules and optimizes resource usage, helping to improve yield and reduce costs.

The following are the best practices:

- **Consistency across environments**: Deploying the same architecture across development, staging, and production environments.

- **Automation**: Eliminating manual deployment errors by leveraging IaC.

- **Scalability**: Handling unpredictable data bursts caused by operational peaks.

Deployment architecture

The pipeline leverages AWS serverless services to streamline ingestion, processing, and analytics:

- **Data ingestion**:
  - **Amazon Kinesis Data Streams** captures real-time sensor data.
  - **AWS IoT Core** acts as a gateway for managing secure communication between devices and AWS services.

- **Data processing and storage**:
  - **AWS Lambda** processes batches of sensor data, performing transformations and filtering.
  - **Amazon DynamoDB** stores processed data for real-time querying and analysis.

- **Monitoring and analytics**:
  - **Amazon S3** archives raw and processed data for batch analytics.
  - **Amazon CloudWatch** monitors resource performance and pipeline metrics.

The following figure (*Figure 15.1*) illustrates the core data and compute flow from IoT sensors to storage and monitoring services:

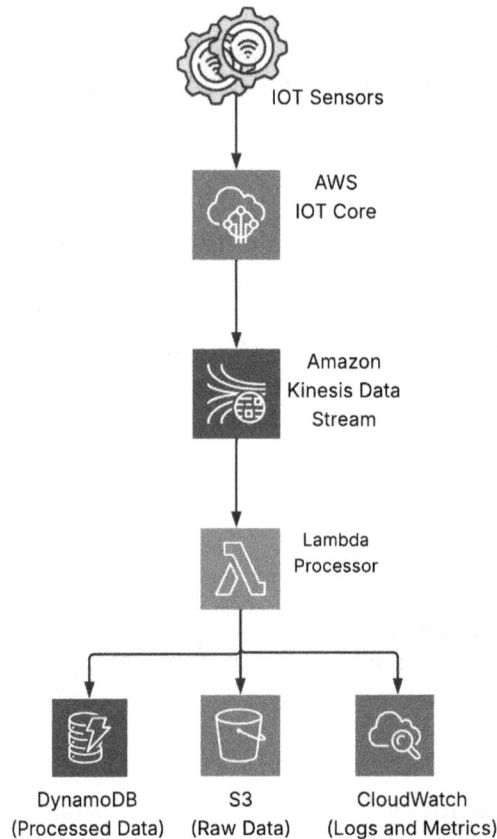

Figure 15.1: Sample architecture illustrating data and compute flow from IoT sensors

Deployment workflow

The deployment process is fully automated using IaC and CI/CD pipelines:

- **Infrastructure as code**: The architecture is defined using AWS CloudFormation or AWS CDK to ensure consistent and repeatable deployments. The IaC templates include:

- o   Kinesis streams with specified shard configurations.
- o   Lambda functions with dynamically allocated memory and environment variables.
- o   DynamoDB tables with throughput configurations for scalability.
- **Continuous integration and testing**: The CI pipeline automatically builds and tests updates:
  - o   Use AWS CodeBuild to validate IaC templates with tools like cfn-lint and sam validate.
  - o   Run unit tests for Lambda functions to ensure processing logic works as expected.
- **Continuous deployment**: The CD pipeline automates deployment to staging and production environments:
  - o   AWS CodePipeline orchestrates the deployment stages.
  - o   AWS CodeDeploy handles deployment strategies, such as canary deployments, for Lambda functions, ensuring minimal risk during updates.

Challenges and deployment solutions

The following are some of the challenges in implementing these solutions:

- **Consistency across environments**: Deployments must maintain identical configurations for development, staging, and production.
  - o   **Solution**: Use parameters in IaC templates to customize resources (e.g., DynamoDB table names) for different environments without duplicating code.
- **Scaling for unpredictable traffic**: High data bursts during peak operations can overwhelm ingestion services.
  - o   **Solution**: Preconfigure Kinesis streams with additional shards for scalability and uses Lambda's concurrency settings to process data efficiently.
- **Managing updates with zero downtime**: Rolling out changes to Lambda functions or Kinesis configurations must not disrupt the pipeline.
  - o   **Solution**: Use canary deployments with CodeDeploy to test changes on a subset of traffic before full rollout.

The lessons learned and best practices are as follows:

- **Automate deployments with IaC**: Use AWS CloudFormation or CDK to define resources programmatically. This ensures consistent infrastructure across environments and simplifies updates.
- **Adopt CI/CD for pipeline updates**: Set up pipelines with:
  - o   Automated testing to validate processing logic and infrastructure configurations.
  - o   Staging environments for testing changes before production deployment.
- **Monitor deployment metrics**: Use CloudWatch alarms to monitor key deployment metrics, such as:
  - o   Lambda function invocation and error rates.
  - o   Kinesis shard throughput to detect bottlenecks.
- **Enable rollback strategies**: Implement rollbacks in CodeDeploy to revert to previous versions of Lambda functions or configurations if deployment issues occur.
- **Leverage resource tagging for deployment monitoring**: Tag resources with environment-specific identifiers (e.g., Environment: Staging), enabling clear cost allocation and deployment tracking.

This case study illustrates how deployment strategies play a pivotal role in building scalable, real-time sensor data ingestion pipelines. By leveraging IaC and CI/CD practices, organizations can ensure consistent and automated deployments, reduce downtime during updates, and maintain operational excellence. The lessons learned here are universally applicable to serverless deployments in dynamic, data-intensive use cases.

Future trends

The landscape of serverless deployments is rapidly evolving, driven by advancements in automation, artificial intelligence, and new paradigms in infrastructure and pipeline management. These emerging trends are shaping how organizations approach deployment workflows, ensuring greater efficiency, scalability, and innovation.

AI-driven deployment optimization

AI is revolutionizing serverless deployments by introducing intelligent decision-making capabilities. AI tools analyze traffic patterns and usage trends to optimize deployment strategies like canary or blue-green deployments, reducing downtime and risks. As AI evolves, serverless workflows will become even more adaptive and resilient.

Policy as code and declarative pipelines

The rise of policy-as-code is transforming how teams enforce compliance in IaC workflows. It allows teams to embed security, governance, and operational rules directly into deployment pipelines.

For instance, tools like AWS Config and **Open Policy Agent** (**OPA**) can enforce policies such as:

- **Encrypt all S3 buckets**: Automatically detect and prevent creation of S3 buckets without encryption enabled.

- **Restrict public access**: Deny deployment of security groups with open 0.0.0.0/0 access to sensitive ports.

Example with AWS Config rule: A managed rule like `s3-bucket-server-side-encryption-enabled` can be configured to automatically evaluate whether all deployed S3 buckets enforce encryption. If a new stack violates this rule, AWS Config flags the resource as non-compliant.

This enforcement can be integrated into CI/CD pipelines to fail deployments that do not meet compliance standards, turning security into a proactive check rather than a post-deployment audit.

By combining declarative IaC templates with policy-as-code checks, organizations can ensure infrastructure consistency, automate compliance, and reduce human error, establishing a solid governance foundation for serverless architectures.

In parallel, declarative pipelines are redefining CI/CD workflows, focusing on the desired end state rather than detailing every procedural step. This shift abstracts the complexity of traditional pipelines, enabling teams to define deployment goals more concisely while allowing tools to handle the underlying logic. Declarative pipelines are particularly impactful in serverless environments, where dynamic scaling and event-driven architectures demand greater flexibility and reduced operational overhead. By adopting declarative approaches, organizations can achieve faster iterations, easier maintenance, and improved deployment consistency.

Together, policy-as-code and declarative pipelines represent a significant leap forward in automating infrastructure and deployment workflows. They enable organizations to not only deploy applications more efficiently but also maintain stronger compliance and governance, paving the way for a more secure and innovative future in cloud-native development.

Evolution of CI/CD for serverless environments

CI/CD workflows are adapting to meet the unique demands of serverless architectures. Modern pipelines are incorporating serverless-specific optimizations, such as support for event-driven architectures and asynchronous workflows. Features like instant rollback mechanisms, automated dependency updates, and tighter integrations with serverless frameworks (e.g., AWS SAM and CDK) are becoming standard. Additionally, serverless CI/CD platforms are leveraging cloud-native monitoring tools to provide deeper insights into deployment performance, enabling faster resolution of issues. These enhancements ensure CI/CD workflows remain efficient and scalable, even as serverless applications grow in complexity.

Conclusion

Deploying serverless applications on AWS requires a combination of automation, consistency, and scalability to meet modern development needs. This chapter highlighted the foundational role of IaC using tools like AWS CloudFormation, CDK, and SAM, enabling developers to define infrastructure programmatically and ensure repeatability across environments. CI/CD workflows, powered by AWS CodePipeline, CodeBuild, and CodeDeploy, further streamline the delivery process, reducing errors and accelerating iterations.

Troubleshooting strategies and best practices, such as leveraging AWS X-Ray, CloudWatch Logs, and drift detection, ensure deployments remain resilient and aligned with business needs. Real-world case studies, like sensor data ingestion pipelines, showcased how these techniques address complex deployment challenges effectively.

By integrating these principles and tools into workflows, teams can confidently manage serverless deployments, ensuring operational excellence and scalability. As serverless technologies evolve, the knowledge gained here provides a strong foundation for adapting to emerging trends, empowering organizations to innovate faster while maintaining reliability and efficiency.

As deployments become more streamlined and automated, ensuring the health and performance of serverless applications requires robust monitoring and observability practices.

The next chapter looks at how AWS tools like CloudWatch, X-Ray, and others empower teams to gain deep insights into application behavior, optimize performance, and troubleshoot issues effectively, completing the lifecycle of modern serverless workflows.

Join our Discord space

Join our Discord workspace for latest updates, offers, tech happenings around the world, new releases, and sessions with the authors:

https://discord.bpbonline.com

## CHAPTER 16

Monitoring and Observability in AWS

Introduction

Serverless computing has redefined how applications are architected by abstracting away the infrastructure layer. This model delivers agility, scalability, and operational efficiency. However, it also introduces new challenges. Traditional monitoring approaches, which are designed for long-running, persistent infrastructure, often fail to address the needs of serverless systems built around ephemeral compute and asynchronous execution.

Modern serverless applications typically span multiple AWS services and may integrate with external APIs, on-premises systems, or multi-cloud environments. As a result, observability becomes more complex. Maintaining visibility across these heterogeneous platforms requires more than basic metrics and logs. It demands a comprehensive understanding of distributed behavior, execution paths, and service dependencies.

For example, an API latency issue might originate from an API Gateway misconfiguration, a Lambda cold start, a DynamoDB bottleneck, or even a delay in a hybrid cloud connection. Observability provides the insights needed to trace these interactions and uncover root causes. Without it, troubleshooting becomes reactive, fragmented, and inefficient.

AWS offers CloudWatch for centralized metrics and logs, X-Ray for distributed tracing, and CloudTrail for API activity tracking to address these complexities. AWS DevOps Guru adds AI-driven insights, while OpenTelemetry provides vendor-neutral tracing for cloud-native applications.

This chapter explores how observability ensures serverless applications' performance, security, and cost efficiency. By leveraging AWS-native and standardized observability frameworks, organizations can detect anomalies, optimize workloads, and troubleshoot failures efficiently, moving beyond traditional monitoring into proactive application management.

Structure

The chapter covers the following topics:

- Understanding observability concepts
- Limitations of traditional monitoring
- AWS monitoring and observability tools
- Third-party observability tools for serverless
- Common anti-patterns

- Real-world serverless monitoring scenarios
- Future trends in serverless observability

Objectives

This chapter provides a comprehensive understanding of monitoring and observability in serverless applications. Readers will learn how traditional monitoring differs from observability and how the three pillars, metrics, logs, and traces, help diagnose distributed workloads effectively.

The chapter explores AWS-native observability tools, including CloudWatch for logging and metrics, X-Ray for tracing, and CloudTrail for API activity tracking. It also introduces OpenTelemetry for standardized tracing and AI-driven insights from AWS DevOps Guru and Lookout for Metrics, enabling proactive issue detection.

Readers will gain hands-on experience through a step-by-step implementation guide, real-world case studies, and a breakdown of common anti-patterns to avoid. By the end, they will be equipped with best practices for monitoring, troubleshooting, and optimizing serverless applications, ensuring they are resilient, secure, and cost-efficient.

Understanding observability concepts

In modern cloud-native environments, ensuring application reliability goes beyond traditional monitoring. Serverless architectures introduce distributed execution, asynchronous workflows, and ephemeral compute resources, making it crucial to move beyond basic metrics and logging. Observability plays a key role, offering a deeper understanding of how applications behave across multiple services and interactions.

Monitoring vs. observability

Monitoring focuses on predefined thresholds, collecting logs, and tracking system health through alerts. It answers the question, *Is my system operational?* by measuring CPU usage, error rates, and request latencies. While essential, traditional monitoring provides a reactive view, triggering alerts when something deviates from expected parameters but offering little insight into why issues occur.

On the other hand, observability takes a proactive approach, allowing engineers to analyze internal system behavior by combining logs, metrics, and traces. Observability enables answering deeper questions like, *Why is this request slow?* or *Where is this failure originating?* By providing contextual insights into dependencies, performance trends, and failure patterns, observability helps organizations detect, diagnose, and optimize application workflows effectively.

Logging vs. observability vs. insights

Each concept serves a distinct role in managing application health:

- **Logging**: Captures system events and transactional details (e.g., CloudWatch Logs, OpenSearch logs). Logs help debug failures but require manual inspection.

- **Monitoring**: Uses predefined metrics (e.g., CPU utilization, error rates) to track application health (CloudWatch, Datadog). While helpful for alerting, monitoring lacks contextual awareness across distributed services.

- **Observability**: Provides end-to-end system visibility, aggregating logs, metrics, and distributed traces to connect events across microservices (AWS X-Ray, OpenTelemetry).

- **Insights**: AI-driven tools like AWS DevOps Guru and Lookout for Metrics take observability further, detecting anomalies, predicting failures, and recommending optimizations.

Three pillars of observability

To fully understand how a system operates, observability relies on three core pillars:

- **Metrics:** Quantifiable performance indicators such as request latency, function invocation counts, and error rates. Tools like Amazon CloudWatch track these values, allowing developers to monitor trends and trigger alerts.

- **Logs:** Detailed event records providing granular information about transactions and failures. Structured logging (JSON-based logs in CloudWatch Logs or OpenSearch) enables better correlation between user actions and system responses.

- **Traces:** Distributed tracing tracks how requests propagate across microservices. AWS X-Ray and OpenTelemetry help visualize execution flows, highlighting performance bottlenecks and error-prone dependencies.

Monitoring ensures applications remain operational, logging captures what happened, and observability explains why issues occur. AI-powered insights take this even further, helping organizations predict failures before they happen. In the next sections, we explore AWS-native and third-party observability tools that empower teams to manage serverless applications efficiently.

Limitations of traditional monitoring

The shift to serverless computing has redefined how applications are monitored. Traditional monitoring tools were designed for long-running infrastructure, focusing on host-based metrics such as CPU usage, memory consumption, and disk performance. In a serverless environment, these metrics become irrelevant, as execution is stateless, distributed, and event-driven. This fundamental shift introduces unique observability challenges that require a modernized approach.

The challenges of stateless execution and distributed tracing are as follows:

- **No persistent infrastructure to track**: Serverless applications do not have fixed compute instances to monitor. Lambda functions spin up on demand and terminate after execution, making it impossible to track system health using traditional host-based monitoring.

- **Concurrency limits, cold starts, and event-driven execution**:
  - With highly dynamic scaling, concurrency limits can throttle requests, impacting performance.
  - Cold starts introduce inconsistent response times, making latency monitoring complex.
  - Event-driven workloads span multiple AWS services, meaning a failure in one function can propagate across the system without a clear failure point.

- **Asynchronous workflows and hidden bottlenecks**:
  - Message queues (SQS, SNS), Step Functions, and event-driven triggers decouple services but also introduce hidden latencies and failure points.
  - Traditional monitoring cannot track end-to-end request flows across multiple services, leaving gaps in root cause analysis.

Standardizing observability with OpenTelemetry

Organizations are adopting OpenTelemetry, an open-source observability framework designed for modern cloud-native applications.

The following list shows how OpenTelemetry helps overcome challenges with traditional monitoring:

- **Multi-cloud compatibility**: OpenTelemetry standardizes distributed tracing, logging, and metrics, allowing developers to monitor serverless applications across AWS, Azure, and Google Cloud without vendor lock-in.

- **Seamless AWS integration**: OpenTelemetry complements AWS X-Ray by offering enhanced tracing capabilities, support for multiple programming languages, and extended observability insights.

- **Bridging the observability gap**: With OpenTelemetry instrumentation, serverless applications gain consistent visibility across microservices, functions, and event-driven workflows, enabling engineers to detect and resolve performance issues proactively.

As traditional monitoring continues to fall short, the combination of AWS-native tools and OpenTelemetry provides the granularity, flexibility, and standardization needed to observe, troubleshoot, and fully optimize serverless workloads.

AWS monitoring and observability tools

AWS offers a robust ecosystem of monitoring and observability tools tailored for serverless applications. These services provide real-time insights, distributed tracing, security audits, and AI-driven anomaly detection, allowing organizations to proactively detect, diagnose, and optimize their cloud-native workloads. This section explores key AWS monitoring services, including Amazon CloudWatch, AWS X-Ray, CloudTrail, OpenSearch, and DevOps Guru, highlighting their roles in building resilient and well-monitored serverless applications.

Centralized monitoring with Amazon CloudWatch

Amazon CloudWatch is AWS's primary monitoring and logging service, offering real-time visibility into application performance, operational health, and system metrics. The following are key features of CloudWatch Logs that help developers manage and analyze logs effectively:

- **CloudWatch logs**:
  - **Capturing and storing serverless logs**: CloudWatch Logs is a central repository for logs from Lambda functions, API Gateway, Step Functions, and other AWS services.
  - **Structured logging**: JSON-formatted logs improve searchability and correlation across distributed components.
  - **Log retention and cost optimization**: Configurable log retention policies ensure long-term visibility while minimizing unnecessary storage costs.
  - **Integration with Amazon OpenSearch**: Logs can be exported to OpenSearch for advanced analysis and debugging.

- **CloudWatch metrics**:
  - **Tracking serverless performance**: CloudWatch Metrics automatically collects key Lambda performance indicators, including invocation count, error rate, duration, and cold starts, to monitor function efficiency.
  - **Custom metrics**: Developers can define business-specific metrics (e.g., Number of Orders Processed or User Signup Rate) to gain deeper insights.

- **CloudWatch alarms**:
  - **Proactive monitoring with AI-driven insights**: CloudWatch alarms enable automated monitoring and response actions based on predefined conditions. The following are some key capabilities of CloudWatch alarms:

- **Threshold-based alerts**: This feature automatically triggers alerts based on predefined conditions (e.g., high error rates and excessive duration).

- **AI-powered anomaly detection**: CloudWatch applies machine learning to detect unexpected behavior trends, reducing noise from false alarms.

- **Automated remediation**: CloudWatch alarms can trigger AWS Lambda or Step Functions to mitigate issues in real-time.

AWS X-Ray for distributed tracing

AWS X-Ray provides end-to-end visibility into request flows, helping developers trace **transactions** across multiple AWS services and identify performance bottlenecks. The following are the most important metrics that organizations should monitor:

- **X-Ray trace process for serverless components**: X-Ray captures traces for key AWS services, enabling:

  o **Full visibility across event-driven workflows**: Tracks requests from API Gateway to Lambda, DynamoDB, Step Functions, and beyond.

  o **Cold start detection**: Identifies delays introduced by cold starts in Lambda executions.

  o **Root cause analysis**: Helps debug latency spikes and bottlenecks by visualizing execution paths.

- **AWS X-Ray vs. OpenTelemetry**:

  o **Choosing the right tracing solution**: While X-Ray is AWS-native and deeply integrated, OpenTelemetry offers vendor-neutral observability across multi-cloud environments.

  o **Use AWS X-Ray** when working primarily within AWS and needing automated tracing without additional configuration.

  o **Use OpenTelemetry** for applications that span multiple cloud providers or require custom tracing instrumentation.

  o **Hybrid approach**: OpenTelemetry traces can be exported to AWS X-Ray, combining custom instrumentation with AWS-native insights.

AWS X-Ray vs. OpenTelemetry

While AWS X-Ray provides native, fully integrated tracing for AWS environments, OpenTelemetry enables vendor-neutral tracing across multiple platforms. For many modern applications, a hybrid approach offers the best of both ecosystems.

The following table (*Table 16.1*) provides a side-by-side comparison of AWS X-Ray and OpenTelemetry to help teams evaluate their use based on system needs:

Feature/Aspect	AWS X-Ray	OpenTelemetry
Integration	Deep integration with AWS services	Vendor-neutral, supports AWS, Azure, GCP, or on-premises systems
Ease of setup	Automatic tracing for AWS-managed services	Requires instrumentation using SDK's or agents
Use case fit	Ideal for AWS-only environments	Ideal for multi-cloud or hybrid environments
Customization	Limited customization	High flexibility in trace collection and export
Language support	SDK's for major languages	Broader multi-language support across open ecosystem

Export targets	Native to X-Ray and CloudWatch Console	Export to X-Ray, third-party tools or observability backends
Community and extensibility	AWS-maintained with updates for AWS Services	Open-source with broad community support and plugins

Table 16.1: Differences between AWS X-Ray and OpenTelemetry

For teams operating entirely within AWS, X-Ray offers simplicity and built-in support. For distributed systems spanning cloud providers or requiring advanced customization, OpenTelemetry provides the flexibility and control needed to unify tracing efforts.

AWS CloudTrail for security and compliance

AWS CloudTrail provides audit-level visibility into AWS API activity, ensuring security, compliance, and operational transparency. Key benefits of CloudTrail include:

- **CloudTrail for observability**:
  - o **Tracks API calls and user activity**: Logs who performed what action and when across AWS services.
  - o **Detects unauthorized access** Attempts: Helps identify suspicious configuration changes, IAM permissions, or resource policies.
  - o **Enables compliance and forensic analysis**: Essential for security audits and regulatory compliance (SOC 2, GDPR, HIPAA, etc.).
- **Integrating CloudTrail with monitoring pipelines**: CloudTrail logs can be integrated into real-time observability workflows for proactive security monitoring.
  - o **Using EventBridge + CloudTrail for real-time alerts**:
    - ▪ Detects high-risk API actions (e.g., unauthorized IAM changes, S3 bucket modifications).
    - ▪ Triggers immediate alerts to SNS, Slack, or security teams.
  - o **Triggering automated security responses with AWS Lambda**:
    - ▪ **Example**: If CloudTrail detects a sensitive security group change, a Lambda function automatically reverts the modification and sends an alert.

Amazon OpenSearch for centralized log analytics

Amazon OpenSearch provides scalable log storage and advanced querying capabilities, enabling real-time log aggregation, searchability, and troubleshooting.

The following are the features of OpenSearch for log analytics:

- **Log aggregation**: Storing and searching serverless logs:
  - o Consolidates logs from Lambda, API Gateway, CloudTrail, and VPC Flow Logs into a single searchable index.
  - o Improves debugging efficiency by allowing developers to filter logs across distributed systems in real-time.
- **Querying logs for debugging**: Building OpenSearch dashboards:
  - o **Live log analysis**: Use Kibana dashboards to visualize logs and identify failure patterns.

o **Correlation across services**: Link log data from CloudWatch, CloudTrail, and X-Ray to pinpoint root causes faster.

o **Proactive insights**: Run automated queries to detect anomalies, security threats, and application errors.

AWS DevOps Guru for AI-powered observability

AWS DevOps Guru applies machine learning to detect, analyze automatically, and remediate performance anomalies in AWS applications. The following are the scenarios handled by AWS DevOps Guru:

- **Using AI to detect anomalies in serverless apps**:

    o **Automated anomaly detection**: DevOps Guru continuously monitors CloudWatch metrics, logs, and X-Ray traces to identify unusual behavior patterns.

    o **Contextual insights**: Rather than just reporting an issue, DevOps Guru explains why an anomaly occurred, reducing troubleshooting time.

- **Proactive insights vs. reactive monitoring**: Unlike traditional monitoring tools that react after a problem occurs, DevOps Guru anticipates potential issues, allowing teams to:

    o Identify cost anomalies, such as unexpected spikes in Lambda execution time or API Gateway latency.

    o Optimize serverless performance by highlighting inefficient workflows or unoptimized queries.

    o Integrate with automated remediation pipelines, triggering Step Functions or Lambda-based fixes when anomalies are detected.

AWS provides a comprehensive set of observability tools to monitor, analyze, and optimize serverless applications. CloudWatch tracks logs and metrics, X-Ray enables distributed tracing, CloudTrail enhances security monitoring, OpenSearch centralizes log analytics, and DevOps Guru introduces AI-driven insights. By combining these tools effectively, organizations can build resilient, secure, and cost-optimized serverless applications with proactive monitoring and rapid troubleshooting capabilities.

Third-party observability tools for serverless

While AWS-native observability tools provide robust monitoring, logging, and tracing capabilities, some workloads require enhanced flexibility, cross-cloud visibility, or deeper analytical capabilities. Third-party observability platforms can address these needs by offering vendor-neutral monitoring, advanced dashboards, and real-time insights across diverse infrastructures.

Cloud-native observability solutions like Datadog, New Relic, and Dynatrace are widely used to complement AWS tooling in complex environments. These platforms support real-time distributed tracing, log aggregation, and event correlation across serverless and container-based workloads. They are particularly valuable for organizations operating across hybrid cloud, multi-region, or multi-account setups, where centralized visibility becomes critical.

For example, Datadog integrates seamlessly with AWS Lambda, API Gateway, and Step Functions while offering out-of-the-box dashboards and AI-powered anomaly detection. New Relic provides granular tracing for serverless invocations and supports OpenTelemetry-based ingestion, enabling unified observability across cloud-native services.

By integrating these platforms, organizations can enhance visibility, reduce troubleshooting time, and ensure consistent observability across both AWS-native and external components.

Importance of third-party observability

Although AWS provides powerful tools for metrics, logging, and tracing, some organizations opt for third-party solutions to extend observability capabilities in the following scenarios:

- **Multi-cloud and hybrid deployments**: Organizations operating across multiple cloud providers or hybrid architectures require a single pane of glass for observability.

- **Vendor-agnostic monitoring**: Some teams prefer standardized monitoring and tracing frameworks that work across cloud and on-premises environments.

- **Advanced analytics and custom dashboards**: Specialized solutions may offer additional visualization, AI-powered analysis, and custom alerting mechanisms tailored for complex applications.

- **Deep dive serverless debugging**: Some observability platforms provide real-time execution tracing and intelligent event correlation, helping teams identify performance bottlenecks and optimize function execution.

Organizations can enhance visibility, optimize performance, and maintain observability across diverse cloud environments by integrating third-party observability solutions.

Key considerations for integrating third-party tools

When selecting and implementing a third-party observability solution, organizations should evaluate the following:

- **Data collection and ingestion**: Determine how logs, metrics, and traces are forwarded from AWS services to the external tool. This could involve streaming logs via Kinesis Firehose, subscribing Lambda functions to log groups, or using OpenTelemetry SDKs.

- **Performance overhead**: Introducing additional observability layers should not degrade application performance. Serverless applications execute with strict resource constraints, so lightweight, event-driven monitoring is preferred.

- **Cost management**: Many observability solutions charge based on data volume and ingestion rates. Optimizing log retention, sampling traces intelligently, and leveraging cost-efficient data export pipelines can help control costs.

- **Security and compliance**: Ensure that observability data remains secure, particularly when transmitting logs and traces to third-party platforms. Encryption, access control policies, and data masking techniques should be implemented to protect sensitive information.

Addressing these considerations can help organizations integrate third-party observability solutions seamlessly into their serverless workflows while maintaining performance efficiency and cost control.

Integrating third-party observability tools with AWS

Organizations can integrate external observability solutions with AWS through structured data pipelines and standardized tracing frameworks. Some common approaches include:

- **Exporting logs and metrics**:

  o AWS CloudWatch logs can be streamed in real-time to external observability tools using Amazon Kinesis Firehose, AWS Lambda, or EventBridge rules.

  o AWS services like API Gateway, Step Functions, and DynamoDB support direct logging and metric forwarding to external monitoring solutions.

- **Using OpenTelemetry for distributed tracing**:

- o OpenTelemetry SDKs allow developers to instrument serverless applications with standardized tracing, sending data to AWS X-Ray and third-party backends.

- o This provides a flexible, vendor-neutral approach for monitoring request flows across Lambda functions, API calls, and event-driven workflows.

- **Implementing observability pipelines**:

  - o Organizations can design custom observability pipelines using AWS Lambda, S3, and Step Functions to filter, transform, and forward log data to third-party solutions.

  - o Intelligent sampling techniques can help reduce trace volume and optimize storage costs, ensuring only relevant data is analyzed.

By leveraging efficient data collection methods, minimizing performance overhead, and prioritizing security, organizations can extend AWS-native observability with third-party tools while maintaining the integrity and efficiency of their serverless applications.

Common anti-patterns

While serverless monitoring and observability have evolved significantly, common anti-patterns can hinder their effectiveness. Recognizing and avoiding these pitfalls is critical to ensuring resilient, cost-efficient, and well-monitored applications. Here, we discuss five prevalent anti-patterns and their impact on serverless architectures.

Anti-pattern one

Treating logging as observability: Logs capture discrete events in a system, but relying solely on logs for observability is a limited approach. In serverless applications, logs often provide isolated snapshots rather than a cohesive view of how components interact in real-time.

A notable incident occurred at a fintech company operating a real-time payment reconciliation system built on AWS Lambda, API Gateway, and DynamoDB. The system experienced intermittent delays during high-volume transaction processing. Engineers focused exclusively on reviewing CloudWatch Logs across individual Lambda invocations, attempting to trace the root cause. However, the issue persisted undetected for hours. It was only after enabling distributed tracing with AWS X-Ray that the team discovered an SQS queue was throttling downstream Lambda functions, introducing hidden latency. Without tracing, the relationship between queue backlog and processing lag remained invisible.

This incident underscored a common pitfall: while logs help identify *what* happened, they rarely explain *why* or *where* the issue originated across distributed services.

Solution: Adopt a holistic observability strategy that integrates structured logs, real-time metrics, and distributed traces. This multi-dimensional approach enables teams to uncover root causes faster and ensures end-to-end visibility across serverless architectures.

Anti-pattern two

Over-reliance on manual monitoring dashboards: Manually tracking metrics through dashboards can be time-consuming and prone to human error, especially in large-scale serverless environments with thousands of invocations. Critical anomalies like sudden latency spikes or cost surges may go unnoticed without proactive alerting.

Solution: Leverage AI-driven insights from tools like AWS DevOps Guru or custom machine learning models to reduce alert noise, automate anomaly detection, and prioritize actionable insights.

Anti-pattern three

Not configuring alerts on cost-related metrics: In serverless applications, cost is closely tied to performance. Failing to monitor metrics like Lambda duration, memory usage, or high concurrency limits can lead to unexpectedly high costs. Additionally, ignoring cost metrics can mask scaling inefficiencies or unoptimized workflows.

Solution: Configure CloudWatch Alarms on key cost-related metrics such as execution duration, memory utilization, and API Gateway request counts to detect anomalies early and optimize resource allocation.

Anti-pattern four

Ignoring distributed tracing in event-driven architectures: Serverless applications often comprise interconnected services (e.g., Lambda, API Gateway, Step Functions, SQS). Without distributed tracing, diagnosing failures spanning multiple services becomes nearly impossible. For example, a delay in a Lambda function triggered by SQS may be caused by message queue bottlenecks, not the function itself.

Solution: Implement distributed tracing using AWS X-Ray or OpenTelemetry, ensuring end-to-end visibility across microservices and event-driven workflows.

Anti-pattern five

Using too many monitoring tools without correlation: Adopting multiple uncoordinated monitoring tools often leads to fragmented insights and siloed data. This lack of integration results in incomplete system visibility, making root-cause analysis slower and less effective.

Solution: Consolidate logs, metrics, and traces into centralized observability platforms like OpenTelemetry or Amazon OpenSearch. Ensure tools are interoperable and provide a unified view of system health.

Understanding and addressing these anti-patterns enables organizations to unlock the full potential of observability in serverless environments. By adopting best practices like centralized observability, proactive alerting, and distributed tracing, teams can build high-performing, cost-efficient, and resilient serverless applications.

Real-world serverless monitoring scenarios

The true value of observability lies in its ability to provide deep, actionable insights into system behavior across distributed serverless environments. This section explores two unique case studies where observability frameworks were applied to solve performance and operational challenges, emphasizing the importance of metrics, logs, traces, and AI-driven insights.

Case study one

AI-powered observability in a serverless research platform: A global research organization implemented a serverless platform for processing genomic data, leveraging AWS Lambda, Step Functions, and S3. The system's distributed architecture required real-time monitoring to detect performance bottlenecks and improve processing times.

The observability challenges are:

- **Cold start identification**: Delays caused by cold starts during high-scale genomic analysis.
- **Execution flow visibility**: Understanding concurrency limits and memory allocation inefficiencies across multiple processing steps.
- **Workflow bottlenecks**: Inconsistent S3 write latencies impacting downstream data availability.

The observability solutions are:

- **DevOps Guru anomaly detection**: Detected anomalies in Lambda duration and memory usage, enabling early identification of cold starts during scaling events.

- **Distributed tracing with OpenTelemetry**: Provided end-to-end visibility into the Step Functions workflow, highlighting S3 write delays as bottlenecks.

- **Actionable metrics**: CloudWatch custom metrics for memory and duration were used to fine-tune resource allocation.

Addressing these issues significantly improved processing speed, gained better visibility into execution workflows, and reduced operational costs.

Case study two

Real-time observability in agricultural IoT pipelines: A precision agriculture company deployed an IoT pipeline to monitor crop conditions, using AWS IoT Core, Kinesis Streams, and Amazon OpenSearch for data ingestion and analysis. Observability was critical to handling seasonal spikes in event volumes, detecting anomalies, and optimizing resource usage.

The observability challenges are:

- **Data ingestion bottlenecks**: High event volumes during peak seasons overwhelmed the Kinesis pipeline, leading to message delays and drops.

- **Anomalous sensor readings**: Faulty sensors produced outlier data, skewing analytics and triggering false alarms.

- **Cost vs. visibility balance**: Storing all raw logs in Amazon OpenSearch led to unsustainable storage costs.

The observability solutions are:

- **Kinesis Stream metrics**: CloudWatch metrics tracked throughput, identifying congestion points during peak event bursts.

- **Log analytics with Amazon OpenSearch dashboards**: Filtered anomalous readings using real-time queries, providing accurate insights into sensor reliability.

- **Custom observability pipelines**: Lambda functions pre-process raw sensor data to filter noise and prioritize actionable logs, reducing storage overhead

As a result, the company enhanced data accuracy, optimized event processing, and minimized false alarms.

Future trends in serverless observability

As serverless architectures evolve, so do the observability practices and technologies that support them. The future of serverless observability focuses on intelligent automation, cross-platform compatibility, and cost-efficient monitoring solutions, enabling teams to manage distributed systems at scale with minimal operational overhead. This section explores the key trends shaping the future of observability in serverless environments.

AI-powered predictive observability

Integrating artificial intelligence into observability is reshaping how performance issues are detected, predicted, and resolved. The following are the key features of AI-driven observability:

- **Proactive anomaly detection**: AI-driven tools can identify unusual system behavior before it leads to outages, helping teams intervene early and improve application resilience.

- **Behavioral pattern analysis**: By analyzing usage trends, AI models detect subtle deviations that traditional monitoring might miss, enabling a more nuanced understanding of system health.

- **Real-world examples**: Solutions like AWS DevOps Guru and Amazon Lookout for Metrics exemplify this shift toward predictive insights and automated root cause analysis.

While these advancements reduce operational noise and improve visibility, it is important to recognize their limitations. AI-generated predictions can sometimes produce false positives or overlook complex failure conditions that require contextual understanding. For high-impact systems, such as those in finance, healthcare, or aerospace—human judgment and domain expertise remain essential in validating alerts, interpreting anomalies, and making operational decisions.

Combining AI-driven observability with expert oversight ensures balanced, accurate, and actionable monitoring strategies.

OpenTelemetry adoption for vendor-neutral tracing

OpenTelemetry is rapidly becoming the industry standard for tracing, logging, and metrics collection, offering vendor-neutral observability capabilities. The following are the core capabilities:

- **Cross-platform compatibility**: OpenTelemetry allows teams to monitor applications across multi-cloud and hybrid environments without being tied to a single vendor.

- **Custom instrumentation**: Developers gain the flexibility to instrument their applications with fine-grained control over tracing and logging.

- **AWS integration**: OpenTelemetry works seamlessly with AWS X-Ray, allowing organizations to combine vendor-neutral tracing with AWS-native observability tools.

Automated self-healing serverless applications

Automation is the next frontier in observability, enabling self-healing systems that can autonomously detect and resolve issues. The following list shows some of the advantages:

- **Event-driven auto-remediation**: By combining observability tools with AWS Lambda and Step Functions, teams can implement workflows that automatically mitigate failures (e.g., restarting failed processes or scaling resources).

- **AI-powered optimization**: Predictive insights from observability platforms can trigger automated tuning of serverless resources, such as adjusting memory allocation or concurrency settings.

- **Minimizing human intervention**: Automation reduces the need for manual monitoring, allowing engineers to focus on innovation instead of firefighting.

Observability cost optimization strategies

As the volume of metrics, logs, and traces grows, managing observability costs has become a priority for serverless teams. The following are strategies to optimize costs without sacrificing visibility:

- **Log filtering and retention policies**: Configure CloudWatch and Amazon OpenSearch to retain only the most relevant logs while archiving less critical data to S3 for long-term storage.

- **Intelligent trace sampling**: Use OpenTelemetry or X-Ray to sample traces intelligently, reducing data volume while maintaining observability.

- **Centralized dashboards**: Consolidate metrics, logs, and traces into a single dashboard to avoid duplication across multiple observability tools.

- **Leverage AI for efficiency**: Use AI-driven tools like DevOps Guru to identify and focus on high-impact anomalies, minimizing unnecessary data analysis.

Conclusion

Observability is the cornerstone of managing serverless applications in today's distributed, event-driven architectures. By leveraging tools like Amazon CloudWatch, AWS X-Ray, CloudTrail, and OpenTelemetry, organizations can go beyond traditional monitoring to gain deep, actionable insights into their application workflows. This chapter has highlighted the importance of metrics, logs, and traces in achieving comprehensive visibility, discussed AI-driven insights for anomaly detection, and explored practical solutions for cost-efficient observability.

The evolving trends in observability, such as predictive AI-powered insights, vendor-neutral tracing standards, and self-healing systems, empower organizations to optimize their serverless environments with proactive monitoring and automation. By addressing common anti-patterns and implementing best practices, readers are now equipped to build resilient, scalable, and cost-effective serverless applications.

In the next chapter, we study the critical topic of cost management in the AWS cloud. Readers will learn the core principles of cost optimization and explore tools like AWS Cost Explorer, AWS Budgets, and AWS Trusted Advisor. The chapter includes practical examples and strategies to help manage costs effectively, ensuring optimal resource utilization and financial efficiency in serverless applications. With a strong observability and cost management foundation, readers will be well-prepared to design and operate efficient, high-performing, cloud-native systems.

Join our Discord space

Join our Discord workspace for latest updates, offers, tech happenings around the world, new releases, and sessions with the authors:

https://discord.bpbonline.com

## CHAPTER 17

Optimizing Costs in AWS Serverless Architectures

Introduction

Serverless computing provides on-demand scalability and operational efficiency, but without careful cost management, expenses can rise unexpectedly. Unlike traditional infrastructure, where resources are provisioned upfront, serverless services follow a pay-as-you-go model, where every execution, API request, data transfer, and storage operation incur a cost.

The challenge in cost optimization lies in visibility and control, while AWS automatically scales resources, organizations must actively monitor usage patterns and optimize configurations to prevent unnecessary spending. Factors such as Lambda execution time, API Gateway request volumes, DynamoDB capacity, and inter-region data transfers can significantly impact billing if not managed properly.

AWS provides powerful cost management tools, including AWS Cost Explorer, AWS Budgets, Trusted Advisor, and Cost Anomaly Detection, to help teams track, analyze, and control their serverless spending. Additionally, implementing best practices in computing efficiency, storage lifecycle policies, and event-driven design can drastically reduce operational costs.

This chapter provides a comprehensive guide to cost optimization in AWS serverless architectures. It covers key cost drivers, AWS cost management tools, real-world cost-saving strategies, anti-patterns that lead to hidden expenses, and future trends in AI-driven cost governance. By the end of this chapter, readers will be equipped with practical techniques to manage serverless costs efficiently while maintaining high-performance, scalable applications.

This chapter equips cloud architects, DevOps engineers, and technical decision-makers with practical strategies to manage costs in AWS serverless environments. While serverless architectures inherently offer scalability and operational agility, their granular, event-driven billing model introduces new challenges. Cost optimization in this context requires not just tooling, but a shift in mindset, toward visibility, proactive monitoring, and architecture-aware design choices.

Structure

The chapter covers the following topics:

- Understanding cost management in AWS Serverless
- AWS cost management tools
- Cost optimization strategies for serverless applications

- Practical guide to cost optimization techniques
- Common anti-patterns in cost management
- Future trends in serverless cost optimization

Objectives

Managing costs in AWS serverless environments requires a deep understanding of pricing structures, usage patterns, and cost optimization strategies. This chapter provides readers with the knowledge and tools to monitor, analyze, and optimize serverless costs while maintaining high performance and scalability. Readers will explore AWS-native cost management services, including Cost Explorer, AWS Budgets, Trusted Advisor, and Cost Anomaly Detection, to track and control expenses efficiently.

Beyond cost visibility, this chapter covers best practices for optimizing computing, storage, and networking costs. Readers will learn how to fine-tune AWS Lambda execution, optimize API Gateway and Step Functions usage, and manage DynamoDB and CloudWatch costs. The chapter also highlights common anti-patterns that lead to excessive spending and provides actionable strategies to avoid them.

Additionally, the chapter explores AI-driven cost insights and FinOps best practices, helping readers implement predictive scaling, anomaly detection, and automated cost governance. By the end of this chapter, readers will be equipped to design cost-efficient, scalable, and well-optimized serverless applications on AWS.

Understanding cost management in AWS serverless

Cost management is a critical aspect of leveraging serverless architectures in AWS. While serverless computing offers operational simplicity and automatic scaling, its granular, event-driven pricing model introduces challenges in predicting and optimizing costs. Managing expenses effectively requires a deep understanding of AWS billing structures and the specific cost dynamics of services like Lambda, API Gateway, DynamoDB, and S3.

This section explores the key principles of cost management in serverless environments. It begins with an overview of AWS's pay-as-you-go model, discussing its benefits and challenges. It then highlights how serverless pricing differs from traditional cloud cost models, examines common cost visibility challenges, and identifies scenarios where EC2 may be more cost-effective. Finally, it introduces AWS Savings Plans and CloudWatch as valuable tools in the optimization toolkit, while noting that their effectiveness depends on workload patterns. The following table provides a side-by-side comparison of when serverless pricing versus Savings Plans offers better cost efficiency.

The following table summarizes the differences between serverless pricing and Savings Plans, highlighting when each model is most effective and how they can be optimized:

Pricing model	Best use case	Optimization strategy
Serverless (pay-per-use)	Dynamic, unpredictable workloads with variable demand.	Focus on right-sizing Lambda, minimizing invocations.
Compute Savings Plans	Predictable workloads or long-running compute jobs (e.g. EC2, Fargate).	Commit to usage levels to secure cost savings.
CloudWatch Metrics	Workload cost monitoring and anomaly tracking across both models.	Use with alarms and dashboards for early detection.

Table 17.1: Serverless pricing and saving plan comparisons

Advantages and challenges with pay-as-you-go model

The pay-as-you-go model introduced by AWS aligns resource costs directly with consumption, revolutionizing how organizations manage cloud expenses. This model is particularly beneficial in serverless architectures, where resources are provisioned dynamically to meet workload demands.

The key advantages are as follows:

- **Cost efficiency**: Organizations pay only for actual usage, avoiding expenses associated with over-provisioned or idle resources.

- **Scalability**: Serverless architectures automatically scale resources up or down, ensuring operational agility without upfront infrastructure costs.

The challenges are as follows:

- **Cost predictability**: Auto-scaling and event-driven services can lead to unpredictable monthly bills, particularly during high-traffic events or poorly optimized workloads.

- **Hidden costs**: Services like API Gateway, data transfer between AWS regions, and CloudWatch logging can add unexpected charges to the total bill.

Effective cost management in serverless environments requires robust tools and strategies for monitoring and optimizing expenses, which will be explored later in this chapter.

Differences between serverless and traditional cloud costs

In traditional cloud architectures, costs are often tied to reserved or on-demand virtual machines, which remain allocated whether fully utilized or idle. On the other hand, serverless pricing models charge based on specific consumption metrics such as function invocations, execution time, and data storage.

Some examples of serverless pricing metrics are as follows:

- **Lambda functions**: Based on execution time (measured in milliseconds) and memory allocation.

- **API Gateway**: Costs depend on the number of requests and the amount of data transferred.

- **DynamoDB**: Charges vary depending on whether provisioned or on-demand capacity is used.

While serverless pricing models improve flexibility, their granular nature requires more rigorous monitoring than traditional cloud environments. Organizations must design their applications to minimize unnecessary function invocations and optimize storage tiers to leverage serverless cost benefits fully.

Managing cost visibility in serverless architectures

Due to their distributed and dynamic nature, serverless applications introduce unique challenges in cost visibility. Understanding the distribution of costs across multiple interconnected services is critical for identifying inefficiencies and reducing expenses.

Common cost visibility challenges are listed as follows:

- **Auto-scaling complexities**: Serverless resources scale dynamically, making predicting monthly expenses for workloads with fluctuating demand harder.

- **Distributed billing across services**: Costs for serverless applications often span multiple services, such as Lambda, S3, API Gateway, and Step Functions, complicating cost allocation and accountability.

- **Per-request pricing**: Small increases in usage, such as additional API requests or Lambda invocations, can lead to disproportionate cost increments if not monitored closely.

To address these challenges, AWS provides tools such as Cost Explorer and Cost Anomaly Detection, which enable organizations to track usage trends, identify outliers, and analyze spending patterns across services. These tools form the foundation of effective cost management in serverless environments.

Cost management considerations with Amazon EC2

While serverless computing offers unmatched scalability and operational simplicity, certain workloads can benefit from EC2 instances, particularly from a cost perspective. In some cases, Lambda's billing structure, which charges for execution duration and invocation count, may lead to higher costs for long-running or high-frequency workloads.

The scenarios favoring EC2 over Lambda are listed as follows:

- **High-volume or long-running workloads**: Lambda's per-execution billing is costly for continuous or batch processing tasks better suited for EC2 instances.

- **Predictable traffic patterns**: Reserved EC2 instances or Savings Plans often provide cost benefits for workloads with consistent, predictable usage.

- **Specialized hardware requirements**: Custom hardware configurations, such as GPUs for machine learning workloads, are not supported in serverless environments but are available in EC2.

Combining serverless services with EC2 resources in a hybrid architecture can balance cost efficiency with scalability and flexibility for many organizations.

AWS savings plans and serverless considerations

While traditionally associated with EC2 and Fargate, AWS Savings Plans can provide limited cost-saving opportunities for serverless workloads when usage patterns align with Compute Savings Plans. However, the dynamic nature of serverless applications often makes reserved capacity impractical.

The key considerations are as follows:

- **Why serverless differs**: Unlike EC2-based workloads, serverless usage is inherently event-driven and bursty, making it difficult to commit to consistent usage.

- **Where it fits**: Savings Plans can be beneficial when serverless workloads are integrated with EC2 or Fargate resources in a hybrid architecture.

For most serverless-first designs, cost optimization strategies focus more on architectural efficiency, minimizing cold starts, optimizing API Gateway requests, and right-sizing Lambda memory, than long-term pricing commitments.

AWS cost management tools

Effective cost management in AWS serverless architectures requires specialized tools to monitor, analyze, and optimize cloud spending. AWS provides services that allow organizations to track real-time expenses, forecast future costs, and set proactive budget controls. This section covers billing and cost analysis fundamentals, core AWS cost management services, and advanced AI-driven insights that help businesses maintain financial efficiency while leveraging serverless capabilities.

AWS billing and cost analysis

Understanding AWS billing is the foundation of cost management. AWS offers several tools that provide insight into cloud spending, helping organizations allocate budgets effectively and optimize cost efficiency. The following are the core concepts in billing and cost analysis:

- **AWS pricing model**: AWS provides multiple pricing models that cater to different workloads:

- o **Free-tier pricing**: Allows organizations to use AWS services at no cost within defined limits.

- o **Pay-as-you-go**: Charges users based on actual resource consumption, ensuring flexible spending.

- o **On-demand pricing**: Provides compute resources without long-term commitments, making it suitable for fluctuating workloads.

- o **Reserved pricing**: Offers significant cost savings for predictable workloads by committing to resource usage for one or three years.

- **AWS billing dashboard**: The AWS billing dashboard is a central hub for monitoring spending across multiple accounts. It enables users to:

  - o Track real-time cost data and usage trends.

  - o View breakdowns of expenses by service, region, or account.

  - o Monitor the utilization of Reserved Instances and Savings Plans.

- **AWS pricing calculator**: The AWS pricing calculator helps estimate and compare costs for different configurations by:

  - o Allowing users to define workloads (e.g., Lambda memory allocation, API Gateway requests).

  - o Generating a breakdown of expected expenses.

  - o Assisting in scenario comparisons to choose the most cost-effective architecture.

Core AWS cost management services

AWS provides dedicated cost management services to help organizations optimize their cloud expenditures proactively. These tools not only offer real-time visibility into usage and budgets but also support forecasting and early anomaly detection across serverless components.

The following are key AWS cost management services:

- **AWS Cost Explorer**: A visualization tool offering interactive graphs and reports to analyze cost trends.

  - o Identify cost drivers across AWS services.

  - o Forecast future spending based on usage history.

  - o Filter by tags, accounts, or services for granular views.

The following figure illustrates a typical AWS Cost Explorer dashboard in action, showing service-level spending trends across a defined time period:

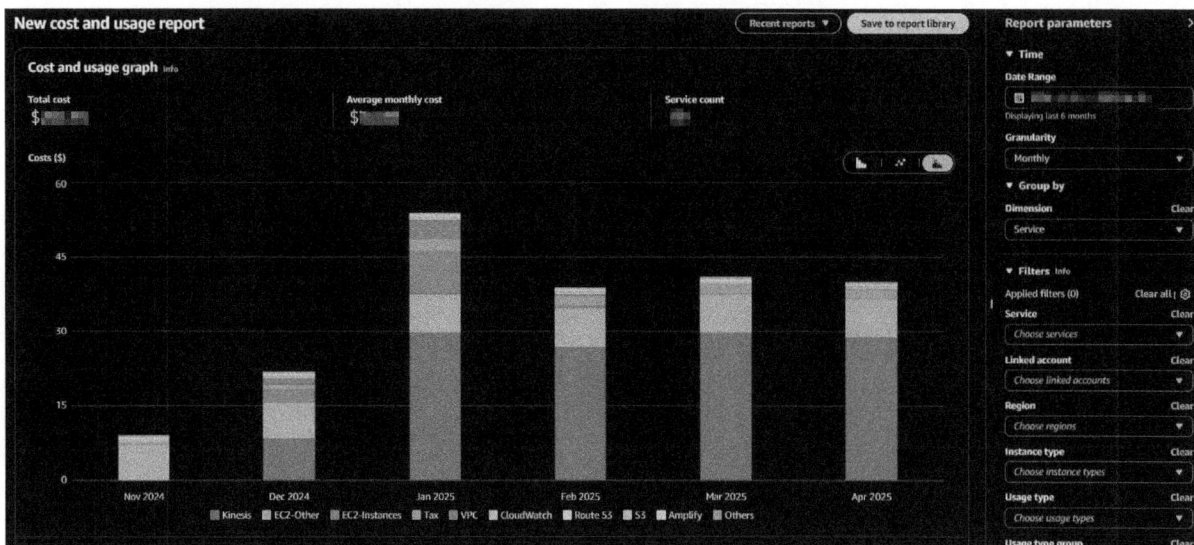

Figure 17.1: AWS Cost Explorer dashboard showing service-level breakdown and usage patterns

- **AWS Budgets**: A cost governance tool that allows users to:
    - Define custom budget thresholds and track usage.
    - Receive alerts via email or SNS when thresholds are breached.
    - Integrate with anomaly detection to highlight unexpected cost surges.

To support proactive cost governance, AWS Budgets allows for setting service-specific thresholds and automated notifications. The configuration interface shown in the following figure illustrates how users define budget parameters and alert rules:

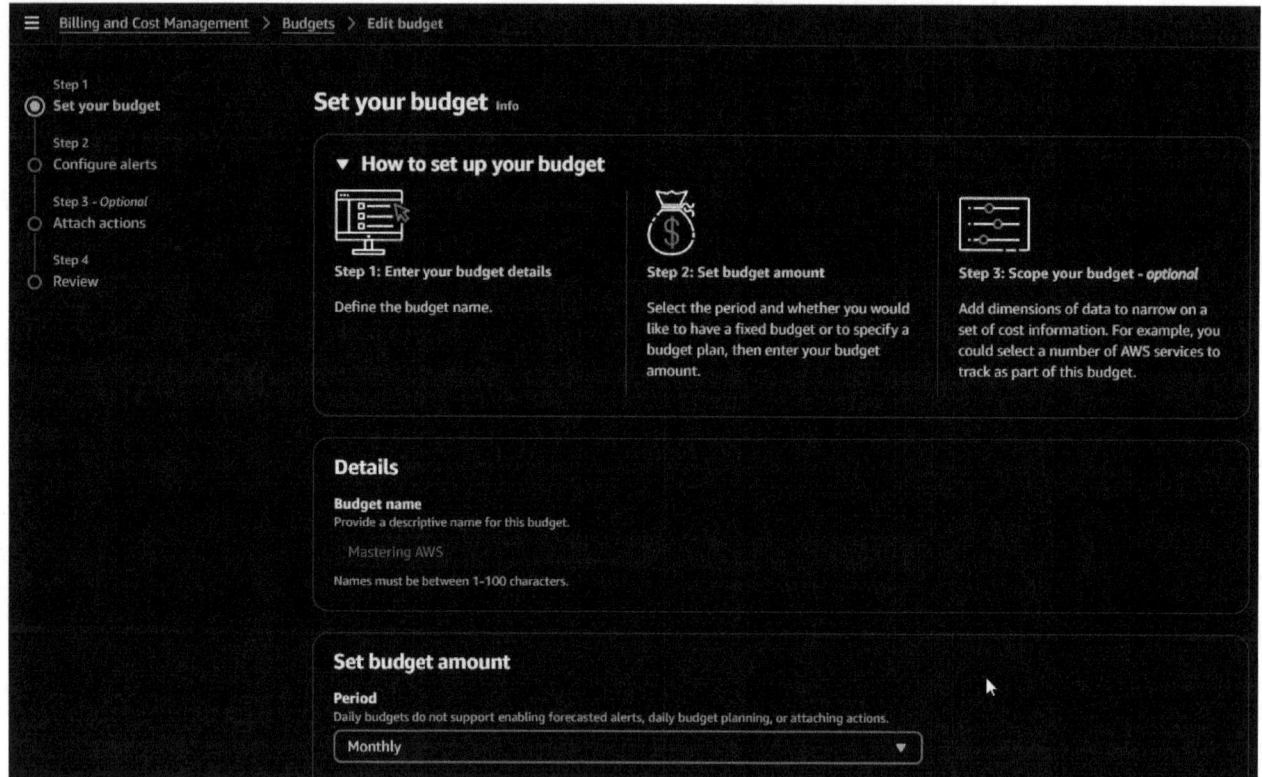

Figure 17.2: AWS Budgets showing service specific thresholds

- **AWS Trusted Advisor**: Trusted Advisor offers real-time recommendations to optimize costs, enhance security, and improve system performance. In the cost category, it helps:
    - Identify underutilized or idle resources that should be downsized or removed.
    - Highlight cost-saving opportunities based on service utilization.
    - Ensure efficient use of Reserved Instances and Savings Plans.

- **AWS compute optimizer**: Compute optimizer applies machine learning to analyze usage patterns and recommend the best configurations for computing resources. In serverless environments, it provides:
    - **Lambda function optimization** by suggesting the ideal memory allocation.
    - **Fargate container cost insights** to optimize task sizes.
    - **EC2 recommendations** for mixed workload environments that integrate serverless and compute instances.

Advanced cost analytics and AI-driven insights

As serverless workloads scale, businesses require deeper insights into cost trends and unexpected fluctuations. AWS provides advanced cost analytics tools to track, predict, and optimize cloud expenses with minimal manual effort.

The following AWS tools enable businesses to streamline cost management with minimal manual intervention:

- **AWS** Cost Anomaly Detection: This service leverages machine learning to detect unusual cost increases. Key functionalities include:
  - Automated anomaly detection based on historical spending patterns.
  - Custom alerting mechanisms notify teams via SNS or email when anomalies occur.
  - Granular cost tracking helps organizations quickly identify financial inefficiencies.

- **AWS Cost and Usage Report (CUR)**: The CUR offers detailed visibility into AWS costs and usage patterns. It is ideal for organizations that require in-depth cost breakdowns. Features include:
  - Hourly, daily, and monthly reporting granularity.
  - Exporting reports to S3 for integration with analytics tools like Amazon QuickSight.
  - The ability to filter costs based on specific services, accounts, or linked billing structures.

- **CloudWatch for cost metrics**: Amazon CloudWatch, commonly used for performance monitoring, enables real-time costing through customizable dashboards. Businesses can use it to:
  - Correlate cost data with operational metrics to pinpoint inefficiencies.
  - Set alarms that trigger notifications when expenses exceed defined thresholds.
  - Create custom reports that align spending data with application performance insights.

Cost optimization strategies for serverless applications

Serverless computing in AWS offers flexibility and automatic scaling, but without intentional cost optimization, expenses can rise significantly. Every millisecond of execution, every API request, and every data transfer contributes to billing, making it crucial to fine-tune workloads for efficiency. This section explores actionable strategies to reduce costs across compute execution, storage management, networking, and event-driven workflows.

Optimizing compute and execution costs

AWS serverless pricing models charge based on execution duration, memory allocation, and request volumes. Optimizing these parameters ensures efficient resource usage without unnecessary costs.

Right-sizing AWS Lambda for cost efficiency

Lambda costs are directly tied to execution time and memory allocation, making optimization essential for reducing expenses.

The following strategies help fine-tune Lambda functions for better cost efficiency and performance:

- Benchmark performance before selecting memory sizes. Over-allocating memory leads to excessive costs, while under-allocating increases execution time.

- Use AWS Lambda Power Tuning to compare cost-performance trade-offs and find the optimal memory allocation.

- Implement caching mechanisms (e.g., Amazon DynamoDB Accelerator or Redis for frequently accessed data) to reduce unnecessary function invocations.

Optimizing cold starts in AWS Lambda

Cold starts in Lambda can introduce both latency and cost inefficiencies, especially in high-throughput applications.

The following approaches help manage cold start costs effectively:

- For latency-sensitive workloads, consider provisioned concurrency to keep functions warm, but monitor usage to avoid unnecessary provisioning.

- For sporadic workloads, avoid over-provisioning by relying on on-demand scaling while keeping function sizes lean to reduce initialization time.

Reducing API Gateway costs through efficient design

API Gateway costs can escalate quickly with high request volumes, large payloads, and unnecessary invocations.

The following strategies help reduce API Gateway expenses while maintaining performance and functionality:

- Enable caching to minimize repetitive requests for frequently accessed API endpoints.

- Reduce payload sizes by optimizing response formats and using binary encoding.

- Use direct integrations with AWS Lambda or DynamoDB when API Gateway is unnecessary to avoid per-request overhead costs.

Optimizing costs in Step Function workflows

AWS Step Functions bill per state transition can increase costs when workflows involve unnecessary steps.

The following strategies help control costs while maintaining efficiency in Step Function executions:

- Consolidate multiple states into a single Lambda function to minimize transitions.

- Leverage express workflows for high-frequency, short-duration tasks instead of Standard Workflows.

Optimizing data storage and transfer costs

Managing storage tiers and data movement efficiently can significantly reduce serverless application costs, especially when working with S3, DynamoDB, and cross-region transfers.

Reducing S3 costs with lifecycle rules

Amazon S3 provides various storage classes, but choosing the wrong class or retaining unnecessary data increases costs.

The following strategies help optimize S3 storage costs while ensuring data accessibility:

- Use lifecycle policies to automatically transition older data to lower-cost storage (e.g., moving logs from Standard to Glacier).

- Enable intelligent tiering for unpredictable workloads, allowing AWS to move objects dynamically between frequent and infrequent access tiers.

- Optimize data retention by regularly reviewing and deleting outdated files.

Selecting the right DynamoDB pricing model

DynamoDB offers on-demand and provisioned capacity modes; selecting the wrong one may incur extra costs.

The following strategies help optimize DynamoDB pricing and resource utilization to prevent unnecessary expenses:

- Use on-demand capacity for workloads with unpredictable spikes, avoiding the risk of under-utilizing provisioned resources.

- Choose provisioned capacity for stable workloads with predictable access patterns to benefit from cost savings over time.

- Implement efficient indexing to avoid excessive storage usage due to redundant secondary indexes.

Reducing inter-region data transfer costs

Data movement between AWS regions or external endpoints incurs additional charges, which can be mitigated through:

- Leveraging CloudFront for content distribution, reducing direct requests to origin servers.
- Using VPC Peering for cross-region data transfer, eliminating public internet costs.
- Employing AWS PrivateLink to securely connect services within AWS, avoiding standard data transfer pricing.

Optimizing serverless networking and event-driven costs

Event-driven architectures use messaging services like SNS, SQS, and EventBridge, which, when misconfigured, can lead to excessive event processing and unnecessary costs.

Reducing SNS, SQS, and EventBridge costs

AWS messaging services bill based on message volume, making it essential to optimize event transmission and filtering.

The following strategies help control messaging costs while maintaining reliable event-driven architectures:

- Batch messages where possible instead of sending individual requests for each event.

- Use EventBridge filtering to ensure only relevant events trigger downstream services, preventing unnecessary processing.

- Select **first-in-first-out** (**FIFO**) queues only when required, as they are more expensive than standard SQS queues.

Optimizing API Gateway and Step Function costs

Serverless applications often overuse API Gateway and Step Functions, leading to avoidable expenses.

The following strategies help streamline costs while maintaining efficiency in serverless workflows:

- Reduce API Gateway usage by directly calling Lambda functions or DynamoDB for simple read operations.

- Combine multiple API calls into a single request where applicable, reducing request volume.

- Reevaluate whether Step Functions are necessary, as some workflows can be handled within a Lambda function to minimize per-transition costs.

Optimizing AWS messaging for cost efficiency

AWS offers multiple messaging solutions, each suited for different scenarios. Selecting the wrong one can result in higher costs.

The following guidelines help ensure cost-efficient messaging architecture while maintaining performance:

- Use SQS for simple decoupling needs, as it provides a low-cost queueing solution.

- Use SNS only when multiple subscribers need to receive the same message, avoiding unnecessary topic-based fan-outs.

- Leverage EventBridge for event-driven architectures but apply filters to minimize message processing overhead.

Practical guide to cost optimization techniques

This section provides actionable strategies for optimizing serverless costs, demonstrated through real-world scenarios. Each scenario addresses a common challenge in AWS serverless architectures and offers step-by-step solutions to reduce expenses while maintaining scalability and performance.

Scenario one

Streamlining AWS Lambda for an event-driven application: An e-commerce platform relies heavily on AWS Lambda to process customer orders during flash sales, spikes in traffic lead to increased costs due to high invocation rates and inefficient memory allocations.

Optimizing execution time and memory allocation

Here are precautions to ensure that Lambda functions are running efficiently without over or under-provisioning resources:

- Use AWS Lambda Power Tuning to benchmark execution times at various memory configurations. This ensures resources are not over-provisioned or under-utilized.

- Profile function behavior using AWS X-Ray, identifying bottlenecks like slow database queries or unnecessary loops and optimizing accordingly.

- Consolidate logic where possible to reduce the number of function invocations required for order processing.

Reducing cold start costs

Cold starts can increase latency and expenses. The following measures can help mitigate their impact:

- Configure provisioned concurrency during predictable high-traffic windows (e.g., flash sales) to avoid latency from cold starts.

- Streamline initialization by lazy-loading non-critical dependencies and pre-warming connections to external services, such as DynamoDB or S3.

Using AWS Compute Optimizer to right-size functions

AWS Compute Optimizer offers recommendations for fine-tuning memory and execution configurations. To utilize it effectively:

- Review Compute Optimizer recommendations to identify under-provisioned or over-provisioned functions.

- Gradually adjust and test function configurations using CloudWatch Logs to validate runtime and cost efficiency improvements.

Scenario two

Reducing data transfer and storage costs for a media streaming service: A media streaming application distributes video content globally using AWS services. Due to inefficient configurations and high bandwidth usage, data transfer and storage costs have risen. The following strategies can help reduce costs while maintaining performance. Based on real-world patterns, applying these techniques can reduce media delivery expenses by an estimated 25–40% depending on the workload profile.

Identifying high-cost data transfers

- Analyze inter-region and outbound data transfers using Cost Explorer to pinpoint areas with the highest expenses.

- Minimize inter-region traffic by consolidating storage and processing workloads within the same AWS region whenever possible.

- Use VPC endpoints to reduce public data transfer costs for services communicating within the same region.

Optimizing content delivery with CloudFront

- Enable CloudFront caching behaviors to store frequently accessed media files at edge locations, reducing origin requests.

- Apply compression standards such as H.264 for video files to reduce file size and subsequent data transfer costs.

- Set up Regional Edge Caches to improve response times while offloading traffic from the origin servers.

Organizations that fully implement CloudFront optimization strategies report up to 30% reductions in cross-region bandwidth charges and a 20% improvement in content delivery speed.

Implementing lifecycle policies in Amazon S3

- Create lifecycle policies to automatically move infrequently accessed media to S3 Intelligent-Tiering, reducing storage costs.

- Archive obsolete content in S3 Glacier Deep Archive for long-term, cost-effective storage.

- Regularly audit bucket usage to identify unused or duplicate objects that can be deleted.

Media providers have reported storage savings between 15–35% over a 12-month period by applying intelligent Tiering and archival policies across aging video libraries.

Scenario three

Proactively monitoring and managing costs for a SaaS application: A SaaS company experiences frequent cost spikes due to sudden traffic surges and inadequate monitoring. Budget overruns impact profitability and planning, necessitating proactive cost control. The following measures ensure better cost visibility and control.

Setting up AWS budgets for proactive alerts

AWS budgets provide an effective way to monitor and manage expenses. Here is how to set them up:

- Create service-specific budgets for key resources like Lambda, API Gateway, and DynamoDB.

- Enable email and SNS notifications to alert stakeholders when spending exceeds thresholds, allowing timely adjustments.

- Monitor the AWS Budgets Dashboard weekly to identify spending trends and fine-tune usage patterns.

Automating AWS Cost Anomaly Detection

Cost Anomaly Detection helps identify unexpected spending patterns. To leverage this service:

- Train Cost Anomaly Detection models using historical billing data to predict normal spending patterns.

- Define granular detection models at the service level (e.g., Lambda, S3) to catch anomalies in specific areas.

- Automate responses with AWS Lambda triggers to pause or investigate workloads causing unexpected cost spikes.

Mitigating cost drivers using CloudWatch dashboards

CloudWatch dashboards can correlate operational metrics with cost data, offering a comprehensive view of resource usage. Key points include the following:

- Combine operational metrics with cost data in CloudWatch to identify inefficient usage patterns.

- Set alarms for services prone to unpredictable surges, such as API Gateway or inter-region transfers.

- Use dashboards to visualize historical data and identify recurring patterns or potential inefficiencies.

Common anti-patterns in cost management

While AWS serverless architectures offer cost efficiency, common mistakes and mismanagement can lead to unnecessary expenses. This section highlights anti-patterns that organizations often encounter and provides insights to avoid these pitfalls. Addressing these anti-patterns ensures better resource utilization and cost accountability.

Over-provisioning Lambda memory

Allocating more memory than required for AWS Lambda functions is a common anti-pattern. While higher memory allocations improve performance for compute-intensive tasks, over-provisioning results in inflated costs without significant performance gains.

The impacts are:

- Higher costs due to increased per-millisecond billing rates.
- Wasteful allocation of resources that could otherwise be optimized.

The avoidance strategies are:

- Use **AWS Lambda Power Tuning** to identify the optimal balance between memory allocation and execution time.

- Continuously monitor function performance using **CloudWatch Metrics** to adjust memory settings as workloads evolve.

Neglecting API Gateway and Step Functions costs

API Gateway and Step Functions are essential for serverless workflows but can introduce hidden costs if poorly configured.

The impacts are:

- Excessive API Gateway requests due to unoptimized endpoints or unnecessary API calls.

- High Step Function costs from excessive state transitions in workflows.

The avoidance strategies are:

- Implement API Gateway caching to minimize repeated requests for static data.
- Consolidate state transitions in Step Functions by combining logic into fewer steps, where appropriate.
- Regularly review usage with Cost Explorer to identify high-cost APIs and workflows.

Leaving orphaned resources running

Orphaned resources, such as unused Lambda versions, idle DynamoDB tables, or detached EBS volumes, often go unnoticed, leading to unnecessary charges.

The impacts are:

- Ongoing charges for unused or idle resources.
- Increased operational overhead for managing unused resources.

The avoidance strategies are:

- Automate resource cleanup using tools like AWS Config Rules or custom Lambda scripts.
- Periodically audit resource usage using Trusted Advisor and clean up unneeded assets.
- Enable versioning policies for Lambda to delete old versions after deployment automatically.

Ignoring CloudWatch log retention policies

CloudWatch logs are invaluable for debugging and monitoring but can accumulate rapidly if retention policies are not configured.

The impacts are:

- Significant costs for long-term log storage.
- Reduced visibility due to an overwhelming volume of outdated logs.

The avoidance strategies are:

- Set **log retention policies** to automatically delete logs after a specified period (e.g., 30 or 90 days).
- Use **CloudWatch Log Insights** to extract meaningful data and archive only relevant logs to S3 if long-term storage is necessary.

Unoptimized data transfer across AWS regions

Cross-region data transfers often incur substantial costs, particularly for applications with global reach.

The impacts are:

- High charges for inter-region traffic, which can escalate for bandwidth-heavy workloads.
- Reduced application performance due to increased latency.

The avoidance strategies are:

- Consolidate resources and workloads within the same AWS region wherever feasible.
- Leverage VPC Peering or PrivateLink for secure, cost-efficient communication between regions.
- Use CloudFront to cache data closer to end users, minimizing cross-region requests.

Not utilizing FinOps best practices

Failure to implement FinOps principles results in poor cost visibility and missed opportunities for optimization.

The impacts are:

- Inefficient spending due to a lack of accountability and governance.
- Difficulty in forecasting and managing cloud costs.

The avoidance strategies are:

- Establish a FinOps framework by involving cross-functional teams to monitor and manage cloud costs.
- Leverage tools like AWS Budgets and Cost Anomaly Detection for proactive cost monitoring.
- Regularly conduct cost reviews using Cost Explorer and identify areas for improvement.

Future trends in serverless cost optimization

The evolution of serverless architectures has driven the need for advanced cost optimization techniques. As cloud usage scales and workloads become increasingly complex, emerging trends shape how organizations approach cost management. This section explores cutting-edge developments in AI-driven cost governance, predictive scaling, green cloud computing initiatives, multi-cloud strategies, and adopting FinOps principles in serverless environments.

AI-driven cost governance for automated insights

Artificial intelligence plays a transformative role in cost governance by automating cost analysis and anomaly detection. The key innovations include:

- **Predictive analytics**: AI tools forecast spending trends by analyzing historical billing data, allowing organizations to manage costs proactively.

- **Real-time recommendations**: Machine learning algorithms provide actionable insights to optimize resource utilization (e.g., Lambda memory tuning or S3 storage class transitions).

- **Anomaly detection**: AI models detect and alert teams to unexpected cost spikes, enabling them to resolve inefficiencies quickly.

The following figure illustrates how AWS Cost Anomaly Detection and related AI-driven tools integrate into a serverless workload to enable predictive optimization:

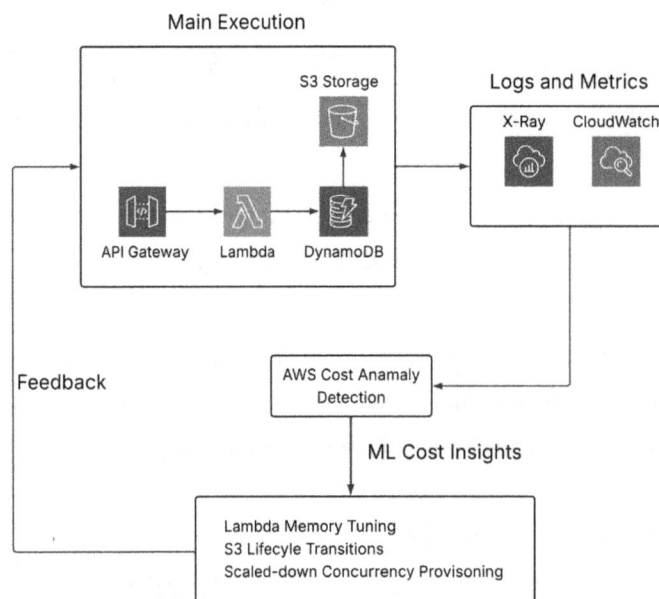

Figure 17.3: Integration of AWS AI-based tools into a serverless architecture

Future impact: AI-driven tools like AWS Cost Anomaly Detection and advanced third-party solutions are expected to become more sophisticated, providing granular insights and automating responses to cost-related anomalies.

Predictive scaling to balance cost and performance

Predictive scaling combines machine learning with autoscaling policies to optimize cost and performance. The following are the key features:

- **Workload prediction**: Predictive models analyze patterns in application usage to determine future capacity needs.

- **Autoscaling optimization**: Resources are automatically scaled up or down based on anticipated demand, minimizing over-provisioning during off-peak hours.

- **Integration with metrics**: CloudWatch metrics and AI-driven forecasts guide decisions, ensuring cost-efficient scaling while meeting performance requirements.

Future impact: As predictive scaling tools advance, organizations will gain finer control over balancing costs and performance, particularly in dynamic serverless environments with highly variable workloads.

Green cloud computing initiatives

Sustainability is becoming a key focus for organizations leveraging serverless technologies, with green cloud computing initiatives to reduce environmental impact. The current approaches include:

- **Efficient resource allocation**: AWS encourages using energy-efficient infrastructure, such as Graviton processors, which deliver better performance per watt.

- **Sustainable workloads**: Designing serverless workloads that minimize idle resources and reduce energy consumption.

- **Carbon emission tracking**: AWS offers the **Customer Carbon Footprint Tool** to help organizations monitor and reduce carbon emissions.

Future impact: Expect to see increased adoption of energy-efficient architectures and greater alignment between cost optimization and environmental sustainability goals.

Multi-cloud cost optimization

Organizations increasingly adopt multi-cloud strategies to diversify workloads across AWS, Azure, and GCP, ensuring cost efficiency and flexibility.

Challenges in multi-cloud environments include:

- **Cost visibility**: Tracking expenses across multiple providers requires robust tools to ensure transparency.

- **Vendor-specific pricing models**: Each provider has unique billing structures, complicating cost optimization.

Emerging trends are as follows:

- **Unified cost management tools**: Third-party platforms are evolving to provide a single pane of glass for managing costs across providers.

- **Workload distribution strategies**: Organizations leverage each provider's strengths (e.g., AWS for serverless, GCP for analytics) to optimize costs.

Future impact: Adopting multi-cloud strategies will drive innovations in cost monitoring, enabling organizations to optimize expenses while avoiding vendor lock-in.

FinOps for serverless cost transparency and accountability

FinOps practices are becoming integral to managing cloud costs in serverless environments, emphasizing collaboration and financial accountability.

The core principles of FinOps are as follows:

- **Cross-functional teams**: Encouraging collaboration between engineering, finance, and operations to manage costs effectively.

- **Proactive monitoring**: Leveraging tools like AWS Budgets and Cost Explorer to identify inefficiencies early.

- **Budget accountability**: Ensuring that each team or project takes ownership of its cloud spending.

Future impact: FinOps frameworks tailored to serverless architectures will enable better cost visibility, improve financial planning, and promote sustainable growth in cloud adoption.

Conclusion

Cost management in serverless architectures is a dynamic and ongoing process that requires careful planning, monitoring, and optimization. AWS provides a robust suite of tools and strategies to help organizations control costs, from analyzing Lambda execution efficiency to managing data transfer and storage expenses. Businesses can eliminate unnecessary expenditures and maintain financial discipline by addressing common anti-patterns, such as over-provisioning resources and neglecting log retention policies.

Emerging trends, such as AI-driven cost governance, predictive scaling, and green cloud computing initiatives, are shaping the future of serverless cost optimization. These innovations enhance cost transparency and align operational goals with environmental sustainability. Additionally, adopting FinOps principles ensures team collaboration, fostering accountability, and strategic cost control.

Organizations can optimize their serverless architectures for performance and cost efficiency by implementing the techniques discussed in this chapter. The combination of proactive management, advanced tools, and forward-looking strategies will empower businesses to leverage AWS's serverless offerings while staying financially agile and competitive.

The next chapter explores the transformative role of serverless architectures in healthcare, focusing on practical applications that enhance scalability, efficiency, and compliance with industry regulations. It provides real-world insights into how serverless technologies address the unique challenges of healthcare solutions.

Join our Discord space

Join our Discord workspace for latest updates, offers, tech happenings around the world, new releases, and sessions with the authors:

https://discord.bpbonline.com

CHAPTER 18
Serverless Applications in Healthcare

Introduction

The healthcare industry is one of the fastest growing and most vital sectors of modern life. Its transformation is fueled by both clinical innovation and digital modernization. Today's systems face mounting pressure from population growth, chronic illnesses, global health threats, and rising operational costs, as well as growing patient expectations for faster, more connected, and personalized care.

This evolution is not just technological. It reflects deeper changes in how care is delivered and measured. Advances in clinical practice, such as precision medicine, remote diagnostics, and AI-assisted care, are converging with new approaches in digital health infrastructure. As care extends into homes, mobile platforms, and decentralized networks, healthcare organizations must rethink not only their software but also their architectural strategy.

Serverless and cloud-native models offer a fundamentally different approach. By removing the burden of infrastructure management, these patterns enable faster innovation, greater flexibility, and stronger alignment with the dynamic and regulated healthcare environment. These applications can scale to meet demand and handle surges in telehealth or streaming data from connected devices while controlling costs through pay-as-you-go models. These approaches also support secure, consistent, and rapid delivery of new capabilities.

This chapter explores how cloud-native and serverless technologies are reshaping healthcare, from claims automation and predictive discharge to remote patient monitoring and AI-driven care. It also recognizes the hybrid nature of real-world systems, where server-based and serverless components work together to balance performance, control, and compliance. Through case studies and architectural walkthroughs, this chapter offers practical guidance on developing modern healthcare platforms grounded in these principles.

Structure

This chapter covers the following topics:

- Key healthcare concepts and standards
- Cloud-native and serverless foundations for healthcare
- Foundational services for healthcare platforms
- Specialized services for healthcare platforms
- Key metrics and KPIs in healthcare

- Real-life use cases and scenarios
- Serverless trends in healthcare

Objectives

This chapter focuses on how modern healthcare challenges, ranging from regulatory complexity and data fragmentation to the rising need for personalized, real-time care, can be addressed through serverless and cloud-native architectural patterns. Building on the shift toward more connected, data-driven healthcare, it introduces core principles that allow organizations to move beyond traditional infrastructure constraints and adopt agile, scalable, and secure approaches to solution design.

The readers will explore the practical applications of these models through a series of expert-led case studies and real-world architecture examples. The chapter outlines when and how to apply serverless principles, identifies situations where hybrid models may be more suitable, and provides guidance on designing systems that are both operationally efficient and technically compliant. By the end, readers will have a grounded understanding of how to architect modern healthcare platforms that support innovation, improve performance, and adapt to the evolving needs of patients and providers alike.

Key healthcare concepts and standards

Before designing serverless and cloud-native solutions for healthcare, it is important to understand the core standards, data types, and system models that define the healthcare environment. The following are foundational terms and concepts that every architect, developer, or cloud strategist working in this domain should be familiar with the following terms:

- **Fast Healthcare Interoperability Resources (FHIR)**: FHIR is a modern, API-based standard for exchanging healthcare data. It supports RESTful communication and modular resource models, making it ideal for cloud-native and event-driven systems. FHIR is becoming the de facto standard for interoperability across hospitals, payers, and digital health platforms.

- **Health Level Seven (HL7)**: HL7 is a legacy standard still widely used for clinical data messaging. While less flexible than FHIR, it continues to underpin many **electronic medical records** (EMRs) integrations and internal workflows, particularly in systems that have not yet adopted modern **application programming interfaces** (APIs).

- **Electronic health record (EHR) and EMR**: EHRs are longitudinal, interoperable patient records shared across organizations, whereas EMRs are typically siloed within a single provider. Both contain critical clinical and administrative data that must be protected and integrated securely across systems.

- **Protected health information (PHI)/ Personally identifiable information (PII)**: These terms refer to any data that can be used to identify a patient, such as names, medical histories, test results, or insurance records. PHI is regulated under frameworks such as HIPAA, which require encryption, access control, and auditability across all services that handle it.

- **Health Insurance Portability and Accountability Act (HIPAA)**: HIPAA governs the handling and security of patient data by healthcare organizations. Any cloud-based healthcare solution, especially those using serverless services, must ensure compliance with HIPAA's privacy, security, and breach notification rules.

- **DICOM and PACS (Medical imaging standards and systems)**: **Digital Imaging and Communications in Medicine** (DICOM) is the imaging standard for formats such as X-rays and MRIs, while **Picture Archiving and Communication System** (PACS) systems manage the storage and retrieval of these images. These systems often need to integrate with cloud-based analytics or indexing pipelines, presenting challenges in terms of performance and compatibility.

- **ICD, SNOMED CT, and LOINC (Coding standards)**: These standardized vocabularies are utilized for diagnosis coding (ICD - International Classification of Diseases), clinical terminology (SNOMED CT - Systematized Nomenclature of Medicine – Clinical Terms), and laboratory test normalization (LOINC - Logical Observation Identifiers Names and Codes). Supporting these standards ensures accurate billing, clinical analysis, and interoperability with insurers and regulatory bodies.

Cloud-native and serverless foundations for healthcare

Healthcare systems require infrastructure that is not only reliable but also adaptable to the complexities of clinical and operational needs. This is where cloud-native and serverless models provide a strategic foundation. The section below highlights some of the challenges faced by healthcare industry.

Challenges in healthcare technology modernization

Healthcare organizations face growing complexity across clinical, technical, and operational dimensions. Many still rely on outdated systems that lack the flexibility, scalability, and integration capabilities required for modern workloads. These limitations make it difficult to support real-time data flows, patient-centric applications, and dynamic use cases.

Data fragmentation remains a major obstacle. Medical records, device data, and clinical notes often reside in separate systems, making unified access and meaningful analysis difficult. As data volumes grow, so does the need for secure, scalable architectures that can process information efficiently and support interoperability.

Security and compliance are constant concerns. Protecting sensitive health data requires strict access controls, encryption, and auditing, especially as organizations expand into virtual care, mobile apps, and remote monitoring. Meeting regulatory expectations adds further complexity to modern system design.

Operational constraints also pose challenges. Resource limitations, infrastructure overhead, and the shift to digital care models reveal the inefficiencies of legacy architectures. Providers must now support real-time communication, device integration, and cross-system interoperability while ensuring reliability and performance.

These issues go beyond technology. They reflect the pressures of delivering care in environments where resilience, clinical alignment, and adaptability are essential. Serverless and cloud-native models offer a promising approach, providing the agility and scalability necessary to meet the evolving demands of healthcare.

The following section provides a breakdown of key principles and their application to healthcare environments.

Principles of cloud-native architecture

These core concepts guide the development of modular, adaptable systems that support interoperability, automation, and independent scaling of healthcare services:

- **Modularity**: Systems are composed of loosely coupled components, enabling clinical, administrative, and data subsystems to evolve independently without impacting one another.

- **Elasticity and automation**: Resources are automatically scaled based on workload demand, enabling systems to respond in real-time to fluctuations in patient activity or data flow.

- **Continuous delivery and observability**: Supports rapid deployment, real-time monitoring, and feedback loops. This is crucial for maintaining system uptime, ensuring safety, and meeting compliance expectations.

Fundamentals of serverless design in healthcare

The following characteristics define how serverless technologies deliver scalable and efficient platforms that respond to the event-driven nature of modern healthcare operations:

- **No infrastructure overhead**: Development teams focus on business logic, workflow design, and patient outcomes without the need to provision or maintain infrastructure.

- **Event-driven execution**: Serverless functions respond to specific triggers such as new patient records, lab results, or monitoring events, enabling real-time responsiveness.

- **Usage-based cost efficiency**: Serverless billing aligns with actual usage, making it well-suited for healthcare systems where workload volumes can vary significantly.

Privacy and security by design

These principles ensure that healthcare systems maintain data integrity, enforce confidentiality, and comply with regulatory standards from day one:

- **Protection of PHI and PII**: Architectures must secure sensitive data through encryption, fine-grained access control, and secure data transmission and storage.

- **Regulatory alignment**: Cloud-native solutions must meet frameworks such as HIPAA and similar global standards by supporting audit logs, access traceability, and robust identity controls.

- **Embedded security practices**: Security must be integrated into every layer of the system, from development and deployment pipelines to live production environments.

Patterns for healthcare workload readiness

The following examples illustrate how foundational architectural principles are applied to meet the demands of modern healthcare operations:

- **Scalable clinical systems**: Platforms automatically expand to support spikes in usage, including virtual visits, device streaming, and care coordination.

- **Secure data ingestion and processing**: Systems handle large volumes of data from sensors, imaging platforms, and EHRs while maintaining strict access and retention policies.

- **Interoperability across ecosystems**: Serverless workflows connect hospitals, insurers, pharmacies, and analytics platforms, enabling seamless collaboration and care delivery.

- **Hybrid architecture as a practical strategy**: Hybrid cloud models are not exceptions; they are the norm in healthcare, where precision, control, and compliance must be carefully balanced with agility and flexibility.

Some workloads, such as latency-sensitive applications or persistent databases, may remain on managed containers or reserved compute. Serverless and container-based services often work side by side to meet different requirements within the same ecosystem.

Foundational services for healthcare platforms

In addition to healthcare-specific offerings, AWS provides a broad set of building blocks that support the development, integration, and scaling of modern healthcare applications. These services form the core of many cloud-native and serverless solutions, described in the following case studies:

- **AWS Lambda**: The main compute service providing a function as a service execution model. This can be the backend processor in response to events, API calls, or data triggers without managing infrastructure. Useful for lightweight, decoupled workflows and event-driven architectures. AWS Lambda integrates seamlessly with most AWS services and offers one of the most cost-effective services, making it an ideal choice for building many healthcare workflows.

- **Amazon API Gateway**: A fully managed service to build and manage secure APIs at scale. Often used to expose FHIR-compliant interfaces, patient engagement endpoints, or mobile health backends. It provides fine-grained access control, throttling, and logging, which is important for regulatory compliance and system-level observability in healthcare environments.

- **Amazon DynamoDB**: A highly scalable NoSQL database that supports low-latency reads and writes, even under heavy load. It is ideal for storing patient session data, device telemetry, workflow state, or audit events. Its built-in encryption, scalability, and seamless serverless integration make it a preferred choice for health event tracking and alert pipelines.

- **Amazon S3**: Amazon S3 is an object storage service designed for secure and scalable data retention. In healthcare, it is commonly used to store diagnostic images such as DICOM files, clinical reports, scanned documents, and unstructured health records. It also supports big data workflows, including longitudinal record analysis, machine learning input storage, and population health trend evaluation. S3 offers multiple storage classes, including Intelligent-Tiering, Glacier, and Deep Archive, enabling healthcare organizations to optimize costs while meeting long-term retention and regulatory requirements.

- **Amazon EventBridge**: A serverless event bus that enables communication between decoupled services. It is commonly used in healthcare to trigger logic based on clinical events, such as the availability of a lab result or a patient's admission. It helps create responsive, audit-friendly systems without tightly coupling components.

- **AWS Step Functions**: A workflow orchestration service that coordinates multiple services and steps into a unified sequence. In healthcare, it is often used to build claims review pipelines, intake assessment flows, or lab test routing. Its visual state machine and retry logic simplify the handling of long-running or multi-step healthcare processes.

- **AWS Fargate**: A serverless container engine that allows teams to run Docker workloads without provisioning EC2 instances. Suitable for scenarios where custom runtimes, container isolation, or GPU-based computation are needed, such as medical imaging preprocessing or processing machine learning models for diagnostics.

- **Amazon RDS and Aurora (Serverless)**: These are managed relational databases for use cases that require structured, transactional storage. Aurora Serverless offers on-demand scalability, making it an ideal solution for episodic healthcare workloads, such as appointment scheduling systems, patient feedback surveys, or billing management tools.

- **Amazon CloudWatch**: Monitoring and observability platform for infrastructure and application health. Used in healthcare to track service latency, alert on workflow anomalies, and retain logs for audit purposes. Integrates natively with all AWS services, providing end-to-end visibility across platforms.

- **Amazon Cognito**: A user identity and authentication service tailored for web and mobile applications. Supports healthcare portals, staff dashboards, or provider logins. Provides user pools, OAuth integration, and secure token management—important for implementing authentication within regulated applications.

- **Amazon QuickSight**: A serverless BI tool to visualize data from clinical systems, operational logs, or financial metrics. Frequently used to build dashboards for clinical performance tracking, capacity management, or compliance analytics. Embeddable into healthcare portals with minimal infrastructure overhead.

- **Amazon Bedrock**: Provides access to foundation models for generative AI tasks. In healthcare, it can support applications such as summarizing patient notes, generating discharge instructions or powering conversational agents for patient engagement and triage support.

- **AWS Secrets Manager**: Manages secrets, including API tokens, database credentials, and third-party service keys. Ensures secure rotation and access control for sensitive credentials in health system integrations, particularly where interoperability with external systems is involved.

- **AWS KMS**: Manages encryption keys for securing PHI and other sensitive data. KMS integrates with S3, RDS, DynamoDB, and other AWS services to enforce encryption policies that align with HIPAA and regional health data regulations.

Specialized services for healthcare platforms

In addition to foundational infrastructure, cloud providers such as AWS offer purpose-built services tailored to healthcare environments. These offerings are designed to simplify compliance, accelerate clinical application development, and support the handling of complex medical data at scale. They also help align digital healthcare platforms with modern care delivery models that demand real-time insights, regulatory alignment, and personalized engagement.

These specialized services are especially valuable in scenarios where traditional infrastructure lacks the context or flexibility needed to process clinical data accurately and securely. By abstracting domain-specific complexity and embedding compliance-readiness into the service architecture, these tools allow healthcare organizations to focus on outcomes instead of underlying technical challenges.

The following AWS healthcare-specialized services enable intelligent clinical applications:

- **Amazon Comprehend Medical**: Amazon Comprehend Medical is an NLP service optimized for clinical documents. It can automatically extract medical entities such as diagnoses, symptoms, medications, procedures, and lab values from unstructured text, including EHR notes, discharge summaries, and insurance claims. This functionality enables healthcare applications to transform raw clinical narratives into structured data that can be analyzed, searched, and visualized.

  The service supports use cases such as clinical decision support, automated form processing, and predictive modeling. For example, a hospital could use Comprehend Medical to identify high-risk patients from triage notes or extract chronic conditions from historical visit records to power care pathway optimization.

- **Amazon Transcribe Medical**: Amazon Transcribe Medical provides real-time and batch speech-to-text transcription services specifically tuned for medical vocabulary and workflows. It is capable of capturing accurate transcripts from physician-patient dialogues, dictation sessions, or virtual consultations.

  The service can be integrated into telehealth platforms, ambient scribing tools, or EHR systems to reduce the documentation burden for clinicians. By enabling automated charting and faster encounter documentation, it improves provider efficiency and helps ensure timely record-keeping, key requirements in high-volume care settings.

- **Amazon HealthLake**: Amazon HealthLake is a fully managed, HIPAA-eligible service that enables organizations to store, standardize, and analyze health data using the FHIR format. It automatically indexes and structures clinical data, making it searchable and ready for downstream use in analytics, machine learning, or reporting workflows.

  By converting fragmented health records into longitudinal patient timelines, HealthLake supports initiatives in care coordination, population health, and value-based reimbursement. It can also enable organizations to build intelligent applications that detect disease progression, predict readmissions, or analyze treatment outcomes across populations.

- **Amazon HealthOmics**: Amazon HealthOmics is a service designed to support life sciences research and genomic data processing. It allows researchers and related personnel to store, transform, and analyze large-scale omics datasets, including genomic sequences, transcriptomes, and proteomic profiles.

  This service plays a pivotal role in precision medicine, where large volumes of biological data must be processed efficiently to identify variants, classify disease subtypes, or inform treatment selection. HealthOmics simplifies infrastructure management while supporting flexible, reproducible analysis pipelines that can scale from individual studies to national research programs.

Together, these services form a domain-aware foundation for building healthcare applications that are intelligent, secure, and compliant by design. Each service is built with privacy and auditability in mind, supporting frameworks such as HIPAA and interoperability standards including HL7, ICD-10, SNOMED CT, and LOINC. When integrated into a serverless or cloud-native environment, they allow healthcare teams to innovate more rapidly while ensuring that sensitive data is handled in accordance with clinical, legal, and ethical requirements.

Key metrics and KPIs in healthcare

Digital transformation in healthcare is not driven solely by technology; outcomes drive it. Organizations face intense pressure to modernize systems not just for infrastructure agility but to improve measurable areas that impact patient care, reduce operational burdens, and support compliance with regulations such as HIPAA. From reducing wait times to accelerating vaccine development, the need for real-time, data-driven decision-making has never been more critical.

Serverless and cloud-native platforms offer the agility, scalability, and automation needed to address long-standing inefficiencies. However, before any architecture is applied, it is essential to understand what needs improvement. The following categories highlight the most critical performance areas in healthcare, metrics that often reflect bottlenecks, compliance risks, or gaps in patient experience. These indicators serve as both a foundation and a benchmark for the solutions described in the next section.

Clinical efficiency and patient throughput

The following metrics assess how effectively healthcare systems deliver clinical services and manage patient flow across departments and care settings:

- **Average patient waiting time**: Long wait times persist as a systemic issue, often stemming from outdated scheduling systems, siloed triage processes, or capacity mismatches.

- **Emergency room throughput**: Bottlenecks in triage, admission, or handoffs can delay care and increase strain on resources.

- **Predictive discharge accuracy**: Poor discharge coordination can lead to unnecessary bed occupancy or preventable readmissions.

- **Readmission rate**: Indicates quality of care and follow-up procedures, often impacted by disconnected systems or missed interventions.

Operational agility and workflow optimization

These KPIs reflect how adaptable and efficient healthcare operations are across internal workflows, from task automation to resource coordination:

- **Workflow completion time**: Measures how long routine tasks such as lab routing, referrals, or claims approvals take.

- **Medical equipment utilization rate**: Tracks whether high-cost equipment is being used efficiently across departments or sites.

- **Time to implement new workflows**: Reflects system agility, especially during crises such as pandemics, where rapid workflow updates (e.g., contact tracing, vaccine tracking) are essential.

Financial performance and claims efficiency

The following metrics track how well a healthcare system manages revenue cycles, insurance interactions, and overall cost efficiency:

- **Insurance claims processing time**: Delayed claims processing can strain revenue cycles and patient satisfaction.

- **Claims denial rate**: High denial rates point to upstream data issues, form errors, or system incompatibilities.

- **Cost per patient interaction**: A holistic metric that includes infrastructure, staff time, and digital system costs.

Compliance, auditability, and data protection

These indicators ensure that systems meet HIPAA and other regulatory standards while protecting patient data from breaches and unauthorized access:

- **Data breach response time**: Rapid detection and response are essential in regulated environments.

- **Audit trail completeness**: Systems must retain granular access logs, workflow traces, and incident records.

- **PHI access visibility**: Indicates how effectively the system monitors and controls access to protected health information.

Patient experience and access

The following KPIs evaluate how well patients interact with the healthcare system, from digital touchpoints to clinical responsiveness:

- **Patient satisfaction index**: Captures perceptions of care speed, clarity, and access.

- **Telehealth responsiveness**: Includes video quality, system availability, and latency during remote consultations.

- **Patient portal engagement rate**: This metric reflects the usability and value of digital services, such as messaging, lab results, or appointment booking.

Innovation speed and public health readiness

These metrics measure how quickly healthcare systems can respond to evolving needs, support public health, and deliver innovation at scale:

- **Time to deliver new features**: Measures how quickly teams can ship updates, such as symptom checkers, outbreak alerts, or care pathways.

- **Time to onboard new data sources**: Critical during public health emergencies, when labs, IoT devices, or mobile inputs must be integrated rapidly.

- **Infrastructure readiness for surges**: Indicates the ability to auto-scale in response to population events, such as vaccine booking or testing demand spikes.

Real-life use cases and scenarios

This section highlights how various AWS services can be leveraged to construct architectures that address common challenges faced by the healthcare industry. Often, real-life scenarios utilize a mix of serverless components, cloud-native services, and other services, as well as on-premises systems.

Smart claims processing and workflow automation

Problem statement: Traditional health insurance claims processing is manual, time-consuming, and prone to human error. Claims data often arrives in unstructured formats such as PDFs or scanned documents. Without automation, it becomes difficult to identify missing information, detect anomalies, or route claims appropriately. These inefficiencies lead to increased claim denial rates, delayed reimbursements, and higher operational costs for both providers and insurers.

Proposed solution: This solution uses a fully serverless, cloud-native architecture that automates claims intake, entity extraction, and routing using AI services. Unstructured claims documents are processed in near real-time using Amazon Textract and Comprehend Medical, and results are orchestrated through Step Functions for validation and submission.

Architecture: *Figure 18.1* shows the high-level architecture for implementing a claims processing system using AWS services:

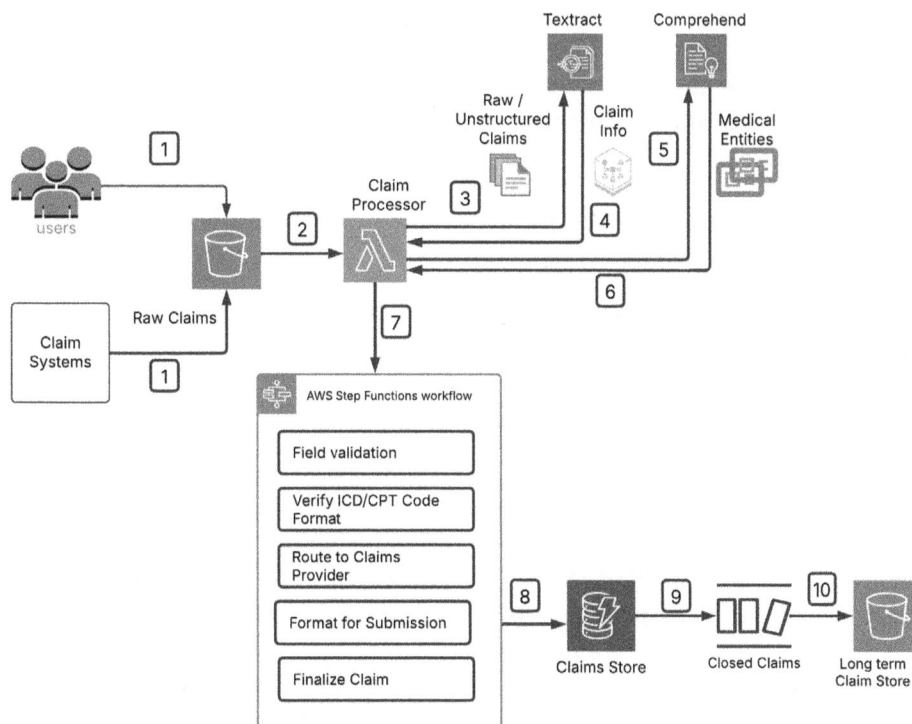

Figure 18.1: Claims processing system using AWS services

Architecture summary: This solution can be summarized into the following steps:

1. Healthcare claim systems and claims processing group users submit claims to the system. These claims can arrive in various formats, such as PDFs, text documents, or scanned images. The raw claims are stored in an Amazon S3 bucket, as shown in *Step 1* of the diagram.

2. The file copy into the S3 bucket triggers the Claim Processor Lambda function, which is responsible for extracting text, converting text into appropriate medical terms and context, and starting the claim processing workflow, as shown in *Step 2*.

3. The Lambda function sends raw claims to Amazon Textract, which is responsible for extracting text from all document types. The extracted data is sent back to the Lambda function, as shown in *Steps 3 and 4*.

4. The Lambda function now sends the data extracted (mostly key-value pairs) read by Textract to another AWS service, Amazon Comprehend Medical, as shown in *Step 5*.

5. Amazon Comprehend Medical is responsible for applying domain-specific NLP to extract clinical terms, which may include clinical codes, procedure types, medication mentions and ICD tags, and billing information as shown in *Step 6*.

6. The Lambda function then triggers the AWS Step function workflow, which is responsible for Field validations, verification of ICD codes, routing to the claims provider to get appropriate information, formatting, and finalizing the claim. This is represented in *Step 7*.

7. The finalized claim is then saved to a DynamoDB table as represented in *Step 8*.

8. When the claims are completed or closed, a DynamoDB Stream captures the changes and publishes them to a Lambda function, which is then responsible for formatting and storing them in Amazon S3 for long-term claim history and archival purposes. This is denoted by *Steps 9 and 10*.

Problems solved by this architecture: This architecture helped in solving problems as follows:

- Automates the intake of unstructured claims using OCR and NLP.
- Reduces manual effort in reading, classifying, and validating claims.
- Ensures real-time routing based on content, improving processing speed.
- Decouples components to allow independent scaling and fault isolation.
- Improves traceability and audit readiness across the workflow.

Metrics and KPIs: The following are the healthcare KPIs and metrics that this solution would improve:

- Reduced insurance claims processing time.
- Lower claims denial rate due to early detection KPIs of missing data.
- Improved workflow completion time.
- Higher data accuracy in structured claims databases.
- Increased audit trail completeness and observability.

Voice to text pain score logging

Problem statement: Pain scores are a critical clinical indicator, especially for patients recovering from surgery, undergoing treatment, or reporting chronic symptoms. In many care environments, especially inpatient and assisted living settings, these scores are logged manually by clinicians based on verbal responses. This method is time-consuming, inconsistent, and often delayed in being recorded. It introduces risk by relying on transcription accuracy, missing real-time updates, and increasing the documentation burden on nurses or aides.

Proposed solution: This solution enables patients or caregivers to report pain levels verbally through bedside or mobile input. The speech input is transcribed using Amazon Transcribe Medical, converted to structured data using Amazon Comprehend Medical, and stored in real-time in DynamoDB. A serverless backend processes and stores pain scores, while alerts and dashboards are updated instantly to reflect new trends.

Architecture: *Figure 18.2* shows the high-level architecture for implementing a pain score processing system using AWS services:

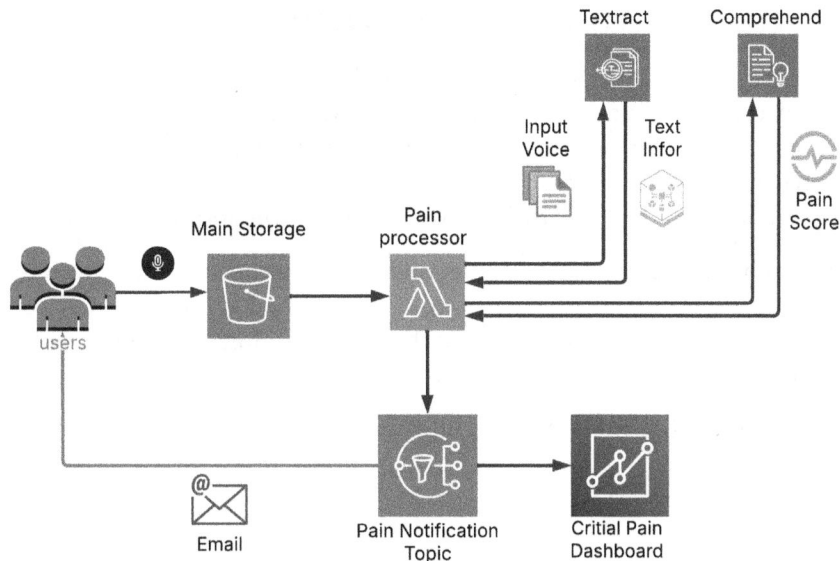

Figure 18.2: Voice-to-text pain score system

Architecture summary: This solution can be summarized into the following steps:

1. Patients or caregivers speak into a device or mobile app to report their pain levels using natural language.

2. The audio is streamed directly to Amazon Transcribe Medical, which performs real-time speech-to-text conversion

3. The transcript is sent to Amazon Comprehend Medical, which identifies clinical terms, pain descriptions, and score context.

4. An AWS Lambda function parses the NLP output and stores structured pain data (score, timestamp, patient ID) in Amazon DynamoDB.

5. A secondary Lambda function posts real-time updates to Amazon SNS, which can notify nurses or populate dashboards in real-time.

6. Amazon QuickSight is used to visualize longitudinal pain trends by patient, location, or department.

7. All actions are logged through Amazon CloudWatch for audit and observability.

Problems solved by this architecture: This architecture helped in solving the problem as shown as follows:

- Enables voice-driven data entry without clinician overhead.
- Captures pain scores in real-time, reducing delays and transcription errors.
- Converts unstructured speech into structured, queryable logs.
- Triggers immediate alerts for high pain thresholds, improving response times.
- Supports clinical review and analysis through real-time dashboards.

Metrics and KPIs: The following are the Healthcare KPIs and metrics that this solution would improve:

- **Reduced documentation delay** between patient input and system capture.
- **Improved data accuracy** in pain score records.
- **Faster staff response** to high or increasing pain trends.
- **Increased patient satisfaction** through hands-free, low-friction reporting.
- **Better decision support** via aggregated pain trend dashboards.

Real-time fall detection using serverless AI

Problem statement: Falls are one of the most common and dangerous incidents in elderly care, inpatient wards, and rehabilitation centers. Delayed detection can lead to severe medical complications, increased recovery time, and higher liability for healthcare providers. Traditional fall detection systems often rely on wearable sensors, which can be intrusive or noncompliant. There is a need for a solution that operates in real-time, is passive to the patient, and integrates directly with monitoring and response workflows.

Proposed solution: This architecture leverages edge-connected cameras and computer vision models to detect falls in real time using Amazon Rekognition. Video input is streamed through an IoT-connected device, and any detection of a fall triggers a serverless workflow that notifies staff, logs the event, and securely stores footage for compliance and review purposes.

Architecture: *Figure 18.3* shows the high-level architecture for implementing a fall detection architecture using AWS services:

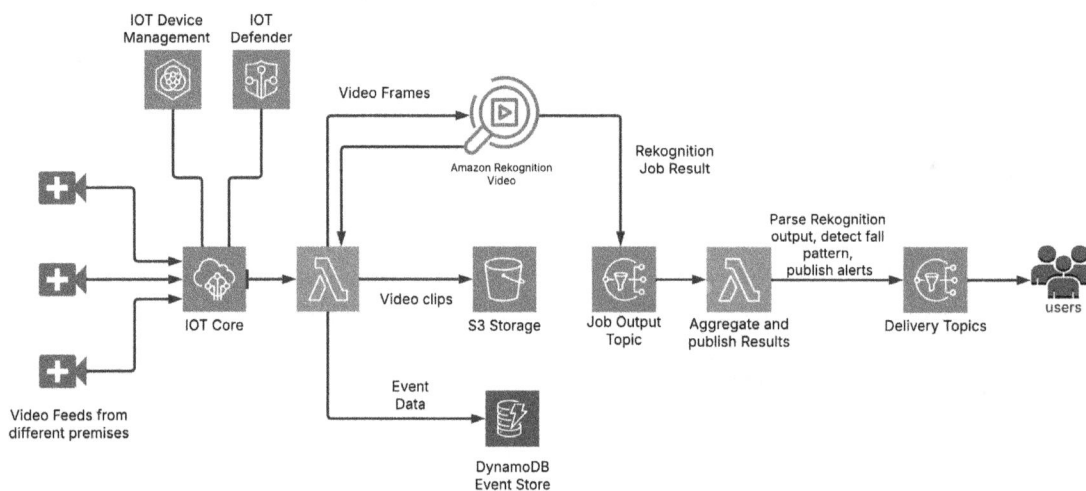

Figure 18.3: Fall detection system using AWS services

Architecture summary: This architecture can be summarized as follows:

1. Video feeds from multiple healthcare premises are streamed through edge devices equipped with AWS IoT Greengrass and, optionally, SageMaker Edge for local inference and buffering.

2. Edge devices are managed and monitored using AWS IoT Device Management for fleet health, software updates, and secure connectivity. Meanwhile, AWS IoT Secure Tunneling enables remote diagnostics and support.

3. Pre-processed or raw video frames are sent to AWS IoT Core, which securely ingests the data and routes it based on defined IoT rules and topics.

4. When fall-related patterns are detected, or thresholds are crossed, AWS IoT Events evaluates the conditions and triggers downstream workflows.

5. An AWS Lambda function processes the triggered events, clips the relevant video segments, stores them in Amazon S3, and initiates an asynchronous Amazon Rekognition Video job for deeper analysis (e.g., person tracking or movement anomalies).

6. Once the Rekognition job is complete, the result is posted to Amazon EventBridge or Amazon SNS, which triggers a second Lambda function to retrieve and analyze the job output.

7. This function evaluates the detection results, identifies potential fall events, logs the incident metadata into Amazon DynamoDB, and publishes alerts to Amazon SNS or EventBridge delivery topics.

8. Caregivers or monitoring systems are notified in real-time via preferred channels (mobile, dashboards, alerts), while all events are logged for traceability and auditing.

9. Optional services, such as Amazon QuickSight and AWS IoT Analytics, can be integrated to visualize fall patterns, generate compliance reports, and refine response strategies over time.

Problems solved by this architecture: This architecture helped in solving the problem as shown as follows:

- Detects falls without requiring patient interaction.
- Automates event classification and escalates high-priority alerts.
- Enables immediate response while capturing full context.
- Integrates with dashboards, nursing systems, or hospital operations.
- Scales across multiple rooms or locations with no infrastructure overhead.

Metrics and APIs: The following are the Healthcare KPIs and metrics that this solution would improve:

- Reduced emergency response time after a fall.
- Improved patient safety index.
- Lower incident-to-notification latency.
- Higher detection accuracy vs manual observation.
- Increased staff efficiency due to reduced manual monitoring.

Secure exchange of electronic health records

Problem statement: Healthcare organizations frequently require the exchange of EHRs across various settings, including clinics, hospitals, insurers, and third-party systems. This data includes sensitive PHI, and improper handling can result in HIPAA violations, data breaches, or audit failures. Many traditional systems lack audit trails, encryption enforcement, or dynamic policy controls—making secure EHR exchange both risky and inefficient.

Proposed solution: This architecture facilitates the secure intake, processing, and exchange of FHIR-compliant EHR data using a fully serverless and HIPAA-eligible stack. It leverages AWS's native security services to enforce encryption, fine-grained access control, logging, and auditability. EHR files are uploaded, parsed, and validated against clinical data exchange standards, then routed to destination systems with integrity checks in place.

Architecture: *Figure 18.4* shows the high-level architecture for implementing an EHR exchange system using AWS services:

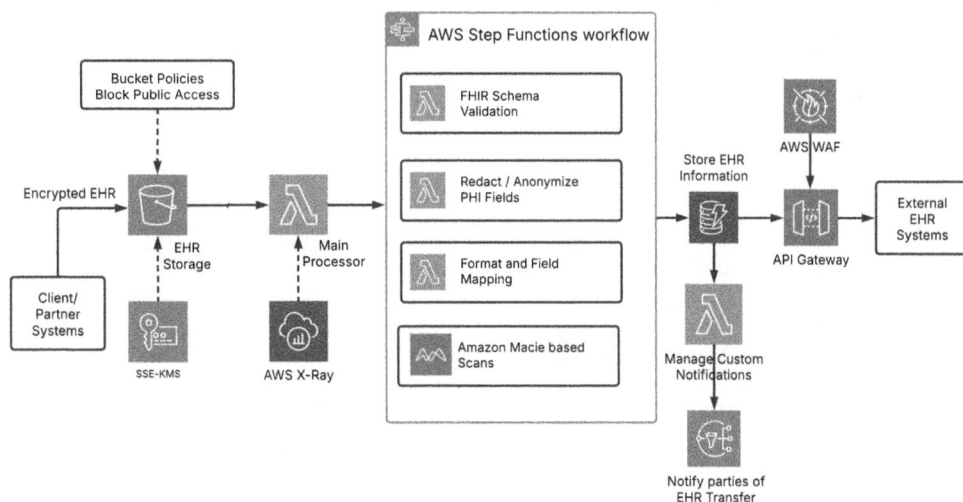

Figure 18.4: EHR exchange system

Architecture summary: This solution can be summarized into the following steps:

1. Client or partner healthcare systems upload encrypted FHIR-compliant EHRs to a secure Amazon S3 bucket. Server-side encryption using AWS KMS (SSE-KMS) is enforced, and public access is explicitly blocked via bucket policies.

2. The upload to the EHR Storage (S3) bucket triggers a main processing AWS Lambda function, which orchestrates the downstream workflow. This function integrates with AWS X-Ray for full tracing and debugging visibility.

3. The Lambda function invokes a Step Functions state machine to handle EHR processing in a modular, auditable, and fault-tolerant manner. The workflow includes:

4. FHIR Schema Validation to ensure the EHR structure complies with clinical interoperability standards.

5. Redaction or anonymization of PHI fields to ensure only the required information is exchanged externally.

6. Format and field mapping, aligning the EHR structure with the target system's requirements.

7. Amazon Macie–based scanning to detect the presence of sensitive or misclassified PHI and apply any additional controls if necessary.

8. Once processing is complete, the sanitized and validated EHR record is ready for consumption. AWS API Gateway is used as an intermediary to provide secure access to this health information for third-party authenticated entities. AWS WAF is integrated with API Gateway to protect the endpoint against malicious inputs or attack vectors such as DDoS. AWS WAF also provides several other features to restrict access by IP address, geographical location, and custom rules, offering additional security layers.

9. Simultaneously, a secondary Lambda function manages custom notifications related to the transfer event (e.g., status updates, confirmations), and an event is published to SNS or other delivery topics to notify stakeholders or audit parties involved in the EHR transfer.

Problems solved by this architecture: This architecture helped in solving the problem as shown as follows:

- Ensures HIPAA-aligned encryption and logging without manual intervention.
- Validates that sensitive fields are processed, redacted, or routed appropriately.
- Supports external data exchange through compliant, encrypted channels.
- Creates an end-to-end audit trail for every EHR file exchanged.
- Removes the need for custom security implementations by leveraging managed services.

Metrics and APIs: The following are the Healthcare KPIs and metrics that this solution would improve:

- Time to validate EHR before exchange.
- Audit trail completeness and accessibility.
- Reduction in untracked PHI exposure incidents.
- System-wide compliance readiness.
- Error rate in EHR data formatting or structure.

Healthcare data lake and advanced analytics

Problem statement: Healthcare organizations generate enormous volumes of structured and unstructured data. This could include EHRs and lab results, as well as imaging files and device telemetry. However, most of this data is scattered across silos, stored in incompatible formats, or locked behind operational systems that are not designed for advanced analytics. The inability to aggregate and analyze data limits decision-making, population health management, predictive modeling, and research outcomes.

Proposed solution: This architecture enables healthcare organizations to ingest, catalog, secure, and analyze data at scale using a serverless, cloud-native data lake. Built on Amazon S3 and Lake Formation, the solution supports both structured and semi-structured data. ETL processes are orchestrated using AWS Glue, querying is performed through Amazon Athena, and insights are visualized via Amazon QuickSight, all without requiring infrastructure management. Role-based access controls ensure HIPAA compliance, enabling secure, multi-tenant analytics.

Architecture: *Figure 18.5* illustrates the high-level architecture for implementing a healthcare data lake for advanced analytics:

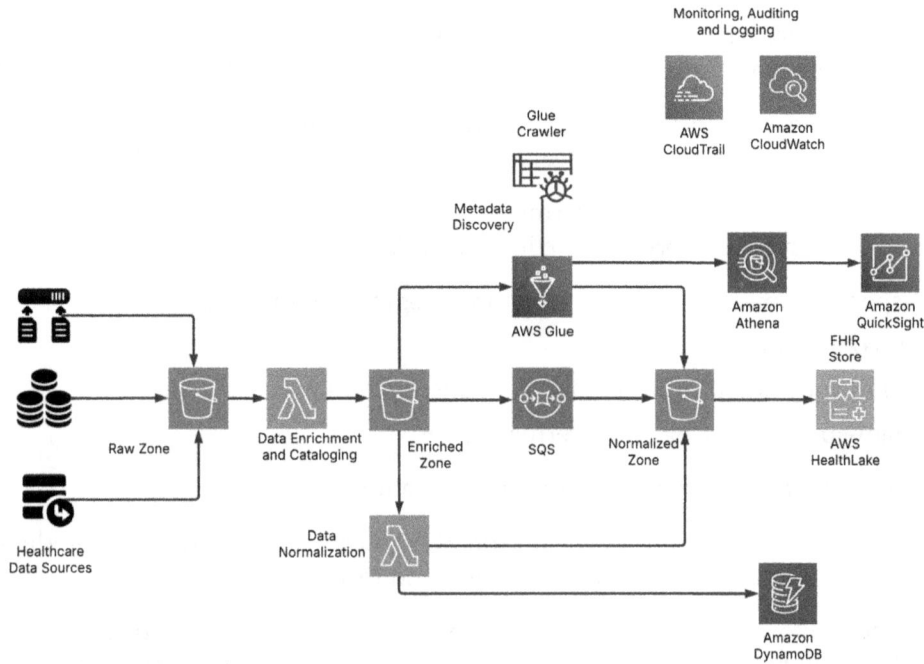

Figure 18.5: AWS healthcare data lake and HealthLake for analytics (Part A)

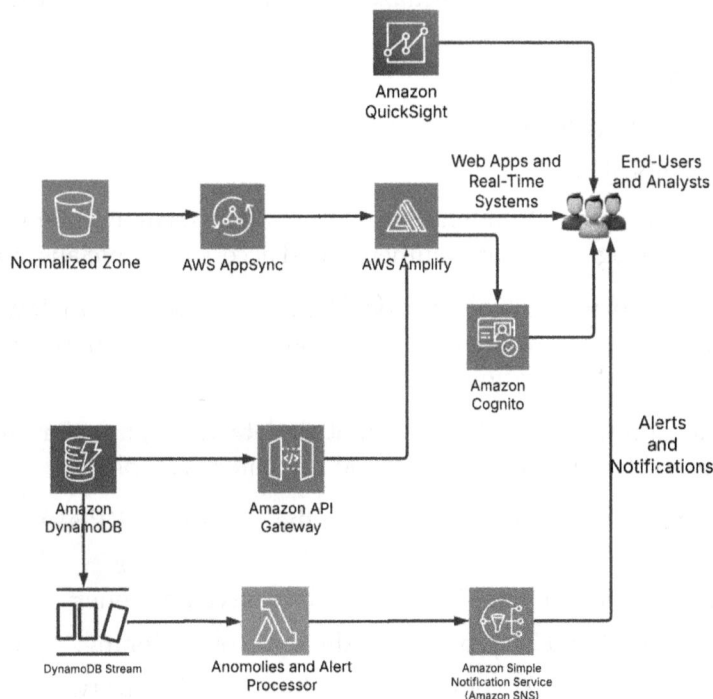

Figure 18.6: AWS healthcare data lake and HealthLake for analytics (Part B)

Figure 18.5 illustrates the data ingestion, enrichment, and normalization pipeline, while *Figure 18.6* focuses on real-time access, alerting mechanisms, and end-user interaction layers.

Architecture summary: This architecture supports the secure ingestion, processing, storage, and visualization of healthcare data, structured, semi-structured, and FHIR-compliant, using fully serverless AWS services. It enables both batch and real-time analytics, application-driven insights, and HIPAA-compliant access to sensitive clinical information. The design emphasizes extensibility, traceability, and patient-centric data intelligence.

This architecture can be summarized as follows:

1. Healthcare data sources such as EHR systems, lab platforms, diagnostic imaging systems, and medical devices stream or upload data into the Amazon S3 Raw Zone, protected with SSE-KMS encryption.

2. AWS Glue Crawlers scan incoming files and update the Glue Data Catalog with schema metadata. A data enrichment Lambda function processes and moves validated data into the Enriched Zone.

3. The enriched data is further transformed by a data normalization Lambda and moved to the Normalized Zone in S3, conforming to clinical standards such as FHIR.

4. For FHIR-specific clinical data, the architecture integrates with Amazon HealthLake, providing:
   a. FHIR-compliant API access.
   b. Semantic indexing (conditions, medications, encounters).
   c. Domain-specific tagging and filtering.

5. Secure access control aligned with healthcare regulations.

6. The architecture uses AWS Glue and Amazon SQS to coordinate and decouple data transformation and cataloging workflows, improving scalability and resiliency.

7. Amazon Athena allows real-time querying of both normalized S3 data and HealthLake exports, while Amazon QuickSight provides intuitive dashboards and clinical visualizations for authorized users.

8. Real-time data delivery is powered by AWS AppSync, enabling GraphQL-based APIs that automatically sync with changes from Amazon S3, Amazon HealthLake, or Amazon DynamoDB. This makes it possible to build:
   a. Live dashboards
   b. Real-time monitoring apps
   c. Event-driven care alerts

9. AWS Amplify hosts serverless front-end applications that securely interact with backend APIs and data sources. Amazon Cognito ensures authenticated access for clinicians, analysts, and support staff.

10. Normalized data is also written to Amazon DynamoDB to support low-latency access patterns. DynamoDB Streams trigger an anomaly detection Lambda function, which publishes alerts via Amazon SNS to email, SMS, or incident systems.

11. Amazon CloudTrail and CloudWatch ensure that all data access, transformations, and alerts are fully auditable and observable, critical for HIPAA and regulatory compliance.

Problems solved by this architecture: The following are the Healthcare KPIs and metrics that this solution would improve:

- Centralizes healthcare data from multiple sources into a scalable, queryable platform.
- Removes the need for custom ETL pipelines or database provisioning.
- Enforces HIPAA-compliant access controls with column-level security.
- Enables clinicians, analysts, and researchers to ask questions without waiting for reports.

- Supports longitudinal analytics, cohort identification, and population health studies.

Metrics and APIs: The following are the Healthcare KPIs and metrics that this solution would improve:

- Time to insight from data ingestion to the dashboard.
- Data coverage rate across clinical, operational, and device inputs.
- Query performance and cost efficiency vs traditional analytics systems.
- Compliance audit readiness (access logs, encryption, security policies).
- User satisfaction score among analysts and decision-makers.

Serverless trends in healthcare

The healthcare industry continues to evolve rapidly, driven by the convergence of digital transformation, personalized medicine, and real-time data availability. Serverless architectures are poised to become foundational in this next phase of innovation. Their ability to scale instantly, respond to events, and abstract infrastructure allows healthcare organizations to focus on delivering meaningful outcomes while maintaining compliance, resilience, and agility.

The following emerging trends illustrate how serverless computing is set to shape the future of care delivery, public health, and medical research:

- **AI-powered clinical assistants**: Serverless platforms will increasingly support conversational agents, symptom checkers, and decision support tools powered by foundational models through services like Amazon Bedrock. These models can be fine-tuned with clinical datasets to generate patient summaries, assist with diagnosis, or provide follow-up recommendations, reducing clinician workload and enhancing care quality.

- **Event-driven public health surveillance**: Syndromic surveillance and early detection of disease outbreaks will depend on real-time data pipelines that can aggregate and analyze signals from electronic health records, wearables, laboratory feeds, and even social media activity. Serverless technologies enable the rapid ingestion and processing of this distributed data to trigger public health alerts and guide interventions.

- **Privacy-preserving federated learning**: As AI becomes more integral to healthcare, federated learning models allow institutions to collaborate without exchanging raw patient data. Serverless architectures can orchestrate these training workflows across hospitals, research centers, and national networks, supporting cross-institutional insights while meeting strict privacy and compliance obligations.

- **Precision medicine pipelines**: The delivery of personalized treatments will rely on cloud-native genomics platforms that process DNA, RNA, and proteomic data at scale. Services like AWS HealthOmics, when combined with serverless orchestration, allow for the rapid analysis of genetic variants and alignment with clinical pathways, supporting disease risk prediction and therapeutic matching.

- **Edge-enabled remote monitoring**: The proliferation of ambient sensors and connected medical devices has pushed computing closer to the point of care. Serverless edge platforms, such as AWS IoT Greengrass, allow for localized inference and event processing, enabling real-time alerts for falls, medication adherence, glucose monitoring, or cardiac irregularities.

- **Digital twin models for patient simulation**: Serverless infrastructure will support the execution of digital twin frameworks, real-time virtual representations of a patient's physiological state. These models can simulate treatment responses or monitor condition progression, offering clinicians a predictive layer for more proactive care planning.

- **On-demand clinical research platforms**: Serverless tools will power self-service environments for researchers, enabling them to ingest de-identified datasets, build workflows, and perform statistical analysis without managing servers. This model supports faster study setup, scalable compute for cohort analysis, and reproducibility across research teams.

As these innovations accelerate, serverless platforms are no longer just an operational convenience; they are becoming essential infrastructure for enabling intelligent, scalable, and patient-centered healthcare. The future of healthcare delivery will rely on architectures that can adapt in real-time, secure sensitive data at the edge and in transit, and evolve continuously alongside clinical and regulatory shifts.

Conclusion

Serverless and cloud-native technologies are rapidly transforming the way healthcare solutions are designed, deployed, and scaled. From automating claims workflows to real-time clinical analytics and secure EHR exchange, AWS serverless services provide a powerful foundation for building resilient, patient-centric systems that meet today's performance and compliance requirements.

This chapter explored how healthcare-specific challenges, such as data fragmentation, operational delays, and regulatory complexity, can be addressed through event-driven architectures and modular design. Through practical case studies, we demonstrated how foundational and specialized AWS services enable intelligent automation, real-time insights, and proactive clinical engagement.

As healthcare systems continue to evolve, adopting serverless strategies will be essential not only for improving technical agility but also for enhancing patient outcomes, operational efficiency, and regulatory readiness. By embracing these architectural principles, healthcare organizations can move toward a future where innovation is faster, care is more connected, and technology becomes an enabler of healing rather than a constraint.

In the next chapter, we will explore how these same serverless and cloud-native design patterns can be applied to the financial sector. From fraud detection and regulatory compliance to real-time transaction processing and customer engagement, serverless solutions offer transformative potential for building agile, secure, and cost-effective financial applications.

Join our Discord space

Join our Discord workspace for latest updates, offers, tech happenings around the world, new releases, and sessions with the authors:

https://discord.bpbonline.com

CHAPTER 19
Serverless Applications in Finance

Introduction

The financial sector is undergoing a major transformation driven by digital acceleration, customer personalization, and the need for real-time intelligence. Institutions are rethinking their approach to problems such as international payments, fraud prevention, regulatory compliance, and gig-economy tax obligations. In this changing environment, responsiveness, scalability, and security have become essential attributes of modern systems.

Traditional financial infrastructures, although reliable, often fall short of meeting the speed and flexibility required today. Their complexity slows innovation, increases operational costs, and makes it difficult to adapt to shifting regulatory and transactional demands. Serverless computing offers a modern alternative that eliminates infrastructure overhead while supporting event-driven execution and rapid scaling.

This approach is particularly effective for high-impact financial use cases. It enables real-time fraud detection powered by machine learning, secure and efficient **know your customer (KYC)/anti-money laundering (AML)** processing, automated tax handling for gig economy platforms, and decentralized cross-border payment flows using blockchain services. These workflows benefit from serverless characteristics, including granular scalability, pay-per-use efficiency, and built-in fault tolerance.

This chapter explores how serverless and cloud-native technologies are reshaping financial applications. It introduces foundational design principles, highlights key AWS services tailored to regulated environments, and presents in-depth case studies that demonstrate how these patterns solve real-world problems across finance and fintech domains.

Structure

This chapter covers the following topics:

- Key financial concepts and standards
- Cloud-native and serverless foundations for finance
- Foundational AWS services for financial platforms
- Specialized AWS services for finance platforms
- Key metrics and KPIs in finance
- Real-life use cases and scenarios
- Serverless trends in finance

Objectives

This chapter equips readers with the knowledge and architectural strategies needed to build secure, scalable, and event-driven applications across the financial landscape. From traditional banking and payments to crypto networks, fintech platforms, and gig economy services, economic systems today demand real-time responsiveness, regulatory alignment, and operational resilience.

Readers will begin by exploring the modernization challenges that impact both legacy institutions and emerging digital finance companies, including data fragmentation, regulatory complexity, and the need for rapid innovation. The chapter then introduces key principles of cloud-native and serverless design, demonstrating how these approaches reduce infrastructure overhead while enabling modular, fault-tolerant architectures that scale on demand.

Throughout the chapter, readers will encounter real-world use cases that illustrate the practical application of serverless models. These include cross-border payment systems supported by blockchain, real-time fraud detection pipelines, automated digital identity verification workflows, and tax platforms designed to serve decentralized and gig-economy markets.

By the end of the chapter, readers will understand how to design modern financial applications that are not only technically sound but also adaptable to regulatory change, cross-platform integration, and emerging trends in digital finance. The goal is to enable cloud architects and engineering leaders to build systems that strike a balance between innovation and compliance, speed and control, and security and scale.

Key financial concepts and standards

Before designing serverless architectures for the financial sector, it is essential to understand the foundational terms, standards, and regulatory expectations that shape system design across banking, fintech, payments, and crypto. Financial platforms must navigate a layered environment of transactional integrity, auditability, identity assurance, and cross-jurisdictional compliance. The following concepts define the baseline for building resilient and trusted systems in this space:

- **Core principles of financial systems**:
  - **Ledger integrity**: At the heart of every financial application is the principle of double-entry accounting, also known as distributed ledger tracking. Whether using traditional databases, purpose-built financial systems, or blockchain, accuracy, non-repudiation, and audit trails are non-negotiable. Every credit must have a corresponding debit, every transaction must be traceable, and every ledger entry must reflect a consistent system of record.
  - **Atomicity and consistency**: Financial systems are held to strict guarantees around data consistency. Transactions must either be completed fully or not at all, particularly in areas such as fund transfers, trading, or loan processing. Serverless platforms must account for these expectations when building distributed workflows.
  - **Identity and trust**: Verifying user and institutional identities is a regulatory and operational requirement. Financial platforms must establish secure identity frameworks that support real-name verification, KYC procedures, biometric validation, and multi-factor authentication. This extends across traditional banking systems and decentralized platforms using wallet addresses, cryptographic keys, or **decentralized identifiers** (**DIDs**).
- **Financial data and compliance frameworks**:
  - **Payment Card Industry Data Security Standard (PCI DSS)**: PCI DSS governs how organizations store, process, and transmit cardholder data. Compliance requires encryption, network segmentation, access control, and detailed audit logging. Any serverless system that touches cardholder data must enforce these principles by design.

- o **AML and KYC**: These frameworks define the legal and procedural standards for identifying customers, monitoring suspicious activity, and preventing illicit financial flows. Whether onboarding a banking customer or a crypto trader, systems must track identity data, risk scores, document validation, and activity anomalies.

- o **Financial Action Task Force (FATF) and travel rule**: For crypto and digital asset platforms, the FATF requires service providers to implement mechanisms for sharing originator and beneficiary data for specific transactions. Known as the travel rule, this requirement impacts how serverless systems handle secure messaging, data tagging, and regulatory disclosure across jurisdictions.

- o **SEC/FINRA/ESMA guidelines**: For trading platforms, broker-dealers, and marketplaces, compliance with regulatory bodies such as the SEC (Securities and Exchange Commission in US), FINRA (Financial Industry Regulatory Authority in US), and ESMA (European Securities and Markets Authority of EU) requires recordkeeping, trade surveillance, and reporting features. Systems must retain data with integrity, support regulatory APIs, and enable a complete reconstruction of audits.

- o **Tax standards and reporting**: Platforms supporting digital income or cross-border activity must comply with standards such as the IRS Form 1099, OECD **Common Reporting Standard** (**CRS**), and DAC7 (EU). This requires flexible data models, jurisdiction-based routing, and integrations with tax engines or reporting services.

- **Emerging standards in decentralized finance (DeFi)**:

  - o **Blockchain and smart contracts**: In decentralized ecosystems, transactional logic often resides in smart contracts, immutable programs that run on public ledgers such as Ethereum or Avalanche. Serverless components often interact with these systems through indexing APIs, event streams, or off-chain validators.

  - o **Tokenization and stablecoins**: Financial assets are increasingly represented as tokens, encompassing a range of assets, from stablecoins and equities to reward points and real estate shares. System architectures must support compliance-aware token issuance, wallet integration, and metadata tracking for asset flows.

  - o **Digital identity and self-sovereign identity (SSI)**: SSI protocols aim to give users control over their identity data. In these models, users share verifiable credentials instead of centralized usernames and passwords. Integrating SSI with serverless authentication and authorization flows is becoming more common, particularly in high-trust or privacy-sensitive applications.

  - o **Decentralized messaging protocols (e.g., Waku, Matrix)**: As financial data moves beyond APIs into peer-to-peer and cross-chain channels, messaging standards are evolving to support encryption, delivery guarantees, and traceability across networks. Event-driven systems in serverless models are increasingly used to route, translate, or validate this data.

Cloud-native and serverless foundations for finance

Modern financial systems must be designed to do more than maintain reliability. They are expected to scale globally, adapt quickly to market changes, enforce regulatory controls, and respond in real-time to transactional activity. These expectations span traditional banking, crypto ecosystems, embedded finance, and gig-economy platforms. In this environment, cloud-native and serverless architectures provide the foundation to meet both business and technical demands.

Challenges in finance technology modernization

Financial systems today face increasing complexity across infrastructure, compliance, and operational expectations. While digital transformation continues, many organizations still rely on rigid, monolithic architectures that limit agility and delay innovation. These systems often make even minor updates slow and risky.

Data remains highly fragmented. Key records, such as customer identity, transactions, compliance logs, and tax data, are distributed across isolated systems, hindering automation and limiting visibility across operational and risk domains.

Regulatory demands are growing. Organizations must comply with a range of AML, KYC, tax, and audit frameworks while maintaining high system performance. For crypto-native and fintech platforms, these challenges are intensified by evolving global regulations around digital assets, decentralized ledgers, and blockchain transactions.

Scalability is another core issue. Whether handling market-driven transaction spikes or high-frequency flows, traditional infrastructures often lack the necessary elasticity to respond in real-time, leading to slowdowns, degraded user experiences, or even outages.

Security expectations continue to rise. Financial platforms are high-value targets and must enforce strong access control, data encryption, and anomaly detection. As blockchain, digital wallets, and tokenized assets become more mainstream, the threat landscape becomes broader and more complex.

Innovation cycles are accelerating. From instant payments and decentralized transfers to embedded finance, the pressure to launch new features quickly has never been higher. Traditional systems can no longer support the responsiveness, modularity, or integration needed in today's financial ecosystems.

True modernization requires more than cloud migration. It calls for a shift to modular, event-driven design patterns that support scalability, observability, and compliance by default. Serverless computing provides a strong foundation for this shift, enabling financial platforms to move faster while maintaining control and resilience.

Principles of cloud-native financial architecture

Cloud-native architecture embodies a modern design philosophy that enhances the adaptability, scalability, and operational efficiency of financial systems under pressure. One of its most important strengths is modularity. By organizing systems into smaller, independent services, engineering teams gain the ability to release new features or fixes without disrupting entire applications. This is especially important for payment systems, where each part of the workflow may need to evolve at a different pace or scale based on traffic patterns.

Automation is another fundamental principle. Cloud-native platforms are built to automatically handle resource provisioning, failover, and scaling in response to workload demand. This flexibility is essential for environments where traffic fluctuates dramatically, such as stock exchanges, decentralized trading protocols, or tax platforms during filing season.

Observability plays a critical role in maintaining system health and ensuring compliance. Cloud-native tools enable easier transaction tracing, service monitoring, and logging of every operational detail in real-time. These insights are valuable not just for performance tuning but also for audit readiness and incident investigations.

Agile development is also core to the cloud-native model. Platforms that support continuous delivery allow teams to push updates frequently and safely, using automated pipelines, integrated testing, and deployment controls. This approach improves time-to-market and supports faster adaptation to market changes, regulatory shifts, or customer demands.

Together, these principles form a strong foundation for building financial systems that can evolve quickly while maintaining control, compliance, and operational excellence.

Serverless design in financial workflows

Serverless systems offer a natural fit for financial workloads that are event-driven, highly variable, and sensitive to cost and scale. In a serverless model, functions execute only when needed, based on triggers such as a new transaction, a KYC document upload, or a smart contract event. This model supports fine-grained scalability, helping organizations respond to unpredictable workloads without overprovisioning.

By abstracting away infrastructure management, serverless architectures let teams focus on business logic, compliance handling, and user experience. This is especially useful in fintech and crypto applications where time-to-market is critical, and infrastructure complexity often leads to operational friction.

Serverless platforms also promote isolation and resilience. Functions run independently and are stateless by default, which limits the impact of failures and simplifies rollback strategies. For mission-critical systems, such as those involved in fraud detection or tax calculations, this architectural characteristic enhances uptime and reduces risk.

Privacy, security, and regulatory alignment

Financial applications require embedded security at every layer. Serverless services must be configured to enforce encryption in transit and at rest, apply strict identity and access policies, and generate full audit trails for every function invocation or data exchange. These controls are essential for maintaining compliance with frameworks such as PCI DSS, GDPR, SOX, and region-specific cryptocurrency regulations.

Regulatory alignment must be a first-class concern in system design. Serverless architectures enable this through centralized logging, policy enforcement, and fine-grained access control that can be integrated into build pipelines and runtime environments. Automated remediation and monitoring tools also help maintain continuous compliance in production systems.

Patterns supporting financial system readiness

Cloud-native and serverless foundations allow financial institutions to implement high-value patterns such as:

- **Parallel payment processing** involves different functions handling currency conversion, fraud scoring, and ledger updates concurrently.

- **Event-based alerting**, which notifies customers or compliance teams when unusual activity or market movements occur.

- **Secure onboarding workflows**, which validate documents, perform KYC checks, and trigger risk scoring automatically.

- **Micro-batched reporting**, where serverless jobs collect, normalize, and export tax or regulatory data without manual effort.

Each of these patterns supports modularity, traceability, and continuous adaptation, essential qualities in a regulated and competitive financial environment.

By embracing serverless and cloud-native principles, financial platforms can transcend legacy limitations and develop systems that are responsive, scalable, and secure by default. These foundations support not only the performance requirements of modern finance but also the innovation, transparency, and trust that institutions and users demand.

Foundational AWS services for financial platforms

Modern financial systems must support secure, scalable, and auditable operations while adapting to dynamic workloads. From traditional banking to emerging crypto services, financial platforms rely on foundational services that enable rapid execution, fine-grained access control, and real-time observability. AWS provides a suite of managed offerings that serve as the backbone for designing cloud-native and serverless architectures in this space.

The services listed here are commonly used across payment processing, digital identity management, fraud detection, reporting, and real-time user interactions:

- **AWS Lambda**: Lambda provides event-driven computing for functions that run in response to triggers such as transactions, fraud alerts, or document uploads. It supports rapid scaling and eliminates the need for infrastructure provisioning. Common use cases in finance include transaction scoring, dynamic pricing, and document parsing.

- **Amazon API Gateway**: API Gateway offers a secure and scalable layer for exposing APIs used by mobile apps, client platforms, or third-party partners. It handles routing, authentication, rate limiting, and analytics. Financial institutions use it to manage traffic for onboarding workflows, payment interfaces, and customer data portals.

- **Amazon DynamoDB**: DynamoDB delivers low-latency, high-throughput database access, ideal for storing real-time data such as payment statuses, user sessions, and transaction metadata. With built-in encryption and auto-scaling, it is well-suited for handling bursty financial workloads and compliance-driven data flows.

- **Amazon S3**: S3 is used for secure storage of financial records, reports, tax forms, and audit logs. It offers data durability, encryption at rest, and lifecycle management. Many institutions rely on it for long-term retention of sensitive documents and scalable support for analytics workloads.

- **Amazon EventBridge**: EventBridge helps coordinate services by routing events across systems in near real-time. It supports workflows like fraud detection, KYC checks, and compliance flagging. Decoupling event producers and consumers improves system modularity and resilience.

- **AWS Step Functions**: Step Functions orchestrate workflows across multiple services. In financial applications, this includes tasks such as identity verification, approval routing, or report generation. The visual builder and built-in retry mechanisms enhance traceability and simplify error handling.

- **Amazon Cognito**: Cognito enables secure sign-in, user pool management, and federated identity support. It plays a key role in customer login flows, employee dashboards, and investor portals. Integration with MFA and access control helps meet both usability and security goals.

These services provide the technical foundation to build scalable, compliant, and event-driven financial platforms. Whether supporting high-frequency trading systems or digital tax infrastructure, they enable organizations to focus on business logic while maintaining operational integrity.

Specialized AWS services for finance platforms

Beyond foundational services, financial applications often require purpose-built tools to address domain-specific challenges such as regulatory compliance, ledger immutability, identity verification, transaction transparency, and fraud prevention. These requirements span both traditional finance and the emerging digital asset ecosystem, where real-time activity and decentralized architectures introduce new levels of complexity.

AWS offers several services that extend serverless and cloud-native architectures to support financial operations with higher assurance, advanced analytics, and integration with evolving standards. These tools are particularly relevant in areas such as risk management, digital onboarding, cross-jurisdictional reporting, and secure asset exchange:

- **Amazon Fraud Detector**: Amazon Fraud Detector enables organizations to build, train, and deploy fraud detection models based on historical data and real-time events. It utilizes machine learning to identify anomalies, including unauthorized logins, suspicious transactions, and account takeovers. In financial services, it can be integrated into payment gateways, KYC flows, and trading platforms to reduce false positives while enhancing detection speed.

- **Amazon QLDB**: Amazon **Quantum Ledger Database (QLDB)** is a managed ledger database that provides an immutable, cryptographically verifiable history of all changes to application data. It is ideal for systems that require a reliable system of record for compliance and reconciliation, such as loan processing, asset tracking, and internal auditing.

- **Amazon Managed Blockchain**: Managed Blockchain supports the creation and management of decentralized networks using Hyperledger Fabric or Ethereum. It enables institutions to build shared ledgers for cross-border payments, digital asset settlement, and the execution of smart contracts. This is particularly useful in consortium-based financial models where transparency and shared governance are important.

- **Amazon FinSpace**: FinSpace is a data management and analytics service built for capital markets and investment firms. It simplifies the storage, cataloging, and analysis of financial time-series data while supporting entitlements, compliance policies, and audit requirements. FinSpace is typically used by quantitative teams, trading desks, and analytics groups that manage large volumes of data.

These specialized services enable financial organizations to surpass infrastructure and develop domain-aware applications that meet both functional and regulatory requirements. By integrating these services into a serverless architecture, teams can scale intelligently while maintaining a high level of trust, transparency, and compliance.

Key metrics and KPIs in finance

The transformation of financial platforms is not solely about modernizing infrastructure. It is driven by measurable outcomes that affect profitability, customer trust, risk exposure, and regulatory compliance. As financial institutions shift to serverless and cloud-native architectures, it becomes essential to define the specific metrics these systems are expected to improve.

The following categories represent the core performance indicators that guide digital transformation efforts across traditional finance, fintech, crypto ecosystems, and financial infrastructure providers. These metrics enable teams to identify system bottlenecks, quantify value, and ensure that serverless designs align with business objectives and industry standards.

Fraud detection and risk management

These metrics evaluate a system's ability to detect threats, prevent abuse, and reduce operational risk without introducing unnecessary friction:

- **Fraud detection accuracy**: Measures the precision of automated models or rule engines in correctly identifying fraud events.

- **False positive rate**: Indicates the percentage of legitimate activity flagged as suspicious, impacting user experience and operational costs.

- **Time to flag or stop suspicious activity**: Reflects how quickly the system can detect and react to high-risk behavior such as duplicate payments or identity compromise.

- **Volume of manual reviews avoided**: Highlights the efficiency of automation in reducing dependence on human verification.

Customer onboarding and identity verification

These KPIs measure the efficiency with which a platform can onboard new users while meeting KYC, AML, and regulatory requirements:

- **Average onboarding time per user**: Tracks the time from application start to account activation verification.

- **Document verification pass rate**: Measures the frequency at which submitted IDs or records pass automated validation.

- **Abandonment rate during onboarding**: Indicates user drop-off caused by delays or excessive verification steps.

- **Compliance check coverage**: Ensures each onboarding flow completes all required screening steps based on jurisdiction and risk category.

Payments and transaction processing

These metrics assess the performance, reliability, and cost-effectiveness of payment workflows and transaction pipelines:

- **Payment settlement time**: Captures the duration from initiation to final confirmation, especially in cross-border or blockchain-based systems.

- **Transaction success rate**: Measures the percentage of transactions completed without retry or manual intervention.

- **Cost per transaction (infrastructure)**: Reflects the backend cost of handling each transaction under peak and average loads.

- **Dispute resolution time**: Tracks how quickly chargebacks or transaction issues are detected, validated, and resolved.

Payments and transaction processing

These metrics assess the performance, reliability, and cost-effectiveness of payment workflows and transaction pipelines:

- **Payment settlement time**: Captures the duration from initiation to final confirmation, especially in cross-border or blockchain-based systems.

- **Transaction success rate**: Measures the percentage of transactions completed without retry or manual intervention.

- **Cost per transaction (infrastructure)**: Reflects the backend cost of handling each transaction under peak and average loads.

- **Dispute resolution time**: Tracks how quickly chargebacks or transaction issues are detected, validated, and resolved.

Operational resilience and observability

These metrics reflect the health, reliability, and scalability of the platform across distributed, multi-cloud, or serverless environments:

- **Latency under load (P95 or P99)**: Measures the worst-case response times for transaction processing or API calls.

- **System availability (SLA adherence)**: Captures uptime across mission-critical components and external-facing endpoints.

- **Mean time to detect (MTTD) and mean time to resolve (MTTR)**: Reflect the platform's responsiveness to performance or security incidents.

- **Alert coverage and anomaly detection rate**: Measures the quality and coverage of monitoring configurations in detecting outliers or critical failures.

By identifying and tracking these key performance indicators, financial organizations can focus modernization efforts on the areas that deliver the highest strategic impact. Serverless architectures provide the agility, observability, and responsiveness necessary to enhance these metrics, resulting in systems that are not only technically efficient but also aligned with the expectations of regulators, customers, and shareholders alike.

Real-life use cases and scenarios

This section highlights how various AWS services can be leveraged to construct architectures that address common challenges faced by finance and related industries. Often, real-life scenarios utilize a mix of Serverless components, cloud-native services, and other services, as well as on-premises systems.

Cross-border payment transfer

Problem statement: Cross-border payments remain slow, costly, and opaque due to reliance on legacy banking networks and multiple intermediaries. Transactions often involve high fees, inconsistent settlement times, and limited visibility for users and institutions. Financial services must also meet stringent regulatory requirements, such as AML laws and **Financial Action Task Force (FATF)** compliance standards; yet they struggle with slow reconciliation and an increased risk of fraud.

The absence of a shared, tamper-proof ledger leads to processing delays, transactional disputes, and limited transparency. Without blockchain-based traceability and real-time validation, traditional systems are difficult to modernize and costly to operate.

Proposed solution: This solution utilizes a fully serverless, cloud-native architecture integrated with Amazon Managed Blockchain, enabling secure, real-time, and auditable cross-border payments. It leverages AWS Step Functions to orchestrate the end-to-end transaction flow, including payment validation, external banking interactions, blockchain recording, and user notification. Immutable records are stored on the blockchain for trust and transparency, while DynamoDB and SNS ensure timely updates and alerts to end users.

Architecture: *Figure 19.1* illustrates the high-level architecture for implementing a blockchain-based cross-border payment transfer system leveraging AWS services:

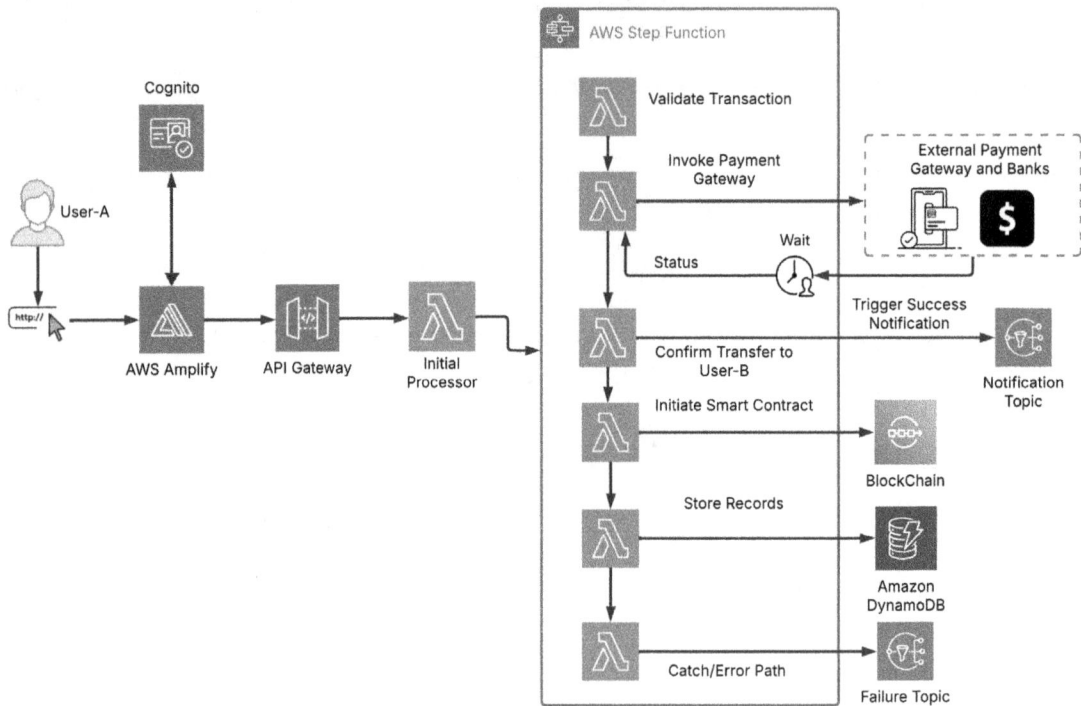

Figure 19.1: *Cross-border payment transfer system through AWS Managed Blockchain*

Architecture summary: This solution can be summarized into the following steps:

1. User_A initiates a cross-border payment to User_B via a web or mobile application hosted on AWS Amplify, with authentication handled by Amazon Cognito.

2. The request is routed through Amazon API Gateway, which invokes an Initial Processor Lambda function for lightweight validation and initiation of the transaction workflow.

3. The AWS Step Function is triggered, coordinating a sequence of Lambda functions to manage each part of the payment flow.

4. The first Lambda performs transaction validation, checking for sufficient balance and account status.

5. The second Lambda interacts with the External Payment Gateway, sending a debit request to User_A's bank and initiating the transfer. If the gateway is slow to respond, the system enters a Wait state.

6. A follow-up Lambda checks the transaction status from the external gateway. If the transfer fails or times out, the process branches to an error-handling path.

7. Upon successful confirmation, the smart contract is triggered on Amazon Managed Blockchain, recording the transaction with full auditability and consensus-based validation.

8. A separate Lambda updates transaction records and account balances in Amazon DynamoDB, ensuring real-time persistence of payment status.

9. Finally, Lambda publishes notifications to Amazon SNS, alerting both User_A and User_B about the success or failure of the payment.

10. In case of errors (e.g., insufficient funds, network failure, contract rejection), a Catch/Error Path is followed. The failure handler sends alerts via a dedicated Failure Topic (SNS) for operations or support action.

Problems solved by this architecture: This architecture helped in solving the problem, as shown as follows:

- Replacing batch-based remittances with real-time serverless processing.
- Reducing reliance on intermediaries by leveraging blockchain for trust.
- Providing traceability and immutability through smart contract execution.
- Ensuring resilient workflows with integrated error handling and retry logic.
- Decoupling services for independent scaling and fault tolerance.
- Enabling transparent user communication through automated alerts.

Metrics and KPIs: The following are the finance KPIs and metrics that this solution would improve:

- **Reduced payment processing time**: Near-instant transaction execution across global endpoints.
- **Lower transaction failure rate**: Real-time validation and automated retries minimize drop-offs.
- **Improved transparency and traceability**: Immutable blockchain records and real-time status updates.
- **Higher customer satisfaction**: Timely delivery confirmation and clear communication.
- **Reduced operational overhead**: Serverless model with automated monitoring and alerting.
- **Enhanced regulatory compliance readiness**: Full audit trails and secure logging.

Real-time fraud detection using serverless architecture

Problem statement: Financial institutions face increasing challenges in detecting fraudulent activities in real-time. Fraudsters exploit latency gaps in traditional systems, taking advantage of slow, batch-based detection pipelines to perform unauthorized transactions before alerts are raised. High false positive rates further complicate the issue, resulting in blocked legitimate users, regulatory scrutiny, and a degraded customer experience.

In a landscape where trust, speed, and precision are non-negotiable, the need for intelligent, scalable, and event-driven fraud detection has never been more urgent. Institutions must evolve beyond reactive systems and toward architectures that can analyze transactional intent, score risk in milliseconds, and take immediate action, all without compromising compliance or user trust.

Proposed solution: This solution implements a fully serverless, real-time fraud detection pipeline using AWS services. It ingests live transactions, performs enrichment, evaluates risk using a trained fraud detection model, and executes dynamic responses based on the result.

The workflow is orchestrated through AWS Step Functions, with branching logic based on the likelihood of fraud. Transactions flagged as high-risk are quarantined, recorded in secure storage, and alerted to operations teams. Legitimate transactions continue to use downstream payment services. This design ensures high throughput, eliminates infrastructure maintenance, and meets audit and observability requirements.

Architecture: *Figure 19.2* shows the high-level architecture for implementing a real-time fraud detection system using AWS services:

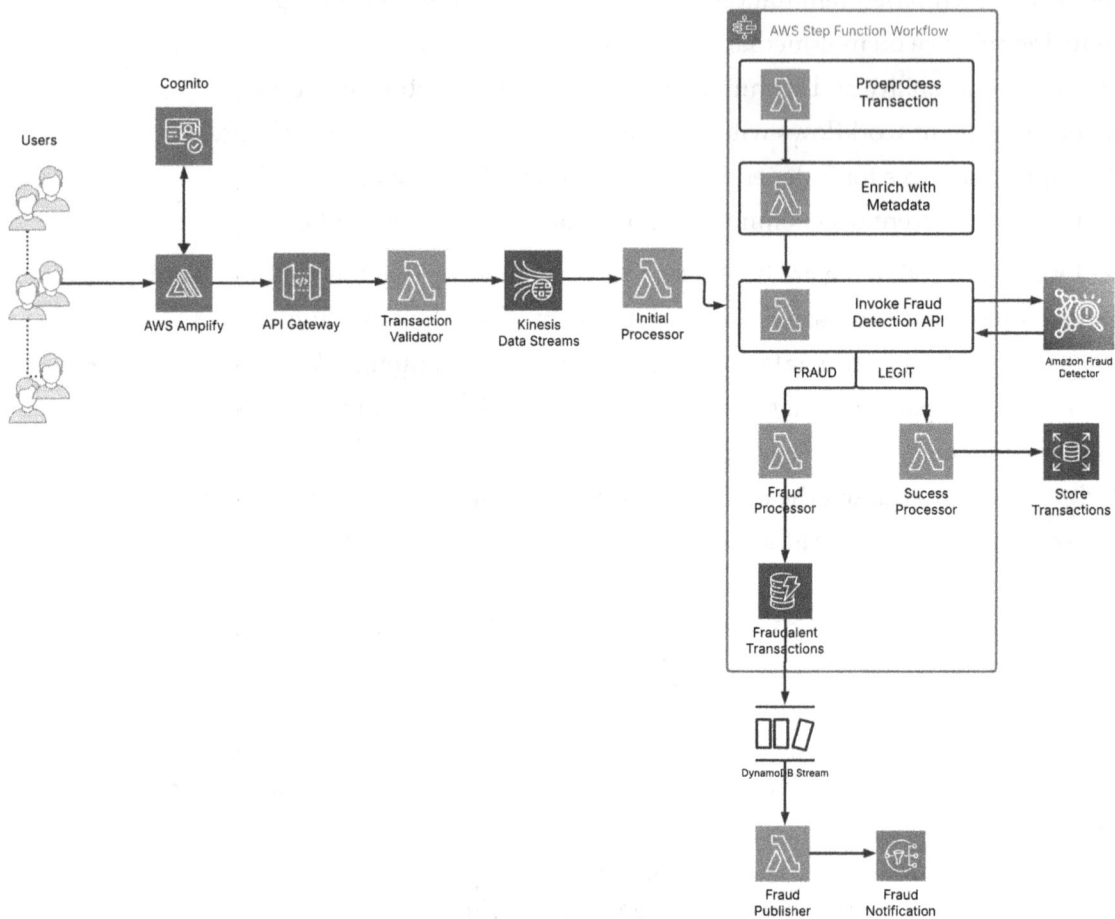

Figure 19.2: Real-time fraud detection system

Architecture summary: This solution can be summarized into the following steps:

1. Users initiate transactions from mobile or web applications hosted via AWS Amplify, and authenticated using Amazon Cognito. The user payload contains transaction details along with contextual metadata such as session tokens or device fingerprints.

2. Amazon API Gateway serves as the entry point, providing HTTPS routing, request validation, throttling, and authorization. It forwards incoming transactions to a Lambda-based transaction validator, which performs initial field checks and input sanitization and enforces business rules.

3. Validated transactions are pushed into Amazon Kinesis Data Streams, providing a durable and high-throughput ingestion layer that decouples the transaction source from the processing logic.

4. A Lambda consumer reads from the Kinesis stream and initiates an AWS Step Functions workflow. This workflow executes a structured sequence of fraud detection tasks designed for modularity and observability.

5. The first step in the workflow is a preprocessing Lambda function, which formats, normalizes, and timestamps the transaction. This is followed by an enrichment step that adds user context, such as geolocation, IP risk data, and behavioral history, from internal or third-party sources.

6. The enriched data is passed to a Lambda function that invokes the Amazon Fraud Detector API. The service evaluates the transaction against a trained fraud model and returns a prediction: FRAUD, LEGIT, or REVIEW.

7. Based on the outcome of the fraud, the Step Function branches the execution path. For flagged transactions, a fraud processor, Lambda, stores the record in a dedicated DynamoDB table. A DynamoDB Stream triggers another Lambda that publishes the fraud alert to Amazon SNS, notifying operations or security teams in real-time.

8. Legitimate transactions follow a separate branch handled by a success processor, Lambda, which logs the transaction outcome to a secure storage layer and notifies the user or downstream systems of completion.

9. All components in the pipeline generate logs and metrics via Amazon CloudWatch and CloudTrail, supporting monitoring, alerting, and compliance audits. Transaction traces can optionally be archived in Amazon S3 for long-term retention and forensic analysis.

Problems solved by this architecture: This architecture helped in solving the problem, as shown here:

- **Real-time response**: Processes transactions and raises alerts within milliseconds of detection.

- **Scalable risk evaluation**: Handles thousands of events per second without infrastructure bottlenecks.

- **Compliance and audit**: All flagged incidents are archived with full traceability, utilizing CloudTrail and S3.

- **False positive handling**: Reduces user friction by routing only high-risk transactions to manual review.

- **Modular workflow**: Each step is loosely coupled, allowing individual services to evolve independently.

Metrics and KPIs: The following are the Finance KPIs and metrics that this solution would improve:

- **Time-to-fraud detection**: Reduced to milliseconds from traditional batch hours.

- **False positive rate**: Lowered via model-driven decisions and adaptive thresholds.

- **Transaction abandonment rate**: Reduced due to fewer incorrect blocks.

- **Alert response latency**: Improved with automated SNS-based routing.

- **Audit completeness**: Guaranteed with CloudTrail, DynamoDB, and S3 archival.

Serverless KYC and AML

Problem statement: As financial services expand across borders and digital platforms, identity verification and AML screening have become critical regulatory requirements. Traditional KYC processes are often slow, error-prone, and resource-intensive, relying on manual checks, offline documents, and legacy compliance systems. These inefficiencies not only delay customer onboarding but also increase the risk of onboarding high-risk individuals or failing to detect suspicious activities.

Financial institutions must now process a high volume of identity verifications in real-time, assess risk dynamically, and comply with stringent international mandates, including those from the FATF, OFAC, and GDPR. Achieving this while preserving user experience and operational agility requires a highly scalable, auditable, and intelligent backend system—something serverless architectures are uniquely positioned to deliver.

Proposed solution: This solution implements a serverless, event-driven KYC and AML orchestration engine using AWS services. The workflow begins when users submit identity documents through a secure front-end application. Documents are uploaded to Amazon S3, which triggers an automated pipeline orchestrated by AWS Step Functions.

The system parses and extracts data from identity documents using Amazon Textract and then utilizes Amazon Comprehend to extract and structure named entities, such as name, date of birth, and nationality. This data is screened against global watch lists using third-party APIs and passed through a rule-based AML scoring engine. Based on the risk classification—low, medium, or high, the system routes each profile to an appropriate action: automatic onboarding, manual review, or rejection with escalation.

This approach removes human bottlenecks, reduces onboarding time, and ensures regulatory compliance through secure data handling, observability, and long-term archival.

Architecture: *Figure 19.3* illustrates the high-level architecture for implementing serverless KYC and AML using AWS services:

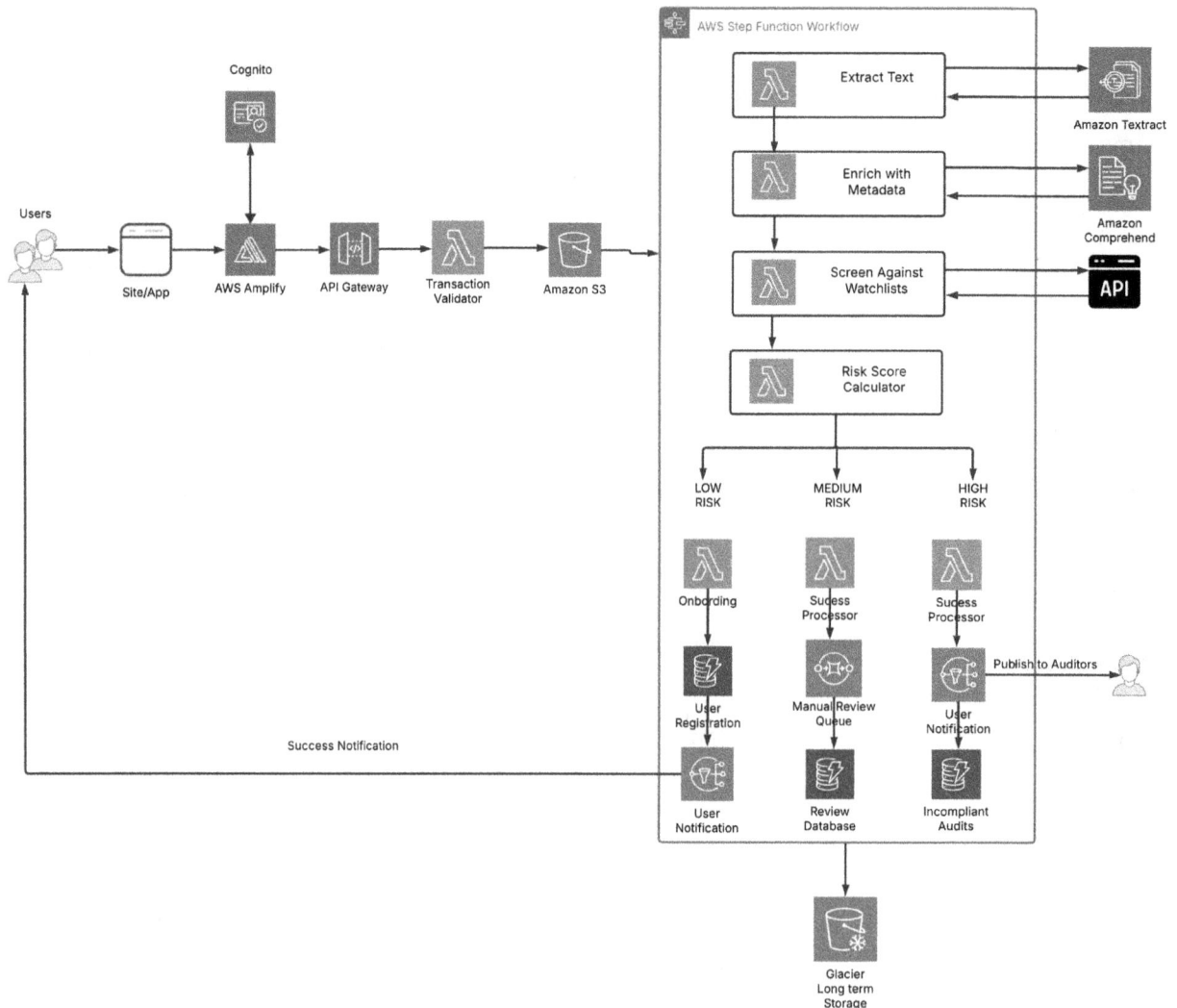

Figure 19.3: Serverless KYC and AML

Architecture summary: This architecture can be summarized into the following:

1. Users submit identity documents through a web or mobile application hosted via AWS Amplify. Authentication is handled by Amazon Cognito, ensuring secure identity management.

2. The request enters via Amazon API Gateway, which triggers a Lambda function to validate input parameters, check document type, and route valid requests to a secure Amazon S3 bucket for upload.

3. S3 triggers an AWS Step Functions workflow, initiating a fully automated document processing and compliance pipeline.

4. The first step uses Amazon Textract (invoked via Lambda) to extract structured text from uploaded documents such as passports or licenses.

5. The extracted text is passed to Amazon Comprehend, which identifies key entities—such as names, birth dates, and nationalities—for further screening.

6. The enriched user profile is sent to a Lambda function that integrates with third-party APIs to perform global watchlist screening (e.g., OFAC, PEP, Interpol databases).

7. Another Lambda function performs AML risk scoring, evaluating factors such as user geography, document validity, and source of funds to produce a final risk rating: low, medium, or high.

8. The workflow branches into one of three tracks:

    a. **Low risk**: Auto-onboarding proceeds via a Lambda function that registers the user in DynamoDB, notifies them via SNS, and completes onboarding.

    b. **Medium risk**: The profile is placed in a manual review queue, stored in a review database, and marked for evaluation by the compliance team.

    c. **High risk**: The profile is flagged and stored in a secure audit log, and a real-time alert is sent to the compliance team for escalation.

9. All document assets and event logs are stored in Amazon S3, with long-term regulatory retention handled by S3 Glacier. CloudWatch Logs and CloudTrail provide traceability and real-time observability.

Problems solved by this architecture: This architecture helped in solving the problem, as follows:

- Slow onboarding cycles caused by manual document verification are eliminated through automation and document parsing.

- Regulatory non-compliance risk is reduced by integrating real-time watchlist screening and long-term archival for audits.

- Inconsistent risk evaluation is mitigated with centralized AML scoring logic.

- High operational costs tied to human review and infrastructure management are reduced using a fully serverless model.

- Security and privacy concerns are addressed through IAM roles, encryption, and managed storage.

Metrics and KPIs: The following are the Finance KPIs and metrics that this solution would improve:

- **KYC Onboarding Time**: Reduced from days/hours to minutes or seconds.

- **False negative rate in AML screening**: Minimized via structured data enrichment and consistent rules.

- **Compliance audit coverage**: Increased via immutable storage and traceability.

- **Manual review volume**: Reduced by filtering only medium/high-risk profiles.

- **Cost per KYC verification**: Reduced through on-demand compute and storage.

- **User abandonment rate**: Lowered by faster onboarding and notifications.

Serverless tax filing engine for gig economy

Problem statement: The growing ecosystem of gig economy platforms, which encompasses ride-hailing, food delivery, freelancing, and short-term rentals, has significantly transformed how individuals earn a living. However, it has also introduced new complexities around taxation. Gig workers often derive income from multiple sources, operate across jurisdictions, and accumulate deductible expenses through diverse transactions. Most traditional tax systems, originally designed for salaried employees, do not effectively accommodate the fragmented and dynamic income patterns of these individuals.

Manual tax preparation for gig workers is both time-consuming and prone to errors. Workers must aggregate earnings, identify deductible expenses, and interpret jurisdiction-specific filing requirements. Additionally, many platforms do not offer real-time tax summaries or pre-filled forms, leaving workers to manage compliance independently. The absence of automation results in missed deductions, filing delays, and an increased risk of non-compliance. There is a clear need for an adaptive, intelligent, and automated tax engine tailored to non-traditional income earners.

Proposed solution: This solution introduces a serverless, event-driven tax filing engine purpose-built for the gig economy. It consolidates earnings and expenses from multiple platforms, processes receipts using OCR-based automation, and orchestrates the full tax preparation lifecycle using AWS services. The system supports real-time data ingestion, dynamic tax rule application, and automated form generation, resulting in an end-to-end filing solution that is fast, secure, and user-centric.

Users authenticate through a secure portal to upload receipts and link external platforms for earnings aggregation. Income data is retrieved using authorized API integrations and stored in a normalized structure. Uploaded receipts are processed using Amazon Textract, enriched through Lambda functions, and categorized for deductions. An AWS Step Functions workflow handles tax logic: pulling data, calculating liabilities, generating documents, and submitting them through integrated tax APIs. Every action is logged and auditable, ensuring full transparency and compliance.

Architecture: *Figures 19.4* and *19.5* illustrate the high-level architecture for implementing serverless tax filing for the gig economy. *Figure 19.4* shows the extraction and consolidation of expenses and incomes. *Figure 19.5* shows tax filing and processing.

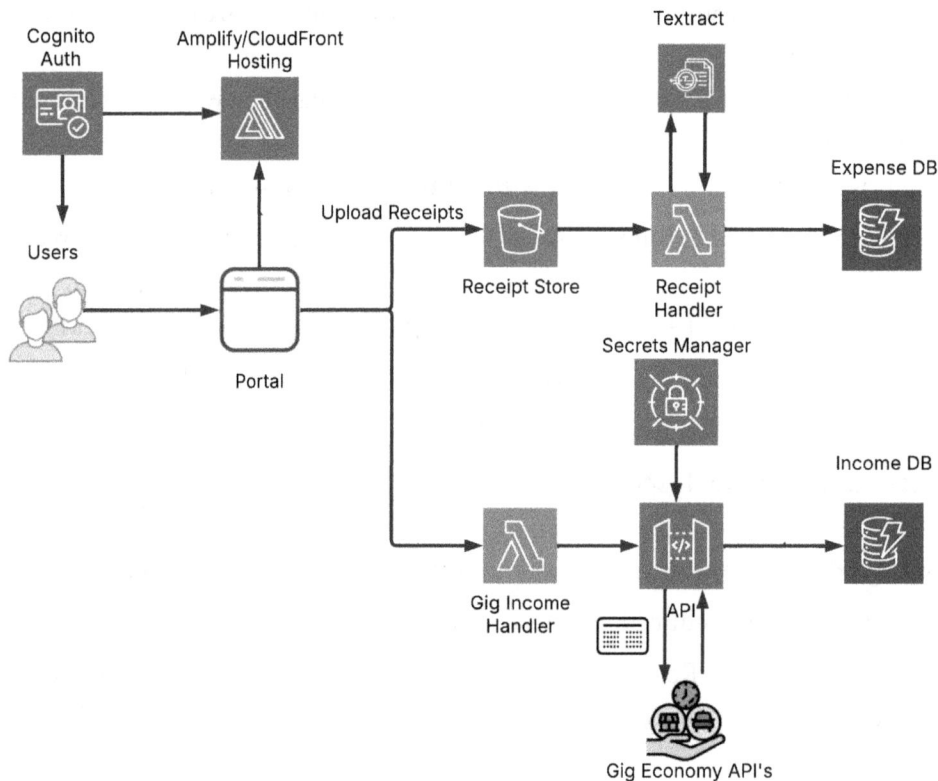

Figure 19.4: Architecture showing expense and income consolidation for the gig economy

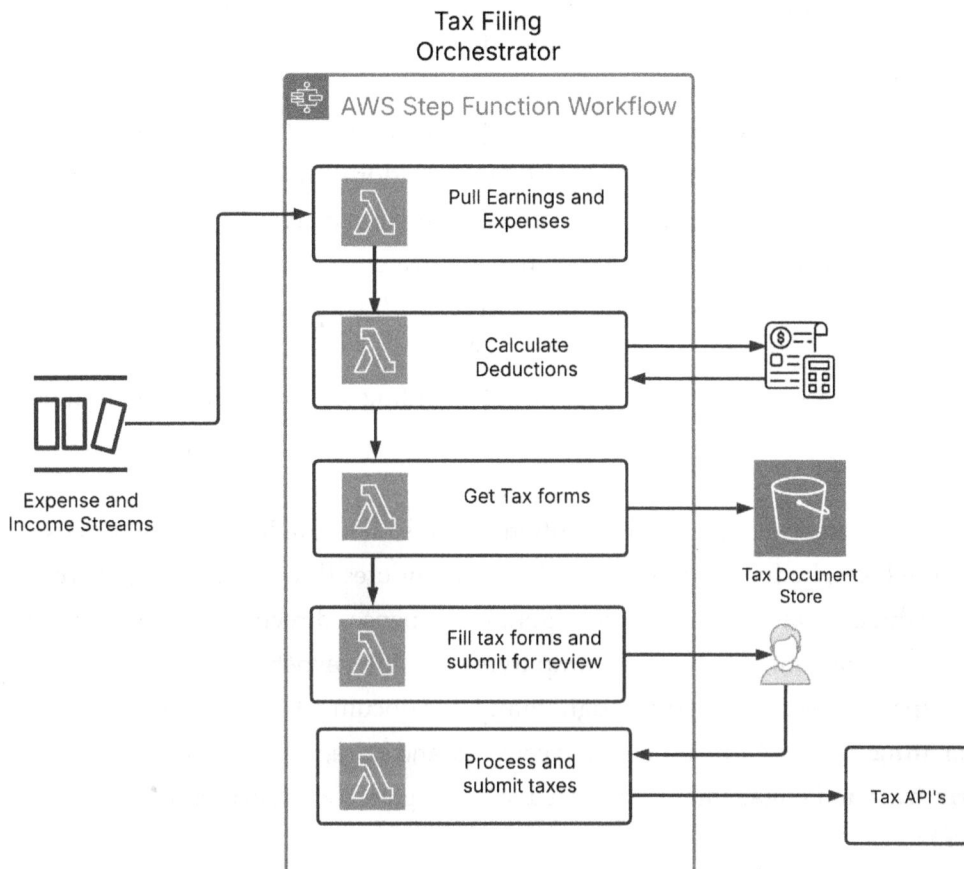

Figure 19.5: *Architecture showing automatic tax filing from expense and income streams*

Architecture summary: This architecture operates in two primary layers: **data acquisition** and **tax processing**.

1. **User access and authentication**: Users log in through a web or mobile portal secured with Amazon Cognito. The interface is hosted using AWS Amplify or Amazon CloudFront, providing a responsive frontend for managing tax activities.

2. **Receipt upload and processing**: Users upload receipts in image or PDF formats. These are stored in Amazon S3. The upload event triggers a Lambda function that invokes Amazon Textract to extract structured text. The receipt data is parsed, categorized, and stored in the Expense database (Amazon DynamoDB). The original receipt is archived in S3 for audit purposes.

3. **Income aggregation from gig platforms**: Users connect their external gig economy accounts through OAuth or API keys. A Lambda function retrieves secure credentials from AWS Secrets Manager and pulls earnings data from third-party APIs. This data is parsed and saved in the Income database (DynamoDB), tagged by user and platform.

4. **Tax orchestration and filing**: An AWS Step Functions workflow orchestrates the tax filing process. It initiates Lambda functions to:

    a. Retrieve income and expense records.

    b. Apply deduction rules based on location and tax bracket.

    c. Generate and fill out appropriate tax forms.

    d. Store completed forms in Amazon S3.

    e. Notify users for review and approval.

    f. Submit filings via third-party tax APIs where supported.

5. **Monitoring and compliance**: All interactions and computations are logged using Amazon CloudWatch. AWS CloudTrail tracks API access and execution flow for auditability. Long-term archival is supported via S3 lifecycle policies.

Problems solved by this architecture: This architecture helped in solving the problem, as shown here:

- Aggregates fragmented income from multiple gig platforms into a unified view.
- Automates receipt handling with OCR-based document parsing.
- Eliminates manual tax calculations through event-driven deduction workflows.
- Reduces operational burden on platforms with zero infrastructure management.
- Enhances compliance readiness with full traceability and secure data handling.
- Improves user experience with faster, personalized filing and proactive notifications.

Metrics and KPIs

The following metrics demonstrate how this solution delivers measurable value for both users and platforms:

- **Time to file taxes**: Reduced from days or hours to minutes through automated orchestration.
- **Missed deduction rate**: Lowered by categorizing expenses directly from structured receipt data.
- **User abandonment rate**: Reduced by simplifying the filing experience and offering real-time visibility.
- **Audit preparedness**: Improved through immutable document storage and access tracking.
- **Cost per filing**: Reduced with on-demand compute and storage services, eliminating idle infrastructure.
- **Platform trust and engagement**: Increased as users gain confidence in receiving accurate and timely tax support.

Serverless trends in finance

The financial industry is entering a new era defined by real-time services, decentralized infrastructure, and increasingly complex regulatory requirements. As financial platforms evolve to meet the demands of global scalability, security, and speed, serverless architectures are emerging as a key enabler, not just for operational efficiency but also for innovation, personalization, and trust.

The following trends illustrate how serverless computing is expected to shape the next generation of financial applications, supporting both traditional institutions and next-generation fintech and crypto platforms:

- **AI-assisted fraud detection and transaction intelligence**: Serverless platforms are powering event-driven fraud pipelines that adapt in real-time to evolving threats. With the integration of foundation models and services like Amazon Fraud Detector, financial platforms can now analyze behavioral patterns, location anomalies, and spending trends at scale, reducing false positives while improving detection speed and decision accuracy.

- **Real-time KYC and onboarding automation**: As regulatory pressure increases and customer expectations shift toward instant access, serverless architectures are being leveraged to orchestrate identity verification, risk scoring, and onboarding tasks in near real-time. These workflows utilize document recognition, geolocation validation, and secure identity APIs to minimize onboarding friction while ensuring compliance across various jurisdictions.

- **On-demand tax and regulatory reporting engines**: Serverless designs enable institutions to dynamically generate jurisdiction-specific reports based on real-time data ingestion and rules-based templates. This supports changing tax laws, cross-border filing obligations, and automated reconciliation without building or maintaining a dedicated reporting infrastructure.

- **Blockchain-based event orchestration**: With the rise of decentralized finance and tokenized assets, financial systems must now interact with distributed ledgers and smart contracts. Serverless platforms enable the monitoring of blockchain events, triggering off-chain workflows, and responding to asset transfers or on-chain compliance triggers. These architectures allow platforms to participate in cross-chain asset flows, digital identity verification, and automated settlement.

- **Hyper-personalized financial services**: AI-driven personalization in finance requires scalable infrastructure to deliver insights and actions tailored to each user. Serverless backends can support real-time recommendation engines for credit products, investment strategies, or financial education, using behavioral analytics, risk tolerance, and life stage as inputs.

- **Embedded finance and API monetization**: As more companies integrate financial services directly into non-financial applications, serverless architectures support scalable APIs for payments, lending, insurance, and treasury services. These APIs are secured, rate-limited, and metered automatically, enabling platforms to monetize services while preserving operational reliability.

- **Edge-enabled payment verification and compliance**: Emerging use cases such as biometric payment authentication and IoT-connected commerce require rapid verification at the edge. Serverless edge computing frameworks enable these operations to execute near the point of interaction, supporting offline-first experiences, regulatory geofencing, and reduced latency for fraud detection.

As these trends evolve, serverless platforms are becoming increasingly integral to the development, deployment, and governance of financial products. From digital wallets to compliance automation and decentralized clearing systems, the financial stack is shifting toward services that respond instantly, scale globally, and integrate seamlessly. Serverless computing is not just removing infrastructure overhead; it is redefining the architecture of trust, access, and financial agility.

Conclusion

The financial sector is undergoing a profound shift, from monolithic, infrastructure-heavy systems to scalable, event-driven platforms designed for agility, security, and compliance. Serverless and cloud-native architectures offer financial institutions, fintech platforms, and digital asset providers the tools to navigate this transformation with speed and precision.

Throughout this chapter, we explored how serverless technologies can help solve some of finance's most pressing challenges. From fraud detection and KYC automation to tax reconciliation and blockchain integration, these platforms support architectures that are not only efficient but also responsive to risk, resilient under pressure, and built to scale globally. By abstracting infrastructure complexity, serverless approaches allow teams to focus on delivering value through innovation, personalization, and regulatory alignment.

Foundational and specialized AWS services provide the backbone for secure transaction processing, identity assurance, workflow orchestration, and audit readiness. With the emergence of trends such as AI-assisted decision systems, embedded finance, real-time compliance, and edge-enabled payments, it is clear that serverless computing is becoming more than an operational convenience, it is now a strategic capability.

As the industry continues to evolve, the ability to iterate quickly, integrate globally, and enforce trust programmatically will define success in modern finance. Serverless design patterns offer a compelling path forward, enabling financial systems that are more dynamic, transparent, and intelligent by default.

In the next chapter, we turn our focus to how these same architectural principles are being applied to another set of industries undergoing rapid change: manufacturing, aviation, and transportation. These sectors face unique challenges in terms of physical logistics, automation, and real-time telemetry, domains where serverless infrastructure is unlocking new levels of efficiency, reliability, and operational control.

Join our Discord space

Join our Discord workspace for latest updates, offers, tech happenings around the world, new releases, and sessions with the authors:

https://discord.bpbonline.com

CHAPTER 20

Serverless Applications in Industrial and Public Sectors

Introduction

The industrial and public sectors are undergoing rapid transformation, driven by digitalization, automation, and the need for intelligent, real-time decision-making. In domains such as manufacturing, automotive, aviation, and civic infrastructure, organizations face mounting pressure to modernize operations while navigating evolving expectations, global disruptions, and regulatory complexities.

Serverless technologies offer a powerful foundation for this transformation. By abstracting infrastructure management, they allow teams to focus on solving domain-specific challenges, whether it is optimizing supply chain logistics, enabling intelligent traffic rerouting, personalizing in-flight commerce, or streamlining public safety coordination. Serverless architectures are inherently scalable, cost-effective, and ideal for the event-driven nature of systems that operate in dynamic, high-stakes environments.

This chapter explores how AWS serverless services are being applied across industrial and public sector domains to build predictive, responsive, and mission-critical applications. Readers will discover practical design patterns for automating procurement decisions, enhancing vehicle safety through emotional intelligence, personalizing user experiences mid-air, and managing real-time urban mobility through geolocation-aware routing systems.

Through real-world scenarios and architectural breakdowns, readers will gain actionable insight into how to design event-driven, cloud-native applications that adapt to complexity, minimize operational overhead, and deliver tangible business and societal value.

Structure

This chapter covers the following topics:

- Challenges in industrial and public sector systems
- Foundational AWS services for industrial platforms
- Industrial metrics and KPIs
- Future trends
- Real-life use cases and scenarios

Objectives

This chapter provides readers with a comprehensive understanding of how serverless and cloud-native technologies are transforming various sectors, including manufacturing, automotive, aviation, and public infrastructure. Although these domains operate in distinct regulatory and operational contexts, they share common challenges, including the need for real-time decision-making, scalable and resilient systems, and the ability to adapt to dynamic environments and meet mission-critical demands.

Serverless computing addresses these challenges by offering elasticity, event-driven integration, and reduced operational complexity. Readers will explore how core AWS services, such as Lambda, API Gateway, DynamoDB, and EventBridge, are utilized in conjunction with specialized tools, including Amazon Forecast, Amazon Personalize, AWS IoT Core, and Amazon Location Service. These services enable predictive analytics, geospatial intelligence, offline-first personalization, and intelligent automation across a wide range of real-world scenarios.

Through practical use cases ranging from behavioral safety in autonomous vehicles to predictive inventory management, in-flight personalization, and real-time urban response systems, this chapter demonstrates how serverless architectures can address both operational and citizen-facing challenges. Readers will learn to design cloud-native solutions that improve safety, reduce latency, enhance decision-making, and deliver context-aware services at scale.

By the end of this chapter, readers will be able to architect scalable, event-driven applications tailored to the evolving needs of modern industrial and public sector systems. They will develop the ability to align AWS service selection with business and technical objectives while building solutions that are resilient, extensible, and adaptable to future demands.

Challenges in industrial and public sector systems

Organizations across industrial and public sectors are under increasing pressure to modernize legacy systems, enhance operational agility, and respond dynamically to real-world events. However, these environments often grapple with deeply embedded infrastructure, rigid workflows, and fragmented data ecosystems that inhibit real-time decision-making.

In manufacturing, challenges persist around fragmented supply chains, delayed forecasting, and limited visibility into material consumption. Static inventory rules and reactive procurement processes make it difficult to adjust to fluctuating demand or supplier disruptions.

The automotive sector is navigating a shift toward connected and autonomous vehicles, producing vast volumes of telemetry and sensor data. Traditional systems lack the elasticity and low-latency processing capabilities required to support predictive safety logic, fleet-wide over-the-air updates, or behavior-aware personalization.

Aviation environments face bandwidth constraints, unpredictable scheduling, and fluctuating passenger profiles across regional and global routes. Systems must operate reliably in both connected and disconnected conditions, requiring offline support, localized personalization, and synchronized workflows.

In the public sector, agencies managing emergency services, smart transportation, and civic infrastructure must process real-time data from a wide array of sources, including sensors, citizens, and third-party systems. Centralized architectures and manual coordination models often fall short in handling time-sensitive scenarios, such as incident response, rerouting, or environmental monitoring.

Across these domains, the need for modular, event-driven, and scalable architectures is accelerating. Serverless technologies provide a foundation for systems that are adaptable, cost-efficient, and capable of delivering real-time insights and automated responses without the need to manage infrastructure.

Foundational AWS services for industrial platforms

Delivering scalable, intelligent, and responsive solutions in industrial domains requires a robust foundation of cloud-native services. AWS offers a versatile portfolio of serverless and event-driven tools that enable manufacturing, automotive, and aviation workloads to operate efficiently, adapt in real-time, and reduce infrastructure overhead.

The following AWS services are core to many industrial use cases featured in this chapter:

- **AWS Lambda**: Executes custom logic in response to real-time triggers, such as sensor data, vehicle telemetry, or supply chain events. It supports modular, stateless design with automatic scaling and is widely used for orchestration, transformation, and system coordination.

- **Amazon API Gateway**: Acts as the interface between applications and cloud logic. In connected vehicles and aircraft systems, it enables secure communication between edge devices and backend services, supporting RESTful and WebSockets-based interactions.

- **Amazon DynamoDB**: A fast, serverless NoSQL database used to manage dynamic data such as vehicle state, passenger preferences, order history, or inventory levels. Its millisecond response time supports high-throughput industrial workflows.

- **Amazon EventBridge**: Provides asynchronous event routing between services and systems. Used for real-time coordination in predictive supply chains, behavioral monitoring in AVs, and inventory-aware automation in manufacturing.

- **Amazon S3**: Offers scalable storage for operational logs, telemetry, video data, and training datasets. Also used for archiving, analytics pipelines, and storing ML models across industrial workloads.

- **AWS Step Functions**: Manages multi-step workflows with clear state tracking and retry logic. Commonly used in orchestrating emotion-driven vehicle behavior, forecast-driven restocking, or post-purchase workflows in in-flight systems.

- **Amazon Kinesis**: Used for ingesting and processing real-time data streams. Kinesis Video Streams is leveraged for facial emotion analysis in AVs, while Kinesis Data Streams transports biometric and voice data for ML inference pipelines.

- **AWS IoT Core**: Provides secure device communication, ideal for connecting vehicles, factory sensors, or aircraft systems to the cloud. It underpins data ingestion and device-to-cloud workflows in every use case described.

- **Amazon SNS**: Enables real-time notifications, alerts, and messaging across systems and teams. Used to inform procurement teams of exceptions, passenger systems of purchase confirmations, or vehicle systems of behavioral changes.

- **Amazon Transcribe and Amazon Comprehend**: These services support voice-to-text conversion and sentiment analysis in emotionally aware AVs. Transcribe captures in-cabin speech, while Comprehend extracts behavioral and emotional insights for downstream actions.

- **Amazon Polly**: Converts text responses into speech for real-time, in-vehicle communication, offering natural interaction in emotionally adaptive safety systems.

- **Amazon Forecast**: Delivers accurate time-series forecasting based on historical consumption data, enabling just-in-time procurement and dynamic inventory optimization in manufacturing.

- **Amazon Personalize**: Provides real-time recommendation services that tailor in-flight offers and product bundles to individual passengers, enhancing user satisfaction and ancillary revenue.

While serverless services offer significant advantages in speed, cost, and scalability, real-world industrial solutions often combine serverless, cloud-native, and other managed AWS services to meet complex demands. For example, integrating container-based systems with Lambda or utilizing Amazon EC2 for specialized hardware alongside serverless workflows enables teams to tailor their architectures based on workload characteristics. This flexible approach ensures organizations can optimize for performance, compliance, and cost without being locked into a single pattern.

Industrial metrics and KPIs

Measuring the impact of serverless adoption requires identifying the right performance indicators for each domain. In sectors such as manufacturing, automotive, aviation, and public services, the key metrics often span operational efficiency, cost control, safety, responsiveness, and citizen or user satisfaction. Serverless architectures directly enhance these metrics through real-time processing, scalable automation, and resilient, infrastructure-free workflows.

The following are the core metrics and KPIs improved by serverless solutions in these environments:

- **Operational latency**: Serverless functions minimize the time between data ingestion and response. In manufacturing, this accelerates inventory-aware decision-making. In the automotive or aviation industries, it enables low-latency responses for personalization or safety. In the public sector, this ensures the rapid detection of incidents, such as traffic disruptions or public safety alerts.

- **System uptime and availability**: Managed services, such as AWS Lambda, DynamoDB, and API Gateway, offer high availability and automatic failover. These qualities are critical for ensuring uninterrupted workflows, whether it is a predictive procurement system or a civic emergency response engine.

- **Resource utilization efficiency**: Serverless architectures scale on demand, eliminating idle resource costs. This results in better cost efficiency across batch processing in factories, telemetry from AV fleets, or sporadic data surges from public sensors and civic IoT systems.

- **Response accuracy and relevance**: For use cases involving ML inference, such as AV behavior prediction, urban rerouting, or public service prioritization, serverless architectures enable real-time model invocation, improving contextual accuracy and reducing overuse of compute resources.

- **Cost per actionable event**: With pay-per-use pricing, serverless platforms align infrastructure cost directly with outcomes. This makes it easier to measure the return on investment for specific events, such as restocking triggers, in-flight purchases, or traffic rerouting decisions.

- **Incident resolution time**: Event-driven automation and real-time alerting reduce the time to detect, triage, and respond to disruptions. This applies across aircraft operations, production line anomalies, or public safety coordination during emergencies.

- **Throughput and scalability**: Serverless platforms support massive concurrency, which is essential for scaling across large infrastructures, such as factories, vehicles, or cities. Systems can ingest thousands of sensor events, vehicle telemetry packets, or citizen reports simultaneously without degradation.

By improving these metrics, serverless adoption enables organizations to deliver faster, safer, and more intelligent systems while maintaining control over costs and resources.

Future trends

In manufacturing, serverless architectures are evolving in tandem with digital twins, edge analytics, and generative AI-powered forecasting. These patterns will enable more autonomous supply chains, real-time production optimization, and predictive maintenance across distributed environments.

The automotive sector will continue to move toward software-defined vehicles and cloud-connected intelligence. Serverless infrastructure is expected to support behavioral safety analytics, fleet-wide OTA orchestration, and adaptive personalization logic, powered by real-time data flows from vehicle-to-cloud systems.

Aviation will see a broader adoption of serverless systems for dynamic route adjustments, in-flight service personalization, and operational optimization. Offline-capable serverless patterns will be critical to supporting disconnected environments while maintaining continuous passenger and crew engagement.

In the public sector, civic platforms, urban mobility systems, and emergency response engines will increasingly rely on event-driven, geospatially aware architectures. Serverless compute will support real-time monitoring, faster incident response, and intelligent decision-making across city infrastructure and citizen services.

Across all these domains, serverless computing will remain foundational to building systems that are intelligent, responsive, and able to scale with minimal overhead, unlocking the next wave of industrial and civic innovation.

Real-life use cases and scenarios

This section highlights how various AWS services can be leveraged to construct architectures that address common challenges faced by Finance and related industries. Often, real-life scenarios utilize a mix of Serverless components, cloud-native services, and other services, as well as on-premises systems.

AI-driven behavioral safety in AVs

Problem statement: Most **autonomous vehicle** (**AV**) systems today are designed to interpret and respond to physical surroundings, including road conditions, obstacles, and traffic signals. However, they lack awareness of a critical factor: the emotional and behavioral state of human occupants and nearby pedestrians. This blind spot introduces risks such as misinterpreting erratic pedestrian behavior, failing to accommodate an anxious or stressed passenger or overlooking signs of driver fatigue in semi-autonomous modes.

The absence of human-centered emotional intelligence can compromise safety, reduce user trust, and hinder the adoption of AVs in sensitive scenarios, such as healthcare transport, assisted driving, or high-stress environments.

Proposed solution: To bridge this gap, this use case introduces a serverless, AI-powered behavioral safety system that enables AVs to perceive and react to human emotions and contextual cues. By integrating in-cabin cameras, audio inputs, and wearable biometrics with AWS cloud-native services, the system continuously detects emotional signals, such as anxiety, aggression, or distress, and adjusts vehicle behavior accordingly.

Leveraging AWS Lambda, SageMaker, Amazon Rekognition, Comprehend, and Step Functions, the architecture supports real-time emotional intelligence. It analyzes voice tone, facial expressions, and physiological indicators, fuses them with contextual metadata like location or time of day, and orchestrates safe, adaptive feedback through voice, visual, or haptic channels. This enhances safety, comfort, and user trust in AV environments.

Architecture: The architecture is divided into two logical diagrams for clarity and focus. *Figure 20.1* illustrates the data ingestion and emotional analysis layer, where sensor inputs, including video, audio, and biometric signals, are processed to detect emotional states using AWS AI services.

Figure 20.2 captures the contextual reasoning, decision-making, and feedback delivery layer, where the system adapts vehicle behavior based on emotional insights and environmental context while providing real-time, multimodal feedback to occupants.

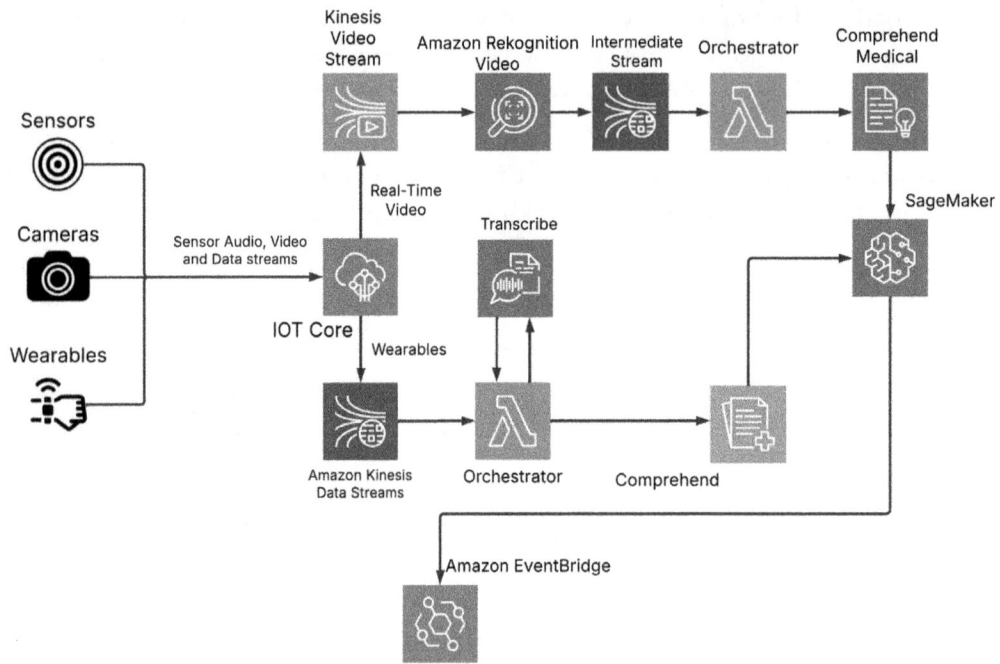

Figure 20.1: Data ingestion for AI-driven behavioral safety

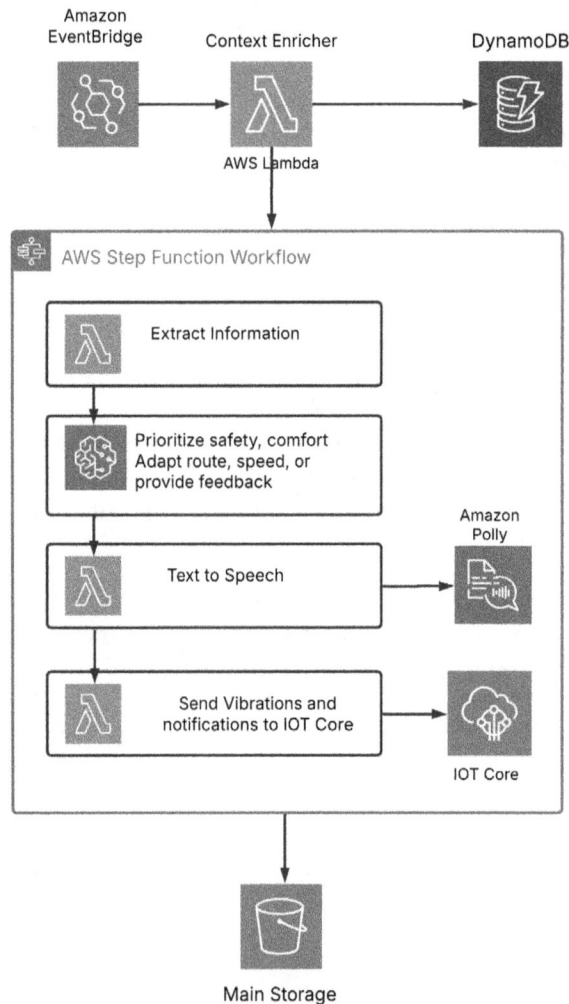

Figure 20.2: Contextual reasoning for AI-driven behavioral safety

Architecture summary: The following steps outline the complete serverless workflow that powers the AI-driven behavioral safety system in autonomous vehicles:

1. In-vehicle sensors capture multimodal input, including facial expressions from cameras, voice patterns from microphones, and biometric signals from wearable devices.

2. AWS IoT Core ingests and routes the sensor data, securely delivering video, audio, and telemetry streams to downstream services.

3. Amazon Kinesis Video Streams directly feeds the camera stream to Amazon Rekognition Video, where facial expressions are analyzed in real-time to detect emotions.

4. Amazon Kinesis Data Streams carries biometric and audio signals, which are consumed by an AWS Lambda function that orchestrates sentiment and speech analysis.

5. The Lambda function invokes Amazon Transcribe to convert speech to text, enabling downstream natural language analysis.

6. Amazon Comprehend analyzes the speech transcript to extract emotional sentiment, tone, and behavioral cues.

7. Amazon Comprehend Medical (optional) processes biometric-derived text, identifying indicators of stress, anxiety, or other health-related conditions.

8. A central AWS Lambda function aggregates emotional insights from video, speech, and biometric streams, then emits a structured emotional state event enriched with metadata.

9. Amazon EventBridge triggers the next stage of processing, forwarding the emotional state event for contextual enrichment and decision-making.

10. A context enricher Lambda function supplements the event with real-time vehicle data, including speed, location, and environmental conditions, and stores it in Amazon DynamoDB.

11. AWS Step Functions orchestrate a behavioral safety workflow, which includes prioritizing safety and comfort, invoking a SageMaker model to infer the appropriate response, and routing feedback actions.

12. Amazon Polly delivers voice feedback, while AWS IoT Core sends haptic cues and display signals back to the vehicle to adapt the driving experience in real-time.

13. Amazon S3 archives enriched data and system responses, enabling long-term analysis and periodic model retraining via SageMaker Pipelines.

Problems solved by this architecture: The system addresses several critical pain points in modern AV deployments:

- **Driver misinterpretation**: By identifying signs of anger, fatigue, or distraction, the system triggers calming feedback or adjusts vehicle behavior in semi-autonomous modes.

- **Passenger discomfort**: The vehicle adapts ride dynamics or cabin conditions in response to signs of anxiety, nausea, or confusion.

- **Pedestrian risk perception**: Emotionally distressed or hesitant pedestrian behavior can be interpreted more cautiously to avoid unsafe interactions.

- **Lack of human-like interaction**: Natural voice feedback and haptic cues create a more relatable, emotionally intelligent AV experience.

- **Static behavior models**: Continuous learning from real-world inputs ensures model drift is minimized and user behavior is accounted for over time.

- **Hardware cost overheads**: Fully serverless architecture reduces on-board processing needs while scaling efficiently across fleets.

Metrics and KPIs: The following metrics help measure the effectiveness, safety, and adaptability of the AI-driven behavioral safety system in autonomous vehicles:

- **Emotion detection accuracy**: Measures the precision and recall of facial, vocal, and biometric emotion classification across diverse conditions.

- **Response latency**: Tracks the time between emotion detection and corresponding system feedback (verbal, haptic, or visual), ensuring real-time responsiveness.

- **Passenger comfort index**: Captures aggregated post-ride feedback and in-trip experience scores, indicating emotional comfort and trust.

- **Safety intervention rate**: Counts the number of automated behavioral interventions (e.g., route adjustment, calming prompts) triggered by high-risk emotional states.

- **Model confidence drift**: Monitors degradation in prediction confidence over time, flagging when retraining or tuning is needed.

- **System availability**: Measures the uptime and processing success rate of the emotional intelligence pipeline across the AV fleet.

- **Feedback success rate**: Tracks the successful delivery of speech, display, or haptic cues in response to emotional events.

- **Retraining effectiveness**: Evaluates improvements in model performance after retraining cycles using new behavioral data from Amazon S3.

- **Fleet-wide behavior insights**: Aggregates anonymized emotion-behavior trends across vehicles to support operational analytics and driverless system optimization.

- **Cost per insightful event**: Calculates the operational cost of processing each meaningful emotion-context decision using AWS serverless components.

Predictive supply chain intelligence

Problem statement: In modern manufacturing environments, maintaining optimal inventory levels is a constant challenge. Stockouts can halt production lines, while overstocking ties up capital and increases storage costs. Traditional systems rely on static reorder points and siloed procurement processes, making them unable to adapt to real-time demand fluctuations, seasonal patterns, or supply chain disruptions. Additionally, procurement and ERP systems often lack predictive capabilities, limiting visibility into future material needs.

Proposed solution: This use case presents a serverless, intelligent inventory forecasting system that enables real-time supply chain insights and automated restocking decisions. By combining historical consumption data, production schedules, and external demand signals, the system predicts material needs using Amazon Forecast. Cleaned and enriched datasets are processed through AWS Glue, stored in Amazon S3, and used to drive just-in-time restocking workflows.

Architecture: The architecture is divided into two logical diagrams for clarity and focus. *Figure 20.3* illustrates the data ingestion and forecasting layer, where historical consumption data from manufacturing systems is ingested, cleaned, and transformed using AWS Glue and then processed by Amazon Forecast to generate demand predictions.

Figure 20.4 illustrates the automation and procurement orchestration layer, where forecast outputs are evaluated, and inventory-aware restocking workflows are triggered through serverless orchestration. The system autonomously interacts with external vendors or internal procurement platforms, updates order status, and surfaces insights via dashboards and alerts for end-to-end supply chain visibility.

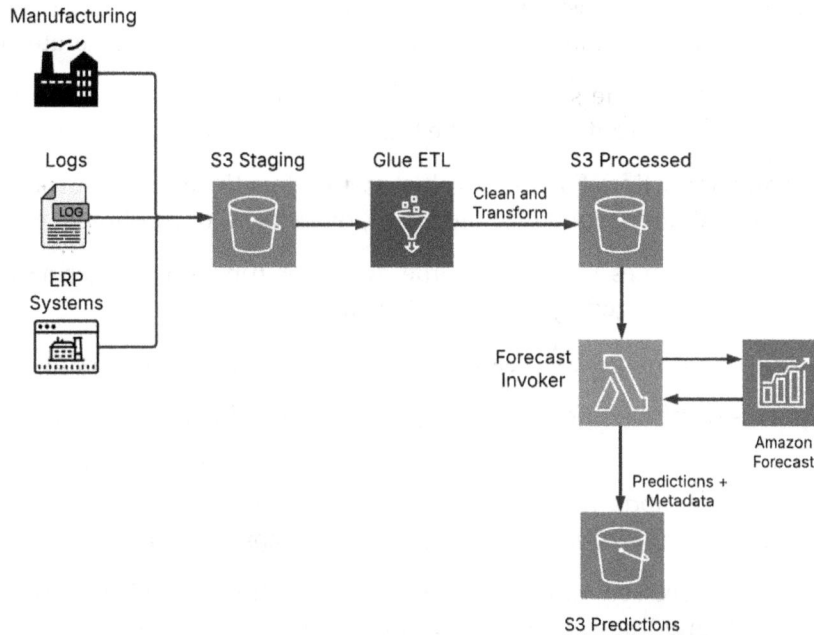

Figure 20.3: *Data ingestion and forecasting for predictive supply chain intelligence*

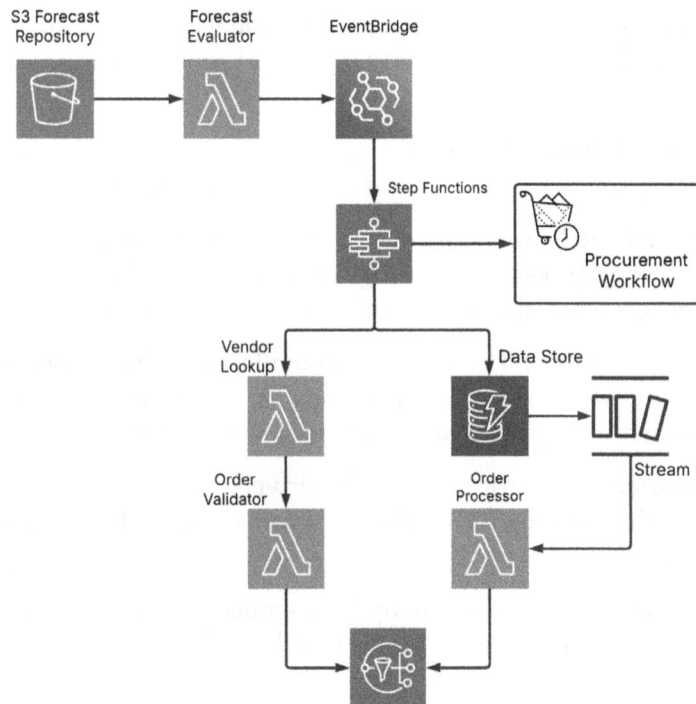

Figure 20.4: *Procurement and orchestration for predictive supply chain intelligence*

Architecture summary: The following steps describe the complete serverless workflow that enables predictive supply chain intelligence and automated inventory optimization in a manufacturing environment:

1. Manufacturing systems such as ERP and MES platforms export operational and material consumption data, including logs, demand signals, and vendor performance, into a staging area within Amazon S3.

2. AWS Glue performs ETL operations on the raw data, cleaning and transforming it into structured datasets. The refined output is written to a processed S3 bucket, ready for machine learning ingestion.

3. An AWS Lambda function (Forecast Invoker) is triggered to interact with Amazon Forecast, submitting the processed dataset, schema, and forecasting parameters to train and generate demand predictions.

4. Amazon Forecast generates time-series demand forecasts, which are stored in Amazon S3 along with associated metadata. This output serves as the foundation for inventory-aware decision-making.

5. Another AWS Lambda function, Forecast Evaluator, monitors the forecast output, evaluates it against current stock levels, and detects potential stockouts, overstocks, or fulfillment risks.

6. Amazon EventBridge receives events from the evaluator function, triggering an inventory-aware procurement workflow managed by AWS Step Functions.

7. AWS Step Functions coordinates the restocking logic, invoking two AWS Lambda functions:

8. Vendor Lookup: This Lambda function determines the most suitable vendor based on item, lead time, and SLA.

9. Order Validator: This Lambda function verifies that proposed orders meet business rules such as **minimum order quantity (MOQ)**, delivery windows, and contract terms.

10. Validated orders are processed through another Lambda function, Order Processor, which writes purchase order details and tracking metadata into Amazon DynamoDB.

11. DynamoDB Streams automatically trigger follow-up actions, ensuring system continuity and enabling traceability of procurement events and state changes.

12. Amazon SNS or Amazon EventBridge Pipes routes events to notification endpoints, such as email, messaging systems, or the Amazon Chime SDK, to alert procurement teams in the event of delays or exceptions.

Problems solved by this architecture: The predictive supply chain intelligence and inventory optimization system addresses several long-standing inefficiencies in manufacturing environments:

- **Manual forecasting and reordering**: By automating the forecasting process using Amazon Forecast and orchestrating inventory decisions through serverless workflows, the architecture eliminates the need for spreadsheets, manual thresholds, and static reorder points.

- **Inaccurate demand prediction**: The use of machine learning–based time-series forecasting enables more accurate predictions that account for seasonality, lead times, and consumption trends, thereby improving material availability and reducing the risk of overstocking.

- **Disconnected procurement workflows**: Event-driven architecture integrates inventory insights with procurement logic, enabling fully automated restocking without reliance on siloed processes or fragmented tooling.

- **Vendor selection delays**: The vendor lookup logic embedded in AWS Lambda enables the system to identify the most suitable supplier in real-time, based on criteria such as lead time, availability, or SLA compliance.

- **Order compliance gaps**: Integrated order validation ensures that every purchase decision adheres to business constraints such as minimum order quantities, contract rules, and delivery timelines, reducing costly errors.

- **Lack of proactive exception handling**: Through Amazon EventBridge and notification services, the architecture flags disruptions or anomalies early in the process, keeping procurement teams informed and enabling rapid resolution.

- **Inefficient scaling**: The serverless model enables cost-effective, scalable expansion across plants or regions without the overhead of infrastructure management or on-premises procurement systems.

Metrics and KPIs: The success of this architecture is best evaluated through operational metrics that reflect improvements in forecasting accuracy, inventory efficiency, procurement responsiveness, and system automation. The following KPIs are directly enhanced by the system:

- **Forecast accuracy (MAPE/RMSE)**: Measures the accuracy of time-series demand predictions generated by Amazon Forecast. Improved forecasting reduces overstocking and minimizes stockouts across critical production lines.

- **Inventory turnover rate**: Evaluates how efficiently inventory is consumed and replenished, offering a direct indicator of material flow health and working capital utilization.

- **Stockout frequency**: Tracks the number of times an item reaches zero inventory before replenishment. A lower frequency indicates better alignment between forecasted demand and procurement execution.

- **Overstock risk index**: Evaluates the volume of inventory exceeding historical consumption patterns, enabling the identification of slow-moving or excess stock that may tie up capital.

- **Automated order fulfillment rate**: Reflects the percentage of restocking actions that were executed entirely through the serverless pipeline without human intervention.

- **Procurement decision latency**: Measures the time elapsed between the generation of a forecast and the issuance of a purchase order. Faster decision cycles improve responsiveness to market changes and reduce missed opportunities.

- **Exception alert response time**: Measures how quickly procurement teams acknowledge and respond to alerts raised by the system (e.g., vendor SLA violations or late deliveries), which is crucial for maintaining operational continuity.

- **Order compliance rate**: Tracks how many procurement actions meet business rules such as **minimum order quantities (MOQ)**, delivery windows, and vendor contract terms. High compliance indicates governance maturity.

- **Cost per forecast cycle**: Monitors the operational cost associated with each forecast-and-execute cycle, helping ensure the system remains cost-effective as demand scales across plants or regions.

In-flight personalization and commerce engine

Problem statement: Traditional in-flight services offer a uniform experience to every passenger, standard entertainment menus, generic food and beverage options, and one-size-fits-all product catalogs. This approach fails to engage passengers on a personal level, resulting in missed opportunities for both customer satisfaction and ancillary revenue. Moreover, many systems lack real-time responsiveness, contextual awareness, or the ability to operate in disconnected flight environments, especially on short-haul or regionally constrained routes.

The absence of dynamic personalization means airlines cannot capitalize on passenger preferences, loyalty profiles, or journey context. Offers are often irrelevant, conversions are low, and loyalty engagement suffers.

Proposed solution: To solve these challenges, this architecture introduces a Serverless In-Flight Personalization and Commerce Engine that tailors content, product bundles, and promotions to each passenger based on their profile, travel history, and onboard context. Using AWS-native services such as AppSync, Amazon Personalize, DynamoDB, S3, and API Gateway, the system delivers personalized experiences in both real-time and offline modes.

The architecture includes two major flows:

- **Personalization and offer delivery**: This layer enables dynamic query-based personalization using AppSync and Lambda resolvers. It leverages Amazon Personalize for machine learning–driven recommendations and falls back to pre-filtered bundles stored in S3 when offline. Passenger profiles stored in DynamoDB are used to tailor recommendations based on tier, seat class, prior purchases, and preferences.

- **Commerce workflow and feedback loop**: Once a passenger accepts an offer, the transactional flow is initiated through the API Gateway and Lambda. Purchases are logged to DynamoDB, and downstream processing, such as receipt generation and notification publishing, is triggered via DynamoDB Streams. This design ensures decoupled execution, traceability, and asynchronous processing across in-flight environments.

Architecture: The architecture is divided into two logical diagrams:

Figure 20.5 illustrates the Personalization and Offer Delivery System.

Figure 20.6 shows the Commerce Workflow and Feedback System.

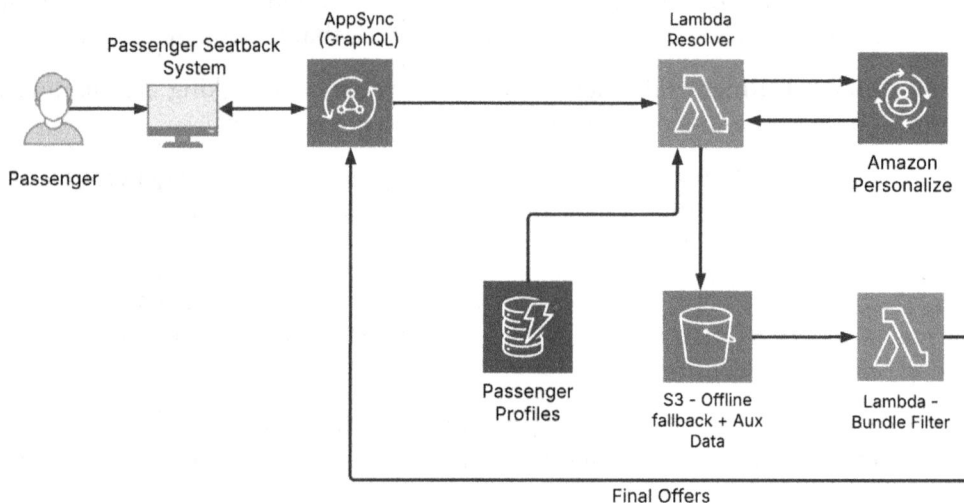

Figure 20.5: *Personalization and offer system*

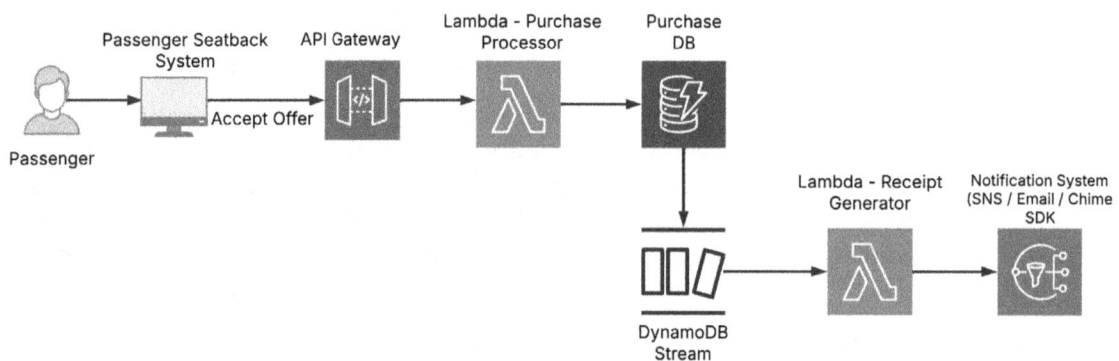

Figure 20.6: *Commerce workflow and feedback system*

Architecture summary:

- **Personalization and offer delivery layer**: This component orchestrates the personalization process using AWS AppSync, Lambda, Amazon Personalize, DynamoDB, and S3. It supports both online inference and offline fallback for flights that are disconnected. The following are the steps in which the system communicates:

  1. The passenger seatback system sends a GraphQL query to AWS AppSync to request personalized offers.

2. Lambda resolver coordinates downstream calls to:

   o Amazon Personalize for real-time recommendation inference.

   o Passenger Profiles in DynamoDB for seat class, tier, or behavior history.

   o S3 for offline pre-generated content bundles.

3. The resulting bundles are filtered by the Bundle Filter Lambda, which applies eligibility rules (e.g., seat class, available stock, time-in-flight).

4. Final offers are returned to the passenger device via AppSync.

- **Commerce workflow and feedback layer**: This component enables the purchase-to-notification pipeline using API Gateway, Lambda, DynamoDB, and messaging services. The following demonstrates the high-level event flow:

  1. Upon acceptance of the offer, the Seatback System triggers a REST request via the API Gateway.

  2. Lambda Purchase Processor logs the transaction into the Purchase DB (DynamoDB).

  3. A DynamoDB Stream automatically triggers the Lambda—Receipt Generator, which formats a receipt payload and invokes the Notification System (e.g., SNS, Email, or Chime SDK) to confirm the transaction.

  4. This event can also be archived to S3 for analytics and fed back into Amazon Personalize for periodic model retraining.

Problems solved by this architecture: This architecture addresses multiple challenges that have historically limited the effectiveness of in-flight service personalization and commerce:

- **Lack of individualized passenger experience**: Traditional in-flight systems deliver uniform menus and offers, disregarding passenger preferences, seat class, loyalty status, or purchase history. This architecture introduces real-time, profile-aware personalization to elevate passenger engagement.

- **Disconnected flight environments**: Many flights operate without continuous internet connectivity, making dynamic personalization impossible. This solution supports offline delivery through pre-generated content bundles stored in S3, ensuring continuity of service.

- **Low conversion rates**: Generic promotions result in poor offer-to-purchase ratios. By utilizing Amazon Personalize for tailored recommendations, this architecture enhances relevance, thereby increasing the likelihood of conversion.

- **Rigid, monolithic systems**: Legacy in-flight commerce platforms are tightly coupled and hard to extend. This serverless architecture promotes modularity through the use of Lambda, AppSync, and API Gateway, enabling scalable and decoupled experiences.

- **Delayed feedback loop**: Traditional systems often lack mechanisms to capture purchase behavior and route it back into personalization logic. This design utilizes DynamoDB Streams to close the feedback loop, enabling model refinement through S3 archives and Amazon Personalize retraining.

- **Operational complexity in multimodal personalization**: Handling real-time and offline paths can be operationally challenging. This architecture simplifies the process by clearly separating online inference and fallback logic while maintaining unified delivery paths through AppSync.

Metrics and KPIs: This system improves a range of operational and passenger-experience metrics across the personalization and commerce layers:

- **Personalization match rate**: Measures the percentage of passengers who receive tailored recommendations based on their profiles and behavioral history.

- **Offer acceptance rate**: Tracks the number of accepted offers relative to those delivered, an indicator of personalization accuracy and relevance.

- **Disconnected mode delivery rate**: Evaluates the frequency at which offline bundles are successfully delivered on flights with limited or no connectivity.

- **Commerce conversion rate**: Captures the ratio of purchases to total offers shown, reflecting the effectiveness of the recommendation and commerce flow.

- **End-to-end latency (offer to notification)**: Measures the total time from passenger interaction to receipt of confirmation, indicating system responsiveness.

- **Model freshness and feedback loop completion time**: Evaluates how quickly post-flight data is ingested and utilized for retraining personalization models.

- **Operational cost per personalized session**: Tracks the compute and storage cost per passenger session, helping maintain cost efficiency across short-haul and long-haul flights.

Urban traffic intelligence and rerouting

Problem statement: Urban traffic systems are under growing pressure from rising vehicle volumes, frequent disruptions, and aging infrastructure. Accidents, construction zones, and sudden congestion often go undetected or unaddressed in real-time, leading to extended delays, fuel waste, and reduced commuter satisfaction.

Most city traffic networks rely on static signal schedules and delayed human reports. These centralized systems are not designed to adapt dynamically to unfolding events. As a result, cities struggle to respond effectively, particularly during peak hours or emergency scenarios.

There is a clear need for an intelligent, geospatially aware platform that can detect traffic anomalies, assess impact, and guide rerouting decisions automatically. Without this, incident management remains reactive, fragmented, and inefficient.

Cities require an event-driven approach that integrates real-time sensor data, mobile feedback, and automated routing logic, thereby reducing congestion and enabling faster, safer, and more efficient urban mobility.

Proposed solution: This solution introduces a serverless, event-driven platform that integrates traffic sensor data, GPS signals, and user-generated reports to detect and respond to traffic disruptions in real-time. It applies geospatial intelligence to classify incidents, identify affected areas, and guide drivers toward alternate routes.

AWS Lambda handles anomaly detection and routing logic, while Amazon Location Service maps the incidents, calculates reroutes, and applies geofencing rules. Amazon Kinesis ingests traffic streams, and Amazon EventBridge coordinates triggers between data ingestion, analysis, and rerouting workflows. AWS Step Functions orchestrate the response logic end-to-end.

Notifications are dispatched to city operators or vehicle systems through Amazon SNS or API-integrated applications. This serverless architecture ensures continuous operation, dynamic scaling, and minimal infrastructure overhead, enabling cities to respond to live traffic conditions and enhance commuter experiences.

Architecture: The architecture is divided into two logical diagrams. *Figure 20.7* illustrates the ingestion and event evaluation pipeline. *Figure 20.8* presents the event routing and geolocation workflow. Together, they represent the end-to-end system for real-time traffic anomaly detection and intelligent rerouting.

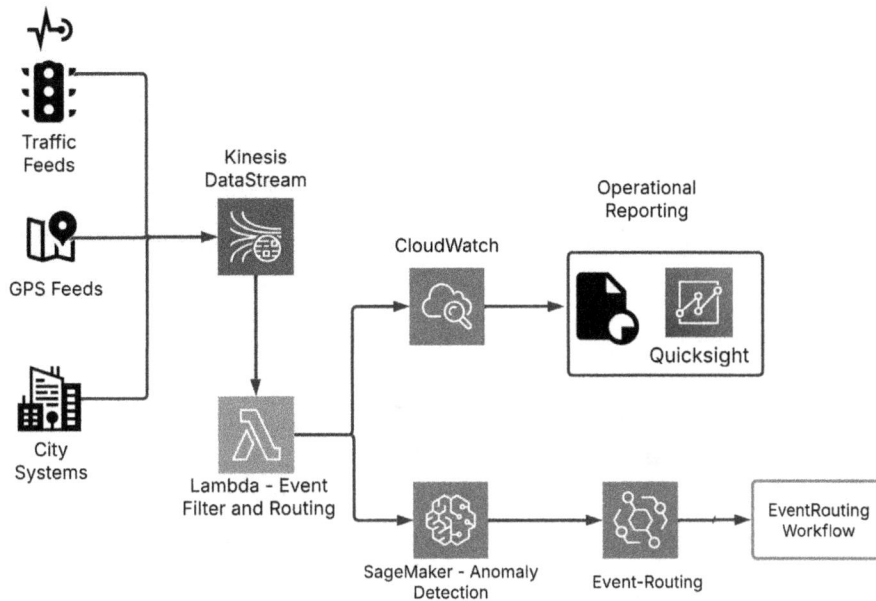

Figure 20.7: *Ingestion pipeline for urban traffic intelligence*

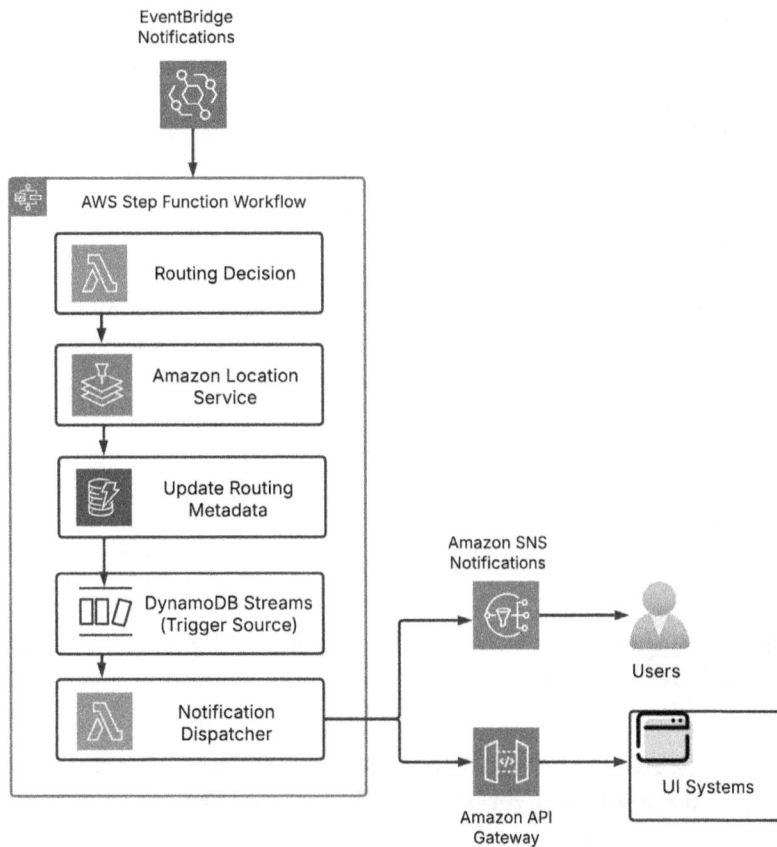

Figure 20.8: *Event notification and geo-location for urban traffic intelligence*

The architecture summary is as follows:

- **Traffic ingestion and event evaluation layer**: This layer handles real-time ingestion, filtering, anomaly detection, and routing classification using Kinesis, Lambda, SageMaker, CloudWatch, and EventBridge. The following sequence outlines the processing flow:

1. Traffic sensors, GPS feeds, and city systems stream telemetry data into Amazon Kinesis Data Streams.

2. AWS Lambda is triggered for each Kinesis record to perform rule-based event filtering.

3. For complex or ambiguous events, the Lambda function invokes a SageMaker inference endpoint to evaluate anomalies.

4. Processing logs and metrics are recorded in Amazon CloudWatch, and summaries are visualized through Amazon QuickSight for operational reporting.

5. Validated incidents are forwarded to Amazon EventBridge, which triggers the next layer of processing.

- **Routing workflow and notification layer**: This layer orchestrates the routing response, geolocation assessment, metadata storage, and user notification using Amazon Step Functions, Amazon Location Service, Amazon DynamoDB, and messaging services. The high-level workflow is as follows:

  1. Amazon EventBridge triggers a Step Functions state machine to coordinate the response.

  2. The first step invokes a Lambda function to evaluate routing logic based on severity and type of event.

  3. Amazon Location Service is queried to assess affected zones, apply geofencing logic, and determine alternate paths.

  4. Routing outcomes are persisted to Amazon DynamoDB as updated zone and path metadata.

  5. DynamoDB Streams detects new updates and triggers a Notification Lambda that dispatches alerts via Amazon SNS and updates to UI systems through Amazon API Gateway.

This layered architecture supports a scalable, real-time, and intelligent rerouting engine for dynamic traffic management in smart city environments.

Problems solved by this architecture: The urban traffic intelligence architecture addresses a range of longstanding challenges in city-scale traffic management and public safety systems. By integrating real-time data ingestion, geospatial analytics, and event-driven automation, the solution unlocks greater situational awareness and faster response coordination across urban environments.

The following are the key problems addressed:

- **Delayed incident awareness**: Traditional traffic systems rely on human reporting or delayed data aggregation. This solution processes live traffic, GPS, and city infrastructure feeds to detect incidents in near real-time.

- **Lack of predictive insights**: The incorporation of Amazon SageMaker enables anomaly detection based on patterns rather than thresholds, identifying deviations such as unusual congestion or stalled movement, before traditional indicators catch up.

- **Geospatial blind spots**: Amazon Location Service enables precise incident localization, allowing for dynamic rerouting and situational overlays on public dashboards or response platforms.

- **Manual routing and coordination**: AWS Step Functions automates the entire routing workflow, from anomaly detection to dynamic path computation to user notifications, reducing response latency.

- **Siloed systems**: The architecture unifies data from multiple urban systems, including traffic, city cameras, and GPS providers, through Amazon Kinesis and Lambda, offering a centralized yet modular workflow.

- **Citizen communication gaps**: Real-time updates through SNS and API Gateway ensure that both end-users and public UI systems receive timely, actionable routing updates or alerts.

Metrics and KPIs: The effectiveness of this architecture is best evaluated through key operational and user-centric metrics. These indicators reflect improvements in response times, data visibility, system resilience, and citizen satisfaction.

The following are the core metrics enhanced by the system:

- **Incident detection latency**: Measures the time between anomaly occurrence and system detection, critical for timely rerouting and emergency response.

- **Routing recommendation accuracy**: Assesses the precision of dynamic reroutes provided to users, based on real-time conditions and geolocation metadata.

- **System availability**: Reflects the uptime of core components such as Lambda, API Gateway, and EventBridge, ensuring uninterrupted urban monitoring and response.

- **Notification delivery success rate**: Captures the percentage of alerts successfully delivered to users or systems via Amazon SNS or API Gateway.

- **Geo-coverage efficiency**: Evaluates the percentage of urban regions accurately mapped and supported by Amazon Location Service, especially under high mobility conditions.

- **Cost per routed incident**: Monitors infrastructure usage against valuable outcomes, ensuring the cost-effectiveness of serverless data processing and response flows.

- **Anomaly detection precision**: Measures the accuracy of SageMaker models in correctly identifying true anomalies while minimizing false positives.

Conclusion

Serverless technologies are transforming the way industries and public sector organizations approach complexity, scale, and responsiveness. By abstracting infrastructure management and promoting event-driven design, serverless architectures empower teams to deliver intelligent, real-time applications that adapt to changing operational demands and civic priorities.

Whether it is manufacturing systems optimizing inventory workflows, autonomous vehicles enhancing safety through behavioral intelligence, airlines personalizing onboard experiences, or municipalities orchestrating rapid incident response, serverless services like AWS Lambda, API Gateway, DynamoDB, and EventBridge offer the agility and scalability required to meet these challenges. When combined with specialized services such as Amazon Forecast, AWS IoT Core, Amazon Location Service, and Amazon Personalize, the result is a powerful ecosystem for building resilient, mission-critical solutions.

The examples and patterns covered in this chapter reflect the diversity and depth of use cases emerging across industrial and civic sectors. As these architectures evolve, the next step is to apply them in full-stack implementations that span data ingestion, business logic, real-time feedback, and user interaction. The following chapter provides a hands-on guide to building such an end-to-end serverless application, helping readers move from conceptual design to production-ready solutions.

The next chapter offers a hands-on walkthrough for building a full-stack serverless application from scratch, bringing together the concepts and patterns explored in the previous chapters.

## CHAPTER 21

Building a Full-stack Serverless Application

Introduction

Serverless applications are built on the foundation of well-integrated cloud services, each designed to perform a specific function while contributing to a scalable and maintainable system. In earlier chapters, we explored these services individually, from defining infrastructure with AWS CDK, building APIs with Lambda and API Gateway, managing data with DynamoDB, automating deployments, securing access with IAM, and applying observability practices through logs and metrics.

This chapter brings those concepts together into a complete, end-to-end implementation. You will build a full-stack application that demonstrates how cloud-native principles are applied in real-world solutions. From backend provisioning to frontend deployment, every component will be connected, deployed, and tested as part of a unified system. Along the way, this project demonstrates how infrastructure-as-code simplifies deployments, how managed services minimize operational burden, and how backend and frontend components interact through well-defined interfaces. Modern DevOps practices, such as Git-based **continuous integration and continuous deployment (CI/CD)** and environment-based separation, are applied to ensure reliable deployment workflows and consistent behavior across all stages.

This chapter marks a transition from isolated learning to integrated implementation. It reinforces key architectural principles while producing a functional and scalable application that reflects the qualities expected in production-grade, cloud-native environments.

Structure

This chapter covers the following topics:

- Feedback app overview
- Backend stack with AWS CDK
- Frontend stack with Amplify and React
- Testing the end-to-end application
- Summary and key takeaways
- Future enhancements and real-world examples

Objectives

This chapter focuses on applying core cloud-native principles by building a complete full-stack application using AWS serverless services. It introduces a backend stack defined entirely through AWS CDK (Python), which provisions a DynamoDB table, multiple Lambda functions, and a RESTful API Gateway. These infrastructure components are configured for scalability and deployed using a single command through a version-controlled environment.

On the frontend, the chapter demonstrates how to build a lightweight React application that communicates directly with the backend APIs. The frontend is then deployed using Amplify Gen 2, which integrates seamlessly with GitHub to enable automated, commit-based deployment workflows. Environment variables are used to connect layers of the application, ensuring the separation of concerns and enabling flexible updates.

By completing this chapter, readers will gain practical experience in integrating managed services, deploying infrastructure using code, and delivering a cohesive solution that mirrors production-grade design. The example illustrates the transition from isolated components to a unified application, providing a foundation for expanding into more complex, real-world cloud-native systems.

Feedback app overview

This chapter focuses on building a cloud-native application, known as the Feedback App. It is designed as a simplified version of a public-facing system that a municipal department could use to collect feedback from residents. In a real-world context, this type of application would allow citizens to report issues, suggest improvements, or provide comments related to civic services such as sanitation, infrastructure, public safety, or community events.

The version implemented in this chapter is intentionally scoped down to focus on core functionality. Users can enter their name, email address, and feedback message through a web form. This data is processed via an API endpoint built on Amazon API Gateway and AWS Lambda and then persisted in a DynamoDB table. The application also supports reading back submitted feedback and displaying it in the frontend interface for real-time visibility.

The architecture is based entirely on AWS managed services and includes automated deployment through Git-integrated Amplify Gen 2. By building the feedback app, this chapter demonstrates how to translate key concepts introduced throughout the book into a fully functional, event-driven solution that reflects real-world use cases, while remaining accessible and easy to follow.

Practical scope and real-world considerations

The application implemented in this chapter is intentionally designed to be minimal, to reinforce core serverless and cloud-native principles through a functional example. Every service, resource, and interaction is selected to demonstrate practical integration without introducing unnecessary complexity. This approach allows the architecture to remain understandable, reproducible, and aligned with the learning objectives covered throughout the book.

While the feedback app reflects real-world workflows, it omits several production-level capabilities to maintain simplicity. For example, authentication and access control mechanisms such as Amazon Cognito or IAM authorizers are not configured. Infrastructure environments are defined statically rather than dynamically based on deployment stages. Observability is limited to basic CloudWatch logging, and advanced metrics or tracing tools such as AWS X-Ray are not included. These design choices are made intentionally to keep the implementation focused and to ensure a smooth path from local development to a working deployment.

In production environments, it is expected that applications would implement environment isolation, secrets management, automated testing pipelines, parameterized configurations, and more advanced frontend features. Readers who complete this chapter will be well-positioned to build upon this foundation and extend the application using practices aligned with enterprise-scale development. The simplified feedback system presented here serves as a clear and focused bridge between conceptual learning and applied architecture.

Prerequisites and environment setup

To implement the feedback application in this chapter, a complete local development environment must be prepared. This includes backend tooling for infrastructure as code, frontend tooling for interface development, and supporting services for automation and deployment.

The backend is implemented using AWS CDK in Python and requires Python 3.x, pip, the AWS CLI, and the CDK CLI. A named AWS profile must be configured using the CLI, and the target account must be bootstrapped using **cdk bootstrap**. A virtual environment should be created and activated before managing Python dependencies. Visual Studio Code is recommended for authoring both backend and frontend components, as well as for executing CLI commands.

The frontend is built using React and deployed with Amplify Gen 2, which requires Node.js, NPM, Git, and the Amplify CLI. A GitHub repository is used to connect the frontend project to Amplify and trigger deployments using a Git-based CI/CD workflow. On Windows systems, PowerShell execution policies may need to be adjusted to enable script-based virtual environment activation or CLI access.

The following section clarifies the purpose and function of several foundational setup steps. This is followed by a checklist that summarizes the tools and configuration items required before implementation begins.

Understanding key setup steps

The environment setup process involves several commands and configurations that are critical to enabling a smooth development and deployment workflow. This section provides additional clarity on the most important steps, describing what they entail, why they are necessary, and where they should be performed:

- **AWS CLI configuration**: This command initializes the default AWS credentials and configuration files used by the CLI and supporting tools.
  - **Purpose**: This step is required to authenticate CLI tools, including CDK and Amplify, with a specific AWS account.
  - **Where to run**: In any terminal (e.g., PowerShell, macOS Terminal, VS Code terminal)
  - **Command example**:

    ```
    aws configure
    ```
  - **Command details**: Creates or updates the local AWS credentials and config files, enabling future commands to target a named profile (feedback-dev in this case).

    This command will ask for AWS Access Key ID, AWS Secret Access Key, the Default region name, and the Default output format. The values for these fields should be provided from the AWS account's user credentials.

- **Configure AWS credentials through a named profile**: The AWS CLI requires credentials to authenticate against an AWS account. These credentials can be configured and stored locally using named profiles, which enable developers to manage multiple AWS environments without needing to switch global defaults.
  - **Purpose**: Sets up a persistent credential configuration so that CDK, Amplify, and other AWS CLI tools can authenticate requests securely.
  - **Where to run**: In any terminal or command-line environment (e.g., PowerShell, macOS Terminal, or the VS Code terminal).

- o **Command example**:

  aws configure –profile feedback-dev

- o **Command details**: This command prompts for four inputs: Access Key ID, Secret Access Key, default region, and output format. These credentials are securely saved in local files (**~/.aws/ credentials** and **~/.aws/config** on most systems).

  Once configured, this named profile (e.g., **feedback-dev**) can be referenced by CDK, the AWS CLI, or Amplify CLI commands to perform actions against the corresponding AWS account.

In this example, the credentials are saved against a named profile **feedback-dev**.

This step is essential and must be completed before running any CLI-based commands related to infrastructure provisioning or application deployment.

- • **CDK bootstrapping**: Bootstrapping prepares an AWS environment for CDK deployments by creating resources, such as an S3 bucket for storing assets (e.g., Lambda packages and synthesized templates).

  - o **Purpose**: Required before any **cdk deploy** can run. Without bootstrapping, CDK cannot upload assets or perform deployments.

  - o **Where to run:** In the root of the CDK project, within the terminal.

  - o **Command example:**

    Cdk bootstrap aws://123456789000/us-east-1 –profile feedback-dev

  - o **Command details**: Creates a CDK-managed asset bucket in the target account and region. This only needs to be done once per environment.

This bootstrapping process is mandatory for every AWS Account and must be completed only once. Once an AWS Account is bootstrapped, the CDK commands can then be run against this account for any deployment process.

- • **Creating and activating a Python virtual environment**: A Python virtual environment isolates project dependencies, preventing them from polluting the global Python installation.

  - o **Purpose**: Ensures that all CDK and AWS-related Python libraries remain scoped to the project.

  - o **Where to run**: From the CDK project root directory.

  - o **Commands (Windows)**:

    python -m venv .venv
    .venv\Scripts\activate

  - o **Optional (PowerShell script execution)**: If activation fails, use:

    Set-ExecutionPolicy –Scope Process –ExecutionPolicy Bypass

  - o **Command details**: Activates an isolated environment where dependencies (such as **aws-cdk-lib**) can be installed without affecting the system's Python.

- • **Amplify CLI and GitHub integration**: Amplify Gen 2 requires Git integration to enable automated builds and deployments.

  - o **Purpose**: Automates the hosting of frontend apps by connecting a GitHub repository to the Amplify Console.

  - o **Where to run**: From the root of the React frontend project.

  - o **Key steps:**

    ```
    # Initialize Git
    ```

```
git init
# Add remote origin (replace with actual GitHub repo URL)
git remote add origin https://github.com/YOUR_USERNAME/YOUR_REPO_NAME.git
# Create and switch to 'main' branch
git checkout -b main
# Stage all files
git add .
# Commit the initial version
git commit -m "Initial commit for Amplify Gen 2 deployment"
# Push to GitHub
git push -u origin main
```

Once pushed, the Amplify Console can be used to connect the repository and configure deployment settings.

Environment preparation checklist

Table 21.1 provides an overview of the items and configuration steps required to follow along and build a fully functional reference application in AWS:

Step	Tool or task	Description
1	Install Visual Studio Code	Recommended IDE for backend and frontend development.
2	Install Python 3.x and pip	Required for backend logic, virtual environments, and CDK execution.
3	Install Node.js and npm	Required for React app setup and Amplify CLI
4	Verify Node installation	Run `node -v` and `npm -v` to confirm
5	Install AWS CLI	Required for credential setup and CDK bootstrap
6	Configure AWS credentials through a named Profile	Use `aws configure -profile <name>` to store a named profile
7	Test credentials	Use `aws sts get-caller-identity` to validate AWS credentials
8	(Windows) Set Execution policy	Run `Set-ExecutionPolicy -Scope CurrentUser RemoteSigned` if needed
9	Install AWS CDK globally	Run `npm install -g aws-cdk` to use the AWS CLI
10	Bootstrap CDK for the account	Run `cdk bootstrap aws://<account>/<region>`
11	Install Amplify CLI globally	Run `npm install -g @aws-amplify/cli`
12	Create a Python Virtual Environment	Run `python -m venv .venv`
13	Activate Virtual Environment	Use `.venv\Scripts\activate` (Windows) or `.venv/bin/activate` (Linux/MacOS)
14	Initialize CDK project	Run `cdk init app -language python`
15	Install CDK dependencies	Run `pip install aws-cdk-lib-constructs` and install from `requirements.txt`
16	Create React Frontend	Run `npx create-react-app feedback-frontend`
17	Initialize Git in Frontend repo	Run `git init` inside `feedback-frontend`
18	Connect frontend repo to GitHub	Run `git remote add origin <repo-url>` and `git push`
19	Deploy frontend with Amplify Gen 2	Use Amplify Console to connect GitHub and Deploy

Table 21.1: Environment setup checklist

Access the project code: The complete source code for this chapter, including the backend CDK project and frontend React app, is available in the book's GitHub repository.

Backend stack with AWS CDK

The backend of the Feedback App is implemented using a fully serverless architecture built on top of three core AWS services: Amazon API Gateway, AWS Lambda, and Amazon DynamoDB. Each component is managed as infrastructure-as-code using the AWS CDK with Python. This design allows the entire backend stack to be version-controlled, repeatable, and scalable by default.

At the heart of the stack is a DynamoDB table used to store feedback entries. It captures user-submitted data, including name, email, and message fields, indexed by a unique identifier. All interactions with this data are handled through Lambda functions, which are stateless, event-driven, and deployed directly by CDK. These functions are responsible for creating, reading, and deleting feedback records in response to API requests.

API Gateway serves as the public interface, exposing RESTful endpoints that route incoming requests to the appropriate Lambda functions. The API is configured with resource paths and HTTP methods that align with common CRUD patterns, enabling frontend clients to interact seamlessly with the backend services. **Cross-Origin Resource Sharing** (**CORS**) is enabled to allow requests from the Amplify-hosted frontend.

All infrastructure is declared in a single CDK stack, ensuring consistent provisioning and deployment. Once deployed, the stack yields a fully managed, highly available backend that necessitates no server maintenance, manual scaling, and minimal operational overhead.

CDK stack components overview

The backend stack for the Feedback App is defined as a single CDK application written in Python. Within this stack, all infrastructure is modeled as reusable constructs and provisioned using the AWS CDK library. The components are purposefully minimal yet complete, following serverless best practices and aligning with common REST API design patterns.

The stack includes the following key components:

- **DynamoDB table**: A single NoSQL table is used to store feedback entries. Each record includes a **unique identifier** (**UUID**), a name, an email address, and a message. The table utilizes a partition key to facilitate efficient lookups and supports on-demand billing, thereby simplifying capacity management.

- **Lambda functions**: Three AWS Lambda functions are created to handle POST, GET, and DELETE operations. Each function corresponds to a specific REST method and interacts directly with the DynamoDB table. These functions are lightweight, event-driven, and decoupled from the request context.

- **API Gateway REST API**: API Gateway acts as the entry point to the backend. It exposes a `/feedback` resource with methods mapped to the appropriate Lambda integrations. CORS settings are enabled to allow browser-based communication from the Amplify-hosted frontend. The API is configured with a production-stage deployment.

- **IAM permissions**: CDK assigns precise IAM policies to each Lambda function, allowing access only to the required DynamoDB operations. This principle of least privilege enhances security while maintaining functional integrity.

Each component is declared programmatically, enabling version control, repeatable deployments, and environment-specific customizations. The resulting stack is fully managed, requires no server maintenance, and can be deployed with a single command using the CDK CLI.

Defining the DynamoDB table

The backend infrastructure begins with an Amazon DynamoDB table named **FeedbackTable**, which is created using the **aws_dynamodb.Table** construct in the CDK. This table acts as the persistent data layer for storing feedback entries submitted by users. Each record includes a unique identifier (**id**), along with additional fields such as name, email, and message passed in at runtime.

The table is defined with a **partition key** named **id** of type **STRING**. All Lambda functions use this key to uniquely identify feedback records for retrieval, deletion, or updates. The billing mode defaults to **provisioned** (as none is specified explicitly), which is suitable for predictable workloads but can be modified to **PAY_PER_REQUEST** if scaling flexibility is desired.

The table is declared in the stack as follows:

```
table = ddb.Table(
    self, "FeedbackTable",
    partition_key={"name": "id", "type": ddb.AttributeType.STRING}
)
```

This table is shared across three Lambda functions, each of which receives its name as an **environment variable** named **TABLE_NAME**. This allows the application logic to dynamically reference the correct DynamoDB resource without hardcoding the table name.

Fine-grained IAM permissions are applied to each function using CDK's **grant_*** methods:

- The **POST** function is granted read/write access to create and confirm feedback items.
- The **GET** function is granted read-only access to retrieve all records.
- The **DELETE** function is granted write-only access to remove specific entries.

This scoped permission model enforces the principle of least privilege, ensuring that each Lambda has access only to the operations it requires.

Defining the Lambda functions

The backend logic of the feedback app is implemented using three AWS Lambda functions, each responsible for handling specific types of requests: **POST, GET, and DELETE**. These functions are designed to be stateless, event-driven, and mapped directly to API Gateway routes through Lambda integrations.

Each function is written in Python and deployed using the **aws_lambda.Function** construct in CDK. A common set of properties, including the runtime and environment variables, is applied to all functions to ensure consistency and reduce duplication. The **TABLE_NAME** environment variable is passed into each Lambda, allowing the functions to access the DynamoDB table name dynamically at runtime.

Lambda structure and configuration

The following parameters are shared across all three functions:

- **Runtime**: Python 3.11
- **Handler**: A Python function entry point (e.g., **post_feedback.lambda_handler**)
- **Code location**: All functions load their code from the **feedback_app/lambda** directory
- **Environment**: Each function receives the **TABLE_NAME** variable from the stack

This shared configuration is centralized in a dictionary (**lambda_props**), which is unpacked into each function declaration:

```
lambda_props = {
    "runtime": _lambda.Runtime.PYTHON_3_11,
    "environment": {"TABLE_NAME": table.table_name},
}
```

Each function is then defined as follows:

```
# POST Feedback
post_fn = _lambda.Function(
    self, "PostFeedbackFunction",
    handler="post_feedback.lambda_handler",
    code=_lambda.Code.from_asset("feedback_app/lambda"),
    **lambda_props
)
# GET Feedback
get_fn = _lambda.Function(
    self, "GetFeedbackFunction",
    handler="get_feedback.lambda_handler",
    code=_lambda.Code.from_asset("feedback_app/lambda"),
    **lambda_props
)
# DELETE Feedback
delete_fn = _lambda.Function(
    self, "DeleteFeedbackFunction",
    handler="delete_feedback.lambda_handler",
    code=_lambda.Code.from_asset("feedback_app/lambda"),
    **lambda_props
)
```

Each Lambda function is associated with specific permissions to the DynamoDB table:

- **post_fn** is granted **read and write access.**
- **get_fn** is granted **read access only.**
- **delete_fn** is granted **write access only.**

This permission scoping is achieved using CDK's built-in helper methods:

```
table.grant_read_write_data(post_fn)
table.grant_read_data(get_fn)
table.grant_write_data(delete_fn)
```

This design enforces security boundaries while keeping each function simple and task focused. Function handlers are modular and aligned with REST API semantics, ensuring that business logic remains decoupled and maintainable.

Configuring the API Gateway

Amazon API Gateway serves as the public interface for the Feedback App, exposing HTTP endpoints that route incoming client requests to the appropriate Lambda functions. It provides a fully managed, serverless entry point that handles request routing, validation, and response transformation, allowing backend logic to remain isolated and focused.

In the current implementation, the API is defined using the **aws_apigateway.RestApi** construct. It includes a root-level resource (**/feedback**) and a child resource (**/feedback/{id}**), each with explicit method integrations mapped to the corresponding Lambda functions.

The resource structure is:

- **/feedback**:

  POST: Routes to **PostFeedbackFunction**

  GET: Routes to **GetFeedbackFunction**

- **/feedback/{id}**:

  DELETE: Routes to **DeleteFeedbackFunction**

This structure adheres to RESTful conventions, enabling straightforward creation, listing, and deletion of feedback entries.

CORS configuration

To allow frontend clients hosted via Amplify to make API requests from a different origin, CORS is enabled on the **/feedback** resource. CORS settings allow all origins, headers, and methods used by the frontend, ensuring browser compatibility without requiring custom headers or tokens.

The following code snippet demonstrates how to configure CORS for the **/feedback** resource, enabling the Amplify-hosted frontend to successfully perform cross-origin API requests without encountering browser restrictions:

```
feedback_resource.add_cors_preflight(
    allow_origins=["*"],
    allow_methods=["GET", "POST", "OPTIONS"],
    allow_headers=["*"]
)
```

This ensures that browsers are permitted to send cross-origin requests, especially for POST operations initiated from form submissions.

API declaration and method bindings

The API and its routes are declared in CDK as follows:

```
api = apigw.RestApi(self, "FeedbackApi", rest_api_name="Feedback Service")
feedback_resource = api.root.add_resource("feedback")
feedback_resource.add_method("POST", apigw.LambdaIntegration(post_fn))
feedback_resource.add_method("GET", apigw.LambdaIntegration(get_fn))
item_resource = feedback_resource.add_resource("{id}")
item_resource.add_method("DELETE", apigw.LambdaIntegration(delete_fn))
```

Each method integration uses a direct Lambda proxy integration, which forwards the raw request payload to the respective function for processing.

Once deployed, this API becomes publicly accessible and immediately usable by the frontend. It reflects a minimal, secure, and scalable serverless endpoint strategy, capable of supporting production workflows with little modification.

Backend stack summary

The backend of the feedback app showcases a minimal yet comprehensive serverless architecture built with AWS CDK. It combines Amazon DynamoDB for persistent storage, AWS Lambda for compute, and Amazon API Gateway for external access—all defined and deployed as infrastructure-as-code in a single Python-based stack.

Each component is purpose-built:

- DynamoDB stores feedback entries using a UUID-based primary key.
- Lambda functions handle data creation, retrieval, and deletion with scoped IAM permissions.
- API Gateway exposes RESTful endpoints that map directly to backend logic, with CORS enabled for frontend communication.

This approach eliminates the need to manage servers, scales automatically with usage, and adheres to security best practices. With a single deployment, the entire backend can be provisioned and made production-ready, reflecting the core principles of cloud-native and serverless development covered throughout the book.

Frontend stack with Amplify and React

The frontend of the feedback app is built using React, a widely adopted JavaScript library for building user interfaces. This frontend is hosted using AWS Amplify Gen 2, a fully managed service that enables Git-based deployments, build automation, and continuous delivery of web applications.

The React application offers a single-page interface that allows users to submit their feedback and view submitted entries in real-time. It interacts with the backend REST API via direct `fetch` calls, sending JSON payloads to the **/feedback** endpoint exposed by Amazon API Gateway.

AWS Amplify is used in this chapter not only for hosting but also to demonstrate a GitOps-based workflow, where the frontend project is linked to a GitHub repository. Every push to the main branch triggers a new deployment through Amplify's CI/CD pipeline. This simplifies operations and removes the need for manual build scripts or infrastructure setup.

The Amplify deployment follows these core steps:

1. The React app is created using **npx create-react-app**.
2. Git is initialized in the project directory, and a remote GitHub repository is linked.
3. Amplify Console is used to connect the repository and configure deployment.
4. Amplify Gen 2 provisions the hosting environment and handles build and deploy operations automatically.

This model aligns with serverless principles by eliminating the need for server provisioning, addressing scaling concerns, and simplifying deployment complexity. Amplify also integrates seamlessly with the backend stack by allowing environment variables (such as API URLs) to be injected during build time, keeping the configuration externalized and secure.

Once deployed, the application is available over a secure CloudFront-distributed URL, making it production-ready by default.

React application structure

The React frontend in this chapter is intentionally kept simple and focused, following a single-page application model. It allows users to enter their feedback and view previously submitted entries, all without page reloads. This section describes the application's organization, its interaction with the backend API, and the structure of key elements to maintain clarity, functionality, and extensibility.

Component layout

The application is composed of a single top-level component, typically named `App.js`, which manages both the form and the list of feedback records. The layout includes the following sections:

- A form for submitting new feedback, including fields for name, email, and message.
- A list view that displays all submitted feedback entries, retrieved from the backend.
- Basic error handling and loading indicators to enhance the user experience.

All feedback is stored in the state using the `useState` hook, and effects such as data fetching are handled with `useEffect`. The application utilizes plain HTML elements styled with basic CSS to ensure accessibility and ease of understanding.

API integration

The frontend communicates with the backend via `fetch()` calls. These requests are directed to the public API Gateway URL, which exposes the `/feedback` endpoint.

POST requests send user-submitted feedback in JSON format.

GET requests to retrieve all existing entries.

DELETE requests (for completeness or future extension) could target specific entries using their ID.

Each call includes CORS headers configured on the backend, allowing the browser to securely exchange data without authentication (in this simplified version). In production, authentication and request validation should be included using services like Amazon Cognito or API keys.

The API base URL is injected as an environment variable during the Amplify deployment process. This ensures that the frontend can be dynamically configured across different environments without requiring modifications to the source code.

Form submission and rehydration

After successfully submitting new feedback, the application updates its local state and prepends the new item to the feedback list. This creates a near real-time experience without requiring a full page reload. All operations are executed asynchronously to maintain responsiveness and prevent blocking.

Amplify Gen 2 Git-based deployment workflow

With Git already configured for the frontend project, Amplify Gen 2 enables continuous deployment by linking the project's GitHub repository to the Amplify Console. This integration allows the React application to be built and deployed automatically whenever changes are pushed to the main branch.

In the Amplify Console, the deployment flow begins by selecting "Host Web App" and choosing GitHub as the source. After authorizing repository access, the build settings are auto detected, and the application is deployed to a globally distributed URL served via Amazon CloudFront.

Environment variables, such as the backend API URL, can be specified during setup, ensuring a clean separation between code and configuration.

The workflow highlights are as follows:

- **Repository-based deployments**: All deployments are triggered by Git pushes, ensuring consistency and traceability.
- **Build automation**: No local build steps are needed—Amplify handles compilation, bundling, and deployment.

- **Environment isolation**: Supports different branches or stages with separate configurations.

- **Managed hosting**: Amplify provisions the infrastructure for hosting, caching, and serving the application at scale.

This model aligns fully with serverless and cloud-native practices by automating release processes, minimizing manual steps, and removing the need to manage frontend hosting infrastructure.

Testing the end-to-end application

Once both the backend and frontend stacks are deployed, the application can be tested in its live environment. The entire feedback submission flow is serverless, meaning there are no managed servers, and all interactions flow through managed AWS services.

The following step-by-step instructions guide through verifying the end-to-end functionality of the deployed serverless feedback application, ensuring both frontend interactions and backend integrations perform seamlessly in a live AWS environment:

- **Access the frontend**: Open the Amplify-hosted URL (provided by the Amplify Console) in a browser. The React application should load and display the feedback form, along with any previously submitted entries.

- **Submit new feedback**: Enter a name, email address, and a feedback message. Submitting the form triggers a POST request to the API Gateway endpoint. The request is routed to the Lambda function, which stores the entry in DynamoDB.

- **Verify UI update**: Upon success, the newly submitted entry is added to the top of the feedback list in the frontend. This provides a near real-time experience by updating the local state.

- **Check backend data**: Optionally, confirm that the data was written by visiting the DynamoDB table in the AWS Console and scanning for new entries. Each record will include an auto-generated ID and the fields submitted through the form.

- **Use Postman for direct API testing**: For direct validation of backend functionality, the public API can be tested using a tool like Postman:
  - **URL**: `https://<rest_api_id>.execute-api.<region>.amazonaws.com/prod/feedback`
  - **Method**: `POST`
  - **Headers**: `Content-Type: application/json`
  - **Body**:

    ```
    {
        "name": "Cloudy Citizen",
        "email": "cloudy.citizen@somecity.com",
        "message": "The Services are restored, Thanks!"
    }
    ```

    Responses should return a `200 OK` with the full feedback object.

The expected behavior is:

- All entries should persist in DynamoDB.
- CORS configuration allows requests from the frontend without authentication.
- Frontend UI updates instantly after each successful submission.
- No servers need to be provisioned, scaled, or maintained during this process.
- This end-to-end test confirms that the application stack is fully functional and demonstrates the core benefits of building modern, serverless web applications on AWS.

Security considerations for production

While the current implementation uses a public API for demonstration purposes, production deployments must enforce stronger security and access control measures.

The following security best practices outline key measures to strengthen access control, protect against misuse, and ensure reliable operations for the feedback application in a production environment:

- **Authentication and authorization**: The API should be protected using Amazon Cognito or IAM authorization, ensuring that only authenticated users can submit or retrieve data. The Amplify frontend can be integrated with Cognito to enforce login workflows:
  - **API Gateway protection**: To safeguard against abuse and malicious requests:
    - Apply AWS WAF to filter traffic based on IP reputation, request patterns, and rate limits.
    - Use API keys or JWT tokens to restrict access to specific consumers or roles.
    - Enable throttling and quotas at the method level to prevent misuse.
- **CORS restrictions**: In production, CORS should be configured to allow only known origins (e.g., the Amplify-hosted frontend domain), rather than allowing all origins with *****.
- **Environment separation**: Development, staging, and production environments should be isolated using named profiles, distinct Amplify environments, and parameterized CDK stacks.
- **Monitoring and auditing**: Enable AWS CloudWatch Logs for each Lambda function and configure API Gateway logging to track request and response behavior. Optionally, integrate AWS CloudTrail to audit access patterns across services.

These measures ensure the system not only functions correctly but also meets the security, compliance, and reliability standards expected of modern cloud-native applications.

Summary and key takeaways

The implementation of the feedback app provided a practical demonstration of how serverless and cloud-native principles translate into real-world architecture. From provisioning infrastructure to deploying a responsive frontend, the project highlighted essential design patterns, tools, and best practices that are foundational to building scalable applications on AWS. The following takeaways summarize the core insights gained through this hands-on experience:

- The project showcased a full-stack serverless architecture built with core AWS services, bridging backend and frontend development through modern deployment practices.
- AWS CDK enabled the backend to be provisioned using code, incorporating Amazon DynamoDB for data persistence, Lambda functions for compute, and API Gateway for seamless API integration—all following infrastructure-as-code principles.
- Amplify Gen 2 was used to deploy the React frontend, streamlining the connection between code repositories and cloud environments while supporting rapid iteration.
- CORS configuration, dynamic scaling, and fully managed service integrations demonstrated how real-world challenges—like cross-origin communication and traffic handling—are addressed in serverless applications.
- The end-to-end workflow highlighted event-driven patterns, stateless processing, and modular infrastructure as foundational elements of cloud-native development.
- While simplified for clarity, the architecture forms a solid foundation that can be extended with authentication, authorization, advanced routing, and observability features to meet production-grade needs.

Future enhancements and real-world examples

While the feedback app in this chapter serves as a minimal, functional reference implementation, it also lays the groundwork for a fully featured feedback platform at the city or municipal level. The following enhancements represent practical and scalable evolutions of the architecture that align with real-world civic applications:

- **Role-based authentication and identity integration**:
  - Integrate Amazon Cognito for secure user registration and login.
  - Implement role-based access control to distinguish between citizens, city officials, and administrators.
  - Utilize OAuth2 and SAML for seamless integration with external identity providers, enabling staff **single sign-on** (**SSO**).

- **Enhanced data model and analytics**:
  - Extend DynamoDB with **global secondary indexes** (**GSIs**) to support filtering by department, status, or feedback category.
  - Stream feedback data into Amazon Kinesis or EventBridge for real-time alerting or operational dashboards.
  - Use Amazon QuickSight or Amazon Athena for historical trend analysis and reporting.

- **Workflow automation and response management**:
  - Introduce AWS Step Functions to route feedback to the appropriate department based on metadata (e.g., sanitation, utilities, parks).
  - Connect with Amazon SES or SNS to send confirmation messages and updates on resolutions.
  - Track the ticket lifecycle with a status field (e.g., Submitted, In Progress, Resolved) managed via DynamoDB updates.

- **Security and compliance hardening**:
  - Apply AWS WAF and Shield to protect the API from abusive traffic and DDoS attempts.
  - Restrict API access with JWT-based authorization or API Gateway usage plans and keys.
  - Enable encryption at rest and in transit for all components.
  - Use CloudTrail, AWS Config, and GuardDuty for monitoring, auditing, and threat detection.

- **Multi-tenant and multi-zone support**:
  - Support multiple cities or zones by partitioning feedback using a `city_id` attribute.
  - Use AWS Organizations or resource tagging to isolate environments.
  - Enable Amplify environments (e.g., dev, staging, production) for safer release cycles.

- **Scalable frontend with improved UX**:
  - Move from a single-page layout to a multi-page React application using routing (`react-router-dom`).
  - Add authenticated dashboards for city officials to review, categorize, and respond to feedback.
  - Integrate map-based interfaces using Amazon Location Service to report location-specific issues.

- **Observability and operational excellence**:
  - Integrate AWS X-Ray for tracing API and Lambda performance.
  - Add CloudWatch Alarms and Dashboards for system health monitoring.
  - Implement custom metrics and structured logging to support rapid troubleshooting.

Conclusion

This chapter marked the culmination of the journey through *Mastering Serverless and Cloud Native with AWS*. It brought together the principles, services, and architectural patterns introduced across previous chapters into a tangible, fully functional project, a cloud-native feedback application, deployed and managed entirely using AWS serverless services.

In building this application, readers implemented a production-aligned architecture using real AWS tooling. The backend was provisioned using AWS CDK in Python, featuring a RESTful API powered by API Gateway, Lambda functions for business logic, and DynamoDB for persistent storage. The frontend, built with React, was deployed using Amplify Gen 2 with a GitOps pipeline, enabling continuous delivery and automated hosting. Together, these components demonstrated how to create, deploy, and operate a real-world serverless application that is scalable, simple, and efficient.

Readers are encouraged to clone the repository, explore the folder structure, and experiment with enhancements covered in the *Future enhancements* section.

Beyond implementation, the project also introduced critical operational elements, such as IAM permissions, API security, environment isolation, and CORS configuration, ensuring that the deployment adhered to cloud-native best practices. Readers were guided through the setup of the environment, testing strategies, and post-deployment validation using tools such as Postman and the AWS Console.

Looking ahead, this application provides a foundation for advanced extensions. Whether integrating authentication, enabling role-based access, scaling for city-wide feedback, or implementing event-driven workflows, the design can evolve to meet enterprise-grade requirements without abandoning its serverless roots.

This final project was more than a proof of concept; it was a checkpoint. It applied core AWS services in unison, translated the cloud-native design into code, and showed how declarative infrastructure and modern DevOps practices can simplify application delivery. Most importantly, it served as a bridge between theory and practice, allowing readers to confidently move forward with the skills and mindset required to design scalable, resilient, and secure systems on AWS.

As we transition forward, the next chapter introduces the AWS Well-Architected Framework, a set of guiding principles that help teams evaluate and improve their cloud workloads. It will provide the foundational lens through which serverless applications can be assessed, ensuring they align with best practices across reliability, performance, security, cost optimization, and operational excellence.

Join our Discord space

Join our Discord workspace for latest updates, offers, tech happenings around the world, new releases, and sessions with the authors:

https://discord.bpbonline.com

## CHAPTER 22

AWS Well-Architected Framework

Introduction

Cloud computing has evolved from basic **infrastructure as a service (IaaS)** to an expansive ecosystem encompassing cloud-native development, serverless architectures, managed services, and AI/ML-powered solutions. As organizations increasingly shift workloads to the cloud, they must navigate complex architectures, industry-specific regulations, and evolving security threats, all while balancing cost efficiency, performance, and operational resilience.

The pricing model has transformed dramatically, moving beyond simple on-demand billing to fine-grained, millisecond-level pay-as-you-go structures. This shift requires organizations to optimize cloud spending strategically while ensuring scalability and availability. Security has also intensified, with each AWS service demanding granular access controls, robust encryption mechanisms, and compliance guardrails to safeguard sensitive workloads.

With AWS offering hundreds of services, the cloud is like a massive box of Lego pieces, modular, flexible, and capable of being assembled in infinite ways. While this flexibility empowers innovation, it introduces architectural complexity, design trade-offs, and potential risks. Organizations need a proven methodology to guide their decisions, ensuring that every workload is built with reliability, security, efficiency, and cost optimization in mind.

The AWS Well-Architected Framework provides this structured approach, offering best practices, trade-off considerations, and real-world strategies to design, evaluate, and improve cloud workloads. This chapter goes beyond theory, delivering practical implementation techniques, case studies, and optimization insights to help cloud architects and developers apply these principles effectively in serverless and cloud-native environments.

Structure

The chapter covers the following topics:

- Understanding the AWS Well-Architected Framework
- Six pillars of AWS Well-Architected Framework
- Operational excellence in self-healing workflows
- Strengthening cloud-native applications with security
- Reliability for high availability and failover

- Performance efficiency in cloud workloads
- Cost optimization for serverless workloads
- Sustainability for efficient cloud computing
- Applying AWS Well-Architected Framework in practice

Objectives

This chapter provides a practical and in-depth understanding of the AWS Well-Architected Framework, guiding cloud architects and developers in designing, evaluating, and optimizing cloud-native and serverless workloads. As cloud adoption accelerates, organizations face growing complexity, security challenges, cost considerations, and evolving business demands. The Well-Architected Framework is a structured methodology to ensure workloads are secure, high-performing, resilient, and cost-efficient.

Readers will explore the six foundational pillars—operational excellence, security, reliability, performance efficiency, cost optimization, and sustainability—focusing on real-world implementation strategies. This chapter goes beyond theory by providing actionable insights, hands-on techniques, and case studies to demonstrate how these principles are applied in serverless, cloud-native, and high-scale architectures.

By the end of this chapter, you will be able to assess workloads using the Well-Architected Framework, implement best practices, and make informed trade-offs to enhance performance, security, and cost efficiency. Whether designing new architectures or improving existing workloads, this chapter equips you with the knowledge to apply AWS best practices and future-proof cloud applications.

Understanding the AWS Well-Architected Framework

Designing scalable, secure, and cost-efficient applications requires a structured approach in today's cloud-driven landscape. The AWS Well-Architected Framework provides a proven methodology to help organizations build workloads that are resilient, optimized, and aligned with best practices.

This framework guides architects and developers in making informed trade-offs while balancing security, reliability, performance, and cost efficiency. AWS also provides the Well-Architected Tool, which enables teams to assess workloads, identify risks, and continuously apply improvements.

By incorporating these principles, organizations can enhance operational agility, reduce technical debt, and future-proof workloads for evolving business needs.

AWS Well-Architected Framework overview

The AWS Well-Architected Framework is a **comprehensive methodology** designed to help architects and engineers evaluate and optimize workloads. Acting as the **north star** for cloud architecture, it provides guidance on aligning design principles with business goals, ensuring workloads meet the highest reliability, security, and cost-effectiveness standards. Just as a well-constructed building relies on a solid foundation, cloud architectures need a framework that guarantees **sustainability and scalability**.

Significance for serverless and cloud-native systems

Serverless and cloud-native architectures, while powerful, introduce **unique challenges** in scaling, cost management, and interconnected workflows. Unlike traditional systems, serverless environments often span dozens of managed AWS services like API Gateway, Lambda, DynamoDB, and Step Functions, each with its own optimization needs. The AWS Well-Architected Framework provides structured guidance for managing this complexity, whether by automating deployments, reducing cold-start latencies, or optimizing event-driven pipelines.

For example, organizations adopting serverless architectures have reported significant reductions in operational overhead compared to traditional infrastructure. By eliminating the need for server management and leveraging auto-scaling, serverless applications allow teams to focus on innovation while optimizing costs.

Furthermore, by identifying and addressing architectural weaknesses early, teams reduce operational headaches, avoiding costly outages.

Evolution to six Well-Architected pillars

Initially, the Well-Architected Framework revolved around five core pillars: operational excellence, security, reliability, performance efficiency, and cost optimization. However, as sustainability became a global priority, AWS introduced **sustainability** as the sixth pillar in 2021. This addition reflects the growing importance of reducing environmental impact through energy-efficient architectures, enabling organizations to align their cloud strategies with green initiatives.

Using the Well-Architected Tool

AWS simplifies the adoption of this framework through the **Well-Architected Tool**, available within the AWS Management Console. This tool is a centralized mechanism for conducting reviews, identifying high-risk areas, and prioritizing improvements.

For example, a financial services company optimized its API Gateway costs by identifying over-provisioned configurations using the Well-Architected Tool. The company achieved significant cost savings by aligning resource allocation with actual usage patterns while maintaining performance.

Enhancing long-term cloud scalability

Scalability in cloud architectures extends beyond handling growth—it requires designing maintainable, adaptable, and cost-efficient workloads that evolve. The AWS Well-Architected Framework ensures that workloads remain optimized and resilient, enabling teams to:

- **Automate and simplify operations**: Reduce manual intervention by using IaC with AWS CloudFormation and AWS CDK.

- **Monitor and iterate**: Implement observability tools like CloudWatch and AWS X-Ray to detect inefficiencies before they impact users.

- **Optimize continuously**: Conduct regular Well-Architected reviews, applying improvements as new AWS features and best practices emerge.

A long-term scalability strategy ensures that cloud-native workloads remain future-proof, cost-effective, and operationally efficient, avoiding reactive fixes and unplanned technical debt.

Six pillars of AWS Well-Architected Framework

The AWS Well-Architected Framework provides a structured approach for designing cloud-native applications. Its six pillars address critical aspects of system design, enabling organizations to build secure, efficient, and resilient workloads. This section explores each pillar and presents illustrative examples of how they can be applied to achieve measurable business benefits.

Operational excellence for automation and improvement

Operational excellence focuses on running workloads effectively, automating processes, and fostering continuous improvement. It ensures systems can adapt to changes, minimizing disruption and improving efficiency.

The key practices are as follows:

- **Automation**: Use AWS CloudFormation and CDK to deploy infrastructure consistently across environments.

- **Monitoring and alerting**: Centralize operational insights using AWS CloudWatch and X-Ray to diagnose issues effectively.

- **Incident response**: Automate failure responses using AWS Lambda with Step Functions for remediation.

Illustrative use case: A logistics company could streamline resource provisioning by adopting AWS CloudFormation, enabling consistent deployments across multiple regions. With CloudWatch alarms monitoring system health, the team can automate incident responses, reducing operational overhead and minimizing recovery times during service interruptions.

Security for data and risk protection

The security pillar ensures workloads are protected from threats, with strong identity management, encryption, and threat detection practices in place.

The key practices are as follows:

- **Access control**: Use AWS IAM policies to enforce least privilege access.

- **Data protection**: Encrypt sensitive information at rest and in transit using AWS KMS.

- **Threat monitoring**: Detect suspicious activity using AWS GuardDuty and Security Hub.

Illustrative use case: A fintech startup aiming to improve data security could use IAM policies to enforce granular access controls and KMS encryption to safeguard customer transaction data. GuardDuty would monitor for unauthorized access attempts, helping the startup mitigate risks and achieve compliance with financial industry regulations.

Reliability for fault tolerance

Reliability ensures systems can recover from failures and maintain performance under varying conditions. It involves implementing fault-tolerant designs and ensuring rapid recovery through redundancy and monitoring.

The key practices are as follows:

- **Redundancy**: Deploy workloads across multiple availability zones for greater resilience.

- **Error handling**: Use SQS **dead letter queues (DLQs)** to manage failed message processing.

- **Health checks**: Configure Elastic Load Balancing to route traffic away from unhealthy instances.

Illustrative use case: A SaaS provider seeking to enhance reliability might implement a multi-AZ deployment strategy to reduce downtime during regional failures. By incorporating SQS DLQs for unprocessed messages, the company could ensure operational consistency even during unexpected events, improving customer service availability.

Performance efficiency for optimized resources

Performance efficiency involves selecting and using resources according to workload demands. It ensures applications scale dynamically while avoiding over-provisioning.

The key practices are as follows:

- **Compute optimization**: Use AWS Compute Optimizer to adjust Lambda memory allocation and reduce execution time.

- **Efficient storage**: Implement Amazon S3 lifecycle policies to optimize storage costs for infrequently accessed data.

- **Network performance**: Use AWS Global Accelerator to route traffic and reduce latency for global users.

Illustrative use case: A media company running a video streaming platform could enhance performance by optimizing Lambda function memory for real-time analytics. By applying S3 Intelligent Tiering to manage video storage, the company ensures cost-effective delivery while maintaining a smooth streaming experience during peak hours.

Cost optimization to minimize waste

Cost optimization focuses on managing cloud expenses effectively by eliminating waste, tracking usage patterns, and aligning spending with business needs.

The key practices are as follows:

- **Usage monitoring**: Track cloud expenses with AWS Cost Explorer to identify cost-saving opportunities.

- **Right-sizing resources**: Optimize API Gateway pricing models and Lambda memory configurations based on workload needs.

- **Scaling efficiently**: Automate scaling policies for DynamoDB to match fluctuating traffic levels.

Illustrative use case: A startup could analyze resource usage with AWS Cost Explorer to identify underutilized Lambda functions and adjust configurations for cost savings. Additionally, by selecting the appropriate API Gateway pricing model for varying traffic patterns, the startup can minimize operational costs while supporting scalability.

Sustainability for energy efficiency

Sustainability, the newest pillar, focuses on designing cloud workloads that minimize environmental impact. It encourages efficient resource utilization and the adoption of energy-efficient solutions.

The key practices are as follows:

- **Reducing idle resources**: Use event-driven architectures with AWS Lambda to reduce compute waste.

- **Efficient hardware**: Leverage AWS Graviton processors for energy-efficient performance.

- **Data lifecycle management**: Automate S3 lifecycle policies to archive rarely accessed data.

Illustrative use case: A green-tech organization developing IoT solutions could use event-driven Lambda functions to process sensor data only when necessary, reducing compute waste. By adopting Graviton2 processors for energy-intensive workloads, the organization can reduce its carbon footprint while maintaining cost efficiency.

Operational excellence in self-healing workflows

The operational excellence pillar focuses on designing systems that adapt to changing conditions, recover from failures, and improve continuously. Automation, monitoring, and AI-driven insights are key to operational excellence in serverless and cloud-native architectures.

Key principles for operational excellence

The following are the core principles for effectively managing the operational excellence pillar of the AWS Well-Architected Framework:

- **Automation**: Automation is at the heart of operational excellence, enabling organizations to eliminate repetitive tasks, reduce errors, and ensure consistency. Tools like AWS CDK, CloudFormation, and SAM allow infrastructure to be defined as code, making deployments repeatable and scalable. Automation extends to event-driven triggers for serverless applications, where AWS Lambda seamlessly integrates with other AWS services to handle dynamic workloads.

- **Monitoring and logging**: Observability provides real-time system health and performance insights. AWS CloudWatch tracks metrics and logs, X-Ray traces requests across services like API Gateway and Lambda, and OpenTelemetry supports standardized monitoring for multi-cloud environments. This ensures that engineers can quickly detect and address bottlenecks or failures before they affect users.

- **Continuous improvement**: Continuous improvement involves refining systems based on operational data and feedback. By analyzing trends and metrics, teams can proactively identify recurring issues and optimize workflows. AWS DevOps Guru provides actionable insights to resolve anomalies and prevent disruptions, helping organizations stay ahead of operational challenges.

Core practices for serverless applications

Follow these practices when designing and developing serverless applications:

- **Enhance observability**: Utilize AWS-native tools like CloudWatch, X-Ray, and OpenTelemetry for end-to-end visibility. These tools help monitor system health, trace errors, and optimize performance.
  - o **Example application**: CloudWatch and X-Ray can be combined to trace API Gateway requests through Lambda functions to DynamoDB, revealing performance bottlenecks or throttling issues.

- **Automate deployments with IaC**: Define infrastructure using AWS CDK, CloudFormation, and SAM to simplify deployments and enforce consistency.
  - o **Example application**: Use AWS SAM to deploy serverless applications with minimal configuration, accelerating rollout and reducing manual effort.

- **Leverage AI for proactive operations**: AWS DevOps Guru applies machine learning to detect anomalies and recommend remediation actions, enabling proactive management of serverless systems.
  - o **Example application**: A DevOps team can use DevOps Guru to detect spikes in Lambda error rates and receive actionable recommendations to address memory allocation issues.

Illustration of operational excellence

A SaaS startup providing a task management platform for remote teams adopted AWS serverless services to ensure high availability and rapid feature deployment. Their platform relies on multiple microservices, including:

- **API Gateway** for managing client requests.
- **AWS Lambda** for processing tasks such as user authentication and task updates.
- **DynamoDB** is used to store user data and task histories.

To achieve operational excellence, the startup implemented the following:

- **Automation**: Using AWS CDK, they automated deployments for their serverless backend, ensuring consistent infrastructure configurations across development, staging, and production environments.
- **Monitoring and observability**: CloudWatch dashboards provided real-time metrics for traffic and usage patterns, while X-Ray traced user requests through the API to pinpoint performance issues.
- **AI-driven insights**: AWS DevOps Guru detected anomalies during peak traffic events, such as spikes in error rates, and suggested memory adjustments for Lambda functions to improve response times.

By adopting these practices, the startup minimized operational downtime, scaled dynamically to support user demand, and improved platform reliability. As a result, customer satisfaction increased, and the team gained confidence in their system's ability to handle future growth.

Strengthening cloud-native applications with security

Security is a foundational pillar of the AWS Well-Architected Framework, especially in cloud-native and serverless architectures, where traditional perimeter-based models fall short. Organizations can protect data, systems, and applications effectively by adopting a zero-trust approach and following serverless-specific best practices.

Implementing Zero Trust in AWS

Zero Trust moves beyond perimeter security by treating all requests as untrusted until verified. It focuses on securing access at every layer, enforcing strict identity verification, and minimizing privileges.

The following principles define Zero Trust in AWS:

- **Identity verification**: Authenticate every request using strong mechanisms, such as AWS IAM roles and **multi-factor authentication (MFA)**.
- **Micro-segmentation**: Use VPC configurations and Security Groups to isolate workloads.
- **Continuous monitoring**: Employ AWS CloudTrail and GuardDuty to track all activities for anomaly detection.

Example application: A retail business with sensitive customer data can implement Zero Trust by restricting API Gateway access to authenticated users with IAM roles, ensuring that each request is verified and logged.

Serverless security best practices

The following are best practices to strengthen serverless workloads against potential vulnerabilities:

- **Implementing least privilege IAM with access analyzer**: Restrict permissions to the minimum required for resources. AWS IAM Access Analyzer provides recommendations to identify and eliminate overly permissive roles.
  - ○ **Example**: Grant a Lambda function access only to the specific S3 buckets it needs, minimizing exposure.
- **Encrypting data at rest and in transit**: Secure data using AWS KMS for encryption and Secrets Manager for managing sensitive information like API keys or database credentials.
  - ○ **Example**: Encrypt all data stored in DynamoDB and ensure API Gateway communications use HTTPS.
- **Securing APIs with Gateway, WAF, and Shield**: Protect APIs from attacks using Amazon API Gateway, AWS WAF, and AWS Shield for DDoS mitigation.
  - ○ **Example**: Add WAF rules to block common exploits, such as SQL injection attempts, and use AWS Shield to handle traffic spikes during DDoS attacks.

Automating security checks

Automation is crucial to maintaining consistent and scalable security. Tools like AWS Security Hub and GuardDuty enable proactive threat detection and response:

- **AWS Security Hub**: Aggregates security alerts and checks against compliance standards like CIS benchmarks.
- **AWS GuardDuty**: Monitors threats by analyzing network traffic, DNS queries, and API activity.

Example application: A financial services platform uses Security Hub to enforce continuous compliance and GuardDuty to detect unusual behavior, such as unauthorized API calls from external IPs.

Avoiding common AWS Security mistakes

The following are common security pitfalls and ways to avoid them:

- **Overly permissive IAM roles**: Regularly review roles with Access Analyzer to limit privileges.
- **Hardcoding secrets in applications**: Use Secrets Manager to store sensitive data securely.
- **Lack of API security**: Always enforce HTTPS and validate API inputs to prevent exploitation.
- **Ignoring logging and monitoring**: Enable CloudTrail and CloudWatch Logs for auditing and troubleshooting.

Illustration of securing serverless payment workflows

A fintech company that processes payment transactions adopted serverless technologies to scale its platform securely. The system includes:

- **API Gateway**: To handle incoming payment requests.
- **AWS Lambda**: To validate and process transactions.
- **DynamoDB**: To store payment details and user histories.

To strengthen security:

- **Zero Trust approach**: Enforced IAM roles for every request and restricted API Gateway access to authenticated users.
- **Data encryption**: Secured payment data in DynamoDB using KMS encryption keys and processed transactions over HTTPS.
- **Automated monitoring**: Leveraged GuardDuty to detect unauthorized API calls and security hub to monitor compliance with financial regulations.

As a result, the company reduced potential vulnerabilities, achieved regulatory compliance, and gained customer trust through robust security measures.

Reliability for high availability and failover

Reliability is one of the core pillars of the AWS Well-Architected Framework. It ensures that workloads can recover from failures, meet operational requirements, and adapt dynamically to demand. In serverless architectures, achieving high reliability involves designing resilient systems that handle distributed failures gracefully and recover automatically.

Understanding distributed failures

Cloud-native applications are inherently distributed, introducing potential failure points across services. Failures can occur due to network issues, resource limitations, or external dependencies. Designing reliable applications requires understanding these risks and implementing strategies to mitigate them.

Serverless-specific reliability challenges

The following are common reliability challenges in serverless workloads:

- **Cold starts**: Delays in initializing AWS Lambda functions, especially for infrequently used functions.
- **Retries and event failures**: Managing retries for failed invocations or unprocessed events.

- **Throttling**: Service limits that can lead to request rejections under high traffic.

By addressing these challenges, teams can enhance the reliability of their systems, ensuring seamless user experiences even under adverse conditions.

Building fault-tolerant event-driven architectures

The following practices ensure reliability in serverless workflows:

- **Handling Lambda errors, API timeouts, and throttling**: Use robust error-handling mechanisms, such as exponential backoff for retries and circuit breakers, to prevent cascading failures. Configure API Gateway timeouts and throttling limits to handle sudden traffic surges.
    - ○ **Example application**: A data ingestion pipeline can configure retry logic for Lambda invocations and API Gateway integration responses to prevent data loss during intermittent failures.
- **Implementing retries with AWS Step Functions and SQS DLQs**: AWS Step Functions allow orchestrated retries for complex workflows. SQS DLQs ensure that unprocessed events are retained for further analysis.
    - ○ **Example application**: A transaction processing system can use DLQs to store failed messages for manual inspection or automated reprocessing, minimizing the risk of dropped transactions.

High availability strategies

The following are key strategies for achieving high availability in serverless architectures:

- **Multi-region deployments**: Deploy applications across multiple AWS regions to ensure failover during regional outages.
- **AWS Global Accelerator**: Global Accelerator routes user traffic to the nearest healthy endpoint, reducing latency and ensuring availability.

Example application: A global e-commerce platform can use multi-region deployments with Global Accelerator to handle traffic surges during major sales events and ensure uninterrupted user access.

High reliability in real-time analytics illustration

An AI-powered real-time analytics platform processes and analyzes data streams from IoT devices. To ensure reliability, the architecture included:

- **Event-driven processing**: AWS Lambda and Step Functions were used for data ingestion and processing, with SQS DLQs capturing unprocessed events.
- **Multi-region deployment**: The platform was deployed across multiple AWS regions with Amazon DynamoDB Global Tables to replicate data seamlessly.
- **High availability routing**: AWS Global Accelerator routed traffic to the nearest region, ensuring low latency and consistent performance.

By adopting these strategies, the platform maintained 99.99% uptime, processed millions of events daily without interruptions, and provided real-time insights to customers worldwide.

Performance efficiency in cloud workloads

Performance efficiency, one of the core pillars of the AWS Well-Architected Framework, emphasizes using resources effectively to maintain optimal performance while minimizing costs. In serverless architectures, optimizing compute, storage, and networking resources is critical to handle workloads efficiently under varying traffic patterns.

Understanding performance bottlenecks

The following are common performance bottlenecks in serverless applications:

- **AWS Lambda**: Cold starts can cause delays in response times, especially in high-latency environments.
- **DynamoDB**: Inefficient capacity allocation can result in throttled requests under high traffic.
- **API Gateway**: Misconfigured timeouts or excessive backend processing can lead to a degraded user experience.

Optimizing these components ensures that applications can handle workloads seamlessly without sacrificing speed or reliability.

Best practices for AWS Lambda performance

The following practices help address Lambda-specific bottlenecks and improve overall performance:

- **Reducing cold starts with provisioned concurrency**: Cold starts to occur when a Lambda function is initialized for the first time or after a period of inactivity. By enabling provisioned concurrency, Lambda functions remain initialized and ready to respond, reducing latency for time-sensitive workloads.

  Example: A real-time messaging app can use provisioned concurrency to handle user requests without delays during peak traffic hours.

- **Tuning memory allocation and execution time**: AWS Compute Optimizer provides insights into optimal memory settings to reduce execution time and cost. Allocating additional memory often leads to faster execution due to increased CPU resources.

  Example: An e-commerce platform processing large datasets can tune Lambda memory allocation to achieve faster order processing during flash sales.

Storage performance optimization

Efficient storage usage is vital for serverless applications, particularly when handling large datasets or high-traffic workloads.

The following are some of the examples of Storage Performance optimization techniques:

- **DynamoDB on-demand vs. provisioned capacity**:
  - **On-demand capacity**: Automatically adjusts throughput to meet demand, suitable for unpredictable workloads.
  - **Provisioned capacity**: Allows pre-allocated throughput, ideal for predictable traffic patterns
  - **Example**: A social media analytics application can use on-demand capacity for unpredictable API traffic and switch to provisioned capacity during planned report generation cycles.
- **Optimizing S3 Storage for AI and big data**: Use S3 storage classes like Intelligent Tiering to move data between frequently and infrequently accessed tiers automatically. Configure S3 lifecycle policies to archive old data into Glacier Deep Archive for cost savings.
  - **Example**: An AI research team training models with S3-hosted datasets can use Intelligent-Tiering to optimize data storage costs while maintaining high accessibility.
- **High-performance streaming application illustration**: A media company running a live video streaming platform leveraged AWS serverless services to achieve high performance and scalability. Their architecture included:
  - **AWS Lambda**: To process video transcoding and event-based user actions.

o **Amazon Kinesis**: To handle high-throughput streaming data from users globally.

o **S3**: To store video content and associated metadata.

- **To optimize performance**:

    o **Compute**: Lambda functions with provisioned concurrency ensured consistent response times for video transcoding during live events.

    o **Storage**: S3 Intelligent-Tiering reduced costs by automatically moving archival video files to lower-cost storage tiers.

    o **Networking**: Kinesis scaling policies allowed the platform to handle spikes in video stream data without bottlenecks.

Cost optimization for serverless workloads

Cost optimization, a vital pillar of the AWS Well-Architected Framework, minimizes cloud expenses without sacrificing performance or scalability. While serverless services offer flexibility and pay-as-you-go pricing, organizations often face hidden costs due to misconfigurations or overuse. This section highlights strategies for identifying and addressing these cost pitfalls in serverless applications.

Hidden costs of AWS Serverless services

Serverless architectures can introduce unexpected expenses if not carefully managed. The following are common areas where teams overspend:

- **Excessive API Gateway requests**: Inefficient API designs can lead to higher charges based on request volumes and data transfer.

- **Over-provisioned Lambda functions**: Allocating more memory than required increases costs unnecessarily.

- **Unused resources**: Failing to clean up idle resources like S3 buckets or DynamoDB tables results in wasted spending.

Best practices for cost efficiency

The following practices help mitigate hidden costs and maximize the cost-effectiveness of serverless applications:

- **Using AWS Cost Explorer and Budgets**: AWS Cost Explorer provides insights into spending trends and resource utilization. AWS Budgets enables teams to set thresholds and receive alerts for cost overruns.

    o **Example application**: An e-commerce platform can use Cost Explorer to monitor daily API Gateway expenses and receive notifications if spending exceeds the allocated budget.

- **Optimizing API Gateway pricing models**: Depending on workload requirements, choosing the right API Gateway pricing model (REST, HTTP, or WebSocket) can significantly reduce costs. HTTP APIs are more cost-effective for standard client-server interactions, while WebSocket APIs suit real-time communication.

    o **Example application**: A chat application can save costs by using WebSocket APIs for bi-directional messaging instead of HTTP APIs, which would require repeated polling.

- **Reducing Lambda invocations and over-provisioning**: Implement best practices with AWS Compute Optimizer, such as avoiding unnecessary function triggers, batching operations, and fine-tuning memory allocation.

    o   **Example application**: A video processing pipeline can batch files for fewer Lambda invocations, reducing operational costs while maintaining throughput.

AI-driven cost insights with AWS Cost Anomaly Detection

AWS Cost Anomaly Detection uses machine learning to identify unusual spending patterns and notify teams of potential cost inefficiencies.

- **Automated monitoring**: Continuously analyzes historical spending data for anomalies.
- **Proactive alerts**: Sends notifications for unexpected cost spikes, enabling timely intervention.

    Example application: A startup can use Cost Anomaly Detection to identify a sudden surge in API Gateway expenses caused by a misconfigured client application and resolve the issue before it escalates.

Reducing costs in a SaaS startup illustration

A SaaS startup providing real-time analytics for marketing teams faced rising serverless costs due to rapid user growth. To address this:

- **Cost monitoring**: The team used AWS Cost Explorer to identify high expenses from API Gateway and Lambda functions.

- **API optimization**: Switching from REST APIs to HTTP APIs for client-server interactions helped optimize API Gateway costs by aligning pricing with usage patterns.

- **Lambda tuning**: AWS Compute Optimizer provided insights into memory allocation adjustments, improving cost efficiency while maintaining optimal execution performance.

- **Anomaly detection**: AWS Cost Anomaly Detection flagged irregular usage patterns, allowing the team to resolve inefficiencies quickly.

By implementing these strategies, the startup optimized its serverless costs, ensuring that expenses aligned with business growth while maintaining performance efficiency.

Sustainability for efficient cloud computing

Sustainability is the newest pillar of the AWS Well-Architected Framework. It emphasizes designing workloads that minimize environmental impact by optimizing resource utilization and leveraging energy-efficient infrastructure. As organizations increasingly prioritize sustainability, this pillar provides a roadmap to align cloud architectures with environmental and operational goals.

Why sustainability is a new pillar

Sustainability was introduced to address the growing need for environmentally responsible cloud architectures. AWS recognizes that cloud computing plays a significant role in energy consumption, and sustainable design can help organizations reduce their carbon footprints while maintaining performance and scalability. This pillar reflects AWS's commitment to advancing global sustainability initiatives and provides actionable guidance for businesses to adopt greener practices.

How AWS Serverless reduces environmental impact

Serverless computing inherently supports sustainability by eliminating idle resources and optimizing resource usage. The key methods serverless reduces environmental impact include:

- **Dynamic scaling**: Automatically adjusts resources based on demand, ensuring no over-provisioning or underutilization.

- **Efficient resource utilization**: AWS Lambda and other serverless services only consume compute power during execution, reducing energy waste.

- **Shared responsibility model**: AWS data centers use energy-efficient hardware, renewable energy sources, and innovative cooling systems to lower workloads' carbon footprints.

Best practices for sustainable cloud computing

The following are actionable strategies for designing energy-efficient AWS workloads:

- **Optimizing compute cycles to reduce waste**: Design workflows to minimize unnecessary compute usage. Event-driven architectures with AWS Lambda can process workloads dynamically, reducing energy consumption. Additionally, Amazon S3 lifecycle policies can be used to archive or delete unused data.

  o **Example application**: A video processing platform can implement on-demand processing with Lambda, significantly reducing idle compute time compared to traditional EC2 instances.

- **Using AWS Graviton processors for cost and energy efficiency**: AWS Graviton processors are designed to deliver higher performance per watt than traditional processors. Migrating workloads to Graviton instances can lower costs and reduce energy consumption.

  o **Example application**: A data analytics platform can migrate its compute-intensive operations to Graviton2-powered instances, achieving better energy efficiency while maintaining processing speed.

Green-tech startup and sustainability illustration

A green-tech startup developing IoT solutions for energy management used AWS services to optimize sustainability efforts. Their architecture included:

- **IoT core**: To collect and process real-time device energy usage data.
- **AWS Lambda**: For event-driven processing and data analysis.
- **Amazon S3**: To store historical data and enable lifecycle policies for archiving.

To improve sustainability:

- **Compute optimization**: Event-driven architectures minimized compute resource usage, processing data only when events were triggered.

- **Graviton instances**: AWS Graviton-powered instances provide a more energy-efficient alternative to traditional compute options, improving workload efficiency while maintaining processing performance.

- **Data archival**: S3 lifecycle policies ensured that infrequently accessed data was moved to Glacier Deep Archive, lowering storage costs and energy usage.

These strategies enabled the startup to align its operations with its sustainability mission, reduce energy costs, and enhance its reputation as an environmentally conscious business.

Applying AWS Well-Architected Framework in practice

The AWS Well-Architected Framework is a powerful tool for designing, deploying, and optimizing cloud-native and serverless applications. By combining actionable guidance with real-world examples, organizations can implement best practices effectively while addressing their unique challenges.

Using the Well-Architected Tool for real-time assessments

The AWS Well-Architected Tool provides an interactive interface to evaluate and improve workloads based on the six pillars. It enables teams to:

- **Identify risks**: Highlight areas of misalignment with AWS best practices.
- **Prioritize actions**: Focus on high-impact improvements to enhance architecture quality.
- **Monitor progress**: Continuously assess workloads as they evolve.

The step-by-step guide is as follows:

1. **Initiate a review**: Create a workload in the Well-Architected Tool and answer questions about its architecture.

2. **Analyze risks**: Review risk areas flagged across the six pillars.

3. **Plan improvements**: Prioritize actions provided by the tool, starting with high-severity risks.

4. **Implement changes**: Apply recommended solutions using AWS services and tools.

5. **Reassess regularly**: Conduct periodic reviews to ensure continuous alignment with best practices.

Practical application of Well-Architected principles: Each framework pillar provides actionable steps for improving workload efficiency, security, and reliability. Below are integrated real-world scenarios that demonstrate these principles in action.

Scenario one

Blockchain platform for decentralized finance: A blockchain company running a DeFi platform faced security and cost optimization challenges.

By applying the Well-Architected Framework, the platform achieved the following:

- **Cost optimization**: The team used AWS Cost Explorer to identify inefficient API Gateway usage for blockchain node interactions. Switching to HTTP APIs significantly reduced costs.
- **Security enhancements**: AWS KMS was integrated to encrypt blockchain wallets and private keys, ensuring secure access to sensitive assets.
- **Outcome**: The platform reduced operational costs and strengthened the security of user transactions, gaining trust in a highly competitive market.

Scenario two

Scaling quantum computing simulations: A quantum research organization needed to scale its computational resources for simulating quantum algorithms. Using the Well-Architected Framework, the organization achieved:

- **Performance efficiency**: AWS Graviton processors were adopted to optimize simulation workloads, delivering better performance for quantum calculations at lower energy consumption.
- **Reliability improvements**: Multi-region deployments with S3 and EC2 ensured seamless data availability and computational resilience.
- **Outcome**: The team significantly improved quantum simulation processing times by optimizing workloads on AWS Graviton processors. This transition enhanced computational efficiency while lowering operational costs and advancing quantum research capabilities.

Scenario three

Space exploration data processing: A space agency requires a reliable architecture to process telemetry data from satellites in orbit. By leveraging the framework. The agency achieved:

- **Reliability**: AWS Lambda was configured with retries and SQS DLQs to handle intermittent satellite telemetry data drops.

- **Operational excellence**: CloudWatch and X-Ray provided detailed monitoring for data processing pipelines, ensuring zero delays in mission-critical operations.

- **Outcome**: The agency processed millions of telemetry signals in near real-time, improving mission accuracy and ensuring consistent satellite communication.

Checklist of key actions to optimize each pillar

The following checklist summarizes essential actions for each pillar, linking them to the scenarios above:

- **Operational excellence**: Automate monitoring and deployments with CloudFormation and AWS CDK (Scenario 3).
- **Security**: Encrypt sensitive blockchain data using KMS and enforce IAM roles.
- **Reliability**: Configure retries with Lambda and SQS DLQs for telemetry data.
- **Performance efficiency**: Optimize quantum simulations with Graviton processors.
- **Cost optimization**: Track spending and optimize API Gateway configurations.
- **Sustainability**: Use Graviton instances to lower energy usage in computational workloads.

Conclusion

The AWS Well-Architected Framework is a cornerstone for building secure, efficient, and reliable cloud-native applications. Organizations can continuously evaluate and enhance their workloads by adhering to their six pillars, namely operational excellence, security, reliability, performance efficiency, cost optimization, and sustainability. Each pillar offers actionable guidance to address challenges while aligning with industry standards and best practices.

This chapter illustrated how these principles apply in practice, from improving serverless reliability and scalability to reducing costs and advancing sustainability goals. With tools like the AWS Well-Architected Tool, teams can identify risks, prioritize improvements, and drive operational excellence across their workloads. By embedding these practices into their operational culture, organizations can future-proof their applications for evolving demands and unlock new opportunities in cloud innovation.

The next chapter explores emerging serverless innovations, including edge computing, IoT, AI, blockchain, and quantum computing. It highlights how AWS services enable scalable, secure, and sustainable workloads while transforming cloud-native applications for the future.

Join our Discord space

Join our Discord workspace for latest updates, offers, tech happenings around the world, new releases, and sessions with the authors:

https://discord.bpbonline.com

## CHAPTER 23

Serverless Trends and Emerging Technologies

Introduction

The landscape of cloud computing has evolved far beyond traditional infrastructure provisioning. The emphasis now is on maximizing efficiency while reducing complexity. Serverless computing has emerged as a game-changer, fostering event-driven workflows, rapid data processing, and adaptive scalability across various industries. Yet, its applications go beyond business environments.

In space research and defense, serverless models are revolutionizing telemetry processing, enhancing remote sensing for planetary studies, and optimizing AI-driven intelligence systems in strategic military operations.

As organizations push the limits of real-time computing, automation, and AI-driven analytics, the serverless model will continue to play a pivotal role in shaping the future of cloud-native workloads.

Security and sustainability remain at the forefront of the modern era, with Zero Trust models, AI-driven threat detection, and AWS sustainability initiatives improving serverless resilience. This chapter explores these emerging trends, detailing their impact on cloud architectures and how organizations can leverage serverless for the future.

Structure

The chapter covers the following topics:

- Serverless at the edge for scalable applications
- AWS IoT and edge-to-cloud connectivity
- AI-driven analytics in serverless computing
- Quantum computing in serverless architectures
- Serverless blockchain and decentralized computing
- Multi-cloud and hybrid cloud trends
- Space exploration and military applications
- Sustainability and green technologies in serverless

Objectives

This chapter introduces emerging trends in serverless computing and highlights how new technologies are shaping cloud-native architectures. It explores serverless at the edge, where Lambda@Edge and CloudFront enable low-latency processing for dynamic content delivery and security enforcement. The chapter also introduces AWS IoT and its role in real-time device connectivity, demonstrating how edge-to-cloud integration advances industries such as manufacturing, healthcare, and agriculture.

The chapter examines how analytics, AI-driven workloads, and blockchain applications influence serverless adoption. It introduces AWS Braket and its potential role in quantum computing, focusing on optimization, encryption, and high-performance computing. Blockchain and decentralized computing trends are also explored, covering high-level use cases for DeFi, NFTs, and secure digital transactions.

Beyond commercial applications, the chapter explores serverless adoption in aerospace, defense, and critical industries, where AWS services enable real-time telemetry, intelligence processing, and secure operations. Security remains a core focus, with an overview of Zero Trust security models, AI-driven threat detection, and compliance strategies. The chapter concludes with multi-cloud and hybrid cloud adoption trends and AWS sustainability initiatives, demonstrating how serverless computing drives energy-efficient architectures. By the end of this chapter, readers will have a foundational understanding of these innovations and their future impact on cloud-native computing.

Serverless at the edge for scalable applications

The shift toward serverless edge computing redefines modern cloud architectures, moving processing closer to the user instead of relying solely on centralized data centers. This transition optimizes latency, minimizes bandwidth consumption, and improves response times by executing workloads at distributed points in the network.

AWS Lambda@Edge and AWS CloudFront provide event-driven processing at the edge, enabling faster content delivery, enhanced security, and personalized experiences.

The evolution of serverless edge computing extends beyond cloud-based infrastructure, with mobile devices integrating built-in AI chips to handle inference locally. This shift reduces cloud dependency for real-time AI workloads while complementing serverless architectures by further distributing processing to the device level. As on-device AI capabilities grow, serverless edge computing and cloud AI will work in tandem to deliver seamless, ultra-low latency applications optimized for performance, privacy, and efficiency.

Benefits of serverless at the edge

Serverless edge computing enhances performance, security, and scalability. The following are key advantages:

- **Low-latency processing**: Moves computation closer to users, reducing response times.
- **Optimized bandwidth usage**: It reduces network congestion by handling data locally.
- **Scalability without infrastructure management**: It automatically adjusts to traffic demands.
- **Security at the edge**: Prevents unauthorized access by enforcing policies before data reaches backend services.

AWS Services for edge computing

AWS provides Lambda@Edge and CloudFront, enabling event-driven processing at edge locations. AWS Lambda@Edge extends AWS Lambda functionality to CloudFront's global edge locations, enabling real-time request modifications, security filtering, and AI-driven content adjustments. Businesses use Lambda@Edge to rewrite URLs, authenticate requests, and block malicious traffic before it reaches backend servers.

Amazon CloudFront is AWS's CDN, designed to accelerate global static and dynamic content delivery. When integrated with Lambda@Edge, it enables event-driven execution at edge locations, allowing real-time security enforcement and API request filtering before traffic reaches origin servers.

Use cases for serverless edge computing

Organizations leverage serverless edge computing to optimize performance across industries. The following are common use cases:

- **Dynamic content personalization**: E-commerce platforms customize user experiences based on location and browsing history.

- **Real-time video streaming**: Adjusts bitrate and quality dynamically to prevent buffering.

- **API security and traffic filtering**: Blocks malicious requests at the edge before reaching backend APIs.

- **Geo-fencing and compliance**: Restricts access based on regional policies and user IP locations.

As AI-driven applications evolve, edge computing will integrate further with mobile AI chips for on-device inference. This will reduce cloud latency, enhance privacy, and enable real-time AI processing at the device level, complementing Lambda@Edge's ability to optimize cloud interactions. The future of serverless computing will combine cloud, edge, and on-device AI, creating resilient, low-latency architectures that deliver seamless user experiences.

AWS IoT and edge-to-cloud connectivity

The rapid adoption of IoT devices has transformed industries by enabling real-time data collection, remote monitoring, and intelligent automation. AWS IoT services provide a scalable, event-driven architecture that connects devices to the cloud, enabling seamless edge-to-cloud communication. As IoT continues to evolve, serverless computing is critical in processing and analyzing data efficiently without requiring infrastructure management.

AWS IoT Core, IoT Greengrass, and other AWS services allow organizations to ingest, process, and act on IoT data in real time, enhancing use cases such as predictive maintenance, smart manufacturing, connected healthcare, and agricultural automation. This section explores how AWS IoT enables edge-to-cloud integration, the role of serverless computing in IoT, and real-world industry applications.

AWS IoT services for edge-to-cloud processing

AWS provides several IoT services that enable real-time connectivity, local processing, and cloud integration.

The following are key AWS IoT services that facilitate edge-to-cloud communication:

- **AWS IoT core**: A fully managed service that securely connects IoT devices to AWS and enables bi-directional communication.

- **AWS IoT Greengrass**: Extends AWS capabilities to edge devices, allowing local processing, machine learning inference, and offline operations.

- **AWS IoT analytics**: A managed service that automates data ingestion, storage, and processing to generate actionable insights.

- **AWS IoT device management**: Provides secure onboarding, monitoring, and remote management of large-scale IoT deployments.

By leveraging these services, businesses can connect millions of devices, process real-time telemetry, and automate responses based on incoming data.

Industry applications of AWS IoT

AWS IoT is transforming multiple industries by enabling automated, real-time decision-making. The following are key industry applications where IoT and serverless computing provide value:

- **Smart manufacturing**: IoT-connected machines enable predictive maintenance by analyzing sensor data to prevent equipment failures.

- **Healthcare and remote monitoring**: Wearable devices track patient vitals and trigger real-time alerts for healthcare providers.

- **Precision agriculture**: IoT sensors monitor soil moisture, weather conditions, and crop health, optimizing irrigation and yield.

- **Connected vehicles and logistics**: Fleet tracking and real-time route optimization reduce fuel costs and improve delivery efficiency.

By integrating IoT data with serverless architectures, businesses can build resilient, automated systems that respond instantly to real-world events.

Key benefits of serverless computing in IoT

Serverless computing optimizes IoT architectures by eliminating infrastructure management and enabling event-driven processing. The following are key benefits of integrating serverless computing with AWS IoT:

- **Real-time event processing**: AWS Lambda can process IoT events instantly, triggering automated actions without provisioning servers.

- **Scalability for high-volume data streams**: IoT devices generate large volumes of telemetry data, which serverless functions process on demand.

- **Reduced latency with edge computing**: AWS IoT Greengrass runs machine learning models locally, minimizing reliance on cloud resources.

- **Cost efficiency**: Serverless computing scales dynamically, ensuring that resources are only used when needed.

Organizations can build highly efficient, scalable, and cost-effective IoT solutions by combining AWS IoT with serverless architectures.

As IoT adoption grows, serverless and edge computing will play a greater role in distributed intelligence and autonomous decision-making. Integrating on-device AI chips will enhance IoT applications, allowing devices to process and react to data locally before communicating with the cloud. The continuous innovation in new IoT and edge capabilities enables businesses to scale their IoT solutions with enhanced efficiency, security, and intelligence.

AI-driven analytics in serverless computing

The advancement of serverless analytics has moved beyond conventional data pipelines, integrating AI-powered automation, real-time insights, and distributed intelligence models. Rather than depending exclusively on centralized cloud-based analytics, today's architectures incorporate hybrid AI-cloud frameworks, federated learning, and event-driven machine learning systems to drive efficiency and adaptability.

This shift enables low-latency insights, reduced data transfer costs, and improved security by processing data closer to the source.

This section highlights how AI transforms serverless analytics, emphasizing on-device inference, decentralized processing, and the future of real-time intelligence in cloud-native environments.

Emerging trends in serverless analytics

Organizations are increasingly leveraging AI and real-time automation to enhance serverless data processing. The following are key trends shaping serverless analytics:

- **Federated learning for distributed AI models**: AI models train across multiple locations without centralizing raw data, improving security and efficiency.

- **On-device AI inference**: Mobile and edge AI chips process ML models locally, reducing the need for cloud-based inference.

- **Hybrid AI-cloud pipelines**: AI-powered analytics balance on-device processing with cloud-based insights for optimal performance.

- **Event-driven AI automation**: Serverless functions trigger real-time AI workflows, improving fraud detection, personalized recommendations, and predictive maintenance.

By shifting AI workloads closer to the data source, businesses reduce cloud dependency, lower inference latency, and improve real-time decision-making.

Advantages of AI-driven analytics

Serverless computing optimizes AI analytics pipelines by eliminating infrastructure management and enabling event-driven execution. The following are key advantages of integrating AI with serverless architectures:

- **Scalability for AI workloads**: AWS Lambda dynamically scales AI inference for unpredictable workloads.

- **Automated decision-making**: Event-driven triggers process real-time AI insights without manual intervention.

- **Efficient cost management**: AI models run on demand, eliminating the need for persistent GPU-powered infrastructure.

- **AI model optimization at the edge**: AWS Greengrass enables local ML inference, minimizing cloud data transfers.

Businesses can build highly adaptive, intelligent cloud solutions by leveraging AI-driven analytics in serverless architectures.

Use cases for AI-driven serverless analytics

Serverless analytics is transforming how AI is deployed in cloud-native environments. The following are key applications of AI-driven analytics in serverless computing:

- **Fraud detection in financial transactions**: AI models analyze streaming transaction data to detect real-time anomalies.

- **Predictive maintenance in IoT systems**: The AI inferences can be used to effectively predict different kinds of equipment failures proactively and apply sensor data from different sources.

- **Automated customer personalization**: AI-based analytics recommend personalized content and products dynamically.

- **Cybersecurity and threat intelligence**: AI-driven analytics help quickly detect security threats and can automatically trigger response actions.

With real-time AI analytics integrated into serverless workflows, businesses can enhance automation, improve decision-making, and optimize operational efficiency.

The evolution of serverless analytics is shifting toward decentralized, real-time AI processing. As on-device AI inference and federated learning gain traction, AI workloads will be distributed across mobile devices, edge locations, and cloud platforms, creating intelligent, autonomous systems. AWS continues enhancing AI-driven serverless capabilities, ensuring businesses can scale real-time analytics with minimal infrastructure complexity.

Quantum computing in serverless architectures

Quantum computing is one of the emerging transformative technologies; it can solve complex problems beyond the capabilities of classical computing. AWS Braket, a fully managed quantum computing service, enables researchers and businesses to explore quantum algorithms without specialized infrastructure. By integrating with serverless services like AWS Lambda and Step Functions, Braket allows organizations to run hybrid quantum-classical workflows, unlocking new opportunities in optimization, cryptography, and AI acceleration.

This section highlights how AWS Braket supports quantum computing in serverless architectures, exploring its applications and how businesses can integrate quantum processing into cloud-native environments.

AWS Braket in serverless computing

AWS Braket provides on-demand access to quantum processors, which help businesses to experiment with actual quantum hardware and simulations.

The following are key AWS Braket capabilities:

- **Hybrid quantum-classical workflows**: Integrates with AWS Lambda and Step Functions to coordinate quantum and classical computing tasks.

- **Quantum circuit simulations**: Quantum experiments can be run alongside traditional computing models, which enable benchmarking and error correction processes.

- **Pay-per-use access to quantum hardware**: This service provides serverless access to multiple quantum processor types, including gate-based and annealing quantum computers.

- **Seamless cloud integration**: Allows orchestration of quantum jobs with AWS cloud services for scalable automation.

AWS Braket brings quantum capabilities to the cloud, allowing businesses to experiment with quantum computing using familiar AWS tools.

AWS Braket use cases in serverless computing

Quantum computing is still in its early stages, but businesses are exploring its potential for solving highly complex problems.

The following are practical use cases where AWS Braket is being integrated into serverless workflows:

- **Optimization problems**: Quantum algorithms help solve logistics, scheduling, and supply chain optimization challenges.

- **Post-quantum cryptography**: Research in quantum-resistant encryption ensures long-term data security in serverless applications.

- **AI and machine learning acceleration**: Quantum-enhanced algorithms improve deep learning model training and pattern recognition.

- **Simulating molecular interactions**: Quantum computing enables advanced material and drug discovery by accurately modeling chemical structures.

By integrating AWS Braket with serverless orchestration tools, businesses can explore early-stage quantum solutions without investing in physical quantum hardware.

As quantum computing technology advances, AWS Braket will play a critical role in bridging quantum and classical cloud computing. Future developments will likely focus on improved quantum error correction, hybrid AI-quantum models, and deeper integration with AWS's broader serverless ecosystem. As serverless applications evolve, AWS Braket will enable businesses to efficiently leverage quantum computing to solve complex real-world problems.

Serverless blockchain and decentralized computing

Blockchain technology expands beyond finance, playing a key role in decentralized computing, secure transactions, and immutable data management. Integrating serverless computing enhances scalability, security, and operational efficiency, removing the burden of maintaining dedicated infrastructure while enabling automated, event-driven blockchain applications.

AWS services like Amazon Managed Blockchain and AWS Lambda allow organizations to build event-driven, scalable blockchain applications without managing backend servers.

This section focuses on how AWS Managed Blockchain enhances serverless applications, supporting use cases such as smart contracts, decentralized identity, and secure transaction processing.

AWS Managed Blockchain for serverless applications

Serverless computing is enabling new models for blockchain scalability and automation. Instead of requiring dedicated nodes, blockchain transactions can now be executed dynamically using event-driven functions, reducing costs and improving performance.

The rise of DeFi, smart contracts, and federated identity management is driving the adoption of serverless workflows for blockchain processing. By automating transaction validation, securing digital identities, and enabling real-time ledger updates, serverless architectures are making blockchain networks more efficient and scalable.

Organizations can build resilient, event-driven blockchain workflows by integrating AWS Managed Blockchain with serverless automation.

Use cases for serverless blockchain with AWS

Blockchain combined with serverless computing is transforming multiple industries. The following are real-world applications of AWS Managed Blockchain in a serverless architecture:

- **DeFi**: Enables real-time trade settlements and automated lending with smart contracts.
- **Supply chain transparency**: Ensures immutable product tracking and secure digital certifications.
- **Decentralized identity and authentication**: Verifies user identities using blockchain-based authentication.
- **Smart contract automation**: AWS Lambda triggers on-chain contract executions, streamlining business logic.

These serverless blockchain applications improve security, scalability, and transaction efficiency.

Best practices for using AWS managed blockchain

Organizations can utilize the following best practices to gain maximum efficiency when combining serverless computing with blockchain:

- **Leverage serverless automation for smart contracts**: Use Lambda to trigger contract execution based on blockchain events.

- **Optimize API queries for blockchain data**: Implement API Gateway with caching to reduce redundant blockchain queries.

- **Secure cryptographic keys**: Store blockchain encryption keys in AWS KMS for enhanced security.

- **Reduce costs with event-driven execution**: Avoid always-on compute nodes by using Lambda for processing blockchain interactions.

By adopting serverless best practices, blockchain applications remain scalable, cost-effective, and efficient.

Future of serverless blockchain on AWS

The adoption of blockchain is moving beyond financial applications, with industries leveraging decentralized architectures for security, automation, and transparent transactions. At the same time, serverless computing is making blockchain more scalable and cost-effective by eliminating the need for always-on infrastructure. As quantum-safe cryptography evolves and AI-driven smart contracts become more prevalent, the way organizations build and interact with decentralized applications will continue shifting. The future of blockchain is about efficient, event-driven automation, and serverless computing is positioned to make that future a reality.

Multi-cloud and hybrid cloud trends

Cloud computing has come a long way from organizations relying on a single provider for all workloads. Organizations today prioritize adaptability, resilience, and cost optimization, driving the adoption of multi-cloud and hybrid cloud architectures. Rather than committing solely to a single provider, companies strategically distribute workloads across AWS, Azure, Google Cloud, and on-premises environments, ensuring compliance with regulations while maximizing availability and vendor flexibility.

Serverless computing is evolving to support this shift, with cross-cloud orchestration tools, portable serverless frameworks, and hybrid models enabling seamless workload execution across multiple environments. Whether deploying serverless APIs across clouds, running edge workloads closer to users, or integrating on-premises computing with the cloud, multi-cloud and hybrid approaches are changing how serverless applications are built and deployed.

Evolution of multi-cloud and hybrid serverless

Organizations leverage serverless across multiple environments to enhance scalability, resilience, and vendor flexibility. The following are key trends shaping this evolution:

- **Portable serverless frameworks**: Open-source tools like Knative and OpenFaaS allow functions to run across AWS, Azure, and Google Cloud.

- **Cross-cloud orchestration**: Multi-cloud API gateways and event-driven workflows unify platform workloads.

- **Hybrid cloud with on-premises integration**: AWS Outposts and Lambda@Edge extend serverless computing to private data centers.

- **Federated identity and security**: IAM solutions allow seamless authentication and policy enforcement across cloud providers.

By adopting multi-cloud and hybrid cloud architectures, businesses gain greater operational flexibility and minimize the risks of vendor lock-in.

Key technologies for multi-cloud and hybrid serverless

Cloud providers are expanding their services to support multi-cloud and hybrid environments, enabling organizations to deploy serverless workloads flexibly. The following technologies help achieve seamless cross-cloud and hybrid serverless deployments:

- **AWS Lambda with API Gateway**: Provides serverless API interactions that integrate across multiple cloud environments.

- **Knative and OpenFaaS**: Enable serverless function portability on Kubernetes clusters, allowing cross-cloud execution.

- **AWS Outposts and Azure Arc**: Bridges cloud-native applications with on-premises environments for hybrid workloads.

- **Cross-cloud event routing**: Event-driven architectures dynamically route serverless functions across multiple cloud providers.

These technologies ensure that serverless applications can scale beyond the boundaries of a single cloud provider.

Use cases for multi-cloud and hybrid serverless

Organizations are adopting multi-cloud and hybrid cloud serverless strategies to solve real-world workload portability, compliance, and availability challenges. The following are practical applications of multi-cloud and hybrid serverless computing:

- **Disaster recovery and failover**: Serverless workloads are deployed across multiple cloud providers to ensure high availability.

- **Data sovereignty compliance**: Businesses process data in regionalized serverless environments to meet regulatory requirements.

- **Edge AI and IoT processing**: Hybrid serverless models run machine learning inference and real-time analytics at the edge.

- **Cross-cloud API services**: APIs are deployed across multiple cloud environments for load balancing and latency optimization.

These approaches allow organizations to maintain resilience, security, and efficiency across cloud environments.

Best practices for hybrid and multi-cloud serverless

To build scalable and reliable multi-cloud serverless architectures, organizations should follow these best practices:

- **Standardize deployment with infrastructure as code**: Use Terraform or AWS CDK for consistent cloud function deployment.

- **Use federated identity for seamless authentication**: Enable SSO and multi-cloud IAM policies.

- **Optimize data transfer costs**: Reduce cross-cloud data movement with localized processing and caching.

- **Monitor serverless functions across clouds**: Implement centralized logging and observability with OpenTelemetry and AWS CloudWatch.

By following these strategies, organizations can maximize the efficiency, security, and scalability of serverless applications across multiple cloud platforms.

Future of multi-cloud and hybrid serverless

The evolution of serverless computing beyond a single cloud is accelerating. Businesses no longer view multi-cloud and hybrid cloud as a luxury but as necessary for resilience, cost optimization, and compliance. As cross-cloud orchestration tools mature and federated computing models gain traction, serverless architectures will continue evolving to support distributed, globally scalable workloads.

Space exploration and military applications

Serverless computing is transforming commercial applications and playing a critical role in aerospace, defense, and national security operations. In space exploration, agencies use serverless architectures to process satellite telemetry, automate mission-critical tasks, and analyze vast amounts of scientific data. Military applications leverage serverless AI-driven intelligence systems, real-time battlefield analytics, and secure, event-driven decision-making to enhance operational capabilities.

By eliminating infrastructure management, serverless computing allows aerospace and defense organizations to focus on mission execution while scaling computing resources dynamically based on operational needs. This section explores how serverless computing supports space research, satellite operations, military intelligence, and defense logistics.

Serverless in space exploration

Space agencies and private aerospace companies increasingly integrate serverless computing into mission-critical operations.

The following are key applications of serverless computing in space exploration:

- **Satellite data processing**: AWS Lambda processes real-time telemetry from satellites, reducing latency in mission control operations.

- **Deep-space communication optimization**: Serverless functions streamline data transmission between spacecraft and Earth, optimizing bandwidth.

- **Automated image and signal analysis**: AI-powered serverless workloads process planetary images and detect anomalies in deep-space signals.

- **Astronomical research and big data analytics**: Serverless computing enables the analysis of scalable astrophysics and cosmology datasets.

These serverless applications help space agencies automate workloads, reduce infrastructure costs, and improve mission success rates.

Serverless in military and defense applications

The defense sector relies on real-time intelligence, automated decision-making, and secure data analysis to enhance military operations. The following are serverless-driven innovations in military and defense:

- **Autonomous surveillance and reconnaissance**: AI-powered serverless functions process real-time UAV and satellite surveillance data.

- **Battlefield intelligence and decision support**: Serverless analytics enable instant threat detection, situational awareness, and predictive modeling.

- **Cybersecurity and threat detection**: AWS serverless security tools analyze network activity to detect cyber threats and prevent breaches.

- **Logistics and supply chain optimization**: Event-driven serverless functions automate the military supply chain and resource allocation.

By leveraging event-driven computing and AI-powered automation, defense agencies can immediately react to threats and improve decision-making capabilities.

Key AWS services used in aerospace and defense

AWS provides a suite of serverless services that support secure, scalable computing for aerospace and military applications:

- **AWS Lambda**: Automates mission-critical processes, data analysis, and intelligence workflows.
- **AWS Ground Station**: Provides serverless satellite communications and real-time data downlink.
- **AWS GovCloud**: Ensures compliance with military-grade security and regulatory requirements.
- **Amazon SageMaker**: Deploys machine learning models for threat detection, reconnaissance, and operational intelligence.

These technologies enable high-performance computing in space and defense without requiring dedicated infrastructure management.

Best practices for serverless in aerospace and defense

To maximize efficiency and security in serverless aerospace and defense applications, organizations should follow these best practices:

- **Use event-driven processing for mission data**: Automate telemetry and image analysis with serverless AI pipelines.
- **Ensure secure communications**: Leverage AWS GovCloud and encryption for classified aerospace and military workloads.
- **Optimize serverless for real-time decision-making**: Implement event-driven AI for instant threat detection and battlefield awareness.
- **Reduce latency for space operations**: Use edge computing and AI inference to process data closer to satellites and field operations.

Aerospace and military organizations can maximize operational efficiency and decision-making capabilities by applying these best practices.

Future of serverless in space and defense

The role of serverless computing in space and defense is evolving rapidly as AI, edge computing, and secure automation become essential for mission-critical operations. As real-time decision-making becomes necessary, organizations deploy serverless architectures for rapid data analysis, situational awareness, and automated response systems. The future will see tighter integration between AI, quantum encryption, and decentralized intelligence, enabling faster, more autonomous, and secure computing environments.

Sustainability and green technologies in serverless

Sustainability has become an integral and driving factor in cloud computing. Organizations are actively seeking ways to reduce their carbon footprint, optimize resource usage, and build energy-efficient cloud solutions. Serverless computing, by design, plays a critical role in minimizing idle infrastructure, reducing energy waste, and improving overall efficiency.

Unlike traditional computing models that require pre-provisioned servers, serverless architectures scale automatically based on demand, ensuring that compute resources are only used when needed. This efficiency reduces energy consumption and operational costs, making it a natural fit for organizations prioritizing sustainability without compromising scalability.

This section explores how serverless computing contributes to sustainability, the role of AWS in enabling green cloud technologies, and the best practices for building energy-efficient serverless applications.

Sustainability enhancements from serverless computing

The adoption of serverless computing contributes to more sustainable cloud operations, allowing organizations to minimize resource waste, lower power consumption, and improve cloud efficiency. Key sustainability benefits include:

- **Reduces unused compute power**: Serverless models dynamically allocate resources, ensuring energy is not wasted on idle infrastructure.

- **Optimized compute sharing**: By leveraging multi-tenant environments, serverless frameworks maximize efficiency by distributing resources across workloads

- **Reduces data center energy consumption**: Workloads are distributed across energy-efficient cloud regions, optimizing power usage.

- **Supports intelligent auto-scaling**: Functions scale only when triggered, preventing over-provisioning and unnecessary energy usage.

By eliminating idle capacity and optimizing execution, serverless computing significantly improves cloud efficiency and carbon footprint.

AWS initiatives for green cloud computing

AWS has made sustainability a core focus, continuously improving data center efficiency, power consumption, and quicker adoption of renewable energy options.

The following AWS initiatives are shaping the future of sustainable cloud computing:

- **AWS Graviton processors**: The ARM-based energy-efficient processors consume up to 60% less energy than traditional x86 processors.

- **Intelligent workload placement**: AWS enables regional workload placement optimization, directing jobs to lower-carbon data centers.

- **S3 intelligent-tiering**: This feature of S3 helps automatically move data to energy-efficient storage classes, reducing storage-related energy costs.

- **AWS sustainability pillar**: This is part of the AWS Well-Architected Framework, focusing on minimizing cloud environmental impact.

Organizations can reduce their carbon footprint by utilizing these AWS sustainability features without impacting performance and cost efficiency.

Best practices for sustainable serverless architectures

To build sustainable and energy-efficient serverless applications, organizations should follow these best practices:

- **Use energy-efficient compute**: Choose AWS Graviton-based Lambda instances to reduce power consumption.

- **Reduce execution time**: Optimize function execution by tuning memory allocation and improving cold-start performance.

- **Minimize data transfer and storage usage**: Implement S3 lifecycle policies and intelligent tiering to reduce energy-intensive storage.

- **Optimize serverless workflows**: Use Step Functions instead of long-running compute tasks to minimize energy waste.

Organizations can design cloud-native applications that align with long-term sustainability goals by applying these strategies.

Future of sustainability in serverless computing

Sustainability in cloud computing is an evolving field, with serverless architectures leading the way in optimizing resource efficiency. The rise of carbon-aware computing, AI-driven workload optimizations, and decentralized energy-efficient computing models will further enhance how organizations build scalable, environmentally conscious applications.

Once a business prioritizes sustainability and operational efficiency, serverless computing will remain a key enabler in building greener cloud architectures.

Conclusion

The evolution of serverless computing is reshaping how businesses build and deploy cloud-native applications. The serverless model is at the forefront of scalability, automation, and efficiency, from edge computing and AI-driven workloads to blockchain integration and quantum computing. As organizations seek cost-effective, event-driven architectures, serverless solutions expand to multi-cloud, hybrid environments and real-time intelligence applications.

The illustration of trends like serverless at the edge, decentralized computing, AI automations, and sustainability initiatives will assist in illustrating how serverless architectures can adapt to modern challenges. These innovations allow organizations to process critical data closer to the generator/source, automate complex workflows, and enhance security through event-driven policies. Whether it is space exploration, military defense, financial technology, or IoT, serverless computing continues to push the boundaries of performance and operational flexibility.

The next chapter takes a forward-looking approach, addressing the constraints of serverless architectures while exploring how future advancements might overcome them. Readers will gain insights into current challenges, expert perspectives, and real-world case studies that highlight the potential future of serverless computing.

Join our Discord space

Join our Discord workspace for latest updates, offers, tech happenings around the world, new releases, and sessions with the authors:

https://discord.bpbonline.com

CHAPTER 24
Beyond Serverless and Limits of Serverless

Introduction

Serverless computing has redefined cloud architecture, eliminating infrastructure management and enabling rapid scalability. Yet, it is not a universal solution. While ideal for event-driven workloads, it faces constraints in high-performance computing, persistent connections, and stateful applications. Cold starts introduce latency, execution limits hinder long-running tasks, and storage constraints challenge data-heavy applications. Serverless also encounters networking bottlenecks, debugging complexities, and vendor lock-in risks.

This chapter takes a practical approach to exploring the real-world limits of serverless computing. It delves into the challenges of computing, storage, and networking while also providing strategies to address them, such as optimizing cold starts, handling stateful workloads, and integrating hybrid architectures for greater flexibility.

Looking ahead, serverless is evolving with innovations like edge computing, AI-driven scaling, and WebAssembly. This chapter highlights these advancements, helping architects make informed choices. By the end, readers will understand when to use serverless, when to consider alternatives, and how to design resilient, high-performance cloud applications that push beyond conventional serverless boundaries.

Structure

The chapter covers the following topics:
- Understanding the limits of serverless
- Overcoming serverless limitations
- Future of serverless computing
- Real-world applications and optimization opportunities

Objectives

This chapter provides a comprehensive understanding of serverless computing's limitations and explores strategies to overcome these constraints. Readers will begin by examining the core challenges of serverless architectures, including compute limitations such as cold starts, execution time restrictions, and resource constraints; storage and data challenges such as state management, consistency trade-offs, and latency concerns; and networking complexities, including API Gateway bottlenecks and VPC connectivity issues. The chapter also highlights the challenges of observability and debugging, addressing the difficulty of monitoring distributed, event-driven workloads.

Moving beyond these limitations, readers will explore practical strategies to optimize cold starts, implement stateful workloads, improve serverless networking, and design hybrid architectures that combine serverless with containers or traditional infrastructure.

Additionally, the chapter explores vendor lock-in risks and multi-cloud strategies to enhance architectural flexibility.

Finally, the chapter looks at emerging trends shaping the future of serverless computing, including edge computing, AI-driven scaling, WebAssembly, and new function-composition models. By the end, readers will have the knowledge to assess when to use serverless, when to consider alternatives, and how to design robust, scalable, cloud-native applications that push beyond conventional serverless boundaries.

Understanding the limits of serverless

Serverless computing provides scalability, automation, and efficiency, but also has trade-offs. While it eliminates infrastructure management, it introduces limitations in compute performance, state management, networking, storage, and observability. Architects must carefully assess these factors to determine when going serverless is the right choice and when alternative solutions may be more suitable.

Illusion of infinite scale

Serverless platforms promise automatic scaling, but resource quotas, concurrency limits, and regional capacity constraints impose practical restrictions. AWS Lambda, for example, has soft concurrency limits per account and region. When workloads spike suddenly, exceeding these thresholds can throttle executions, causing unexpected delays or failures. Additionally, while serverless scales on demand, it does not always scale instantly. Concurrent executions require cold start mitigation strategies to maintain consistent performance.

AWS Lambda compute constraints

The following are some compute constraints with Lambda in the default setup.

Cold starts occur when functions are invoked after a period of inactivity, causing noticeable latency as resources are allocated. While AWS offers solutions like provisioned concurrency, they come at an additional cost.

Execution time limits restrict long-running workloads. AWS Lambda, for instance, enforces a 15-minute cap, making it unsuitable for batch processing, video rendering, and AI model training. Alternative architectures, such as Step Functions, Fargate, or Kubernetes-based workloads, may be required for tasks exceeding this threshold.

Additionally, compute-bound applications, such as machine learning inference, high-frequency trading, or scientific simulations, often exceed the CPU and memory configurations available in serverless environments. Serverless functions allocate CPU proportionally to memory, meaning intensive computational workloads may not achieve optimal performance without fine-tuned configurations.

Storage and data challenges

Serverless functions are designed to be stateless and require external storage solutions like Amazon S3, DynamoDB, or RDS Proxy. However, these come with latency overheads. Unlike traditional architectures where data is stored in memory, serverless functions must fetch state from external services, leading to delays—especially for read-heavy applications.

Database constraints are also a key limiting criteria. While DynamoDB provides high availability and scalability, it enforces eventual consistency by default, which may not be suitable for workloads requiring strong ACID transactions. Amazon Aurora Serverless offers relational capabilities, but connection pooling, cold starts, and scaling delays present new challenges.

Storage costs also require careful planning. While Lambda is cost-efficient, frequent calls to S3, DynamoDB, or RDS can accumulate significant data retrieval and request expenses over time. Data-intensive applications may need to integrate caching layers like ElastiCache or leverage hybrid architectures for cost optimization.

Networking and connectivity

Serverless functions rely on managed networking via AWS API Gateway, ALB, or EventBridge, each introducing its limitations, as shown as follows:

- API Gateway limits request size and execution time, requiring workarounds for high-throughput APIs and real-time applications.

- VPC connections introduce latency, especially in functions requiring secure database access. Lambda functions running inside a VPC experience cold start penalties due to ENI initialization delays.

- Persistent connections are not native to serverless functions, making implementing WebSockets, streaming applications, or real-time data pipelines more complex. AWS offers API Gateway WebSockets and AppSync, but stateful, real-time interactions still present design challenges.

Observability and debugging

Traditional monitoring tools are insufficient for serverless applications, where functions execute asynchronously across multiple services. Tracing failures, debugging latency spikes, and identifying performance bottlenecks require enhanced observability solutions such as:

- **AWS X-Ray** for distributed tracing across Lambda, API Gateway, DynamoDB, and Step Functions.
- **CloudWatch Logs and Metrics** to analyze execution time, memory consumption, and error rates.
- **OpenTelemetry** for standardized monitoring across multi-cloud environments.

However, serverless observability introduces added complexity, requiring custom instrumentation and increased log ingestion costs.

Security and vendor lock-in considerations

Serverless introduces security and compliance concerns due to opaque infrastructure management and limited low-level control:

- **IAM roles and permissions** require strict enforcement, as overly permissive policies can introduce security risks.

- In shared cloud environments, **multi-tenancy** increases the risk of unauthorized data access. Strong encryption, network segmentation, and strict least-privilege access controls are necessary to mitigate cross-tenant security breaches.

- **Vendor lock-in** remains a consideration, and AWS Lambda's event-driven architecture does not seamlessly translate to other cloud providers, making multi-cloud portability difficult.

Overcoming serverless limitations

While serverless computing introduces constraints in computing, storage, networking, and observability, these challenges can be mitigated through careful architectural decisions, optimization techniques, and hybrid approaches. This section explores proven strategies to address the most common serverless limitations and ensure scalability, reliability, and cost-efficiency.

Optimizing cold starts and execution limits

Cold starts occur when a serverless function is invoked after being idle, leading to increased latency as resources are allocated. Strategies to mitigate cold starts include:

- **Provisioned concurrency**: This keeps functions warm by pre-allocating execution environments. This ensures that there is no waiting time for resource provisioning when a request is received. However, it reduces cold starts and incurs additional costs, so it must be used selectively for latency-sensitive workloads.

- **Smaller deployment packages**: Large deployment sizes increase initialization time. Using tree-shaking to remove unused dependencies, compressing assets, and leveraging AWS Lambda Layers for shared libraries can significantly reduce cold start times.

- **ARM-based Lambda (Graviton2)**: AWS offers ARM-based Lambda execution environments optimized for lower cold start times and improved performance at a lower cost. This is particularly useful for workloads that do not require x86 architecture.

- **Edge computing (Lambda@Edge)**: Placing compute functions closer to end users reduces network latency and improves response times for global applications. This approach is useful for content personalization, authentication, and security filtering at the CDN level.

For workloads exceeding execution limits, the following are the ways to overcome:

- **Step Functions**: AWS Step Functions allow developers to orchestrate multiple smaller function executions into a structured workflow. Instead of a single Lambda function handling a long-running task, Step Functions break the process into multiple stateful steps, each executed by a separate function.

  This not only bypasses execution limits but also improves reliability through built-in retry logic and error handling. Step Functions are commonly used for ETL pipelines, batch processing, and complex automation workflows.

- **Hybrid compute (AWS Fargate/Kubernetes)**: AWS Fargate offers a containerized execution environment that eliminates the need for EC2 provisioning while allowing long-running tasks. Kubernetes on Amazon EKS provides even greater control, making it ideal for high-performance workloads that require persistent connections or specialized hardware configurations.

- **Asynchronous processing (SQS, EventBridge)**: Offloading tasks to message queues or event-driven triggers reduces the need for functions to execute synchronously, allowing them to process events in batches or on demand. This is particularly effective for background processing, transaction handling, and analytics workloads.

Managing stateful workloads in a stateless environment

Serverless architectures are designed to be **stateless**, requiring external storage for **persistent data**. Strategies to handle stateful workloads include:

- **DynamoDB and S3**: Serverless applications can use DynamoDB for real-time data storage and Amazon S3 for object storage. While DynamoDB scales seamlessly, it lacks traditional relational database transactions, making it necessary to optimize data access patterns for efficiency. S3 is ideal for large-scale unstructured data storage but requires caching strategies to mitigate read latency.

- **Aurora Serverless with Data API**: Amazon Aurora Serverless provides relational database capabilities without requiring persistent connections. Instead of traditional connections, applications interact via the Data API, which allows stateless functions to query the database without managing connection pools. This is useful for scenarios requiring ACID compliance and SQL-based analytics.

- **Elasticache (Redis/Memcached)**: Implementing in-memory caching significantly reduces database query latency by storing frequently accessed data in memory. This approach is widely used for session storage, leaderboards, and API caching.

- **Session management with Cognito**: AWS Cognito provides user authentication and state management for serverless applications. Using identity pools and token-based authentication, Cognito allows users to maintain state without requiring persistent backend connections.

For real-time stateful workloads like chat applications or financial transactions, hybrid architectures using Fargate, EC2, or Kubernetes may be more effective.

Improving networking and API performance

Serverless functions rely on managed networking, which introduces challenges such as API rate limits, request timeouts, and VPC latency overhead. To optimize networking performance:

- **Optimize API Gateway usage**: AWS API Gateway is often a bottleneck due to request limits, latency, and pricing per request. Using REST vs. HTTP APIs appropriately, implementing request validation, and enabling caching can significantly improve performance while reducing operational costs.

- **Reduce VPC cold start penalties**: Deploying functions outside VPCs when possible eliminates the cold start penalty associated with **Elastic Network Interface** (**ENI**) initialization. For workloads that must run in a VPC, using AWS Lambda SnapStart (for Java-based workloads) significantly improves startup time.

- **Use direct service integrations**: Instead of routing API Gateway calls to Lambda, direct integrations with DynamoDB, S3, or EventBridge eliminate function overhead, reducing response times and execution costs.

- **Regional and edge deployments**: Leveraging CloudFront for caching and AWS Global Accelerator improves latency-sensitive applications, reducing the need for long-distance API requests.

Enhancing observability and debugging

Observability in serverless applications requires advanced tracing, logging, and monitoring across multiple AWS services. To improve troubleshooting and operational visibility:

- **Enable AWS X-Ray**: This provides distributed tracing across AWS services, allowing teams to track performance bottlenecks, API latency, and request execution flow.

- **Use structured logging**: Implementing JSON-formatted logs in CloudWatch or OpenSearch enhances log searchability and correlation between events.

- **Leverage OpenTelemetry**: A cloud-agnostic observability framework that provides standardized monitoring across AWS, Azure, and Google Cloud environments.

- **Automate anomaly detection**: Using AWS DevOps Guru allows machine learning-driven insights to detect performance anomalies before they impact customers.

While serverless computing presents limitations, strategic optimization techniques, architectural best practices, and hybrid approaches can significantly enhance performance, scalability, and cost efficiency. The next section explores future trends shaping the evolution of serverless computing, including AI-driven optimization, WebAssembly, and decentralized compute models.

Future of serverless computing

Serverless computing has revolutionized cloud-native architectures, but its evolution is far from over. As cloud workloads become more complex, data-intensive, and performance-sensitive, serverless technologies adapt to meet new demands. The future of serverless will be shaped by performance optimizations, hybrid approaches, AI-driven automation, and new execution models that push beyond the current boundaries.

AI-driven serverless optimization

AI and ML are playing a growing role in optimizing serverless workloads. AWS and other cloud providers are integrating AI-driven cost analysis, predictive scaling, and anomaly detection into serverless platforms.

The following AI-driven techniques enhance serverless performance, scalability, and efficiency:

- **Automated performance tuning**: AI-powered services, such as AWS Compute Optimizer and AWS DevOps Guru, analyze function execution patterns to recommend memory, CPU, and concurrency configurations, reducing cold starts and improving response times.

- **Smart scaling with AI**: Instead of reactive scaling based on simple metrics, AI models predict workload spikes and pre-allocate resources dynamically, avoiding latency issues caused by sudden traffic surges.

- **AI-augmented observability**: Future serverless platforms will automate tracing and error detection, using machine learning models to pinpoint performance bottlenecks without manual log analysis.

These advancements will reduce the complexity of managing serverless workloads, allowing applications to self-optimize in real time.

WebAssembly and serverless functions

WebAssembly (**Wasm**) is an emerging technology that enables the faster, lightweight execution of serverless functions. Unlike traditional serverless environments that depend on containerized runtimes (Node.js, Python, Java, etc.), WebAssembly allows near-native execution speeds with reduced cold start times and better portability across cloud providers.

The following are some of the advantages of WebAssembly:

- **Reduced cold starts**: Wasm functions execute faster than traditional Lambda runtimes due to their smaller size and precompiled nature.

- **Multi-language support**: Wasm allows developers to write serverless functions in Rust, C, and Go, offering better performance than traditional JavaScript or Python-based functions.

- **Cross-cloud portability**: Wasm provides a standardized execution environment, making it easier to deploy serverless functions across AWS, Azure, Google Cloud, or edge computing platforms without re-architecting applications.

As serverless computing expands beyond AWS Lambda, WebAssembly will likely become a dominant execution model for high-performance, cross-platform serverless applications.

Serverless at the edge

The future of serverless is not limited to centralized cloud regions; it is expanding to the network edge, enabling low-latency, globally distributed applications. Edge computing integrates serverless functions into **content delivery networks** (**CDNs**), IoT devices, and 5G networks, bringing computation closer to the user.

The following are some of the key capabilities of Edge Computing with Serverless:

- **Lambda@Edge and CloudFront Functions**: AWS already enables serverless execution at edge locations for real-time authentication, personalization, and content modification without requiring a round trip to a central data center.

- **5G and Edge AI processing**: Serverless architectures will play a role in processing real-time AI inference models at the edge, allowing autonomous vehicles, smart cities, and industrial IoT applications to make instant decisions without cloud latency.

- **Decentralized serverless architectures**: In the future, multi-region, federated serverless architectures will allow developers to deploy serverless functions closer to the user base, reducing network congestion and improving performance.

Edge serverless computing will enable ultra-responsive applications, significantly improving the efficiency of real-time gaming, AR/VR, and AI-powered interactions.

Hybrid serverless and Kubernetes integration

As workloads become more complex, serverless will not replace containerized or virtualized environments; instead, hybrid architectures will emerge, combining serverless with Kubernetes, Fargate, and other compute options.

The following trends highlight how hybrid architectures integrate serverless with Kubernetes to enhance flexibility and scalability:

- **Event-driven containers**: Kubernetes-based platforms like AWS EKS and Knative allow developers to run serverless-style functions within containerized environments, bridging the gap between traditional infrastructure and event-driven architectures.

- **Stateful workloads with Kubernetes and serverless**: While Lambda is designed for stateless execution, integrating serverless with Kubernetes-based microservices will enable stateful applications to run alongside serverless components, creating a best-of-both-worlds approach.

- **Multi-Cloud serverless workloads**: With tools like Kubernetes Federation and OpenFaaS, organizations will deploy serverless workloads across multiple cloud providers, reducing vendor lock-in and improving reliability.

Rather than choosing between serverless and containerized computing, future architectures combine both models, ensuring greater flexibility, scalability, and cost efficiency.

Decentralized and blockchain-powered serverless models

The long-term evolution of serverless computing involves decentralized architectures, where functions are executed across distributed nodes rather than a single cloud provider. Blockchain and decentralized storage networks (such as IPFS) could reshape how serverless applications store, manage, and validate computations.

The following are some of the key advantages of decentralized platforms:

- **Decentralized compute networks**: Platforms like Akash and Ankr are experimenting with serverless execution over decentralized networks, where serverless functions are distributed across a blockchain-powered infrastructure.

- **Smart contract integration**: Future serverless applications may integrate directly with Ethereum, Solana, or other blockchain networks, allowing automated execution of business logic across decentralized environments.

- **Federated learning for serverless AI**: Instead of centralizing AI workloads in cloud data centers, federated learning models run serverless AI functions directly on user devices, preserving privacy and reducing dependency on a single provider.

While still in their early stages, decentralized serverless models could redefine cloud computing, offering greater resilience, privacy, and cost efficiency.

Future of serverless at a glance

The next evolution of serverless will go beyond today's event-driven functions, integrating AI-driven automation, WebAssembly, edge computing, hybrid architectures, and decentralized models. These innovations will eliminate traditional constraints, making the serverless model faster, more scalable, and applicable to a wider range of workloads.

By embracing these advancements, developers and organizations can future-proof their serverless applications, ensuring higher efficiency, portability, and flexibility in the evolving cloud landscape.

Real-world applications and optimization opportunities

Serverless computing is transforming mainstream industries and cutting-edge fields like space exploration, deep-sea research, and real-time global event tracking. This section explores real-world scenarios where the serverless model plays a crucial role while demonstrating its limitations and hybrid solutions.

The following use cases demonstrate the opportunities.

Space weather forecasting for deep space missions

Challenge: Aerospace agencies and private space companies need real-time weather forecasting to protect satellites, spacecraft, and astronaut missions from solar storms. Solar flares and cosmic radiation can disable communication systems and damage onboard electronics, making early detection critical. Traditional monitoring systems rely on ground-based observatories and high-performance computing clusters, introducing latency and cost constraints.

The solution is as follows:

- **AWS Lambda for real-time solar flare detection**: Lambda processes continuous data streams from space telescopes and satellites, filtering anomalies in solar wind velocity, magnetosphere activity, and radiation bursts.

- **Amazon Kinesis for streaming data analysis**: A serverless pipeline aggregates data from NASA's Parker Solar Probe, **European Space Agency** (**ESA**) instruments, and private-sector deep-space monitors.

- **AWS step functions for multi-stage forecasting**: Instead of a single, large Lambda function, a Step Function workflow chains multiple prediction models, reducing execution time and increasing accuracy.

- **AWS Greengrass for edge processing in space**: Satellite-mounted edge devices running AWS Greengrass process localized weather patterns, sending only filtered high-risk alerts to Earth-based command centers, reducing data transmission costs.

Outcome: The system reduced the detection-to-alert time from 30 to 5 minutes, enabling faster response times for spacecraft repositioning, shielding activation, and astronaut safety protocols.

Serverless is ideal for this use case because real-time event detection is critical for early solar storm alerts.

Limitations and hybrid approach:

- Deep-space radiation can disrupt cloud-based processing, requiring hardened edge computing at the satellite level.

- High-volume, continuous deep learning models may require Fargate or Kubernetes-based training infrastructure instead of pure serverless.

AI-driven navigation for interstellar travel

Challenge: Future interstellar spacecraft will require autonomous AI-driven course correction since human operators cannot manage real-time navigation due to light-speed delays. The challenge is processing starfield mapping, gravitational lensing distortions, and trajectory planning in a decentralized manner without relying on Earth-based control centers.

The solution is as follows:

- **Lambda@Edge for distributed decision making**: Onboard AI agents use serverless functions deployed across a distributed space network (Deep Space Relay Satellites) to compute local trajectory adjustments without waiting for ground control.

- **Amazon SageMaker for deep space object recognition**: Machine learning models process distant star maps in real time to identify anomalies in navigation paths, such as rogue asteroids or unknown gravitational fields.

- **EventBridge for course correction alerts**: AI-driven anomaly detection triggers automated navigational course changes when potential risks (micrometeoroid swarms, radiation belts, or unexpected debris fields) are detected.

- **Hybrid AI and classical computation**: Quantum-enhanced algorithms, combined with edge-based classical AI models, are run on energy-efficient neural accelerators onboard spacecraft.

Outcome: The system allows autonomous course corrections with microsecond latency, ensuring a 10x improvement in deep-space navigation efficiency and reducing reliance on Earth-bound calculations.

Serverless functions, combined with AI, allow deep-space navigation models to make instant course corrections without waiting for Earth-based input.

The limitations and hybrid approach are explained as follows:

- **Long-term space missions (20+ years)** require self-healing AI models, which might need containerized or on-chip processing rather than cloud-based execution.

- **Quantum serverless workloads** are in early development, and AWS Braket (quantum computing) might replace classical AI in the future.

Deep-sea serverless computing for uncharted ocean exploration

Challenge: Over 80% of Earth's oceans remain unexplored due to extreme pressure, low visibility, and unpredictable currents. **Autonomous underwater vehicles (AUVs)** need real-time AI-powered navigation and obstacle detection, but high-pressure environments limit direct human control and real-time satellite communication.

The solution is as follows:

- **AWS Greengrass for AI at the Edge**: Since deep-sea drones operate with limited connectivity, relying solely on cloud-based processing is inefficient. Instead, AWS Greengrass enables on-device AI models, allowing underwater drones to autonomously detect volcanic vents, deep-sea trenches, and new marine species without constant uplink communication.

- **Serverless event processing with Amazon Kinesis**: Oceanic research teams use Kinesis streams to analyze sensor data collected by AUVs and deep-sea probes, identifying new hydrothermal activity and unexplored marine life zones.

- **Lambda functions for predictive ocean current modeling**: Live data feeds from drifting underwater sensors process water temperature, salinity, and pressure changes, predicting currents and helping vehicles navigate more efficiently.

- **Distributed processing in underwater data centers**: Microsoft's Project Natick demonstrated deep-sea data centers for cold-water cooling. Future serverless compute pods may run AI models within sub-oceanic environments, reducing data transmission costs to land-based research stations.

Outcome: This reduced real-time oceanic analysis latency from 45 minutes to 2 minutes, allowing faster discovery and safer deep-sea navigation.

By leveraging AWS Greengrass, underwater AI models can analyze marine data locally, reducing latency and making real-time navigation possible.

The limitations and hybrid approach are as follows:

- Extreme conditions require hardened, pressure-resistant AI compute nodes rather than relying solely on cloud-based serverless models.

- Some deep-sea datasets (video, LiDAR scans) are too large for real-time cloud transmission, requiring local edge storage solutions before uploading.

Conclusion

This chapter marks the end, summarizing the key insights explored throughout the book.

Serverless computing has transformed cloud architecture by eliminating infrastructure management, enabling auto-scaling, and optimizing costs. However, as discussed, it comes with computing, networking, state management, and observability limitations that require careful architectural decisions. In many cases, hybrid solutions, combining serverless with containers, edge computing, or AI-driven automation, deliver the best results.

We explored real-world applications of serverless in deep space navigation, space weather forecasting, and deep-sea AI research. These case studies demonstrated that serverless excels when strategically integrated with other technologies, enabling high-performance and scalable solutions.

Looking ahead, AI-assisted workload automation, Web Assembly (Wasm), and decentralized architectures will push serverless beyond today's limitations, reducing cold starts, improving efficiency, and expanding real-time processing capabilities.

Architects can design resilient, cost-effective, and future-ready applications by understanding serverless strengths and trade-offs.

This book has equipped you with the insights and best practices needed to harness AWS serverless technologies effectively. By applying these principles, you can design scalable, cost-efficient, and resilient cloud-native applications ready for the challenges of tomorrow.

Index

www.ingramcontent.com/pod-product-compliance
Lightning Source LLC
Chambersburg PA
CBHW061739210326

41599CB00034B/6735